THE SCHILLINGER SYSTEM
OF MUSICAL COMPOSITION

Da Capo Press Music Reprint Series

MUSIC EDITOR
BEA FRIEDLAND
Ph.D., City University of New York

THE SCHILLINGER SYSTEM
OF
MUSICAL COMPOSITION

by

JOSEPH SCHILLINGER

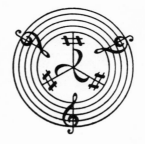

IN TWO VOLUMES

Volume I: Books I-VII

Volume II: Books VIII-XII

DA CAPO PRESS • NEW YORK • 1978

Library of Congress Cataloging in Publication Data

Schillinger, Joseph, 1895-1943.
    The Schillinger system of musical composition.

    (Da Capo Press music reprint series)
    Reprint of the 1941 ed. published by C. Fischer, New
York.
    1. Composition (Music) I. Title.
MT40.S315 1978   781.6'1   77-21709
ISBN 0-306-77552-2

This Da Capo Press edition of
THE SCHILLINGER SYSTEM OF MUSICAL COMPOSITION Volume II
is an unabridged republication of the first edition
published in New York in 1941.
It is reprinted by arrangement with Carl Fischer, Inc.

Published by Da Capo Press, Inc.
A Subsidiary of Plenum Publishing Corporation
227 West 17th Street, New York, N.Y. 10011

THE SCHILLINGER SYSTEM
OF MUSICAL COMPOSITION

THE SCHILLINGER SYSTEM

OF

MUSICAL COMPOSITION

by

JOSEPH SCHILLINGER

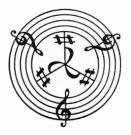

IN TWO VOLUMES

Volume I: Books I-VII
Volume II: Books VIII-XII

CARL FISCHER, Inc., NEW YORK

03359 B

VOLUME II

CONTENTS

BOOK VIII

BOOK IX

BOOK X

BOOK XI

BOOK XII

THE SCHILLINGER SYSTEM

OF

MUSICAL COMPOSITION

by

JOSEPH SCHILLINGER

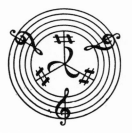

BOOK VIII

INSTRUMENTAL FORMS

BOOK EIGHT

INSTRUMENTAL FORMS

CHAPTER 1

MULTIPLICATION OF ATTACKS

INSTRUMENTAL form will mean, so far as this discussion is concerned, a modification of the original melody and/or harmony which renders them fit for execution on an instrument. *Instrumental* can thus be regarded as an *applied* form of *pure* music. Depending on the degree of virtuosity which can be expected from singers, instrumental forms may be applied to vocal music as well as orchestral.

The main technical characteristic of the instrumental (i.e., of applied, as against pure) form is that it emphasizes the *development of quantities (multiplication) and the forms of attacks* from the original attack. We shall here be concerned only with the former—i.e., with quantities and their uses in composition—and leave the latter, the forms of attack (such as durable, abrupt, bouncing, oscillating, etc.), to that branch of this theory called *orchestration*.

Multiplication of attacks may be applied directly to single pitch-units as well as to pitch-assemblages. The number of instrumental forms available is dependent upon the number of pitch-units in an assemblage. When the number of pitch-units (parts) in an assemblage is few, the number of instrumental forms is low. When the pitch-units (parts) in an assemblage are abundant, the number of instrumental forms is high, permitting greater variety in a composition insofar as its instrumental aspect is concerned.

The paucity of instrumental forms derivable from but one pitch-unit (part) often compels us to resort to *couplings*. By the addition of one coupling to one part, we achieve a two-part setting with all its instrumental implications. Likewise, the addition of two couplings to one part transforms the latter into a three-part assemblage, etc.

What we are to discuss here is all forms of arpeggio and their applications in the field of melody, harmony, and correlated melodies.

A. Nomenclature:

Σ—score (group of instrumental strata)
S—stratum (instrumental stratum)
p—part (function, coupling)
a—attack

Preliminary Data:

(1) $p = a$; $p = 2a$; . . . $p = na$
(2) $S = p$; $S = 2p$; . . . $S = np$
(3) $\Sigma = S$; $\Sigma = 2S$; . . . $\Sigma = nS$

B. SOURCES OF INSTRUMENTAL FORMS

(a) Multiplication of S is achieved by $1 : 2 : 4 : 8 : \ldots$ ratio (i.e., by the octaves).

(b) Multiplication of p in S is achieved by coupling or by harmonization. It is applicable to melody (p), to correlated melodies $(2p, \ldots np)$, and to harmony $(2p \ldots 4p)$. The material for p is to be found in my previous exposition of the *Theory of Pitch-Scales*[*] and the *Theory of Melody*.[**] The material for $2p, \ldots np$ acting as melodies was discussed in the theory of correlated melodies (*Counterpoint*).[***] The material for $2p, \ldots np$ acting as parts of harmony is presented in the previous *Special Theory of Harmony*,[****] and in the discussion that is to come on the *General Theory of Harmony*.[*****]

(c) Multiplication of a is achieved by repetition and sequence of p's (arpeggio).

(d) Different S's and different p's, as correlated melodies of Σ, may have independent instrumental forms.

C. DEFINITION OF INSTRUMENTAL FORMS:

I. (a) *Instrumental Forms of Melody*: I $(M = p)$:

Repetition of pitch-units represented by the duration-group and expressed through its common denominator. The number of a equals the number of t.

$$\text{If } \frac{1}{nt} = nt, \text{ then } nt = na$$

Rhythmic composition of durations assigned to each attack.

(b) *Instrumental Forms of Melody*: I $(M = np)$:

Repetition of pitch-units (p_I) and their couplings $(p_{II}, p_{III}, \ldots p_N)$ and transition (sequence) from one p to another, represented by the duration group and expressed through its common denominator. Instrumental groups of p's consisting of repetitions and sequences are subject to permutations.

(α) *Instrumental Forms of the Simultaneous Groups of Melody*:

$$M = \frac{p_{II}}{p_I}; \ \frac{p_I}{p_{II}}; \ \frac{\frac{p_{III}}{p_I}}{p_{II}}; \ \frac{\frac{p_{II}}{p_I}}{p_{III}}; \ \frac{\frac{p_I}{p_{II}}}{p_{III}}; \ \frac{\frac{p_I}{p_{III}}}{p_{II}}; \ \frac{\frac{p_{III}}{p_{II}}}{p_I}; \ \frac{\frac{p_{II}}{p_{III}}}{p_I}; \ \ldots$$

(β) *Instrumental Forms of the Sequent Groups of Melody*:

$M = p_I + p_{II}; \ p_{II} + p_I; \ p_I + p_{II} + p_{III}; \ p_I + p_{III} + p_{II}; \ p_{III} + p_I + \newline + p_{II}; \ p_{II} + p_I + p_{III}; \ p_{II} + p_{III} + p_I; \ p_{III} + p_{II} + p_I.$

$M = p_I + p_{II} + p_I; \ p_I + p_{II} + p_{III} + p_I; \ p_I + p_{II} + p_{III} + p_{II}; \newline p_I + p_{II} + p_{III} + p_{III} , \ldots .$

---

*See Vol. I, p. 101 ff. **See Vol. I, p. 227 ff. ***See Vol. I, p. 708 ff. ****See Vol. I, p. 359 ff. *****See p. 1063 ff.

(γ) *Instrumental Forms of the Combined Groups of Melody*:

$$M = \frac{P_{II}}{p_I} + \frac{P_{III}}{P_I} + \frac{P_{III}}{P_{II}}; \frac{P_{II}}{P_I} + \frac{P_{III}}{P_I} + \frac{P_{IV}}{P_I} + \frac{P_{III}}{P_{II}} + \frac{P_{IV}}{P_{II}} + \frac{P_{IV}}{P_{III}}; \cdots$$

$$M = \frac{P_{III}}{P_{II}} + \frac{P_{IV}}{P_{II}} + \frac{P_{IV}}{P_{III}} + \frac{P_{IV}}{P_{III}}; \cdots$$
$$ \frac{P_{II}}{p_I} + \frac{P_{II}}{p_I} + \frac{P_{II}}{p_I} + \frac{P_{III}}{P_{II}}; \cdots$$

II. *Instrumental Forms of Correlated Melodies*:

(a) $I\left(\dfrac{M_{II} = p}{M_I = p}\right)$: correlation of instrumental forms of the two uncoupled

melodies (M_I and M_{II}) by means of correlating their a's.

M_I (nt = na); M_{II} (nt = 2na; 3na; . . . mna)

$$\frac{M_{II}\ (t = a)}{M_I\ (t = 2a)}; \frac{M_{II}\ (t = 2a)}{M_I\ (t = a)}; \frac{M_{II}\ (t = a)}{M_I\ (t = 3a)}; \frac{M_{II}\ (t = 3a)}{M_I\ (t = a)}$$

$$\frac{M_{II}\ (t = 2a)}{M_I\ (t = 3a)}; \frac{M_{II}\ (t = 3a)}{M_I\ (t = 2a)}; \frac{M_{II}\ (t = a)}{M_I\ (t = 4a)}; \frac{M_{II}\ (t = 4a)}{M_I\ (t = a)};$$

$$\frac{M_{II}\ (t = 2a)}{M_I\ (t = 4a)}; \frac{M_{II}\ (t = 4a)}{M_I\ (t = 2a)}; \frac{M_{II}\ (t = 3a)}{M_I\ (t = 4a)}; \frac{M_{II}\ (t = 4a)}{M_I\ (t = 3a)}; \cdots$$

$$\cdots \ \frac{M_{II}\ (t = na)}{M_I\ (t = ma)}$$

(b) $I\left(\dfrac{M_{II} = np}{M_I = mp}\right)$: this form corresponds to combinations of (α), (β) and

(γ).of I (b).

$$\frac{M_{II}\ (\alpha)}{M_I\ (\alpha)}; \frac{M_{II}\ (\alpha)}{M_I\ (\beta)}; \frac{M_{II}\ (\beta)}{M_I\ (\alpha)}; \frac{M_{II}\ (\beta)}{M_I\ (\beta)};$$

$$\frac{M_{II}\ (\alpha)}{M_I\ (\gamma)}; \frac{M_{II}\ (\gamma)}{M_I\ (\alpha)}; \frac{M_{II}\ (\beta)}{M_I\ (\gamma)}; \frac{M_{II}\ (\gamma)}{M_I\ (\beta)}; \frac{M_{II}\ (\gamma)}{M_I\ (\gamma)}.$$

III. *Instrumental Forms of Harmony*:

I (S = p, 2p, 3p, 4p): this corresponds to one-part harmony, which is the equivalent of M; two-part harmony, which is the equivalent of two correlated uncoupled melodies; three-part harmony, which is the equivalent of three correlated uncoupled melodies; four-part harmony, which is the equivalent of four correlated uncoupled melodies.

The source of the harmony may be the *Theory of Pitch-Scales*, the *Special Theory of Harmony*, and the *General Theory of Harmony*.* Parts (p's) in their simultaneous and sequent groupings correspond to a, b, c, d.

$$P_I = a; P_{II} = b; P_{III} = c; P_{IV} = d.$$

*See Vol. I, p. 101 ff.; p. 359 ff. and Vol. II, p. 1063 ff.

CHAPTER 2

STRATA OF ONE PART

THERE being, by definition, but one part to strata of this type, we need not classify the attack forms in any general way, but may proceed at once to discuss the instrumental forms for S = p. The material for these forms is:

    (a) melody;
    (b) any one of the correlated melodies;
    (c) one part harmony;
    (d) harmonic form of one unit scale;
    (e) one part of any harmony.

I = a; 2a; 3a; ma; A var.
      nt = na

Figure 1. Melody.

(b) Theme

Figure 2. Correlated melody (continued).

Var. I $\left(\frac{M_{II}}{M_I}\right)$: $\begin{array}{l} a = t \\ a = 2t \end{array}$

Figure 2. Correlated melodies (concluded).

(c) Theme

Var. I (B): a = t

Figure 3. One-part harmony (continued).

Var. I (B): A = 3a + a + 2a + 2a + a + 3a; T″: $\frac{4}{4}$ series

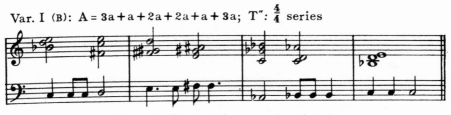

Figure 3. One-part harmony (concluded).

(d) Ped. Point. Theme

Var. I (p): a = t

Figure 4. Harmonic form of one-unit scale.

(e) Theme

Var. I (s): a = t + 2t + t; T″: $\frac{8}{8}$ series

Var. I (ABTS): a = t; T″ $\frac{8}{8}$ series

Figure 5. One part of any harmony.

CHAPTER 3

STRATA OF TWO PARTS

A. General Classification of I (S = 2p)
    (*A table of the combinations of attacks for a and b.*)

A = a; 2a; 3a; 4a; 5a; 6a; 7a; 8a; 12a.*

I give here a complete table of all forms of I (S = 2p). Included are *all the combinations and permutations* for 2, 3, 4, 5, 6, 7, 8 and 12 attacks.

A = 2a; *a + b.*
$$P_2 = 2! = 2$$
        Total of general permutations: 2
        Total of circular permutations: 2

A = 3a; *2a + b; a + 2b.*
$$P_3 = \frac{3!}{2!} = \frac{6}{2} = 3$$
Each· of the above 2 permutations of the coefficients has 3 general permutations.

        Total: $3 \cdot 2 = 6$
        The total number of cases: A = 3a
        General permutations: 6
        Circular permutations: 6

A = 4a
Forms of the distribution of coefficients:
    4 = 1+3; 2+2 ; 3+1
A = a + 3b; 3a + b.
$$P_4 = \frac{4!}{3!} = \frac{24}{6} = 4$$
Each of the above 2 permutations of the first form of distribution of the coefficients of recurrence has 4 general permutations.
        Total: $4 \cdot 2 = 8$
A = 2a + 2b
$$P_4 = \frac{4!}{2! \, 2!} = \frac{24}{2 \cdot 2} = 6$$
The above invariant form of distribution has 6 general permutations.
        The total number of cases: A = 4a
        General permutations: $8 + 6 = 14$
        Circular permutations: $4 \cdot 3 = 12$

*In this chapter and several ensuing chapters we are to be concerned with tables of combinations; it should be said that the tables are included not merely as items of interest, but as actual sources on which the composer or arranger may draw—above all, if he is insufficiently familiar with the techniques of making permutations, combinations, and related groups. (Ed.)

A = 5a

Forms of the distribution of coefficients:

$$5 = 1+4; \ 2+3.$$
$$A = a + 4b; \ 4a + b$$
$$P_5 = \frac{5!}{4!} = \frac{120}{24} = 5$$

Each of the above 2 permutations of the first form of distribution has 5 general permutations.

Total: $5 \cdot 2 = 10$

$A = 2a + 3b; \ 3a + 2b$
$$P_5 = \frac{5!}{2! \ 3!} = \frac{120}{2 \cdot 6} = 10$$

Each of the above 2 permutations of the second form of distribution has 10 general permutations.

Total: $10 \cdot 2 = 20$
The total number of cases: $A = 5a$
General permutations: $10 + 20 = 30$
Circular permutations: $5 \cdot 4 = 20$

A = 6a

Forms of the distribution of coefficients:

$$6 = 1+5; \ 2+4; \ 3+3.$$

$A = a + 5b; \ 5a + b.$
$$P_6 = \frac{6!}{5!} = \frac{720}{120} = 6$$

Each of the above 2 permutations of the first form of distribution has 6 general permutations.

Total: $6 \cdot 2 = 12$

$A = 2a + 4b; \ 4a + 2b.$
$$P_6 = \frac{6!}{2! \ 4!} = \frac{720}{2 \cdot 24} = 15$$

Each of the above 2 permutations of the second form of distribution has 15 general permutations.

Total: $15 \cdot 2 = 30$

$A = 3a + 3b$

$$P_6 = \frac{6!}{3! \ 3!} = \frac{720}{6 \cdot 6} = 20$$

The above invariant (third) form of distribution has 20 general permutations.

> The total number of cases: $A = 6a$
> General permutations: $12 + 30 + 20 = 62$
> Circular permutations: $6 \cdot 5 \qquad \quad = 30$

A = 7a

Forms of the distribution of coefficients:

> $7 = 1+6; \ 2+5; \ 3+4.$

$A = a + 6b; \ 6a + b.$

$$P_7 = \frac{7!}{6!} = \frac{5040}{720} = 7$$

Each of the above 2 permutations of the first form of distribution has 7 general permutations.

> Total: $7 \cdot 2 = 14$

$A = 2a + 5b; \ 5a + 2b.$

$$P_7 = \frac{7!}{2! \ 5!} = \frac{5040}{2 \cdot 120} = 21$$

Each of the above 2 permutations of the second form of distribution has 21 general permutations.

> Total: $21 \cdot 2 = 42$

$A = 3a + 4b; \ 4a + 3b.$

$$P_7 = \frac{7}{3! \ 4!} = \frac{5040}{6 \cdot 24} = 35$$

Each of the above 2 permutations of the third form of distribution has 35 general permutations.

> Total: $35 \cdot 2 = 70$
> The total number of cases: $A = 7a$
> General permutations: $14 + 42 + 70 = 126$
> Circular permutations: $7 \cdot 6 \qquad \quad = 42$

A = 8a

Forms of the distribution of coefficients:

> $8 = 1+7; \ 2+6; \ 3+5; \ 4+4.$

$A = a + 7b; 7a + b.$

$$P_8 = \frac{8!}{7!} = \frac{40,320}{5,040} = 8$$

Each of the above 2 permutations of the first form of distribution has 8 general permutations.

Total: $8 \cdot 2 = 16$

$A = 2a + 6b; 6a + 2b.$

$$P_8 = \frac{8!}{2! \; 6!} = \frac{40,320}{2 \cdot 720} = 28$$

Each of the above 2 permutations of the second form of distribution has 28 general permutations.

Total: $28 \cdot 2 = 56$

$A = 3a + 5b; 5a + 3b.$

$$P_8 = \frac{8!}{3! \; 5!} = \frac{40,320}{6 \cdot 120} = 56$$

Each of the above 2 permutations of the third form of distribution has 56 general permutations.

Total: $56 \cdot 2 = 112$

$A = 4a + 4b$

$$P_8 = \frac{8!}{4! \; 4!} = \frac{40,320}{24 \cdot 24} = 70$$

The above invariant (fourth) form of distribution has 70 general permutations.

The total number of cases: $A = 8a$
General permutations: $16 + 56 + 112 + 70 = 254$
Circular permutations: $8 \cdot 7 = 56$

A = 12a

Forms of the distribution of coefficients:

$12 = 1 + 11; \; 2 + 10; \; 3 + 9; \; 4 + 8; \; 5 + 7; \; 6 + 6$

$A = a + 11b; 11a + b.$

$$P_{12} = \frac{12!}{11!} = \frac{479,001,600}{39,916,800} = 12$$

Each of the above 2 permutations of the first form of distribution has 12 general permutations.

Total: $12 \cdot 2 = 24$

$A = 2a + 10b; 10a + 2b.$

$$P_{12} = \frac{12!}{2! \; 10!} = \frac{479,001,600}{2 \cdot 3,628,800} = 66$$

Each of the above 2 permutations of the second form of distribution has 66 general permutations.

Total: $66 \cdot 2 = 132$

$A = 3a + 9b; 9a + 3b.$

$$P_{12} = \frac{12!}{3! \; 9!} = \frac{479,001,600}{6 \cdot 362,880} = 220$$

Each of the above 2 permutations of the third form of distribution has 220 general permutations.

Total: $220 \cdot 2 = 440$

$A = 4a + 8b; 8a + 4b.$

$$P_{12} = \frac{12!}{4! \; 8!} = \frac{479,001,600}{24 \cdot 40,320} = 495$$

Each of the above 2 permutations of the fourth form of distribution has 495 general permutations.

Total: $495 \cdot 2 = 990$

$A = 5a + 7b; 7a + 5b.$

$$P_{12} = \frac{12!}{5! \; 7!} = \frac{479,001,600}{120 \cdot 5,040} = 792$$

Each of the above 2 permutations of the fifth form of distribution has 792 general permutations.

Total: $792 \cdot 2 = 1584$

$A = 6a + 6b$

$$P_{12} = \frac{12!}{6! \; 6!} = \frac{479,001,600}{720 \cdot 720} = 924$$

The above invariant (sixth) form of distribution has 924 general permutations.

The total number of cases: $A = 12a$
General permutations: $24 + 132 + 440 + 990 + 1584 + 924 = 4094$.
Circular permutations: $12 \cdot 11 = 132$

The interval of an octave may be changed to any other interval. For the groups with more than 6 attacks, only circular permutations are included. See figures 6-12 inclusive.

A = a   A = 2a; 2 forms   A = 3a: 2a+b; a+2b.   2 combinations.

3 permutations each. Total 2·3 = 6

Figure 6. A = 2a.

A = 4a: 3a+b: 2a+2b; a+3b

4 forms

6 forms

4 forms

Total: 4+6+4 = 14

Figure 7. A = 4a.

A = 5a: 4a+b: 3a+2b· 2a+3b; a+4b

5 forms

5 forms

10 forms

10 forms

5 forms

Total: 5+10+10+5 = 30

Figure 8. A = 5a.

A = 6a: 5a+b; 4a+2b; 3a+3b; 2a+4b; a+5b

Total: 6+15+20+15+6 = 62

Figure 9. A = 6a.

A = 7a: 6a+b; 5a+2b; 4a+3b; 3a+4b; 2a+5b; a+6b

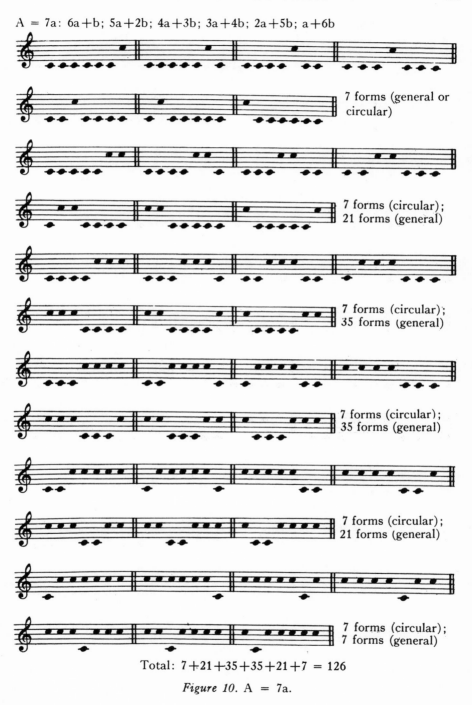

Total: 7+21+35+35+21+7 = 126

Figure 10. A = 7a.

A = 8a: 7a + b; 6a + 2b; 5a + 3b; 4a + 4b; 3a + 5b; 2a + 6b; a + 7b

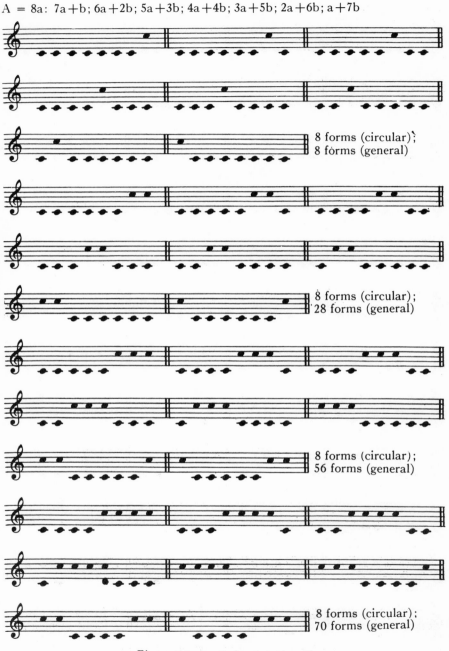

Figure 11. A = 8a. (continued).

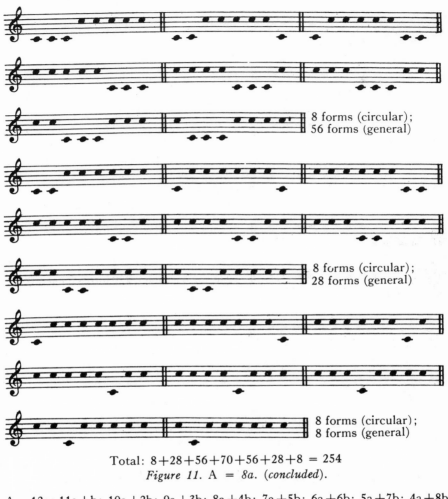

8 forms (circular);
56 forms (general)

8 forms (circular);
28 forms (general)

8 forms (circular);
8 forms (general)

Total: 8+28+56+70+56+28+8 = 254
Figure 11. A = *8a.* (*concluded*).

A = 12a: 11a+b; 10a+2b; 9a+3b; 8a+4b; 7a+5b; 6a+6b; 5a+7b; 4a+8b;
3a+9b; 2a+10b; a+11b

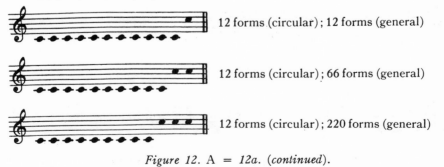

12 forms (circular); 12 forms (general)

12 forms (circular); 66 forms (general)

12 forms (circular); 220 forms (general)

Figure 12. A = *12a.* (*continued*).

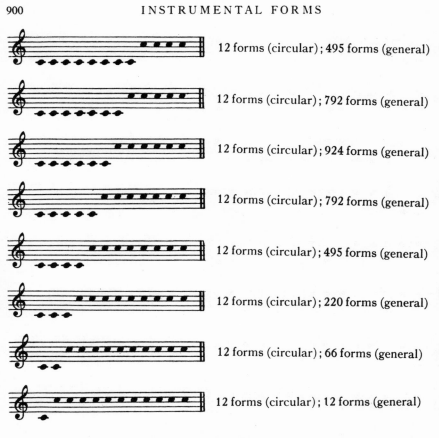

12 forms (circular); 495 forms (general)

12 forms (circular); 792 forms (general)

12 forms (circular); 924 forms (general)

12 forms (circular); 792 forms (general)

12 forms (circular); 495 forms (general)

12 forms (circular); 220 forms (general)

12 forms (circular); 66 forms (general)

12 forms (circular); 12 forms (general)

Total: $12+66+220+495+792+924+792+495+220+66+12 = 4094$

Figure 12. A $= 12a$. *(concluded).*

Examples of the polynomial attack-groups (coefficients of recurrence).

A $= r_{3 \div 2}$ A $= r_{4 \div 3}$

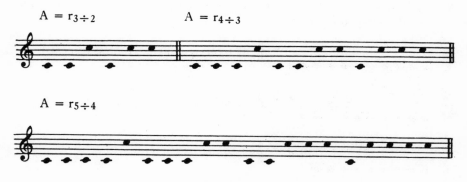

A $= r_{5 \div 4}$

Figure 13. Polynomial attack-groups (continued).

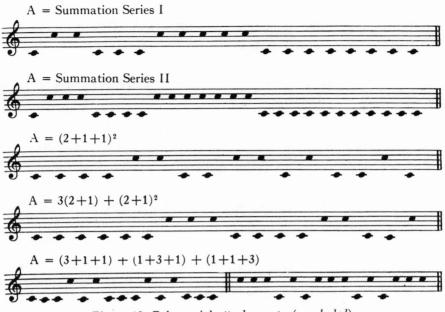

A = Summation Series I

A = Summation Series II

A = $(2+1+1)^2$

A = $3(2+1) + (2+1)^2$

A = $(3+1+1) + (1+3+1) + (1+1+3)$

Figure 13. Polynomial attack-groups (concluded).

B. INSTRUMENTAL FORMS OF S = 2p

The material for these forms is:

(a) coupled melody: M $(\frac{p_I}{p_{II}})$;

(b) harmonic forms of two-unit scales;

(c) two-part harmony;

(d) two-parts of any harmony.

$$I = a: \frac{p_{II}}{p_I}, \frac{p_I}{p_{II}}; \frac{a_2}{b_2} + \frac{b_2}{a_2}; \frac{ma_2}{mb_2} + \frac{nb_2}{na_2}$$

I = ab, ba: permutations of the higher orders.

Coefficients of recurrence: 2a+b; a+2b; . . .

. . . ma + nb.

(a) **Var.**

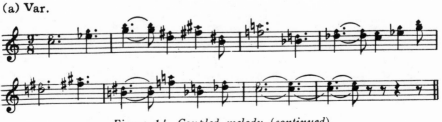

Figure 14. Coupled melody (continued).

Var.

Var.

Figure 14. Coupled melody (concluded).

(b) Scale

$M = 2a_2 + 2b_2 + a_2 + b_2 + 2a_2 + 2b_2; d_0 + d_2 + d_1$ $T = r_5 \div 2;$ $T'' = 8t$

Theme

d₁ begins

Figure 14A. Harmonic forms of two-unit scales (continued).

Figure 14A. Harmonic forms of two-unit scales (concluded).

Var. I: $\dfrac{2a_2 + 2b_2 + a_2 + b_2 + 2a_2 + 2b_2}{2b_2 + 2a_2 + b_2 + a_2 + 2b_2 + 2a_2}$

Figure 14B. Harmonic forms of two-unit scales (continued).

Figure 14B. Harmonic forms of two-unit scales (concluded).

(c) Theme: $S = 2p$

Var. I = $3a_2 + b_2$

Var. I = $3a_2 + b_2$; $T = r_{4 \div 3}$; $T'' = 12t$; $t = \flat$

$T'' = 16t$; $t = \flat$

Var. I $\dfrac{2a_2 + 2b_2}{2b_2 + 2a_2} + \dfrac{2b_2 + 2a_2}{2a_2 + 2b_2}$

Figure 15. Two-part harmony (continued).

When the progression of chords ($H^{\rightarrow}$) has an assigned duration group, instrumental form (I) can be carried out through t.

Theme

Var. I = $a_4 + b_4$; t = ♪

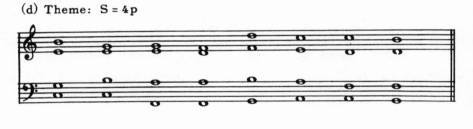

Figure 15. Two-part harmony (concluded).

(d) Theme: S = 4p

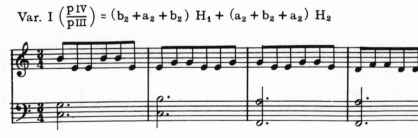

Var. I $\left(\dfrac{\text{p IV}}{\text{p III}}\right)$ = $(b_2 + a_2 + b_2)$ H_1 + $(a_2 + b_2 + a_2)$ H_2

Figure 16. Two parts of any harmony. (continued).

Var. I $\left(\dfrac{pII}{pI}\right)$ = $(a_2 + b_2 + a_2)\ H_1 + (b_2 + a_2 + b_2)\ H_2$

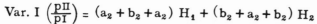

Var.: the two preceding variations combined

Theme: $T = r_{5 \div 4}$

Figure 16. Two parts of any harmony (continued).

Var. I $\left(\dfrac{p\,\mathrm{III},\ p\,\mathrm{IV}}{p\,\mathrm{I},\ p\,\mathrm{II}}\right) = \dfrac{2\,a_2 + b_2 + a_2 + 2\,b_2}{2\,b_2 + a_2 + b_2 + 2\,a_2}$; $t = \eighthnote$

Figure 16. Two parts of any harmony (concluded).

Individual attacks emphasizing one or two parts can be combined into one attack-group of any desirable form.

Example:

$$\qquad\qquad \text{b} \quad \text{bb} \quad \text{bb bbb} \quad\quad \text{bbbb b}$$
1 $(S = 2p)$: aa ; aaaa ; aaa aa ; aa a aa ; . . .

Theme

Var.: $\begin{smallmatrix} \text{b} & \text{b b} \\ \text{a a} & \text{a} \end{smallmatrix}$

Var.: $\left(\begin{smallmatrix} & \text{b b b b} \\ \text{a a a} & \text{a} \end{smallmatrix}\right)$ H.

Figure 17. I (S = 2p.) (continued).

Figure 17. I (S = 2p) (concluded).

CHAPTER 4

STRATA OF THREE PARTS

A. General Classification of I (S = 3p)
  (*A table of the combinations of attacks for a, b, and c*)

A = a; 2a; 3a; 4a; 5a; 6a; 7a; 8a; 12a.

The following is a complete table of all forms of I(S = 3p). It includes *all the combinations and permutations* for 2, 3, 4, 5, 6, 7, 8 and 12 sequent attacks.*

(1) I = ap (one part, one attack).

Three invariant forms: a or b or c.
A = ap, 2ap, . . . map.
This is equivalent to I(S = p).

(2) I = a2p$^{\rightarrow}$ (one attack to a part, two sequent parts)

Three invariant forms: ab, ac, bc.
Each invariant form produces 2 attacks and has 2 permutations.
This is equivalent to I(S = 2p).
Further combinations of ab, ac, bc are not necessary as it corresponds to the forms of (3).

(3) I = a3p$^{\rightarrow}$ (one attack to a part, three sequent parts).

One invariant form: abc.
The invariant form produces 3 attacks and has 6 permutations:
  abc, acb, cab, bac, bca, cba.
All other attack groups (A = 3 + n) develop from this source by means of the coefficients of recurrence.

---

*Here, as on other occasions, Schillinger uses convenient and brief rather than the full mathematical expressions to indicate relationships. For example, in an expression like S = p the coefficients are understood to be 1, i.e., 1 S = 1 p. It does *not* mean, as it would in strict mathematical form, that the number— any number—of strata equals the number of parts. Nor does the juxtaposition of, say, *a* and *p* as in *ap* imply multiplication; on the contrary, it means, as the text makes clear, "one attack to one part"—which would be expressed in rigid mathematical form as

$$\frac{A_1 p}{_1 p} = 1. \qquad \text{(Ed.)}$$

I(S = 3p): attack-groups for one simultaneous p.

A = 3p

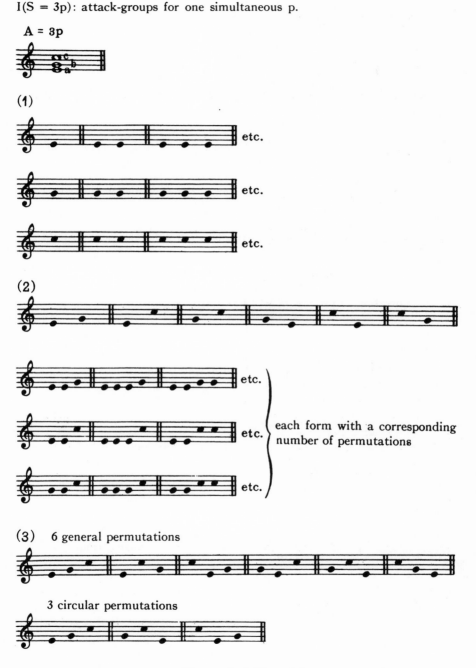

(1)

etc.

etc.

etc.

(2)

etc.

etc. } each form with a corresponding

etc. } number of permutations

(3) 6 general permutations

3 circular permutations

Figure 18. I (S = 3p)

B. Development of Attack-Groups by Means of the Coefficients of Recurrence

$A = 4a;\ 2a+b+c;\ a+2b+c;\ a+b+2c.$

$$P_4 = \frac{4!}{2!} = \frac{24}{2} = 12$$

Each of the above 3 permutations of the coefficients has 12 general permutations.

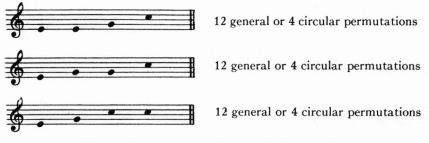

12 general or 4 circular permutations

12 general or 4 circular permutations

12 general or 4 circular permutations

Figure 19. $A = 4a;\ 2a+b+c;\ a+2b+c;\ a+b+2c$

Total in general permutations: $12+12+12 = 36$
Total in circular permutations: $4+4+4 = 12$

$A = 5a.$

Forms of the distribution of coefficients:
$$5 = 2+2+1 \text{ and } 5 = 1+1+3$$
$$A = 2a+2b+c;\ 2a+b+2c;\ a+2b+2c$$
$$P_5 = \frac{5!}{2!\ 2!} = \frac{120}{2\cdot2} = 30$$

Each of the 3 permutations of the first form of distribution has 30 general permutations. Total: $30\cdot3 = 90$.

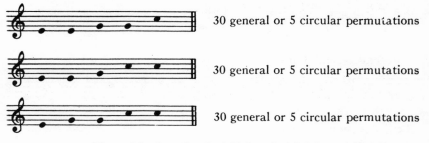

30 general or 5 circular permutations

30 general or 5 circular permutations

30 general or 5 circular permutations

Figure 20. $A = 5a;\ 2a+2b+c;\ 2a+b+2c;\ a+2b+2c$

Total in general permutations: $30+30+30 = 90$
Total in circular permutations: $5+5+5 = 15$

$$A = a+b+3c; \ a+3b+c; \ 3a+b+c.$$
$$P_5 = \frac{5!}{3!} = \frac{120}{6} = 20$$

Each of the above 3 permutations of the second form of distribution has 20 general permutations. Total: $20 \cdot 3 = 60$.

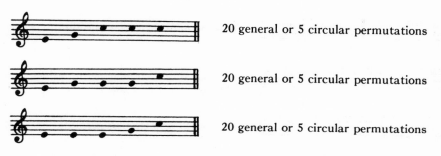

20 general or 5 circular permutations

20 general or 5 circular permutations

20 general or 5 circular permutations

Figure 21. A = 5a; a+b+3c; a+3b+c; 3a+b+c.

Total in general permutations: $20+20+20 = 60$
Total in circular permutations: $5+5+5 = 15$
The entire total for 5 attacks: in general permutations: 150
in circular permutations: 30

A = 6a.

Forms of the distribution of coefficients:
$$6 = 1+1+4; \ 1+2+3; \ 2+2+2.$$
$$A = a+b+4c; \ a+4b+c; \ 4a+b+c.$$
$$P_6 = \frac{6!}{4!} = \frac{720}{24} = 30$$

Each of the above 3 permutations of the first form of distribution has 30 general permutations.

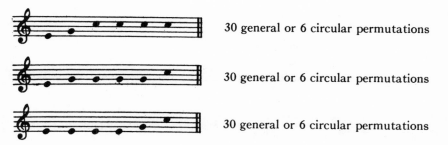

30 general or 6 circular permutations

30 general or 6 circular permutations

30 general or 6 circular permutations

Figure 22. A = 6a; a+b+4c; a+4b+c; a+b+4c.

Total in general permutations: $30 \cdot 3 = 90$
Total in circular permutations: $6 \cdot 3 = 18$

$$A = a+2b+3c; \ a+3b+2c; \ 3a+b+2c; \ 2a+b+3c; \ 2a+3b+c; \ 3a+2b+c.$$

$$P_6 = \frac{6!}{2! \ 3!} = \frac{720}{2 \cdot 6} = 60$$

Each of the above 6 permutations of the second form of distribution has 60 general permutations.

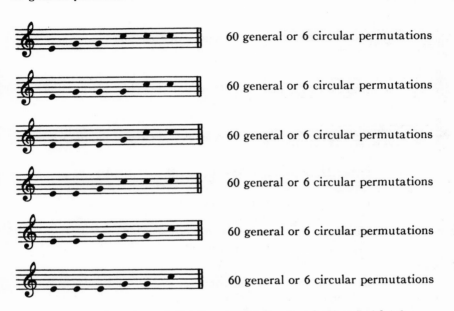

60 general or 6 circular permutations

60 general or 6 circular permutations

60 general or 6 circular permutations

60 general or 6 circular permutations

60 general or 6 circular permutations

60 general or 6 circular permutations

Figure 23. A = 6a; a+2b+3c; a+3b+2c; 3a+b+2c; 2a+b+3c; 2a+3b+c; 2a+2b+c

Total in general permutations: $60 \cdot 6 = 360$
Total in circular permutations: $6 \cdot 6 = 36$

$$A = 2a+2b+2c.$$

$$P_6 = \frac{6!}{2! \ 2! \ 2!} = \frac{720}{2 \cdot 2 \cdot 2} = 90$$

The third form of distribution (invariant) has 90 general permutations

90 general or 6 circular permutations

Figure 24. A = 6a: 2a+2b+2c.

The entire total for 6 attacks: in general permutations: 540
in circular permutations: 60

A = 7a.

Forms of the distribution of coefficients:

$$7 = 1+1+5; \ 1+2+4; \ 2+2+3; \ 3+3+1$$
$$A = a+b+5c; \ a+5b+c; \ 5a+b+c,.$$
$$P_7 = \frac{7!}{5!} = \frac{5040}{120} = 42$$

Each of the above 3 permutations of the first form of distribution has 42 general permutations.

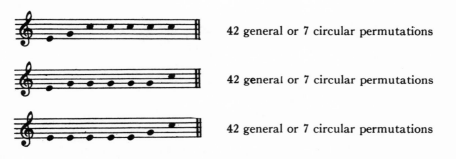

42 general or 7 circular permutations

42 general or 7 circular permutations

42 general or 7 circular permutations

Figure 25. A = 7a; a+b+5c; a+5b+c; 5a+b+c.

Total in general permutations: $42 \cdot 3 = 126$
Total in circular permutations: $7 \cdot 3 = 21$

$$A = a+2b+4c; \ a+4b+2c; \ 4a+b+2c; \ 2a+b+4c; \ 2a+4b+c; \ 4a+2b+c.$$
$$P_7 = \frac{7!}{2! \ 4!} = \frac{5040}{2 \cdot 24} = 105$$

Each of the above 6 permutations of the second form of distribution has 105 general permutations.

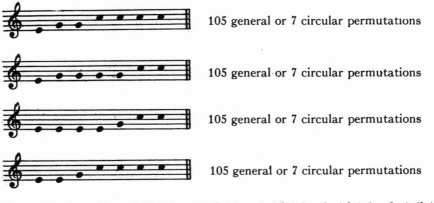

105 general or 7 circular permutations

105 general or 7 circular permutations

105 general or 7 circular permutations

105 general or 7 circular permutations

Figure 26. A = 7a; a+2b+4c; a+4b+2c; 4a+b+2c; 2a+b+4c; 2a+4b+c;
4a+2b+c (continued).

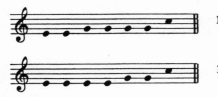

105 general or 7 circular permutations

105 general or 7 circular permutations

Figure 26. A = 7a; a+2b+4c; a+4b+2c; 4c+b+2c; 2a+b+4c; 2a+4b+c; 4a+2b+c (concluded).

Total in general permutations: 105·6 = 630
Total in circular permutations: 7·6 = 42

$A = 2a+2b+3c; \ 2a+3b+2c; \ 3a+2b+2c.$

$$P_7 = \frac{7!}{2! \ 3! \ 2!} = \frac{5040}{2 \cdot 6 \cdot 2} = 210$$

Each of the above 3 permutations of the third form of distribution has 210 general permutations.

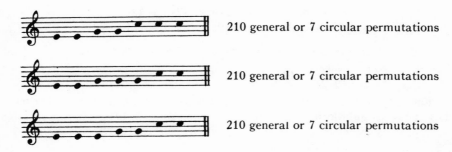

210 general or 7 circular permutations

210 general or 7 circular permutations

210 general or 7 circular permutations

Figure 27. A = 7a; 2a+2b+3c; 2a+3b+2c; 3a+2b+2c.

Total in general permutations: 210·3 = 630
Total in circular permutations: 7·3 = 21

$A = 3a+3b+c; \ 3a+b+3c; \ a+3b+3c.$

$$P_7 = \frac{7!}{3! \ 3!} = \frac{5040}{6 \cdot 6} = 140$$

Each of the above 3 permutations of the fourth form of distribution has 140 general permutations.

See Figure 28 on the following page.

140 general or 7 circular permutations

140 general or 7 circular permutations

140 general or 7 circular permutations

Figure 28. A = 7a; 3a+3b+c; 3a+b+3c; a+3b+3c.

Total in general permutations: $140 \cdot 3 = 420$
Total in circular permutations: $7 \cdot 3 = 21$

The entire total for 7 attacks: in general permutations: 1806
in circular permutations: 105

A = 8a.

Forms of the distribution of coefficients:

$$8 = 1+1+6; 1+2+5; 1+3+4; 2+2+4; 2+3+3$$

$$A = a+b+6c; a+6b+c; 6a+b+c.$$

$$P_8 = \frac{8!}{6!} = \frac{40,320}{720} = 56$$

Each of the two above 3 permutations of the first form of distribution has 56 general permutations.

Total: $56 \cdot 3 = 168$

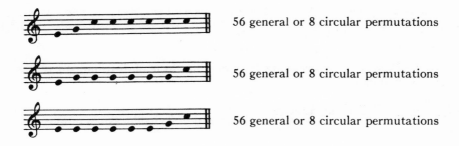

56 general or 8 circular permutations

56 general or 8 circular permutations

56 general or 8 circular permutations

Figure 29. A = 8a; a+b+6c; a+6b+c; 6a+b+c.

Total in general permutations: $56 \cdot 3 = 168$
Total in circular permutations: $8 \cdot 3 = 24$

$$A = a+2b+5c; \ a+5b+2c; \ 5a+b+2c; \ 2a+b+5c; \ 2a+5b+c; \ 5a+2b+c.$$

$$P_8 = \frac{8!}{2! \ 5!} = \frac{40,320}{2 \cdot 120} = 168$$

Each of the above 6 permutations of the second form of distribution has 168 general permutations.

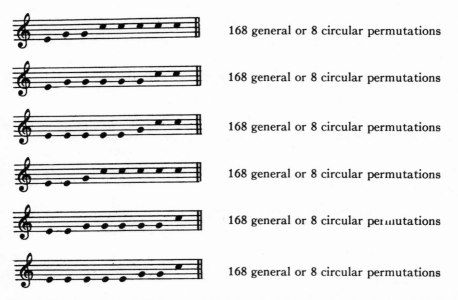

168 general or 8 circular permutations

168 general or 8 circular permutations

168 general or 8 circular permutations

168 general or 8 circular permutations

168 general or 8 circular permutations

168 general or 8 circular permutations

Figure 30. $A = 8a; \ a+2b+5c; \ a+5b+2c; \ 5a+b+2c; \ 2a+b+5c; \ 2a+5b+c;$
$5a+2b+c.$

Total in general permutations: $168 \cdot 6 = 1008$
Total in circular permutations: $8 \cdot 6 = \quad 48$

$$A = a+3b+4c; \ a+4b+3c; \ 4a+b+3c; \ 3a+b+4c; \ 3a+4b+c; \ 4a+3b+c.$$

$$P_8 = \frac{8!}{3! \ 4!} = \frac{40,320}{6 \cdot 24} = 280$$

Each of the above 6 permutations of the third form of distribution has 280 general permutations.

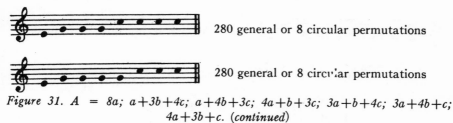

280 general or 8 circular permutations

280 general or 8 circular permutations

Figure 31. $A = 8a; \ a+3b+4c; \ a+4b+3c; \ 4a+b+3c; \ 3a+b+4c; \ 3a+4b+c;$
$4a+3b+c.$ (*continued*)

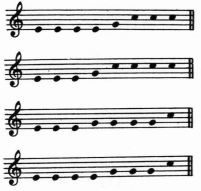

280 general or 8 circular permutations

280 general or 8 circular permutations

280 general or 8 circular permutations

280 general or 8 circular permutations

Figure 31. A = 8a; a+3b+4c; a+4b+3c; 4a+b+3c; 3a+b+4c; 3a+4b+c;
4a+3b+ c (concluded).

Total in general permutations: 280·6 = 1680
Total in circular permutations: 8·6 =   48

$A = 2a+2b+4c;\ 2a+4b+2c;\ 4a+2b+2c$

$$P_8 = \frac{8!}{2!\ 2!\ 4!} = \frac{40,320}{2·2·24} = 420$$

Each of the above 3 permutations of the fourth form of distribution has 420 general permutations.

420 general or 8 circular permutations

420 general or 8 circular permutations

420 general or 8 circular permutations

Figure 32. A = 8a; 2a+2b+4c; 2a+4b+2c; 4a+2b+2c.

Total in general permutations: 420·3 = 1260
Total in circular permutations: 8·3 =   24

$A = 2a+3b+3c;\ 3a+2b+3c;\ 3a+3b+2c$

$$P_8 = \frac{8!}{2!\ 3!\ 3!} = \frac{40,320}{2·6·6} = 560$$

Each of the above 3 permutations of the fifth form of distribution has 560 general permutations.

See Figure 33 on the following page.

560 general or 8 circular permutations

560 general or 8 circular permutations

560 general or 8 circular permutations

Figure 33. A = 8a; 2a+3b+3c; 3a+2b+3c; 3a+3b+2c.

Total in general permutations: 560·3 = 1680
Total in circular permutations: 8·3 =   24

The total number of cases: A = 8a
General permutations: 168 + 1008 + 1680 + 1260 + 1680 = 5796
Circular permutations: 24 + 48 + 48 + 24 + 24 = 168

A = 12a.

Forms of the distribution of coefficients:

8 = 1+1+10; 1+2+9; 1+3+8; 1+4+7; 1+5+6; 2+2+8;
    2+3+7; 2+4+6; 2+5+5; 3+3+6; 3+4+5; 4+4+4.

$A = a+b+10c; a+10b+c; 10a+b+c$

$$P_{12} = \frac{12!}{10!} = \frac{479,001,600}{3,628,800} = 132$$

Each of the above 3 permutations of the first form of distribution has **132** general permutations.

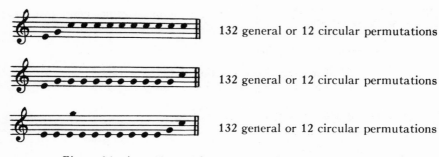

132 general or 12 circular permutations

132 general or 12 circular permutations

132 general or 12 circular permutations

Figure 34. A = 12a; a+b+10c; a+10b+c; 10a+b+c.

Total in general permutations: 132·3 = 396
Total in circular permutations: 12·3 =   36

$A = a+2b+9c; a+9b+2c; 9a+b+2c; 2a+b+9c; 2a+9b+c; 9a+2b+c.$

$$P_{12} = \frac{12!}{2!\ 9!} = \frac{479,001,600}{2 \cdot 362,880} = 660$$

Each of the above 6 permutations of the second form of distribution has 660 general permutations.

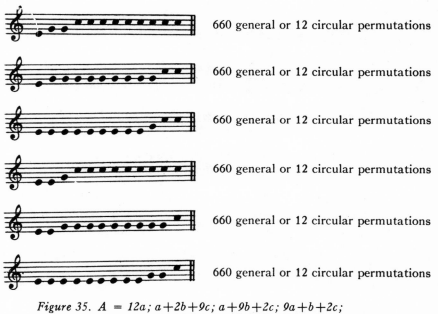

660 general or 12 circular permutations

660 general or 12 circular permutations

660 general or 12 circular permutations

660 general or 12 circular permutations

660 general or 12 circular permutations

660 general or 12 circular permutations

Figure 35. A = 12a; a+2b+9c; a+9b+2c; 9a+b+2c;
2a+b+9c; 2a+9b+c; 9a+2b+c.

Total in general permutations: $660 \cdot 6 = 3960$
Total in circular permutations: $12 \cdot 6 = 72$

$A = a+3b+8c; a+8b+3c; 8a+b+3c; 3a+b+8c; 3a+8b+c; 8a+3b+c.$

$$P_{12} = \frac{12!}{3!\ 8!} = \frac{479,001,600}{6 \cdot 40,320} = 1980$$

Each of the above 6 permutations of the third form of distribution has 1980 general permutations.

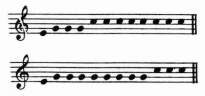

1980 general or 12 circular permutations

1980 general or 12 circular permutations

Figure 36. A = 12a; a+3b+8c; a+8b+3c; 8a+b+3c; 3a+b+8c; 3a+8b+c;
8a+3b+c (continued).

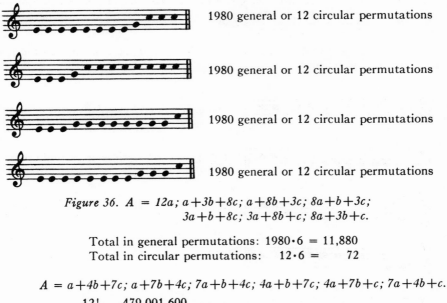

Figure 36. *A* = *12a; a+3b+8c; a+8b+3c; 8a+b+3c;*
3a+b+8c; 3a+8b+c; 8a+3b+c.

Total in general permutations: 1980·6 = 11,880
Total in circular permutations: 12·6 =   72

$$A = a+4b+7c;\ a+7b+4c;\ 7a+b+4c;\ 4a+b+7c;\ 4a+7b+c;\ 7a+4b+c.$$

$$P_{12} = \frac{12!}{4!\ 7!} = \frac{479,001,600}{24\cdot 5,040} = 3960$$

Each of the above 6 permutations of the fourth form of distribution has 3960 general permutations.

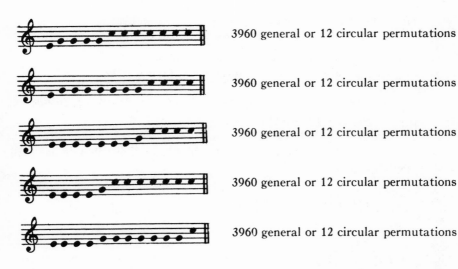

Figure 37. *A* = *12a; a+4b+7c; a+7b+4c; 7a+b+4c; 4a+b+7c; 4a+7b+c;*
7a+4b+c (continued).

 3960 general or 12 circular permutations

Figure 37. $A = 12a;\ a+4b+7c;\ a+7b+4c;\ 7a+b+4c;\ 4a+b+7c;\ 4a+7b+c;$
$7a+4b+c.$ (*concluded.*)

Total in general permutations: $3960 \cdot 6 = 23,760$
Total in circular permutations: $12 \cdot 6 = 72$

$A = a+5b+6c;\ a+6b+5a;\ 6a+b+5c;\ 5a+b+6c;\ 5a+6b+c;\ 6a+5b+c.$

$$P_{12} = \frac{12!}{5!\ 6!} = \frac{479,001,600}{120 \cdot 720} = 5544$$

Each of the above 6 permutations of the fifth form of distribution has 5544 general permutations.

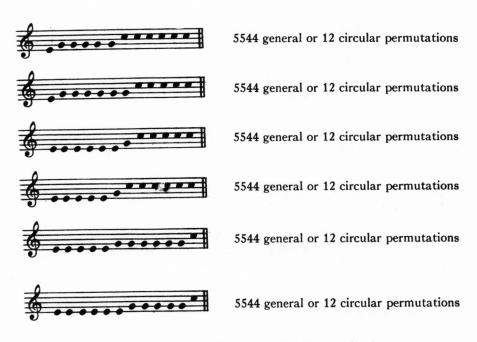

5544 general or 12 circular permutations

5544 general or 12 circular permutations

5544 general or 12 circular permutations

5544 general or 12 circular permutations

5544 general or 12 circular permutations

5544 general or 12 circular permutations

Figure 38. $A = 12a;\ a+5b+6c;\ a+6b+5c;\ 6a+b+5c:$
$5a+b+6c;\ 5a+6b+c;\ 6a+5b+c.$

Total in general permutations: $5544 \cdot 6 = 32,264$
Total in circular permutations: $12 \cdot 6 = 72$

$$A = 2a+2b+8c; \; 2a+8b+2c; \; 8a+2b+2c.$$

$$P_{12} = \frac{12!}{2! \; 2! \; 8!} = \frac{479,001,600}{2 \cdot 2 \cdot 40,320} = 2970$$

Each of the above 3 permutations of the sixth form of distribution has 2970 general permutations.

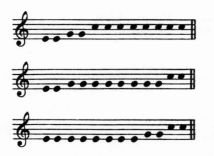

2970 general or 12 circular permutations

2970 general or 12 circular permutations

2970 general or 12 circular permutations

Figure 39. $A = 12a; \; 2a+2b+8c; \; 2a+8b+2c; \; 8a+2b+2c$

Total in general permutations: $2970 \cdot 3 = 8910$
Total in circular permutations: $\quad 12 \cdot 3 = \quad 36$

$$A = 2a+3b+7c; \; 2a+7b+3c; \; 7a+2b+3c; \; 3a+2b+7c;$$
$$3a+7b+2c; \; 7a+3b+2c.$$

$$P_{12} = \frac{12!}{2! \; 3! \; 7!} = \frac{479,001,600}{2 \cdot 6 \cdot 5,040} = 7920$$

Each of the above 6 permutations of the seventh form of distribution has 7920 general permutations.

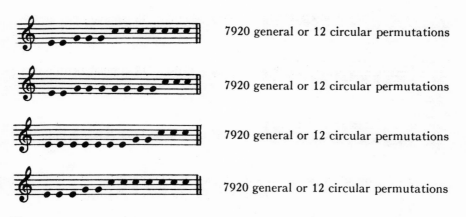

7920 general or 12 circular permutations

7920 general or 12 circular permutations

7920 general or 12 circular permutations

7920 general or 12 circular permutations

Figure 40. $A = 12a; \; 2a+3b+7c; \; 2c+7b+3c; \; 7a+2b+3c; 3a+2b+7c; \; 3c+7b+2c;$
$7a+3b+2c.$ (continued).

 7920 general or 12 circular permutations

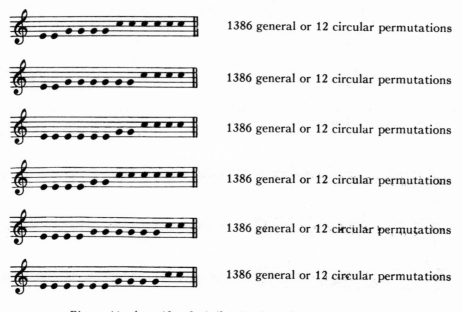

7920 general or 12 circular permutations

Figure 40. A = 12a; 2a+3b+7c; 2a+7b+3c; 7a+2b+3c; 3a+2b+7c;
3a+7b+2c; 7a+3b+2c. (concluded).

Total in general permutations: $7920 \cdot 6 = 47,520$
Total in circular permutations: $12 \cdot 6 = \qquad 72$

$A = 2a+4b+6c; 2a+6b+4c; 6a+2b+4c; 4a+2b+6c;$
$4a+6b+2c; 6a+4b+2c.$

$$P_{12} = \frac{12!}{2!\ 4!\ 6!} = \frac{479,001,600}{2 \cdot 23 \cdot 720} = 1386$$

Each of the above 6 permutations of the eighth form of distribution has 1386 general permutations.

1386 general or 12 circular permutations

1386 general or 12 circular permutations

1386 general or 12 circular permutations

1386 general or 12 circular permutations

1386 general or 12 circular permutations

1386 general or 12 circular permutations

Figure 41. A = 12a; 2a+4b+6c; 2a+6b+4c; 6a+2b+4c;
4a+2b+6c; 4a+6b+2c; 6a+4b+2c.

Total in general permutations: $1386 \cdot 6 = 8316$
Total in circular permutations: $12 \cdot 6 = \qquad 72$

$$A = 2a+5b+5c; \ 5a+2b+5c; \ 5a+5b+2c.$$

$$P_{12} = \frac{12!}{2! \ 5! \ 5!} = \frac{479,001,600}{2 \cdot 120 \cdot 120} = 16,632$$

Each of the above 3 permutations of the ninth form of distribution has 16,632 general permutations.

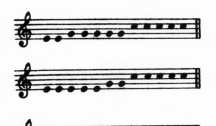

16,632 general or 12 circular permutations

16,632 general or 12 circular permutations

16,632 general or 12 circular permutations

Figure 42. A = 12a; 2a+5b+5c; 5a+2b+5c; 5a+5b+2c.

Total in general permutations: $16,632 \cdot 3 = 49,896$
Total in circular permutations: $\quad 12 \cdot 3 = \quad 36$

$$A = 3a+3b+6c; \ 3a+6b+3c; \ 6a+3b+3c.$$

$$P_{12} = \frac{12!}{3! \ 3! \ 6!} = \frac{479,001,600}{6 \cdot 6 \cdot 720} = 18,480$$

Each of the above 3 permutations of the tenth form of distribution has 18,480 general permutations.

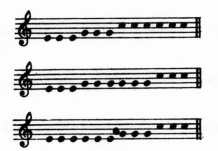

18,480 general or 12 circular permutations

18,480 general or 12 circular permutations

18,480 general or 12 circular permutations

Figure 43. A = 12a: 3a+3b+6c: 3a+6b+3c: 6a+3b+3c

Total in general permutations: $18,480 \cdot 3 = 55,440$
Total in circular permutations: $\quad 12 \cdot 3 = \quad 36$

$A = 3a+4b+5c;\ 3a+5b+4c;\ 5a+3b+4c;$
$\quad 4a+3b+5c;\ 4a+5b+3c;\ 5a+4b+3c.$

$$P_{12} = \frac{12!}{3!\ 4!\ 5!} = \frac{479,001,600}{6\cdot24\cdot120} = 27,720$$

Each of the above 6 permutations of the eleventh form of distribution has 27,720 general permutations.

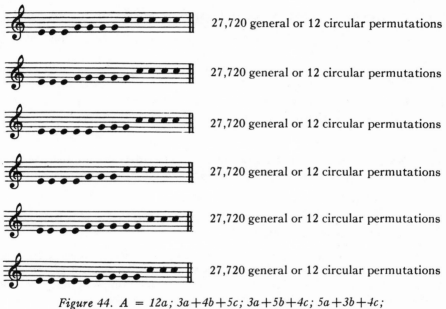

27,720 general or 12 circular permutations

27,720 general or 12 circular permutations

27,720 general or 12 circular permutations

27,720 general or 12 circular permutations

27,720 general or 12 circular permutations

27,720 general or 12 circular permutations

Figure 44. $A = 12a;\ 3a+4b+5c;\ 3a+5b+4c;\ 5a+3b+4c;$
$\quad 4a+3b+5c;\ 4a+5b+3c;\ 5a+4b+3c.$

Total in general permutations: $27,720\cdot6 = 166,320$
Total in circular permutations: $\quad\ 12\cdot6 = \quad\quad 72$

$A = 4a+4b+4c$

$$P_{12} = \frac{12!}{4!\ 4!\ 4!} = \frac{479,001,600}{24\cdot24\cdot24} = 34,650$$

34,650 general or 12 circular permutations

Figure 45. $A = 12a;\ 4a+4b+4c.$

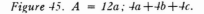

The total number of cases: A = 12a.

General permutations: 396 + 3960 + 11,880 + 23,760 + 32,264 + 8910 +
+ 47,520 + 8316 + 49,896 + 55,440 + 166,320 +
+ 34,650 = 443,312.

Circular permutations: 36 + 72 + 72 + 72 + 72 + 36 + 72 + 72 + 36 + 36 +
+ 72 + 12 = 660

(4) I = a2p (one attack to a combination or two simultaneous parts).*

The three invariant forms of (2) become elements of the second order:

$$\frac{b}{a} = a_2 \; ; \quad \frac{c}{a} = b_2 \; ; \quad \frac{c}{b} = c_2$$

Further combinations in sequence necessitate the inclusion of all three parts.
Sequent combinations by two:

$$a_2 + b_2 \; ; \; a_2 + c_2 \; ; \; b_2 + c_2$$

This corresponds to two consecutive attacks. The growth of attack-groups is
achieved by means of the coefficients of recurrence:

$$2a_2 + b_2 \; ; \; 3b_2 + c_2 \; ; \; 2a_2 + 3b_2 \; ; \; 2a_2 + c_2 + a_2 + 2c_2$$

ᴛhe latter, in turn, become subject to permutations (general or circular), as well
as to permutations of the higher orders.

Sequent combination by three (there is only one such combination): $a_2 +$
$+ b_2 + c_2$. The latter with its permutations becomes an element of the third
order: $a_2 + b_2 + c_2 = a_3$. The development of attack groups by means of the
coefficients of recurrence corresponds to figures 19-45 inclusive in classification
and quantity.

Table of $I(S = 3p) = a2p$.

2 permutations to each combination

Figure 46. I (S = 3p) = a2p (continued).

---

*We are here concerned no longer with
I = a2p→, in which the 2p→ denotes two
sequent parts, but with I = a2p, in which
the absence of the → denotes two simultaneous
parts. (Ed.)

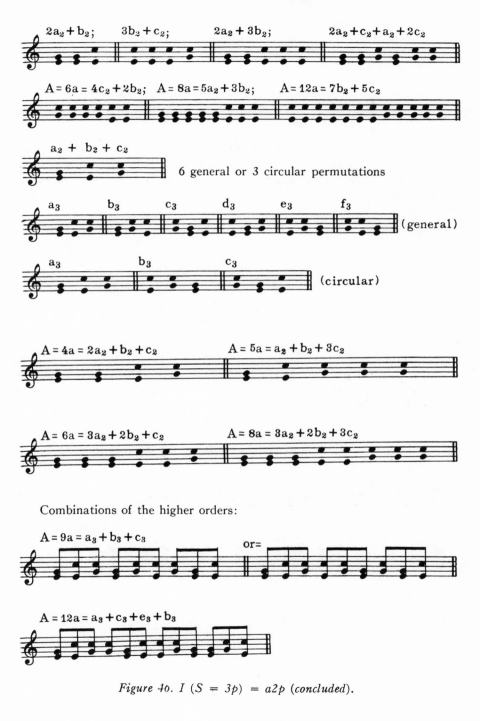

Figure 40. I (S = 3p) = a2p (concluded).

(5) I = a3p (one attack to a combination of three simultaneous parts)

One invariant form: $\dfrac{\genfrac{}{}{0pt}{}{c}{b}}{a} = a_2$

Multiplication of attacks is achieved by direct repetition: A = a_2; $2a_2$; $3a_2$; . . . ma_2.

Further variations may be obtained by means of permutations of the vertical (simultaneous) arrangement of parts. The extreme $p^{\rightarrow}$ of a given position must serve as a limit, that is, for a position above the original, c is the limit for the lower function, and for a position below the original, a is the limit for the upper function.

The original position, in relation to all the upper and all the lower positions, is:

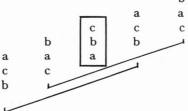

The positions indicated by the brackets are *identical but in different octaves.* It is desirable to use the adjacent positions in a sequence. From the above variations of the original position, any number of attacks can be devised.

Table of I(S = 3p) = a3p

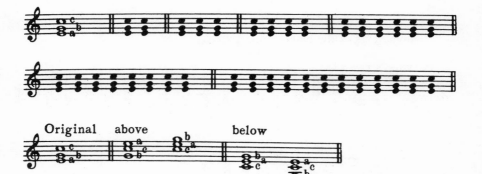

Figure 47. I (S = 3p) = a3p (continued).

Figure 47. I (S = 3p) = a3p (concluded).

C. Instrumental Forms of S = 3p

Material:

(1). melody with two couplings: $M \begin{pmatrix} P_{III} \\ P_{II} \\ P_{I} \end{pmatrix}$;

(2). harmonic forms of three-unit scales;

(3). three-part harmony;

(4). three parts of any harmony.

$$I = a: \frac{\begin{array}{c}p_{III}\\p_{II}\\p_{I}\end{array}}{} \quad \text{(6 general or 3 circular permutations)};$$

$$\frac{\begin{array}{c}c_2\\b_2\\a_2\end{array}}{} \quad \text{(6 general or 3 circular permutations)};$$

$$\frac{mc_2}{mb_2} + \frac{nc_2}{nb_2} + \frac{pc_2}{pb_2} \quad \text{(6 general or 3 circular permutations of the coefficients m, n, p)}$$

1. Melody with two couplings: M $\left(\frac{p_{III}}{\frac{p_{II}}{p_{I}}}\right)$. Illustrated by a theme and six variations. See figures 48 to 54 inclusive.

Examples of application of the I(S = 3p)

Figure 48. Theme.

Figure 49. Variation: abc constant.

Figure 50. Variation: abc + bca + cab.

Figure 51. Variation: 2a + b + a + 2c

Figure 52. Variation: $a_2 + b_2 + c_2$ (continued).

Figure 52. Variation: $a_2 + b_2 + c_2$ (concluded).

Figure 53. Variation: $(2a_2 + b_2 + c_2) + (a_2 + 2b_2 + c_2) + (a_2 + b_2 + 2c_2)$

Figure 54. Variations: a_3 (continued).

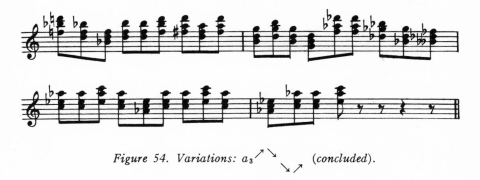

Figure 54. Variations: a_3 (concluded).

2. Harmonic forms of three-unit scales.

Illustrated by a series of themes and variations. See figures 55, 56 and 57.

Theme:

T= r 4 ÷ 3

Var.: $2a_2 + b_2 + c_2$

Var.: $2a_2 + b_2 + c_2$ T = 12t

Figure 55. Theme and two variations.

Figure 56. *Theme and variation.*

Figure 57. *Theme and variation.*

3. Three-part harmony. Illustrated by themes and variations. See figures 58 to 67 inclusive.

Theme:

Var.: $I = a_2 + b_2 + c_2$

Var.: I (abc + abc + ab) + (bca + bc + bca) + (ca + cab + cab)

etc.

Var.: $I = 3\flat = \dfrac{\dfrac{2c_2}{2b_2}}{2a_2} + \dfrac{\dfrac{a_2}{c_2}}{b_2} + \dfrac{\dfrac{3b_2}{3a_2}}{3c_2}$

Figure.58.·Theme and variations (continued).

Figure 58. Theme and Variations I = 3p⃗ (concluded).

Var.: $I = 6p^{\rightarrow}$ (general permutations); $A = 5a = a+2b+2c$.

Sequent circular permutations of the coefficients:

$(a+2b+2c) + (2a+c+2b) + (2c+2a+b) +$
$+ (b+2a+2c) + (2b+c+2a) + (2c+2b+a)$.

$T = 6t = (2+1+1+1+1) + (1+1+2+1+1) + (1+1+1+1+2)$

Figure 59. Variation. I = 6p⃗ (continued).

Figure 59. Variation. T = 6p→ (concluded).

Var.: I = a2p: $(2a_2 + b_2 + c_2) + (a_2 + 2b_2 + c_2) + (a_2 + b_2 + 2c_2)$

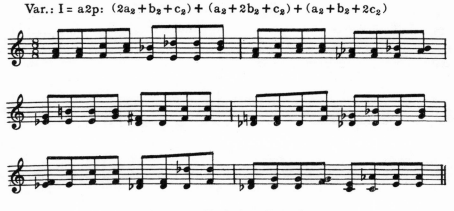

Figure 60. Variation. I = a2p.

Var.: I = a2p: $3a_2 + 2b_2 + c_2$. Three simultaneous parts in circular permutations: $(3a_2 + 2b_2 + c_2) + (2b_2 + c_2 + 3a_2) + (c_2 + 3a_2 + 2b_2)$.

Figure 61. Variation. I = a2p (continued).

Figure 61. Variation. I = a2p (concluded).

Var.: I = a2p: $a_2+b_2+c_2+d_2+e_2+f_2$ in simultaneous general permutations.
T = 2+1+1. T'' = 8t.

Figure 62. Variation. I = a2p (continued).

Figure 62. Variation. I = a2p (concluded).

Var.: I = a3p; A = 6a:

Figure 63. Variation. I = a3p.

FAST MOTION *without final recurrence of the original position* must follow the **ORIGINAL SCHEME** of voice-leading.

Figure 64. Variation. I = a3p.

SLOW MOTION *without final recurrence of the original position* must follow the voice-leading of the **ADJACENT POSITIONS**.

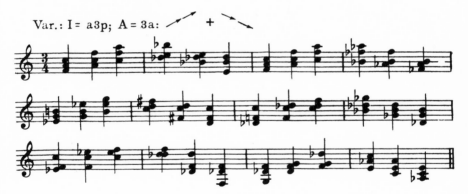

Figure 65. Variation. I = a3p.

Figure 66. Theme.

Var.: I = ap: $a_2 + b_2 + c_2$ in circular permutations

Var.: I = a2p: conditions as above

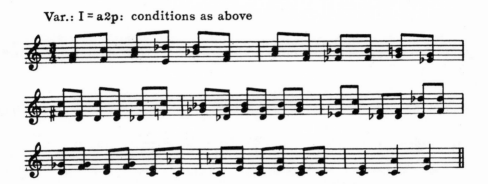

Var.: I = a3p:

Figure 67. Variations. I = a3p.

4. Three parts of any harmony.   Illustrated with a theme and variations. See figure 68.

Theme: $\Sigma = 2S$

Var.: $\left[(a+b+2c)+(a+2b+c)+(2a+b+c)\right]S_1$

Var.: $\left[\left(\begin{smallmatrix} & c & \\ b & & b \\ & a & \end{smallmatrix}\right)H_1 +\left(\begin{smallmatrix} & c & \\ b & & \\ & a & \end{smallmatrix}\right)H_2\right] S_2$

Figure 68. Theme $\Sigma = 2S$ *(continued).*

Var.: The two preceding variations combined

Figure 68. Theme Σ = 2S (concluded).

Individual attacks emphasizing one, two, or three parts may be combined into one attack-group of any desirable form.

Examples

```
              c    cc  cc    c   c cc  c
              b b  b    b b    b  bb     bb
I(S = 3p):   a  aa  aa      ; a  a   aa a      ;
```

```
    c cc c c    c ccccc   c ccc
    b  bbbb    bbbb b   bbb b
    aaaa    a ; aaa   a aa ; aa a a ;
```

```
    c        ccccccc
    bbbbbb    bbb
    aaaaa   aaa a   ; • • •
```

```
    b
    aaa
    ccccc  c c  c
    bb b b bb bb
    a       aaaaa  ; • • •
            c
```

Theme:

Figure 69. Theme and variations (continued).

Figure 69. Theme and Variations.

CHAPTER 5

STRATA OF FOUR PARTS

A. General Classification of $I(S = 4p)$
    (*Table of the combinations of attacks for a, b, c and d*).

A = a; 2a; 3a; 4a; 5a; 6a; 7a; 12a.

The following is a complete table of all forms of $I(S = 4p)$. It includes *all the combinations and permutations* for 2, 3, 4, 5, 6, 7, 8 and 12 attacks.

(1) I = ap (one part, one attack).

Four invariant forms: a, b, c, d. [*See figure 70 (1)*]
A = ap, 2ap, . . . map.
This is equivalent to $I(S = p)$.

(2) I = a2p→ (one attack to a part, two sequent parts).

Six invariant forms: ab, ac, ad, bc, bd, cd. [*See figure 70 (2)*]
Each invariant form produces 2 attacks and has 2 permutations.
This is equivalent to $I(S = 2p)$.

(3) I = a3p→ (one attack to a part, three sequent parts).

Four invariant forms: abc, abd, acd, bcd. [*See figure 70 (3)*]
Each invariant form produces 3 attacks and has 6 general or 3 circular
    permutations.

(4) I = a4p→ (one attack to a part, four sequent parts).

One invariant form: abcd.
The invariant form produces 4 attacks and has 24 general or 4 circular
    permutations. [*See figure 70 (4)*]
All other attack-groups $(A = 4+n)$ develop from this source by means of
    the coefficients of recurrence.

$I(S = 4p)$: attack-groups for one simultaneous p.

A = 4p

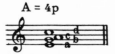

Figure 70. I (S = 4p) (continued).

[948]

(1)

(2)

Each form with a corresponding number of permutations.

Figure 70. I (S = 4p) (continued).

(3)

Each of the above forms has 6 general or 3 circular permutations

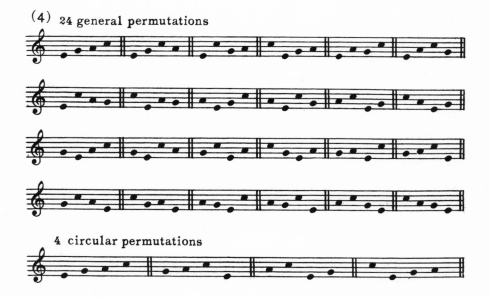

Each form with a corresponding number of permutations

(4) 24 general permutations

4 circular permutations

Figure 70. I (S = 4p) (concluded).

B. DEVELOPMENT OF ATTACK-GROUPS BY MEANS OF
COEFFICIENTS OF RECURRENCE

A = 5a; a+b+c+2d; a+b+2c+d; a+2b+c+d; 2a+b+c+d.

$$P_5 = \frac{5!}{2!} = \frac{120}{2} = 60$$

Each of the above 4 permutations of the coefficients has 60 general per--
mutations.

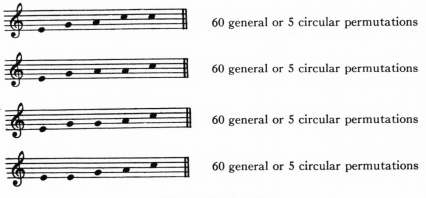

60 general or 5 circular permutations

60 general or 5 circular permutations

60 general or 5 circular permutations

60 general or 5 circular permutations

Figure 71. A = 5a.

Total in general permutations: 60·4 = 240
Total in circular permutations: 5·4 = 20

A = 6a

Forms of the distribution of coefficients:

6 = 1+1+1+3; 1+1+2+2

A = a+b+c+3d; a+b+3c+d; a+3b+c+d; 3a+b+c+d

$$P_6 = \frac{6!}{3!} = \frac{720}{6} = 120$$

Each of the above 4 permutations of the first form of distribution has 120
general permutations.

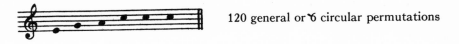

120 general or 6 circular permutations

Figure 72. A = 6a. Permutations of 1+1+1+3 (continued).

120 general or 6 circular permutations

120 general or 6 circular permutations

120 general or 6 circular permutations

Figure 72. A = 6a. Permutations of 1+1+1+3. (concluded).

Total in general permutations: $120 \cdot 4 = 480$
Total in circular permutations: $6 \cdot 4 = 24$

A = a+b+2c+2d; a+2b+2c+d; 2a+2b+c+d; 2a+b+c+2d;
    a+2b+c+2d; 2a+b+2c+d.

$$P_6 = \frac{6!}{2!\ 2!} = \frac{720}{4} = 180$$

Each of the above 6 permutations of the second form of distribution has 180 general permutations.

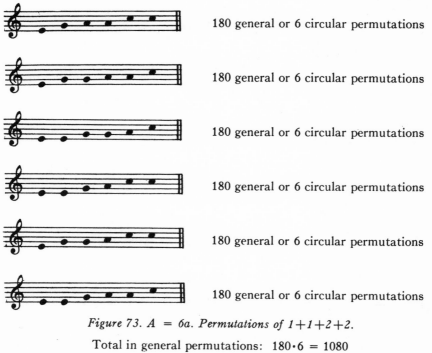
180 general or 6 circular permutations

180 general or 6 circular permutations

180 general or 6 circular permutations

180 general or 6 circular permutations

180 general or 6 circular permutations

180 general or 6 circular permutations

Figure 73. A = 6a. Permutations of 1+1+2+2.

Total in general permutations: $180 \cdot 6 = 1080$
Total in circular permutations: $6 \cdot 6 = 36$

The total number of cases: A = 6a
   General permutations: 480 + 1080 = 1560
   Circular permutations: 24 + 36 = 60

A = 7a

Forms of the distribution of coefficients:

$$7 = 1+1+1+4; \; 1+1+2+3; \; 1+2+2+2$$
$$A = a+b+c+4d; \; a+b+4c+d; \; a+4b+c+d; \; 4a+b+c+d$$

$$P_7 = \frac{7!}{4!} = \frac{5040}{24} = 210$$

Each of the above 4 permutations of the first form of distribution has 210 general permutations.

210 general or 7 circular permutations

210 general or 7 circular permutations

210 general or 7 circular permutations

210 general or 7 circular permutations

Figure 74. A = 7a. Permutations of 1+1+1+4.

Total in general permutations: 210·4 = 840
Total in circular permutations: 7·4 =   28

$$A = a+b+2c+3d; \; a+2b+3c+d; \; 2a+3b+c+d; \; 3a+b+c+2d;$$
$$a+b+3c+2d; \; a+3b+2c+d; \; 3a+2b+c+d; \; 2a+b+c+3d;$$
$$a+2b+c+3d; \; 2a+b+3c+d; \; a+3b+c+2d; \; 3a+b+2c+d$$

$$P_7 = \frac{7!}{2! \; 3!} = \frac{5040}{2 \cdot 6} = 420$$

Each of the above 12 permutations of the second form of distribution has 410 general permutations. See Figure 75 on the following page.

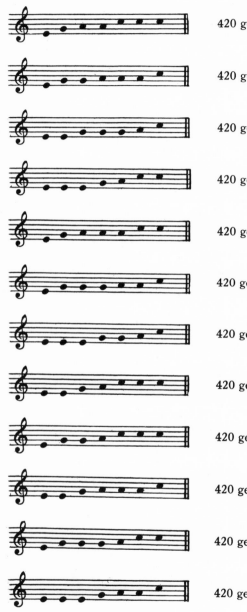

420 general or 7 circular permutations

420 general or 7 circular permutations

420 general or 7 circular permutations

420 general or 7 circular permutations

420 general or 7 circular permutations

420 general or 7 circular permutations

420 general or 7 circular permutations

420 general or 7 circular permutations

420 general or 7 circular permutations

420 general or 7 circular permutations

420 general or 7 circular permutations

420 general or 7 circular permutations

Figure 75. A = 7a. Permutations of 1+1+2+3.

Total in general permutations: $420 \cdot 12 = 5040$
Total in circular permutations: $7 \cdot 12 = 84$

$A = a+2b+2c+2d;\ 2a+b+2c+2d;\ 2a+2b+c+2d;\ 2a+2b+2c+d$

$$P_7 = \frac{7!}{2!\ 2!\ 2!} = \frac{5040}{8} = 630$$

Each of the above 4 permutations of the third form of distribution has 630 general permutations.

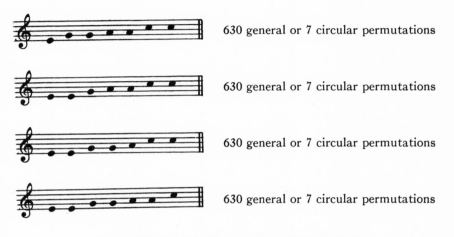

630 general or 7 circular permutations

630 general or 7 circular permutations

630 general or 7 circular permutations

630 general or 7 circular permutations

Figure 76. A = 7a. Permutations of 1+2+2+2.

Total in general permutations: 630·4 = 2520
Total in circular permutations: 7·4 =   28

The total number of cases: A = 7a
   General permutations: 840 + 5040 + 2520 = 8400
   Circular permutations: 28 + 84 + 28 = 140

A = 8a

Forms of the distribution of coefficients:

$8 = 1+1+1+5;\ 1+1+2+4;\ 1+1+3+3;\ 1+2+2+3;\ 2+2+2+2$
$A = a+b+c+5d;\ a+b+5c+d;\ a+5b+c+d;\ 5a+b+c+d$

$$P_8 = \frac{8!}{5!} = \frac{40,320}{120} = 336$$

Each of the above 4 permutations of the first form of distribution has 336 general permutations. See Figure 77 on the following page.

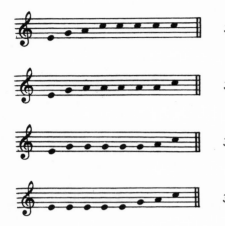

336 general or 8 circular permutations

336 general or 8 circular permutations

336 general or 8 circular permutations

336 general or 8 circular permutations

Figure 77. A = 8a. Permutations of 1+1+1+5.

Total in general permutations: 336·4 = 1344
Total in circular permutations: 8·4 =   32

A = a+b+2c+4d; a+2b+4c+d; 2a+4b+c+d; 4a+b+c+2d;
    a+b+4c+2d; a+4b+2c+d; 4a+2b+c+d; 2a+b+c+4d;
    a+2b+c+4d; 2a+b+4c+d; a+4b+c+2d; 4a+b+2c+d.

$$P_8 = \frac{8!}{2! \ 4!} = \frac{40,320}{2·24} = 840$$

Each of the above 12 permutations of the second form of distribution has 840 general permutations.

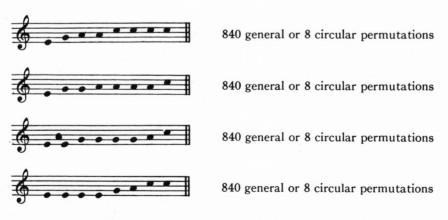

840 general or 8 circular permutations

840 general or 8 circular permutations

840 general or 8 circular permutations

840 general or 8 circular permutations

Figure 78. A = 8a. Permutations of 1+1+2+4 (continued).

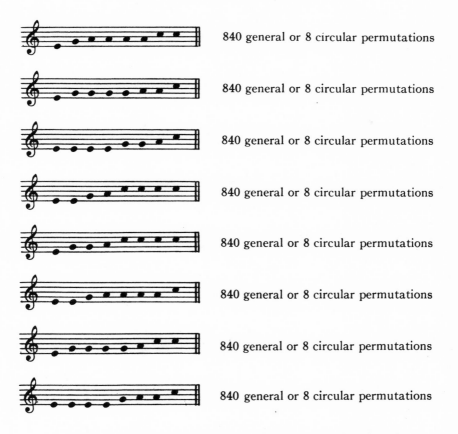

840 general or 8 circular permutations

840 general or 8 circular permutations

840 general or 8 circular permutations

840 general or 8 circular permutations

840 general or 8 circular permutations

840 general or 8 circular permutations

840 general or 8 circular permutations

840 general or 8 circular permutations

Figure 78. A = 8a. Permutations of 1+1+2+4 (concluded).

Total in general permutations: 840·12 = 10,080
Total in circular permutations: 8·12 = 96

A = a+b+3c+3d; a+3b+3c+d; 3a+3b+c+d; 3a+b+c+3d;
   a+3b+c+3d; 3a+b+3c+d.

$$P_8 = \frac{8!}{3!\ 3!} = \frac{40,320}{6 \cdot 6} = 1120$$

Each of the above 6 permutations of the third form of distribution has 1120 general permutations.

 1120 general or 8 circular permutations

Figure 79. A = 8a. Permutations of 1+1+3+3 (continued).

1120 general or 8 circular permutations

1120 general or 8 circular permutations

1120 general or 8 circular permutations

1120 general or 8 circular permutations

1120 general or 8 circular permutations

Figure 79. A = 8a. Permutations of 1+1+3+3 (concluded).

Total in general permutations: 1120·6 = 6720
Total in circular permutations: 8·6 =   48

A = a+2b+2c+3d; 2a+2b+3c+d; 2a+3b+c+2d; 3a+b+2c+2d;
    a+2b+3c+2d; 2a+3b+2c+d; 3a+2b+c+2d; 2a+b+2c+3d;
    a+3b+2c+2d; 3a+2b+2c+d; 2a+2b+c+3d; 2a+b+3c+2d.

$$P_8 = \frac{8!}{2!\ 2!\ 3!} = \frac{40,320}{2\cdot2\cdot6} = 1680$$

Each of the above 12 permutations of the fourth form of distribution has 1680 general permutations.

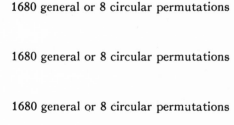

1680 general or 8 circular permutations

1680 general or 8 circular permutations

1680 general or 8 circular permutations

1680 general or 8 circular permutations

Figure 80. A = 8a. Permutations of 1+2+2+3 (continued).

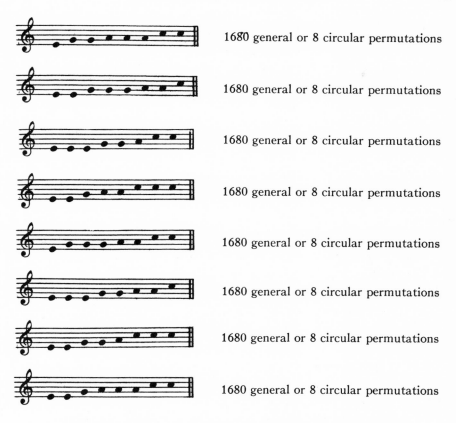

1680 general or 8 circular permutations

1680 general or 8 circular permutations

1680 general or 8 circular permutations

1680 general or 8 circular permutations

1680 general or 8 circular permutations

1680 general or 8 circular permutations

1680 general or 8 circular permutations

1680 general or 8 circular permutations

Figure 80. A = 8a. Permutations of 1+2+2+3 (concluded).

Total in general permutations: $1680 \cdot 12 = 20{,}160$
Total in circular permutations: $8 \cdot 12 = 96$

$A = 2a + 2b + 2c + 2d$

$$P_8 = \frac{8!}{2!\ 2!\ 2!\ 2!} = \frac{40{,}320}{2 \cdot 2 \cdot 2 \cdot 2} = 2520$$

The above invariant (fifth) form of distribution has 2520 general permutations.

2520 general or 8 circular permutations

Figure 81. A = 8a. 2a+2b+2c+2d.

The total number of cases: A = 8a
    General permutations: 1344 + 10,080 + 6720 + 20,160 +
                      + 2520 = 40,824
    Circular permutations: 32 + 96 + 48 + 96 + 8 = 280

A = 12a

Forms of the distribution of coefficients:

$1+1+1+9$; $1+1+2+8$; $1+1+3+7$; $1+1+4+6$; $1+1+5+5$; $1+2+2+7$;
$1+2+3+6$; $1+2+4+5$; $1+3+3+5$; $1+3+4+4$; $2+2+2+6$; $2+2+3+5$;
$2+2+4+4$; $2+3+3+4$; $3+3+3+3$.

$A = a+b+c+9d$; $a+b+9c+d$; $a+9b+c+d$; $9a+b+c+d$

$$P_{12} = \frac{12!}{9!} = \frac{479,001,600}{362,880} = 1320$$

Each of the above 4 permutations of the first form of distribution has 1320 general permutations.

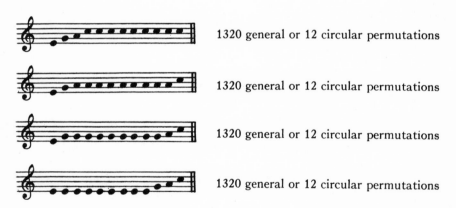

1320 general or 12 circular permutations

1320 general or 12 circular permutations

1320 general or 12 circular permutations

1320 general or 12 circular permutations

Figure 82. A = 12A. Permutations of 1+1+1+9.

Total in general permutations: 1320·4 = 5280
Total in circular permutations: 12·4 =   48

$A = a+b+2c+8d$; $a+2b+8c+d$; $2a+8b+c+d$; $8a+b+c+2d$;
    $a+b+8c+2d$; $a+8b+2c+d$; $8a+2b+c+d$; $2a+b+c+8d$;
    $a+8b+c+2d$; $8a+b+2c+d$; $a+2b+c+8d$; $2a+b+8c+d$.

$$P_{12} = \frac{12!}{2! \; 8!} = \frac{479,001,600}{2 \cdot 40,320} = 5940$$

Each of the above 12 permutations of the second form of distribution has 5940 general permutations. See Figure 83 on the following page.

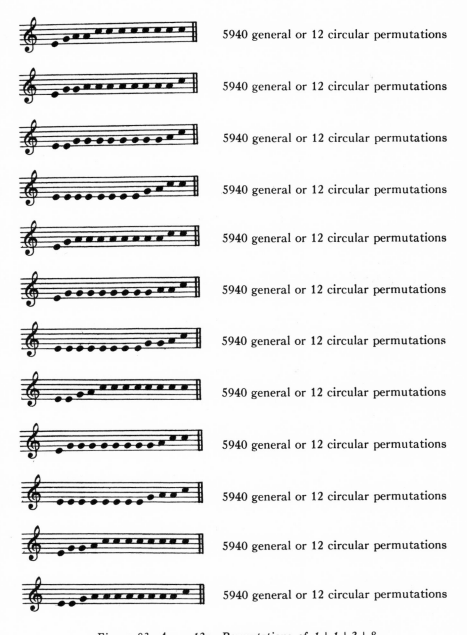

5940 general or 12 circular permutations

5940 general or 12 circular permutations

5940 general or 12 circular permutations

5940 general or 12 circular permutations

5940 general or 12 circular permutations

5940 general or 12 circular permutations

5940 general or 12 circular permutations

5940 general or 12 circular permutations

5940 general or 12 circular permutations

5940 general or 12 circular permutations

5940 general or 12 circular permutations

5940 general or 12 circular permutations

Figure 83. A = 12a. Permutations of 1+1+2+8.

Total in general permutations: 5940·12 = 71,280
Total in circular permutations: 12·12 =   144

A = a+b+3c+7d; a+3b+7c+d; 3a+7b+c+d; 7a+b+c+3d;
　　a+b+7c+3d; a+7b+3c+d; 7a+3b+c+d; 3a+b+c+7d;
　　a+3b+c+7d; 3a+b+7c+d; a+7b+c+3d; 7a+b+3c+d.

$$P_{12} = \frac{12!}{2!\ 7!} = \frac{479,001,600}{6 \cdot 5040} = 15,840$$

Each of the above 12 permutations of the third form of distribution has 15,840 general permutations.

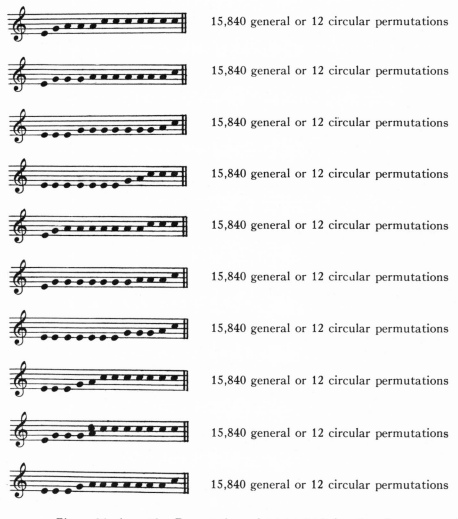

15,840 general or 12 circular permutations

15,840 general or 12 circular permutations

15,840 general or 12 circular permutations

15,840 general or 12 circular permutations

15,840 general or 12 circular permutations

15,840 general or 12 circular permutations

15,840 general or 12 circular permutations

15,840 general or 12 circular permutations

15,840 general or 12 circular permutations

15,840 general or 12 circular permutations

Figure 84. A = 12a. Permutations of 1+1+3+7 (continued).

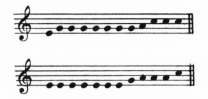 15,840 general or 12 circular permutations

15,840 general or 12 circular permutations

Figure 84. A = 12a. Permutations of 1+1+3+7 (concluded).

Total in general permutations: 15,840·12 = 190,080
Total in circular permutations: 12·12 =   144

$$A = a+b+4c+6d;\ a+4b+6c+d;\ 4a+6b+c+d;\ 6a+b+c+4d;$$
$$a+b+6c+4d;\ a+6b+4c+d;\ 6a+4b+c+d;\ 4a+b+c+6d;$$
$$a+4b+c+6d;\ 4a+b+6c+d;\ a+6b+c+4d;\ 6a+b+4c+d.$$

$$P_{12} = \frac{12!}{4!\ 6!} = \frac{479,001,600}{24\cdot720} = 27,720$$

Each of the above 12 permutations of the fourth form of distribution has 27,720 general permutations.

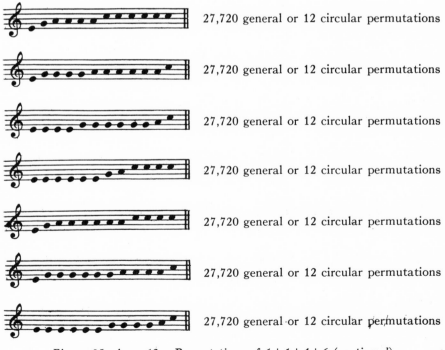

27,720 general or 12 circular permutations

27,720 general or 12 circular permutations

27,720 general or 12 circular permutations

27,720 general or 12 circular permutations

27,720 general or 12 circular permutations

27,720 general or 12 circular permutations

27,720 general or 12 circular permutations

Figure 85. A = 12a. Permutations of 1+1+4+6 (continued).

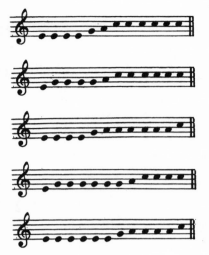

27,720 general or 12 circular permutations

27,720 general or 12 circular permutations

27,720 general or 12 circular permutations

27,720 general or 12 circular permutations

27,720 general or 12 circular permutations

Figure 85. A = 12a. Permutations of 1+1+4+6 (concluded).

Total in general permutations: $27,720 \cdot 12 = 332,640$
Total in circular permutations: $12 \cdot 12 = 144$

$A = a+b+5c+5d$; $a+5b+5c+d$; $5a+5b+c+d$; $5a+b+c+5d$;
$a+5b+c+5d$; $5a+b+5c+d$.

$$P_{12} = \frac{12!}{5! \; 5!} = \frac{479,001,600}{120 \cdot 120} = 33,264$$

Each of the above 6 permutations of the fifth form of distribution has 33,264 general permutations.

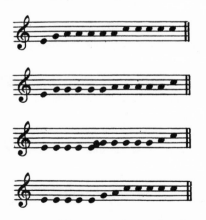

33,264 general or 12 circular permutations

33,264 general or 12 circular permutations

33,264 general or 12 circular permutations

33,264 general or 12 circular permutations

Figure 86. A = 12a. Permutations of 1+1+5+5 (continued).

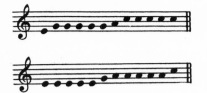

33,264 general or 12 circular permutations

33,264 general or 12 circular permutations

Figure 86. A = 12a. Permutations of 1+1+5+5 (concluded).

Total in general permutations: 33,264·6 = 199,584
Total in circular permutations: 12·6 =   72

A = a+2b+2c+7d; 2a+2b+7c+d; 2a+7b+c+2d; 7a+b+2c+2d;
    a+2b+7c+2d; 2a+7b+2c+d; 7a+2b+c+2d; 2a+b+2c+7d;
    7a+2b+2c+d; 2a+2b+c+7d; 2a+b+7c+2d; a+7b+2c+2d.

$$P_{12} = \frac{12!}{2!\ 2!\ 7!} = \frac{479,001,600}{2\cdot2\cdot5040} = 23,760$$

Each of the above 12 permutations of the sixth form of distribution has 23,760 general permutations.

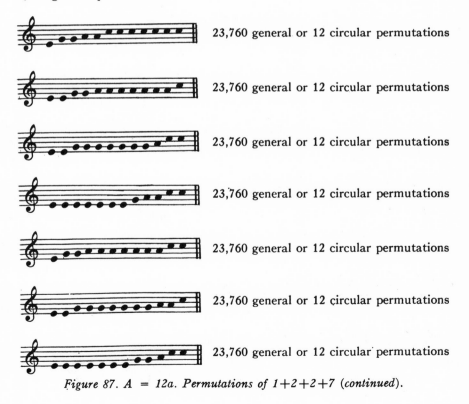

23,760 general or 12 circular permutations

23,760 general or 12 circular permutations

23,760 general or 12 circular permutations

23,760 general or 12 circular permutations

23,760 general or 12 circular permutations

23,760 general or 12 circular permutations

23,760 general or 12 circular permutations

Figure 87. A = 12a. Permutations of 1+2+2+7 (continued).

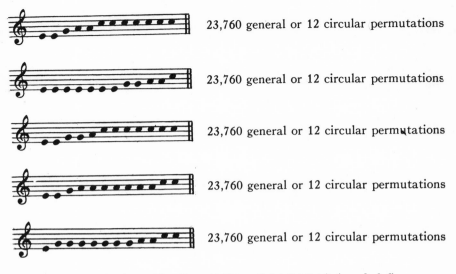

23,760 general or 12 circular permutations

23,760 general or 12 circular permutations

23,760 general or 12 circular permutations

23,760 general or 12 circular permutations

23,760 general or 12 circular permutations

Figure 87. A = 12a. Permutations of 1+2+2+7 (concluded).

Total in general permutations: $23{,}760 \cdot 12 = 285{,}120$
Total in circular permutations: $12 \cdot 12 = 144$

A = a+2b+3c+6d; a+2b+6c+3d; a+6b+2c+3d; 6a+b+2c+3d;
   a+3b+2c+6d; a+3b+6c+2d; a+6b+3c+2d; 6a+b+3c+2d;
   3a+b+2c+6d; 3a+b+6c+2d; 3a+6b+c+2d; 6a+3b+c+2d;
   2a+b+3c+6d; 2a+b+6c+3d; 2a+6b+c+3d; 6a+2b+c+3d;
   2a+3b+c+6d; 2a+3b+6c+d; 2a+6b+3c+d; 6a+2b+3c+d;
   3a+2b+c+6d; 3a+2b+6c+d; 3a+6b+2c+d; 6a+3b+2c+d.

$$P_{12} = \frac{12!}{2!\ 3!\ 6!} = \frac{479{,}001{,}600}{2 \cdot 6 \cdot 720} = 55{,}440$$

Each of the above 24 permutations of the seventh form of distribution has 55,440 general permutations.

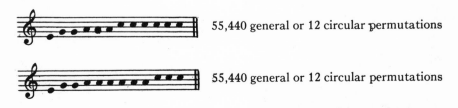

55,440 general or 12 circular permutations

55,440 general or 12 circular permutations

Figure 88. A = 12a. Permutations of 1+2+3+6 (continued).

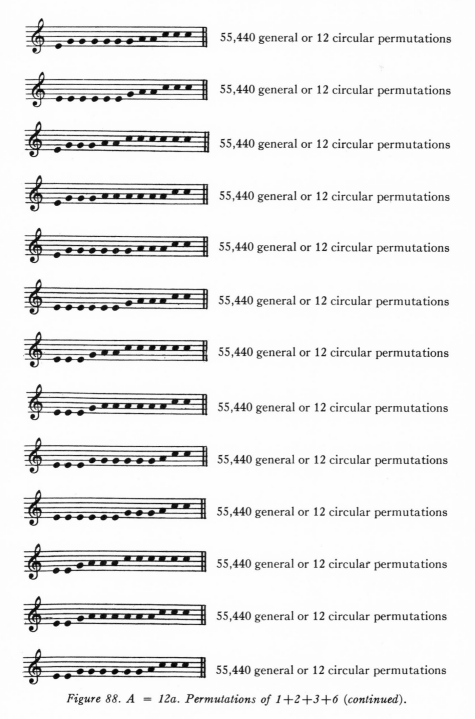

55,440 general or 12 circular permutations

55,440 general or 12 circular permutations

55,440 general or 12 circular permutations

55,440 general or 12 circular permutations

55,440 general or 12 circular permutations

55,440 general or 12 circular permutations

55,440 general or 12 circular permutations

55,440 general or 12 circular permutations

55,440 general or 12 circular permutations

55,440 general or 12 circular permutations

55,440 general or 12 circular permutations

55,440 general or 12 circular permutations

55,440 general or 12 circular permutations

Figure 88. A = 12a. Permutations of 1+2+3+6 (continued).

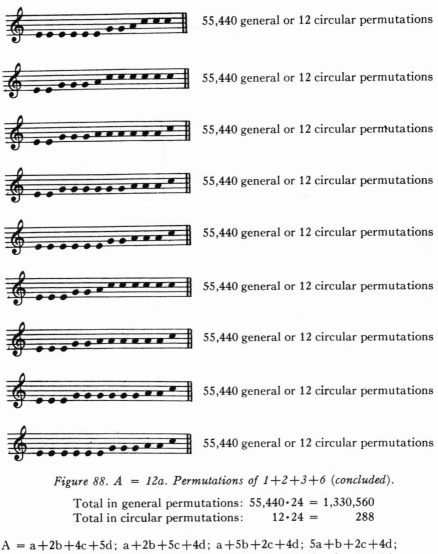

55,440 general or 12 circular permutations

55,440 general or 12 circular permutations

55,440 general or 12 circular permutations

55,440 general or 12 circular permutations

55,440 general or 12 circular permutations

55,440 general or 12 circular permutations

55,440 general or 12 circular permutations

55,440 general or 12 circular permutations

55,440 general or 12 circular permutations

Figure 88. A = 12a. Permutations of 1+2+3+6 (concluded).

Total in general permutations: 55,440·24 = 1,330,560
Total in circular permutations: 12·24 =   288

A = a+2b+4c+5d; a+2b+5c+4d; a+5b+2c+4d; 5a+b+2c+4d;
    a+4b+2c+5d; a+4b+5c+2d; a+5b+4c+2d; 5a+b+4c+2d;
    4a+b+2c+5d; 4a+b+5c+2d; 4a+5b+c+2d; 5a+4b+c+2d;
    2a+b+4c+5d; 2a+b+5c+4d; 2a+5b+c+4d; 5a+2b+c+4d;
    2a+4b+c+5d; 2a+4b+5c+d; 2a+5b+4c+d; 5a+2b+4c+d;
    4a+2b+c+5d; 4a+2b+5c+d; 4a+5b+2c+d; 5a+4b+2c+d.

$$P_{12} = \frac{12!}{2!\ 4!\ 5!} = \frac{479,001,600}{2 \cdot 24 \cdot 120} = 83,160$$

Each of the above 24 permutations of the eighth form of distribution has 83,160 general permutations. See Figure 89 on next page.

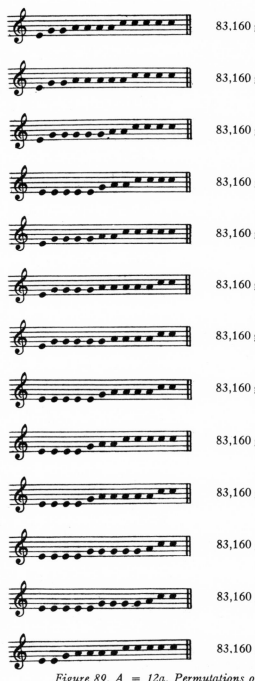

83,160 general or 12 circular permutations

83,160 general or 12 circular permutations

83,160 general or 12 circular permutations

83,160 general or 12 circular permutations

83,160 general or 12 circular permutations

83,160 general or 12 circular permutations

83,160 general or 12 circular permutations

83,160 general or 12 circular permutations

83,160 general or 12 circular permutations

83,160 general or 12 circular permutations

83,160 general or 12 circular permutations

83,160 general or 12 circular permutations

83,160 general or 12 circular permutations

Figure 89. A = 12a. Permutations of 1+2+4+5 (continued).

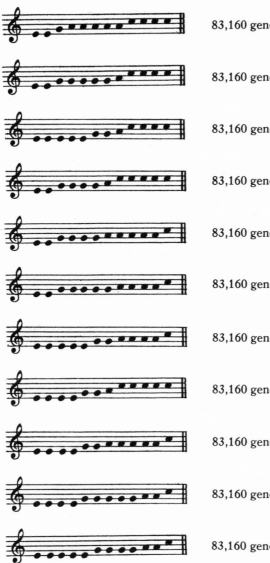

83,160 general or 12 circular permutations

83,160 general or 12 circular permutations

83,160 general or 12 circular permutations

83,160 general or 12 circular permutations

83,160 general or 12 circular permutations

83,160 general or 12 circular permutations

83,160 general or 12 circular permutations

83,160 general or 12 circular permutations

83,160 general or 12 circular permutations

83,160 general or 12 circular permutations

83,160 general or 12 circular permutations

Figure 89. A = 12a. Permutations of 1+2+4+5 (concluded).

Total in general permutations: 83,160·24 = 1,995,840
Total in circular permutations: 12·24 =   288

A = a+3b+3c+5d; 3a+3b+5c+d; 3a+5b+c+3d; 5a+b+3c+3d;
  a+3b+5c+3d; 3a+5b+3c+d; 5a+3b+c+3d; 3a+b+3c+5d;
  5a+3b+3c+d; 3a+3b+c+5d; 3a+b+5c+3d; a+5b+3c+3d.

$$P_{12} = \frac{12!}{3!\ 3!\ 5!} = \frac{479{,}001{,}600}{6 \cdot 6 \cdot 120} = 110{,}880$$

Each of the above 12 permutations of the ninth form of distribution has 110,880 general permutations.

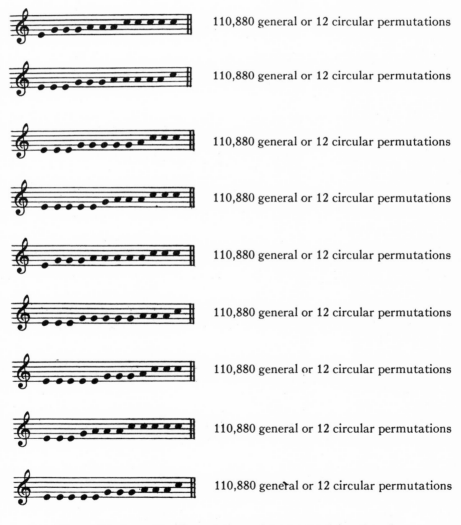

110,880 general or 12 circular permutations

110,880 general or 12 circular permutations

110,880 general or 12 circular permutations

110,880 general or 12 circular permutations

110,880 general or 12 circular permutations

110,880 general or 12 circular permutations

110,880 general or 12 circular permutations

110,880 general or 12 circular permutations

110,880 general or 12 circular permutations

Figure 90. A = 12a. Permutations of 1+3+3+5 (continued).

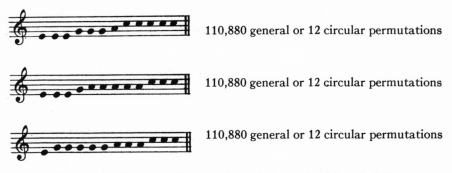

110,880 general or 12 circular permutations

110,880 general or 12 circular permutations

110,880 general or 12 circular permutations

Figure 90. A = 12a. Permutations of 1+3+3+5 (concluded).

Total in general permutations: 110,880·12 = 1,330,560
Total in circular permutations: 12·12 =   144

A = a+3b+4c+4d; 3a+4b+4c+d; 4a+4b+c+3d; 4a+b+3c+4d;
3a+b+4c+4d; a+4b+4c+3d; 4a+4b+3c+d; 4a+3b+c+4d;
a+4b+3c+4d; 4a+3b+4c+d; 3a+4b+c+4d; 4a+b+4c+3d.

$$P_{1z} = \frac{12!}{3! \; 4! \; 4!} = \frac{479,001,600}{6 \cdot 24 \cdot 24} = 138,600$$

Each of the above 12 permutations of the tenth form of distribution has 138,600 general permutations.

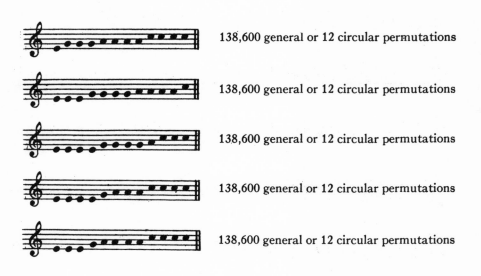

138,600 general or 12 circular permutations

138,600 general or 12 circular permutations

138,600 general or 12 circular permutations

138,600 general or 12 circular permutations

138,600 general or 12 circular permutations

Figure 91. A = 12a. Permutations of 1+3+4+4 (continued).

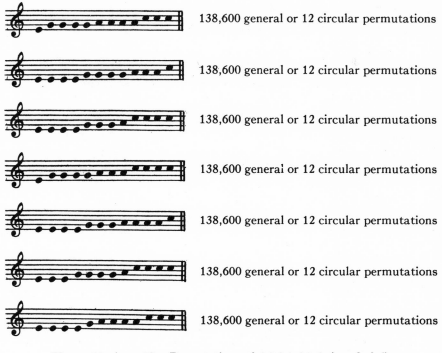

138,600 general or 12 circular permutations

138,600 general or 12 circular permutations

138,600 general or 12 circular permutations

138,600 general or 12 circular permutations

138,600 general or 12 circular permutations

138,600 general or 12 circular permutations

138,600 general or 12 circular permutations

Figure 91. A = 12a. Permutations of 1+3+4+4. (concluded).

Total in general permutations: $138,600 \cdot 12 = 1,663,200$
Total in circular permutations: $12 \cdot 12 = 144$

$A = 2a+2b+2c+6d; \ 2a+2b+6c+2d; \ 2a+6b+2c+2d; \ 6a+2b+2c+2d$

$$P_{12} = \frac{12!}{2! \ 2! \ 2! \ 6!} = \frac{479,001,600}{2 \cdot 2 \cdot 2 \cdot 720} = 83,160$$

Each of the above 4 permutations of the eleventh form of distribution has 83,160 general permutations.

83,160 general or 12 circular permutations

83,160 general or 12 circular permutations

83,160 general or 12 circular permutations

Figure 92. A = 12a. Permutations of 2+2+2+6 (continued).

 83,160 general or 12 circular permutations

Figure 92. A = 12a. Permutations of 2+2+2+6 (concluded).

Total in general permutations: 83,160·4 = 332,640
Total in circular permutations: 12·4 =   48

A = 2a+2b+3c+5d; 2a+3b+5c+2d; 3a+5b+2c+2d; 5a+2b+2c+3d;
    2a+2b+5c+3d; 2a+5b+3c+2d; 5a+3b+2c+2d; 3a+2b+2c+5d;
    2a+3b+2c+5d; 3a+2b+5c+2d; 2a+5b+2c+3d; 5a+2b+3c+2d.

$$P_{12} = \frac{12!}{2!\ 2!\ 3!\ 5!} = \frac{479,001.600}{2\cdot2\cdot6\cdot120} = 166,320$$

Each of the above 12 permutations of the twelfth form of distribution has 166,320 general permutations.

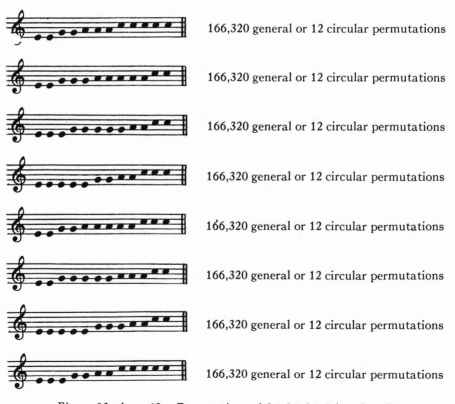

Figure 93. A = 12a. Permutations of 2+2+3+5 (continued).

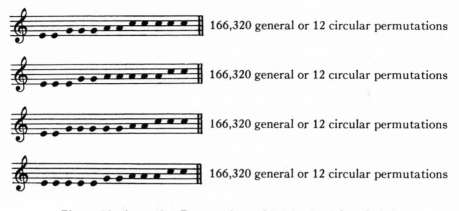

166,320 general or 12 circular permutations

166,320 general or 12 circular permutations

166,320 general or 12 circular permutations

166,320 general or 12 circular permutations

Figure 93. A = 12a. Permutations of 2+2+3+5 (concluded).

Total in general permutations: $166,320 \cdot 12 = 1,995,840$
Total in circular permutations: $12 \cdot 12 = 144$

A = 2a+2b+4c+4d; 2a+4b+4c+2d; 4a+4b+2c+2d; 4a+2b+2c+4d;
2a+4b+2c+4d; 4a+2b+4c+2d.

$$P_{12} = \frac{12!}{2! \ 2! \ 4! \ 4!} = \frac{479,001,600}{2 \cdot 2 \cdot 24 \cdot 24} = 207,900$$

Each of the above 6 permutations of the thirteenth form of distribution has 207,900 general permutations.

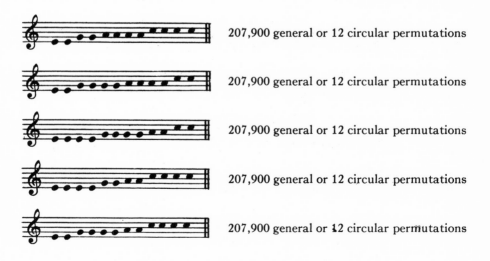

207,900 general or 12 circular permutations

207,900 general or 12 circular permutations

207,900 general or 12 circular permutations

207,900 general or 12 circular permutations

207,900 general or 12 circular permutations

Figure 94. A = 12a. Permutations of 2+2+4+4 (continued).

 207,900 general or 12 circular permutations

Figure 94. A = 12a. Permutations of 2+2+4+4 (concluded).

Total in general permutations: 207,900·6 = 1,247,400
Total in circular permutations: 12·6 =   72

A = 2a+3b+3c+4d; 3a+3b+4c+2d; 3a+4b+2c+3d; 4a+2b+3c+3d;
    2a+3b+4c+3d; 3a+4b+3c+2d; 4a+3b+2c+3d; 3a+2b+3c+4d;
    4a+3b+3c+2d; 3a+3b+2c+4d; 3a+2b+4c+3d; 2a+4b+3c+3d.

$$P_{12} = \frac{12!}{2!\ 3!\ 3!\ 4!} = \frac{479{,}001{,}600}{2\cdot6\cdot6\cdot24} = 277{,}200$$

Each of the above 12 permutations of the fourteenth form of distribution has 277,200 general permutations.

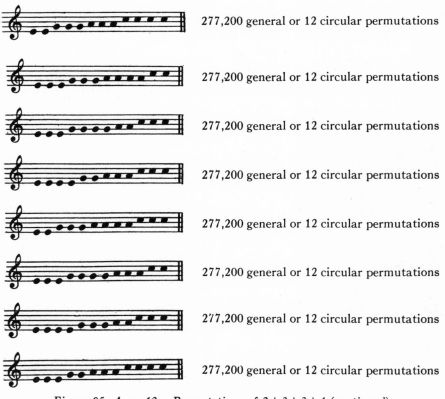

277,200 general or 12 circular permutations

277,200 general or 12 circular permutations

277,200 general or 12 circular permutations

277,200 general or 12 circular permutations

277,200 general or 12 circular permutations

277,200 general or 12 circular permutations

277,200 general or 12 circular permutations

277,200 general or 12 circular permutations

Figure 95. A = 12a. Permutations of 2+3+3+4 (continued).

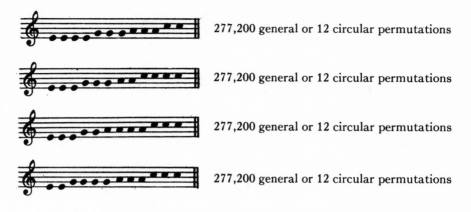

Figure 95. A = 12a. Permutations of 2+3+3+4 (concluded).

Total in general permutations: $277,200 \cdot 12 = 3,326,400$
Total in circular permutation: $12 \cdot 12 =$ 144

$A = 3a+3b+3c+3d$

$$P_{12} = \frac{12!}{3!\ 3!\ 3!\ 3!} = \frac{479,001,600}{6 \cdot 6 \cdot 6 \cdot 6} = 369,600$$

The above invariant (fifteenth) form of distribution has 369,600 general permutations.

369,600 general or 12 circular permutations

Figure 96. A = 12a. 3a+3b+3c+3d.

The total number of cases: A = 12a

General permutations: 5280 + 71,280 + 190,080 + 332,640 + 199,584 + + 285,120 + 1,330,560 + 1,995,840 + 1,330,560 + 1,663,200 + 332,640 + + 1,995,840 + 1,247,400 + 3,326,400 + 369,600 = 14,646,024

Circular permutations: 48 + 144 + 144 + 144 + 72 + 144 + 288 + 288 + + 144 + 144 + 48 + 144 + 72 + 144 + 12 = 1960

(5) I = a2p (one attack to a combination of two simultaneous parts).

The six invariant forms of (2) become elements of the second order:

$$\frac{b}{a} = a_2; \quad \frac{c}{a} = b_2; \quad \frac{d}{a} = c_2; \quad \frac{c}{b} = d_2; \quad \frac{d}{b} = e_2; \quad \frac{d}{c} = f_2$$

Table of $I(S = 4p) = a2p$

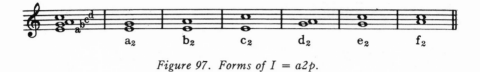

Figure 97. Forms of I = a2p.

Combinations of these forms in sequence, within the limits of a to c or b to d, require the inclusion of the three lower or the three upper parts.

Combinations of these forms in sequence, within the limit of a to d, require the inclusion of all four parts.

Sequent combinations by two:

$a_2 + b_2; \; a_2 + c_2; \; a_2 + d_2; \; a_2 + e_2; \; a_2 + f_2;$
$\quad b_2 + c_2; \; b_2 + d_2; \; b_2 + e_2; \; b_2 + f_2;$
$\quad\quad c_2 + d_2; \; c_2 + e_2; \; c_2 + f_2;$
$\quad\quad\quad d_2 + e_2; \; d_2 + f_2;$
$\quad\quad\quad\quad e_2 + f_2.$

Figure 98. Sequent combinations by 2.

The table above corresponds to two consecutive attacks. Each of the above combinations has 2 permutations.

Further development of attacks is achieved by means of the coefficients of recurrence:

$2a_2 + b_2; \; 3a_2 + 2c_2; \; . \; . \; .$
$2b_2 + d_2 + b_2 + 2d_2; \; 3c_2 + f_2 + 2c_2 + 2f_2 + c_2 + 3f_2; \; . \; . \; .$

Figure 99. Coefficients of recurrence.

The latter, in turn, become subject to permutations (general or circular), as well as to permutations of the higher orders:

$a_2 + b_2$; $b_2 + a_2$; $a_2 + c_2$; $c_2 + a_2$; . . .

$a_2 + b_2 = a_3$; $b_2 + a_2 = b_3$; . . .

Sequent combinations by three:

$a_2 + b_2 + c_2$; $a_2 + b_2 + d_2$; $a_2 + b_2 + e_2$; $a_2 + b_2 + f_2$;
$a_2 + c_2 + d_2$; $a_2 + c_2 + e_2$; $a_2 + c_2 + f_2$;
$a_2 + d_2 + e_2$; $a_2 + d_2 + f_2$;
$a_2 + e_2 + f_2$;
$b_2 + c_2 + d_2$; $b_2 + c_2 + e_2$; $b_2 + c_2 + f_2$;
$b_2 + d_2 + e_2$; $b_2 + d_2 + f_2$;
$b_2 + e_2 + f_2$;
$c_2 + d_2 + e_2$; $c_2 + d_2 + f_2$;
$c_2 + e_2 + f_2$;
$d_2 + e_2 + f_2$.

Figure 100. Sequent combinations by 3.

The above corresponds to three consecutive attacks. Each of the above combinations has 6 general or 3 circular permutations. The latter may develop still further through permutations of the higher orders:

$a_2 + b_2 + c_2 = a_3$; $a_2 + c_2 + b_2 = b_3$; . . . $c_2 + b_2 + a_2 = f_3$;
or:
$a_2 + b_2 + c_2 = a_3$; $b_2 + c_2 + a_2 = b_3$; $c_2 + a_2 + b_2 = c_3$.

Further development of attacks is achieved by means of the coefficient-groups, which may assume any form, i.e., trinomials, polynomials whose terms are divisible by 2, or interference groups:

$3a_2 + b_2 + 2c_2$; $3a_2 + c_2 + 2e_2 + 2a_2 + c_2 + 3e_2$;

$2b_2 + d_2 + 2f_2 + b_2 + 2d_2 + f_2$; . . .

See Figure 101 on the following page.

Figure 101. Coefficients of recurrence.

The latter, in turn, become subject to permutations (general or circular) as well as to permutations of the higher orders.

Sequent combinations by four:

$$a_2 + b_2 + c_2 + d_2;\ a_2 + b_2 + c_2 + e_2;\ a_2 + b_2 + c_2 + f_2;$$
$$a_2 + b_2 + d_2 + e_2;\ a_2 + b_2 + d_2 + f_2;$$
$$a_2 + b_2 + e_2 + f_2;$$
$$a_2 + c_2 + d_2 + e_2;\ a_2 + c_2 + d_2 + f_2;$$
$$a_2 + c_2 + e_2 + f_2;$$
$$a_2 + d_2 + e_2 + f_2;$$
$$b_2 + c_2 + d_2 + e_2;\ b_2 + c_2 + d_2 + f_2;$$
$$b_2 + c_2 + e_2 + f_2;$$
$$b_2 + d_2 + e_2 + f_2;$$
$$c_2 + d_2 + e_2 + f_2.$$

Figure 102. Sequent combinations by 4.

The above corresponds to four consecutive attacks. Each of·the above combinations has **24** general or **4** circular permutations. The latter may develop still further through permutations of the higher orders:

$$a_2 + b_2 + c_2 + d_2 = a_3;\ a_2 + b_2 + d_2 + c_2 = b_3;\ \ldots$$
or:
$$a_2 + b_2 + c_2 + d_2 = a_3;\ b_2 + c_2 + d_2 + a_2 = b_3;\ \ldots$$

Further development of attacks is achieved by means of the coefficient-groups, which may assume any form, i.e., quadrinomials, polynomials divisible by 4, or interference groups:

$$4a_2 + b_2 + 3c_2 + 2d_2;\ 2a_2 + b_2 + c_2 + 2d_2;\ 3a_2 + b_2 + 3c_2 + d_2;$$
$$4a_2 + b_2 + 3c_2 + 2d_2 + 2a_2 + 3b_2 + c_2 + 4d_2;$$
$$3a_2 + b_2 + 2c_2 + 3d_2 + a_2 + 2b_2 + 3c_2 + d_2 + 2a_2 + 3b_2 + c_2 + 2d_2;\ \ldots$$

See Figure 103 on the following page

Figure 103. Coefficients of recurrence.

The latter, in turn, become subject to permutations (general or circular), as well as to permutations of the higher orders.

Sequent combinations by five:

$$a_2 + b_2 + c_2 + d_2 + e_2; \; a_2 + b_2 + c_2 + d_2 + f_2; \; a_2 + b_2 + c_2 + e_2 + f_2;$$
$$a_2 + b_2 + d_2 + e_2 + f_2;$$
$$a_2 + c_2 + d_2 + e_2 + f_2;$$
$$b_2 + c_2 + d_2 + e_2 + f_2.$$

Figure 104. Sequent combinations by 5.

The above corresponds to five consecutive attacks. Each of the above combinations has 120 general or 5 circular permutations. The latter may develop still further through permutations of the higher orders:

$$a_2 + b_2 + c_2 + d_2 + e_2 = a_3; \; a_2 + b_2 + c_2 + e_2 + d_2 = b_3; \; \ldots$$
or:
$$a_2 + b_2 + c_2 + d_2 + e_2 = a_3; \; b_2 + c_2 + d_2 + e_2 + a_2 = b_3; \; \ldots$$

Further development of attacks is achieved by means of coefficient-groups, which may assume any form, i.e., quintinomials, polynomials divisible by 5, or interference groups:

$$2a_2 + b_2 + 2c_2 + d_2 + 2e_2;$$
$$5a_2 + b_2 + 4c_2 + 2d_2 + 3e_2 + 3a_2 + 2b_2 + 4c_2 + d_2 + 5e_2;$$
$$3a_2 + b_2 + 3c_2 + d_2 + 3e_2 + a_2 + 3b_2 + c_2 + 3d_2 + e_2; \; \ldots$$

See Figure 105 on the following page

Figure 105. Coefficients of recurrence.

The latter, in turn, become subject to permutations (general or circular), as well as to permutations of the higher orders.

The sequent combination by six $(a_2 + b_2 + c_2 + d_2 + e_2 + f_2)$ has 720 general or 6 circular permutations.

Figure 106. Sequent combinations by 6.

The latter may develop still further through permutations of the higher orders:

$a_2 + b_2 + c_2 + d_2 + e_2 + f_2 = a_3;\ a_2 + b_2 + c_2 + d_2 + f_2 + e_2 = b_3;\ \ldots$

or:

$a_2 + b_2 + c_2 + d_2 + e_2 + f_2 = a_3;\ b_2 + c_2 + d_2 + e_2 + f_2 + a_2 = b_3;\ \ldots$

Further development of attacks is achieved by means of the coefficient-groups, which may assume any form, i.e., sextinomials, polynomials divisible by 6, or interference groups:

$3a_2 + b_2 + 2c_2 + 2d_2 + e_2 + 3f_2;$

$3a_2 + b_2 + 2c_2 + 2d_2 + 3e_2 + f_2 + 2a_2 + 2b_2 + 3c_2 + d_2 + 2e_2 + 2f_2;$

$5a_2 + 4b_2 + 3c_2 + 2d_2 + e_2 + 5f_2 + 4a_2 + 3b_2 + 2c_2 + d_2 + 5e_2 + 4f_2 +$

$+ 3a_2 + 2b_2 + c_2 + 5d_2 + 4e_2 + 3f_2 + 2a_2 + b_2 + 5c_2 + 4d_2 + 3e_2 +$

$+ 2f_2 + a_2 + 5b_2 + 4c_2 + 3d_2 + 2e_2 + f_2;\ \ldots$

Figure 107. Coefficients of recurrence (continued).

Figure 107. Cofficients of recurrence (concluded).

The latter, in turn, become subject to permutations (general or circular), as well as to permutations of the higher orders.

(6) I = a3p (one attack to a combination of three simultaneous parts).

The four invariant forms of (3) become elements of the second order:

$$\frac{\frac{c}{b}}{a} = a_2; \quad \frac{\cdot\frac{d}{b}}{a} = b_2; \quad \frac{\frac{d}{c}}{a} = c_2; \quad \frac{\frac{d}{c}}{b} = d_2.$$

Figure 108. Forms of I = a3p.

Any combination of these forms in sequence requires the inclusion of all four parts.

Sequent combinations by two:

$a_2 + b_2;\ a_2 + c_2;\ a_2 + d_2;$
$\qquad b_2 + c_2;\ b_2 + d_2;$
$\qquad\qquad c_2 + d_2.$

Figure 109. Sequent combinations by 2.

The above corresponds to two consecutive attacks. Further development of attacks is achieved by means of the coefficients of recurrence.

Each of the preceding combinations has 2 permutations. The latter may develop further through permutations of the higher orders:

$$a_2 + b_2 = a_3; \quad b_2 + a_2 = b_3.$$

Further development of attacks is achieved by means of the coefficient-groups, which may assume any form, i.e., binomials, polynomials divisible by 2, or interference groups:

$$2a_2 + b_2; \; 3a_2 + 2b_2; \; \ldots$$
$$2a_2 + b_2 + a_2 + 2b_2; \; \ldots$$
$$3a_2 + 2b_2 + a_2 + 3b_2 + 2a_2 + b_2; \; \ldots$$

Figure 110. Coefficients of recurrence.

The latter in turn become subject to permutations (general or circular), as well as to permutations of the higher orders.

Sequent combinations by three:

$$a_2 + b_2 + c_2; \; a_2 + b_2 + d_2; \; a_2 + c_2 + d_2; \; b_2 + c_2 + d_2.$$

Figure 111. Sequent combinations by 3.

These correspond to three consecutive attacks. Further development of attacks is achieved by means of the coefficients of recurrence. Each of the above combinations has 6 general or 3 circular permutations. The latter may develop further through permutations of the higher orders:

$$a_2 + b_2 + c_2 = a_3; \quad a_2 + c_2 + b_2 = b_3; \; \ldots$$
or:
$$a_2 + b_2 + c_2 = a_3; \quad b_2 + c_2 + a_2 = b_3; \; \ldots$$

Further development of attacks is achieved by means of the coefficient-groups, which may assume any form, i.e., trinomials, polynomials divisible by 3, or interference groups:

$$3a_2 + b_2 + 2c_2; \; \ldots$$
$$3a_2 + b_2 + 2c_2 + 2a_2 + b_2 + 3c_2; \; \ldots$$
$$2a_2 + b_2 + c_2 + a_2 + 2b_2 + c_2 + a_2 + b_2 + 2c_2; \; \ldots$$

See Figure 112 on the following page.

Figure 112. Coefficients of recurrence.

The latter, in turn, become subject to permutations (general or circular), as well as to permutations of the higher orders.

The sequent combination by four $(a_2 + b_2 + c_2 + d_2)$ has 24 general or 4 circular permutations.

Figure 113. Sequent combination by 4.

The latter may develop further through permutations of the higher orders:

$a_2 + b_2 + c_2 + d_2 = a_3;\ a_2 + b_2 + d_2 + c_2 = b_3;\ \ldots$
or:
$a_2 + b_2 + c_2 + d_2 = a_3;\ b_2 + c_2 + d_2 + a_2 = b_3;\ \ldots$

Further development of attacks is achieved by means of the coefficient-groups, which may assume any form, i.e., quadrinomials, polynomials divisible by 4, or interference groups:

$4a_2 + b_2 + 3c_2 + 2d_2;$
$5a_2 + b_2 + 4c_2 + 2d_2 + 2a_2 + 4b_2 + c_2 + 5d_2;\ \ldots$
$2a_2 + b_2 + c_2 + 2d_2 + a_2 + b_2 + 2c_2 + d_2 + a_2 + 2b_2 + c_2 + d_2;\ \ldots$

Figure 114. Coefficients of recurrence.

(7) **I = a4p (one attack to a combination of four simultaneous parts).**

One invariant form: $\dfrac{\underline{\underline{\underline{\dfrac{d}{\dfrac{c}{\dfrac{b}{a}}}}}}}{} = a_2.$

Multiplication of attacks is achieved by direct repetition: $A = a_2$; $2a_2$; $3a_2$; . . . ma_2.

Figure 115. Multiplication of attacks.

Further variations may be obtained by means of permutations of the vertical (simultaneous) arrangement of parts. The extreme $p^{\rightarrow}$ of a given position must serve as a limit, that is, for a position above the original, the function, d, is the limit for the lower function. For a position below the original, the function, a, is the limit for the upper function.

The original position in relation to all the upper and all the lower positions is as follows:

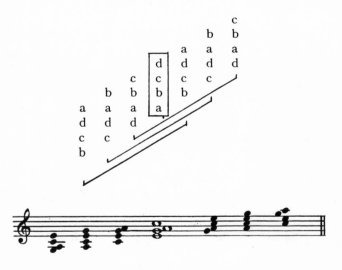

Figure 116. Relation to original position.

Positions indicated by the brackets are identical in the different octaves.

It is desirable to use the adjacent positions in sequence.

From the above variations of the original position, any number of attacks may be devised.

Voice-leading from the adjacent positions
(long durations)

Voice-leading from the original positions
(short durations)

Figure 117. Voice-leading.

From the above variations of the original position any number of attacks may be devised.

Figure 118. Multiplication of attacks (continued).

Figure 118. Multiplication of attacks (concluded).

C. INSTRUMENTAL FORMS OF S = 4p

Material:

(1) melody with three couplings:

$$M \begin{bmatrix} p_{IV} \\ p_{III} \\ p_{II} \\ p_I \end{bmatrix}$$

(2) harmonic forms of four-unit scales;
(3) four-part harmony;
(4) four part stratum (S) of any compound harmony (Σ)

$$I = a: \quad \frac{\begin{matrix} p_{IV} \\ p_{III} \\ p_{II} \end{matrix}}{p_I} \quad \text{(24 general or 4 circular permutations)}$$

$$\frac{\begin{matrix} d_2 \\ c \\ b_2 \end{matrix}}{a_2} \quad \text{(24 general or 4 circular permutations)}$$

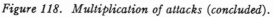

$$\begin{matrix} md_2 + nd_2 + pd_2 + qd_2 \\ mc_2 + nc_2 + pc_2 + qc_2 \\ mb_2 + nb_2 + pb_2 + qb_2 \\ ma_2 \quad na_2 \quad pa_2 \quad qa_2 \end{matrix} \quad \text{(24 general or 4 circular permutations of the coefficients m, n, p, q).}$$

1. Melody with three couplings. Illustrated by theme and variations. See figures 119 to 125 inclusive.

Figure 119. Theme.

Figure 120. Theme with couplings.

Figure 121. Variation I.

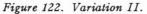

Figure 122. Variation II.

Figure 123. Variation III.

Figure 124. Variation IV.

Figure 125. Variation V.

2. Harmonic forms of four-unit scales. Illustrated by theme and ten variations. See figures 126 to 136 inclusive.

Figure 126. Theme.

Figure 127. Variation I.

Figure 128. Rhythmic variation of the theme.

Figure 129. Variation III. (The two best reciprocals)

Figure 130. Variation IV. (Eight p→: 4 and 4 reciprocals)

Figure 131. Variation V.

Figure 132. Variation VI.

Figure 133. Variation VII.

Figure 134. Variation VIII.

Figure 135. Variation IX.

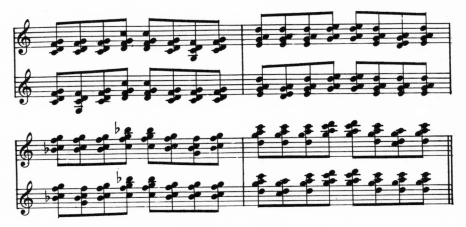

Figure 136. Variation X.

3. Four-part harmony. Illustrated by a theme and six variations. See figures 137 to 143 inclusive.

Figure 137. Theme and rhythmic variation.

Figure 138. Variation I. $I = 2a_2 + b_2 + c_2 + 2d_2$.

Figure 139. Variation II. Theme in rhythmic variation.

$$I = 2a_2 + b_2 + c_2 + 2d_2$$

Figure 140. Variation III. $I = a_2 + b_2 + c_2 + d_2 + e_2 + f_2.$

Figure 141. Variation IV. Theme in rhythmic variation.
$$I = a_2 + b_2 + c_2 + d_2$$

Figure 142. Variation V.

Figure 143. Variation VI.

(4) Four-part stratum (S) of any compound harmony (Σ). Illustrated by a theme and three variations. See figures 144 to 147 inclusive.

Figure 144. Theme.

Figure 145. Variation I.

Figure 146. Variation II.

Figure 147. Variation III.

Individual attacks emphasizing one, two, three or four parts can be combined into one attack-group of any desirable form.

Examples:

```
          d        d     d dddd      ddd
        c c       ccc    c c  c     cccc
        b b b    bbb b    b  b  b   bbbb
I(S = 4p): aaaaaa ;   aa a  a ;  aaa  aa ;   aa  a ;
```

```
d ddd ddddd      dddddd      d d ddd     d       d     d d    d ;
ccc ccc ccc      cc ccccc     c ccc c    c cc          c c    c
bb b bbbbb b      bbbb bbb     bbb b b    bbb b          bb bb b
aaaaaa a a a ;   aaaaaa a ;   aa a a a ;  aa a a    ;   aa aa a ;
                                                              d c
                                                              c d
```

```
                       a
        ddddd      dddd d   d
      ccccccc      ccc ccc cc
     bbbbbbb       bb b bbb b
aaaaaa              ;   a    aaaaaa ; . . .
                       d
```

Figure 148. Combining individual attacks.

Figure 149. Theme and variations.

CHAPTER 6

THE COMPOSITION OF INSTRUMENTAL STRATA

A. IDENTICAL OCTAVE-POSITIONS

IN order to employ various instrumental groups as strata (S) in a simultaneous coordinated performance, it is necessary to arrange these instrumental strata into *identical octave-positions*—a requirement which must be carried out with utmost rigidity, as any deviation from it will result in a loss of acoustical quality, particularly when one is dealing with orchestration.

When simultaneous pitch assemblages are in identical positions, their harmonics and their combination-tones (tones of the difference)* are **similar**. When such assemblages are in non-identical positions, their harmonics and their combination-tones do not appear in acoustical balance, the latter being achieved only when the ratio between all audible tones bearing identical names equals 2 or 4 or 8, etc.

This principle refers to all cases when the strata constitute a multiplication of *one harmonic stratum*. However, when different *harmonic strata* are used in superimposition (as I shall shortly show when I discuss my general theory of harmony),** their positions are independent; but if any of the superimposed harmonic strata of a harmonic Σ (compound harmonic structure) are duplicated in adjacent octaves as *instrumental* strata, the principle of *identical positions* for one harmonic stratum holds true.

To achieve acoustical balance between clockwise ("open") and counter-clockwise ("close") positions of the assemblages, it is necessary to align both instrumental strata in such a way that their *upper instrumental functions will be identical*.

If we designate the lower instrumental stratum as S_1 and the upper adjacent stratum as S_2, then the instrumental score (Σ) takes on the following form:

$$S = 2p; \quad \Sigma = 2S$$

$$\Sigma \begin{bmatrix} S_2 \begin{bmatrix} \dfrac{b}{a} \\[4pt] \dfrac{b}{a} \end{bmatrix} \\[16pt] S_1 \end{bmatrix} \text{identical positions}$$

---

*Tones of the difference—or differential tones—are tones produced by pairs of other tones. The frequency of a differential tone is equal to the frequency of the higher tone minus that of the lower tone. The differential tone is a real tone and may be heard clearly on instruments producing nearly "pure" frequencies.
—(Ed.)

**See pp. 1074 ff., 1110 ff., 1139 ff.

Superimposition of two *non-identical* positions for S = 2p is obviously impossible; there is, however, another variant for the identical positions:

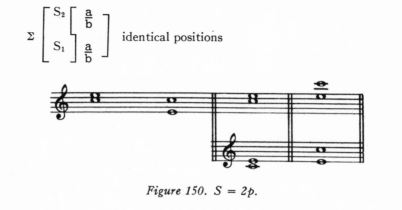

Figure 150. S = 2p.

Theme:

Instrumental octave-coupling

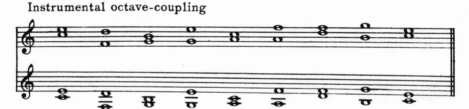

Instrumental Variation I.

Figure 151. Theme and instrumental variations (continued).

Instrumental Variation II.

Figure 151. Theme and instrumental variations. (concluded)

In three-part assemblages both identical and non-identical positions may be used in the octave-couplings.

$$S = 3p; \quad \Sigma = 2S$$

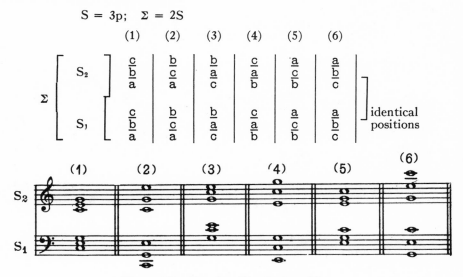

Figure 152. S = 3p. Identical positions.

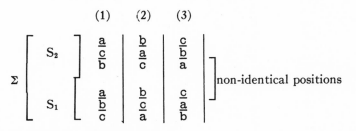

See Figure 153 on the following page.

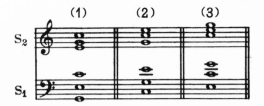

Figure 153. Non-identical positions.

The principles on which close and open positions of the same assemblage, S, can be brought into octave coordination, may be expressed as follows:

(1) both instrumental strata are in close position;
(2) both instrumental strata are in open position;
(3) the lower instrumental stratum (S_1) is in open position, and the upper instrumental stratum (S_2) is in close position.

Figure 154. Theme and instrumental octave-coupling.

The reversal of (3) conflicts with the normal distribution of harmonics, which will deprive the Σ of its acoustical clarity. This means: whatever the number of instrumental strata aligned in octave coordination, *there must never be an open position above a close.*

Instrumental Variation I.

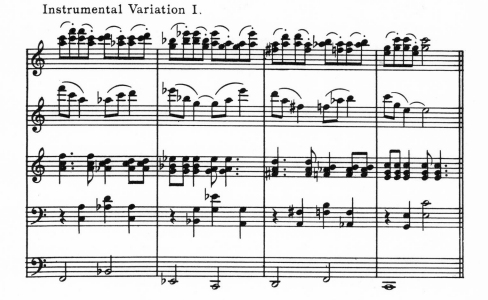

Instrumental Variation II.

Figure 155. Two instrumental variations.

All the above described principles and regulations hold true for the four-part assemblages as well.

$$S = 4p; \; \Sigma = 2S$$

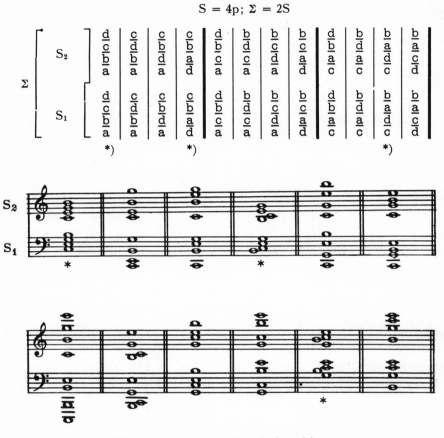

Figure 156. S = 4p. Identical positions.

See Figure 157 on the following page.

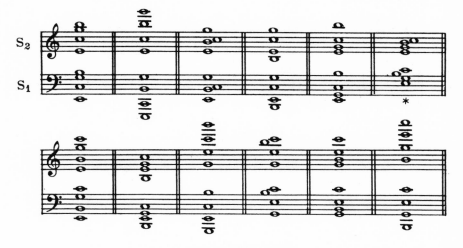

Figure 157. Identical Positions.

The above table shows all cases of identical positions. The forms marked by the asterisk are the practical ones for general use, as the distribution of all four functions is confined to a one-octave range. This permits more than one octave-duplication when necessary. All other positions of this table are practical mostly for one stratum instrumental forms, particularly for fingerboard and keyboard instruments.

Non-identical positions with identical upper functions are most practical when constructed from the preceding forms marked by the asterisk (the latter are clockwise circular permutations when read upward):

$$
\Sigma
\begin{bmatrix}
S_2 & \begin{matrix} d\\c\\b\\a \end{matrix} & \begin{matrix} a\\d\\c\\b \end{matrix} & \begin{matrix} b\\a\\d\\c \end{matrix} & \begin{matrix} c\\b\\a\\d \end{matrix} & \begin{matrix} d\\c\\b\\a \end{matrix} & \begin{matrix} a\\d\\c\\b \end{matrix} & \begin{matrix} b\\a\\d\\c \end{matrix} & \begin{matrix} c\\b\\a\\d \end{matrix} \\
S_1 & \begin{matrix} d\\a\\b\\c \end{matrix} & \begin{matrix} a\\b\\c\\d \end{matrix} & \begin{matrix} b\\c\\d\\a \end{matrix} & \begin{matrix} c\\d\\a\\b \end{matrix} & \begin{matrix} d\\b\\c\\a \end{matrix} & \begin{matrix} a\\c\\d\\b \end{matrix} & \begin{matrix} b\\d\\c\\a \end{matrix} & \begin{matrix} c\\d\\b\\a \end{matrix}
\end{bmatrix}
$$

$$
\Sigma
\begin{bmatrix}
S_2 & \begin{matrix} d\\c\\b\\a \end{matrix} & \begin{matrix} a\\d\\c\\b \end{matrix} & \begin{matrix} b\\a\\d\\c \end{matrix} & \begin{matrix} c\\b\\a\\d \end{matrix} & \begin{matrix} d\\c\\b\\a \end{matrix} & \begin{matrix} a\\d\\c\\b \end{matrix} & \begin{matrix} b\\a\\d\\c \end{matrix} & \begin{matrix} c\\b\\a\\d \end{matrix} & \begin{matrix} d\\c\\b\\a \end{matrix} & \begin{matrix} a\\d\\c\\b \end{matrix} & \begin{matrix} b\\a\\d\\c \end{matrix} & \begin{matrix} c\\b\\a\\d \end{matrix} \\
S_1 & \begin{matrix} d\\b\\a\\c \end{matrix} & \begin{matrix} a\\c\\b\\d \end{matrix} & \begin{matrix} b\\c\\a\\d \end{matrix} & \begin{matrix} c\\b\\d\\a \end{matrix} & \begin{matrix} d\\c\\a\\b \end{matrix} & \begin{matrix} a\\d\\b\\c \end{matrix} & \begin{matrix} b\\a\\d\\c \end{matrix} & \begin{matrix} c\\a\\d\\b \end{matrix} & \begin{matrix} d\\a\\c\\b \end{matrix} & \begin{matrix} a\\d\\c\\b \end{matrix} & \begin{matrix} b\\a\\c\\d \end{matrix} & \begin{matrix} c\\a\\b\\d \end{matrix}
\end{bmatrix}
$$

See Figure 158 on the following page.

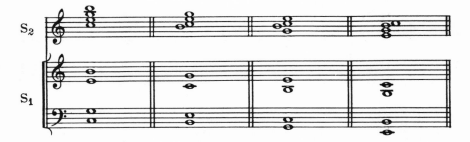

Figure 158. Most practical forms of the non-identical positions.

The above table represents matched pairs of S, the upper (S_2) being in close—and the lower (S_1) in open position. The choice of one or another form depends on its suitability to the type of orchestration—considerations of range, register, and adaptability to instrumental execution.

It is desirable that, in the case of octave duplication of an open position, all instrumental strata (in the open position) be *identical.*

If extra parts are added to a three-part or a four-part assemblage, such individual consecutive parts form their own instrumental strata and may be subjected to couplings for such a purpose. Whether the added part appears *below* or *above* the assemblage, its couplings must be always constructed *in the outward direction.* Thus, melody appearing above harmony must have couplings above its original functions:

$$M = \frac{p_{II}}{p_I}; \; \frac{\dfrac{p_{III}}{p_{II}}}{p_I}; \; . \; . \; .,$$ where p_I is the original function of melody and p_{II}, p_{III}, . . . are its couplings.

The *bass*, on the contrary, must have couplings *below* its original functions:

$$B = \frac{p_I}{p_{II}}; \; \frac{\dfrac{p_I}{p_{II}}}{p_{III}}; \; . \; . \; .,$$ where p_I is the original function of the bass and p_{II}, p_{III}, . . . are its couplings.

Forms of instrumental strata appearing in simultaneous coordination may assume *different degrees of density.* For instance:

(1)

$$\Sigma \begin{bmatrix} I\,(S_3) = a3p \\ I\,(S_2) = a2p \\ I\,(S_1) = ap \end{bmatrix}$$

(2)

$$\Sigma \begin{bmatrix} I\,(S_4) = a4p \\ I\,(S_3) = a3p \\ I\,(S_2) = ap \\ I\,(S_1) = a2p \end{bmatrix}$$

$$(3)$$

$$\Sigma \left] \begin{array}{l} I\ (S_3) = ap \\ I\ (S_2) = a2p \\ I\ (S_1) = a3p \end{array} \right.$$

$$(4)$$

$$\Sigma \left] \begin{array}{l} I\ (S_4) = ap \\ I\ (S_3) = a2p \\ I\ (S_2) = a3p \\ I\ (S_1) = a4p \end{array} \right.$$

Different instrumental strata may have different arrangements of time elements—including durations, rests, etc.

B. ACOUSTICAL CONDITIONS FOR SETTING THE BASS

The form, $S = 3p$, either appears independently or in octave duplications. To such three-part harmony, a fourth part may be added and it is usually the harmonic bass, which is actually *an added part* and must be treated as an independent $S = p$ when it has no couplings. This fourth part may also be subjected to outward couplings. Neither the bass nor any of its couplings should ever cross any of the functions of the adjacent upper assemblage.

$S = 4p$ appears independently or in octave duplications. In hybrid five-part harmony, the bass is an added part and must be treated as an independent $S = p$; as in the preceding case, it may acquire outward couplings, but neither its original functions nor the couplings should ever cross any of the functions of the adjacent upper assemblage.

When four-part harmony appears independently, that is, without a bass as such, the entire S must be subjected to octave-coupling, but never any individual functions nor any combinations thereof. This principle applies to close positions. Harmony appearing in open position and in the lower instrumental stratum may have an octave doubling of its lower function (i.e., the bass voice of four-part harmony), whichever meaning this function may assume harmonically. This does not prevent us from doubling the entire stratum in the adjacent upper stratum either in open or in close position.

Theme:

Figure 159. Theme and instrumental octave-coupling (continued).

Instrumental octave-coupling

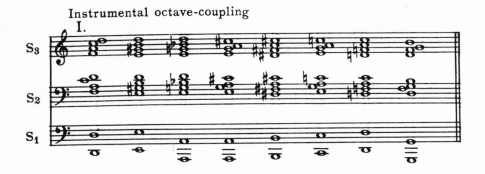

Figure 159. Instrumental octave coupling (continued).

IV.

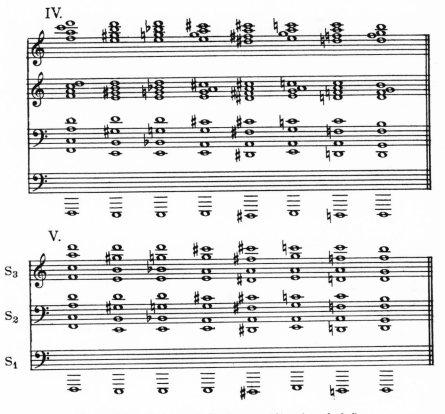

V.

Figure 159. Instrumental octave coupling (concluded).

Instrumental Variation I.

I = 3abcbcd + bcdabc.

Figure 160. Five instrumental variations (continued).

Figure 160. Instrumental variation I = 3abcbcd + bcdabc

Instrumental Variation II.

Figure 160. Instrumental variations (continued).

Instrumental Variation III.

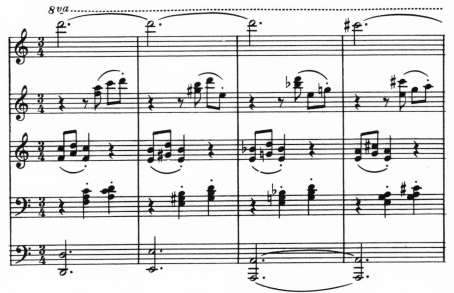

Figure 160. Instrumental variations (continued).

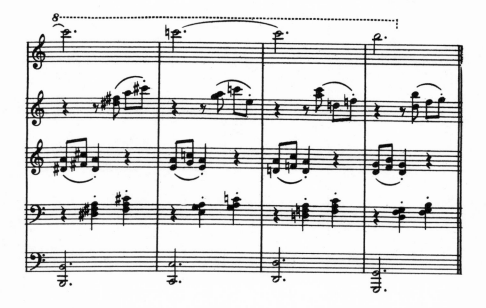

Instrumental Variation IV.

Figure 160. Instrumental variations (continued).

Instrumental Variation V.

Figure 160. Instrumental variations (concluded).

It is obvious that instrumental variations of Figure 160 are complete and self-sufficient scores of harmonic accompaniments. They may be subjected to orchestration without their forms being changed.

CHAPTER 7

SOME INSTRUMENTAL FORMS OF ACCOMPANIED MELODY

NOW that a systematic classification of all instrumental forms—I(S = p, 2p, 3p and 4p)—and their applications to individual fields of melody and harmony has been completed, we shall evolve some of the most typical forms of combined applications. The most universal of the latter is, undoubtedly, *melody with harmonic accompaniment*, and this involves both harmonization and melodization.

A. MELODY WITH HARMONIC ACCOMPANIMENT

The following considerations specifically pertain to this problem:

(1) The melody should not cross any of the harmonic parts; it may be placed above, between, or below any of the harmonic strata—the various styles of melodization and harmonization being each subject to limitations. When the melody is below the lower instrumental stratum of harmony, any harmonic bass must be completely eliminated. The number of instrumental strata depends on the range of melody (or of melody with its couplings). None of the couplings of melody should ever cross any of the parts of the adjacent harmonies, whether above or below.

(2) Couplings added to the original melody may be placed above it, or below it, or they may surround it. The number of couplings is optional. The most common form of coupling is the octave. Other intervals—as well as the filling in of the octave with other intervals—may also be used. Consonant as well as dissonant harmonic intervals may be used, the selection of one or the other being a matter of style. The 19th century favored thirds and sixths; the 20th century, on the contrary, features fourths, fifths, sevenths, and seconds as couplings. All couplings of melody accompanied by harmony must be *diatonic*, i.e., they must conform to the pitches of accompanying harmonic structure (auxiliary tones being neglected). Thus, if a third is selected as the coupling, it may be major against some chords and minor against some other chords.

Instrumental Variation of Accompanied Melody

Figure 161. Theme. Melodization of harmony of figure 108 (continued).

Figure 161. Melodization of harmony of figure 108 (concluded).

Figure 162. Instrumental variation I.

Figure 163. Instrumental variation II (continued).

Figure 163. Instrumental variation II (concluded).

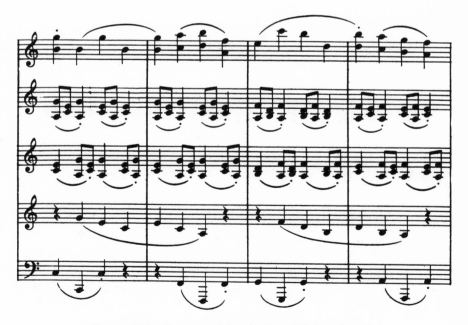

Figure 164. Instrumental variation III (continued).

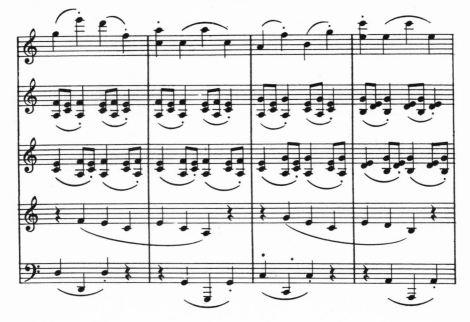

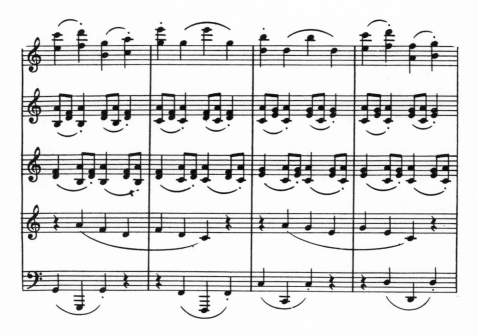

Figure 164. Instrumental variation III (continued).

Figure 164. Instrumental variation III (concluded).

B. INSTRUMENTAL FORMS OF DUET WITH HARMONIC ACCOMPANIMENT

The principles on which instrumental variations of an accompanied duet may be devised are:

(1) If M_I and M_{II} do not cross each other at any point, then *diatonic* couplings may be used in either or in both parts. If both parts are coupled, their respective couplings may be either identical or non-identical. Neither of the two melodies nor any of their couplings may cross any of the parts of accompanying harmony. Crossing melodies should have no couplings.

(2) The harmonic bass may be used only if both melodies are placed above the harmony; in all other cases, such a bass must be eliminated. All the following positions are acceptable ($H^{\rightarrow}$ referring to harmony without bass):

$$
\text{(a)} \ \frac{M_I}{\underset{M_{II}}{H^{\rightarrow}}} \quad
\text{(b)} \ \frac{\overset{M_I}{M_{II}}}{\underset{\text{Bass}}{H^{\rightarrow}}} \quad
\text{(c)} \ \frac{\overset{H^{\rightarrow}}{M_I}}{M_{II}} \quad
\text{(d)} \ \frac{\overset{H^{\rightarrow}}{M_I}}{\underset{M_{II}}{H^{\rightarrow}}} \quad
\text{(e)} \ \frac{\overset{M_I}{H^{\rightarrow}}}{\underset{H^{\rightarrow}}{M_{II}}}
$$

Instrumental Variation of Accompanied Duet.

Figure 165. Theme. Two part melodization of figure 3.

Instrumental Variation

Figure 166. Instrumental variation (continued).

Figure 166. Instrumental variation (concluded).

CHAPTER 8

THE USE OF DIRECTIONAL UNITS IN
INSTRUMENTAL FORMS OF HARMONY

ONCE the auxiliary tones to be used have been pre-set, they may be used as a part of the general technique of instrumental forms. There are no limitations to the *sequent* use of auxiliary tones in instrumental strata. Any instrumental stratum may or may not have directional units. In the case of one instrumental stratum, this proposition will always hold true; in the case of several instrumental strata broken into various forms of arpeggio in sequence (single, double, triple and quadruple attacks), it is preferable to adhere to the acoustical set, i.e., to use directional units in the uppermost stratum.

In simultaneous groups of strata, directional units may be used in strata of identical octave-duplication of simultaneous assemblages *only* when such strata belong to *different* tone-qualities; otherwise the subsequent orchestration will lack clarity. In some instances, a compromise may be affected by juxta-position of contrasting attacks or by extremely contrasting speeds in the two respective instrumental strata. For example, a part with directional units may be played *legato*, and a part with neutral units only may be played *staccato*; or one part may move by sustained half-notes while the other produces instrumental figuration in eighth-notes, with the latter using the directional units.

All other forms of melodic figuration—such as suspensions, anticipations, and passing tones—must either not be used at all, or else be treated as chordal functions, which would mean they should be in the instrumental strata evolved through octave-duplication.

Examples of the Instrumental Forms of Harmony
Containing Melodic Figuration

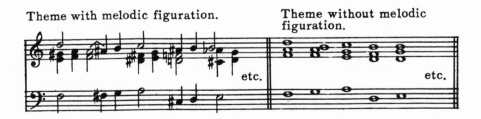

Theme with melodic figuration.   Theme without melodic figuration.

Figure 167. Theme and instrumental variations (continued).

Instrumental Variation I.

Instrumental Variation II.

etc.

Instrumental Variation III.

Figure 167. Instrumental variations (continued).

Instrumental Variation IV.

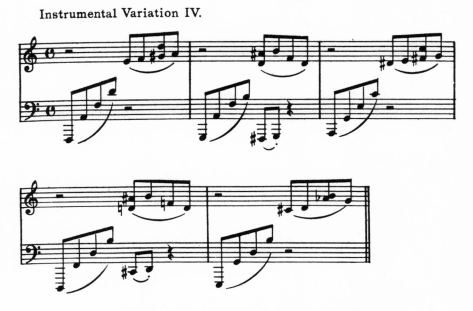

Figure 167.   Instrumental variations (concluded).

Theme: suspended, passing and anticipated tones applied to a given chord-progression.

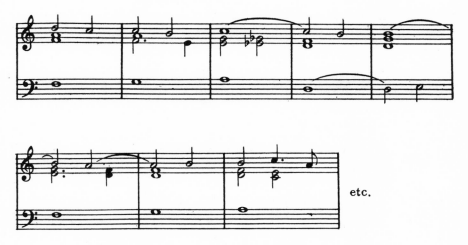

etc.

Figure 168.   Theme and instrumental variations (continued).

Instrumental Variation

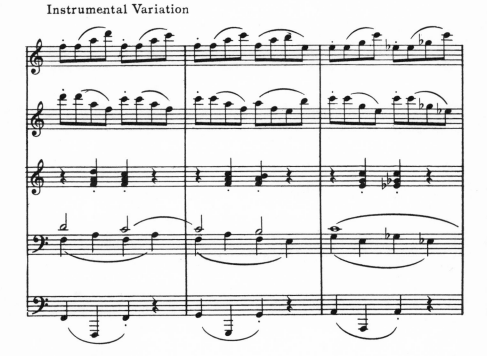

Figure 162   Instrumental variations(continued)

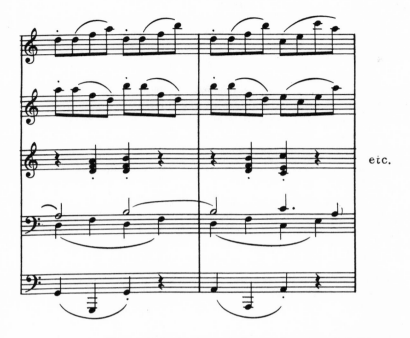

Figure 168. Instrumental variations (concluded).

CHAPTER 9

INSTRUMENTAL FORMS OF TWO-PART COUNTERPOINT

THE principles we have already established for instrumental forms of accompanied duet, apply to an unaccompanied duet as well. Thus, a canon or a fugue may be subjected to instrumental variation. However, as polyphonic duets have a considerable degree of mobility, the main aspect of this technique lies in the utilization of *couplings* as such.

When correlated melodies are unaccompanied their couplings become *automatic*, i.e., once the coupling has been selected, its form—or their forms—does not vary throughout the entire composition. Couplings of M_I and M_{II} may have independent forms. Selection of the automatic couplings is left to the composer's discretion. Such couplings attribute to the counterpoint a certain persistent harmonic flavor. It is to be expected that the two contrapuntal parts supplied with couplings will frequently clash with each other; but without this, the music would lack harmonic contrasts.

The number of couplings added to each part is also optional. The two contrapuntal parts may each have a different number of couplings. For ordinary purposes, the addition of one or two couplings to each part suffices, and doing this attributes to the polyphonic texture a definite and individual harmonic quality.

With a considerable number of couplings added to each contrapuntal part, composition of continuity based on variable density (low, medium, high) becomes possible. Schemes of density variation may be worked out in a fashion similar to that used in the treatment of density as described in my earlier discussion of two-part melodization.* All the more detailed and elaborate forms of continuity based on coupled polyphony will be discussed when I come later to the general theory of composition. For the time being, many valuable results may be obtained through the use of initiative in combining factorial continuity with couplings and instrumental forms.

Below is a table which suggests in detail the system by which more forms of couplings may be obtained. As in most cases there is a definite predominance of a certain harmonic interval occurring as between M_I and M_{II}, it is advisable to select a specific coupling which satisfies some particular occasion in relation to this predominant interval; then the chances of producing this particular harmonic sonority will increase.

Couplings, as in all earlier cases, may be distributed below or above the original pitch unit. Pitch units as well as their couplings are subject to octave-couplings.

*See Vol. I, p. 700.

Figure 169. Exemplary table of automatic couplings.

The couplings are marked by the black notes. Similar tables may be developed with regard to other harmonic intervals. We shall now refer to examples of application of this technique.

Fugue with Automatic Couplings
(Two Parts)

Two Part Fugue*
Type III: Superimposed Coupling

$$5T\frac{0}{CF} + 5T\frac{CF}{CP} + 5T\frac{CF+cpl}{CP} + 5T\frac{CF}{CP+cpl}\ \text{etc.}$$

by Richard Benda

Form: cpl

Figure 170. Fugue by student Richard Benda (continued).

Figure 170. Fugue by student Richard Benda (continued).

Figure 170. Fugue by student Richard Benda (continued).

Figure 170. Fugue by student Richard Benda (continued).

Figure 170. Fugue by student Richard Benda (concluded).

Homophonic Compositions Developed from Two-Part Counterpoint

(1) Original; (2) Couplings; (3) Instrumental forms: Var. I and II.

Figure 171. Two-part counterpoint..

(3) Var. I.

Figure 172.   Variation (continued).

Figure 172. Variation (concluded).

(3) Var. II.

Figure 173. Variation (continued).

Figure 173. Variation (concluded).

CHAPTER 10

INSTRUMENTAL FORMS FOR PIANO COMPOSITIONS

WRITING for the pianoforte requires a highly specialized technique because of peculiarities in execution of music for this instrument. Human beings are bi-fold; they have right and left arms and hands, and they have two sets of fingers arranged in bi-fold symmetry. Because of the strength of the thumb and the relative weakness of some of the other fingers, an extensive exercise system has been developed for the purpose of equalizing the striking power of the various fingers. But this equalization has never been completely achieved. The better pianists, however, have a fair approximation to uniformity in this respect—close enough for practical purposes.

Nevertheless, certain characteristics remain invariant owing to the bi-foldness of the finger arrangement. One of these characteristics is the excessive striking power of the thumb; it leads to an adaptation of some patterns of instrumental forms to piano writing. For example, it is easy and natural in a consecutive group of arpeggio figures to single out the *lower* instrumental function (producing the effect of self-accompanied melody) when such figures are played by the *right hand*, or to single out the *upper* function, when played by the left hand.

This fact and existing piano literature—to which techniques of execution are more or less adjusted (e.g., the convention that instrumental forms of harmony are to played mostly with the left hand)—have created a whole system of digital habits which are so crystallized by now that very few composers—particularly if they are pianists themselves—can develop any really independent style of piano writing.

The purpose of this discussion is to demonstrate the inexhaustible resources of instrumental forms and possibilities, so as to enable the composer to develop any number of his own individual styles.

The principles of natural acoustical arrangement, i.e., the contraction of harmonic intervals in the direction of increasing frequencies (upward direction of pitch) and the octave duplication of identical positions of assemblages combined with the principle of outward coupling, hold true in piano writing as well. The use of directional units remains the same as in all other instrumental forms previously described.

The only peculiarity which is typical of piano writing is the execution of melody in octave coupling filled out by other functions of the same assemblage. In some cases, not all of the functions of an assemblage are used, although certain fingers will remain unengaged. The most customary forms are the thirds from the upper or the lower instrumental function, or the third from one function and the fourth from another. However, these conventional forms of duplication are influenced by their common origin, which is *harmonic*, i.e., the use of S(5) and its inversions.

This viewpoint is well confirmed by present-day American dance music (it has many trade names: jazz,* swing, blues, boogie, etc.), in which it is customary to fill any octave coupling with the remaining functions of S(7), or S(5) with added 13th. This method of coupling melody has become so universal that its use is a permanent feature of many arrangements and orchestrations under the trade name of "block-harmony." This leads me to the belief that the first arrangers and orchestrators of such music were *pianists*, for the orchestral conception of these instrumental strata couplings is acoustically much more sound; the latter correspond to the forms described in this branch.

Many pianist-composers of the past, such as Chopin and Schumann, had very chaotic styles of piano writing, from both the acoustical and the harmonic standpoints. This is due to the fact that their compositions emerged from piano-improvising—and the latter was based, in their cases, on comfortable positions of hands, which in many instances conflicted with the standards of voice-leading. And although the piano acoustically can stand almost anything because it is primarily a percussive instrument (i.e., an instrument whose sounds fade out very rapidly), the orchestral works of these pianist-composers show how they had to pay the penalty. Chopin's own scores of his piano concertos, for example, are not played in the composer's own orchestration!

As the piano is a frequent participant in ensembles and orchestra, being used both as a solo and as an accompanying instrument, it is very desirable indeed to apply only such instrumental couplings as are used in orchestral writing. It would be of great advantage, both harmonically and acoustically, if the amateurish "block-harmony" were eliminated and piano writing were restricted to the general forms of instrumental couplings.

This requirement may be met by following either of these two procedures:

(1) an octave coupling of melody may be used only in the absence of other couplings of the same melody;

(2) any assemblage may be coupled in identical positions in the adjacent octave; *all* units of the assemblage must be included in the instrumental octave coupling if the latter takes place.

Octave coupling of melody or bass is a comfortable interval for most hands. It can be struck without much danger of being missed—hence the popularity of octave coupling on the keyboard.

---

*Schillinger has suggested that, inasmuch as pre-swing jazz is performed in rhythms deriving from $\frac{8}{8}$ series, and swing—although written in $\frac{8}{8}$—is actually performed in $\frac{12}{8}$ series rhythms, the term "jazz" be reserved for $\frac{8}{8}$ style and "Swing" be used to denote $\frac{12}{8}$ style. See his article in *Metronome*, July, 1942. The outstanding feature of boogie-woogie is the *basso ostinato*; it must also always be in $\frac{12}{8}$ series—i.e., the characteristic group is (as written in $\frac{8}{8}$) the triplet, ♪♪♪ , instead of the eighth, ♪♪ .
(Ed.)

Examples of Conventional Instrumental Piano Forms.

Figure 174. Theme. Melodization of harmony.

Instrumental Variation I.

Figure 175. Instrumental variation I.

Instrumental Variation II.

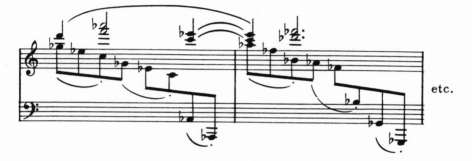

Instrumental Variation III.

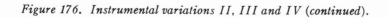

Figure 176. Instrumental variations II, III and IV (continued).

Instrumental Variation IV.

Figure 176. Variation (concluded).

The reader may use his own researches to verify how the problem of the instrumental form for piano writing was solved by Chopin, Mendelssohn, Schumann, Liszt, Rachmaninov. Scriabine, Debussy, and Ravel. Observe the evolution of piano styles toward normal acoustical forms* from Scarlatti, Clementi, etc., down to Liszt and Rachmaninov. Particular attention should be paid to the piano compositions of Nicholas Medtner.**

All problems pertaining to the piano's possibilities as to tone qualities, forms of attacks, and dynamics will be discussed when we come to a discussion of orchestration.

The main subject of the present study is the systematization of piano forms in their relation both to hands and the keyboard.

*See p. 1043.
**Nicolas Medtner is a contemporary Russian composer who was born in Moscow in 1880 and is now living in London. He served as professor of pianoforte at the Moscow Conservatory for a period of years and has toured England, France, and the United States as concert pianist. His best-known compositions are for the piano. (Ed.)

A. The Positions of Hands (R and L) with Respect to the Keyboard

Designating the right hand as R and the left hand as L, we shall evolve and demonstrate the inexhaustible possibilities and diversity of piano styles.

Fundamental principles:

(1) L is located below R; or
(2) L is located above R, crossing over it; or
(3) R is located below L, crossing over it;
(4) there are different *registral* positions for both L and R, and *each* such position emphasizes and corresponds to *one* instrumental stratum.
(5) The reasons for crossing R and L are:
   (a) excessive mobility of the instrumental form;
   (b) more comfortable control over a certain instrumental stratum (often the melody);
(6) avoidance of overloading each hand with too many scalewise passages.

The latter principle was strictly followed by Debussy, but was neglected by his predecessors. The utilization of five fingers (and therefore five points) in one passage is a very sound and economical principle, quite in contrast to the old-fashioned, conventional finger-twisting. To be sure, not too much can be done toward revising the fingering in old compositions, but we are here concerned with the writing of *new* works rather than with the execution of old ones.

The positions of R and L in their different distributions through the strata may refer either to melody, or to harmony, or to a combination of both, as well as to two or more correlated melodies; the following examples of positions, in other words, may be applied in more than one way.

The different levels in the table represent the different instrumental strata The time sequence of the different positions is represented in the usual manner i.e., from left to right. Time periods for the different sequent positions are not specified. The entire scheme is evolved geometrically and is based on level, ascending, and descending directions—and on the number of instrumental strata involved.

*Classification of R and L with Respect to Keyboard, Time
Sequence and the Number of Instrumental Strata.*

$\Sigma = 2S$; Two Staves

Form: ═══

	(1)	(2)	(3)	(4)	(5)	(6)
top	R	L	R	R	L	L
bottom	L	R	L	L	R	R

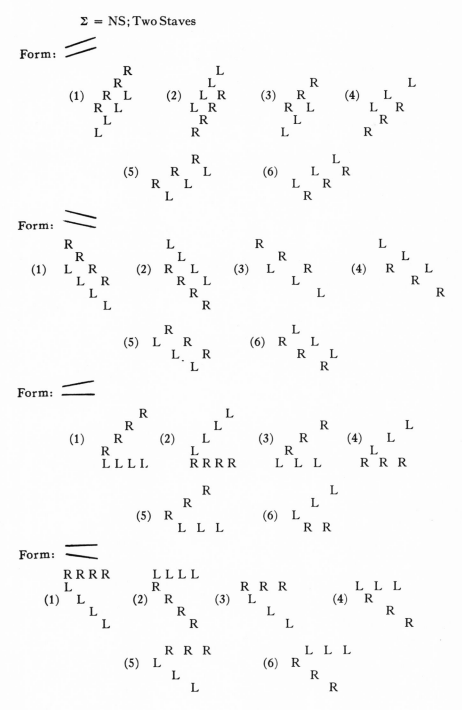

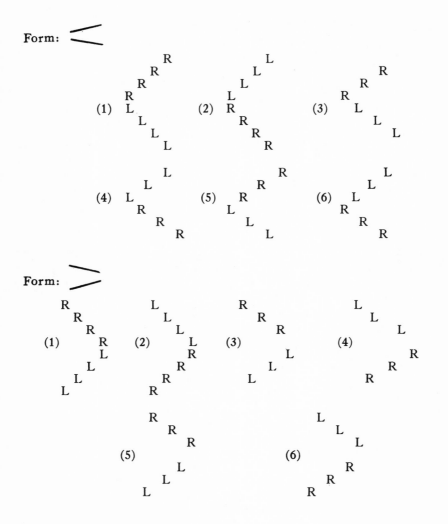

Form:

(1) (2) (3)

(4) (5) (6)

Form:

(1) (2) (3) (4)

(5) (6)

Σ = 3S; Three Staves

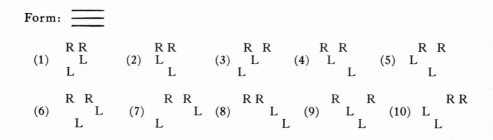

Form:

(1) R R   (2) R R   (3) R R   (4) R R   (5) R R
    L   L   L   L   L
  L   L   L   L   L

(6) R R   (7) R R   (8) R R   (9) R R   (10) R R
      L   L   L   L   L
  L   L   L   L   L

```
        R R                  R R                R   R                  R R
(11)  L                (12)       L      (13)   L          (14)        L
           L                   L                L                      L


      L L                L L              L  L              L L                L L
(15)    R        (16)    R        (17)     R       (18)     R         (19)    R
      R                    R              R                   R                   R


      L  L              L L                LL               L   L
(20)      R      (21)      R       (22)      R       (23)   R
        R                R                     R                  R


         LL                LL               LL              L   L
(24)  R          (25)  R           (26)       R     (27)    R
         R                   R              R                  R


         LL                L              L                L               L
(28)  R          (29)  R R        (30)  R R        (31)  R R       (32)  R  R
      R                L                I                  L                    L


      L                    L                L                L
(33)    R   R      (34)  R   R     (35)  R   R     (36)    RR
          L                L                L                L


      L                    L                L                L
(37)    RR  L      (38)  RR  L     (39)  R   R     (40)     RR
                                           L                L


         L                  L                R                R
(41)    RR         (42)  R   R     (43)  L L       (44)  LL
      L                    L                R                  R


         R                  R                R                   R
(45)  L  L         (46)  L  L      (47)  L L       (48)  L  L
      R                     R               R                  R


         R                  R                R                  R
(49)  L   L        (50)  R  LL     (51)  LL        (52)  LL
      R                 R                   R                 R


         R                  R                R                R
(53)  L   L        (54)  R  LL     (55)  LL        (56)  L   L
         R              R                R                  R
```

Σ = NS; 3 Staves

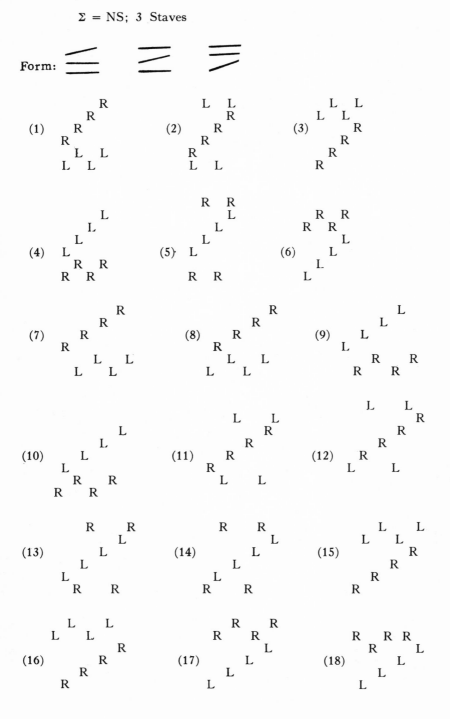

In a similar way, simultaneous and sequent groups of R and L may be developed from the following forms:

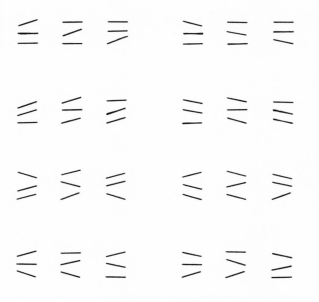

Figure 176. Positions of R and L.

A still greater degree of complexity may be achieved by means of four-staff positions for R and L. It is not necessary to tabulate such forms; they are not likely to be used frequently and may be selected for each particular use, if and when desirable.

Many of the cases, which contain several instrumental strata, become sufficiently complex to be represented on more than the two customary piano staves. Depending on the position of hands which predominates in each particular case, different combinations of staves with regard to R and L may be considered practical. For instance, a harmonic accompaniment, emphasizing two or three instrumental strata played by the L, with melody above it played by the R requires three staves, the lower two (bass and treble clefs) being executed by L; the upper, by R. The case in which L plays the lower and the upper strata while R plays the middle stratum requires three staves also, the two extreme staves should refer to L; the middle staff, to R.

A number of composers have utilized the three-staff arrangement. We find, moreover, a four-staff arrangement in Rachmaninov's *Prelude* in C#-minor, and a five-staff arrangement in N. Cherepnin's First Piano Concerto. In the latter case, in my opinion, three staves would have been entirely adequate.

Figure 177. Theme and instrumental variations (continued).

Figure 177. Instrumental variation (concluded).

THE SCHILLINGER SYSTEM

OF

MUSICAL COMPOSITION

by

JOSEPH SCHILLINGER

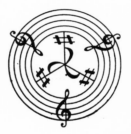

BOOK IX

GENERAL THEORY OF HARMONY

(STRATA HARMONY)

BOOK NINE

GENERAL THEORY OF HARMONY:
STRATA HARMONY

INTRODUCTION TO STRATA HARMONY

My general theory of harmony denotes the whole manifold of techniques, which enable the composer to write *directly* for groups of instruments or voices. Every score (chamber music, symphonic, choral or operatic) consists of parts for such individual instruments as piano, harp, or organ, and for those instruments which generally appear in groups, such as clarinets, violins, or trombones.

To evolve the required techniques for composing these scores, it is necessary to discover, first, the principles which control the behavior of individual parts and groups; and, second, the principles by which these individual parts and groups may be coordinated.

We also know that the field to which the theory of the behavior of groups or assemblages of pitch-units belongs is the field we call harmony. Therefore, the solution to this whole problem lies in the *generalization of harmonic principles*. This generalization must emphasize structures, their coordination in simultaneity and continuity, progressions, and directional units; it must generalize *structure* to such an extent that *sequent* structures will be *convertible* into *simultaneous* structures and vice versa. This means the introduction of scientific system in place of the old musical dualism of melody and harmony. Our theory must also enable us to coordinate any number of melodies, the derivation of which is harmonic. Thus we see that the manifold of harmonic techniques, although it is immense in its scope *per se*, becomes merely a subsidiary propedeutics to the *art of composing for groups*.

My general theory of harmony, I may say, satisfies all of the requirements just stated; it is the first scientific system crossing the threshold of the *sanctum sanctorum* of musical creation.

Contrary to what was the case in my special theory of harmony, this system has not been based on observation and analysis of existing musical facts only; it is entirely *inductive*. General harmony does not conflict with any of the principles of special harmony, but it gives them a broader interpretation instead. As a system, then, special harmony is but one case of general harmony.

The *General Theory of Harmony* discloses the real principles of harmonic creation.* It is particularly gratifying to me that, being an inductive system, this theory gives us direct interpretations of musical facts found in such remote regions of musical creation as the polyphony of Palestrina, the symphonic style of Mozart, the "bizarre" harmonies of Ravel, or the tone-clusters of some of our

*"The main purpose of the *General Theory of Harmony: Strata Harmony*," Schillinger writes in Chapter 7 of the present book, "is to satisfy demands for the scoring of all possible combinations of instruments, voices, or both . . . " In other words, the present book lays the groundwork and presents some of the basic principles of Schillinger's Theory of Orchestration. One aspect of orchestration not included in this book is the assigning of instrumental combinations to harmony "where the mobility of the instrumental form of a part defines the quantity of harmonic parts": i.e., where one instrument may perform an instrumental form of 2, or 3, or 4 part harmony. Nevertheless, the arrangements made by students who had completed this book were so rich and arresting that other students, who had not yet reached this book, assumed that such arrangements had been made on the basis of the *Theory of Orchestration*.(Ed.)

[1063]

contemporaries. Besides covering all known styles of music, both in folklore and in the creations of individual composers, it shows that an inexhaustible number of *new* individual styles is available, and that the possibilities of the twelve-unit equal temperament scale can outlive the life-span of music itself.

The nomenclature I shall use is:

p, 2p, 3p, and 4p = simultaneous pitch-units (parts).

S = simultaneous structure, stratum.

Σ (sigma) = compound structure of strata.

Σ (Σ) (the sigma of a sigma) = complex compound structure (compound structure of sigmae).

P_I, P_{II}, P_{III}, etc. = parts of simultaneity ≡ a, b, c, . . . etc.

S_I, S_{II}, S_{III}, etc. = structures of simultaneity.

$Σ_I$, $Σ_{II}$, $Σ_{III}$, etc. = structures of simultaneity.

S_1, S_2, S_3, etc. = structures of continuity.

$Σ_1$, $Σ_2$, $Σ_3$, etc. = structures of continuity.

i   = pitch-interval unit (semitone).

I   = pitch-interval group (of semitones).

$p_{\rightarrow}$ = ascending directional unit ($a_{\rightarrow}$, $b_{\rightarrow}$, $c_{\rightarrow}$, $d_{\rightarrow}$).

$p^{\rightarrow}$ = descending directional unit ($a^{\rightarrow}$, $b^{\rightarrow}$, $c^{\rightarrow}$, $d^{\rightarrow}$).

$p_{\rightarrow}$ = sequent part (sequent pitch unit).

$S^{\rightarrow}$ = sequent structure (pitch-scale, directional pitch-scale).

$Σ^{\rightarrow}$ = sequent compound structure (pitch-scale derived from all strata of the Σ).

H_1, H_2, H_3, etc. = chords in successive enumeration.

$H^{\rightarrow}$ = progression of chords.

CHAPTER 1

ONE-PART HARMONY

A. One Stratum of One-Part Harmony (S = p)

THE Sp represents a constant or a variable function of a potential assemblage, Σ. It may also have an independent existence, in which case it represents a constant *function a*, since it is a root-tone. In both cases, it becomes a melody harmonically defined.

Progressions of Sp may be evolved through any desirable scale selected from any of the four groups. Either tonal cycles or simply permutations of the pitch-units may control such progressions. It follows from the foregoing statement that progressions of Sp may be either diatonic or symmetric. (It is correct to think of all the diatonic scales as *special cases* of symmetry—where symmetric roots are 2, 4, 8, ... n, i.e., where they are arranged in an octave or in a multiple-octave recurrence).

A one-unit scale of the first (and *ipso facto* of the second) group constitutes the progression known as pedal point.* A one-unit scale of the third or the fourth group constitutes a progression consisting of a group of successive pedal points, each pedal point representing a root of symmetry.**

All other forms of Sp progressions, in most known instances, represent a *basso continuo* (so-called general bass, figured bass, or thorough bass). Under the conditions of general harmony, Sp may appear in any vertical relationship to any other S of the Σ, which means that when Sp assumes the role of a bass, it is simply one special case among the possible cases. In special harmony, Sp progressions appeared as a constant root-tone in harmony composed of S(5) in the classical system, and as a variable chordal function of S(5) in harmony of S(6) and $S(^6_4)$, as the third or the fifth of the chord.

As one chordal function cannot reciprocate with itself, it has no transformations. Its variability depends on a potential Σ, as in the cases described above. Yet, as we learned from the theory of melodization, a constant function, a, may become a constant function b, or c, or d . . . etc., which is dependent on the potential Σ.

The meaning of these constant chordal functions in the light of special harmony is confined to function a's being the root, function b's being the third, function c's being the fifth, etc. But one must now bear in mind that the root, the third, the fifth, etc., are nothing but the degrees of certain seven-unit scales in their E_1. Therefore, the constancy of a chordal function may refer to any degree of any scale in any of the four groups.

We shall make extensive use of Sp progressions in this study as a desirable —and often necessary—supplement to other strata of the Σ. No illustrations of independent progressions of Sp are necessary.

---

*That is to say, when the scale is a one-note scale, the progressions available are: *one*. A single-note progression, so far as one-part harmony goes, is a pedal point. (Ed.)

**The reference here is to the four groups of scales described in Vol. I, pp. 103, 133, 148 and 155. (Ed.)

CHAPTER 2

TWO-PART HARMONY

A. One Stratum of Two-Part Harmony (S = 2p)

ASSEMBLAGES which serve as two-part harmonic structures are the two pitches of two-unit scales brought into simultaneity. As the number of two-unit pitch-scales is eleven,* there are that many two-part harmonic structures.

Illustrations of S = 2p

All structures of S2p

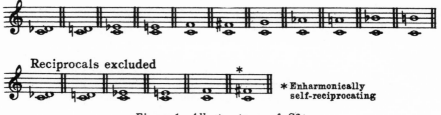

Reciprocals excluded

*Enharmonically self-reciprocating

Figure 1. All structures of S2p.

Each scale, as we know, may be expressed through the quantities of interval-units; if we enumerate the possible structures as S_1, S_2, S_3, . . . we obtain their equivalents in the forms of I.

$$I(S_1) = i; \ I(S_2) = 2i; \ I(S_3) = 3i; \ . \ . \ . \ I(S_{11} = 11i)$$

Progressions of S2p for any one of the eleven forms of S may be evolved through any desirable scale from all four groups. Either tonal cycles or permutation of pitch-units may control such progressions, which may be executed in any form of symmetry, including generalized symmetry as well. It is expedient, for this reason, to develop progressions of S2p under different diatonic and symmetric conditions. However, only the seven-unit scales with non-identical pitches permit the use of all types of structure in diatonic progressions —and even then "all structures" means *all structures within the diatonic scale.*

In this system we shall regard all the possible diatonic structures as consisting of adjacent pitch-units in a given scale under a certain form of tonal expansion. Therefore, the structures of E_0 of a natural major are all seconds: $\frac{d}{c}, \frac{e}{d}, \frac{f}{e}, \ . \ . \ .$, etc. Likewise, all structures of E_1, in the same scale are all *thirds;* $\frac{e}{c}, \frac{f}{d}, \frac{g}{e}, \ . \ . \ .$, etc.

*That is, 11 within the limits of a 12-semitone octave. (Ed.)

Structures, diatonic with respect to natural major.

$S(E_3)$, $S(E_4)$, $S(E_5)$ constitute reciprocity

Structures, diatonic with respect to Chinese Pentatonic.

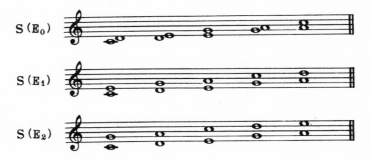

$S(E_3)$ reciprocates with $S(E_0)$

Figure 2. Diatonic structures.

As the number of diatonic structures (i.e., structures corresponding to combinations of musical names and not to the exact quantities of i) corresponds to the number of tonal expansions (including E_0), the number of such structures in any of the above defined seven-unit scales is six:

$$S(E_0) \equiv \text{second}; \quad S(E_1) \equiv \text{third}; \quad S(E_2) \equiv \text{fourth};$$
$$S(E_3) \equiv \text{fifth}; \quad\;\; S(E_4) \equiv \text{sixth}; \quad S(E_5) \equiv \text{seventh}.$$

This number has to be reduced practically to three, for the six forms include three mutually reciprocating pairs in octave-inversion.

Whether $S(E_1)$ be assumed to be $\frac{c}{a}$—causing $S(E_4)$ to be merely an inversion of $S(E_1)$, or whether it is the opposite, makes a purely theoretical difference. Once the transformations take place, the forms begin to reciprocate, and the question as to whether the sixth is an inversion of the third, or the third is an inversion of the sixth, is a metaphysical rather than real one.

It is easy to see from the above discussion that scales with fewer than seven units (providing they are diatonic and not symmetric) do not provide diatonically constant structures under any desirable tonal expansion.

For this reason, whenever the composer wishes to use a constant diatonic structure in a diatonic progression, he should evolve his harmonic progressions from the seven-unit scales with non-identical pitches.

In all other types of harmonic progression we shall use any of the eleven forms of S2p, whatever the stylistic authenticity may be with regard to the progression itself.

Transformations

Transformations* of two-part assemblages of *diatonically identical* structures are reduced to one possible form: $a \circlearrowright b$, i.e., a transforms into b, while b transforms into a. This concerns both the positions and voice-leading. A two-part assemblage of any form may be called a *diad*.

Transformations of two-part assemblages of *diatonically non-identical* structures have an additional const. ab transformation: $a \to a^1$ and $b \to b^1$—i.e., the a-function of the first structure transforms into the a-prime function of the following structure, and the b-function of the first structure transforms into the b-prime function of the following structure. Once the transformation is performed, H_2 is assumed to be the original structure (i.e., $\frac{b}{a}$ and not $\frac{b^1}{a^1}$)—so that H_3, the subsequent structure, in turn may be $\frac{b}{a}$ or $\frac{b^1}{a^1}$, depending on the diatonic identity with the preceding structure.

Structures, diatonic with respect to I = 2i + 3i.

$$S(E_0)$$

$S(E_1)$ reciprocates with $S(E_0)$

Figure 3. $S(E_0)$, $S(E_1)$, and $S(E_2)$ (continued).

---

*If the reader happens to have forgotten it, Schillinger uses the term *transformations* to mean *voice-leading*, so far as general (and special) harmony is concerned. A 2-part structure, $\frac{a}{b}$, transforms—i.e., its voices lead—into a structure, $\frac{b}{a}$. For example, if a=1, b=3, and two successive roots are C & F, then $\frac{a}{b}$ ($\frac{1}{3}$) on C is $\frac{C}{E}$, which transforms to $\frac{b}{a}$ ($\frac{3}{1}$) on F, or $\frac{A}{F}$. In other words the upper voice leads from C to A, while the lower voice leads from F to C, the cycle (C, F) being C_5. Transformations are the general form of *all* voice-leading, of no matter what kind—and the student who grasps this single principle will never have any trouble with even the most complex problems of this sort.
(Ed.)

All the following examples are reversible.

Examples of Diatonic Progressions in Natural Major

Figure 3. $S(E_0)$, $S(E_1)$, and $S(E_2)$ (continued).

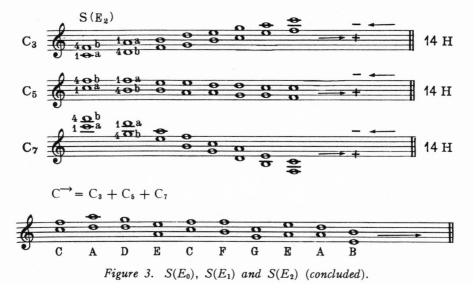

$$C^{\rightarrow} = C_3 + C_5 + C_7$$

Figure 3. S(E₀), S(E₁) and S(E₂) (concluded).

Diatonic-Symmetric Progressions.

(1)

Structure: I = 2i

Structure: I = 3i

Structure: I = 4i

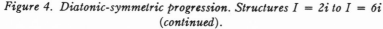

Figure 4. Diatonic-symmetric progression. Structures I = 2i to I = 6i (continued).

Structure: I = 5i

Structure: I = 6i

Figure 4. Diatonic-symmetric progression. Structures I = 2i to I = 6i (concluded).

(2)

Scale: Progression:

Structure: I = 2i

Structure: I = 3i

Structure: I = 4i

Structure: I = 5i

Structure: I = 6i

Figure 5. Diatonic-symmetric progressions. Structures I = 2i to I = 6i.

Figure 6. Diatonic-symmetric progression. Structure I = 2i to I = 6i.

Symmetric Progressions.

Generalized Progression

Figure 7. Symmetric and generalized progression. I(S) = 2i.

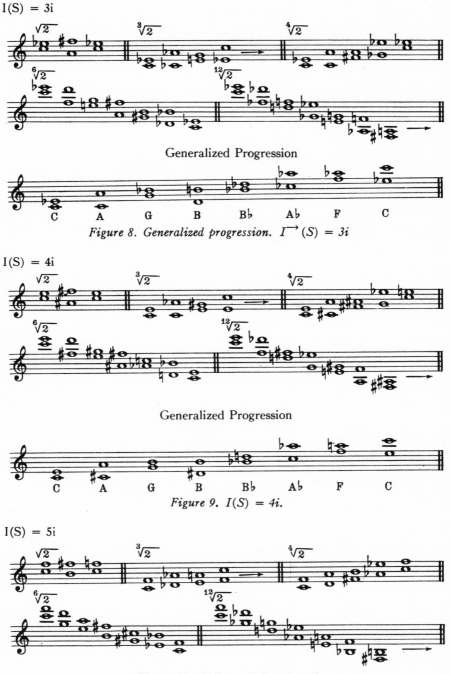

Figure 8. Generalized progression. $\overrightarrow{I}(S) = 3i$

Figure 9. $I(S) = 4i$.

Figure 10. $I(S) = 5i$ (continued).

Generalized Progression

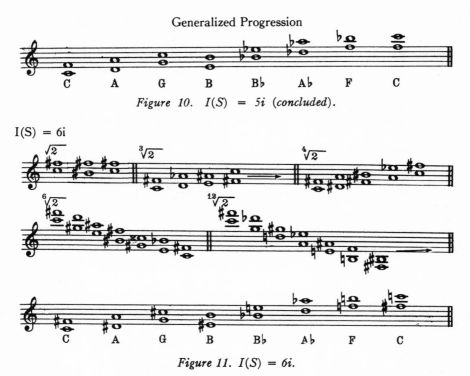

Figure 10. $I(S) = 5i$ (concluded).

$I(S) = 6i$

Figure 11. $I(S) = 6i$.

B. SEQUENCE OF VARIABLE STRUCTURES IN ONE TWO-PART STRATUM

Variable structures may appear in any type of harmonic progression.

Diatonic variable structures may be referred to the different forms of tonal expansion: $S(E_0)$, $S(E_1)$, $S(E_2)$, . . ., etc., which may be selected in any desirable quantities and forms of distribution. However, in view of our auditory habits, it is advisable to use low coefficients of recurrence.

To simplify the notation, we shall represent the correspondence between structures and forms of expansion as follows:

$$\Sigma_1 = S(E_0); \; \Sigma_2 = S(E_1); \; \Sigma_3 = S(E_2); \; . \; . \; .$$

In composing the continuity of structures, we may select a coefficient-group from any source discussed in the *Theory of Rhythm.**

Examples of composition of the structure-groups:

(1) $\overrightarrow{\Sigma} = \Sigma_2 + \Sigma_1$; (2) $\overrightarrow{\Sigma} = \Sigma_3 + \Sigma_1 + \Sigma_2$; (3) $\overrightarrow{\Sigma} = 2\Sigma_1 + \Sigma_2$;

(4) $\overrightarrow{\Sigma} = 3\Sigma_1 + \Sigma_3 + 2\Sigma_2$; (5) $\overrightarrow{\Sigma} = 2\Sigma_2 + \Sigma_3 + \Sigma_2 + 2\Sigma_3$;

(6) $\overrightarrow{\Sigma} = 3\Sigma_1 + \Sigma_2 + 2\Sigma_3 + 2\Sigma_1 + \Sigma_2 + 3\Sigma_3$;

(7) $\overrightarrow{\Sigma} = 4\Sigma_1 + 2\Sigma_2 + 2\Sigma_1 + \Sigma_2$;

*See Vol. I, p. 12 ff.

(8) $\Sigma^{\rightarrow} = 9\Sigma_3 + 3\Sigma_1 + 3\Sigma_3 + \Sigma_1;$

(9) $\Sigma^{\rightarrow} = 4\Sigma_1 + 2\Sigma_2 + 2\Sigma_3 + 2\Sigma_1 + \Sigma_2 + \Sigma_3 + 2\Sigma_1 + \Sigma_2 + \Sigma_3;$

(10) $\Sigma^{\rightarrow} = \Sigma_2 + 2\Sigma_1 + 3\Sigma_2 + 5\Sigma_1;$

(11) $\Sigma^{\rightarrow} = \Sigma_3 + 2\Sigma_1 + 4\Sigma_3 + 8\Sigma_1.$

Structures of seven-unit scales with non-identical pitches produce *diatonically*-identical structures, i.e., Σ_1 are seconds, Σ_2 are thirds, Σ_3 are fourths. In other scales, structures of one expansion are diatonically non-identical. Yet it is better, and a more general method, to select diatonic structures with respect to their expansions.

The choice of general structures (out of the manifold of eleven) may be made freely, and any combination of structures in any form of distribution is acceptable. Such a use of eleven structures in any combinations and arrangement is applicable to progressions of type II, III, and the generalized forms of consecutive symmetry.

Examples of Progressions with Variable Structures

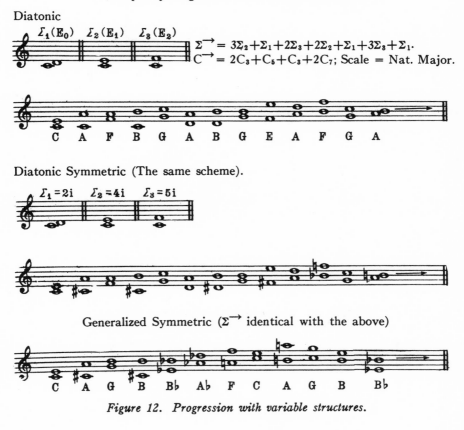

Figure 12. Progression with variable structures.

C. Two Hybrid Strata

$$\Sigma = 2S; S_I = p; S_{II} = 2p$$

The addition of an Sp to any form of S2p progressions produces a *hybrid* three-part harmony.

Actual selection of a function for Sp is a matter of the style of the harmonic structures. Depending on the structure of S2p, the addition of a function of Sp may produce either greater tension or less tension.

It is easy to compute the actual quantity of all possible forms of the three-part hybrid structures. The total quantity of Sp structures is eleven. The latter are built from the twelve symmetric pitch units of equal temperament and represent all combinations by two from the original unit. Assuming that each of the 11 S2p structures may be accompanied by any of the 12 functions of the full tuning scale, we acquire the total of $11 \cdot 12 = 132$ structures.

Out of this total number, all the diatonic structures (with respect to seven musical names) may be classified as well. There are six diatonic structures, corresponding to six expansions of the complete diatonic scale, and seven diatonic units which can be added to any one of them. The total of the diatonic hybrid three-part structures amounts to: $6 \cdot 7 = 42$.

D. Table of Hybrid Three-Part Structures

(a) General and (b) Diatonic

(a)

Figure 13. General hybrid three-part structures (continued).

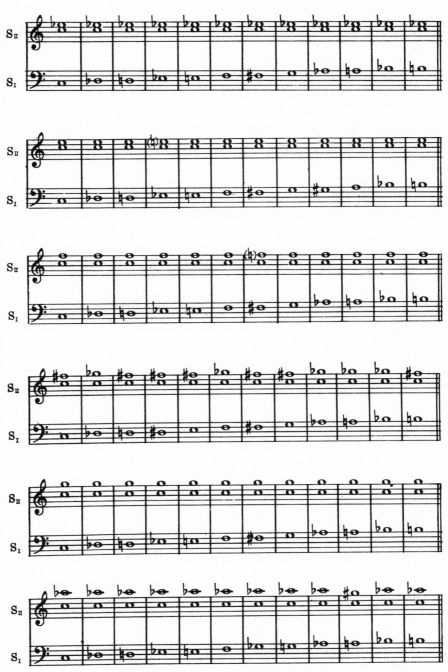

Figure 13. General hybrid three-part structures (continued).

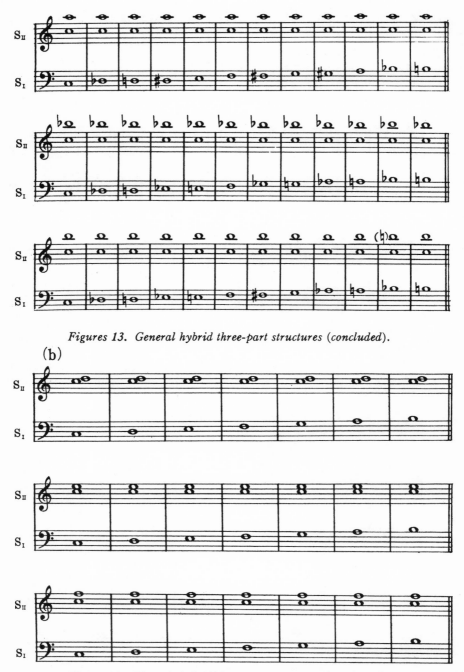

Figures 13. General hybrid three-part structures (concluded).

Figure 14. Diatonic hybrid three-part structures (continued).

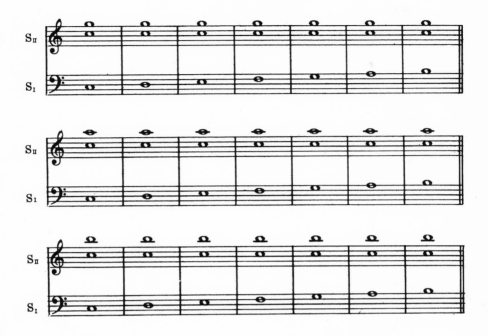

Figure 14. Diatonic hybrid three-part structures (concluded).

All diatonic hybrid three-part structures may acquire *any one system* of accidentals at a time.

Sp may be placed either below or above S2p.

As the sequence of S2p structures may be varied in a progression, the addition of an Sp is a matter of the individual selection of a function for *each* structure of S2p.

In the following notation, we shall use this scheme:

C-chord

(1) Diatonic nomenclature:

c	d	e	f	g	a	b
1	2	3	4	5	6	7

(2) Symmetric nomenclature:

c	c#	d	d#	e	f	f#	g	g#	a	bb	b♮
1	2	3	4	5	6	7	8	9	10	11	12

Let us see how such numerical notation can be applied to either system of structures.

We shall take, for example, $S_{II} = 5i$. This represents: (reading from c) $\frac{f}{c}$, or in numerical notation: $\frac{4}{1}$. If we decided to add d as S_I, the latter becomes const. 2. Therefore the entire Σ may be read as follows:

$$\Sigma = \frac{S_{II} = 1, 4}{S_I = 2 \text{ const.}}$$

which is the *diatonic* form of numerical notation, where $a(S_{II}) = 1$ and $b(S_{II}) = 4$, and where $a(S_I) = 2$. The same case, when represented in the *symmetric* form of numerical notation, assumes the following form:

$$\Sigma = \frac{S_{II} = 1, 6}{S_I = 3 \text{ const.}} \text{, where } a(S_{II}) = 1 \text{ and } b(S_{II}) = 6, \text{ and where } a(S_I) = 3.$$

In case of coincidence in pitch of the function of S_I with either of the functions of S_{II}, only the fundamental form of transformation (a $\circlearrowright$ b) may be used—otherwise consecutive octaves are unavoidable.

E. Examples of Hybrid Three-Part Harmony

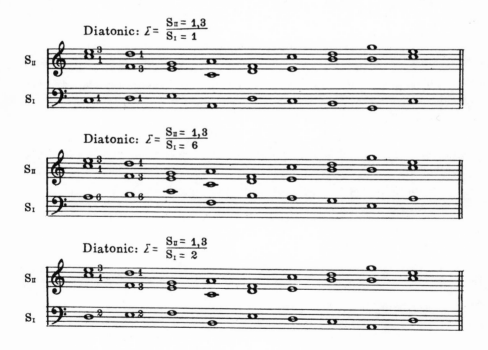

Figure 15. Hybrid three-part harmony (continued).

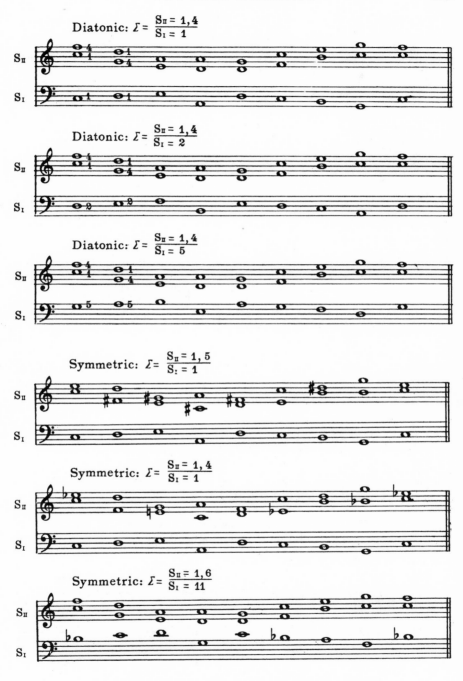

Figure 15. Hybrid three-part harmony (continued).

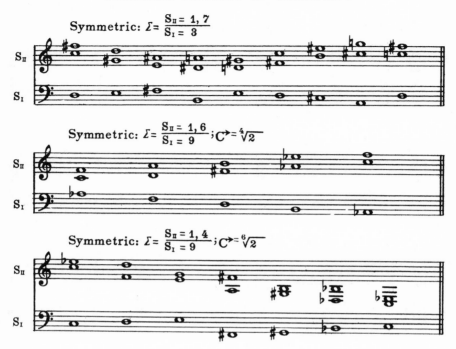

$$\text{Symmetric: } \Sigma = \frac{S_{II} = 1, 7}{S_I = 3}$$

$$\text{Symmetric: } \Sigma = \frac{S_{II} = 1, 6}{S_I = 9}; C^{\rightarrow} = \sqrt[4]{2}$$

$$\text{Symmetric: } \Sigma = \frac{S_{II} = 1, 4}{S_I = 9}; C^{\rightarrow} = \sqrt[6]{2}$$

Figure 15. Hybrid three-part harmony (concluded).

Progressions of Mixed Structures.

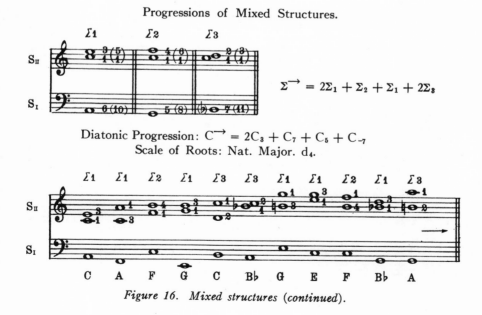

$$\Sigma^{\rightarrow} = 2\Sigma_1 + \Sigma_2 + \Sigma_1 + 2\Sigma_3$$

Diatonic Progression: $C^{\rightarrow} = 2C_3 + C_7 + C_5 + C_{-7}$
Scale of Roots: Nat. Major. d_4.

Figure 16. Mixed structures (continued).

Symmetric Progression on the same Scale of Roots.

Figure 16. Mixed structures (concluded).

F. Two Strata of Two-Part Harmonies

$$\Sigma = 2S; \ S = 2p$$

Two two-part harmonic structures may be coordinated into a simultaneous Σ and subjected to independent transformations in each stratum. The latter result in four-part progressions in which the two component strata act independently. This technique solves many problems in composing for two heterogeneous pairs of instruments. For example, two clarinets may play a stratum not only against another stratum of two French horns, but even against two violin parts. The quality of orchestration can be well affected by different forms of distribution of the same four-part harmony developed into $\Sigma = 2S$.

The number of *general* structures of $\Sigma = 2S2p$ equals the quantity of S2p, times the number of combinations of S2p in the two strata, times the number of possible positions between S_I and S_{II}: $11^3 = 1,331$.

The number of *diatonic* structures (which represents a portion of the total quantity) equals: $6^3 = 216$.

It means that there are 1,331 general and 216 diatonic chord structures from any pitch-unit designated as a starting point (root-tone).

As tabulation of all forms (since the quantity increases so rapidly) becomes impractical, we shall give some samples only of such tables.

Examples of Structures: $\Sigma = 2S2p$

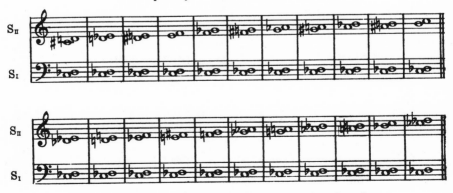

Figure 17. General structures of $\Sigma = 2S2p$ (continued).

Figure 17. *General structures of* $\Sigma = 2S2p$ *(concluded)*.

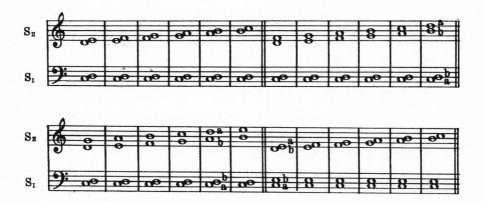

Figure 18. *Diatonic structures of* $\Sigma = 2S2p$ *(continued)*.

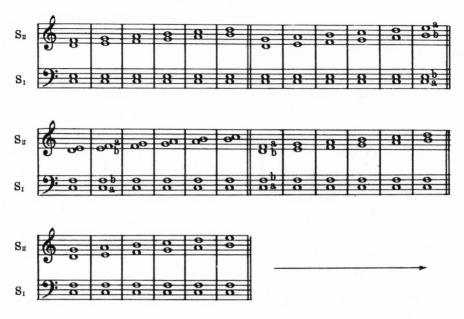

Figure 18. Diatonic structures of $\Sigma = 2S2p$ *(concluded).*

In order to eliminate consecutive octaves between any pair of parts in strata, assign identical pitches to non-identical functions. If, for example, pitch d appears in both strata, one of them should become function ⓐ and the other should become function ⓑ.

G. EXAMPLES OF PROGRESSIONS IN TWO STRATA:

(a) through the different forms of distribution of a given four-part harmony

(a) Theme

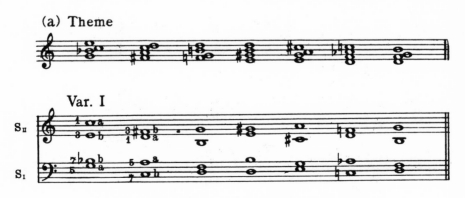

Figure 19. Theme and variations (continued).

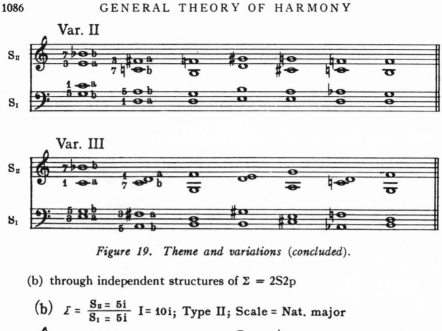

Figure 19. Theme and variations (concluded).

(b) through independent structures of Σ = 2S2p

(b) $\Sigma = \dfrac{S_{II} = 5i}{S_I = 5i}$ I= 10i; Type II; Scale = Nat. major

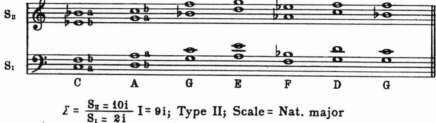

$\Sigma = \dfrac{S_{II} = 10i}{S_I = 2i}$ I= 9i; Type II; Scale = Nat. major

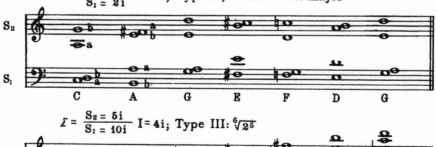

$\Sigma = \dfrac{S_{II} = 5i}{S_I = 10i}$ I= 4i; Type III: $\sqrt[6]{2^5}$

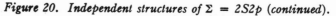

Figure 20. Independent structures of Σ = 2S2p (continued).

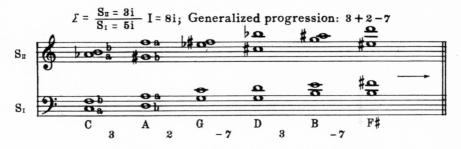

$$\Sigma = \frac{S_{II} = 3i}{S_I = 5i} \quad I = 8i; \text{ Generalized progression: } 3 + 2 - 7$$

Figure 20. Independent structures of Σ = 2S2p (concluded).

In the above examples, the structures are defined by i and I $\left(\dfrac{S_{II}}{S_I}\right)$.

For the time being, we shall use one const. Σ for the entire progression, unless such a progression is the given progression, which can be traced to the sources of special harmony, and which is subject to strata transcription (variation).

H. THREE HYBRID STRATA

$$\Sigma = 3S; \; S_I = p; \; S_{II} = 2p; \; S_{III} = 2p$$

An Sp may be added to Σ = 2S2p. This additional stratum may be either below both S2p, or it may be surrounded by the latter, or it may be above it. This permits three arrangements:

$$(1) \; \Sigma = \frac{S2p}{\dfrac{S2p}{Sp}} \; ; \quad (2) \; \Sigma = \frac{S2p}{\dfrac{Sp}{S2p}} \; ; \quad (3) \; \Sigma = \frac{Sp}{\dfrac{S2p}{S2p}}$$

An interchange of the positions in a written continuity is acceptable only when the total sonority of the Σ does not suffer from such an interchange. Often a high chordal function, originally placed in the upper stratum, sounds unsatisfactory when moved to the bass; such a rearrangement of parts often changes the very meaning of the Σ itself.

In many instances Sp may acquire a constant coupling or two. Such couplings are particularly practical for the extreme positions of Sp, i.e., either below all or above all other strata. Couplings may be constructed either upward or downward from a given function, provided that such coupling does not cross the functions of adjacent stratum. An octave coupling may be considered universal, i.e., applicable to any function. Couplings by perfect fifths for the lower stratum, and couplings by fifths, fourths, and practically all other intervals for the upper stratum are acceptable. The particular choice of couplings should follow to some extent the natural distribution of pitches (upward contraction of intervals). The coupling of a root-tone with the fifth is the commonest after the coupling of a root-tone by its octave.

Some structures, seemingly meaningless by themselves, become powerful tools of harmonic expression when supplemented by an Sp and a coupling.

Examples of Addition to Sp and Coupled Sp to Σ 2S2p

(Originals are taken from Figure 19. Type I progressions may be obtained by cancelling the accidentals, or by superimposing another constant group of accidentals).

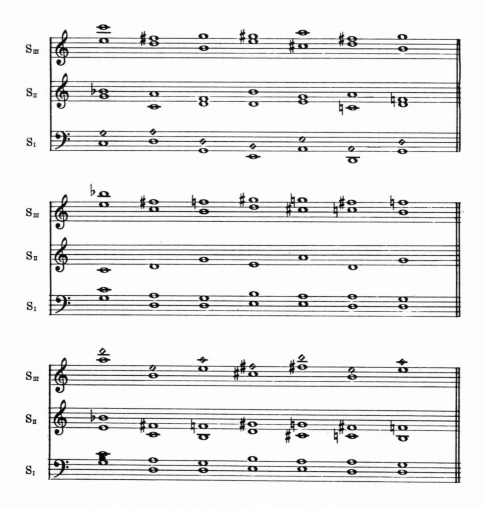

Figure 21. Σ2S2p + Sp + coupled Sp (continued).

Figure 21. Σ2S2p + Sp + *coupled Sp (concluded).*

I. THREE, FOUR AND MORE STRATA OF TWO-PART HARMONIES: HYBRID STRATA

Now that the principle of composing strata and of forming couplings for them has been established, we may proceed with the evolution of more complex forms of Σ.

Since the number of structures grows beyond the practical possibility of exhausting them, we shall refrain from tabulating them any further. We shall confine each case of Σ to a few samples of structures, and we shall choose the latter according to the principle established before, i.e., the structures and the intervals separating the strata will be conceived as forms of tonal expansions, or both will be evolved on the basis of interval symmetry.

In some instances a certain degree of variety may be achieved by alternating the original positions in the adjacent strata. For instance:

$$S_I = \frac{b}{a}; \ S_{II} = \frac{a}{b}; \ S_{III} = \frac{b}{a}; \ S_{IV} = \frac{a}{b} ; \ . \ . \ .$$

The first example of progressions (Fig. 22) compares favorably with six-part counterpoint of the type: $\frac{CP}{CF} = a$.

Examples of Harmonic Structures and
Progressions in Three and more Strata

$\Sigma = 3S2p$

Structures

Diatonic Forms Depend on the Number of Pitch-Units in the Scale.

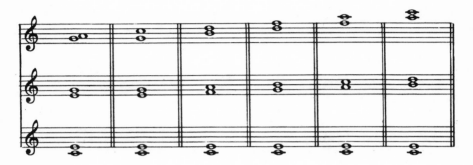

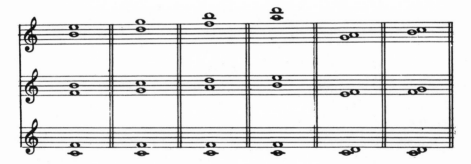

Symmetric Forms have Three or more Roots;

All Symmetric Two-Unit Scales belong to this group.

Figure 22. Structures and progressions of $\Sigma = 3S2p$ *(continued).*

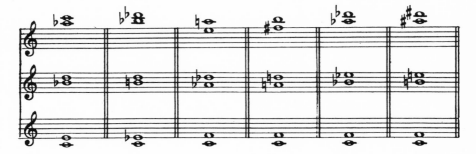

Progressions

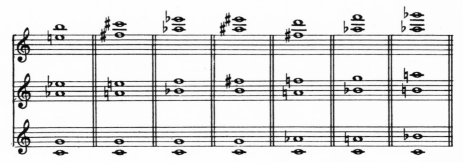

Figure 22. Structures and progressions of Σ = 3S2p (concluded).

$$\Sigma = 3S2pSp$$

Figure 23. $\Sigma = 3S2p\ Sp$.

$\Sigma = 4S2p$

Diatonic Structures

Symmetric structures: 4 or more roots

Figure 24. $\Sigma = 4S2p$ *(continued).*

Progressions

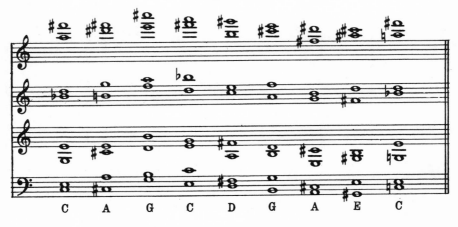

C   A   G   C   D   G   A   E   C

Figure 24. Σ = 4S2p *(concluded)*.

Figure 25. Σ = 4S2pSp.

J. DIATONIC AND SYMMETRIC LIMITS AND THE COMPOUND Σ
OF TWO-PART STRATA

The diatonic limit of a sigma composed from two-part strata may be expressed as Σ = NS2p, where N represents the number of pitch-units of a given scale.

A three-unit scale produces a maximum of three strata, or six parts (even seven parts if one includes a possible added root-tone). A five-unit scale produces Σ = 5S2p, or 10 parts in 5 strata (11 with the added root-tone). A complete seven-unit scale produces Σ = 7S2p, or 14 parts in 7 strata (15 with the added root-tone). Such limit-sigmae may be arranged according to one or another tonal expansion with regard to structures and the intervals between the strata. Selection of one or another tonal expansion controls the range of the Σ.

In practical application such limit-sigmae often require the overlapping of adjacent strata. In orchestration the strata which overlap are assigned to different orchestral groups, a method of tone-quality selection which prevents the score from losing its clarity in actual sound.

Only non-overlapping strata may belong to one orchestral group. For example, assuming that all adjacent strata are overlapping, but that no stratum overlaps the stratum next-but-one, we acquire the following possibilities for orchestration:

S_{IV}	Strings	Wind	Woodwind	Brass	Strings	Brass
S_{III}	Wind	Strings	Brass	Woodwind	Brass	Strings
S_{II}	Strings	Wind	Woodwind	Brass	Strings	Brass
S_{I}	Wind	Strings	Brass	Woodwind	Brass	Strings

More complex forms of sigmae with overlapping adjacent strata are developed in the form of tutti, i.e., with participation of all orchestral groups and often with the addition of soloists and choirs. This device is also practical when one orchestral group is broken into two or more heterogeneous groups by means of variation of instrumental forms—such as a legato against a pizzicato and against a muted tremolo.

In calculating the symmetric limit of a sigma, N represents the number of symmetric roots. Two tonics produce Σ = 2S2p, or two strata in 4 parts (or five parts with the addition of the root-tone). Twelve tonics, being the ultimate symmetric limit produce (Σ = 12S2p), 12 strata in 24 parts, in which case the overlapping of adjacent strata becomes unavoidable (25 parts with the addition of root-tone).

K. Compound Sigmae

I introduce now the concept of a *compound sigma*, or *the sigma of a sigma:* $\Sigma(\Sigma)$.

A compound sigma consists of more than one sigma. Each of the sigmae (i.e., Σ_I, Σ_{II}, Σ_{III}, ... Σ_N) consists of diatonic or of symmetric strata and is combined with another sigma, also consisting of several strata and connected to the first sigma by some form of interval-symmetry. In most cases of $\Sigma(\Sigma)$, overlapping becomes unavoidable. The lower stratum of Σ_I and the lower stratum of Σ_{II} produce a definite interval, which, as a consequence, controls the degree of overlapping.

In $\Sigma (\Sigma)$, diatonic sigmae are connected by a symmetric interval; symmetric sigmae are connected by an interval which is in a mutually excluding form of symmetry* with the structures of strata and the intervals connecting the latter.

The number of strata and of parts in the compound sigma equals the number of strata and of parts in each component sigma multiplied by the number of sigmae. For example, a compound sigma obtained from a five unit scale and three roots of symmetry for each component sigma produces a compound limit of 15 strata in 30 parts (or 31 with an addition of the root of Σ_I):

$$
\Sigma(\Sigma)
\begin{cases}
\Sigma_{III} = \dfrac{S_V}{\dfrac{S_{IV}}{\dfrac{S_{III}}{\dfrac{S_{II}}{S_I}}}} \\[2em]
\qquad\qquad I = \sqrt[3]{4} \\[1em]
\Sigma_{II.} = \dfrac{S_V}{\dfrac{S_{IV}}{\dfrac{S_{III}}{\dfrac{S_{II}}{S_I}}}} \\[2em]
\qquad\qquad I = \sqrt[3]{4} \\[1em]
\Sigma_I = \dfrac{S_V}{\dfrac{S_{IV}}{\dfrac{S_{III}}{\dfrac{S_{II}}{S_I}}}} \quad \text{Only } \Sigma_I \text{ may have an added root-tone.}
\end{cases}
$$

---

*That is, the interval is such as to ensure that the pitch-units composing one Σ do not coincide with those composing another Σ (Ed.)

It follows, from the above, that the limit for a seven-unit scale evolved into $\Sigma\,(\Sigma)$ through 12 symmetric points, becomes $\Sigma\,(\Sigma) = 7S2p \cdot 12 = 84S2p = 168p$.

The ultimate compound sigma composed from two-part strata is $(12S2p \cdot 12 = 144S2p =)$ 288p. This is the ultimate limit for a score composed in twelve-unit equal temperament out of two-part harmonies. Such a score of 289 parts (with an addition of the root-tone) may be used in practice for some group of combined orchestras, or choirs, or both. The place and time for such an occasion would be some such event as a World's Fair, an Eucharistic Congress, a world peace celebration, or an event of similar character calling for resources of such magnitude. With the knowledge of these possibilities, it is pitiful to recollect the experience of New York World's Fair of 1940—with the dozen or so pianos playing the *Second Rhapsody* of Liszt—a la "Roxy" in unison!

*Examples of the Limit-Structures
and the Compound Structures;* $\Sigma\,(\Sigma)$

Diatonic Limit

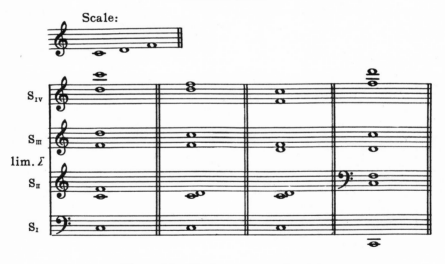

Figure 26. Limit-structures of $\Sigma\,(\Sigma)$.

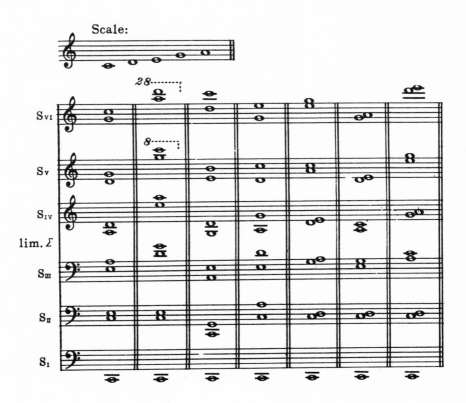

Figure 27. Limit-structures of Σ (Σ).

Figure 28. Limit-structures of Σ (Σ).

Symmetric limit

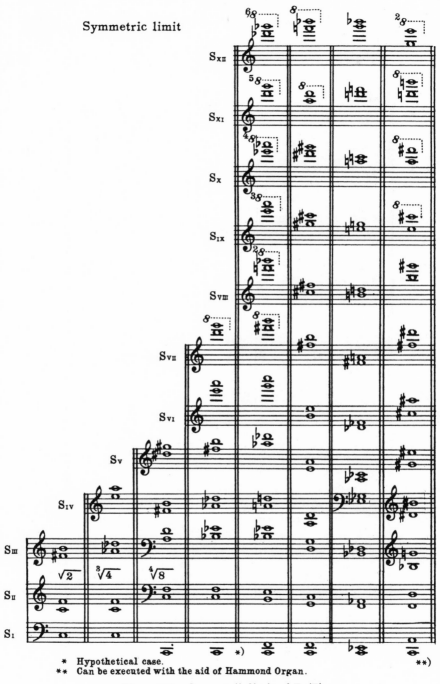

* Hypothetical case.
** Can be executed with the aid of Hammond Organ.

Figure 29. Symmetric limit of Σ (Σ).

Compound Symmetric Limit

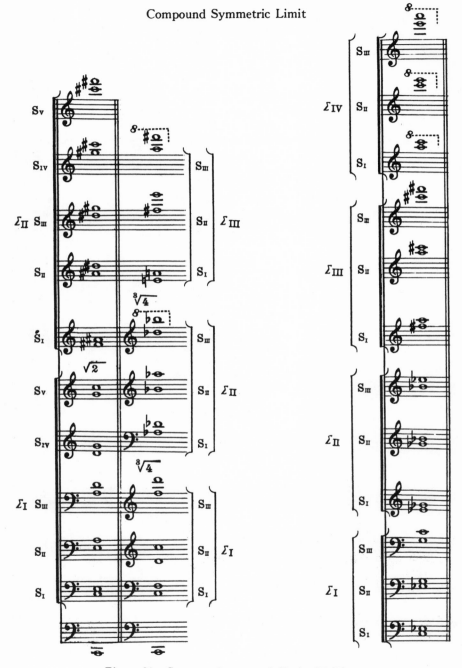

Figure 30. *Compound symmetric limit of Σ (Σ).*

CHAPTER 3

THREE-PART HARMONY

A. One Stratum of Three-Part Harmony (S = 3p)

ASSEMBLAGES which serve as three-part harmonic structures are the pitches of three-unit scales brought into simultaneity. Since the number of three-unit pitch-scales is 55, there are that many harmonic three-part structures. Each structure may be used in its original or in an expanded form, (E_0 and E_1).

All other conditions remain the same as for S2p.

In one stratum, with or without addition of a constant Sp or Sp with a coupling, we shall use either one constant structure or a group of structures belonging to one family. In the latter case, the added Sp must be assigned to each structure individually.

Table of Structures; $\Sigma = S3p$

Figure 31. $\Sigma = S3p$ (continued).

[1103]

Figure 31. Σ = \S3p (concluded).

It is particularly important to approach the study of structures of S3p from the viewpoint of tonal expansions of the complete seven-unit scales. Such an approach makes it possible to acquire six diatonic forms of structure per stratum.

Three-part assemblages of any form may be called *triads*. For this reason it is correct to state that there are 6 forms of diatonic triads which derive from the complete seven-unit scales. Each form of a triad corresponds to the respective expansion.

(1) $S3p \equiv E_0$; (2) $S3p \equiv E_1$; (3) $S3p \equiv E_2$;
(4) $S3p \equiv E_3$; (5) $S3p \equiv E_4$; (6) $S3p \equiv E_5$.

Structures, diatonic with respect to: $I(S) = 2i + 3i$

Structures, diatonic with respect to Chinese Pentatonic.

Figure 32. Diatonic structures (continued).

Structures, diatonic with respect to natural major.

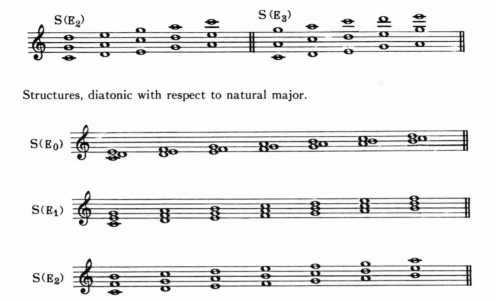

Figure 32. Diatonic structures (concluded).

Of these, the following pairs contain identical pitch-units, in their respective triads, in a different form of distribution:

(1) $S(E_0)$ and $S(E_5)$; (2) $S(E_1)$ and $S(E_4)$; (3) $S(E_2)$ and $S(E_3)$.

B. TRANSFORMATIONS OF S = 3p

Transformations which control three-part assemblages are identical with those described in my discussion of hybrid four-part harmony in the *Theory of Special Harmony*.* They control the positions, (the first two transformations) i.e., the distribution of pitch-units, now serving as chordal functions, and they control voice-leading, (all six) i.e., the transformation of chordal functions in time continuity. The following forms may be used with discretion, depending on the cycles and the possibilities of instrumental execution.

Transformations of S3p

↻	↺	Const. a	Const. b	Const. c	Const. abc
a → b′	a → c′	a → a′	a → c′	a → b′	a → a′
b → c′	b → a′	b → c′	b → b′	b → a′	b → b′
c → a′	c → b′	c → b′	c → a′	c → c′	c → c′

Const. a, Const. b, and Const. c permit the isolation of a heterogeneous instrument from the remaining two, as an independent function, and this solves many important problems in orchestration.

When the structure is constant, a′ = a, b′ = b, c′ = c.

Progressions of Σ = S3p are evolved through the previous means: type I, II, III and the generalized symmetric.

Examples of Transformations
(a) Positions   (b) Voice-leading

Figure 33. Positions (continued).

*See Vol. I. p. 478.

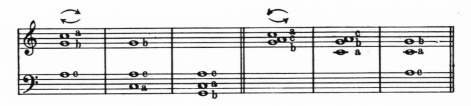

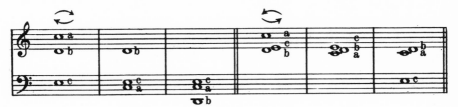

Figure 33. Positions (concluded).

(b)

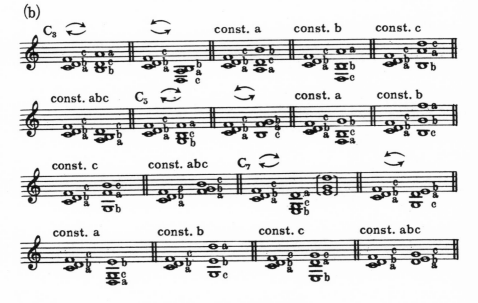

Figure 34. Voice-leading.

It follows from the example—(b) above—that the second chord of the connection appears in all six possible positions developed from any one position of the first chord when all six transformations are applied. For this reason, progressions may be written by selecting any position for the second chord which is adjacent to the given position of the first chord. However, a thorough knowledge of the patterns of motion through all cycles and through all transformations remains very desirable.

Examples of Progressions of S = 3p

Constant and Variable Structures.
Hybrid Four-Part Structures (added Sp and coupled Sp).

S(E₂), nat. major

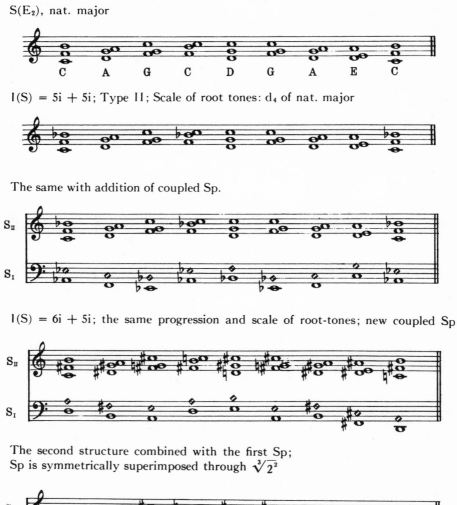

Figure 35. *Added Sp and coupled Sp (continued).*

The first structure combined with the second Sp.

Figure 35. Added Sp and coupled Sp (concluded).

Progression of Structures = $2S_2 + S_3 + S_2 + 2S_1$
Scale of root-tones: d_4 of nat. major

The same with Sp.

The same with coupled Sp.

Figure 36. Added Sp and Coupled Sp.

C. Two Strata of Three-Part Harmonies

$$\Sigma = 2S; \; S = 3p$$

Three-part harmonic structures may be coordinated into a simultaneous Σ and subjected to independent transformations in each stratum. As the number of transformations for S3p is 6, the number of transformations for Σ 2S3p is: $6^2 = 36$.

It is practical to study the fundamental forms first:

$$(1) \; \Sigma \left[\frac{S_{II}\curvearrowright}{S_I \curvearrowright} \right]; \quad (2) \; \Sigma \left[\frac{S_{II}\curvearrowright}{S_I \curvearrowright} \right]; \quad (3) \; \Sigma \left[\frac{S_{II}\curvearrowright}{S_I \curvearrowright} \right]; \quad (4) \; \Sigma \left[\frac{S_{II}\curvearrowright}{S_I \curvearrowright} \right];$$

Σ 2S3p offers solutions to all problems in orchestration in which two groups of three identical instruments are used.

Positions of S_I and S_{II} may be either identical or non-identical. The variety of forms of transformation even permits the use of partly-identical pitch-assemblages in the two strata without producing consecutive octaves as between some of the parts of the two strata.

The number of possible *general* structures of Σ 2S3p equals the quantity of S3p, times the number of combinations of S3p in the two strata, times the number of positions between S_I and S_{II}: $55^2 \cdot 11 = 33,275$ (identical positions of S_I and S_{II} are excluded).

Of these, 216 are *diatonic;* $6^3 = 216$.

Examples of Structures of Σ 2S3p.

(1) Diatonic (all scales of three and more units);
(2) Symmetric (all three-unit scales in all forms of symmetry): (General)

(1)

Figure 37. Structures of Σ 2S3p (continued).

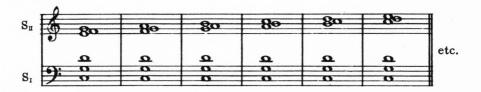

*) A useful form of S(5) with added 13, for a combination of two groups by three, like 3 Trumpets and 3 Trombones.

(2)

Figure 37. Structures of Σ 2S3p (continued).

Figure 37. Structures of Σ2S3p (concluded).

For the time being, use one constant Σ with Σ>S.

*Examples of Progressions of Σ 2S3p and Hybrid Forms Resulting
from the Addition of Sp (uncoupled or coupled).*

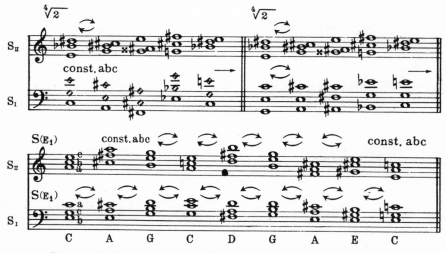

Figure 38. Progressions of Σ 2S3p and hybrid forms (continued).

The same with an added coupled Sp. and identical transformations in both strata

Figure 38. Progression of Σ2S3p and hybrid forms (concluded).

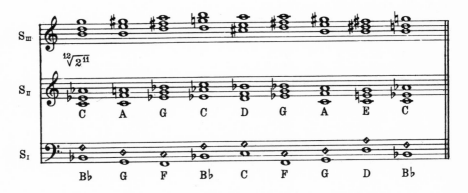

Figure 39. Identical transformations in both strata (continued).

Figure 39. Identical transformations in both strata (concluded).

D. THREE STRATA OF THREE-PART HARMONIES

$$\Sigma = 3S; \ S = 3p$$

Structures of Σ 3S3p may be evolved from diatonic scales with three or more units, and from three-unit symmetric scales having three or more symmetric roots.

Since all principles remain the same as in harmony of the 2S3p type, we shall proceed with the illustrations.

Examples of Structures of Σ 3S3p.

(1) Diatonic;
(2) Symmetric:

(General)

(1)

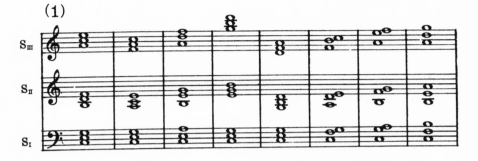

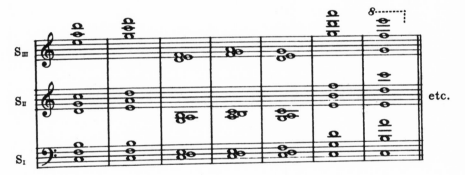

(2)

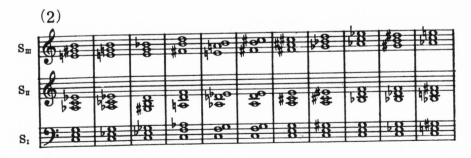

Figure 40.   Structures of Σ3S3p (continued).

Figure 40.   Structures of Σ3S3p (concluded).

*Examples of Progressions of Σ 3S3p and Hybrid Forms Resulting
from the Addition of Sp (uncoupled or coupled).*

Figure 41.   Progressions of Σ3S3p and hybrid forms (continued).

Figure 41. Progressions of Σ3S3p and hybrid forms (concluded).

E. Four and More Strata of Three-Part Harmonies

Structures of $\Sigma = 4S3p$ are available from all diatonic scales having three units and more. They are desirable when it is advantageous to distribute the latter in groups of 3.

In the example presented below, structures of thirds and fourths are offered as characteristic structures and typical forms of arrangement. Structures derived from symmetric scales lend themselves particularly well to distribution in four strata when there are 4 tonics with 3 unit sectional scales. When the number of tonics exceeds 4, the 6 tonic system, also with 3 unit sectional scales, is practical when 4 out of 6 tonics are used. The same concerns scales constructed on 12 tonics with 3 unit scales from each tonic.

$$\Sigma = 4S; \ S = 3p$$

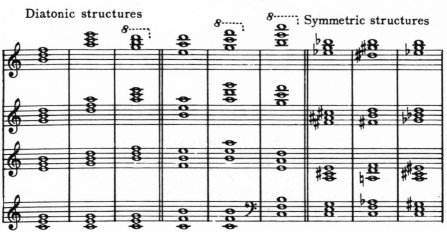

Figure 42. Structures of Σ = 4S3p (continued).

Figure 42. Structures of $\Sigma = 4S3p$ *(concluded).*

When $\Sigma = 5S$ and $S = 3p$, the diatonic arrangement of the groups of 3 usually adheres to the 3rds or the 4ths.

In order to build symmetric strata in five groups, it is necessary to consider the $\sqrt[6]{2}$, and the $\sqrt[12]{2}$ as the practical forms of symmetry without duplication of strata. The following table illustrates the general procedure of building $\Sigma = 5S$.

$\Sigma = 5S$;
Diatonic Structures

$S = 3p$
Symmetric Structures

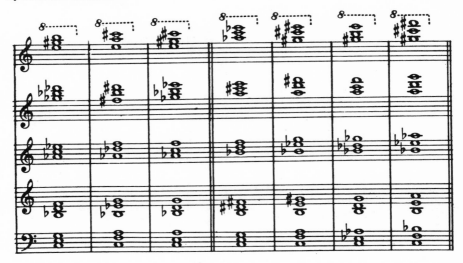

Figure 43. Structures of $\Sigma = 5S3p$.

F. The Limits of Three-Part Harmonies

1. Diatonic Limit

By increasing the number of strata in any diatonic scale, we eventually reach the limit. In any diatonic limit the number of strata equals the number of pitch units in a given scale. When a scale has 3 units, the Σ limit = 3S. When the scale consists of 5 units, the Σ limit = 5S. The commonly used 7 unit diatonic scales have their limit in 7 strata, or 21 parts. The chord structures developed from any diatonic scale for each stratum are derived through tonal expansion. The following table illustrates:

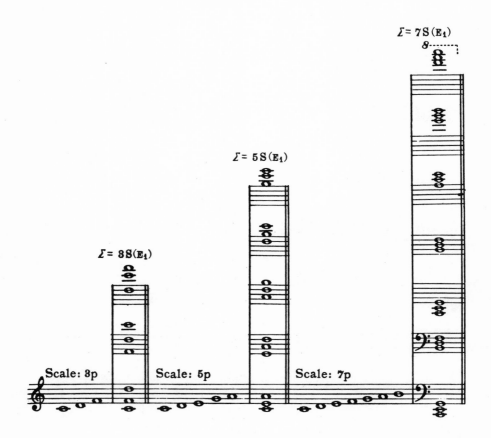

Figure 44. Diatonic limit of S3p.

2. Symmetric Limit

Symmetric limit depends on the number of symmetric roots from which the individual strata are constructed. The two-tonic system produces two strata in 6 parts; the 3-tonic system produces 3 strata in 9 parts; the 4-tonic system produces 4 strata in 12 parts; the 6-tonic system produces 6 strata in 18 parts; and the final symmetric limit on 12 tonics produces 12 strata in 36 parts. The latter is the ultimate symmetric limit.

In the following chart the last bar is a form of re-distribution of strata from the preceding bar. This variation is meant to show a more practical form of vertical arrangement. As a general requirement for satisfactory sonority, the lower stratum must be used in its expanded form (open position) unless it is placed in the middle register or higher.

Figure 45. Symmetric limit of S3p.

3. Compound Symmetric Limit: The Σ (Σ S 3p)

A compound symmetric limit depends on the number of symmetric points from which each individual Σ is constructed. In the following example, Σ consists of 3 strata and is developed from a 3-unit scale, thus representing the diatonic limit for such a scale. The second bar of the example represents a simultaneous vertical arrangement of the original Σ taken thrice through the symmetrical points of the two octave range, $(\sqrt[3]{4})$; thus the first Σ evolves its strata from $\underline{c}$, the second evolves its strata from $\underline{a}\flat$, and the third Σ evolves its strata from $\underline{e}$.

Figure 46. Compound symmetric limit $\Sigma(\Sigma S3p)$.

The limits of Σ (Σ)'s go beyond the practical possibilities of today. It is possible to construct a Σ limit consisting of 12 strata in 36 parts and to arrange 12 of such structures in simultaneity; the Σ (Σ) for such a case, being the absolute compound limit for the groups of 3 parts, equals $12 \times 36 = 432$ parts. The addition of Sp would make it 433 p.

The practical significance of this kind of strata technique is mainly in its application to choral or to orchestral scoring, which is concerned with the individual development of groups and parts, and with a better acoustical quality for the whole sonority of the score.

CHAPTER 4

FOUR-PART HARMONY

A. One Stratum of Four-Part Harmony

$$(S = 4p)$$

ASSEMBLAGES which serve as four-part harmonic structures are the pitches of four-unit scales brought into simultaneity.

There are 165 general S4p structures, which correspond to the 165 four-unit scales. The distribution of functions in any one S4p structure corresponds to E_0, E_1 and E_2.

Four-part assemblages of any form may be called *tetrads*. There are 6 forms of tetrads evolved from the complete seven-unit scales. Each form of a tetrad corresponds to the respective expansion.

(1) $S4p \equiv E_0$; (2) $S4p \equiv E_1$; (3) $S4p \equiv E_2$;
(4) $S4p \equiv E_3$; (5) $S4p \equiv E_4$; (6) $S4p \equiv E_5$.

Table of General Structures of S4p

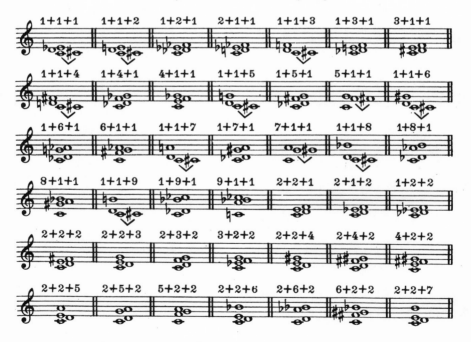

Figure 47. General structures of 4Sp (continued).

[1124]

Figure 47. General structures of S4p (continued).

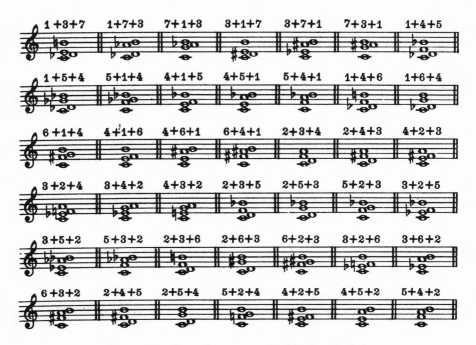

Figure 47. General structures of S4p (concluded).

Table of Diatonic Structures of S4p

Structures, diatonic with respect to: I = 2i + 3i + 2i.

Structures, diatonic with respect to Chinese Pentatonic

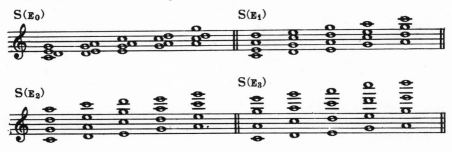

Figure 48. Diatonic structures of S4p (continued).

Structures, diatonic with respect to Natural Major

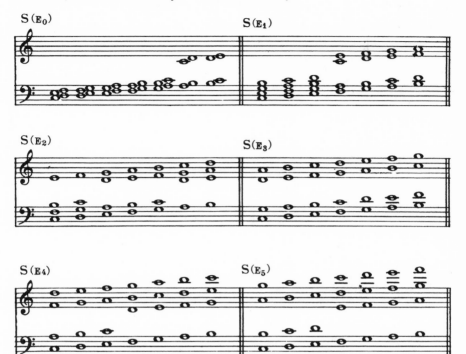

Figure 48. Diatonic structures of S4p (concluded).

Of these, the following pairs contain identical pitch-units, in their respective tetrads, in a different form of distribution:

(1) $S(E_0)$ and $S(E_5)$; (2) $S(E_1)$ and $S(E_4)$; (3) $S(E_2)$ and $S(E_3)$.

B. TRANSFORMATIONS OF $S = 4p$.

The classical system of harmony, based on the postulate of resolving 7th, emphasizes only one form of transformation with each tonal cycle. For example, C_3 requires a ↻ transformation; C_5, ←↑→; and C_7, ↺. But in general forms of transformation not bound to the classical system—i.e., discarding the resolution of the 7th—all forms of transformation may be used with each cycle, giving us three forms for each cycle. In addition to this, one function (either one) of an assemblage may become a constant, producing hybrid 4-part harmony, where the remaining functions are subject to transformations of 3 elements. This produces 4 additional transformations with the ↻ direction for the three functions and one constant, and 4 ↺ transformations for the three functions and one constant.

In addition to this, two functions may become constant, permitting the other two to produce their only possible transformation.

There are six combinations with two constant functions. When the structures are variable, a constant transformation of all 4 functions may become practical. Summing up all forms, we get altogether 18 forms of transformations for each cycle. The following table includes all forms.

Transformations of S4p

↻	↔↕	↺	Const. abc
a → b′ b → c′ c → d′ d → a′	a → c′ c → a′ b → d′ d → b′	a → d′ d → c′ c → b′ b → a′	a → a′ b → b′ c → c′ d → d′
Const. a	**Const. b**	**Const. c**	**Const. d**
a → a′ b → c′ c → d′ d → b′ ↻	b → b′ a → c′ c → d′ d → a′ ↻	c → c′ a → b′ b → d′ d → a′ ↻	d → d′ a → b′ b → c′ c → a′ ↻
Const. a	**Const. b**	**Const. c**	**Const. d**
a → a′ b → d′ d → c′ c → b′ ↺	b → b′ a → d′ d → c′ c → a′ ↺	c → c′ a → d′ d → b′ b → a′ ↺	d → d′ a → c′ c → b′ b → a′ ↺

Const. ab	Const. ac	Const. ad	Const. bc	Const. bd	Const. cd
a → a′ b → b′ c → d′ d → c′	a → a′ c → c′ b → d′ d → b′	a → a′ d → d′ b → c′ c → b′	b → b′ c → c′ a → d′ d → a′	b → b′ d → d′ a → c′ c → a′	c → c′ d → d′ a → b′ b → a′

The above transformations are applicable to all structures of S4p.

The following table represents all transformations in application to S(7). When there is a crossing of voices, a respective crossing pair may be transposed into a different octave as shown on the table.

Certain cases that are undesirable from the viewpoint of orchestral selection may be eliminated. When one has so many cases, it is easy to select the most desirable ones, as well as to cope with all situations of 4-part orchestration of a melody.

Figure 49. All transformations of S(7) (continued).

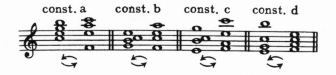

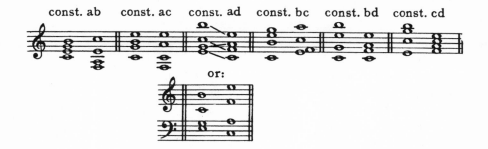

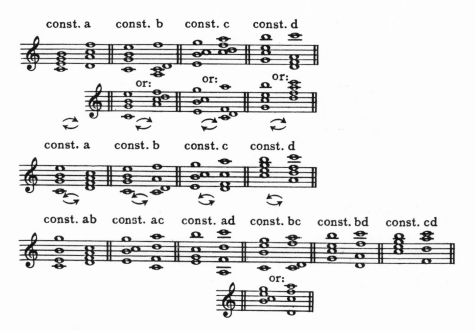

Figure 49. All transformations of S(7) (concluded).

It will be desirable to evolve similar tables for S4p structures in one stratum in all cycles for the following chord structures. An extra Sp may be added to any of these structures in order to obtain a hybrid 5-part harmony.

*After completing the tables, compose continuity selecting any of the following forms as a constant Σ. (—J.S.)

C. Examples of Progressions of S = 4p

Constant and Variable Structures.
Hybrid Five-Part Structures (added Sp and coupled Sp)

At this point, we may observe that the number of transformations can be increased by a *new positional arrangement of the four functions* (a, b, c, d). This is practical for $S(E_2)$ and the wider expansions, where crossing of parts is admissible, since in many instances it becomes unavoidable. The main advantage of having these new transformations in addition to the 18 already offered lies in the fact that in some cases these additional forms give the smoothest voice-leading, i.e., voice-leading with a maximum of common tones and nearest positions. The additional transformations are of the clockwise, the crosswise, and the counterclockwise forms.

For the sake of drawing comparisons between the three fundamental transformations $\left(\circlearrowright, \longleftrightarrow, \circlearrowleft\right)$ in the original positional arrangement of the four functions (abcd) and the two new forms (acdb and acbd), we offer a complete table of 9 transformations for the three positional arrangements.

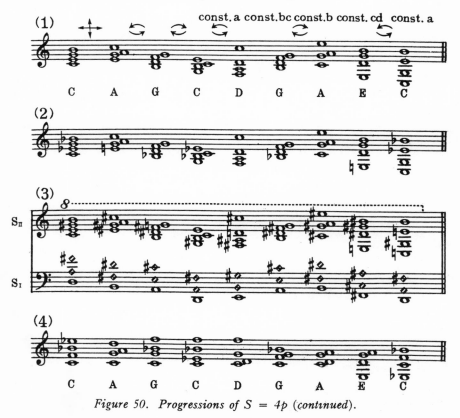

Figure 50. Progressions of S = 4p (continued).

Figure 50. Progressions of S = 4p (concluded).

Fundamental Transformations of S4p in the
Three Positional Arrangements of Functions.

	a d b c	a b c d	a d c b
↻	a → b b → c c → d d → a	a → c c → d d → b b → a	a → c c → b b → d d → a
↔	a → c b → d c → a d → b	a → d c → b d → a b → c	a → b c → d b → a d → c
↺	a → d b → a c → b d → c	a → b c → a d → c b → d	a → d c → a b → c d → b

Some of these forms are used in Fig. 50, (4), (5) and (6).

CHAPTER 5

THE HARMONY OF FOURTHS

HARMONIES built on the intervals of a fourth—which is equivalent to the second tonal expansion of the complete seven-unit scales—still remain practically an unexplored region of musical harmony.

Some composers (Scriabine, Ravel, Hindemith) have used such chord-structures, but they have never subjected the latter to any systematic treatment. Neither have they discovered the principle upon which the progressions and the voice-leading are based.

We have seen, in three-part harmony, that 6 forms of transformation control all the possibilities of voice-leading. Existing music offers more evidence as to the correct way of handling progressions of S3p than the way of handling S4p when they both evolve in E_2; for this reason it is highly practical to present the real foundation for composing four-part harmonies built on fourths.

According to the definitions given in the *Special Theory of Harmony*,* the positive form of structures is the respective tonal expansion of the original scale (E_2 in this case), whereas the scale of chord progressions corresponds to the same set in position ⓑ, i.e., in backward motion. For this reason the functions of the assemblage become *1, 4, 7, 10* and the tonal cycles of the positive form become *cycle of the fourth* (C_4), *cycle of the seventh* (C_7) and *cycle of the tenth* (C_{10}). Cadences evolve as the first and the last steps of the cycles and their combinations.

We shall present now a comparative table of S3p and S4p as they evolve in E_2 of the complete seven-unit scales. Only the fundamental transformations will be used in order to present the matter with the utmost clarity.

HARMONY OF FOURTHS

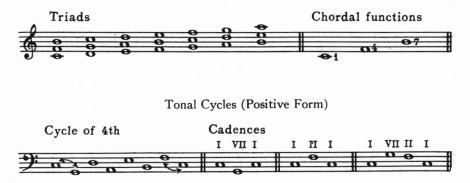

Figure 51. Harmony of fourths (continued).

*See Vol. I, p. 361 ff.

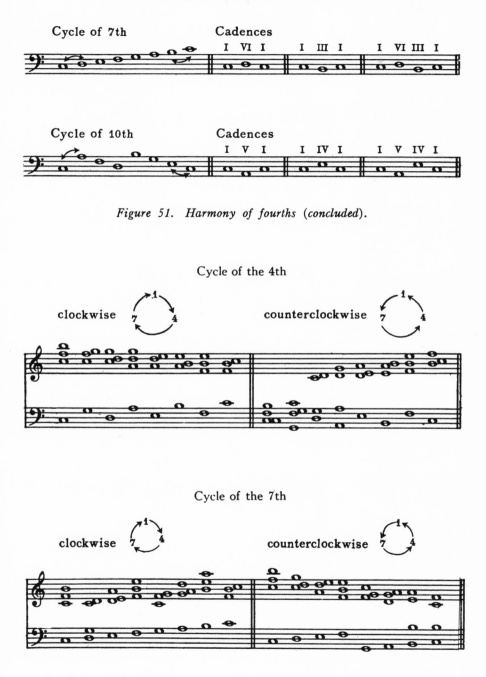

Figure 51. Harmony of fourths (concluded).

Figure 52. Voice-leading, cycle of the 4th, 7th, and 10th (continued).

Cycle of the 10th

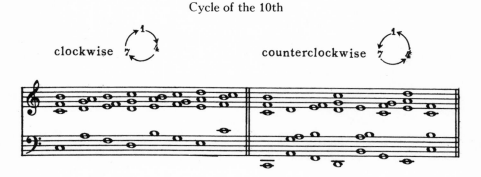

Figure 52. Voice-leading, cycle of the 4th, 7th, and 10th (concluded).

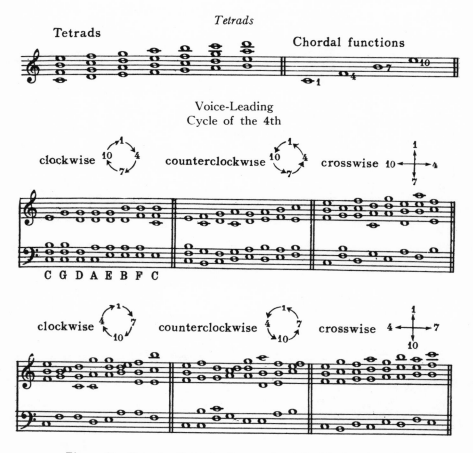

Figure 53. Tetrads. Voice-leading, cycle of the 4ths (continued).

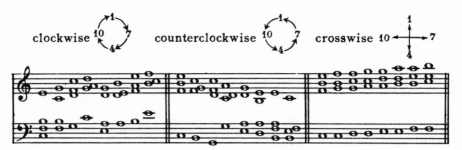

Figure 53. Tetrads. Voice-leading, cycle of the 4ths (concluded).

Cycle of the 7th

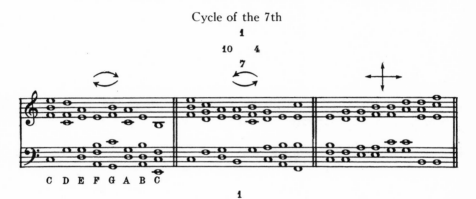

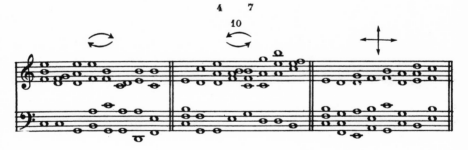

Figure 54. Voice-leading, cycle of the 7th.

Cycle of the 10th

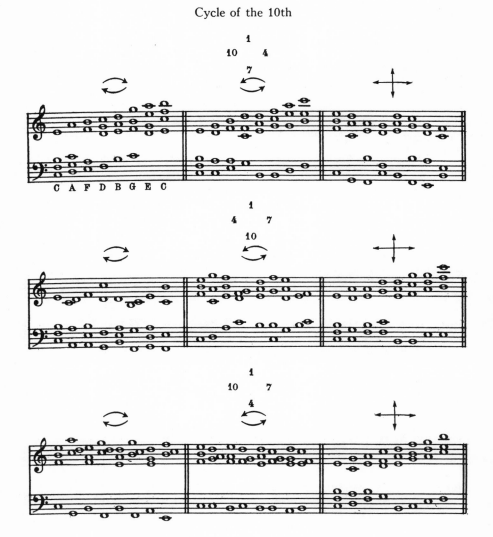

Figure 55. Voice-leading, cycle of the 10th.

CHAPTER 6

ADDITIONAL DATA ON 4-PART HARMONY

A. Special Cases of Four-Part Harmonies in Two Strata

1. Reciprocating Strata

WHEN the number of parts in a harmonic stratum reaches four, it becomes practical to evolve S_{II} to a given S_I by means of inversion of the original stratum. Either the upper or the lower stratum may be·considered original.

Tonal inversion (tonal ⓓ) is appropriate for the diatonic progressions; geometrical inversion ⓓ is appropriate for all other types of progressions. However, type II, III and the generalized may be assigned to a common Σ for both strata (as in figure 56).

The axis of inversion is common for both strata. The cycles are common for both strata but have opposite signs. If one of the strata has a positive progression, the other has a negative progression. However, this does not circumscribe the form of the structure. The structure of a certain stratum may be positive, while its progression may be either positive or negative. The reverse is also true.

If S_{II} has the form of $S(7)$, read 1, 3, 5, 7 from the c-axis (i.e., $c - e - g - b$), S_I, being in the tonal inversion ⓓ, acquires the form of a negative $S(7)$, read 1, -3, -5, -7 from the same axis (i.e., $c-a-f-d$, downward).

It is interesting to note that both strata, when moving through any one cycle, coincide in structure on the dominant (the G-chord in the key of c), which is always an $S(7)$.

In using this technique for progressions type II, III and the generalized, assign one const. Σ, whichever you choose.

The technique of inversions for evolving the second stratum can be extended to all 165 structures.

Examples of Two Mutually Reciprocating Strata.
$\Sigma = 2S4p$.

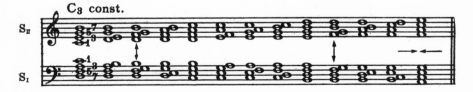

Figure 56. Two mutually reciprocating strata. $\Sigma = 2S4p$ (continued).

C_5 const.

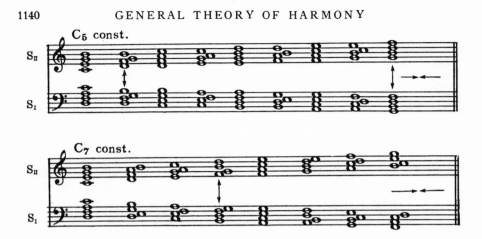

C_7 const.

Diatonic progression $= 2C_3 + C_5 + 2C_7 + C_5$

Diatonic - Symmetric progression: The same cycles.
Scale of roots = Nat. major. $\Sigma = \Sigma$ (13) XIII. Roots in the lower stratum.

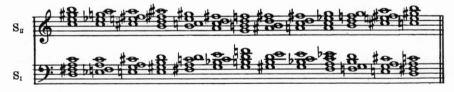

The same progression in $S(E_2)$ structures.

Figure 56. Two mutually reciprocating strata. $\Sigma = 2S4p$ (concluded).

2. Hybrid Symmetric Strata

There is a special case of two strata which deserves particular attention. It offers a technical interpretation of many not quite satisfactory attempts made by Ravel (particularly in the *Daphnis et Chloé* suite) and by Stravinsky (in *Petrouchka, Le Sacre du Printemps* and *Les Noces*) in their urge for *harmonic polytonality*. The latter, in fact, is a *superimposition of two symmetric strata*—to use the terminology of this system. I mention these two composers because they are the only originators of such a harmonic style and because, in the above mentioned works, this tendency of theirs is the more apparent. Ravel is more consistent than Stravinsky in this respect; but neither of the two composers has succeeded in achieving real consistency and clarity in this style—qualities which become possible now with the development of this theory.

Theirs is a special case of adding *Sp constant* as an upper stratum, mostly in $I = \sqrt[4]{2}$, and often with symmetric couplings. The main characteristic of this style, which is to be expected, is the *large S(7)* as a permanent fixture of S_I (the lower stratum).

We shall use this style merely as a basis for building S_{II} as a symmetric superimposition upon S_I of Sp, S2p, S3p and, finally, S4p, when we accumulate the full Σ 2S4p. We shall also adhere to the large S(7) as the structure for S_I. At the same time our S_{II} will be developed in two basic ways:

(1) the structure of S_{II} is a part of $\Sigma(13)$ XIII, applied from one root-tone in the various possible roots of symmetry;

(2) the structure of S_{II} is a part of $\Sigma(13)$ XIII, *transposed* to the respective *root of symmetry.*

Examples of the Special Case of Harmonic Polytonality.

Figure 57. Special case of harmonic polytonality (continued).

Figure 57. Special case of harmonic polytonality (continued).

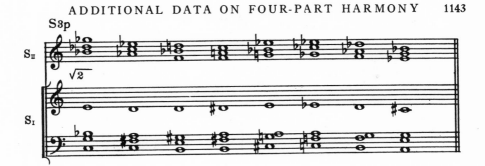

Figure 57. Special case of harmonic polytonality (continued).

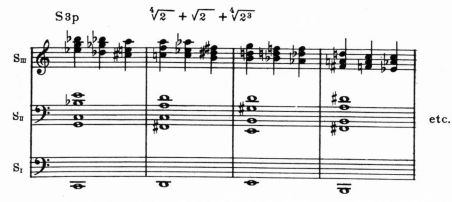

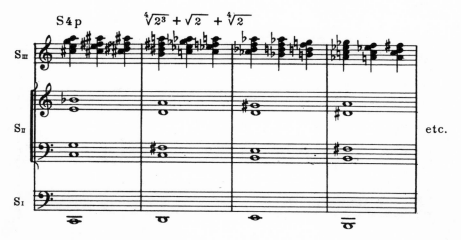

Figure 57. Special case of harmonic polytonality (continued).

$$Sp \quad \sqrt[12]{2} + \sqrt[6]{2}$$

Figure 57. Special case of harmonic polytonality (concluded).

All other cases of two strata belong to the next chapter.

B. TWO STRATA OF FOUR-PART HARMONIES

GENERALIZATION OF THE $\Sigma = 2S$; $S = 4p$

Four-part harmonic structures may be coordinated into a simultaneous Σ and subjected to independent transformation in each stratum. As the number of all transformations for S4p is 24 (18, and the six additional ones), the number of transformations for Σ 2S4p is $24^2 = 576$. Combinations of the 9 fundamental forms alone are sufficient for general use since their quantity amounts to:

$$_9C_2 = \frac{9!}{2!\,(9-2)\,!} = \frac{362,880}{2 \cdot 5040} = 36$$

The latter represent the combinations of $\circlearrowright$, $\longleftarrow\!\!\!\!\!\!\downarrow\!\!\!\longrightarrow$ and $\circlearrowleft$ distributed through two strata and having three forms of the positional arrangement of functions: abcd, acdb and acbd.

All other transformations serve the purpose of isolating one or two parts from the stratum of 4p.

Positions of S_I and S_{II} may be either identical or non-identical. The variety of the forms of transformation permits the use even of completely identical pitch-assemblages, without causing consecutive octaves between any pair of parts of the two strata.

The number of possible *general structures* of Σ 2S4p equals the quantity of S4p, multiplied by the number of combinations of S4p in the two strata, multiplied by the number of positions between S_I and S_{II}: $165^2 \cdot 11 = 299,475$ (excluding identical positions between S_I and S_{II}). Of these 216 are *diatonic;* $6^3 = 216$.

Examples of Structures of Σ 2S4p

(1) Diatonic (all scales with four and more units);

Figure 58. Diatonic structures of Σ 2S4p.

(2) Symmetric (all four-unit scales in all forms of symmetry): (General).

Figure 59. Symmetric structures of Σ 2S4p.

For the time being, use one constant Σ, when Σ>S.

Examples of Progressions of Σ 2S4p and Hybrid Forms Resulting
from the Addition of Sp.
(uncoupled or coupled)

Figure 60. Progressions of Σ2S4p (continued).

Figure 60. Progressions of ΣZS4p (concluded).

C. Three Strata of Four-Part Harmonies

$$\Sigma = 3S; \ S = 4p$$

Structures of Σ 3S4p can be evolved from the diatonic scales with four or more units and from symmetric scales having three or more symmetric roots. All principles remain the same as in the Σ 2S4p.

Examples of Structures of Σ 3S4p

(1) Diatonic;

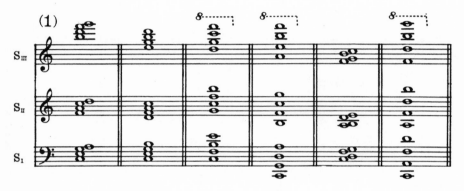

Figure 61. Diatonic structure of Σ 3S4p.

(2) Symmetric:

(General)

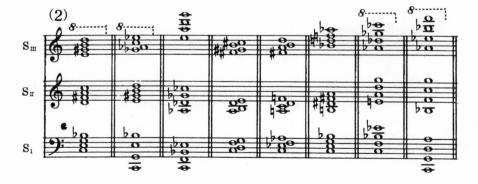

Figure 62. Symmetric structure of Σ 3S4p.

Examples of Progressions of Σ 3S4p and Hybrid Forms Resulting
from the addition of Sp
(uncoupled or coupled)

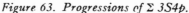

Figure 63. Progressions of Σ 3S4p.

D. Four and More Strata of Four-Part Harmonies

Structures of $\Sigma = 4S4p$ are available from all diatonic scales having four units or more. They are desirable when it is advantageous to distribute the latter in groups of 4. Four-unit sectional scales in four and more tonics serve as material for symmetric structures. To this group belongs one of the forms gaining considerable popularity today. It is the large S(7) distributed through the $\sqrt[4]{2}$.

We shall now offer a few examples of multi-strata structures.

Examples of Structures of Σ 4S4p
(1) Diatonic;

Figure 64. Diatonic structure of Σ 4S4p.

(2) Symmetric:
(General)

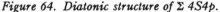

E. The Limits of Four-Part Harmonies

Diatonic limit for S4p is defined by the number of pitch-units, which in this case correspond to the number of strata. The minimum number of units is 4.

The limit for a four-unit scale is Σ 4S4p, i.e., 4 strata in 16 parts (or, with the addition of Sp, 17 parts). The diatonic limit for a seven-unit scale is $\Sigma = $ 7S4p, i.e., 7 strata in 28 parts (or 29 with the addition of Sp).

Overlapping in most cases is unavoidable.

Example of the Diatonic Limits of S4p

Figure 66. Diatonic limits of S4p.

2. Symmetric Limit

Symmetric limit of a Σ is defined by the number of symmetric roots. $\Sigma = Ns4p$ represents the symmetric limits of four-part harmony, equivalent to four-unit scales distributed through N, i.e., the number of symmetric roots.

The symmetric limit for two tonics is: $\Sigma = 2S4p$, i.e., two strata in 8 parts (or 9 with the addition of Sp).

The ultimate symmetric limit for S4p is built on 12 tonics: $\Sigma = 12S4p$, i.e., twelve strata in 48 parts (or 49 with the addition of Sp).

Example of Symmetric Limits of S4p.

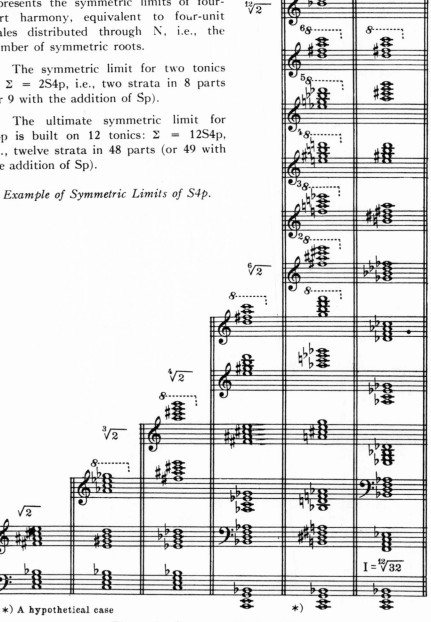

*) A hypothetical case

Figure 67. Symmetric limits of S4p.

3. Compound Symmetric Limit: Σ (Σ S4p)

A compound symmetric limit depends upon the number of symmetric points from which each individual Σ is constructed. Thus, for example, the diatonic limit of a four-unit scale, being used as a Σ structure and being coordinated with another identical Σ from the $\sqrt{2}$, would produce a compound Σ(Σ) = 2Σ4S4p, i.e., two sigmae of four strata each, 16 parts to each sigma, making a total of 32 parts. The same structure, being coordinated through the $\sqrt[12]{2}$, would produce: Σ(Σ) = 12Σ4S4p, i.e., twelve sigmae, four strata each, 16 parts each: 12·4 = 48 strata; 16·12 = 192 parts. The same procedure being applied to a complete seven-unit scale would produce: Σ(Σ) = 12Σ7S4p, i.e., 12·7·4 = 336 parts.

The ultimate compound limit of S4p can be obtained from a twelve unit scale set through twelve points of symmetry: Σ (Σ) = 12Σ12S4p, i.e., 12·12·4 = = 576 parts in 144 four-part strata of the twelve sigmae (or 577 parts with the addition of Sp).

Such is the incredible number of parts possible within the twelve-unit equal temperament scale.

The practical uses of compound symmetric limits require overlapping and serve the purpose of alternate arrangement (distribution) of the superimposed orchestral or vocal groups, in the same way as was described for the compound limits of S2p.

Overlapping is unavoidable because of the limitations of auditory response to a certain frequency range. For this reason it would not be sensible to construct musical instruments (possible through electronics) *for musical purposes*, which exceed the range of audible pitch.

We shall limit the table of structures of the Σ(Σ) to a few practical illustrations. See Figure 68 on the following page.

Examples of Σ (Σ). *S4p*

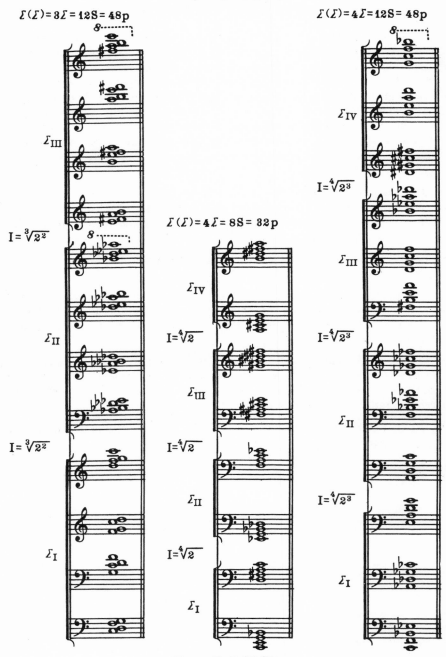

Figure 68. Σ (Σ)*S4p.*

CHAPTER 7

VARIABLE NUMBER OF PARTS IN THE
DIFFERENT STRATA OF A SIGMA

A S the main purpose of the *General Theory of Harmony* is to satisfy demands
for the scoring of all possible combinations of instruments, or voices, or
both, it should be flexible enough to make any instrumental combination practical.

If the score must, for some reason, consist of several orchestral groups
represented by a different number of instruments in each group, harmony must
be evolved for the corresponding number of strata and parts.

A score of 4 violins, 3 clarinets and 2 trombones, fundamentally, requires
a Σ, where $S_I = 2S$, $S_{II} = 3S$ and $S_{III} = 4S$.

There are two ways of assigning instrumental combinations to harmony:
(1) the fundamental way, where each instrument corresponds to one part, and
(2) where the mobility of the instrumental form of a part defines the quantity
of harmonic parts; in the latter conception one instrument produces: Sp, S2p,
S3p or S4p.

The first form is illustrated by the above case of violins, clarinets and
trombones. In the second form *one violin* may perform an instrumental form
of 2, or 3, or 4 part harmony, depending on the degree of mobility required.
For this reason, in cases where chords change at a low rate of speed and the
instrumental form implies high mobility, it is desirable to evolve more than one
harmonic part for one individual orchestral part (which may be an individual
instrument like the clarinet, or a group-unison like that of the violas).

Later on these considerations will be developed into basic principles of the
Theory of Orchestration. At present, we shall look upon this problem as a purely
harmonic one: *correlation of strata into sigma in simultaneity and continuity.*

There is no specific order *per se* in which the number of parts in the various
strata may be distributed. This means that the lower S may have only one or
all four parts. The same is true for any other S. There may be denser harmonic
assemblages in the upper register and more rarified in the middle or lower register,
but the opposite is equally true.

So far as *types of structures* are concerned, there are several considerations
which dictate the means of evolving sigmae:

(1) const. or var. E's as components of the strata structures;
(2) const. or var. E's as intervals between the strata structures;
(3) symmetric arrangement of the strata roots in the vertical monomial
or group symmetry;
(4) identical or non-identical structures in the different symmetric arrangements of roots;
(5) different strata having a different number of parts;
(6) the mirror Σ (inversion of structures by means of an axis of symmetry).

Examples of the Types of Sigmae
(evolved through the above six classifications)

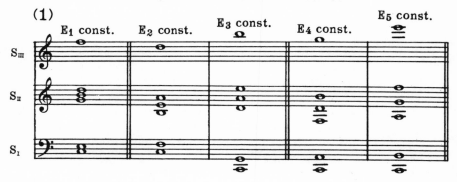

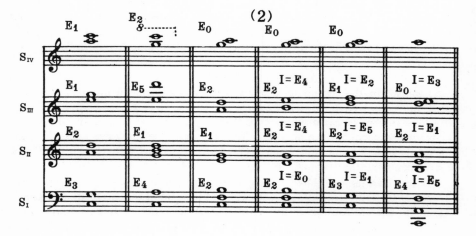

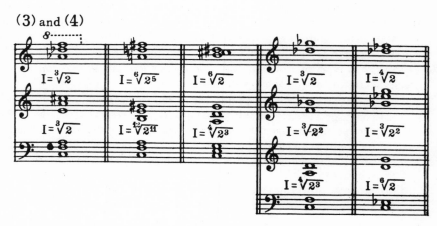

Figure 69. Types of sigmae (continued).

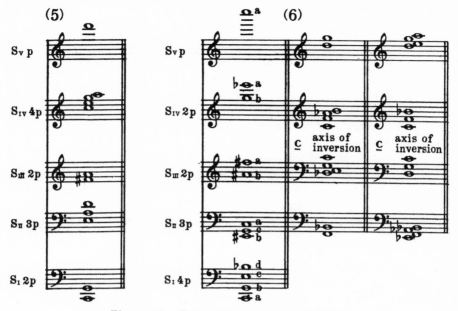

Figure 69. Types of sigmae (concluded).

Examples of Progressions of Σ with a Different Number of Parts in the Different Strata.

Figure 70. Progressions of Σ (continued).

Figure 70. Progressions of Σ *(concluded).*

A. Construction of Sigmae Belonging to One Family (Style)

1. Σ = S.

We shall consider Σ = S as a special case of Σ. The structure of an assemblage representing a chord is defined by the interval-units (i) constituting such a structure. In the case of Σ = S all structures belonging to one family are obtained by means of permutations of interval-groups of the original Σ. Thus a group of sigmae belonging to one family derive from the original Σ as permutation-groups.. Therefore: $\Sigma_1 \equiv \Sigma p_0$, $\Sigma_2 \equiv \Sigma p_1$, $\Sigma_n \equiv \Sigma p_{n-1}$.

We have used this method already in evolving pitch-scales of one family through the permutation of intervals (see *Theory of Pitch-Scales*)* and have applied the same procedure to structures of E_1 (*Special Theory of Harmony*).** For this reason, there is really nothing essentially new in extending the same technique to all Sp, S2p, S3p and S4p structures.

In *diatonic classification*, all structures of one particular expansion *ipso facto* belong to one family, regardless of the number of parts. Thus Sp(E_0), S2p(E_0), S3p(E_0) and S4p(E_0) belong to one family even if their corresponding interval-groups are not identical. Likewise Sp(E_1), S2p(E_1). S3p(E_1) and S4p(E_1) belong to one family. The same is true of all other expansions.

*See Vol. I, p. 117 ff.   **See Vol. I, p. 361.

Examples of the Diatonic Families of $\Sigma = S$
Sigmae of one Family

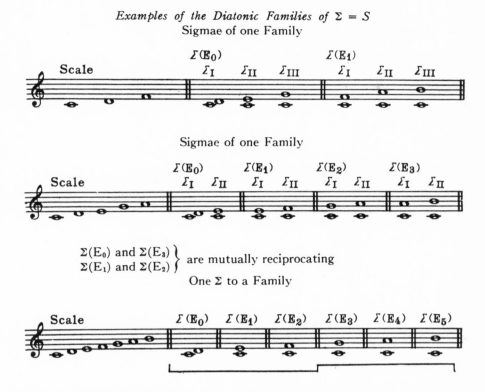

Sigmae of one Family

$\Sigma(E_0)$ and $\Sigma(E_3)$
$\Sigma(E_1)$ and $\Sigma(E_2)$ } are mutually reciprocating

One Σ to a Family

Mutually Reciprocating Pairs: $\Sigma(E_0)$ and $\Sigma(E_5)$; $\Sigma(E_1)$ and $\Sigma(E_4)$; $\Sigma(E_2)$ and $\Sigma(E_3)$.

Figure 81. Diatonic families of $\Sigma = S$.

In the *general classification* of $\Sigma = S$, Sp and S2p do not evolve any structural families: Sp has no interval to go by and S2p has one I(S), thus being invariant in each case. Families of triads (S3p) are based on permutations of two interval-groups in each Σ. Families of tetrads (S4p) are based on permutations of three interval-groups.

The number of families of triads equals the number of combinations of the interval-groups by two and not exceeding eleven semitones as a sum: I ⋗ mi + ni. There are 29 such families, 5 of which contain only one member (Σ).

The number of families of tetrads equals the number of combinations of the interval-groups by three and not exceeding eleven semitones as a sum: I ⋗ mi + + ni + pi. There are 40 such families, 3 of which contain only one member (Σ).

Examples of Triads Belonging to One Family

(1) $I(\Sigma_1) = 2i + 3i$; $I(\Sigma_2) = 3i + 2i$.
(2) $I(\Sigma_1) = 5i + 3i$; $I(\Sigma_2) = 3i + 5i$.
(3) $I(\Sigma_1) = 4i + 3i$; $I(\Sigma_2) = 3i + 4i$.

Examples of Tetrads Belonging to One Family

(1) $I(\Sigma_1) = 3i + 3i + 2i$; $I(\Sigma_2) = 3i + 2i + 3i$;
      $I(\Sigma_3) = 2i + 3i + 3i$.

(2) $I(\Sigma_1) = 2i + 3i + 5i$; $I(\Sigma_2) = 2i + 5i + 3i$;
      $I(\Sigma_3) = 5i + 2i + 3i$; $I(\Sigma_4) = 3i + 2i + 5i$;
      $I(\Sigma_5) = 3i + 5i + 2i$; $I(\Sigma_6) = 5i + 3i + 2i$.

The number of members of one family depends on the number of possible permutations of the interval-groups. If the number of interval-groups is one, there is but one member to a family. If the number of interval-groups is two, and both interval-groups are identical, there is but one member to a family. If both interval groups are non-identical, there are two members to a family. If the number of interval-groups is three, and they are all alike, there is but one member to a family. If the number of interval-groups is three, two of which are identical, there are three members to a family. If the number of interval-groups is three and all three are different, there are six members to a family. Full information on this matter is to be found in my book "Kaleidophone."[*]

Continuity of variable Σ can be composed from combinations of the members of one particular family, arranged in any desirable order and accompanied by coefficients of recurrence.

For instance: $\overrightarrow{\Sigma} = 2\Sigma_2 + \Sigma_1 + 3\Sigma_3$.

2. Σ = NS.

In a compound structure (Σ), *all the substructures* (S) *and the intervals between the latter belong to one family.* The different members of one family of compound structures have interval-groups in the substructures, identical with the corresponding original substructures, and interval-groups between the substructures, identical with that of the original compound structure. The difference between the various members of one particular family of the compound structures *lies in the arrangement* of the original interval-groups; this refers to both the substructures and the intervals between the latter.

It is assumed that the interval between the adjacent strata is either one of the interval-groups of the Σ or 0i (zero i). This 0i refers to the interval between the upper function of S placed immediately below the adjacent upper S and the lower function of the latter, or between the lower function of S placed immediately above the adjacent lower S and the upper function of the latter.

Examples:

(1) S_{III}: a, c $\quad 1 = 0i$
     S_{II} : c, b, a
     S_{I} : b, a, b, a $\quad 1 = 0i$

(2) S_{II}: c, b, a, d $\quad 1 = 0i$
     S_{I} : d, c, b, a

*Published by M. Witmark and Sons, 1940.

We shall evolve now a family of compound structures in which the *Master-Structure* (the original structure) is represented by $I(S) = 5i + 3i + 3i$.

The compound interval-group, which, in this case consists of the variants of three permutations, offers $\Sigma = 3S$ as the most natural solution. From the original Master-Structure we evolve the Compound Master-Structure in three substructures, in which the adjacent functions of adjacent strata are connected by $I = 0i$.

The following is a complete table of the members of this family: $I(S) = 5i + 3i + 3i$.

All numbers express interval-groups.

Σ_1 (Master)	Σ_2	Σ_3	Σ_4	Σ_5	Σ_6	Σ_7	Σ_8	Σ_9
3	3	5	3	3	3	5	3	3
3	5	3	5	3	3	3	3	3
5	3	3	3	5	5	3	5	5
—— 0	—— 0	—— 0	—— 0	—— 0	—— 0	—— 0	—— 0	——- 0
3	3	5	3	3	3	3	5	3
3	5	3	3	5	3	3	3	3
5	3	3	5	3	5	5	3	5
—— 0	—— 0	—— 0	—— 0	—— 0	—— 0	—— 0	—— 0	—— 0
3	3	5	3	3	3	3	3	5
3	5	3	3	3	5	3	3	3
5	3	3	5	5	3	5	5	3

Σ_{10}	Σ_{11}	Σ_{12}	Σ_{13}	Σ_{14}	Σ_{15}	Σ_{16}	Σ_{17}	Σ_{18}
5	3	3	3	3	3	5	3	3
3	5	5	3	5	5	3	3	3
3	3	3	5	3	3	3	5	5
—— 0	—— 0	—— 0	—— 0	—— 0	—— 0	—— 0	—— 0	—— 0
3	5	3	3	3	3	3	5	3
5	3	5	5	3	5	3	3	3
3	3	3	3	5	3	5	3	5
—— 0	—— 0	—— 0	—— 0	—— 0	—— 0	—— 0	—— 0	—— 0
3	3	5	3	3	3	3	3	5
5	5	3	5	5	3	3	3	3
3	3	3	3	3	5	5	5	3

This table is continued on the following page.

Σ_{19}	Σ_{20}	Σ_{21}	Σ_{22}	Σ_{23}	Σ_{24}	Σ_{25}	Σ_{26}	Σ_{27}
3	3	3	5	3	3	5	3	3
5	3	3	3	5	5	3	3	3
3	5	5	3	3	3	3	5	5
— 0	— 0	— 0	— 0	— 0	— 0	— 0	— 0	— 0
3	3	3	3	5	3	3	5	3
3	5	3	5	3	3	3	3	5
5	3	5	3	3	5	5	3	3
— 0	— 0	— 0	— 0	— 0	— 0	— 0	— 0	— 0
3	3	3	3	3	5	3	3	5
3	3	5	3	3	3	5	5	3
5	5	3	5	5	3	3	3	3

This table has four more variants as the interval-groups between the adjacent strata offer the following possibilities:

$\frac{0}{0}$	$\frac{3}{3}$	$\frac{5}{3}$	$\frac{3}{5}$	$\frac{5}{5}$

The total number of Σ — members of this family is: $N(S = 5+3+3) = 27 \cdot 5 = = 135$.

It is hardly necessary, or desirable, to use such an enormous number of structures in one musical composition. Two or three members are perfectly sufficient for such a purpose. It is equally true, however, that one such family may constitute *the life-time harmonic manifold of one composer*, expressing himself in one harmonic style. The harmonic vocabulary of such a composer would positively dwarf that of Bach, Beethoven and Wagner put together.

(The Master Σ)   Some examples from the table

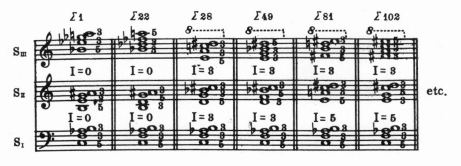

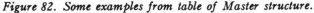

Figure 82. Some examples from table of Master structure.

B. PROGRESSIONS WITH VARIABLE SIGMA

Different sigmae belonging to one family, which can be used in one harmonic continuity, may have a different number of parts in each stratum, but the number does not vary for each individual stratum. For instance:

$$\Sigma_1 = 4S; \; S_I = p, \; S_{II} = 4p, \; S_{III} = 3p, \; S_{IV} = 2p;$$
$$\Sigma_2 = 4S; \; S_I = p, \; S_{II} = 4p, \; S_{III} = 3p, \; S_{IV} = 2p;$$
$$\Sigma_3 = 4S; \; S_I = p; \; S_{II} = 4p, \; S_{III} = 3p, \; S_{IV} = 2p; \; \ldots$$

We shall now present this case in harmonic progression.

Example of a Progression with Variable Sigma and a Different Number of Parts in the Different Strata.

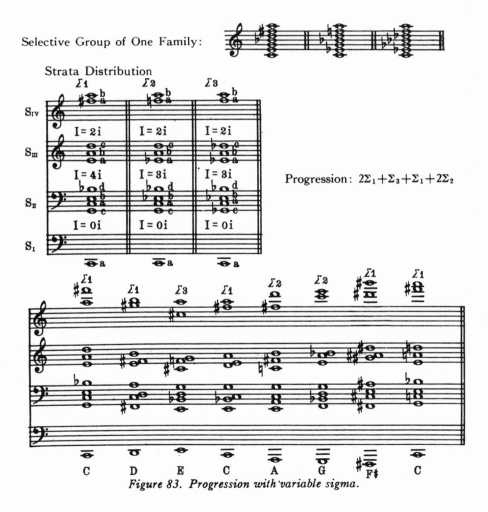

Progression: $2\Sigma_1 + \Sigma_3 + \Sigma_1 + 2\Sigma_2$

Figure 83. Progression with variable sigma.

C. DISTRIBUTION OF A GIVEN HARMONIC CONTINUITY THROUGH STRATA

Strata arrangement of a given harmonic continuity serves as an auxiliary technique for the orchestration of music which has been already written. The common notion of assigning parts existing in the sketch of a composition directly to the instruments and groups of· the orchestra is rather primitive. Since the average sketch contains 2, 3 or 4 and seldom 5 parts, and an average orchestral score contains between 20 and 30 parts, it is no wonder that there is so much duplication of parts. Many instruments are compelled to play identical notes because of the composer's lack of mathematical judgment. Such scores lack acoustical clarity and consume an enormous amount of rehearsing time in order to be made to sound acceptable.

Many prominent composers of the past and present have felt the necessity of individualizing the orchestral parts in a score. Not all of them solved this problem with success. In Mozart's scores we witness a tendency toward rhythmic independence of the duplicated parts, attained by the variation of instrumental forms. In Wagner, the struggle for the individualization of orchestral parts is often achieved by the technique which I call "contrapuntal variation of harmony". But since the advent of the so-called "French Impressionists" (Debussy, Roger-Ducasse, Delage, Ravel), the individualization of orchestral parts by means of *segregation of the harmonic groups* has become a prominent tendency of orchestral writing.

A student of this system can compose his scores directly in harmonic strata. However, whether he plans to use it for the purpose of composing or not, it is necessary for him to know, for the purpose of orchestrating, how to convert a given part-continuity into strata, or how to convert his own sketch of an arrangement into strata, prior to scoring it for the instrumental or vocal combination of parts.

The greater the number of parts in the original continuity, the greater the number of strata which can be developed therefrom. For this reason, if a given harmonic continuity contains too few parts to permit development into the number of parts required by the selection of a larger orchestral combination, it becomes necessary to add one or two more parts to the original harmonic progression before converting it into strata. The selection of functions which are to be added is a matter of harmonic style. But, in the field of transcriptions, paraphrases and arrangements, one style has not infrequently been transformed into another.

Inspecting the trends of existing music, we find that the development of harmony from the few parts into many, which happened in the course of the past few centuries, has relied on two fundamental devices:

(1) the acceptance of auxiliary tones as chordal functions;

(2) the addition of new chordal functions and groups.

Both devices undoubtedly derived from alternation of an auxiliary unit with the respective chordal function (tremolo, legato, trill). In slow motion the auxiliary units often formed suspended tones which later crystallized into chordal functions. In fast motion, alternation of the groups of auxiliary units with chordal functions produced psychological continuity of two *superimposed assemblages*. This gave birth to the simultaneous harmonic polytonality used intentionally by Stravinsky, Malipiero and myself. Facts reveal the systematic use of the strata technique, which I introduced in the United States about 1931, soon became the favorite style in the field of radio and motion-picture music. The sparkling quality of orchestrations, which can be immediately detected by listeners, is due primarily to harmonic factors: reharmonization and strata.

A bold example of the first device (crystallization of auxiliary units into chordal functions) is the cadence in the first movement of Prokofiev's *Piano Sonata* No. 5, which cadence sounds Mozartian when the auxiliary units are discarded.

The chordal functions of a given harmonic continuity (including the new functions or groups of functions, if such have been added) must be assigned before the original continuity is converted into strata. This is particularly important when the original continuity has a variable Σ. As the number of parts in the original remains constant, there is a constant set of letters corresponding to chordal functions. A function may change structurally in its interval value in relation to other functions, yet its functional meaning in the entire Σ assemblage remains constantly represented by the same letter.

For example, $\Sigma_1 S(5) = 1, 3, 5, 13$ and $\Sigma_2 S(7) = 1, 3, 5, 7$ can both be represented by the same assemblage of functions $\Sigma S = a, b, c, d$. However, while the a, b and c functions retain their structural meaning [which in this case is the diatonic $S(E_1)$] of 1, 3 and 5 respectively, function d changes its structural meaning, being the seventh in Σ_2 and the thirteenth in Σ_1. For this reason, transformations in the respective strata are performed by their functional and not by their structural meaning.

The superimposition of a whole new assemblage upon a given one (symmetric superimposition of strata) is equivalent to *harmonization of harmony by another harmony*. While the original sequence of assemblages in this case remains intact, the new added assemblage usually attributes a new quality, in which the original ingredient is still perceptible and yet appears as if it has been differently flavored. Its presence is often detected as timbre and not harmony. This explains why, in scores evolved through strata, the listener often mistakes harmony for orchestration.

Translation of a Given Harmonic Continuity into Strata.
Examples

The Original Progression with Functions Deciphered.

Transcription into Strata: Σ = 4S = 8p

Figure 84. Harmonic continuity into strata. Σ = 4S = 8p.

The Original Progression with a New Function Added.

Figure 85. Harmonic continuity into strata. Σ = 6S = 11p (continued).

Transcription into Strata: $\Sigma = 6S = 11p$.

Figure 85. Harmonic continuity into strata $\Sigma = 6S = 11p$ (concluded).

The Original: $\Sigma = S4p$.

Harmonization of the Given Harmonic Stratum: $\Sigma = 2S = 7p$.

Figure 86. Harmonic continuity into strata. $\Sigma = S4p$ (continued).

Further Strata Development: $\Sigma = 4S = 10p$.

Addition of Two Harmonic Strata to the Original: $\Sigma = 5S = 12p$.

Figure 86. Harmonic continuity into strata. $\Sigma = S4p$ *(concluded).*

CHAPTER 8

GENERAL THEORY OF DIRECTIONAL UNITS
(Melodic Figuration)

ACCORDING to our analysis in the field of the Special Theory of Harmony, passing, suspended and anticipated units actually belong to the assemblage, i.e., they represent either a function present in the chord, or a function which is a potential unit of the sigma. Suspended and anticipated units can be obtained by mere rhythmic variation of harmony which we shall discuss in full detail in the Theory of General ("*Textural*") Composition.* Chromatic passing units are always to be regarded as elements (to be inserted *a posteriori*) of chromatic variation, applicable to any type of harmonic progression.

This leads us to the conclusion that the only authentic element of melodic figuration is the *auxiliary unit*. The latter is not bound to bear any relation either to Σ, or to any substructure of it. An auxiliary unit is selected to be the leading tone to a chordal function. The interval of the *leading unit* from the respective chordal function is limited by the arrangement of the adjacent chordal functions of one S. In the structures of wide expansions it may be 3i, 4i or even greater. However, for practical reasons it is advisable not to exceed $I = 2i$, as habits, partly inherited and partly developed of listeners, obstruct the association of remote pitch-units as leading tones. Our charts, for this reason, will be limited to two forms: $I = i$ and $I = 2i$.

From the viewpoint of melodic figuration, chordal functions will be considered *neutral units* and the auxiliaries will be considered *leading units*. The combination of both, developed into any repetitive form, will be considered a *directional unit*.† A directional unit may start with either the neutral or the leading unit, but it must end with the neutral unit.

Thus the study of melodic figuration as a branch of the *General Theory of Harmony* is confined to the study of directional units in the various forms of S and the coordination of assemblages containing directional units.

A. DIRECTIONAL UNITS OF Sp
(a, a→, a→)

Considering the neutral unit to be a special case of directional units we obtain the following three forms: a, a→ and a→, i.e., the neutral unit, the directional with the lower leading unit (ascending auxiliary) and the directional with the upper leading unit (descending auxiliary).

---

*See p. 1305.
†See **Kaleidophone** by Joseph Schillinger, M. Witmark and sons, 1940. Revised edition, 1945. (Ed.)

The last two forms may have the interval of ascending of i or 2i and the interval of descending also of i or 2i. Thus there are four forms of directional units of Sp:

(1) ╱ i : b̲ →c̲;　　(3) ╲ i : d̲♭→c̲

(2) ╱ 2i : b̲♭→c̲;　　(4) ╲ 2i : d̲ →c̲

Illustrations of Directional Units of Sp

Original: $2C_7 + C_{-3} + C_{-7} + C_5 + C_5$

Figure 87. Directional units of Sp.

B. Directional Units of S2p

(a, b, a→, b→, a⃗, b⃗)

In tabulating the directional units and groups of S2p we shall resort to geometrical representation: neutral unit: — ; ascending directional unit: / and descending directional unit: \.

Using the terminology of the *Theory of Melody*, we can call these three forms: 0, a and b respectively. The three forms in combinations by 2, corresponding to S2p, give: $3^2 = 9$, as each form is combined with itself and with the two remaining forms. The first of these 9 forms represents neutral units in both parts.

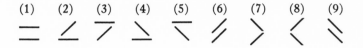

The first form has no interval variation. The second, the third, the fourth and the fifth forms have an interval variation in one part. The remaining forms have an interval variation in both parts.

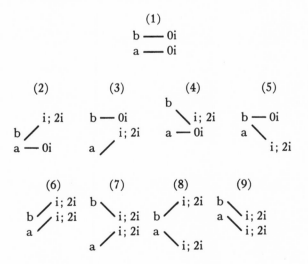

Thus the total number of directional units for any S2p is: one for (1), eight for (2 — 5) and sixteen for (6 — 9), since each of the latter has four variations, i.e., $1 + 8 + 16 = 25$.

In some structures, whose own interval-group is small (they usually belong to E_0 and seldom to E_1), some directional units containing inward motion have to be excluded in order to avoid crossing of the parts. In diatonic progressions, the semitonal precision of directional intervals is not compulsory.

An Exemplary Table of Directional Units Evolved to I(S2p) = 4i

Figure 88. Directional units of I(S2p) = 4i.

Each of the 25 forms of directional units has its own distinct character. Various forms can be selected as a continuity-group of directional units, where each selected form has a definite coefficient of recurrence. It is very desirable, however, to restrict each case to one form, as only such a limitation guarantees perfect unity of style. For this reason our examples will be confined to one form at a time. The following variations should be considered as samples of different styles, and *not* as one sequence.

It is obvious that the directional units must be assigned to each structure when more than one structure is employed.

Directional Harmonic Continuity of S2p and Hybrid
(through addition of Sp)

(1) Original I.

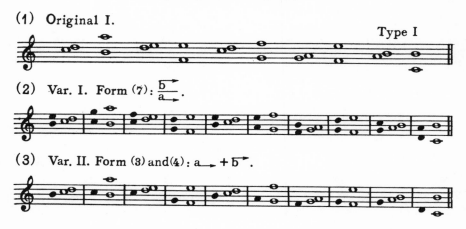

Type I

(2) Var. I. Form (7): $\frac{b}{a}$.

(3) Var. II. Form (3) and (4): a + b.

Figure 89. Directional harmonic continuity of S2p (continued).

Figure 89. Directional harmonic continuity of 2Sp (continued).

Figure 89. Directional harmonic continuity of S2p (continued).

(18)   Var. II. Form (8): $\frac{b \rightarrow i}{a \rightarrow i}$.

$$\Sigma = 2S; \quad S_I = p; \quad S_{II} = 2p$$

Figure 89. Directional harmonic continuity of S2p (concluded).

Original: (4) with added Sp.

Var.: (5)   Form (7): $S_{II} \frac{b \rightarrow i}{a \rightarrow i}$; $S_I a \rightarrow 2i$.

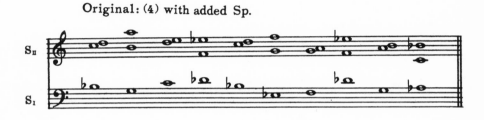

Original: (10) with added Sp.

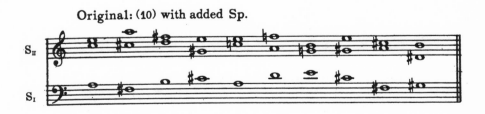

Figure 90. Hybrid harmonic continuity; addition of Sp to S2p (continued).

Var.: (11). Form (6): $S_{II} \dfrac{b \rightarrow i}{a \rightarrow i}$; S_I $a \rightarrow i$.

Original: (16) with added Sp.

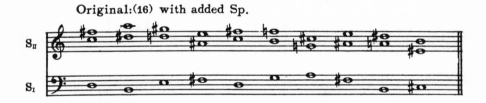

Var.: (17) Form (6): $S_{II} \dfrac{b \rightarrow}{a \rightarrow}$; S_I $a \rightarrow i$.

Figure 90. Hybrid harmonic continuity; addition of Sp to S2p (concluded).

Progression of mixed structures

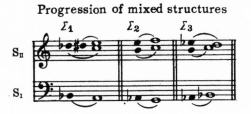

$\overrightarrow{\varSigma} = 2\varSigma_1 + \varSigma_2 + \varSigma_1 + 2\varSigma_3.$
$\overrightarrow{C} = 2C_3 + C_7 + C_5 + C_{-7}.$
Scale of Roots = Nat. major d_4.

Figure 91. Progression of mixed structures.

C. DIRECTIONAL UNITS OF S3p

$$(a, b, c, a_{\rightarrow}, b_{\rightarrow}, c_{\rightarrow}, \overrightarrow{a}, \overrightarrow{b}, \overrightarrow{c})$$

Directional units of S3p consist of the combinations of 0, a and b. As each form is combined with itself as well as with other forms, the total number of the forms of directional and neutral units is: $3^3 = 27$.

For convenience, these forms can be arranged into groups with three identical elements, with two identical elements and with no identical elements.

Table of Directional and Neutral Units of S3p

0	a	b
0	a	b
0	a	b

0	0	a	0	0	b
0	a	0	0	b	0
a	0	0	b	0	0
a	a	0	a	a	b
a	0	a	a	b	a
0	a	a	b	a	a
b	b	0	b	b	a
b	0	b	b	a	b
0	b	b	a	b	b
b	a	a	b	0	0
a	b	0	0	b	a
0	0	b	a	a	b

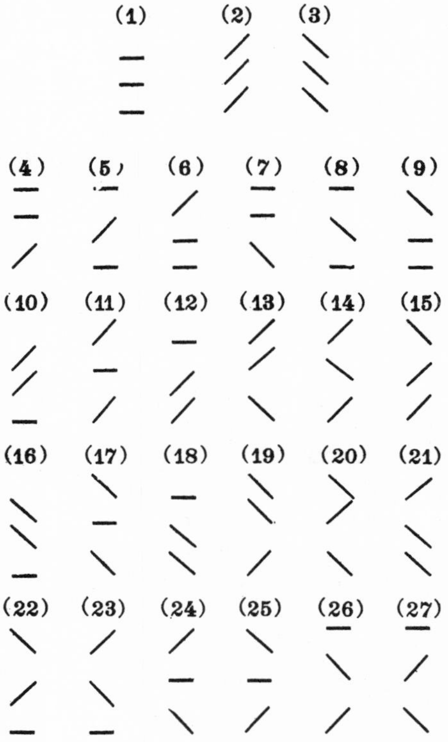

(1) (2) (3)

(4) (5) (6) (7) (8) (9)

(10) (11) (12) (13) (14) (15)

(16) (17) (18) (19) (20) (21)

(22) (23) (24) (25) (26) (27)

Of these 27 forms, (1) has no semitonal variations; the (2) and (3) have 8 variations each (i and 2i participating in each part); the (4), (5), (6), (7), (8) and (9) have 2 variations each; the (10), (11) and (12) have 4 variations each; the (13), (14) and (15) have 8 variations each; the (16), (17) and (18) have 4 variations each; the (19), (20) and (21) have 8 variations each; the remaining 6 forms have 4 variations each.

Thus the 27 forms together with the possible i and 2i variations produce 125 forms of intonation for each given S3p structure.

$1; 2 \cdot 8 = 16; 6 \cdot 2 = 12; 3 \cdot 4 = 12; 3 \cdot 8 = 24; 3 \cdot 4 = 12; 3 \cdot 8 = 24; 6 \cdot 4 = 24.$
$1 + 16 + 12 + 12 + 24 + 12 + 24 + 24 = 125$

An Exemplary Table of Directional Units Evolved
to $I(S3p) = 4i + 3i$

Figure 92. Directional units. $I(S3p) = 4i + 3i$. One movement.

Figure 93. Directional units. $I(S3p) = 4i + 3i$. Two movements.

Three movements

64 cases

Figure 94. Directional units. I(S3p) = 4i + 3i. Three movements.

Similar tables can be devised for any other S3p structure. In spite of the abundance of resources, the composer will do well to assign just one combination to each structure used in a certain continuity. When the structures of one continuity differ in their form, an individual directional group must be assigned to each structure.

Examples of Application of Directional Units
to S3p Progressions

Figure 95. Directional units to S3p progressions (continued).

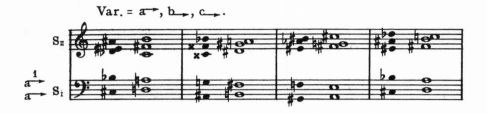

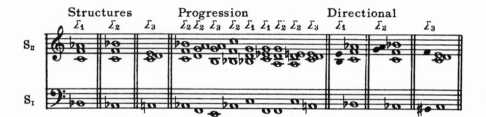

Figure 95. Directional units to S3p progressions (concluded).

D. DIRECTIONAL UNITS OF S4p

$$(a,\ b,\ c,\ d,\ a_{\rightarrow},\ b_{\rightarrow},\ c_{\rightarrow},\ d_{\rightarrow},\ a^{\rightarrow},\ \overrightarrow{b},\ c^{\rightarrow},\ d^{\rightarrow})$$

Directional units of S4p consist of the combinations of 0, a and b. As each form is combined with itself as well as with all other forms, the total number of the forms of directional and neutral units is: $3^4 = 81$.

In the case of variable Σ, it is necessary to assign the directional units to each Σ individually.

Table of Directional and Neutral Units of S4p

0	a	b
0	a	b
0	a	b
0	a	b

0	0	0	a	0	0	0	b	a	a	a	0	a	a	a	b	b	b	b	0	b	b	b	a
0	0	a	0	0	0	b	0	a	a	0	a	a	a	b	a	b	b	0	b	b	b	a	b
0	a	0	0	0	b	0	0	a	0	a	a	a	b	a	a	b	0	b	b	b	a	b	b
a	0	0	0	b	0	0	0	0	a	a	a	b	a	a	a	0	b	b	b	a	b	b	b

a	0	0	a	a	0	b	0	0	b	b	0	b	a	a	b	b	a
a	a	0	0	0	a	b	b	0	0	0	b	b	b	a	a	a	b
0	a	a	0	a	0	0	b	b	0	b	0	a	b	b	a	b	a
0	0	a	a	0	a	0	0	b	b	0	b	a	a	b	b	a	b

b	0	0	a	a	0	0	b	b	0	a	0
a	b	0	0	b	a	0	0	0	b	0	a
0	a	b	0	0	b	a	0	a	0	b	0
0	0	a	b	0	0	b	a	0	a	0	b

b	a	a	0	0	a	a	b	b	a	0	a
0	b	a	a	b	0	a	a	a	b	a	0
a	0	b	a	a	b	0	a	0	a	b	a
a	a	0	b	a	a	b	0	a	0	a	b

a	b	b	0	0	b	b	a	a	b	0	b
0	a	b	b	a	0	b	b	b	a	b	0
b	0	a	b	b	a	0	b	0	b	a	b
b	b	0	a	b	b	a	0	b	0	b	a

See graph presentation of above table on the following page.

(1) (2) (3)

(4) (5) (6) (7) (8) (9) (10) (11) (12) (13) (14) (15) (16) (17) (18) (19)

(20) (21) (22) (23) (24) (25) (26) (27)

(28) (29) (30) (31) (32) (33) (34) (35) (36) (37) (38) (39) (40) (41) (42) (43) (44) (45)

(46) (47) (48) (49) (50) (51) (52) (53) (54) (55) (56) (57)

(58) (59) (60) (61) (62) (63) (64) (65) (66) (67) (68) 69)

(70) (71) (72) (73) (74) (75) (76) (77) (78) (79) (80) (81)

Semitonal variations occurring in one p:

| i | 2i |

2 variations

Semitonal variations occurring in two p's:

i	2i	i	2i
i	i	2i	2i

4 variations

Semitonal variations occurring in three p's:

i	i	i	2i	2i	2i	i	2i
i	i	2i	i	2i	i	2i	2i
i	2i	i	i	i	2i	2i	2i

8 variations

Semitonal variations occurring in four p's:

i	i	i	i	2i	2i	i	i	2i	2i	i	2i	2i	2i	i	2i
i	i	i	2i	i	2i	2i	i	i	i	2i	2i	2i	i	2i	2i
i	i	2i	i	i	i	2i	2i	i	2i	i	2i	i	2i	2i	2i
i	2i	i	i	i	i	i	2i	2i	i	2i	i	2i	2i	2i	2i

On the basis of the above table we find that the 81 forms, tabulated on pages 1183-4, produce the following number of semitonal variations:

(1) has 1 form;

(2) and (3) have . . . . 16 variations each

(4 — 11) have . . . . . . 2 ,, ,,

(12 — 15) have . . . . . . 8 ,, ,,

(16 — 19) have . . . . . 16 ,, ,,

(20 — 23) have . . . . . . 8 ,, ,,

(24 — 27) have . . . . . 16 ,, ,,

(28 — 39) have . . . . . . 4 ,, ,,

(40 — 45) have . . . . . 16 ,, ,,

(46 — 57) have . . . . . . 4 ,, ,,

(58 — 81) have . . . . . 8 ,, ,,

By multiplying the number of forms in each subdivision by its respective number of variations, we find the following:

1

$2 \cdot 16 = 32$

$8 \cdot 2 = 16$

$4 \cdot 8 = 32$

$4 \cdot 16 = 64$

$4 \cdot 8 = 32$

$4 \cdot 16 = 64$

$12 \cdot 4 = 48$

$6 \cdot 16 = 96$

$12 \cdot 4 = 48$

$24 \cdot 8 = 192$

Total: $1 + 32 + 16 + 32 + 64 + 32 + 64 + 48 + 96 + 48 + 192 = 625$

The latter figure represents the number of possibilities for each S4p structure.

It is easy to evolve musical tables for any of the 165 possible S4p structures, taken in any of their three expansions (E_0, E_1 and E_2), by following the chart of 81 forms and the table of semitonal variations.

It is interesting to learn that the manifold of structures of S4p supplied with all the possible directional units produces: $165 \cdot 3 \cdot 625 = 309{,}375$ forms of the c –chord.

Examples of Application of Directional Units to S4p Progressions

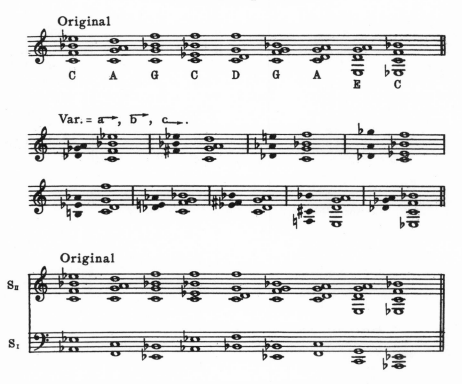

Figure 96. Directional units of S4p progressions (continued).

Figure 96. Directional units of S4p progressions (concluded).

E. Strata Composition of Assemblages Containing Directional Units

Selection of directional units for a Σ depend on several factors:

(1) whether the number of parts is the same or different in the different strata;

(2) if the number of parts is the same in the different strata, it depends on whether the structures in the different strata are identical or not;

(3) whether it is desirable in each individual case to neutralize or to single out the character of the directional units in the different strata.

In case No. 3, the predominant characteristics of the groups of directional units accompanying assemblages are: the *identity* and the *reciprocity* of the patterns. The identity can be carried out with diatonic (with the precision up to 2i) or with general (with the precision up to i), i.e., chromatic precision. Reciprocity can be achieved by means of the axis of inversion. The axis of inversion of a Σ is located at the level of $\frac{\Sigma}{2}$. For example, if a $\Sigma = 2S3p$, it means that $\Sigma = 6p$. Hence $\frac{\Sigma}{2} = \frac{6}{2} = 3$, i.e., the axis is between the two strata.

Under the conditions of such reciprocity, the axis-inversion yields a symmetric arrangement of the directional units throughout the sigma.

If the number of parts in a sigma is: $\Sigma = 2np + 1$ (i.e., an odd number), the part representing the center of the vertical arrangement in a sigma, becomes the axis of inversion.

In such a case, if perfect symmetry is desired in the distribution of directional units throughout the Σ, it is better to leave this part as a *neutral* unit.

Thus, depending on whether $\Sigma = 2np$, or $2np + 1$, the axis of inversion is located between strata, or coincides with a p of the central stratum respectively

Examples of Composition of Directional Units in
Strata; Graphic Representation

$\Sigma = 2S; \; S = 2p.$

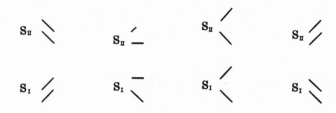

$\Sigma = 2S; \; S = 3p.$

$\Sigma = 2S; \; S = 4p.$

Figure 97. Directional units in strata (continued).

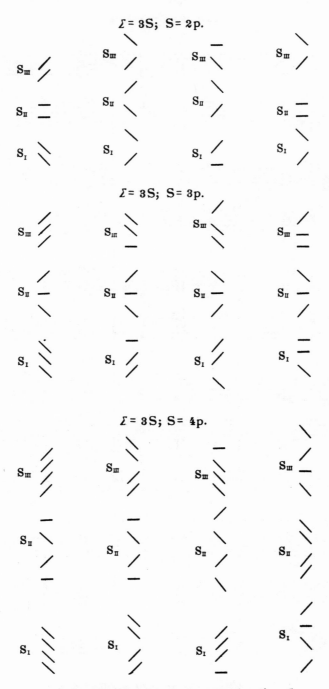

*Figure 97. Directional units in strata*₁*(continued).*

Musical Representation

Figure 97. Directional units in strata (continued).

Figure 97. Directional units in strata (concluded).

In the sigmae with a different number of parts in the different strata, the composer can use his discretion in attempting to evolve symmetric, or nearly symmetric forms, by assigning an axis of inversion.

In many instances directional units are reversible. Whether the structure S is of higher tension than the directional assemblage (i.e., the group of leading units) or vice-versa, both forms can be used. It is analogous in effect to moving from a consonance to a dissonance, or in reverse. As our harmonic progressions are always reversible, the reversal of directional units does not affect the quality of a progression but merely changes its character. Such progressions in position ⓐ and ⓑ are often useful as two themes of one composition.

Example of the Reversal of Directional Units

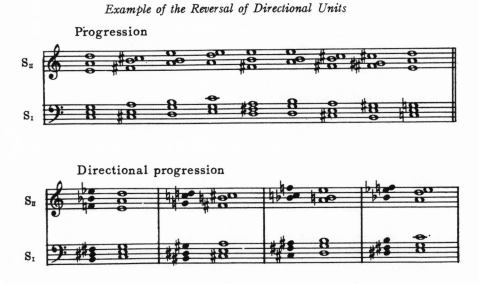

Figure 98. Directional units reversed (continued).

Figure 98. *Directional units reversed (concluded).*

F. SEQUENT GROUPS OF DIRECTIONAL UNITS
(*Leading Units of the Higher Orders*)

The leading units immediately preceding the respective chordal functions can, in turn, be preceded by other leading units which, in turn, can be preceded by still other leading units, etc. Since in most cases the interval of directional units is i; this technique attributes chromatic character to any strata progression to which it is applied.

There are certain limitations to this technique. When the intervals of chord-structures are small, only inward motion of successive leading tones can be achieved. The opposite is true, i.e. outward motion is preferable for widely-spaced intervals; otherwise, the sequent groups of leading units may interfere with adjacent chordal functions. Parallel motion of the sequent leading units is acceptable in all cases, except where such units are assigned to simultaneous chordal functions, undesirable in parallel motion.

The presence of the leading unit to the leading unit, i.e., the leading unit of the second order, can be expressed as follows·

$$a\smile, a\frown, b\smile, b\frown, c\smile, c\frown, d\smile, d\frown$$

Likewise the leading units of the third order can be expressed by introducing still another arrow:

$$a\smile, a\frown, b\smile, b\frown, c\smile, c.\frown, d\smile, d\frown,$$

Examples of Leading Units of the Higher Orders

Figure 99. Leading units of the higher orders.

The conversion of harmony into melody will be discussed in *Applications· of Strata Harmony.*

CHAPTER 9

COMPOSITION OF MELODIC CONTINUITY FROM THE STRATA

EACH individual part of a stratum* can be used as part of a melodic continuity. When harmonic continuity forms a cyclic recapitulating progression, coefficients for the number of attacks on each change of a chord (H) may be set to any desirable type of interference. Thus there are three fundamental types of melodic continuity:

(a) where each part moves through the entire harmonic continuity from beginning to end, after which the next part begins.

(b) where coefficients can be set in such a way that the entire harmonic continuity will serve as a divisor to its own multiple. For example, if the number of chords equals 8, a distribution through $3 + 3 + 2$ produces one cycle. The above coefficients represent the number of H until p changes.

(c) coefficients set as an interference group in relation to the number of H. For example, if H equals 8, and the distribution-group is $r_{5 \div 2}$, then $\frac{10}{8}$ interference will take place.

Theme

$$\Sigma = 3S; \; S_1 = 4p; \; S_2 = 3p; \; S_3 = 2p; \; 1^{\rightarrow} = 3+4+7+11-7-4-3$$

Figure 100. $\Sigma = 3S; \; S_1 = 4p; \; S_2 = 3p; \; S_3 = 2p; \; 1^{\rightarrow} = 3+4+7+11-7-4-3$

*Terminology and nomenclature of this branch corresponds to that used in the *Instrumental Forms* and *General Theory of Harmony*.

A. Melody from One Individual Part of a Stratum

Distributive forms of transitions from p to p and from S to S including $\Sigma^{\rightarrow}$ as a limit. The letters a, b, c, d correspond to chordal functions.

$$M = aS_1\Sigma^{\rightarrow}+bS_1\Sigma.^{\rightarrow}+cS_1\Sigma^{\rightarrow}+dS_1\Sigma^{\rightarrow}+aS_2\Sigma^{\rightarrow}+bS_2\Sigma^{\rightarrow}+cS_2\Sigma^{\rightarrow}+aS_3\Sigma^{\rightarrow}+$$
$$+ bS_3\Sigma^{\rightarrow}$$

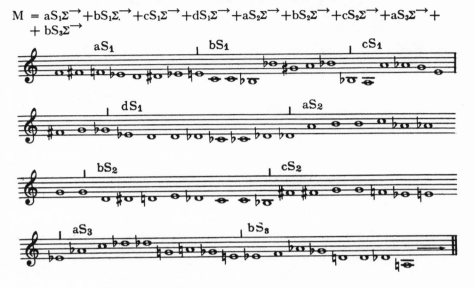

Figure 101. Melody from one part of a stratum.

B. Melody from 2p, 3p, 4p of an S

Each section belongs to a pre-selected quantitative group. Distributive forms of transitions from S to S with respective pre-selected quantitative groups. Permutation of pitch-units within the groups.

$$a \equiv p_I; \; b \equiv p_{II}; \; c \equiv p_{III}; \; d \equiv p_{IV}.$$

(a) $M = ab\;S_1\;H_1 + dc\;S_1\;H_2$

(b) $M = abc\;S_2\;H_1 + bca\;S_2\;H_2 + cab\;S_2\;H_3$

(c) $M = aba\;S_3\;H_1 + bab\;S_3\;H_2$

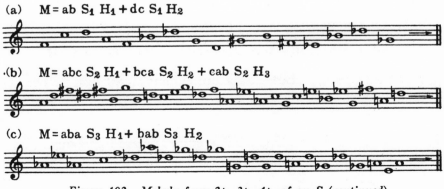

Figure 102. Melody from 2p, 3p, 4p, of an S (continued).

(d) $M = abc\ S_2\ H_1 + dcb\ S_1\ H_2 + abc\ S_1\ H_3 + ba\ S_3\ H_4$

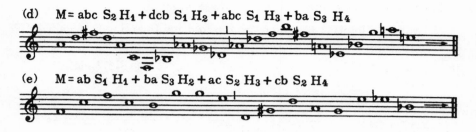

(e) $M = ab\ S_1\ H_1 + ba\ S_3\ H_2 + ac\ S_2\ H_3 + cb\ S_2\ H_4$

Figure 102. Melody from 2p, 3p, 4p, of an S (concluded).

C. Melody from One S

Permutation of pitch-units within one S. Distributive forms of transition from S to S.

a, b, c, d represent instrumental functions.

$M = ab\ S_3\ H_1 + ba\ S_3\ H_2 + dcb\ S_1\ H_3 + cba\ S_1\ H_4 + bab\ S_1\ H_5 + bcd\ S_1\ H_6 +$
$+ abc\ S_2\ H_7 + bca\ S_2\ H_8$

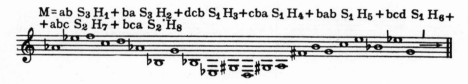

Figure 103. Melody from one S.

D. Melody from 2S, 3S

Each section of melody incorporates a pre-selected quantity and position of S. Permutation of pitch-units within a pre-selected group. Distributive forms of positions and transitions of the groups of S.

a, b, c, d represent instrumental functions.

$M = (abcab\ S_2 + ab\ S_3)\ H_1 + (bcabc\ S_2 + ba\ S_3)\ H_2 + (cabca\ S_2 + ba\ S_3)\ H_3$

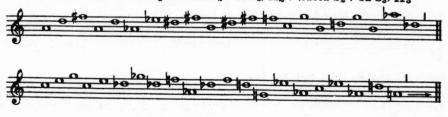

Figure 104. Melody from 2S, 3S . . .

E. GENERALIZATION OF THE METHOD

Σ as the limit becomes a pitch-scale or a melodic form. Permutation of the pitch-units. Transition to the following H occurs after a complete utilization of all p of the preceding H.

a, b, c, d represent instrumental functions.

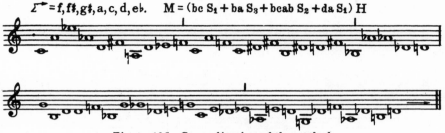

Figure 105. Generalization of the method.

F. MIXED FORMS

Derived through distributive combinations of Paragraphs A, B, C, D, E.

a, b, c, d represent instrumental functions.

$$M = bd\,S_1\,3H + a\,S_2\,4H + dcb\,S_1\,2H + b\,S_3\,3H + (ab\,S_1 + cb\,S_2 + d\,S_1 + bc\,S_2 + ba\,S_3)H$$

Figure 106. Mixed forms.

G. Distribution of Auxiliary Units Through p, S and Σ

Application of auxiliary units to sections A, B, C, D, and E. Permutation of directional units. Composition of continuity where some of the sections of melody contain directional units and some neutral units. Application of coefficients to the above two types of groups. Application of the directional unit technique to Paragraph F.

a, b, c, d represent instrumental functions.

$$M = a{\rightarrow}b{\rightarrow}S_2 3H + b{\rightarrow}a{\rightarrow}S_2 H + b{\rightarrow}aS_3 H + a{\rightarrow}bS_3 H + (bcS_2 + a{\rightarrow}b{\rightarrow}S_3 + c{\rightarrow}b{\rightarrow}S_2)\,2H + d{\rightarrow}c{\rightarrow}abS_1 H + (ac{\rightarrow}b{\rightarrow}S_1 + ac{\rightarrow}S_2 + a{\rightarrow}S_3)\,3H$$

Figure 107. Distribution of auxiliary units through p, S and Σ.

Directional units are one of the most customary forms of variation. Exposition of a theme, followed by variations of it, is a device which is particularly important from the standpoint of mobility. Increase in the number of attacks can be easily achieved through this device.

H. Variation of the Original Melodic Continuity by Means of Auxiliary Tones

a, b, c, d represent instrumental functions.

(Theme: see Fig. 104)

$$M = (abcab\,S_2 + ab\,S_3)\,H_1 + (bcabc\,S_2 + ba\,S_3)\,H_2 + (cabca\,S_2 + ba\,S_3)\,H_3.$$

Figure 108. Variation by means of auxiliary tones (continued).

Variation:

$M = (ab_{\rightarrow} c_{\rightarrow} a_{\rightarrow} b\, S_2 + a_{\rightarrow} b\, S_3)\, H_1 + (bc_{\rightarrow} a_{\rightarrow} b_{\rightarrow} e\, S_1 + ba_{\rightarrow} S_3)\, H_2 + (ca_{\rightarrow} b_{\rightarrow} c_{\rightarrow} a\, S_2 + b_{\rightarrow} a\, S_3)\, H_3$

Figure 108. Variation by means of auxiliary tones (concluded).

There are two ways of assigning a duration-group to such a melodic continuity:

(1) each unit, neutral or leading, corresponds to one attack of the duration group;

(2) directional unit originally corresponds to one attack of the duration-group, afterwards is changed into a split-unit group.

See Theory of Melodization of Harmony: Composition of Durations to a Pre-set Attack-group.*

---

*See Vol. I, p. 649.

CHAPTER 10

COMPOSITION OF HARMONIC CONTINUITY FROM THE STRATA

COMPOSITION of harmonic continuity from a given $\Sigma^{\rightarrow}$ is primarily a method of selecting the different strata with regard to their quantity and the form of distribution. In applying this technique to orchestral writing, the different groups of instruments represent different strata, which permits one to obtain a superior flexibility of harmony with regard to ranges, registers and density. Composition of density as such is a matter of separate study and will be discussed later in this branch. For the time being, it is sufficient to assume that the density may vary gradually or suddenly as well as in an oblique fashion when one stratum alternates with the variable density of remaining strata.

A. HARMONY FROM ONE STRATUM (ANY S OF THE Σ)

Distributive forms of transition from S to S within Σ as a limit. Circular continuity.

$$H^{\rightarrow} = S_2 2H + S_1 H + S_2 H + S_3 2H$$

Figure 109. Harmony from one stratum.

B. Harmony from 2S, 3S, . . .

Distributive method of selecting the groups of S and their sequence in time continuity. Circular continuity.

$$H^{\rightarrow} = (S_1 + S_2)\,2H + (S_2 + S_3)\,4H + (S_3 + S_1)\,2H$$

Figure 110. Harmony from 2S, 3S . . . . .

C. Harmony from $\Sigma(\Sigma^{\rightarrow}$; the Original Layout)

$$H^{\rightarrow} = \Sigma^{\rightarrow}$$

Figure 111. Harmony from Σ.

D. Patterns of Distribution (Variation of Density) from Sections A, B, C
Composition of continuity with variable density.

$$H^{\rightarrow} = S_2\,H + (S_1 + S_2)\,H + S_2\,H + (S_2 + S_3)\,H + S_2 H + (S_1 + S_2 + S_3)\,3H$$

Figure 112. Continuity with variable density (continued).

$$H^{\rightarrow} = S_1\,3H + (S_1+S_2)\,3H + (S_1+S_2+S_3)\,4H + (S_2+S_3)\,3H + S_3\,3H$$

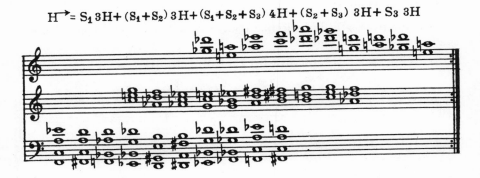

Figure 112. Continuity with variable density (concluded).

E. APPLICATION OF AUXILIARY UNITS AND INSTRUMENTAL FIGURATION OF HARMONY THROUGH ANY OF THE PRECEDING FOUR FORMS OF HARMONIC CONTINUITY OF THE STRATA

Hybrid forms of distribution of the auxiliary tones through strata.

F. VARIATION OF THE ORIGINAL HARMONIC CONTINUITY THROUGH AUXILIARY UNITS

The following example illustrates both Sections E and F, as it may be used in place of a variation on the original theme.

$$H^{\rightarrow} = \varGamma^{\rightarrow};\quad S_1 = \begin{smallmatrix}d^{\rightarrow}\\c^{\rightarrow}\\b^{\rightarrow}\\a\end{smallmatrix}\ \circlearrowleft;\quad S_2 = \begin{smallmatrix}c^{\rightarrow}\\b^{\rightarrow}\\a^{\rightarrow}\end{smallmatrix}\ \text{const.};\quad S_3 = \begin{smallmatrix}b^{\rightarrow}\\a^{\rightarrow}\end{smallmatrix}\ \circlearrowleft$$

a, b, c, d Represent instrumental functions.

Figure 113. Variations of original harmonic continuity (continued).

Figure 113. Variation of original harmonic continuity (concluded).

CHAPTER 11

MELODY WITH HARMONIC ACCOMPANIMENT

All illustrations are based on the theme of figure 100.

(**1**) One S becomes a melody; same S serves as harmony in a different octave.

$$\frac{M}{H} = S \text{ constant}$$

$$\text{(a)} \ \frac{M}{H} = S_1$$

$$\text{(b)} \ \frac{M}{H} = S_2$$

$$\text{(c)} \ \frac{M}{H} = S_3$$

$$\cdots \cdots$$

$$\text{(n)} \ \frac{M}{H} = S_n$$

Example: $\frac{M}{H} = S_1$

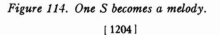

Figure 114. One S becomes a melody.

[1204]

$H^{\rightarrow} = H_12T + H_22T + H_32T + H_42T$

Instrumental form: $(a+b) 2T + bT + aT + (a+b)2T$

$T(M) = (\boxed{t}+t+t+t) + (t+\boxed{t}+t+t) + (t+t+\boxed{t}+t) + (t+t+t+\boxed{t})$

tied over: $T(M) = (\boxed{t}+t+t+t) + (2t+t+t) + (t+2t+t) + (t+t+2t)$

(2) Different individual S's of one Σ become melody with harmonic accompaniment $\left(\dfrac{M}{H} = S \text{ variable}\right)$.

$$\frac{M}{H} = S_1, S_2, S_3, \ldots S_n$$

Example: $\dfrac{M}{H} = S_2H_12T + S_3H_22T + S_2H_3T + S_1H_42T$

Figure 115. $\dfrac{M}{H}$ = *S variable.*

(3) More than one S produce melody; one S produces harmony.

$$\frac{M}{H} = \frac{S_2 + S_3}{S_1}; \quad \frac{M}{H} = \frac{S_2 + S_3 + S_4}{S_1}; \quad \frac{M}{H} = \frac{S_a + \ldots + S_n}{S_1}$$

Example:

$$\frac{M}{H} = \frac{S_2+S_3}{S_1}$$

Rhythm: $\frac{8}{8}$ series: $T = (4+1+1) + (1+4+1) + (1+1+4) +$
$+ (1+1+2+1+1) + (1+2+1+1+1) +$
$+ (2+1+1+1+1)$

See Figure 116 on the following page.

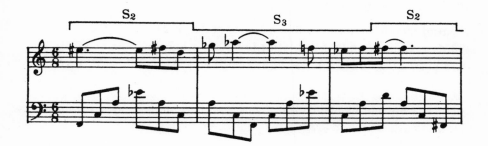

Figure 116. More than one S produces melody.

(4) One S produces melody; more than one S produces harmony.

(5) Several S's produce melody and several other S's (of the same Σ) produce harmony.

(6) Distribution of tension for $\dfrac{M}{H}$ in the preceding cases (H = S_1, M = S_2; H = $S_1 + S_2 + \ldots + S_{n-1}$, M = S_n; H = S_1, M = $S_2 + S_3 + \ldots + S_n$).

$$\frac{M}{H} = \frac{Sa}{Sb}$$

Example: $\dfrac{M}{H} = \dfrac{S_2}{S_1}$

Rhythm: Foxtrot: $\frac{4}{4}$, $\frac{6}{8}$ and $\frac{8}{8}$ series

Instrumental form: $aH_12T + bH_2T + bH_3T + aH_42T$

See Figure 117 on the opposite page.

Figure 117. Distribution of tension for $\frac{M}{H}$.

(**7**) Variable distributive transition from one individual S to another for melody and a constant S or a group thereof for harmony.

(**8**) Constant S or a group thereof for melody and a variable distributive transition from one individual S to another for harmony.

(**9**) Σ for melody; variable density for harmony composed through distributive selection.

(**10**) Melody composed through distributive selection of scales derived from the individual S, the groups of S or the entire Σ; harmony from the entire Σ.

(**11**) All previous cases with application of auxiliary units. M and H without auxiliary units. M with and H without auxiliary units. M without and H with auxiliary units. Both M and H with auxiliary units.

(**12**) All the previous forms of harmonic accompaniment with instrumental figuration.

(**13**) Hybrid forms with respect to density of both melody (scale emphasis) and harmony.

(**14**) Hybrid forms with respect to the presence or absence of auxiliary units in both M and H.

(**15**) Forms of alternating transformations of M into H and vice versa with respect to the selective distribution of strata.

(**16**) Instrumental forms of melody used for the purpose of variation.

(**17**) Intercomposition of the instrumental forms of melody and harmony.

(**18**) Composition of continuity employing the previous devices.

Example:

$$\frac{M}{H} = \frac{\Sigma}{S_3} H_1 3T + \frac{S_2}{\Sigma} H_2 T + \frac{S_3}{S_2} H_3 T + \frac{S_3}{S_1 + S_2} H_3 T + \frac{S_2}{S_1 + S_3} H_4 T +$$

$$+ \frac{S_2}{S_3} H_4 T + \frac{\Sigma}{0} H_5 T + \frac{S_1}{S_1} H_6 T + \frac{S_1 + S_2}{S_1} H_6 T + \frac{S_1 + S_2 + S_3}{S_1} H_6 T$$

Figure 118. Composition of continuity based on previous devices.

CHAPTER 12

CORRELATED MELODIES

CORRELATED Melodies (Transformation of Harmony into Counterpoint by Means of Strata).

The technique of correlating melodies consists of three fundamental processes:

(1) correlation of attacks and durations of two or more melodies;
(2) correlation of melodic forms (axial combinations) of two or more melodies;
(3) correlation of harmonic intervals between two or more melodies (distribution of tension).

The first two processes have been described in the *Theory of Correlated Melodies (Counterpoint)** Here we shall deal with the third procedure as it evolves itself from the technique of strata.

The usual classical conception of a consonance and a dissonance, and the necessity of resolution must give way to the assortment and distribution of harmonic intervals through their respective degrees of tension.

From the harmonic point of view there are the following forms of matching intervals:

(1) a neutral unit against a neutral unit (or units);
(2) a neutral unit against a directional unit (or units);
(3) a directional unit against a neutral unit (or units);
(4) a directional unit against a directional unit (or units).

Taking as illustration the $\Sigma^{\rightarrow}$ used in the previous examples, we may enumerate the following possibilities:

(1) $\dfrac{CP_I}{CP_{II}} = \dfrac{aS_1}{aS_2}$;   (2) $\dfrac{CP_I}{CP_{II}} = \dfrac{bS_1}{aS_2}$;   (3) $\dfrac{CP_I}{CP_{II}} = \dfrac{cS_1}{aS_2}$;   (4) $\dfrac{CP_I}{CP_{II}} = \dfrac{dS_1}{aS_2}$;

(5) $\dfrac{CP_I}{CP_{II}} = \dfrac{aS_1}{bS_2}$;   (6) $\dfrac{CP_I}{CP_{II}} = \dfrac{bS_1}{bS_2}$;   (7) $\dfrac{CP_I}{CP_{II}} = \dfrac{cS_1}{bS_2}$;   (8) $\dfrac{CP_I}{CP_{II}} = \dfrac{dS_1}{bS_2}$;

(9) $\dfrac{CP_I}{CP_{II}} = \dfrac{aS_1}{cS_2}$;   (10) $\dfrac{CP_I}{CP_{II}} = \dfrac{bS_1}{cS_2}$;   (11) $\dfrac{CP_I}{CP_{II}} = \dfrac{cS_1}{cS_2}$;   (12) $\dfrac{CP_I}{CP_{II}} = \dfrac{dS_1}{cS_2}$;

(13) $\dfrac{CP_I}{CP_{III}} = \dfrac{aS_1}{aS_3}$;   (14) $\dfrac{CP_I}{CP_{III}} = \dfrac{bS_1}{aS_3}$;   (15) $\dfrac{CP_I}{CP_{III}} = \dfrac{cS_1}{aS_3}$;   (16) $\dfrac{CP_I}{CP_{III}} = \dfrac{dS_1}{aS_3}$;

(17) $\dfrac{CP_I}{CP_{III}} = \dfrac{aS_1}{bS_3}$;   (18) $\dfrac{CP_I}{CP_{III}} = \dfrac{bS_1}{bS_3}$;   (19) $\dfrac{CP_I}{CP_{III}} = \dfrac{cS_1}{bS_3}$;   (20) $\dfrac{CP_I}{CP_{III}} = \dfrac{dS_1}{bS_3}$;

(21) $\dfrac{CP_{II}}{CP_{III}} = \dfrac{aS_2}{aS_3}$;   (22) $\dfrac{CP_{II}}{CP_{III}} = \dfrac{bS_2}{aS_3}$;   (23) $\dfrac{CP_{II}}{CP_{III}} = \dfrac{cS_2}{aS_3}$;   (24) $\dfrac{CP_{II}}{CP_{III}} = \dfrac{aS_2}{bS_3}$;

(25) $\dfrac{CP_{II}}{CP_{III}} = \dfrac{bS_2}{bS_3}$;   (26) $\dfrac{CP_{II}}{CP_{III}} = \dfrac{cS_2}{bS_3}$.

Each of the above cases may be either a neutral or a directional unit.

*See Vol. I, pp. 730 and 753.

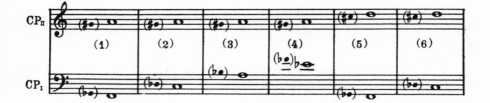

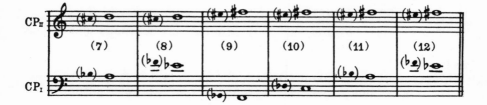

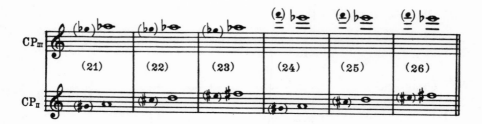

Figure 119. Forms of matching intervals.

Each stratum of harmony may be converted into a melody. The above case of $\Sigma^{\rightarrow}$ makes it possible to obtain a three part counterpoint. Distribution of attacks is the final factor in selecting matching units. Once the units are matched, the harmonic progression produces continuity.

Example:

Composition of attacks (A — attack-group; a — individual attack):

$$\underline{AS_3 = 2aT}$$
$$\underline{AS_2 = 3aT}$$
$$\underline{AS_1 = 6aT}$$

Composition of durations:

$$\underline{TS_3 = 4t + 4t}$$
$$\underline{TS_2 = 4t + 2t + 2t}$$
$$TS_1 = 2t + 2t + t + t + t + t$$

Time in musical notation:

Selection of matched units: (a, b, c, . . . designate chordal functions of the respective strata).

$$\underline{CP_{III} = b4t + a4t}$$
$$\underline{CP_{II} = c4t + a_{\rightarrow}(2t + 2t)}$$
$$CP_I = c^{\rightarrow}(2t + 2t) + a^{\rightarrow}(t+t) + b^{\rightarrow}(t+t)$$

Figure 120. Developing a Σ into 3 part counterpoint.

From this data we evolve the final form of continuity by applying the same selective pattern to the entire $\Sigma^{\rightarrow}$

Figure 121. Final form of continuity.

Composition of contrapuntal continuity can be accomplished from a theme such as the above progression (Figure 121) by means of various techniques.

The most important of these are:

(1) vertical rearrangement of parts;
(2) variation of density;
(3) geometrical inversions.

Figure 122. Composition of contrapuntal continuity (continued).

Figure 122. Composition of contrapuntal continuity (concluded).

The example in Figure 121 is a case of the constant form of duration-groups correlated through three parts. Any other form of distribution deriving from the *Theory of Rhythm* on the basis of compensation or contrast is acceptable for this purpose. The contrasts are particularly effective when several synchronized power-groups are used. The neutral and the directional pitch-units can change their respective octave position. One H may correspond to any time equivalent. $H^{\rightarrow}$ may have any rhythmic distribution of its own. Contrapuntal parts which derive from strata may be coupled and subjected to instrumental variations.

CHAPTER 13

COMPOSITION OF CANONS FROM STRATA HARMONY

AS we have seen, each stratum may become a contrapuntal part. In order to convert a Σ into canonic (continuous) imitation, it is necessary to fulfill the following requirements:

(1) Chord progression must be written in such a way as to permit regular occurrence of the identical chord positions, systematically moving from S to S. This can be accomplished by reciprocation of transformations. The latter must be either clockwise or counterclockwise throughout.
(2) Chord structures must be identical in all strata.
(3) Intervals between the roots of the different strata must be equidistant, i.e., only monomial symmetry is acceptable.
(4) The progression of chords must also be carried out in monomial symmetry of consecutive intervals, but not necessarily in the symmetry of simultaneous roots through which the Σ has been compounded.

So long as there is an interchange of symmetric roots of the same system of symmetry, canonic imitation remains unitonal. Beyond this, the form of imitation with respect to its harmonic correlation depends on the form of consecutive symmetry through which the chords progress.

The advantage of evolving a canon from $\overrightarrow{H}$ lies in the fact that such a canon possesses a definite harmonic characteristic set a priori, which it is impossible to obtain by means of purely contrapuntal technique.

A. Two-Part Continuous Imitation

Such an imitation is based on the reciprocation of the two functions a and b and on the reciprocation of the two symmetric roots of the $\sqrt{2}$.

The initial scheme of harmonic setting for a two-part canon is as follows:

$$CP_I \ (\equiv S_I) = \frac{b}{a}; \ \ CP_{II} \ (\equiv S_{II}) = \frac{a}{b}$$

The scheme of coordinated roots corresponding to the reciprocating positions is as follows:

$$\frac{CP_{II}}{CP_I} = \frac{C + F\sharp}{C + F\sharp + C}$$

The two schemes combined appear as follows:

$$\frac{CP_I}{CP_{II}} = \frac{C \left(\frac{b}{a}\right) + F\sharp \left(\frac{a}{b}\right)}{C \left(\frac{b}{a}\right) + F\sharp \left(\frac{a}{b}\right) + C \frac{b}{a}}$$

From this original scheme the canon follows any form of consecutive symmetry, resulting in a modulating canon. Other roots of symmetry can be used in similar reciprocation as well.

Figure 123. Two-part canon derived from Σ2S2p.

A canon such as this can be further extended by means of quadrant rotation (geometrical inversions). It can be also coupled and subjected to instrumental variations. Any temporal scheme can be used, and T does not necessarily have to equal T''.

B. THREE-PART CONTINUOUS IMITATION

Such an imitation derives from a harmonic scheme, where either clockwise or counterclockwise transformations are applied to both the simultaneous arrangement of strata in the Σ and the continuous progression of $\overrightarrow{H}$.

The initial harmonic scheme must be arranged in the following way:

$$
\begin{array}{ccccccc}
 & a & b & \begin{bmatrix} c \\ b \\ a \end{bmatrix} & \begin{matrix} {}'\,a \\ {}'\,c \\ {}'\,b \end{matrix} & \left.\begin{matrix} b \\ a \\ c \end{matrix}\right) \\
S_{III} & c & a & & & \\
 & b & c & & & \\[2ex]
 & b & \begin{bmatrix} c \\ b \\ a \end{bmatrix} & \begin{matrix} a \\ c \\ b \end{matrix}\Bigr] & \begin{matrix} {}'\,b \\ {}'\,a \\ {}'\,c \end{matrix}\Bigr) & \begin{matrix} c \\ b \\ a \end{matrix} \\
S_{II} & a & & & & \\
 & c & & & & \\[2ex]
 & \begin{bmatrix} c \\ b \\ a \end{bmatrix} & \begin{matrix} a \\ c \\ b \end{matrix}\Bigr] & \begin{matrix} b \\ a \\ c \end{matrix}\Bigr) & \begin{matrix} {}'\,c \\ {}'\,b \\ {}'\,a \end{matrix} & \begin{matrix} a \\ c \\ b \end{matrix} \\
S_{I} & & & & &
\end{array}
$$

This is a clockwise scheme where the sequence of imitation follows from S_I to S_{II} to S_{III}. Similar schemes can be devised for the remaining 5 forms of the sequence of imitation, as well as for the counterclockwise sequent transformations and the 6 forms of the sequence of imitation. Thus the total number of such schemes for $\Sigma 3S3p$ is 12.

The fundamental form of symmetric root-coordination is the $\sqrt[3]{2}$. However' other forms of symmetry may be used as well.

Examples of Schemes of Coordinated Roots

$$
(1)\quad \sqrt[3]{2}\ \begin{matrix} G\# \\ E \\ C \end{matrix}\ \begin{matrix} \dfrac{CP_{III}}{CP_{II}} \\[1ex] \dfrac{}{CP_I} \end{matrix} = \dfrac{\begin{matrix} C + G\# + E + \underline{C} \\ C + G\# + E + C + \underline{G\#} \end{matrix}}{C + G\# + E + C + G\# + E}
$$

$$
(2)\quad \sqrt[12]{2}{}^{\,5}\ \begin{matrix} B\flat \\ F \\ C \end{matrix}\ \begin{matrix} \dfrac{CP_{III}}{CP_{II}} \\[1ex] \dfrac{}{CP_I} \end{matrix} = \dfrac{\begin{matrix} C + B\flat + F + \underline{C} \\ C + B\flat + F + C + \underline{B\flat} \end{matrix}}{C + B\flat + F + C + B\flat + F}
$$

Figure 124. Schemes of coordinated roots.

The scheme of roots, after it is combined with the scheme of transformations, assumes the following form [Fig. 124 (1)]:

$$
\begin{array}{c}
\mathrm{CP_{III}} = \dfrac{\mathrm{C}\begin{pmatrix}c\\b\\a\end{pmatrix} + \mathrm{G\sharp}\begin{pmatrix}a\\c\\b\end{pmatrix} + \mathrm{E}\begin{pmatrix}b\\a\\c\end{pmatrix} + \mathrm{C}\begin{pmatrix}c\\b\\a\end{pmatrix}}{} \\[3em]
\mathrm{CP_{II}} = \dfrac{\mathrm{C}\begin{pmatrix}c\\b\\a\end{pmatrix} + \mathrm{G\sharp}\begin{pmatrix}a\\c\\b\end{pmatrix} + \mathrm{E}\begin{pmatrix}b\\a\\c\end{pmatrix} + \mathrm{C}\begin{pmatrix}c\\b\\a\end{pmatrix} + \mathrm{G\sharp}\begin{pmatrix}a\\c\\b\end{pmatrix}}{} \\[3em]
\mathrm{CP_{I}} \quad \mathrm{C}\begin{pmatrix}c\\b\\a\end{pmatrix} + \mathrm{G\sharp}\begin{pmatrix}a\\c\\b\end{pmatrix} + \mathrm{E}\begin{pmatrix}b\\a\\c\end{pmatrix} + \mathrm{C}\begin{pmatrix}c\\b\\a\end{pmatrix} + \mathrm{G\sharp}\begin{pmatrix}a\\c\\b\end{pmatrix} + \mathrm{E}\begin{pmatrix}b\\a\\c\end{pmatrix}
\end{array}
$$

Figure 124A. Scheme of transformations combined with scheme of roots.

As the scheme of the sequence of imitation for Σ3S3p is sufficiently long by itself, such a scheme may be used as a canonic theme, and be extended further by quadrant rotation. This does not exclude the use of the technique applied to Σ2S2p where the original scheme of H→ was extended by some form of consecutive root-symmetry. The application of the latter produces a modulating canon.

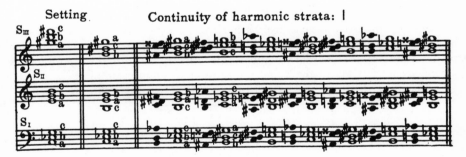

Figure 125. Three-part canon derived from Σ3S3p (continued).

Figure 125. Three-part canon derived from $\Sigma 3S3p$ (concluded).

C. Four-Part Continuous Imitation

Such an imitation derives from a harmonic scheme, where either clockwise or counterclockwise transformations (which correspond to $\circlearrowright$ or to $\circlearrowleft$ circular permutations of the chordal functions) are applied to both the simultaneous arrangement of strata in the Σ and the continuous progression of $H^{\rightarrow}$.

The initial harmonic scheme must be arranged in the following way:

S_{IV}	a	b	c	d	'	a	b	c
	d	a	b	c	'	d	a	b
	c	d	a	b	'	c	d	a
	b	c	d	a	'	b	c	d
S_{III}	b	c	d	a	'	b	c	d
	a	b	c	d	'	a	b	c
	d	a	b	c	'	d	a	b
	c	d	a	b	'	c	d	a
S_{II}	c	d	a	b	'	c	d	a
	b	c	d	a	'	b	c	d
	a	b	c	d	'	a	b	c
	d	a	b	c	'	d	a	b
S_{I}	d	a	b	c	'	d	a	b
	c	d	a	b	'	c	d	a
	b	c	d	a	'	b	c	d
	a	b	c	d	'	a	b	c

Figure 126. Initial harmonic scheme of four-part imitation.

This is a clockwise scheme where the sequence of imitation follows from S_I to S_{II}, to S_{III}, to S_{IV}. Similar schemes can be devised for the remaining 23 forms of the sequence of imitation, as well as for the counterclockwise sequent transformations and their own 24 forms (corresponding to the number of general permutations) of the sequence of imitation. Thus the total number of such schemes for $\Sigma 4S4p$ is 48.

The fundamental form of symmetric root-coordination is the $\sqrt[4]{2}$. However, other forms of symmetry can be used as well.

Example of a Scheme of Coordinated Roots

$$
\sqrt[4]{2}\quad
\begin{array}{ll}
A & CP_{IV} \\
F\# & CP_{III} \\
E\flat & CP_{II} \\
C & CP_{I}
\end{array}
=
\dfrac{\begin{array}{l} C \;+A\; +F\# + E\flat \;+ C \\ \overline{\quad C \;+A\; + F\# + E\flat + C \;+ A\quad} \\ \overline{C + A\; + F\# + E\flat + C \;+ A\; + F\#\quad} \\ C + A + F\# + E\flat + C + A + F\# + E\flat \end{array}}{}
$$

Figure 127. Scheme of coordinated roots.

The scheme of roots, being combined with the scheme of transformations, assumes the following fc   (Fig. 127):

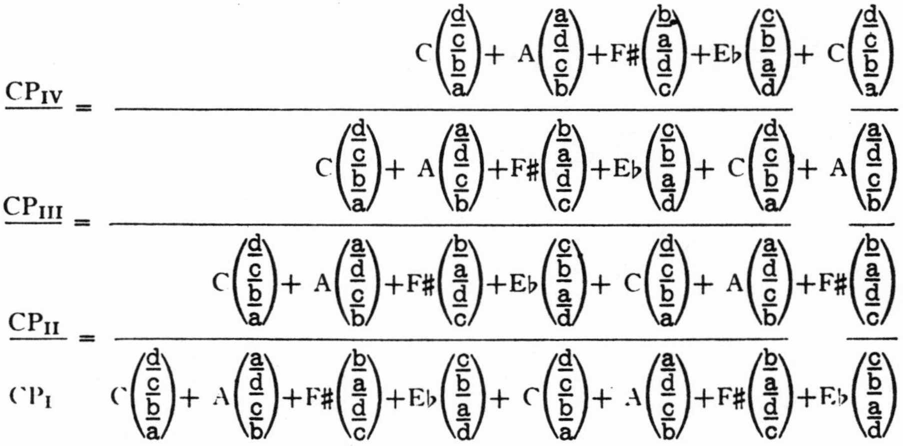

Figure 128. Scheme of transformations combined with scheme of roots.

Such a scheme can serve as a canonic theme, being further extended by· quadrant rotation, or through continuation of $H^{\rightarrow}$ evolved through some form of consecutive symmetry. In the latter case, the canon becomes modulating.

For an obvious technical reason (4p is the limit of S), this method of evolving canons from strata is limited to four parts.

This does not exclude the possibility of writing correlated melodies in any desirable number of parts (corresponding to the number of S in a Σ) in the form of general counterpoint, or counterpoint of discontinuous imitations.

All canonic schemes of the type described in this chapter produce recapitulating canons or *rounds*, providing $H^{\rightarrow}$ does not extend itself beyond the original scheme of symmetric roots.

Figure 129. Four-part canon derived form Σ4S-4p (continued).

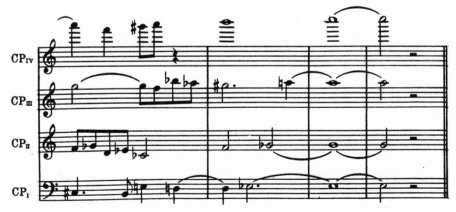

Figure 129. Four-part canon derived form Σ4S4p (concluded).

CHAPTER 14

CORRELATED MELODIES WITH HARMONIC ACCOMPANIMENT

THE fact that harmony can be converted into melody makes it possible to develop such forms as correlated melodies with harmonic accompaniment. There are three main groups into which such techniques may be classified:

Group (1) in which counterpoint and harmonic accompaniment are selected on the basis of identity or non-identity of strata to which the counterpoint and the harmonic accompaniment belong;

Group (2) in which counterpoint and harmonic accompaniment are selected on the basis of neutral or directional units so that either the counterpoint has directional units and the accompanying harmony, neutral units, or vice-versa; or both counterpoint and harmony are based on the same kind of units (i.e., either neutral or directional);

Group (3) in which counterpoint and harmonic accompaniment are inter-composed on the basis of continuity and discontinuity so that either counterpoint or the harmonic accompaniment are either continuous (uninterrupted) or discontinuous (interrupted) , which, at certain times, leaves only one of the two components (i.e., either counterpoint or harmony) and also makes it possible to evolve dialogue-like alternating sequences between the two components; the harmonic accompaniment as well as the counterpoint itself become subject to variation of density (low, medium, high), which may be treated in various forms of reciprocation.

The following classification presents the most important forms of correlated melodies with harmonic accompaniment in their interrelation through the above described three groups:

(1) Correlated melodies with harmonic accompaniment whose strata derivation is identical with that of the counterpoint itself.

(2) Correlated melodies with harmonic accompaniment which derives from strata partly in common with the counterpoint.

(3) Correlated melodies with harmonic accompaniment which derives from strata not participating in the counterpoint.

(4) Counterpoint of constant density accompanied by harmony of constant density.

(5) Counterpoint of variable density accompanied by harmony of constant density.

(6) Counterpoint of constant density accompanied by harmony of variable density.

(7) Counterpoint of variable density accompanied by harmony of variable density:

(a) Counterpoint in increasing density, harmony in increasing density;
(b) Counterpoint in decreasing density, harmony in increasing density;
(c) Counterpoint in increasing density, harmony in decreasing density;
(d) Counterpoint in decreasing density, harmony in decreasing density.

(8) Continuous counterpoint with a continuous harmonic accompaniment.
(9) Discontinuous counterpoint with a continuous harmonic accompaniment.
(10) Continuous counterpoint with a discontinuous harmonic accompaniment.
(11) Discontinuous counterpoint with a discontinuous harmonic accompaniment.
(12) Rhythmic composition of the forms of continuity and discontinuity in both harmony and counterpoint.
(13) Relations of directional and neutral units in the correlated melodies with harmonic accompaniment:

(a) Neutral units in counterpoint, neutral units in harmonic accompaniment;
(b) Directional units in counterpoint, neutral units in harmonic accompaniment;
(c) Neutral units in counterpoint, directional units in harmonic accompaniment;
(d) Directional units in counterpoint, directional units in harmonic accompaniment; in this case the duration-unit of counterpoint has a different value from the duration-unit of harmony.

(14) Composition and coordination of the instrumental forms of harmony and counterpoint.
(15) Composition of continuity based on correlated melodies with harmonic accompaniment, and including the above described devices.

No musical illustrations are necessary, as previous chapters give sufficient guidance for executing these projects.*

---

*Schillinger expected his students to work out each of these suggested procedures as homework. Those who are using the present text as a study-book are urged to do so. (Ed.)

CHAPTER 15

COMPOSITION OF DENSITY IN ITS APPLICATION
TO STRATA

WE have already encountered in the field of harmony and counterpoint certain elementary techniques pertaining to variation of density of the original texture. At the time we found it satisfactory to manipulate density by either employing some distinct degrees of it (like low, medium or high density), or by using harmonic parts as units of density.

Now, in view of the strata technique, with its potential abundance of pa₁ ιs and assemblages, we arrive at the necessity of generalizing a density technique so as to enable the composer to render the utmost plasticity to the density of texture, whether melodic, contrapuntal, harmonic, or combined.

In this branch we shall concern ourselves with the problems of *textural density* alone, as the technique of *instrumental density* belongs to the field of Orchestration.

The behavior of sounding texture in any musical composition is such that it fluctuates between stability and instability, and so remains perpetually in a state of unstable equilibrium. The latter is characteristic of albumen which is chemically basic to all organic forms of nature. For this reason, unstable equilibrium is a manifestation of life itself, and, being applied to the field of musical composition as a formal principle, contributes the quality of life to music.

NOMENCLATURE:

d —density unit $\equiv$ p, S

D— simultaneous density-group $\equiv$ S, 2S, . . . Σ.

$D^{\rightarrow}$—sequent density-group (consecutive D)

Δ (delta) — compound density-group representing density limit in a given score (simultaneous $\Delta \equiv \Sigma$)

$\Delta^{\rightarrow}$ (delta) — sequent compound density group: general symbol for the entire consecutive composition of density: $\Delta^{\rightarrow} = \Sigma$

$\Delta^{\rightarrow} (\Delta^{\rightarrow})$ — the delta of a delta: sequent compound delta.

ϕ (phi) — individual rotation-phase:

$\qquad \phi \, \mathcal{C}$ and $\phi \, \mathcal{G}$ in reference to t or T

$\qquad \phi \, ()$ and $\phi \, ()$ in reference to p or P, or d or D

Θ (theta) — compound rotation-phase, general symbol of the continuity of rotary groups in a given score; it includes both forms of ϕ.

A. TECHNICAL PREMISE

Depending on the degree of refinement with which the composition of density is to be reflected in a score, d may equal p or S. In scores predominantly using individual parts, either as melodic or harmonic parts, it is possible and advisable to make d = p. In scores of predominantly contrapuntal type, where each melody is obtained from a complete S, d = S is a more practical form of assignment.

One of the fundamental forms of variation of the density-groups is rotation of phases.

The *abscissa* (horizontal) *rotation* follows the sequence of harmony ($\circlearrowright$ or $\circlearrowleft$); in it, all pitch-units (neutral or directional) follow the progression originally pre-set by harmony.

The *ordinate* (vertical) *rotation* does not refer to vertical displacement of p or S, but to thematic textures (melody, counterpoint, harmonic accompaniment) only; therefore there is *no vertical rearrangement of harmonic parts at any time*. Such displacement of simultaneously correlated S would completely change the harmonic meaning and the sounding characteristics of the original. Technically such schemes are possible only under the following conditions:

(1) identical interval of symmetry between all strata;
(2) identical structures with identical number of parts in all strata.

The above requirements impose limitations which are unnecessary in orchestral writing, as it means that each orchestral group would have to be represented by the same number of instruments, which is seldom practical.

The idea of *bi-coordinate rotation* (i.e., through the abscissa and through the ordinate) implies that the whole scheme of density in a composition first appears as a graph on a plane, then is folded into a cylindrical (tubular) shape in such a fashion that the starting and the ending duration-units meet, i.e., $\Delta^{\rightarrow} = \text{limit}_1 \leftrightarrow t_m$. Under such conditions the cylinder is the result of bending the graph through ordinate, and the cylinder itself appears in a vertical position. Variations are obtained by rotating this cylinder through abscissa, which corresponds to $\phi \circlearrowright$ and $\phi \circlearrowleft$.

Therefore: $\Delta^{\rightarrow} = \phi \circlearrowright (t_1 \rightarrow t_m), \; \phi \circlearrowleft (t_m \rightarrow t_1)$.

Folding the scheme of density (as it appears on the graph) in such a fashion that the lowest and the highest parts of the score meet, we obtain the limits for p, i.e., $\Delta = \lim p_1 \leftrightarrow p_m$. Under such conditions the cylinder is the result of bending the graph through abscissa, and the cylinder itself appears in horizontal position. Variations are obtained by rotating this cylinder through ordinate, which corresponds to $\phi \, ()$ and $\phi \,)($. Therefore: $\Delta^{\rightarrow} = \phi \, () \begin{pmatrix} pm \\ \uparrow \\ p_1 \end{pmatrix}, \; \phi \,)(\begin{pmatrix} pm \\ \downarrow \\ p_1 \end{pmatrix}$.

Here delta is consecutive as physical time exists during the period of rotation.

B. Composition of Density-Groups

As we have mentioned before, the choice of p and t, or of S and T as density units, depends on the degree of refinement which is to be attributed to a certain particular score. For the sake of convenience and economy of space, we shall express dt as one square unit of cross-section paper. In each particular case, d may equal p or S, and T may equal t or mt. Yet we shall retain the dt unit of the graph in its general form.

Under such conditions a scale of density-time relations can be expressed as follows:

$$\begin{aligned}
D &= d, & D &= 2d, & \ldots \; D &= md \\
D^{\rightarrow} &= dt, & D^{\rightarrow} &= d2t, & \ldots \; D^{\rightarrow} &= dmt \\
D^{\rightarrow} &= dt, & D^{\rightarrow} &= 2dt, & \ldots \; D^{\rightarrow} &= mdt \\
D^{\rightarrow} &= dt, & D^{\rightarrow} &= 2d2t, & \ldots \; D^{\rightarrow} &= mdnt
\end{aligned}$$

The above are monomial density-groups. On the graph they appear as follows:

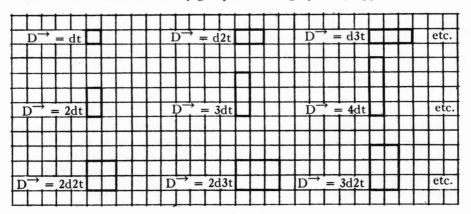

Figure 130. *Monomial density-groups.*

Binomial density-groups can be evolved in a similar way:

$$\Delta^{\rightarrow} = D_1^{\rightarrow} + D_2^{\rightarrow}; \quad D_1^{\rightarrow} = dt; \quad D_2^{\rightarrow} = 2d2t;$$
$$. \; \Delta^{\rightarrow} = dt + 2d2t$$

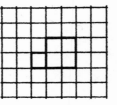

Figure 131. *Binomial density-groups (continued.)*

$$\overrightarrow{\Delta} = \overrightarrow{D_1} + \overrightarrow{D_2}; \quad \overrightarrow{D_1} = d2t; \quad \overrightarrow{D_2} = 2dt;$$
$$\overrightarrow{\Delta} = d2t + 2dt$$

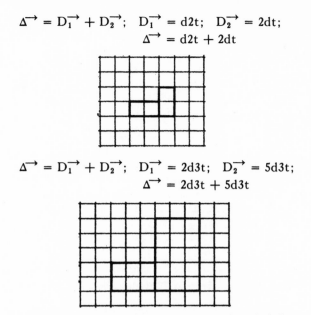

$$\overrightarrow{\Delta} = \overrightarrow{D_1} + \overrightarrow{D_2}; \quad \overrightarrow{D_1} = 2d3t; \quad \overrightarrow{D_2} = 5d3t;$$
$$\overrightarrow{\Delta} = 2d3t + 5d3t$$

Figure 131. Binomial density-groups (concluded).

Polynomial density-groups may be evolved, depending on the purpose, from rhythmic resultants, permutation-groups, involution-groups, series of variable velocities, etc.

$$\overrightarrow{\Delta} = \overrightarrow{D_1} + \overrightarrow{D_2} + \overrightarrow{D_3}; \quad \overrightarrow{D_1} = 3d3t; \quad \overrightarrow{D_2} = dt; \quad \overrightarrow{D_3} = 2d2t;$$
$$\overrightarrow{\Delta} = 3d3t + dt + 2d2t$$

$$\overrightarrow{\Delta} = 4\overrightarrow{D}; \quad \overrightarrow{D_1} = 2d4t + 2d2t + 2d2t + 4d2t$$

Figure 132. Polynomial density-groups.

As it follows from the above arrangement of density-groups, the latter may be distributed in any desirable fashion, preferably in a symmetric one within the range of D. In this particular case D = 4d.

$$\overrightarrow{\Delta} = 6\overrightarrow{D}; \quad \overrightarrow{D_1} = 3d3t; \quad \overrightarrow{D_2} = dt; \quad \overrightarrow{D_3} = 2d2t; \quad \overrightarrow{D_4} = 2d2t;$$
$$\overrightarrow{D_5} = dt; \quad \overrightarrow{D_6} = 3d3t$$
$$\overrightarrow{\Delta} = 3d3t + dt + 2d2t + 2d2t + dt + 3d3t$$

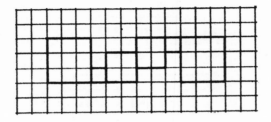

$$\overrightarrow{\Delta} = 4\overrightarrow{D}; \quad \overrightarrow{D_1} = 4dt; \quad \overrightarrow{D_2} = 2d2t; \quad \overrightarrow{D_3} = 2d2t; \quad \overrightarrow{D_4} = d4t;$$
$$\overrightarrow{\Delta} = 4dt + 2d2t + 2d2t + d4t$$

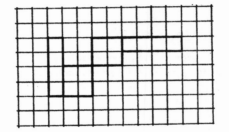

Figure 133. D = 4d.

$$\overrightarrow{\Delta} = 5\overrightarrow{D}; \quad \overrightarrow{D_1} = d8t; \quad \overrightarrow{D_2} = 2d5t; \quad \overrightarrow{D_3} = 3d3t; \quad \overrightarrow{D_4} = 5d2t; \quad \overrightarrow{D_5} = 8dt;$$
$$\overrightarrow{\Delta} = d8t + 2d5t + 3d3t + 5d2t + 8dt$$

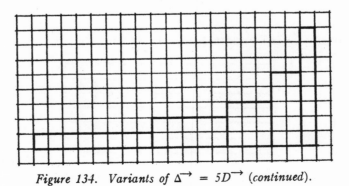

Figure 134. Variants of $\overrightarrow{\Delta} = 5\overrightarrow{D}$ (continued).

Another variant of the same scheme:

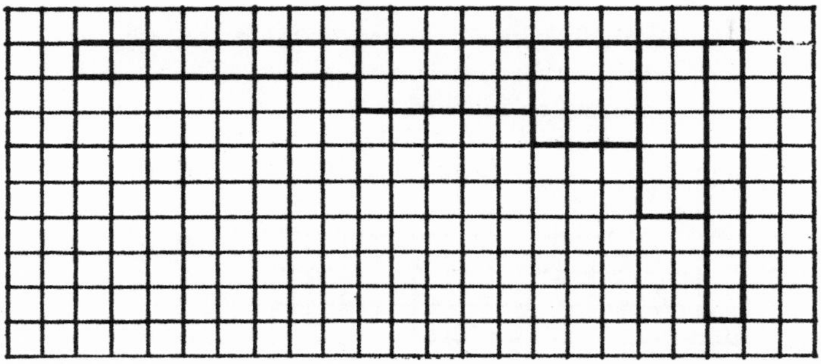

Another variant of the same scheme:

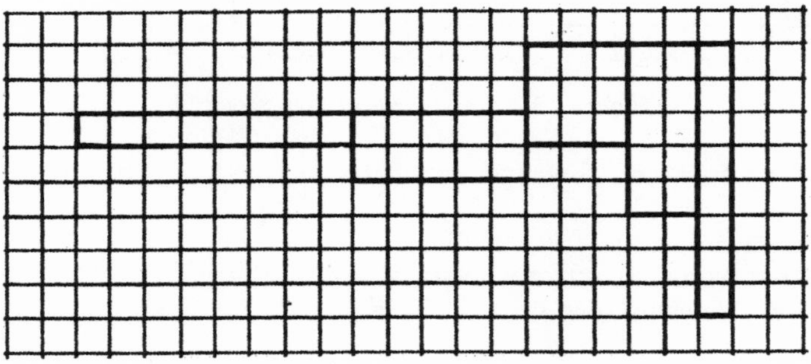

Figure 134.   Variants of $\Delta^{\rightarrow} = 5D^{\rightarrow}$ (concluded).

In all the above cases $\Delta \not> D$, i.e., the compound density-group is not greater than any of the component density groups.

Density groups may be considerably smaller than Δ, in which case there are many more possibilities for the distribution of D's.

$$\Delta = 6D;\ \Delta^{\rightarrow} = 4D;\ D_1^{\rightarrow} = 2d2t;\ D_2^{\rightarrow} = dt;\ D_3^{\rightarrow} = dt;\ D_4^{\rightarrow} = 2d2t;$$
$$\Delta^{\rightarrow} = 2d2t + dt + dt + 2d2t$$

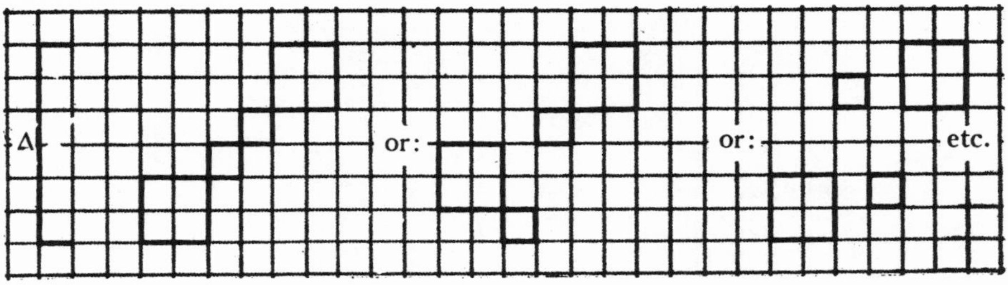

Figure 135.   Density groups smaller than Δ.

The different distributions as in the above Figure can be specified by means of their phasic positions.

If we assume that the lowest d of Δ designates ϕ_0, i.e., the zero phase, then ϕ_1, ϕ_2, . . . designate all the consecutive phases. Thus the first variant of Figure 135 can be expressed as follows:

$$\overrightarrow{\Delta} = (2d2t)\phi_0 + (dt)\phi_2 + (dt)\phi_3 + (2d2t)\phi_4.$$

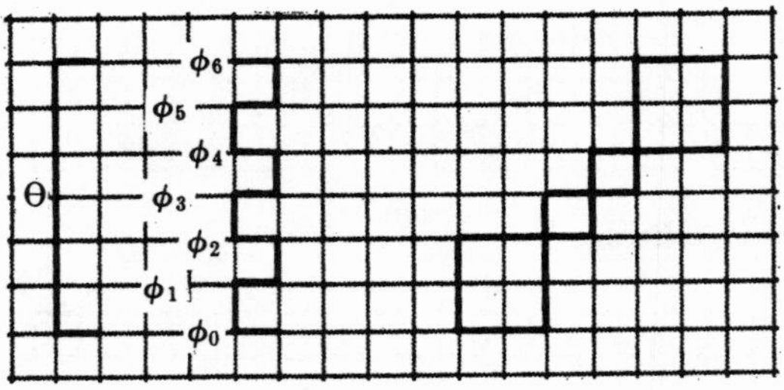

where: $\phi_6 = \phi_0$

Figure 136. First variant of figure 135.

It follows from the above that the first (ϕ_0) and the last (ϕ_6) phases are identical.

C. Permutation of Sequent Density-Groups within the Compound Sequent Density-Group

(Permutations of $\overrightarrow{D}$ within $\overrightarrow{\Delta}$)

Continuity where permutations of $\overrightarrow{D}$'s take place can be designated as a compound sequent group consisting of several other compound sequent density groups, the latter being permutations of the original compound group. Then such a compound density-group yielding n permutations of the original compound sequent density group can be expressed as follows: $\overrightarrow{\Delta}(\overrightarrow{\Delta}) = \overrightarrow{\Delta_0} + \overrightarrow{\Delta_1} + + \overrightarrow{\Delta_2} + ... \overrightarrow{\Delta_n}$.

$$\overrightarrow{\Delta_0} = (3d3t)\overrightarrow{D_1}\phi_0 + (dt)\overrightarrow{D_2}\phi_0 + (2d2t)\overrightarrow{D_3}\phi_0 + (2d2t)\overrightarrow{D_4}\phi_1 +$$
$$+ (dt)\overrightarrow{D_5}\phi_2 + (3d3t)\overrightarrow{D_6}\phi_0, \text{ where } \Delta = 3d.$$

$$\overrightarrow{\Delta}(\overrightarrow{\Delta}) \circlearrowleft = \overrightarrow{\Delta_0} + \overrightarrow{\Delta_1} + \overrightarrow{\Delta_2} + \overrightarrow{\Delta_3} + \overrightarrow{\Delta_4} + \overrightarrow{\Delta_5} =$$
$$= (\overrightarrow{D_1} + \overrightarrow{D_2} + \overrightarrow{D_3} + \overrightarrow{D_4} + \overrightarrow{D_5} + \overrightarrow{D_6}) +$$
$$+ (\overrightarrow{D_2} + \overrightarrow{D_3} + \overrightarrow{D_4} + \overrightarrow{D_5} + \overrightarrow{D_6} + \overrightarrow{D_1}) +$$
$$+ (\overrightarrow{D_3} + \overrightarrow{D_4} + \overrightarrow{D_5} + \overrightarrow{D_6} + \overrightarrow{D_1} + \overrightarrow{D_2}) +$$
$$+ (\overrightarrow{D_4} + \overrightarrow{D_5} + \overrightarrow{D_6} + \overrightarrow{D_1} + \overrightarrow{D_2} + \overrightarrow{D_3}) +$$
$$+ (\overrightarrow{D_5} + \overrightarrow{D_6} + \overrightarrow{D_1} + \overrightarrow{D_2} + \overrightarrow{D_3} + \overrightarrow{D_4}) +$$
$$+ (\overrightarrow{D_6} + \overrightarrow{D_1} + \overrightarrow{D_2} + \overrightarrow{D_3} + \overrightarrow{D_4} + \overrightarrow{D_5})$$

See Figure 137 on opposite page.

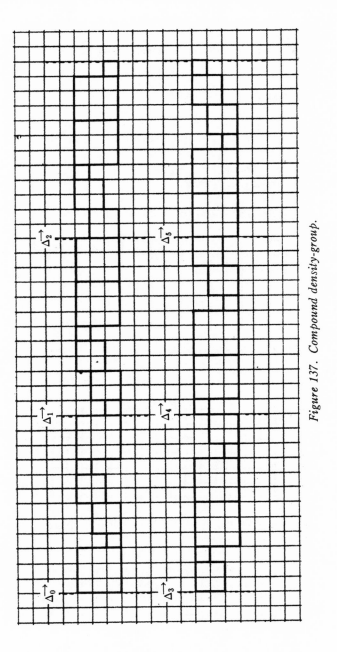

Figure 137. Compound density-group.

The same technique is applicable to all cases where $\Delta > D$, i.e., where delta is greater than any of the simultaneous density-groups.

D. Phasic Rotation of Δ and $\overrightarrow{\Delta}$ through t and d

Assuming $\overrightarrow{\Delta} = \overrightarrow{D} = dt$, we can subject it to rotation:

(1) $\overrightarrow{\Delta}\,\Theta = t\phi_0 + t\phi_1 + \ldots$ and

(2) $\overrightarrow{\Delta}\,\Theta = d\phi_0 + d\phi_1 + \ldots$

The following represents scales of rotation for $\overrightarrow{\Delta}\,\overrightarrow{T} = \overrightarrow{D}\,T = dt$; $\Delta = 4d$; $\overrightarrow{T} = 4t$; $\phi_4 = \phi_0$. $\overrightarrow{T}$ symbolizes the range of duration of D.

The original position: $d\phi_0\ t\phi_0$
The sequence of rotary phases of d:

$$\overrightarrow{\Delta}\Theta = d\phi_0\ t\phi_0 + d\phi_1\ t\phi_0 + d\phi_2\ t\phi_0 + d\phi_3 t\phi_0:$$

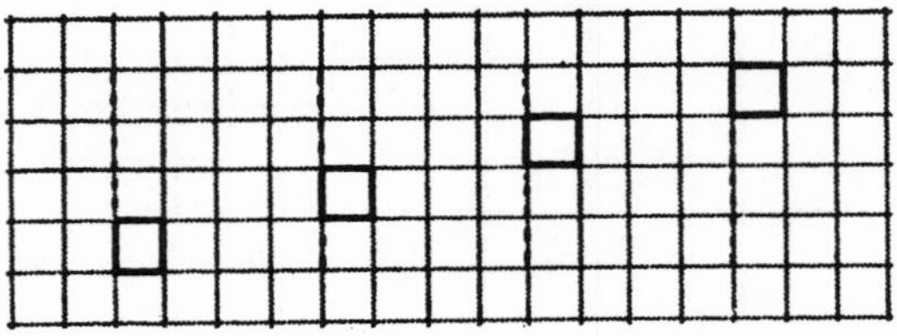

The sequence of rotary phases of t:

$$\overrightarrow{\Delta}\Theta = d\phi_0\ t\phi_0 + d\phi_0\ t\phi_1 + d\phi_0\ t\phi_2 + d\phi_0\ t\phi_3:$$

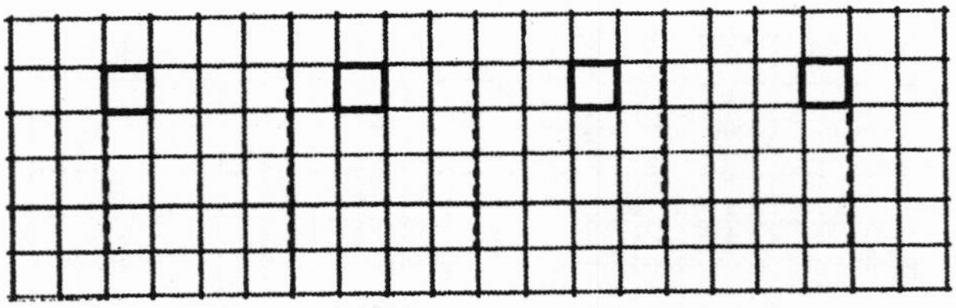

The sequence of rotary phases of dt:

$$\overrightarrow{\Delta}\Theta = d\phi_0\ t\phi_0 + d\phi_1\ t\phi_1 + d\phi_2\ t\phi_2 + d\phi_3\ t\phi_3:$$

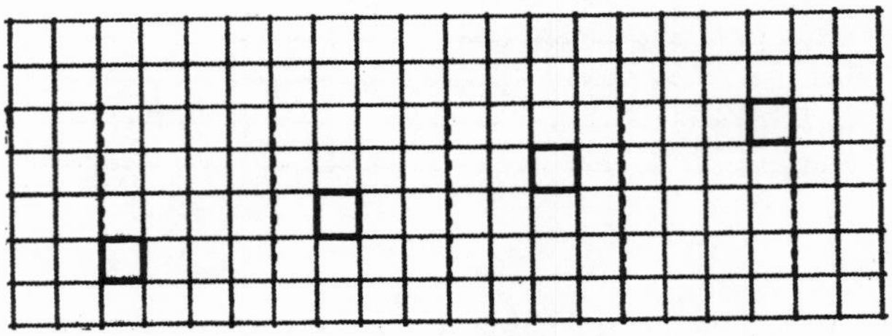

Figure 138. Phasic rotation of Δ and $\overrightarrow{\Delta}$.

The same technique is applicable to a $\Delta^{\rightarrow}$ of any desirable structure.

For example: $\Delta^{\rightarrow} = 3D^{\rightarrow}$; $D_1^{\rightarrow} = 3d3t$; $D_2^{\rightarrow} = dt$; $D_3^{\rightarrow} = 2d2t$;

$\Delta \quad = 3d \quad \Delta_0^{\rightarrow} = (3d3t + dt + 2d2t)\phi_0$;

$T^{\rightarrow} = 6t \quad \Delta_1^{\rightarrow} = \Delta_0^{\rightarrow}\phi_1$; $\Delta_2^{\rightarrow} = \Delta_0^{\rightarrow}\phi_2$; $\Delta_3^{\rightarrow} = \Delta_0^{\rightarrow}\phi_3$; . . .

$\theta \circlearrowleft$ and $\circlearrowright$ $\Delta_0 \quad = (3d + d + 2d)\phi_0$;

$\Delta_1 \quad = \Delta_0\phi_1$; $\Delta_2 = \Delta_0\phi_2$; $\Delta_3 = \Delta_0\phi_3$; . . .

Let $\Delta^{\rightarrow}(\Delta^{\rightarrow})\,\theta = \Delta_0^{\rightarrow}\,(3d\phi_0 3t\phi_0 + d\phi_0 t\phi_0 + 2d\phi_0 2t\phi_0) +$
$\qquad + \Delta_1^{\rightarrow}\,(3d\phi_1 3t\phi_0 + d\phi_1 t\phi_0 + 2d\phi_1 2t\phi_0) +$
$\qquad + \Delta_2^{\rightarrow}\,(3d\phi_2 3t\phi_0 + d\phi_2 t\phi_0 + 2d\phi_2 t\phi_0)\,.$

Then, $\Delta^{\rightarrow}(\Delta^{\rightarrow})\,\theta = \Delta_0^{\rightarrow} + \Delta_1^{\rightarrow} + \Delta_2^{\rightarrow}$ appears as follows:

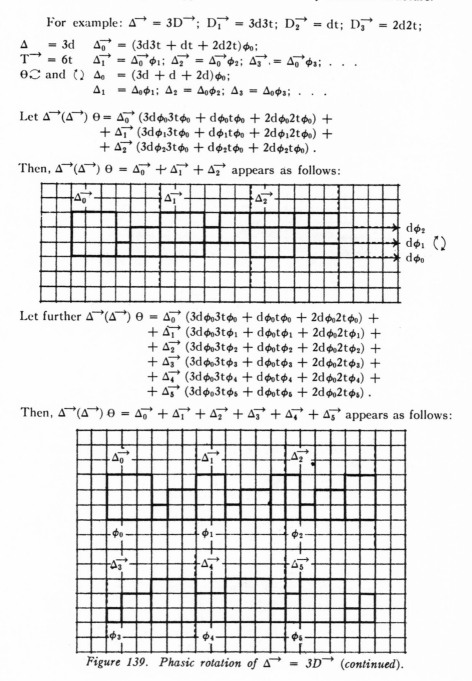

Let further $\Delta^{\rightarrow}(\Delta^{\rightarrow})\,\theta = \Delta_0^{\rightarrow}\,(3d\phi_0 3t\phi_0 + d\phi_0 t\phi_0 + 2d\phi_0 2t\phi_0) +$
$\qquad + \Delta_1^{\rightarrow}\,(3d\phi_0 3t\phi_1 + d\phi_0 t\phi_1 + 2d\phi_0 2t\phi_1) +$
$\qquad + \Delta_2^{\rightarrow}\,(3d\phi_0 3t\phi_2 + d\phi_0 t\phi_2 + 2d\phi_0 2t\phi_2) +$
$\qquad + \Delta_3^{\rightarrow}\,(3d\phi_0 3t\phi_3 + d\phi_0 t\phi_3 + 2d\phi_0 2t\phi_3) +$
$\qquad + \Delta_4^{\rightarrow}\,(3d\phi_0 3t\phi_4 + d\phi_0 t\phi_4 + 2d\phi_0 2t\phi_4) +$
$\qquad + \Delta_5^{\rightarrow}\,(3d\phi_0 3t\phi_5 + d\phi_0 t\phi_5 + 2d\phi_0 2t\phi_5)\,.$

Then, $\Delta^{\rightarrow}(\Delta^{\rightarrow})\,\theta = \Delta_0^{\rightarrow} + \Delta_1^{\rightarrow} + \Delta_2^{\rightarrow} + \Delta_3^{\rightarrow} + \Delta_4^{\rightarrow} + \Delta_5^{\rightarrow}$ appears as follows:

Figure 139. Phasic rotation of $\Delta^{\rightarrow} = 3D^{\rightarrow}$ *(continued).*

Now we shall combine the $\theta\,(\,)$ and the $\theta\,\mathcal{C}$.

Let $\overrightarrow{\Delta}(\overrightarrow{\Delta})\,\theta = \overrightarrow{\Delta_0}D\theta_0\ T\overrightarrow{\ }\theta_0 + \overrightarrow{\Delta_1}D\theta_1T\overrightarrow{\ }\theta_1 + \overrightarrow{\Delta_2}D\theta_2T\overrightarrow{\ }\theta_2 +$
$\qquad\qquad + \overrightarrow{\Delta_3}D\theta_0T\overrightarrow{\ }\theta_3 + \overrightarrow{\Delta_4}D\theta_1T\overrightarrow{\ }\theta_4 + \overrightarrow{\Delta_5}D\theta_2T\overrightarrow{\ }\theta_5$

Then $\overrightarrow{\Delta}(\overrightarrow{\Delta})\,\theta = \overrightarrow{\Delta_0} + \overrightarrow{\Delta_1} + \overrightarrow{\Delta_2} + \overrightarrow{\Delta_3} + \overrightarrow{\Delta_4} + \overrightarrow{\Delta_5}$ appears as follows:

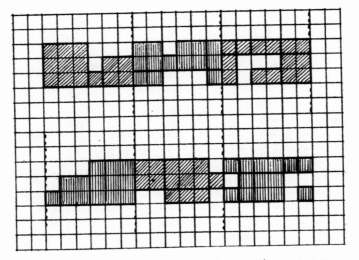

Figure 139. Phasic rotation of $\overrightarrow{\Delta} = 3\overrightarrow{D}$ (concluded).

The diagonal and vertical lines are inserted for clarity.

The addition of positive or negative phases of rotation to any given position of $\overrightarrow{\Delta}$ follows the rules of algebraic addition. Thus if the given position is ϕ_0, the addition of one $\phi\,\mathcal{C}$ or $(\,)$ brings the density-group into position ϕ_1, or: $\phi_0 + \phi = \phi_1$. Likewise $\phi_0 + 2\phi = \phi_2$, $\phi_0 + m\phi = \phi_m$.

As the last phase equals the first phase, or $\phi_n = \phi_0$, negative quantities of phases, or the counterclockwise phases, i.e., $\phi\,\mathcal{C}$ or $\phi\,(\,)$, must be added with the sign minus to the last phase. Thus if the given position is ϕ_0 and the number of phases is n, the addition of one negative phase brings the density-group into position ϕ_{n-1}; or, $\phi_n - \phi = \phi_{n-1}$. Likewise, $\phi_n - 2\phi = \phi_{n-2}$, $\phi_n - m\phi = \phi_{n-m}$.

Problem: find the phase ϕ after the following forms of rotation have been performed from the original ϕ_0, where $\theta = 8\phi$: $2\phi - 3\phi + 5\phi + \phi - 4\phi + 3\phi - \phi$.

Solution: $\phi_x = \phi_0 + 2\phi - 3\phi + 5\phi + \phi - 4\phi + 3\phi - \phi = \phi_0 + 11\phi - 8\phi = \phi_0 + 3\phi = \phi_3$, i.e., the density group appears in its third phase.

This is applicable to both ordinate and abscissa. It follows from the above reasoning that in order to obtain the original position θ_0, after performing a group of phasic rotations, the sum of the coefficients of ϕ must equal zero. As we know from the *Theory of Rhythm,*[*] all resultants with an *even number of terms* have identical terms in both halves of the resultants. If such terms, used as coefficients of ϕ, are supplied with alternating "plus" and "minus", the sum of the whole resultant would be zero. This gives a perfect solution for the cases of variation of density groups, because resultants, being symmetric, produce a perfect form of continuity.

Examples:

$r_{4 \div 3} = 3+1+2+2+1+3$; changing the signs, we obtain:
$$3-1+2-2+1-3 = 6-6 = 0.$$

$r_{5 \div 4} = 4+1+3+2+2+3+1+4$; changing the signs, we obtain:
$$4-1+3-2+2-3+1-4 = 10-10 = 0.$$

$$\Theta(r_{7 \div 2}) = \phi_0 + 2\phi - 2\phi + 2\phi - \phi + \phi - 2\phi + 2\phi - 2\phi =$$
$$= \phi_0 + 7\phi - 7\phi = \phi_0 + 0 = \phi_0.$$

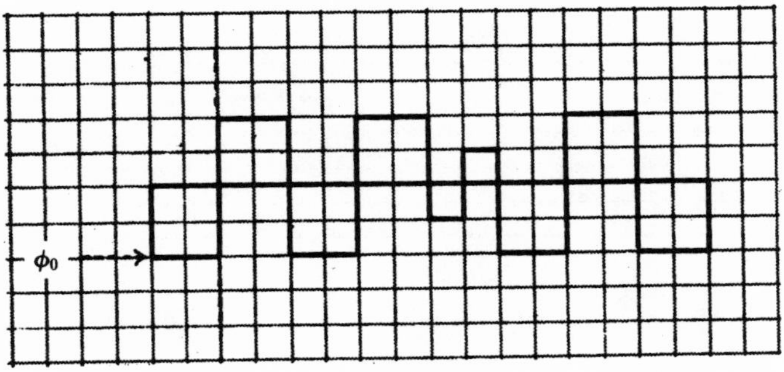

Figure 140. Applying resultants from the theory of rhythm.

Computation of the phasic position Θ_x, which is the outcome of a group of phasic rotation, can be applied to any position Θ_m to which such rotations have been applied. The computation is performed through the use of same technique as before, i.e., through algebraic addition.

Problem: Let the original $\Theta_0 = \phi_3$; find Θ_x after the following group of rotations: $2\phi - 3\phi - \phi + 6\phi$, where $\Theta = 8\phi$.

Solution: $\Theta_x = \phi_3 + 2\phi - 3\phi - \phi + 6\phi = \phi_3 +$
$$+ 8\phi - 4\phi = \phi_3 + 4\phi = \phi_7.$$

*See Vol. I, p. 10 ff.

The original $\overrightarrow{\Delta_0}$: $\overrightarrow{T}$ = 8t

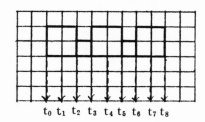

$t_0\ t_1\ t_2\ t_3\ t_4\ t_5\ t_6\ t_7\ t_8$

Variation of continuity: $\overrightarrow{\Delta_x}$ = t_3 + 2t − 3t − t + 6t = t_7

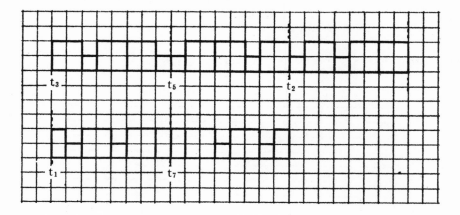

The same group of conditions, as applied to D:

The original $\overrightarrow{\Delta_0}$: Δ = 8d

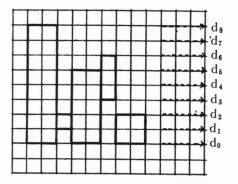

Figure 141. Rotations: $2\phi - 3\phi - \phi + 6\phi$ where $\Theta = 8\phi$.

Variation of continuity: $\overrightarrow{\Delta_x} = d_3 + 2d - 3d - d + 6d = d_7$

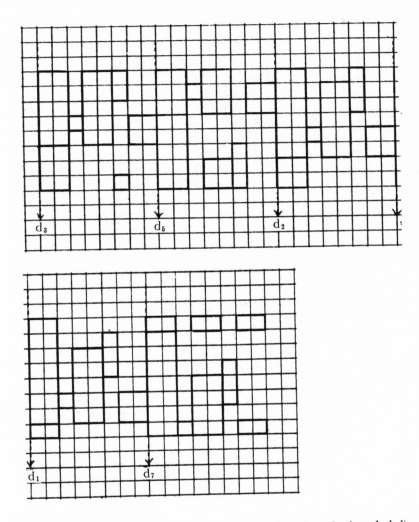

Figure 141. Rotations: $2\phi - 3\phi - \phi + 6\phi$ where $\Theta = 8\phi$ (concluded).

The next step is to combine the phasic rotation of both coordinates. Assuming first that both d and t are in their zero phases, we can express this as follows:

$\overrightarrow{\Delta_0}\,\Theta_0 = d_0 t_0$, i.e., the rotary phase of a consecutive density-group for both coordinates (density and time) is zero. Now we can subject the $\overrightarrow{\Delta_0}\Theta_0$ to variations where the groups of phasic rotation are identical for both coordinates. Using the number values from the preceding example, we obtain the following:

$$\Delta_{\mathbf{x}}^{\rightarrow}\Theta_{\mathbf{x}} = dt\phi_3 + dt2\phi - dt3\phi - dt\phi + dt6\phi = dt\phi_7.$$

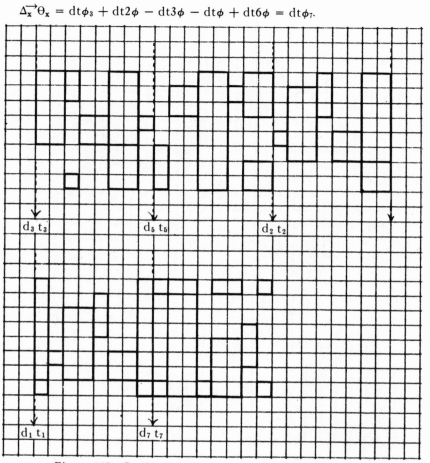

Figure 142. Combining phasic rotation of both coordinates.

When the rotation groups are different for both coordinates, the interference of phases of $\frac{d}{t}$ takes place. After a number of rotations has been performed through both coordinates, their respective resulting phases may be different.

Let $D = 8d$ and $T^{\rightarrow} = 8t$. Let further $\Theta_0 = d_3t_5$.

Now let us subject this group to the following form of phasic rotation:
$d2\phi(\,)t\phi\circlearrowright + d4\phi(\,)t3\phi\circlearrowright + d2\phi(\,)t3\phi\circlearrowright.$

Then: $\Delta_{\mathbf{x}}^{\rightarrow}\Theta_{\mathbf{x}} = d_3t_5 + 2d - t + 4d + 3t - 2d - 3t =$
$= d_3t_5 + 4d - t = d_7t_4.$

Assuming θ to be the limit of a rotation-group (cycle of rotation) and θ^1 the sum of phasic rotations, we encounter the following conditions:

(1) $\theta^1 \not> \theta$ and (2) $\theta^1 \not> \theta$, $\theta^1 \not> 2\theta$, . . . $\theta^1 > m\theta$.

Under the first condition, the sum of phasic rotations does not exceed the total range of rotation, in which case all computations are carried out as shown before:

If $\theta^1 \not> \theta$, then: $\phi_0 + \theta^1 = \phi_{\theta^1}$.

Under the second condition, the sum of phasic rotations does exceed the total range of rotation, in which case the relations of the sum of rotations with the range (limit) are as shown in (2).

In this case, computations must be carried out through use of the following formulae:

If $\theta^1 > \theta$, then: $\phi_0 + \theta^1 = \phi_0 + (\theta^1 - \theta) = \phi_{\theta^1-\theta}$;
If $\theta^1 > 2\theta$, then: $\phi_0 + \theta^1 = \phi_0 + (\theta^1 - 2\theta) = \phi_{\theta^1-2\theta}$;

. . . .

If $\theta^1 > m\theta$, then: $\phi_0 + \theta^1 = \phi_0 + (\theta^1 - m\theta) = \phi_{\theta^1-m\theta}$.

Examples:

(1) $\overset{3}{\underset{0}{\theta}}$ (read: theta to the limit from zero to three)

$\phi_0 + 2\phi = \phi_2$; $\phi_0 + 3\phi = \phi_3 = \phi_0$;
$\phi_0 + 4\phi = 4\phi - 3\phi = \phi_1$, where $\theta^1 = 4\phi$;
$\phi_0 + 5\phi = 5\phi - 3\phi = \phi_2$, where $\theta^1 = 5\phi$.

(2) $\overset{3}{\underset{0}{\theta}}$

$\phi_0 + 6\phi = 6\phi - 2\cdot3\phi = 6\phi - 6\phi = \phi_0$, because if $\theta^1 = 6\phi$, $\theta^1 > 2\theta$;
$\phi_0 + 7\phi = 7\phi - 2\cdot3\phi = 7\phi - 6\phi = \phi_1$, where $\theta^1 = 7\phi$;
$\phi_0 + 8\phi = 8\phi - 2\cdot3\phi = 8\phi - 6\phi = \phi_2$, where $\theta^1 = 8\phi$.

(3) $\overset{3}{\underset{0}{\theta}}$

$\phi_0 + 9\phi = 9\phi - 3\cdot3\phi = 9\phi - 9\phi = \phi_0$, because if $\theta^1 = 9\theta$, $\theta^1 > 3\theta$;
$\phi_0 + 10\phi = 10\phi - 3\cdot3\phi = 10\phi - 9\phi = \phi^1$, where $\theta^1 = 10\phi$.

(4) $\overset{5}{\underset{0}{\theta}}$; $\theta^1 = 3\phi - \phi + 9\phi - 2\phi + 4\phi = 13\phi$;

$\phi_0 + 13\phi = 13\phi - 2\cdot5\phi = 13\phi - 10\phi = \phi_3$.
$\phi_3 + 13\phi = 3\phi + 13\phi - 10\phi = 16\phi - 3\cdot5\phi = 16\phi - 15\phi = \phi_1$,
as θ^1 being added to ϕ_3 equals $3\phi + 13\phi = 16\phi$, in which case $\theta^1 > 3\theta$.

(5) $\overset{5}{\underset{0}{\theta}}$; $\theta^1 = -3\phi + \phi - 9\phi + 2\phi - 4\phi = -13\phi$;

$\phi_0 - 13\phi = -13\phi + 2\cdot5\phi = -13\phi + 10\phi = -3\phi = \phi_{-3}$;
to locate ϕ_{-3} the latter must be subtracted from θ:
$\theta - \phi_{-3} = \theta - 3\phi = 5\phi - 3\phi = 2\phi = \phi_2$.

Figure 143. Sum of phasic rotations.

The technique of phasic rotation of the density-groups can be pursued to any desirable degree of refinement. The phases of d and t can be synchronized when they are subjected to independent rotary groups, in which case we follow the usual formula:

$$\frac{\theta d}{\theta t} = \frac{\theta^1 d}{\theta^1 t} ; \qquad \frac{\theta^1 t \, (\theta d)}{\theta^1 d \, (\theta t)} .$$

In composing the original density-group ($\overrightarrow{\Delta_0}\overrightarrow{T_0}$), it is important to take into consideration the character of $\frac{D}{T}$ relations with regard to the effects such relations produce. In this respect we can rely on the three fundamental forms of correlation, which are mentioned for the first time in the *Theory of Melody*,* i.e., the parallel, the oblique and the contrary.

When they are applied to density-groups, these three forms must be interpreted in the following way:

(1) parallel: identical ratios of the coefficients of ϕd and ϕt;
(2) oblique: non-identical ratios of the coefficients of ϕd and ϕt, where—
    (a) partial coincidence of the coefficients takes place, and/or
    (b) the coefficient of one of the components (either d or t) remains constant;
(3) contrary: identical ratios arranged in inverted symmetry. When the number of coefficients in both coefficient-groups is odd, such case should be classified as *oblique*, due to partial coincidence of coefficients.

E. Practical Application of $\overrightarrow{\Delta}$ to $\overrightarrow{\Sigma}$.

(Composition of Variable Density from Strata)

In its complete form, this subject belongs to the field of Textural Composition and will be treated in this chapter only to the extent necessary in order to make the whole subject more tangible.

The first consideration is that $\overrightarrow{\Delta}$ can be composed to a given $\overrightarrow{\Sigma}$, or $\overrightarrow{\Sigma}$ can be composed to a given $\overrightarrow{\Delta}$. This means that either a progression of chords in strata or a density-group may be the origin of a whole composition. One harmonic progression may be combined with more than one density-group; the opposite is also true, i.e., more than one harmonic progression can be written to the same group of density. For this reason the composer's work on such a scheme may start either with $\overrightarrow{\Sigma}$ or with $\overrightarrow{\Delta}$.

It is practical to consider d = S as the most general form of the density-unit, leaving d = p for cases of particular refinement with regard to density. If d = S it means that one density-unit may consist of p, 2p, 3p or 4p. In actuality, however, harmonic strata acquire instrumental forms, in which case even S4p may sound like rapidly moving melodies. On the other hand, S may be transformed into melody, in which case we also hear one part. The implication

*See Vol. I, p. 275.

is that, in the average case, the density of a melodic line and the density of harmony subjected to instrumental figuration are about the same. Physically and physiologically, and therefore psychologically, *density is in direct proportion to mobility.* This means, for example, that a rapidly moving instrumental form of successive single attacks, which derives from S4p, is nearly as dense as a sustained chord of S4p; the extreme frequency of attacks makes an arpeggio sound like a chord, i.e., in our perception, lines aggregate into an assemblage.

In addition to this, it is important to realize that the insignificant difference, in the case just described, may be completely compensated for by the presence of directional units. In the above illustration, these would counterbalance sustained harmony of S4p by the highly mobile line which derives from 8 units ($\equiv$ 4 directional units, corresponding to 8 attacks, and in an average tempo acquiring high mobility).

As we have seen before, composition of density in its application to strata refers either to melody or harmony as thematic texture. Both melody and harmony can be present in the form of several coordinated parts. For example, there may be 3 correlated melodies and 2 harmonic accompaniments. Of course, any scheme of density may include correlated melodies alone or harmony alone.

The technique of superimposition of $\Delta^{\rightarrow}$ upon $\Sigma^{\rightarrow}$ consists of establishing correspondences between ϕd and p, and between ϕt and H, i.e., between the density-phase, or density-unit, and the number of harmonic parts; and between the duration-phase, or duration-unit, of the sequent density-group and the number of successive chords.

All subsequent techniques pertain to composition of continuity, i.e., to coordination of attacks and durations, instrumental forms, etc.

We shall now evolve an illustration of $\Delta^{\rightarrow}$ correlated with $\Sigma^{\rightarrow}$. To demonstrate this technique beyond doubt, we shall use the most refined form of it, where d = p and t = H.

If Nt = NH, then the cycle of $\Delta^{\rightarrow}$ and $\Sigma^{\rightarrow}$ are synchronized a priori; otherwise, (i.e., if $\frac{Nt}{NH} \neq 1$) they have to be synchronized. This shows that with just a few chords and a relatively brief scheme of density, one can evolve a composition of considerable length, since $\Delta^{\rightarrow}$ itself, in addition to interference with $H^{\rightarrow}$ of $\Sigma^{\rightarrow}$, can be subjected to rotational variations.

Let the original $\Delta_0^{\rightarrow} = \Delta = 8d$ (see Fig. 141).

Let $\Delta_0^{\rightarrow} = \Delta \; \phi_0 2t + d\phi_0 t + 5d\phi_0 2t + 3d\phi_3 t + 2d\phi_0 2t$.

As $\Delta = D = 8d$, Σ must equal 8p.

$T^{\rightarrow} = 8t$ and would require $H^{\rightarrow} = 8H$, unless we wish to introduce a case in which $\dfrac{T^{\rightarrow}}{H^{\rightarrow}} \neq 1$.

We shall introduce such a case.

Let $H^{\rightarrow} = 5H$. Then $\dfrac{T^{\rightarrow}}{H^{\rightarrow}} = \dfrac{8}{5}; \dfrac{5}{8}\dfrac{(8)}{(5)}$.
Hence, $T^{\rightarrow 1} = 8t \cdot 5 = 40t$.

As we intend to use 5 variations of $\Delta^{\rightarrow}$, the entire cycle will be synchronized (completed) in the form: $\Delta^{\rightarrow}(\Delta^{\rightarrow}) = 40t\ 40H$, where $H^{\rightarrow}\ (= 5H)$ appears 8 times.

For the sake of greater pliability of thematic textures, it is desirable to pre-set a directional sigma.

We shall choose the following sigma: $\Sigma = S_I 2p + S_{II} 3p + S_{III} 3p$ and $\Sigma^{\rightarrow} = 5H$.

Let $1^{\rightarrow} = 3i + 2i + 3i + 5i$ and $I(\Sigma) = \dfrac{\sqrt[12]{2}''}{\sqrt[6]{2}}$

We shall now subject the $\Delta_0^{\rightarrow}\theta_s\Sigma_0^{\rightarrow}$ to variations of density evolved in Figure 142.

Further elaboration of the above scheme into thematic textures will be discussed in the Theory of General (Textural) Composition.*

Similar schemes should be evolved by the student with the application of $d = S$.

It would not be entirely premature to convert the $\Delta^{\rightarrow}\Sigma^{\rightarrow}$ schemes into thematic textures, as the last nine chapters contain sufficient information on converting strata into melody and harmony, including instrumental treatment.

Figure 144. $\Delta^{\rightarrow}$ correlated with $\Sigma^{\rightarrow}$ (continued).

*See p. 1279.

Transcription into $\overrightarrow{\Delta_0}$.

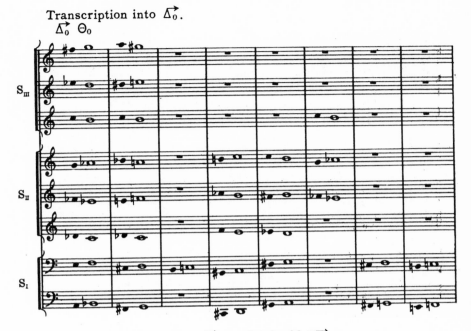

Figure 144. $\overrightarrow{\Delta}$ correlated with $\overrightarrow{\Sigma}$

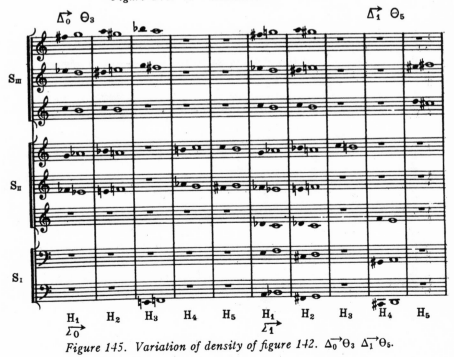

Figure 145. Variation of density of figure 142. $\overrightarrow{\Delta_0}\Theta_3$ $\overrightarrow{\Delta_1}\Theta_5$.

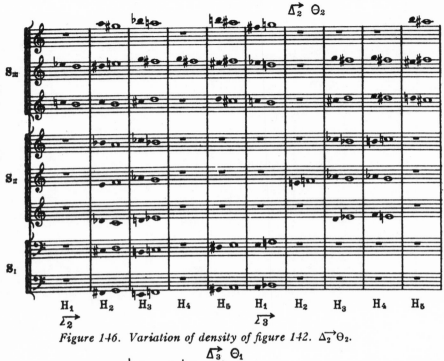

Figure 146. Variation of density of figure 142. $\overrightarrow{\Delta_2}\Theta_2$.

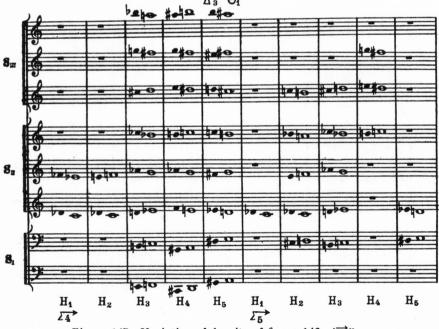

Figure 147. Variation of density of figure 142. $\overrightarrow{\Delta_3}\Theta_1$.

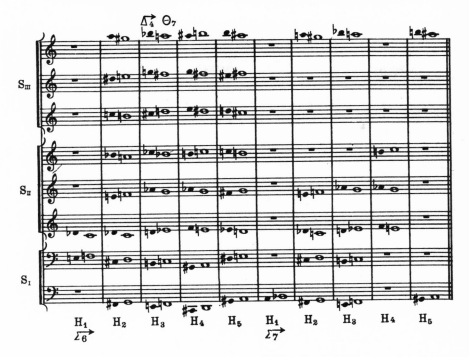

Figure 148. Variation of density of figure 142. $\overrightarrow{\Delta_4}\Theta_1$.

THE SCHILLINGER SYSTEM

OF

MUSICAL COMPOSITION

by

JOSEPH SCHILLINGER

BOOK X

EVOLUTION OF PITCH-FAMILIES
(STYLE)

BOOK TEN

EVOLUTION OF PITCH-FAMILIES (STYLE)

INTRODUCTION

Unity of style evolved in one musical continuity or in a complete composition is, under ordinary circumstances, a task consuming most of a composer's life. To arrive at perfect auditory discrimination and orientation in any new material is a task of great difficulty. Only the greatest composers known were able to mold their own individual styles, and even in these cases, the crystallization of their own styles were actually prepared by a similar effort of their great predecessors.

The problem of unity of style in intonation, when approached from an analytical angle, becomes nothing but a methodological problem. If the factors which contribute to unity of style can be detected, then there is assurance that such unity can be achieved through scientific synthesis.

The factors determining that certain groups of intonation belong to one family are: (1) the identity of pitch-units, and (2) the identity of intervals.

CHAPTER 1

PITCH-SCALES AS A SOURCE OF MELODY

OFTEN styles of intonation can be defined geographically and historically. There may be a certain national style which, in due course of time, undergoes various modifications. These modifications, often associated with the progress of a civilization, can also be looked upon as modernization of the source.

The easiest way to illustrate this viewpoint is by demonstrating the source (*the true primitive*) and its stages of evolution (*the stylized* and *the modernized primitive*). For example, "Dixieland" improvised music of old New Orleans or plantation-songs of the Negroes of the South, or tribal songs of the American Indians, or ritual songs and dances and incantations of the Russian peasants in the sub-arctic north—are all true primitives. The various forms of "jazz" and "swing," the "Indian" music of MacDowell or Cadman or Stravinsky (*Les Noces*), are stylized or modernized primitives—each, of course, in its respective field.

Technically, the source of a *true primitive* is the First Group of Scales (see *Theory of Pitch-Scales*):* particularly, scales with few pitch-units.

The sources of *stylized primitive* are:

(1) derivative scales obtained through permutations of the pitch-units;
(2) derivative scales transposed to one axis;
(3) derivative scales obtained through permutation of the intervals;
(4) derivative scales obtained through direct transposition of the intervals of the original scale to its own consecutive pitch-units;
(5) directional units applied to the above 4 categories.

The sources of *modernized primitive* are:

(1) symmetric scales evolved from the primitive original, by assigning the interval between the extreme pitch-units as the interval of symmetry for the compound scale in which each sectional scale corresponds to the original; the family-scales of the original become the family-scales of the compound symmetric scale;
(2) symmetric superimposition of sectional scales and chords derived therefrom, in which progressions of chords derive from the same compound symmetric scale.

All the above resources are treated independently in their own sub-classifications, where the usual techniques, such as composition of melodic forms by permutation, superimposition of durations, etc., are used.

*See Vol. I, p. 103.

The original primitive:

(1) Stylized primitive:

(2)

(3)

(4)

(5) and others

(1) Modernized primitive:

Progression of roots: etc.

Figure 1. Original, stylized and modernized primitives (continued).

Figure 1. Original, stylized and modernized primitives (concluded).

CHAPTER 2

HARMONY

A. DIATONIC HARMONY

DIATONIC structures, as well as diatonic chord progressions, derive from a pitch scale. Chord structures can be evolved by means of the first tonal expansion, thus serving as accompanying harmony to the original scale. Let us take the fundamental Balinese scale and designate it as E_0. Then E_1 represents the expanded scale. By placing this scale vertically and starting with each consecutive degree of the original E_0 as a root tone, we obtain $\Sigma(E_1)$ on all degrees of the original scale.

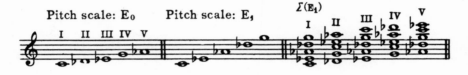

Figure 2. E_0, E_1 and $\Sigma(E_1)$

From these complete forms, partial forms of S2p, S3p or S4p can be obtained, thus offering structures for all degrees of the scale in the form of diads, triads and tetrads.

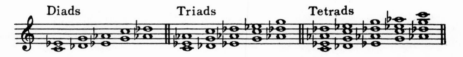

Figure 3. S2p, S3p and S4p.

The fundamental harmony scale is the $E_1\textcircled{6}$ of the original scale. As in all scales which do not contain all 7 musical names, expansions do not produce analogous musical intervals (such as 3rds or 4ths). Diatonic cycles cannot be determined by such names and will be indicated numerically. The fundamental harmony-scale will be referred to as the first cycle (C_1), the second cycle (C_2), and the third cycle (C_3). The second cycle represents the first tonal expansion of the original harmony scale, the third cycle represents the second tonal expansion of the original scale. Cadences are formed by tones adjacent to the tonics, thus producing directional units around the tonic.

In the following table the initial cadences are at the beginning, the final cadences are in the middle and the compound cadences are at the end. The left side of the table represents the fundamental positive cycles of the Balinese scale. By reading this table backwards we obtain the negative system of cycles.

Diatonic Cycles (Positive)

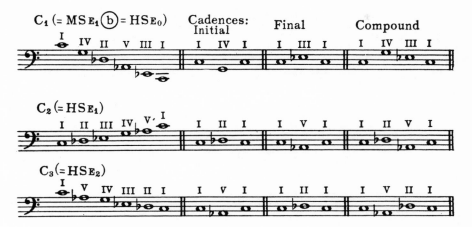

Figure 4. *Diatonic cycles (positive). Read backward for negative.*

Diatonic cycles and their mixtures are applicable to all types of harmony. The first illustration represents the 3 diatonic cycles used individually and in combinations. The form of harmony: hybrid 3-part harmony (functions a, b, and constant a in the bass).

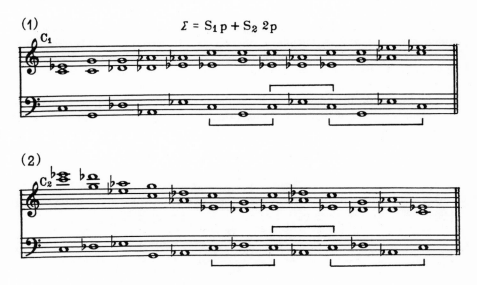

Figure 5. *Hybrid 3-part harmony; functions a, b, and constant a in bass (continued).*

(3)

(4)

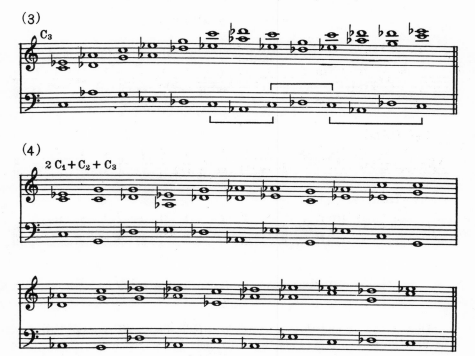

Figure 5. Hybrid 3-part harmony, functions a, b, and constant a in bass (concluded).

Progressions with more parts can emphasize any desirable choice of functions which may or may not include a coincidence of one function with the bass. For example, hybrid 4-part harmony may be constructed on the basis of a–function in the bass, and a, b, c, in the 3 upper parts; or a in the bass, and b, c, d, in the 3 upper parts.

In Figure 6, all progressions have the first form. The sequence of cycles corresponds to that of Figure 5. Transformations are chosen through the nearest pitch positions.

Progressions Type I (Diatonic)

$$\Sigma = \frac{S_{II}\,3p}{S_I\,p}$$

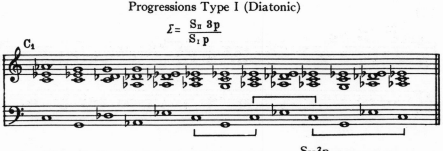

Figure 6. Progressions Type I (Diatonic). $\Sigma = \dfrac{S_{II}3p}{S_{IP}}$ *(continued).*

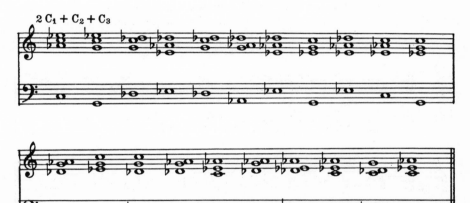

Figure 6. Progressions Type I (Diatonic). $\Sigma = \dfrac{S_{II}3p}{S_{I}p}$ *(concluded).*

B. DIATONIC-SYMMETRIC HARMONY

Evolution of a diatonic-symmetric or a symmetric type of progression must be based on the following principles: the selection of chord structures must be confined to Σ produced by the scale itself; the number of each Σ and its sequence are a matter of selection and distribution.

The best procedure to follow is: first, make a table of all diatonic Σ, then transpose them to one axis. This produces a chart from which it is easy to draw comparisons between the different sonic structures. After an individual selection of structures, as well as their sequence, the coefficients of recurrence can be set.

Progressions Type II (Diatonic-Symmetric)

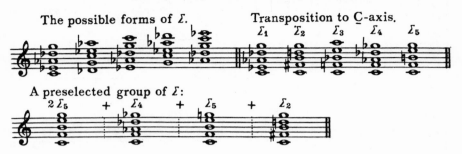

Figure 7. Progressions type II (Diatonic-symmetric).

In the following form of continuity, the sequence of root tones is the same as in the preceding examples. The functions of the upper 3 parts are b, c and d.

Figure 8. Functions of 3 upper parts are b, c, d. Root sequence is as in figure 6

$$2C_1 + C_2 + C_3.$$

C. Symmetric Harmony

Though the choice of intervals for the progression of root-tones in pure symmetric harmony is free, particular satisfaction is obtained when the intervals for the progressions of root-tones are present in the scale itself.

In the following example, the choice of the $\sqrt[4]{2}$ is justified by the relationship $c - eb$ in the original pitch scale.

Progressions Type III (Symmetric).

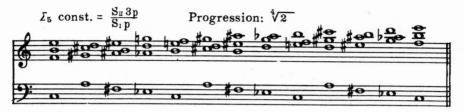

$$\Sigma_5 \ const. = \frac{S_{II}\,3p}{S_I\,p} \qquad Progression:\ \sqrt[4]{2}$$

Figure 9. Progression type III (symmetric).

D. STRATA (GENERAL) HARMONY

For the sake of plasticity of voice leading, and when many voices are employed, it is practical to convert the entire Σ representing the expanded scale into strata. Progressions of strata harmony may be developed through the intervals producing Σ itself, or based on any other form of symmetry.

We shall convert the first expansion of the Balinese scale taken as a Σ into 3 strata where $S_I = p$, $S_{II} = 2p$, $S_{III} = 2p$, and where the progression is based on a descending scale of the Σ itself. Though other forms of symmetry for the chord progressions may be used as well, they represent a further stage of modernization of music.

The following example illustrates the strata described above.

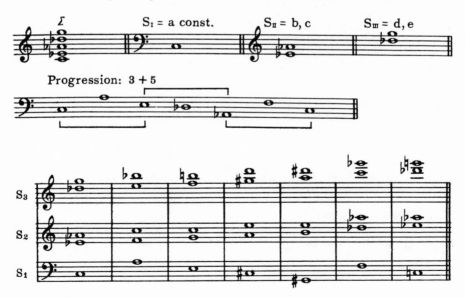

Figure 10. Strata harmony.

E. MELODIC FIGURATION

The problem of melodic figuration, that is, the formation of directional units, is of utmost importance. When such units are set by chance, or free selection, from the general tables of directional units, they may destroy the inherent character of the music as expressed by the given scale. In order to get the proper type of directional units, which are derivative from the original scale, it is necessary to produce permutations either of the pitch-units or of the intervals in the given scale. The procedure is as follows: the original scale, designated as d_0, produces the respective number of derivative scales. These derivative scales furnish leading units to the given scale, after they have been transposed to one axis.

Pitch-units, which are not present in the original scale, become potential leading units. By selecting those nearest the chordal tones (neutral units), a variety of directional units may be secured from which the choice of actual units may be left to the composer.

The following example illustrates the entire procedure as it derives from permutation of pitch-units. See also Evolution of Scale-Families in the *Theory of Pitch-Scales** and in *Kaleidophone.***

Derivative scales obtained through permutation of pitch-units

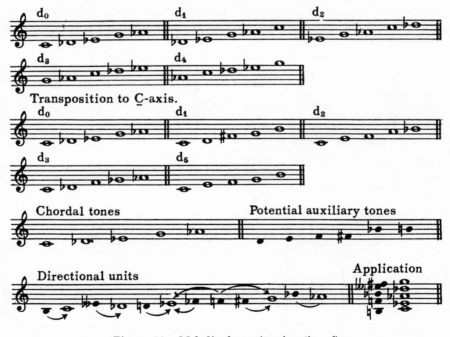

Figure 11. Melodic figuration (continued).

*See Vol. I, p. 115.　　　　**Published by Witmark & Sons, 1940.

Figure 11. Melodic figuration (concluded).

In addition to this, another system based on permutation of intervals, will be found useful.

Derivative scales obtained through permutation of intervals.

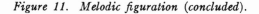

Figure 12. Melodic figuration. Directional units derived from permutation of intervals.

F. TRANSPOSITION OF SYMMETRIC ROOTS OF STRATA

Further modernization of the harmonic style of music may be achieved through transposing the symmetric roots developed from strata. This form is an adaptation of various native intonations to the ultimate development of equal temperament. This type of music is associated with modernity and is usually called "polytonal harmony." Casual and often incoherent examples of this type may be found in the works of Auric, Poulenc, Honegger, Stravinsky, Malipiero, Casella, and many others. Their attempts are in most instances inadequate owing to the fact that they have no definite technique of voice-leading in single strata, and their superimposition of strata is merely a device of placing different keys one above the other. They are unaware of the forms of pitch symmetry. There are a few consistent fragments to be found in Stravinsky's *Petrouchka, Le Sacre du Printemps* and *Les Noces.* Music of the Balinese scale, as developed through symmetric superimposition of strata, still retains its original character in spite of the extreme modernization of harmony.

The following figure illustrates a group of different settings obtained from the Balinese scale.

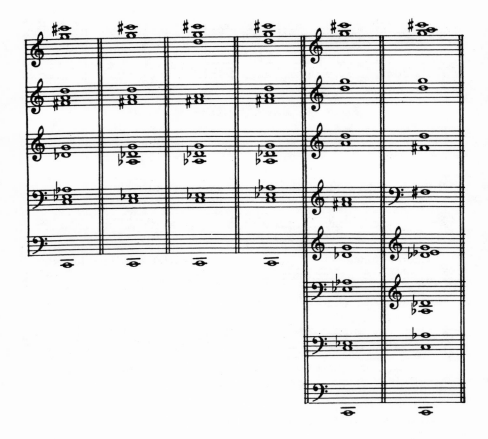

Figure 13. Further modernization through transposing symmetric roots of strata.

G. COMPOUND SIGMA

The development of a compound sigma follows the same procedure as the development of an individual Σ. The combination of two or more sigmae can be coordinated through any desirable form of symmetry.

In the following example, $\sqrt{2}$ is such a form of symmetry. The progression evolves through the form of symmetry used in Figure 10.

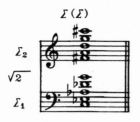

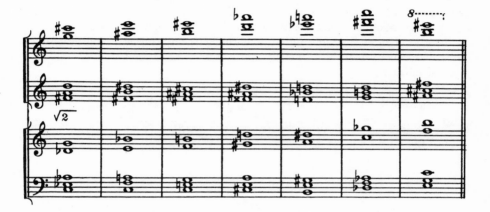

Figure 14. Compound Sigma.

CHAPTER 3

MELODIZATION OF HARMONY

A. DIATONIC MELODIZATION

The general principle of melodization in the diatonic system of harmony is based on an application of the chordal functions with the addition of a successive chordal function which is not present in the chord. Thus the entire system depends on the number of functions in a given harmony and on the number of pitch-units in a given scale.

In the case of two functions (a, b), melody may represent a, b and c functions. In the case of three functions in harmony, melody may consist of four functions. Thus, if harmony is a, b, c, melody consists of a, b, c, d. This is true of any type of harmony.

Figure 15. Where harmony has 3 functions, melody may consist of 4.

In the following example of diatonic melodization, the principle just presented is carried out. The duration-group selected for this example is in conformity with the characteristic Balinese rhythms and is a pure $\frac{8}{8}$ series.

Figure 16. Diatonic melodization (continued).

Figure 16. Diatonic melodization (concluded).

The character of music which is an equivalent of the chromatized pitch-scale of European music and can be recognized through the presence of auxiliary and passing units, can also be developed from scales containing less than seven pitch-units. Not all the steps are truly chromatic, but relatively speaking they are, as the scale has gaps between the pitches and the filling out of these gaps attributes a relatively chromatic character to this music. Some of the directional units which derive from permutation of the original scale are actually chromatic, i.e., they move in semitones.

In the following example of diatonic melodization, including melodic figuration, i.e., directional units, all the added functions are marked by the letter d as they appear in the melody. The chords consist of a, b, and c functions.

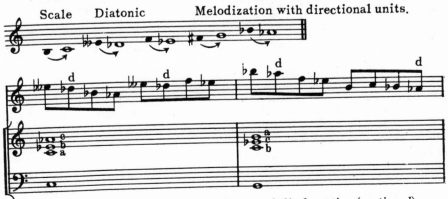

Figure 17. Diatonic melodization includes melodic figuration (continued).

Figure 17. Diatonic melodization includes melodic figuration (concluded).

B. Symmetric Melodization (Harmony Type II and III)

Symmetric melodization, in matching the sonority of the chord, develops on the same principles as diatonic melodization. The difference is that if one chord structure is carried out consistently, all the intonations conform to one pitch scale, which follows the sequence of chords in exact key-axis transposition.

This type of melodization accentuates the inherent character of intonations even more than in diatonic melodization where, owing to the different structures of chords, intonation varies in relation to the chord while the scale remains the same.

In the following example of symmetric melodization, harmony consists of 3 functions and melody is developed with the addition of the function d, which produces its own axis with every chord change.

Figure 18. Symmetric melodization.

Symmetric melodization which acquires chromatic character is analogous to the preceding form of melodization except for the use of directional units. When these two forms are distinctly dissociated, it is possible to use the first form (neutral units only) as an original melody, and the second form (directional units) as a variation of the original melody. The meaning of the second form is that it acquires a more chromatic character than in the case of the application of neutral units only.

In the following figure, the added function d is indicated. The melody itself is constructed through circular permutation of the original pattern.

Figure 19. Symmetric melodization with directional units.

C. CONCLUSION

By reversal of the above described procedures, coupled with the previous experience gained from the Theory of Harmonization, it is easy to obtain harmonizations of melody which are true to style in each specified category.

By combining the technique of the Third and Fourth Group of Pitch-Scales with the knowledge acquired in the branch of harmonic polytonality (*General Theory of Harmony:* S4p*), it is easy to obtain the whole either through harmonization or through transformation of harmony into melody in one of the strata.

Authentic counterpoint, true to style in each of our categories (primitive, stylized, modernized), cannot rely on the classical system of resolutions for these are technically impossible in the field of incomplete scales. The variety of harmonic intervals (within a pre-selected family-set) takes the place of that technique. Utilized with the coordination of attacks, durations and melodic forms (as expressed through axial combinations), pre-selected harmonic intervals in a family-set yield results which can truly be considered perfect.

*See p. 1141.

THE SCHILLINGER SYSTEM

OF

MUSICAL COMPOSITION

by

JOSEPH SCHILLINGER

BOOK XI

THEORY OF COMPOSITION

BOOK ELEVEN

THEORY OF COMPOSITION

PART I

COMPOSITION OF THEMATIC UNITS

PART II

COMPOSITION OF THEMATIC CONTINUITY

[1275]

INTRODUCTION

A S the meaning of the word implies (cum + pono means "to put together"), composition is the process of coordinating raw materials and techniques into a harmonic whole. But the harmonic whole is the most difficult thing for a composer to create, and there are many good reasons for this.

There are three basic approaches in the actual work of a composer. One such approach requires the preparation of all or of most important themes in advance, but without the visualization of the whole. Such themes, being of good quality per se, may not fit into the whole. They may be improperly interrelated with one another as to their character, proportions, etc.

The second approach, typical of soloists and improvisers, requires the composition of a piece in finished form, step by step, from start to finish. In this case the composer can hardly anticipate the whole, as he does not even know what will happen in the next few measures before he gets there. The outcome of such a method of composition, or rather lack of it, is a lack of coherence, lack of proportion, excessive repetition and a generally loose structure.

The third approach involves a great deal of thinking first, the sketching of the whole, at least insofar as the general pace of temporal organization is concerned, and the elaboration of details thereafter. The third approach can be compared with the molding of a sculptured piece.

Each approach contains different ratios of the intuitive and the rational elements by which the process of composition is accomplished. Works of different quality may result from each of these three basic approaches. Often these forms of creation are fused with one another.

I have found, after a thorough and extensive analysis, that the degree of perfection in a work of art, and hence its vitality as a factor of the probability of survival, depends upon the *relation of a tendency to its realization.* If, for example, the tendency in a given work of art is toward a certain form of regularity, we may compute the degree of perfection on the basis of the percentage of adherence of the realized form to such regularity. Of all composers, J. S. Bach scored 100% in some instances. It is equally true that all composers recognized as "great" in the course of time, yield a high degree of perfection (scoring in many instances 80%-90%). In the music of mediocrities (who were in some cases eminent during their lifetime) such scores, on the contrary, are pitifully low.

If the degree of organization and the adequacy of the realization of a tendency constitute the vitality of a work of art, it is only reasonable to seek to evolve works which embody refinement of structural organization, mutual fitness of components and the complete realization of a tendency.

Such a process of reasoning leads us to the necessity of *prefabrication and the assembly of components according to a preconceived design of the whole*, i.e., to the scientific method of art production—in this case, of a musical composition.

PART ONE

COMPOSITION OF THEMATIC UNITS

CHAPTER 1

COMPONENTS OF THEMATIC UNITS

WE shall define a *thematic unit* as a *variable quantity with a constant potential of quantitative aggregation.* Variable quantity in this case refers to the duration of any component and its potential—the tendency by which such a component may grow. A thematic unit, in most cases, consists of more than one component. It evolves, however, from one basic original component, as if from a nucleus, around which all other components (participating in the formation of the thematic unit) develop. We shall call the basic component—major, and all other components—minor.

A major component may be evolved from any technical form. Technical forms, from which both major and minor components may be developed, may be described as follows:

(1) temporal organization (rhythm of factorial and fractional continuity);
(2) family-groups of pitch assemblages (pitch-scale developments);
(3) linear composition (plotted melodies);
(4) composition of simultaneous assemblages (chord structures and progressions);
(5) harmony as a source of melodization;
(6) correlated melodies (counterpoint of attacks, melodic forms, etc.);
(7) orchestral resources (tone-quality, dynamics, density, instrumental forms, attack-forms).

These technical forms correspond to the various branches covered in the present work:

(1) Theory of Rhythm (Book I);
(2) Theory of Pitch-Scales (Book II);
(3) Theory of Melody and Geometrical Projections (Books III and IV);
(4) Harmony, Special and General Theory (Books V and IX);
(5) Melodization and Harmonization (Book VI);
(6) Correlated Melodies (Counterpoint) (Book VII);
(7) Instrumental Forms and Orchestration (Books VIII and XII).

The selection of one or another technique for evolving the nucleus of a thematic unit, i.e., its major component, depends on the technical form which the composer wishes to have dominate over other components of the same thematic unit.

A certain thematic unit may evolve around the major component of temporal rhythm. In such a case temporal rhythm, even after the addition of other components, becomes the dominant characteristic of the thematic unit. In other cases, the dominance of melody may be desired. Then a plotted melody becomes the major component of the thematic unit. Such a melody may be later harmonized, in which case harmony becomes its minor component. On many occasions the dominance of harmony is so important that it becomes practical to evolve chord progressions first—in which case harmony becomes the major component of the thematic unit. A minor component may be evolved later by means of melodization. It is equally obvious that when continuous imitation is desired as the dominant characteristic of a thematic unit, it is best to start with the contrapuntal setting of a canon. The canon itself becomes the major component and its instrumental forms, harmonic accompaniment, etc., become minor components of the thematic unit.

Certain forms of musical expression have dynamics as a dominant characteristic. In such cases dynamic composition becomes the major component of the thematic unit. Harmony and melody in this case play merely a subsidiary role and, therefore, become the minor components. Much of such music is being written for radio-scripts, motion-picture and theatrical productions, and program music in general.

CHAPTER 2

TEMPORAL RHYTHM AS MAJOR COMPONENT

THE process of composing thematic units is both selective and cooordinative.

When the decision is ·to make temporal rhythm the major component of one or more thematic units, the *first selection* refers to the *series of style*. As style can be pure or hybrid, such a correspondence must be established by selection of either a pure series or of a hybrid. The composer may evolve his own hybrids if such hybrids serve the purpose of musical expression best. In other instances, the selection of a hybrid is necessitated by the desire to carry out a certain style whose specifications require such a hybrid.

The second selection deals with *concrete techniques.** Among these are:

(1) Composition of attacks;

(2) Composition of durations to pre-set groups of attacks from the specified series of style;

(3) Direct composition of durations from the various resources** developed in the *Theory of Rhythm*:

　(a) the resultants of interference:

　　$a \div b$, $\underline{a \div b}$, $a \div b \div c$; . . .

　(b) composition of balance, expansion and contraction;

　(c) composition of instrumental interference;

　(d) extension of the T — units by permutation: durations, rests, accents, split-unit groups and groups in general;

　(e) extension of thematic units by permutations of the higher orders;

　(f) composition and coordination of involution-groups belonging to the style-series;

　(g) composition of groups of variable velocity, when the latter becomes the necessary· characteristic of a thematic unit.

All the above techniques apply to both the factorial and the fractional forms of each thematic unit, whose major component is temporal rhythm.

---

*Each of these techniques is illustrated below. Paragraph numbers and sub-letters are correlated with illustrations. (Ed.).
**For details concerning each of the resources (a) to (g) listed above cf. the page indicated after each of the following letters (all references are to Vol. I.: (a) p. 4; (b) p. 21; (c) p. 27; (d) p. 46; (e) p. 63; (f) p. 84; (g) p. 90.

Example: $\frac{4}{4}$ series; summation series: 1, 3, 4, 7, 11, . . .

(1) $A = aT_1 + 2aT_2 + 3aT_3 + 2aT_4$

(2)  $\frac{4}{4}$ ○ | ♩· ♩ | ♩ ♩ ♩ | ♩ ♩· ‖

(3)

  (a) $T^{\rightarrow} = r_{4 \div 3}$; $T'' = 3t$; $\frac{3}{4}$ ♩· | ♩ ♩ | ♩ ♩ | ♩· ‖

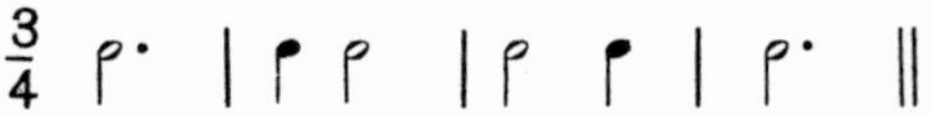

   $T^{\rightarrow} = r_{4 \div 3}$; $T'' = 4t$; $\frac{4}{4}$ ♩· ♩ | ♩ ♩ ♩ | ♩ ♩ ♩ | ♩ ♩· ‖

   $T^{\rightarrow} = r_{7 \div 4 \div 3}$

   $T^{\rightarrow} = r'_{7 \div 4 \div 3}$ $\Big|$ $T'' = 3t$; $T'' = 4t$; $T'' = 7t$

  (b) $T^{\rightarrow} = B_{4 \div 3}$; $T'' = 4t$;
   $T^{\rightarrow} = E_{4 \div 3}$; $T'' = 4t$;
   $T^{\rightarrow} = C_{4 \div 3}$; $T'' = 4t$.

  (c) 12p1 $(A = 2a)$; $T^{\rightarrow} = r_{4 \div 3}$

   $T^{\rightarrow\prime} = \dfrac{4t + 3t + 2t + 3t + 4t}{\boxed{3t} + 2t + 3t + 2t + 3t + 3t}$

   Preliminary: $\frac{4}{4}$ ♩. ♩ | ♩ ♩ ♩ | ♩ ♩ ♩ | ♩. ♩· ‖

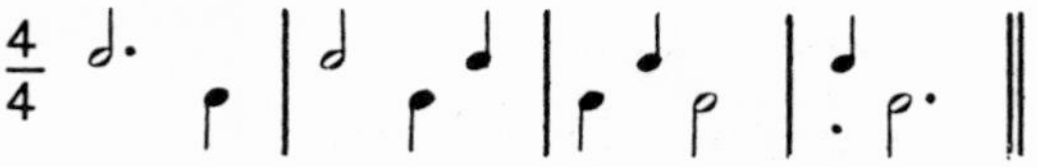

   Final: $\frac{4}{4}$ ○·· ♩♩ ♩ ♩· | ♩ ♩ ♩. ♩♩ ♩ ♩· ‖

Figure 1. ⓐ *Resultants of interference.* ⓑ *Composition of balance, expansion, and contraction.* ⓒ *Composition of instrumental interference.**

The above is applicable to harmony or any instrumental or density-group.

  (d) $T^{\rightarrow} = (3t + t + 2t + 2t) \circlearrowleft$;
   $T^{\rightarrow\prime\prime} = (3t + t + 2t + 2t)T_1 + (t + 2t + 2t + 3t)T_2 +$
    $+ (2t + 2t + 3t + t)T_3 + (2t + 3t + t + 2t)T_4$

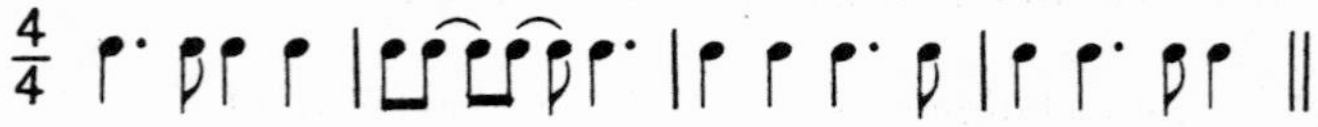

   $\frac{4}{4}$ ♩· ♪♩ ♩ | ♩♩♩♩♩· | ♩ ♩ ♩· ♪ | ♩ ♩· ♪♩ ‖

   $\frac{4}{4}$ ♪ ♩ ♩ ♩ | ♩ ♪ ♩ ♩ | ♩ ♩ ♪ ♩ | ♩ ♩ ♩ ♪ ‖

Figure 2. ⓓ *Extension of T-units by permutation (continued).*

*The letters appearing here are correlated with the letters given above under (3). (Ed.).

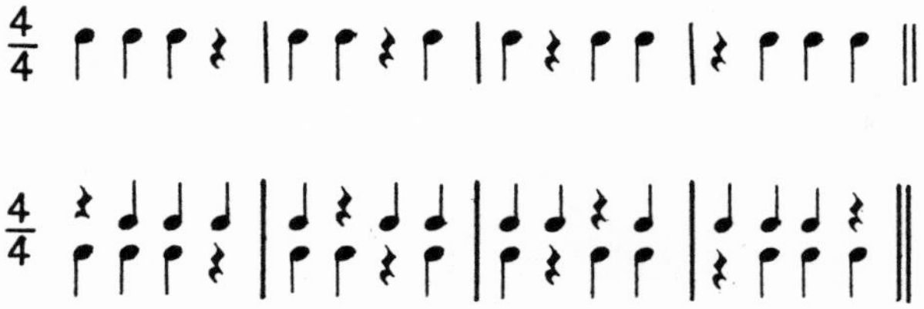

Applicable to melody with harmonic accompaniment, or to counterpoint.

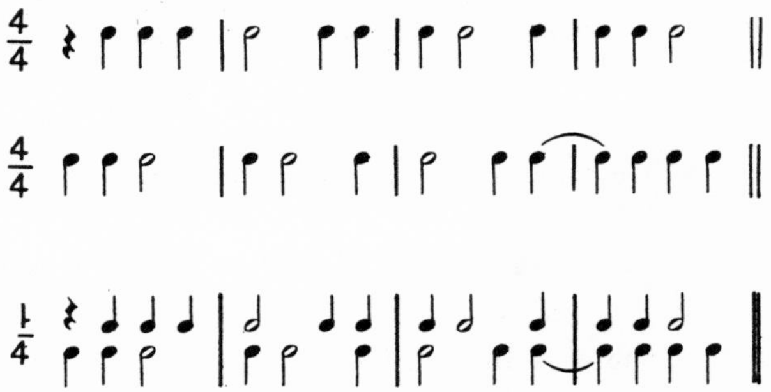

Applicable to $\dfrac{M}{H}\rightarrow$ or $\dfrac{CP_I}{CP_{II}}$

Also general permutations of rests in 4p.

Applicable to $\dfrac{M}{H}\rightarrow$ or $\dfrac{CP_I}{CP_{II}}$

Combinations of the above and also general permutations of accents in 4p.
Applicable to CP4p.

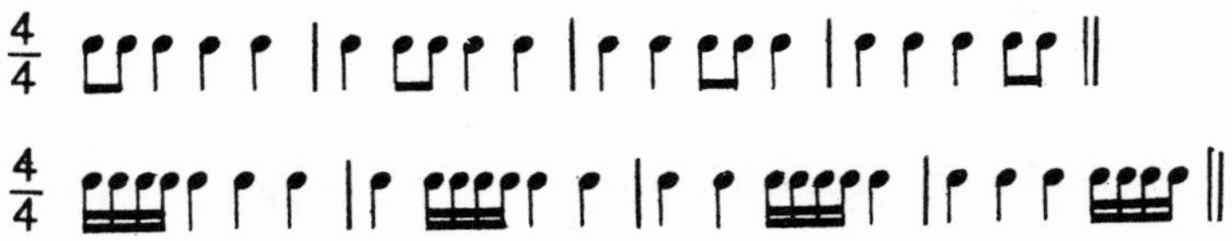

Figure 2. Extension of T-units by permutation (continued).

Applicable to $\dfrac{M}{H\rightarrow}$ and $\dfrac{CP_I}{CP_{II}}$.

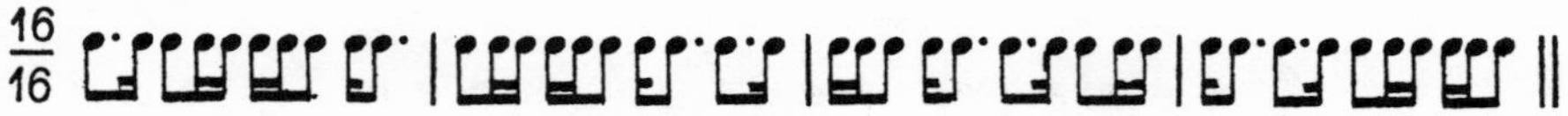

Also $T^{\rightarrow} = 16T$, where $T'' = 4t$.

The same developed in 2p, 3p and 4p.

Figure 2. Extension of T-units by permutation (concluded).

(e) $T^{\rightarrow} = 4t_2{}^{\circ}$ (four T of the second order):

Applicable to $\dfrac{M}{H\rightarrow}$ or CP2p.

Figure 3. (e) Extension of thematic units by permutations of higher orders.

Applicable to: 43p; CP3p; $\dfrac{M}{H2p}$; $\dfrac{M}{M}{H}$ (p, 2p, 3p, . . .np)

Figure 4. (f) Composition of involution groups.

(g) $t + 3t + 4t + 7t + 11t \ldots \leftrightarrow$

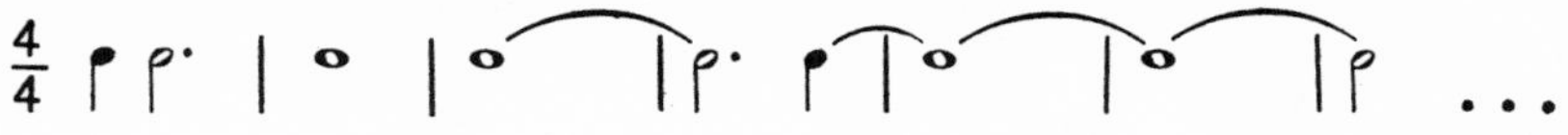

$$r\left(\frac{1+3+4+7+11}{11+7+4+3+1}\right) = 1+3+4+3+4+3+4+3+1$$

The above forms can be combined into 2p and 3p.

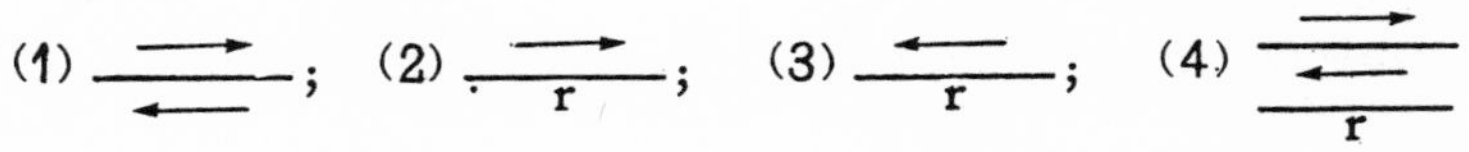

Each combination gives the corresponding number of permutations.

Figure 5. Ⓖ *Composition of groups of variable velocity.*

CHAPTER 3

PITCH-SCALE AS MAJOR COMPONENT

HERE, as in the case of temporal rhythm, the *first selection* refers to the *scale-family*. Such families, as we know from the *Theory of Pitch-Scales*,* can be evolved either on the basis of identity of the pitch-units or on the basis of identity of the interval-units. In the latter case, the sum of interval-units remains constant.

All other techniques, by which further modifications can be obtained, refer to the *second selection*. Among these techniques are the following:

(1) Permutation of pitch units in the selected scale for the purpose of producing MP (master-pattern);**
(2) Transposition of derivative scales to one axis;
(3) Transposition of MP to the consecutive units of the original MP (this also concerns scales as such);
(4) Further modification of MP by permutations of pitch-units, combined with (2) and (3);
(5) Tonal expansions applied to all the preceding techniques;
(6) Selection of the form of distribution of sectional scales through symmetric roots. (The form of symmetry must be constant for the entire family of thematic units used in one composition; such symmetry either is defined a priori, or is based on the limit-interval of the original sectional scale. All the preceding techniques are applicable to this technique.

It is desirable to specify, before composing the thematic units, whether such units will be diatonic or symmetric, as the two styles of intonation conflict. All thematic units of one composition, evolved on the basis of pitch-scales as major component, must be either diatonic or symmetric.

Since all major components require the presence of temporal rhythm as a minor component, it is important in this case to specify the attack-groups of MP in their relation to $\overrightarrow{T}$. Such a relation depends on the desirability of the interference of attacks, i.e., whether $\frac{a\,(M)}{a\,(T)} = 1$, or $\frac{a\,(M)}{a\,(T)} \neq 1$, or whether such an expression is a reducible fraction. Practically, it means that the repetitious character of MP, which may be due to the small number of pitch-units in the scale, can be eliminated by creating interference of $\frac{a\,(M)}{a\,(T)}$. The same is true for the brief duration-groups, whose repetitiousness can be eliminated by the use of MP with many attacks and a scale with many pitch-units.

The use of a pitch-scale as major component does not necessarily mean limiting the thematic unit to melody alone. Part-development can be evolved on the basis of Instrumental Forms, i.e., by reciprocating MP through its own

---

*See Vol. I, p. 101.

**In the illustration given below, figures 6-11, the numbers at the top of each figure are correlated with the paragraph numbers appearing here. (Ed.)

modifications, and may not require harmonization as a new minor component. The latter, in turn, may evolve either from scales or from harmony.

Example:

Figure 6. Permutation of pitch units to produce MP.*

Figure 7. Transposition of derivative scales to one axis.

*The numbers at the top of each illustration in this figure and the succeeding one are correlated with the paragraph numbers on page 1286. (Ed.).

(3)   MP = ecbda (d₀);   MP' = MP

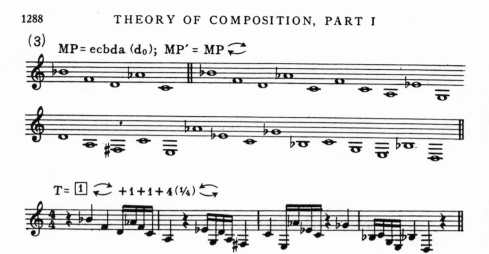

Figure 8. Transposition of MP to consecutive units of original MP.

(4)   MP = acde (d₀)

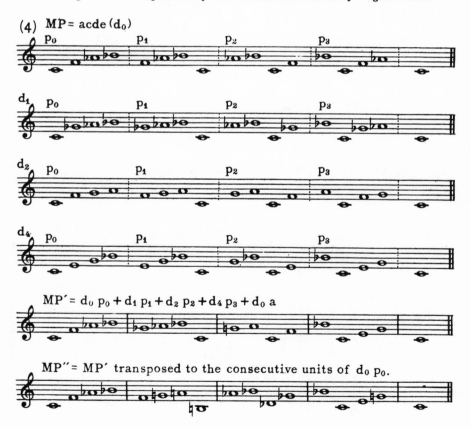

Figure 9. Modification of MP by permutation of pitch-units (continued).

Figure 9. Modification of MP by permutation of pitch-units (concluded

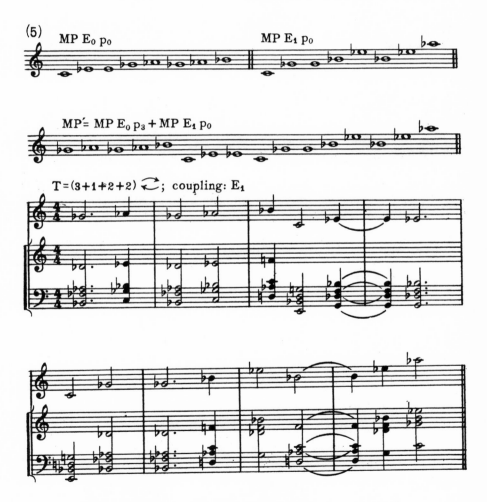

Figure 10. Tonal expansion applied to preceding techniques.

Figure 11. Using symmetric roots for the distribution of sectional scales.

CHAPTER 4

MELODY AS MAJOR COMPONENT

THE use of melody as major component is particularly advantageous when the configurational characteristics of a melodic line are of prime importance. These configurational characteristics correspond to the two forms of selection. The *first selection* refers to *axial combinations* and the *second selection* refers to *trajectorial forms*.

Melodic line as such becomes the dominant factor of a thematic unit. The customary minor components of a melodic line are: temporal rhythm, pitch scale, and, often, either harmonization or coupling.

Composition of thematic units from melody can be accomplished either by plotting or by direct execution in musical notation. The latter requires an MP (master plan) which corresponds to the axial combination and to the intended trajectory. It also necessitates an *a priori* selection of the quantity of pitch-units in which such a trajectory can be realized. Composition of temporal rhythm usually follows this procedure. Finally, a system of accidentals can be chosen and superimposed upon the scale. After this is accomplished, harmonization or coupling may follow.

Example:

Figure 12. Axial combinations in melody composition (continued).

$MP = Ax = O + \frac{c}{c'}$; $S^{\rightarrow} = (h + 2i + h) d_4 \textcircled{d}$; $T = r_{7 \div 4}$; $T'' = 4t$.

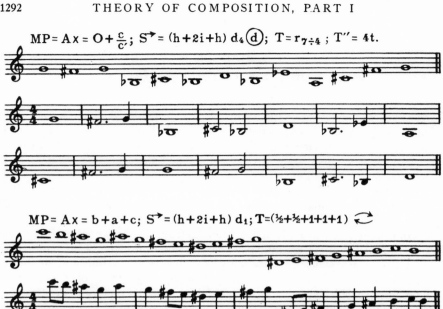

$MP = Ax = b + a + c$; $S^{\rightarrow} = (h + 2i + h) d_1$; $T = (\frac{1}{2} + \frac{1}{2} + 1 + 1 + 1) \circlearrowleft$

Figure 12. Axial combinations in melody composition (concluded).

$T' = T \circlearrowleft abcd$

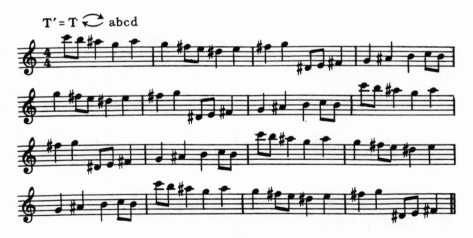

Figure 13. Melody and trajectorial forms.

To achieve unity of harmonic style for several thematic units in one composition all master-structures must be developed from one source. The composer is free to make his decision on the matter of the relationship of $S^{\rightarrow}$ and Σ.

If the general character of the entire composition is diatonic, then the system of progressions must also be diatonic. Once the style of harmonization becomes symmetric, all types of such progressions are acceptable for chords. One may use type II, III, and the generalized. Once the symmetric style of harmonization is accepted, symmetric superimposition may be used as a form of harmonization. To illustrate this, we shall harmonize the thematic units of Figure 12.

In order to achieve contrasts in harmonization of all three thematic units and yet retain unity of harmonic style, we shall subject the first thematic unit to diatonic harmonization in hybrid five-part harmony; we shall employ one of the structures of $S^{\rightarrow}$ as the form of coupling for the second thematic unit; and we shall use the C_0 of the same Σ for the third thematic unit.

Under such conditions, the first thematic unit will have a moderate mobility of harmonic changes; the second thematic unit will have an extreme mobility of harmonic changes (as under couplings $\frac{M}{H}$ = a); and the third thematic unit will have no harmonic changes at all.

As all units of the MP appear four times in permutations according to the structure of the first thematic unit, we shall use the corresponding number of harmonic changes, i.e., four. Under such conditions, any cycle would be acceptable. We shall have $C^{\rightarrow}$ = C_7 const., and assume the first extended duration (d♭) to be 13. Then the first chord is F. Hence: $H^{\rightarrow}$ = H_1F + H_2G + H_3A♭ + + H_4B♭.

The coupling of the second thematic unit will be the $\Sigma(S^{\rightarrow}d_0III)$, i.e., the third degree of the original scale. Each pitch-unit of the melody will become 13 owing to the downward coupling.

The constant structure of the accompaniment of the third thematic unit will be $S(7)S^{\rightarrow}d_0I$, which is a major seventh-chord.

Figure 14. Diatonic harmonization in hybrid five-part harmony (continued).

Figure 14. Diatonic harmonization in hybrid five-part harmony (concluded).

Figure 15. Using one of the structures of S⃗ as a form of coupling.

Figure 16. Using C₀ of same Σ (continued).

Figure 16. Using C_0 of same Σ (concluded).

CHAPTER 5

HARMONY AS MAJOR COMPONENT

HARMONY can be a self-sufficient component not requiring melodization when combined with temporal rhythm. The simplest and most common form of the rhythmization of harmony occurs when each attack of a duration-group emphasizes all parts, resulting in rhythmic unison. Most hymns are composed in such a form. The musical interest of such self-sufficient harmony lies in the fact that, in reality, there is a dominance of one part over the others (usually soprano, sometimes bass, and, originally, tenor). Through the techniques of the *Special Theory of Harmony,** such a dominance of one part, which becomes a melody generated within harmony, can be obtained from various sources. Among them the most important are: groups with passing chords, generalization of the passing seventh, and chromatic variation of the latter.

Another way of evolving thematic units from harmony, and making such harmony self-sufficient consists of the distribution of a duration-group (T) through the instrumental (I) and the attack-group (A). This technique was fully described in the *Theory of Rhythm.*** In its application to harmony, this form of synchronization of attacks, durations and instrumental parts ($S = T \div \div I \div A$), can be accomplished in all cases of $A = ap$ (one attack per part) and in some cases of $A = 2ap$ (two attacks per part).

The selection of a duration-group must satisfy the following requirements:

(1) The number of terms of T must be even;
(2) T must consist either of reciprocating binomials, or of such binomials with an extra binomial (usually the central binomial of $r_{a \div b}$.) consisting of two equal terms.

It is easy to find such T among the various forms of $r_{a \div b}$. The most practical ones are the resultants whose generators have a negligible difference. For example: $3 \div 2$, $4 \div 3$, $5 \div 4$, $6 \div 5$, $7 \div 6$, $8 \div 7$, $9 \div 8$, . . .

The binomials whose first term is greater than the second produce *suspensions*. The binomials whose first term is smaller than the second produce *anticipations*. The extra binomials with two equal terms produce the balanced pace of chord changes. The latter is particularly practical for the bass part, though deviation from this principle is not always undesirable, particularly in variations of the original.

Temporal binomials in reciprocation can be taken also directly from the evolutionary series of rhythm. For example:

$\frac{8}{8}$		$\frac{9}{9}$		$\frac{12}{12}$	
	7+1		7+2		11+1
	1+7		2+7		1+11
	5+3		5+4		7+5
	3+5		4+5		5+7

Figure 17. Temporal binomials.

*See Book V.

**See Book I, Chapter 8, *Coordination of Time Structures.*

Such reciprocating binomials can be vertically re-arranged in any desirable fashion.

For example:

$\frac{8}{8}$	7+1	$\frac{9}{9}$	7+2	$\frac{12}{12}$	11+1
	5+3		5+4		7+5
	3+5		4+5		5+7
	1+7		2+7		1+11

Figure 18. Reciprocating binomials re-arranged.

If the series does not yield a sufficient number of reciprocating binomials, all its values can be multiplied by some common factor. For example: $\frac{3}{3}$ series. The original binomials are: 2+1 and 1+2. By multiplying this series by 2, we acquire two pairs of binomials: 5+1 and 1+5, 4+2 and 2+4. Thus:

$$5+1$$
$$4+2$$
$$2+4$$
$$1+5$$
$$3+3$$

In this case the extra binomial is 3+3. Of course, the result obtained in this way corresponds to $r_{6 \div 5}$, and could have been obtained from the latter directly.

The groups of reciprocating binomials are subject to permutations. This permits a sufficient variety for each individual part of harmony. It should be remembered that the balanced binomial does not participate in permutations affecting all other binomials.

Illustration:

S	$(5+1) + (4+2) + (2+4) + (1+5)$
A	$(4+2) + (2+4) + (1+5) + (5+1)$
T	$(2+4) + (1+5) + (5+1) + (4+2)$
B_I	$(1+5) + (5+1) + (4+2) + (2+4)$
B_{II}	$(3+3) + (3+3) + (3+3) + (3+3)$

Figure 19. Permutation of reciprocating binomials.

The principle of rhythmization of harmony by means of *reciprocating binomials* produces a condition under which every chord in the progression appearing in an odd place has a common attack in all parts. As a result there occurs a complete rectification of all suspensions and anticipations not extending beyond two successive chords. The attack in all parts falls on the succeeding chords of a harmonic progression: $H^{\rightarrow} = H_1 + H_3 + H_5 + \ldots$, between which points the suspensions and the anticipations take place.

The limiting of this principle to binomials is dictated by necessity. It would be difficult to discriminate the dependence of chord-units in a progression where complete rectification of the original structures extended beyond two chords.

Harmony, rhythmicized in such a manner, becomes a self-sufficient thematic unit and does not call for melodization. One of the reasons it appears to be self-sufficient is the presence of the resultants of instrumental interference in each part of the harmony. This attributes to each part an individual rhythmic character.

Rhythmization of harmony by means of reciprocating binomials works for any number of parts (including strata) and in any type of progression. However, it is particularly suited for progressions in which stationary parts are completely or nearly absent. The best progressions for this purpose are the various chromatic types, and particularly the automatic chromatic continuity with alterations of the individual parts. In the non-chromatic types, the constancy, or at least the dominance, of C_7 gives the most satisfactory solution.

Automatic chromatic continuity makes it possible to use T's in addition to those which consist of reciprocating binomials. This principle, when generalized, requires that alterations appear in sequence in each individual attack per part, or that there be an equal distribution of alterations and attacks per part. Thus, each part can have one or two or, on rare occasions, three attacks in succession.

The sequence in which the parts appear is subject to distribution *a priori*. If more than one part moves simultaneously, involving parallel alterations, such harmonic parts must be treated as one rhythmic part. Thus in the following sequence of attacks:

Only two rhythmic parts, i.e., 2pl (I) are necessary.

S		S			S
A			A	A	
	T	T		T	
	B		B		B

Figure 20. Sequence with 2pl (I).

Likewise in the following, only 2pl (I) are necessery:

	S	S			S		S
A			A		A		A
	T		T		T	T	
	B		B	B			B

Figure 21. Sequence with 2pl (I).

For the same reason, the following sequence requires 3 pl (I).

S			S					S		S	
	A			A		A					A
	T				T			T			T
		B	B				B		B		

Figure 22. Sequence with 3pl (I).

All alterations must proceed in one direction until the synchronization of all components (A, T, I, H) is complete.

Examples:

(1)

Figure 23. Rhythmization of harmony.

(2)

Figure 24. Rhythmization of harmony (continued).

Figure 24. Rhythmization of harmony (concluded).

(3)

Var. I: $\mathbf{T}(\mathrm{I})\ 3p = r_{4 \div 3}$ ; $\mathbf{T}'' = 3t.$

Var. II: Variable density by T.

Figure 25. Variable densities in rhythmization of harmony.

$I = 5$ pl.: $pl_V + pl_{IV} + pl_{III} + pl_{II} + pl_I$. $A = ap$; $A' = 5a$; $A(T) = 10a$.
$T' = 16t \cdot 2 = 32t$; $N(T'') = 8$.

Preliminary Scoring.

Final Scoring

Figure 26. Preliminary and final scoring.

(5)

$I = 4$ pl.: $pl_I + pl_{II} + pl_{III} + pl_{IV}$. $A = 2ap$; $A' = 8a$; $A(T) = 20a$;

$A(T') = 40a$; $T' = 32t$

Preliminary Scoring

Figure 27. Preliminary and final scoring (continued).

Final Scoring

Figure 27. Preliminary and final scoring (concluded).

(6)

Figure 28. Preliminary and final scoring (continued).

$I = 3pl.; A = a; A' = 3a; A(T) = 4a; A(T') = 12a; T' = 8t \cdot 3 = 24t; N(T'') = 8.$

Preliminary Scoring

Final Scoring

Figure 28. Preliminary and final scoring ((concluded).

CHAPTER 6

MELODIZATION AS MAJOR COMPONENT

WHILE harmonic progressions, used as a source of melodization, are evolved in one style (one harmonic type) in order to give unity to the entire composition, such progressions may be given a desired amount of contrast in their different thematic units. This is achieved by varying the *type of melodization*.

Thus, for example, a progression evolved in type II (diatonic-symmetric) can be melodized diatonically (by the quantitative scale), symmetrically (by the usual method of Σ—transposition and modulations), or chromatically (by chromatization of either of the first two forms). For this reason, several different thematic units can be evolved from the same type of harmonic progression. Where the chief apparent characteristic becomes the type of melodization, we regard melodization as the major component.

Diatonic harmonic progressions produce their own types of melodization, i.e., the diatonic and the chromatized diatonic. Likewise chromatic harmonic progressions, of various forms and derivation, can be melodized through the two basic techniques assigned to that form, i.e., the acquisition of leading tones from the following chord and the device of quantitative scale.

As both of these techniques can be mixed, and as the diatonic (quantitative) melody can be chromatized, it is possible to devise a large number of thematic units (on the basis of chromatic melodization) which could participate in one composition, yet which would exhibit a noticeable degree of contrast with each other.

In the harmonic strata technique, transformation of a stratum (or strata) into melody is equivalent to melodization.

Examples:

(1)

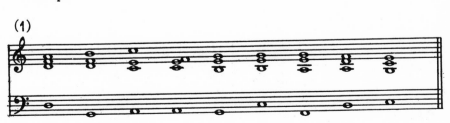

Figure 29. Melodization of harmonic progression (continued).

(a)

Figure 29. Melodization of harmonic progression (continued).

(b)

Figure 29. Melodization of harmonic progression (concluded).

(2)

Quantitative scale

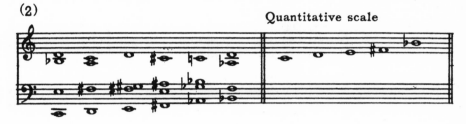

(a)

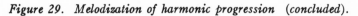

Figure 30. Melodization of harmonic progression (continued).

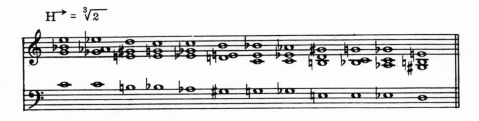

(b) $T = {}^r 4 \div 3$; $T'' = 3t$; $S^{\to}(M) = \Sigma$ XIII E_0. $A(M) = 4a$.

Figure 30. Melodization of harmonic progression (concluded).

(3)   Quantitative scale

Figure 31. Melodization of harmonic progression (continued).

(a)

Figure 31. Melodization of harmonic progression (continued).

Figure 31. Melodization ·of harmonic progression (concluded).

CHAPTER 7

COUNTERPOINT AS MAJOR COMPONENT

THE dominant characteristic of counterpoint becomes particularly noticeable in such forms as imitation, ostinato of a ground melody, and in the contrasting forms of axial correlation. Thematic units evolved as correlated melodies furnish a major component in which the individualization of melodic lines is particularly prominent.

Here major component as such is not confined to any configuration-families. So long as the different thematic units contain their own configurational characteristics, sufficient for the purpose of detectable contrasts, no other requirements are necessary. Unification of style is accomplished through the selection of minor components, such as temporal rhythm, pitch-scale or master-structure (when counterpoint is evolved from strata).

Contrapuntal thematic units can be subjected to harmonization, in which case harmony becomes the unifying factor of style.

It is not advantageous to evolve contrapuntal thematic units by means of part-melodization, as in such a case the forms of correlation are greatly controlled by harmony and therefore force the counterpoint to become a minor component. Part-melodization may be used, however, when the second melody can play a subsidiary (obligato or background) role.

We shall illustrate now the composition of thematic units from counterpoint in its three characteristic aspects:

(1) axial coordination;
(2) canonic imitation;
(3) counterpoint to ground melody.

Example:

(1) $\dfrac{CP_{II}}{CP_{I}} = \dfrac{a}{o}$; Type IV.

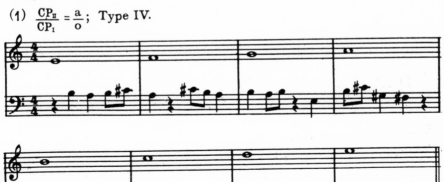

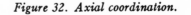
Figure 32. Axial coordination.

[1311]

(2) Type III

Figure 33. Canonic imitation.

(3)

Figure 34. Counterpoint to ground melody (continued).

Figure 34.   Counterpoint to ground melody (concluded).

    All other techniques, such as inversions and expansions, constitute variation and therefore are not applicable to the composition of thematic units. They participate in building up the whole, and for this reason will be considered in the Composition of Thematic Continuity.* This statement concerns all six of the preceding chapters.

*See Part II of this Book. (Ed.).

CHAPTER 8

DENSITY AS MAJOR COMPONENT

DENSITY becomes a dominant factor of the thematic unit when the quantitative distribution of elements (parts) and groups (assemblages) becomes the chief characteristic of such a unit. Nevertheless, the greatest advantage offered by the Theory of Density lies in the composition of continuity from the original group of density by means of positional rotation. It is not difficult for an experienced composer to conceive one density-group as a thematic unit; but the instantaneous composition of melodies and harmonies as textural thematic groups in a considerable temporal extension cannot be solved satisfactorily except by the scientific method. This method which includes both the composition of a density-group and its positional rotation was fully described in Book IX, Chapter 15, Composition of Density in its Application to Strata.

Composition of thematic units or of thematic continuity from density-groups is of particular advantage where large instrumental combinations participate in the score. Chamber, symphonic, choral music, and ensemble music, in general, require such technique.

The student of this theory must realize that positional rotation, as was pointed out before, does not interchange the positions of harmonic strata or their parts, but refers solely and entirely to the positions of thematic textures, i.e., melodies and harmonies conceived as rhythmic and instrumental forms.

The practical outcome of this technique is the projection of thematic textures through harmonic strata of a $\Sigma^{\rightarrow}$, which in itself remains constant. Under such conditions, a certain melody M_I may appear in the different strata or parts of the strata accompanied by another melody M_{II}, which also may appear at different times in the different strata, and which may, in turn, be accompanied by harmony or several harmonies (which are detectable through their temporal and instrumental characteristics).

As positional rotation takes place, all these thematic textures undergo mutations, which change their positions, within strata and parts, individually and reciprocally.

In order to illustrate this technique more fully, we shall demonstrate not only the composition of thematic units from density as a major component, but also the respective form of continuity evolved from such units as the result of positional rotation.

As it was stated in the Theory of Density,* composition of Density-Groups may evolve either from a scheme of density or from a progression of harmonic strata.

*See p. 1227.

We shall use, for our illustration, the $\Delta^{\rightarrow}\Sigma^{\rightarrow}$ scheme offered in Figures 141, 142, 143 and 144 of the Composition of Density.*

Let us assume that the 3S of the Σ, superimposed upon the $\Delta_0\Theta_0$, are assigned in the following manner:

$$S_I \equiv M_I; \ S_{II} \equiv H; \ S_{III} \equiv M_{II}.$$

Then the respective textures controlling the corresponding parts and strata appear as follows:

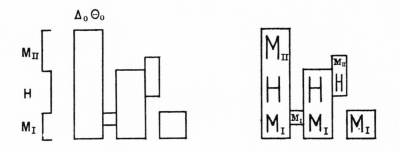

Figure 35. Textures: $S_I \equiv M_I; S_{II} \equiv H; S_{III} \equiv M_{II}.$

This represents a pattern consisting of two melodies and one harmonic accompaniment.

It is to be remembered that $\Delta^{\rightarrow}$ offered in Figure 142 begins with the third phase of dt. For this reason we acquire the following scheme of thematic continuity, based on the three original thematic textures.

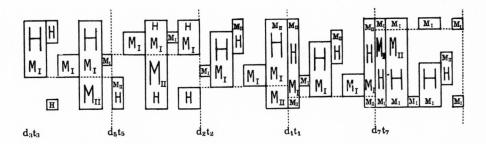

Figure 36. Scheme of thematic continuity. $\Delta^{\rightarrow}$ *begins with third place of dt.*

*See pp. 1238-9, 1240, 1241, 1244.

In order to individualize each thematic texture, we shall assign to each of the textures an individually selected T:

$$T(M_I) = (4+2+2) + (2+2+4)$$
$$T(M_{II}) = (1+1+1+1+3+1) + (3+1+2+2)$$
$$T(H) = 1+1+2+1+1+2$$

Instrumental characteristics may be added to this. We shall equip the harmonic accompaniment with a certain constant form of attacks.

Figure 37. Density as major component (continued).

Figure 37. Density as major component (continued).

Figure 37. Density as major component (continued).

Figure 37. Density as major component (continued).

Figure 37. Density as major component (concluded).

When such a score is orchestrated, melodies which derive from *adjacent* parts of one or more strata are assigned to one or more instruments to play the *continuous* portion of melody in unison. However, for special orchestral effects, where extreme differentiation of tone-qualities is desired, orchestration can follow the fragmentary portions of one continuous melodic extension, assigning a different timbral participant to each fragment (no matter how brief) which derives from an individual part. It should be remembered that this extreme refinement is due, in our example, to the fact that $d = p$. This refinement associates itself, *ipso facto* with the style, where general economy of resources is the fundamental technical premise. Of all composers, Anton von Webern is probably the only one who went as far, as he did, in "splitting" thematic units.

It is easy to see that the effort required in orchestration can be reduced to a minimum by making a density-group the major component of thematic continuity.

CHAPTER 9

INSTRUMENTAL RESOURCES AS MAJOR COMPONENT

THE musical past shows that while some composers were capable of producing a real synthesis of textural and instrumental resources, the majority were not able to produce such a balance of the diversified techniques which constitute a musical composition as a whole. Thus, some creative artists, while in possession of numerous melodic and harmonic devices, were relatively (and sometimes completely) unsuccessful in handling instrumental techniques. At the same time others had very fruitful instrumental ideas and lacked sufficient technique in melodic and harmonic composition.

The dominating and impulsive types, among whom symphonic conductors are usually included, often write what may be called "conductorial music"— for which the Germans have an appropriate term, "Kappelmeister-musik." In many a composition by such men, orchestral versatility of device, coupled with proper use of instruments, usually helps offset the emptiness of intonational forms. The greatest representative of this creative type in the past is Hector Berlioz. At present, however, the sins of conductorial composers might be regarded as virtuous accomplishments with a number of our contemporaries, who, possessing great harmonic and sometimes rhythmic dexterity, lack this particular quality. In some cases, the crudeness of harmonic and melodic technique can be completely overshadowed by the expressiveness of orchestral resources, which in such cases become the major component of the thematic structure.

It is not so much a matter of refinement and skill in orchestration, as it is the simple fact of such a component being prominently present. Such is the case with Beethoven, in whose music, and practically for the first time, dynamics and forms of attack played such an important part.

At any rate, as the student of this system is most luxuriously equipped with all the imaginable techniques, it is time for him to become aware of the importance of *instrumental resources*, as these resources constitute one of the most powerful media of musical expression. The latter consideration makes us believe that a great deal of music written today, interesting as it may be for professionals, is sterile for lack of one of its most vital ingredients.

In writing functional music, i.e., music which is capable of stimulating associations, as most music written for the theatre, cinema, radio and television must be, in order to serve the purpose, instrumental resources most frequently are the major component of a thematic structure.

As details of this subject pertain to the field of orchestration, we shall confine ourselves to essentials for the present. The immediate goal of this discussion is to make the potential composer aware of such resources as instrumental structure offers.

Instrumental resources can be classified into the following fundamental components:

(1) *Density;* symbol: D (density);
(2) *Dynamics*; symbol: V (volume);
(3) *Tone-Quality;* symbol: Q (quality);
(4) *Instrumental Forms;* symbol: I (instrumental);
(5) *Forms of Attack;* symbol: A (attack).

The composer can start to conceive a certain thematic unit with one individual component or with any combination of the above components. But in order to conceive of anything as a definite form in music, two elements are necessary:

(1) configuration of time (T) and
(2) configuration of the special component (in this case: D, V, Q, I or A).

The behavior of the configuration of a special component during an assigned time-period is the basis of composition of thematic units. But in order to evolve configurations, it is necessary to have a scale from which such configurations can be evolved. Then the various degrees òf the respective scales become basic units of the potential configurations.

We have seen before that the mere fact that a certain pitch-scale has two units already implies its configurational versatility. Such versatility is lòw as compared with that of a five-unit scale. But the latter is not nearly as versatile as a seven or eight-unit scale. Thus we arrive at the idea of *low, medium* and *high* versatility. We already have used such an approach more than once. In one instance, it was applied to low, medium and high density, in the branch of Part-Melodization.* Later, this elementary approach was changed to a detailed analytical study. Following this method, we shall deal with instrumental resources in an elementary manner for the present, leaving all strictly technical aspects to our analysis of orchestration.

Density has been thoroughly discussed in the Applications of General Harmony.** Instrumental Forms, likewise, received full attention in the respective branch dedicated to this matter.***

The meaning of composing thematic units, as instrumental forms first, implies the selection of instrumental configurations ruling over a certain simultaneity-continuity [the instrumental sigma: $\Sigma(I)$].

A certain unit, for example, may consist of Iap, while another unit may consist of $I \frac{a2p}{a3p}$, both implying definite time-periods in definite relations. For example:

$T^{\rightarrow}Iap = 4T$ and $T^{\rightarrow}I \frac{a2p}{a3p} = 12T$. In this case their ratio is $1 \div 3$. The harmonic content of both thematic units in this case becomes a minor component. This leaves for our discussion the three new components of instrumental resources: *dynamics, tone-quality* and *attack-forms.*

---

*See Vol. I, p. 700.　　　　**See p. 1226 ff.　　　　***See p. 883.

A. Dynamics

Dynamic scales can be composed within the range of intensity associated with music. As the excitor (amplitude) and the reaction (volume) are, according to the Weber-Fechner law, in logarithmic dependence ($y = \log x$), we can only approximate the designated degrees of volume in musical performance.

We may generally agree that a certain standard of *pp*, *p*, *mf*, *f* and *ff* can be established for practical purposes. But even such an allowance can be admitted only after we specify what instrument or group of instruments we mean. For *f* in a large symphony orchestra is quite different in volume from *f* in a string quartet. Nevertheless, even such a vague definition of dynamic degrees helps to a certain extent when the performer is confronted with interpretation of the composer's intentions.

We can hypothetically assume that the minimum of dynamic flexibility results from a one-unit (one-degree) scale. A one-unit scale can be any degree of the total range of volume. It can be an equivalent of *pp*, *p*, *mf*, *f* or *ff*. There are some forms of folk-music generally performed as *mf*. Then there are dance-bands in the U.S.A. that play everything *f*. When such dance-bands dare to produce two dynamic degrees, such as *p* and *f*, we witness the birth of a two-unit dynamic scale.

We shall replace (only for the composer's use) the customary symbols by the symbols of v and V. These symbols represent a dynamic unit (degree) and a dynamic group respectively. Thus we arrive at the following classification of dynamic scales:

(1) One-unit scales:

$$V = v \equiv v_I, \ v_{II}, \ v_{III}, \ v_{IV}, \ v_V, \ \ldots, \text{ where}$$
$$v_I \equiv pp, \ v_{II} \equiv p, \ v_{III} \equiv mf, \ v_{IV} \equiv f, \ v_V \equiv ff.$$

(2) Two-unit scales:

$$V = 2v \equiv v_I + v_{II}, \ v_I + v_{III}, \ v_I + v_{IV}, \ v_I + v_V,$$
$$v_{II} + v_{III}, \ v_{II} + v_{IV}, \ v_{II} + v_V,$$
$$v_{III} + v_{IV}, \ v_{III} + v_V,$$
$$v_{IV} + v_V.$$

(3) Three-unit scales:

$$V = 3v \equiv v_I + v_{II} + v_{III}, \ v_I + v_{II} + v_{IV}, \ v_I + v_{II} + v_V,$$
$$v_I + v_{III} + v_{IV}, \ v_I + v_{III} + v_V,$$
$$v_I + v_{IV} + v_V,$$
$$v_{II} + v_{III} + v_{IV}, \ v_{II} + v_{III} + v_V,$$
$$v_{II} + v_{IV} + v_V,$$
$$v_{III} + v_{IV} + v_V.$$

(4) Five-unit scales:

$$V = 5v \equiv v_I + v_{II} + v_{III} + v_{IV} + v_V.$$

Of these scales the most practical are the scales of symmetric structure, i.e., with an equidistant arrangement of the units within the total hypothetic range of $V = 5v$. The four-unit scales are entirely omitted, as our classification is based on so-called "normal series," which take place in crystal formations, and with which we are already familiar through the Evolution of Rhythm Series.*

Thus, the best selections from the above table are:

$$V = v \quad \text{any selection}$$
$$V = 2v \quad v_I + v_V; \; v_{II} + v_{IV}$$
$$V = 3v \quad v_I + v_{III} + v_V; \; v_{II} + v_{III} + v_{IV}$$
$$V = 5v \quad \text{one scale}$$

The transition from one dynamic degree to another can be either sudden or gradual. The first form of transition can be indicated in our symbols or in the customary musical symbols as the sequence of the different degrees within a specified time period. For instance:

$$v_I 4t + v_{III} 2t + v_V 2t$$
$$\text{or:} \quad pp4t + mf2t + ff2t$$

Gradual transition (leaving the form of such graduality to the performer) takes place in two directions: from a weaker degree to a stronger degree (known in musical terminology as *crescendo*), and from a stronger degree to a weaker (known as *diminuendo*). The latter are expressed in our notation as follows:

$$(v_I \to v_{III})4t + (v_V \to v_{III})2t + (v_{III} \to v_I)2t, \text{ or in musical notation:}$$
$$(pp < mf)4t + (ff > mf)2t + (mf > pp)2t.$$

The dynamic groups V must be composed with a view to their potential correspondence with other components. For example:

$$T(V) = 16(2 + 1 + 1)$$
$$T(H) = 4(2 + 1 + 1)^2$$
$$T(M) = (2 + 1 + 1)^3$$

Let $V = 3v = v_I + v_{III} + v_V$. Then $\overrightarrow{V}$ (the dynamic continuity-group) can be composed as follows:

$$\overrightarrow{v} = v_V 32T + (v_I \to v_V)16T + (v_V \to v_{III})16T.$$

*See Vol. I, p. 84.

B. Tone-Quality

By the same method, scales of tone-quality can be established. Each degree of quality (q) becomes a unit of the *quality-scale* (Q). From such scales, thematic units can be composed as timbral groups. Intonation and temporal structure can be devised later in order to conform to the temporal organization of the Q–group.

In evolving the scales of quality, we shall consider the following forms: $Q = q$, $Q = 2q$, $Q = 3q$, $Q = 5q$. In some special cases, as in writing for a stringed-bow ensemble, even $Q = 9q$ may be practical.

Since in this chapter we are concerned only with the general forms of timbral composition, our thematic units will be expressed only in terms of Q and not in any concrete selection of instruments. The latter can be superimposed upon any $\overrightarrow{Q}$, i.e., quality continuity-group, and technically belongs to a study of Orchestration. Neither shall we deal with acoustical matters now: they, too, belong to the field of orchestration.

For the present, without attempting to explain quality as phenomenon, we shall resort to the most obvious and, at the same time, the most fundamental conception of the quality-range.

The limits of perceptible quality-range can be defined as *open tone* (lower limit) and *closed* (muted) *tone* (upper limit). Open tone is characterized by a small quantity (sometimes none) of partials and is associated with the tuning fork, flute-stops of an organ, various types of flutes and the upper range of a French horn; also with the string-bow instruments, when played over the fingerboard (*sul tasto*).

Closed tone is characterized by an excessive aggregation of partials within a certain acoustical range and is associated with the heavily muted brass instruments and the string-bow instruments, when the latter are muted and played near the bridge (*sul ponticello*).

It is important to note that the tone production of the open tone is *immediate* (like blowing into the mouth-hole of a flute), while the tone production of the closed tone is *mediate* (as besides the mouthpiece, there is an "acoustical screen" produced by the mute).

In the quality-range of five degrees, the remaining three intermediate degrees appear as follows:

(1) The *single-reed* quality, which is associated with the clarinet and with string-bow instruments bowed in the customary manner. Some physical characteristics affecting this quality are: single-reed mouthpiece, cylindrical bore, and, as a consequence, the presence of *odd* partials.

(2) The *stopped* quality, which can be associated with stopped French horn and the slightly nasal character of the single-reed instruments with a conic bore, such as the saxophones.

(3) The *nasal* quality of prominence, which is associated with the double-reed instruments, such as oboes, bassoons, and with stringed bow instruments when played at the bridge but without a mute; it is also present, ir the customary form of execution, in the high register of the 'cello.

Thus, we arrive at the basic quality-range of five degrees:

    (1) open $\equiv q_I$;   symbol: ○

    (2) single-reed $\equiv q_{II}$;   symbol: R

    (3) stopped $\equiv q_{III}$;   symbol: ⊕

    (4) double-reed (nasal)$\equiv q_{IV}$; symbol: RR

    (5) closed (muted) $\equiv q_V$;   symbol: ●

With extreme skill in orchestration, a certain degree of graduality, in transition from one q to another can be accomplished, but it is more practical as a rule, to conceive the $Q^{\rightarrow}$ schemes with the forms of sudden transitions only. In the year 1932, as a result of my collaboration with Leon Theremin, an electronic organ was constructed (at present it is in the possession of Gerald F. Warburg) on which the closing of an open tone could be accomplished as continuity by means of condensers controlled by pedals.

It is important to realize that the natural instrument of the human voice is capable of such continuous transitions from one q to another by modification of vowels and consonants. This topic will be discussed in orchestration.

Quality-scales can be classified in the same fashion as the dynamic scales, with the only difference that the symbols Q and q take the place of V and v respectively.

An example of $Q^{\rightarrow}$ evolved from $Q = 3q = q_{II} + q_{III} + q_{IV}$.

$$Q^{\rightarrow} = q_{IV}\, 3T + \frac{q_{II}}{q_{IV}}\, T + q_{III}\, 2T + \frac{q_{III}}{q_{II}}\, 2T$$

As it follows from the previous explanation, such $Q^{\rightarrow}$ schemes can be coordinated with M and $H^{\rightarrow}$ on the basis of T, and all three of them, in turn, can be coordinated with $V^{\rightarrow}$

There is a substantial amount of material which can be used for such ultimate forms of complex temporal coordination in the *Theory of Rhythm*, particularly in the Distributive Involution and in the Synchronization of Three and More Generators.[*]

It is to be remembered that the quality-scales must be evolved with the potential instrumental selection in view.

C. FORMS OF ATTACK

Forms of attack can also be classified by the method which we have applied to V and Q.

After the main classification of the.attack-range is established, the composer may evolve a selective scale of attack-forms (A and a). These attack-forms, ultimately arranged into attack-form continuity-groups $(A^{\rightarrow})$ and coupled with T, constitute thematic units, conceived from the viewpoint of a and A.

[*]See Vol. I, p. 70 and p. 24.

The basis on which we establish the fundamental classification of attack-forms is the *durability of attack*. Again, as in the case of V and Q, this subject cannot be subjected to scientific scrutiny, for the present, as, in actuality, no attack-form can be dissociated from its dynamic characteristic. Nevertheless, the composer may derive important benefits from the concept and method of attack-scales, even in their elementary and approximate forms.

We shall define the lower limit of the attack-form range as uninterrupted continuity of sound resulting from one attack and extending over a certain time-period (*legatissimo*, in musical terminology). Then the upper limit of this range becomes a percussive form of attack with a minimum durability (*staccatissimo*, in musical terms, an equivalent of hard staccato, marked as ▪).

Between these two limits we find the basic three intermediate degrees of attack-forms, which are:

(1) the *legato* form, which minimizes the intensity of attack, like the detached (detaché) manner of bowing the stringed-bow instruments.

(2) The *portamento* form, which is discontinuous but not abrupt (marked ‿ for orchestral instruments, and ⌒ for the Piano).

(3) The *staccato* form, which is abrupt and therefore percussive, but is associated with low dynamic degrees. It corresponds to soft staccato (usually marked . . .).

All further refinements of this range would be practical only for the stringed-bow instruments, and will be discussed in Orchestration.

As in the case of other instrumental resources, we can establish scales of attack-forms from which thematic units may be composed.

It should be remembered that this component is fairly new, as compared to the others. It usually has been left to the initiative of the performer.

Scales of attack-forms follow our usual classification: $A = a$, $A = 2a$, $A = 3a$, $A = 5a$, . . .

The respective correspondence of the attack-form degrees are:

(1) *legatissimo:* a_I

(2) *legato:* a_{II}

(3) *portamento:* a_{III}

(4) *staccato:* a_{IV}

(5) *staccatissimo:* a_V

As all known music is quite flexible with regard to the time-periods of ever-hanging a, time units can be specified either in t or T, depending on the degree refinement which the composer intends to impose.

An example of $A^{\rightarrow}$, evolved from $A = 3a = a_{II} + a_{III} + a_{IV}$.

$$A^{\rightarrow} = a_{II}2t + a_{IV}2t + a_{III}4t + a_{IV}4t + a_{III}2t + a_{II}2t.$$

This equipment is fully sufficient for the student-composer to proceed with composition of thematic units as they have been defined in this theory. He may choose any technical form as the major component. He must synchronize this major component with any minor components he may select. It is the coordination itself that is of prime concern. He is free otherwise in making his decisions and selecting his technical resources—choice being controlled only by the composer's decision to evolve this or that type of music.

The next stage of this technique consists of coordinating thematic units into an *a priori* planned musical whole.

PART II

COMPOSITION OF THEMATIC CONTINUITY

CHAPTER 10

MUSICAL FORM

THE term "musical form" is usually applied to casually contrived schemes of thematic sequence. Such schemes are both vague and dogmatic. They are devised solely on a trial-and-error basis. Schemes of thematic sequence usually include two components: the sequent arrangement of subjects and the sequence of keys in which the subjects must follow one another.

While the succession and the recurrence of subjects are intended to achieve some form of symmetry, without regard to the temporal relations of the subjects, the succession of keys in which such schemes are presented is based entirely on antiquated conceptions of tonality. The most convincing proof that such thematic schemes are unsatisfactory, with regard to both their symmetry and key-sequence, lies in the outstanding compositions of the classics. Even Beethoven, who followed these dogmatic schemes more closely than others, had to deviate from the schemes in order to get satisfactory results. This is true of his selection of recurrences, distributions and key-time relations.

Of course, there is no one form that is specifically "musical." Form, conceived as temporal structure evolved from thematic units, most obviously must possess the characteristics inherent in all forms of temporal regularity. But temporal regularity implies both the form of the sequence of units involved and the periodic relationship among such units.

So far as classical schemes of thematic sequence are concerned, we find a few prototypes of such schemes. The latter can be generally classified as *monothematic* (one subject) and *polythematic* (more than one subject). In the monothematic schemes, the subject (thematic unit) repeats itself several times and is usually subjected to variations. Such a form of thematic sequence is usually known as "theme and variations." Polythematic schemes consisting of two subjects usually appear in two forms: in the form of direct repetition: (A + B) + + (A + B) + . . . , like the "lower forms of rondo" and the "old sonata form"; or in the form of triadic symmetry: A + B + A, as in the "three-part song" or the "complex three-part song." In shorter compositions, and particularly in the structures of thematic units, a two-subject scheme adapts itself to the $\frac{4}{4}$ series binomial, i.e., 3+1. It is usually known as a "two-part song" and may have the following scheme: $A_1 + A_2 + B + A_2$. This form of thematic sequence was commonly used for themes from which variations were to be devised, and as a complex structural unit in the form of triadic symmetry—in which case it was used either for A or for B.

It is interesting to note that none of the classical schemes contain symmetric inversion, except in the case of the old sonata form, where symmetric inversion of keys takes place—but not of the sequence of subjects. Designating the key of the tonic as T and the key of the dominant as D, we can represent this scheme as follows: $A(T) + B(D) + A(D) + B(T)$.

Certain schemes of polythematic sequence containing three subjects are referred to as "the higher forms" of the rondo. Whereas the "lower" rondo usually appears in the place of the slow movement in the larger forms (symphony, sonata, quartet, or other chamber ensemble), the "higher" rondo usually is employed for the finale in these forms. What I call the "higher" rondo usually conforms to the following scheme of thematic sequence: $A_1 + B_1 + C + A_2 + B_2$. It is generally agreed that C is longer than A or B taken individually, but not necessarily as long as $A + B$. The chief difference between A_1 and A_2, and B_1 and B_2, respectively, is in the key-relations. The main tendency is the conflict of keys between A_1 and B_1, and the reconciliation between A_2 and B_2. As these relations are workable only in certain forms of tonality, we shall not be concerned with further details pertaining to this matter.

This "higher" rondo may be looked upon as a pentadic form without an axis of inversion. Pentadic forms on a smaller scale are also to be found in some compositions of dance character. In Chopin's waltz No. 7, the scheme could have been a perfect pentadic symmetry, i.e., $A + B + C + B + A$, if not for the composer's passion for repetition, which spoiled the form by adding a "coda" (literally: "tail") consisting of an additional repetition of B.

A special version of triadic symmetry appears as the first movement of a symphony or sonata and is known as "the sonata form," or "the sonata-allegro form". This sectional scheme generally consists of $A_1 + B + A_2$. On the other hand the thematic scheme resembles the pentadic form of the "higher" rondo, with the difference that instead of subject C, there is the so-called "development." The development usually consists of harmonic transpositions of a continuously repeated fragmentary structure (or structures) borrowed from any of the subjects of section A_1. The latter often consists of a large number of subjects. There are, for example, eight of them in the piano sonata No. 4 by Beethoven. Section A_1 is usually known as "exposition"; section B, as "development"; and section A_2, as "recapitulation," which is an abbreviated exposition with a greater key-unification.

Contemporary composers have developed many individual schemes. What they call a "symphony" does not necessarily resemble the classical scheme. Unification of all movements of the sonata form was attempted by Liszt in his "cyclic" piano sonata in B minor. Contemporary composers often have more than one exposition, and the developments are often dissociated from their expositions. In some other cases, each theme undergoes immediately its own development, as in the later sonatas of Scriabine.

Polyphonic forms have schemes of thematic sequence similar to those of the homophonic forms. Thus, a fugue with one subject corresponds to a theme with variations or to a "lower" rondo. A fugue with two subjects is written in the same scheme; the only difference is that both subjects appear simultaneously and are temporarily treated as one subject. In other instances, a fugue with two subjects (see: *The Well-Tempered Clavichord*, Vol. II, No. XVIII) is evolved according to Hegel's triad, i.e., as thesis, antithesis, synthesis, or: $A + B + \frac{A}{B}$.

The manifold forms of thematic sequence in European musical civilization range from continuous repetition of brief thematic structures, which remind one of the repeat-patterns of visual arts, like tiles or wallpaper (Chopin wrote much "wallpaper" music); through continuously flowing broad linear design, constantly varied and syntactically dissociated by cadences, like the Gregorian Chant; to the temporal schemes containing no repetitions and embodying no syntactical cadencing before the end, devised by contemporary Germans (Schoenberg and Hindemith), recognized as a type of *durchkomponierte Musik* (through-composed music) and adopted by contemporaries of other nationalities (Shostakovich). The "through-composed" music is a logical development of the so-called "twelve-tone system," where any repetition of any pitch-unit is taboo until the whole chromatic set has been exhausted.

CHAPTER 11

FORMS OF THEMATIC SEQUENCE

Forms of thematic sequence can be classified into four main groups:

(1) groups of direct recurrence;
(2) groups of symmetric recurrence;
(3) groups of modified recurrence;
(4) groups of progressive symmetry.

Monothematic continuity can be evolved in the form of direct recurrence only. In this case the form of thematic sequence is *monomial periodicity:*

$$A + A + A + \ldots$$

Polythematic continuity based on *two subjects* can be evolved through all four groups:

Group one: $(A + B) + \ldots$ *binomial periodicity*
Group two: $A + B + A$
Group three: $(A + B) + (B + A)$
Group four: $A + (A + B) + B$

Polythematic continuity based on *three subjects* may assume the following forms:

Group one: $(A + B + C) + \ldots$ *trinomial periodicity*
Group two: $A + B + C + B + A$
Group three: $(A+B+C) + (B+C+A) + (C+A+B)$
Group four: $A + (A+B) + (A+B+C) + (B+C) + C$

Polythematic continuity based on *four subjects* may assume the following forms:

Group one: $(A+B+C+D) + \ldots$ *quadrinomial periodicity.*
Group two: $A + B + C + D + C + B + A$
Group three: $(A+B+C+D) + (B+C+D+A) + (C+D+A+B) +$
         $+ (D+A+B+C)$
Group four:
   (1) $A + (A+B) + (A+B+C+D) + (C+D) + D$, i.e., $1+2+4+2+1$
   (2) $A + (A+B+C) + (A+B+C+D) + (B+C+D) + D$, i.e.,
      $1+3+4+3+1$

Polythematic continuity based on *five subjects* may assume the following forms:

Group one: $(A+B+C+D+E) + \ldots$ *quintinomial periodicity*
Group two: $A + B + C + D + E + D + C + B + A$
Group three: $(A+B+C+D+E) + (B+C+D+E+A) +$
         $+ (C+D+E+A+B) + (D+E+A+B+C) +$
         $+ (E+A+B+C+D)$

[1333]

Group four:

(1) A + (A+B) + (A+B+C) + (A+B+C+D+E) + (C+D+E) +
+ (D+E) + E, i.e., 1+2+3+5+3+2+1

(2) A + (A+B+C) + (A+B+C+D+E) + (C+D+E) + E, i.e.,
1+3+5+3+1

Polythematic continuity based on *six subjects* may assume the following forms:

Group one: (A+B+C+D+E+F) + . . . *sextinomial periodicity*

Group two: A+B+C+D+E+F+E+D+C+B+A

Group three: (A+B+C+D+E+F) + (B+C+D+E+F+A) +
+ (C+D+E+F+A+B) + (D+E+F+A+B+C) +
+ (E+F+A+B+C+D) + (F+A+B+C+D+E)

Group four:

(1) A + (A+B+C) + (A+B+C+D+E+F) + (D+E+F) + F, i.e.,
1+3+6+3+1

(2) A + (A+B) + (A+B+C+D) + (A+B+C+D+E+F) +
+ (C+D+E+F) + (E+F) + F, i.e., 1+2+4+6+4+2+1

Polythematic continuity based on *seven subjects* may assume the following forms:

Group one: (A+B+C+D+E+F+G) + . . . *septinomial periodicity*

Group two: A+B+C+D+E+F+G+F+E+D+C+B+A

Group three: (A+B+C+D+E+F+G) + (B+C+D+E+F+G+A) +
+ (C+D+E+F+G+A+B) + (D+E+F+G+A+B+C) +
+ (E+F+G+A+B+C+D) + (F+G+A+B+C+D+E) +
+ (G+A+B+C+D+E+F)

Group four:

(1) A + (A+B+C) + (A+B+C+D) + (A+B+C+D+E+F+G) +
+ (D+E+F+G) + (E+F+G) + G, i.e., 1+3+4+7+4+3+1

(2) A + (A+B+C) + (A+B+C+D+E) + (A+B+C+D+E+F+G)
+ (C+D+E+F+G) + (E+F+G) + G, i.e.,
1+3+5+7+5+3+1

The above forms of thematic sequence range from the most elementary recurrence to the most refined forms of progressive symmetry. Probably the most important characteristic of the latter is the *symmetric interpolation* of subjects. While one subject appears in its last phase, some other subject makes its first appearance. Under such conditions the interpolation of events is similar to that of interpolation of generations. While somebody is in his infancy, somebody else is fully mature, and somebody else is ready to die. The neighboring position of subjects of the different ages makes this form closer to the schemes of actuality than any other form of thematic sequence. It is also important to note that the subjects are symmetrically arranged and form their own hierarchy and ranks. In some of the more developed schemes, different subjects appear a different number of times in the course of entire continuity, the extreme subjects having higher ranks than the middle ones.

CHAPTER 12

TEMPORAL COORDINATION OF THEMATIC SEQUENCE

THE next step in evolving thematic continuity consists of coordinating thematic sequence with temporal forms of regularity. The latter represent the various forms of duration-groups discussed in the *Theory of Rhythm.**

We shall look upon these groups as forms of the temporal organization of thematic sequence. They come from four main sources and serve different purposes respectively:

(1) The resultants of interference;
(2) The permutation-groups;
(3) The involution-groups;
(4) The acceleration-groups.

As any type of duration-group may be superimposed upon any form of thematic sequence, it is important in selecting a temporal group to consider the following points.

If the form of thematic sequence is simple and such simplicity is to be maintained in its temporal organization, the temporal group should be chosen from the simplest forms of temporal regularity, such as monomial or binomial periodicity. If, on the other hand, it is desirable to introduce temporal refinements into a simple form of thematic sequence, any other more complex form of temporal regularity may be used. In order to make such forms of temporal regularity detectable in a monothematic sequence, it is necessary to subject the thematic unit, in each of its appearances, to some form of variation. The latter may be based on quadrant-rotation, tonal expansion, density, instrumental form or modal transposition.

Under such conditions each appearance of the thematic unit is associated with one or another temporal coefficient. Even if the sequence is monothematic and the temporal group is a monomial, each appearance of the thematic unit is recognizable due to the above-described variations.

More complex forms of thematic sequence may be coordinated with the simplest forms of temporal groups when it becomes desirable to accentuate the complexity of thematic sequence by contrasting it with its temporal relations. Yet in some other instances the desired form of expression is such that both the thematic sequence and the temporal form require refinement and complexity.

This theory repudiates the academic point of view, according to which some themes are so unimportant that they function as mere bridges tying the main themes together. If a certain thematic unit is unimportant and insignificant and merely consumes time, it should not participate in a composition. Looking

*See Vol. I, p. 4 to p. 95.

upon thematic continuity as an organic form, the only viewpoint we can accept is: *thematic units have their relative temporal characteristics under which they appear in the sequence.* This implies that whereas in one portion of a composition a certain thematic unit may dominate over others owing to its high temporal co-efficient, in another portion of the composition the same thematic unit may become subordinate owing to its low temporal coefficient and the relatively higher temporal coefficients of other thematic units; ultimately, the first thematic unit may vanish completely, being overwhelmed by other thematic units (this we have already witnessed in the groups of progressive symmetry).

Thus, through selection of temporal coefficients, we can vary the relative importance of any one of the thematic units in any portion of a composition. If the permanent subordination of certain thematic units is desired throughout the entire composition, such thematic units must be assigned to low temporal coefficients.

In the following applications of temporal groups to the forms of thematic sequence, $T^{\rightarrow}$ represents the entire period of a composition and T, coupled with the various coefficients, represents the relative time-values of thematic units in their individual appearances. Thus T is not necessarily one measure, but a unit by which the relative durations are represented. In translating the $T^{\rightarrow}$ into actual measures, additional coefficients are required. These coefficients (or coefficient, speaking of each individual case) are constant for any one $T^{\rightarrow}$.

For example, a temporal continuity-group $T^{\rightarrow}$ may originally have the following form: $T^{\rightarrow} = 3T + T + 2T + 2T$. At the same time, T may be equivalent to T'', $2T''$, $3T''$, . . . NT''. Then, in the actual realization of such a continuity group, we may have a variety of solutions, depending on the correspondence we establish between T and T''.

(1) $T = T''$, then: $T^{\rightarrow} = 3T'' + T'' + 2T'' + 2T''$;

(2) $T = 2T''$, then: $T^{\rightarrow} = 6T'' + 2T'' + 4T'' + 4T''$;

(3) $T = 3T''$, then: $T^{\rightarrow} = 9T'' + 3T'' + 6T'' + 6T''$;

. . . .

(4) $T = NT''$, then: $T^{\rightarrow} = 3NT'' + NT'' + 2NT'' + 2NT''$.

We shall now illustrate the coordination of $T^{\rightarrow}$ with the various forms of thematic sequence.

A. USING THE RESULTANTS OF INTERFERENCE

The simplest form of thematic continuity results from coordinating a mono-thematic sequence with a monomial form of temporal regularity.

$$T^{\rightarrow} (A) = A_1T + A_2T + A_3T + . . .$$

The same form of thematic sequence may be coordinated with a binomial form of temporal regularity. Then:

$$T^{\rightarrow} (A) = (A_1MT + A_2NT) + . . .$$

The values of M and N depend on the style-series of the respective composition. Thus, on being applied to $\frac{4}{4}$ series, such a form offers the following four basic variants:

(1) $T^{\rightarrow}(A) = (A_13T + A_2T) + \ldots$

(2) $T^{\rightarrow}(A) = (A_1T + A_23T) + \ldots$

(3) $T^{\rightarrow}(A) = (A_13T + A_2T) + (A_3T + A_43T) + \ldots$

(4) $T^{\rightarrow}(A) = (A_1T + A_23T) + (A_33T + A_4T) + \ldots$

Further refinement, variety and complexity can be achieved through the selection of resultants associated with the respective style of temporal organization. The following are a few examples which derive from the second summation-series, and therefore are associated with $\frac{4}{4}$ series in the evolution of style.

(1) $T^{\rightarrow} = r_{4 \div 3}$;
$T^{\rightarrow}(A) = A_13T + A_2T + A_32T + A_42T + A_5T + A_63T.$

(2) $T^{\rightarrow} = r_{4 \div 3}$;
$T^{\rightarrow}(A) = A_13T + A_2T + A_32T + A_4T + A_5T + A_6T + A_7T +$
$+ A_82T + A_9T + A_{10}3T.$

(3) $T^{\rightarrow} = r_{7 \div 4}$;
$T^{\rightarrow}(A) = A_14T + A_23T + A_3T + A_44T + A_52T + A_62T +$
$+ A_74T + A_8T + A_93T + A_{10}4T.$

Figure 38.   Derived from second summation-series.

B. Permutation-Groups

The following illustration refers to permutation-groups. Selecting $3 + 1 + 2 + 2$ as an appropriate form of temporal regularity, we shall subject it to circular permutations, thus quadrupling the original period of duration:

$$T^{\rightarrow} = (A_13T + A_2T + A_32T + A_42T) + (A_5T + A_62T + A_72T + A_83T) +$$
$$+ (A_92T + A_{10}2T + A_{11}3T + A_{12}T) + (A_{13}2T + A_{14}3T + A_{15}T +$$
$$+ A_{16}2T).$$

Longer forms of thematic continuity are hardly necessary under ordinary circumstances. In the above case, one thematic unit makes 16 appearances.

C. Involution-Groups

The use of involution-groups as forms of temporal regularity is of particular value, when the proportionate relations between thematic units become the chief characteristic of continuity.

Individual and synchronized involution-groups of different powers can be used in sequence as forms of temporal regularity of $T^{\rightarrow}$.

Examples:

(1) $T^{\rightarrow} = (3+1)^2$;
   $T^{\rightarrow}(A) = A_1 9T + A_2 3T + A_3 3T + A_4 T$.

(2) $T^{\rightarrow} = (2+1+1)^2$;
   $T^{\rightarrow}(A) = (A_1 4T + A_2 2T + A_3 2T) + (A_4 2T + A_5 T + A_6 T) +$
   $+ (A_7 2T + A_8 T + A_9 T)$.

(3) $T^{\rightarrow} = (1+1+2)^2 + 4(1+1+2)$;
   $T^{\rightarrow}(A) = [\,(A_1 T + A_2 T + A_3 2T) + (A_4 T + A_5 T + A_6 2T) +$
   $+ (A_7 2T + A_8 2T + A_9 4T)\,] + (A_{10} 4T + A_{11} 4T + A_{12} 8T)$.

Figure 39. Involution-groups of different powers.

The use of various forms of acceleration (positive and negative) becomes necessary when temporal regularity expresses consistent growth or decline.

In monothematic continuity, a thematic unit either builds itself up with each consecutive appearance or goes into gradual decline.

Examples:

(1) $T^{\rightarrow} = 1 + 2 + 3 + 4 + 5 + 6 + 7 + 8$;
   $T^{\rightarrow}(A) = A_1 T + A_2 2T + A_3 3T + A_4 4T + A_5 5T + A_6 6T +$
   $+ A_7 7T + A_8 8T$.

(2) $T^{\rightarrow} = 8 + 4 + 2 + 1$;
   $T^{\rightarrow}(A) = A_1 8T + A_2 4T + A_3 2T + A_4 T$.

(3) $T^{\rightarrow} = 1 + 3 + 4 + 7$;
   $T^{\rightarrow}(A) = A_1 T + A_2 3T + A_3 4T + A_4 7T$.

Figure 40. Growth and decline in monothematic continuity.

Each form of thematic sequence may assume various forms of temporal coordination, in the same way as indicated for the monothematic thematic sequence. In the form of sequence based on more than one subject, an additional technique may be used: interference between the number of terms of the temporal group and the number of terms of the thematic sequence. This technique is appropriate whenever it is desirable to obtain a rather long continuity for an entire composition, with relatively few thematic units and relatively few appearances of the latter.

We shall now apply some of the forms of temporal regularity to thematic sequences based on two subjects.

Thematic sequence: $(A + B) + \ldots$
$\overrightarrow{T} = 3 + 1$;
$\overrightarrow{T}(A + B) = A_13T + B_1T + A_23T + B_2T + \ldots$

In this case A is always 3 times longer than B.

$\overrightarrow{T} = r_{4 \div 3}$;
$\overrightarrow{T}(A+B) = A_13T + B_1T + A_22T + B_2T + A_3T + B_3T +$
$\qquad + A_4T + B_42T + A_5T + B_53T.$

In this case the period of A goes into decline, while the period of B grows.

Thematic sequence: $A + B + A$.
$\overrightarrow{T} = 3 + 1 + 4$;
$\overrightarrow{T}(A+B+A) = A_13T + BT + A_24T.$

If B is a bridge, such a temporal group is acceptable; otherwise a different variant of the same group would be preferable. For instance:

$\overrightarrow{T} = 3 + 4 + 1$; then:
$\overrightarrow{T}(A+B+A) = A_13T + B4T + A_2T$, in which case
$\overrightarrow{T}(A_1 + A_2) = \overrightarrow{T}(B).$

The use of interference necessitates the recurrence of the entire thematic sequence. For instance:

$\overrightarrow{T} = 3 + 1$;
$\overrightarrow{T}(A+B+A) = (A_13T + B_1T + A_23T) + (A_3T + B_23T + A_4T).$

The use of involution-groups, when applied to thematic sequences, yields the forms of proportionate temporal expansion or contraction for each subject. Thus $A + B$ coordinated with $\overrightarrow{T} = (3+1)^2$ produces the following result:

$\overrightarrow{T}(A+B) = A_19T + B_13T + A_23T + B_2T.$

For opposite effects, the same scheme can be used in reverse, i.e., $\overrightarrow{T} = (1+3)^2$. Then: $\overrightarrow{T}(A+B) = A_1T + B_13T + A_23T + B_29T.$

When more recurrences are desirable in proportionate distribution, involution of higher powers becomes necessary. For instance:

$\overrightarrow{T} = (3+1)^3$;
$\overrightarrow{T}(A+B) = (A_127T + B_19T + A_29T + B_23T) +$
$\qquad + (A_39T + B_33T + A_43T + B_4T).$

It is important to study the effects of coefficient-groups upon schemes of thematic sequence in direct recurrence as compared to permutation-groups obtained from the same schemes.

For example:

Thematic sequence: $3(A + B + C)$;

$$\overrightarrow{T} = 2 + 1 + 1;$$
$$\overrightarrow{T}[3(A+B+C)] = (A_12T + B_1T + C_1T) + (A_22T + B_2T + C_2T) +$$
$$+ (A_32T + B_3T + C_3T).$$

Thematic sequence: $(A + B + C)\circlearrowleft$;

$$\overrightarrow{T} = 2 + 1 + 1;$$
$$\overrightarrow{T}(A+B+C)\circlearrowleft = (A_12T + B_1T + C_1T) + (B_22T + C_2T + A_2T) +$$
$$+ (C_32T + A_3T + B_3T).$$

Figure 41. Effect of coefficient groups.

There is a general way of selecting temporal groups, which becomes particularly practical for the symmetric schemes of thematic sequence consisting of many subjects. As the general characteristic of symmetric groups is reversibility from the center, temporal groups constructed on the same principle and with a corresponding number of terms fit the respective thematic sequence perfectly.

Example:

Thematic sequence: $A + B + C + D + E + D + C + B + A$

As this scheme has five subjects, it requires a five term temporal group. Let it be: $r_{\frac{4 \div 3}{2}}$. Then the temporal group assumes the following appearance:

$$\overrightarrow{T} = 3 + 1 + 2 + 1 + 1 + 1 + 2 + 1 + 3$$

Hence: $\overrightarrow{T}(A+B+C+D+E+D+C+B+A) =$
$$= A_13T + B_1T + C_12T + D_1T + ET + D_2T + C_22T + B_2T + A_23T.'$$

Another important form of correlation of the groups of temporal regularity with the groups of thematic sequence consists of the application of involution-groups to the permutation-groups of thematic sequence. For comparison's sake, we shall offer an illustration of the application of involution-groups to both direct and modified recurrence.

Thematic sequence: $A + B + C$;

$$\overrightarrow{T} = (2+1+1)^2;$$
$$\overrightarrow{T}(A+B+C) = (A_14T + B_12T + C_12T) + (A_22T + B_2T + C_2T) +$$
$$+ (A_32T + B_3T + C_3T).$$

In this case: $A_1 = 4T$; $A_2 = 2T$; $A_3 = 2T$;
$\qquad\qquad B_1 = 2T$; $B_2 = T$; $B_3 = T$;
$\qquad\qquad C_1 = 2T$; $C_2 = T$; $C_3 = T$;

Thematic sequence: $(A + B + C) \circlearrowleft$;

$T^{\rightarrow} = (2+1+1)^2$;

$T^{\rightarrow} (A+B+C) \circlearrowleft = (A_14T + B_12T + C_12T) + (B_22T + C_2T + A_2T) +$
$\qquad\qquad\qquad + (C_32T + A_3T + B_3T)$.

In this case: $A_1 = 4T$; $A_2 = T$; $A_3 = T$;
$\qquad\qquad B_1 = 2T$; $B_2 = 2T$; $B_3 = T$;
$\qquad\qquad C_1 + 2T$; $C_2 = T$; $C_3 = 2T$.

Figure 42. Application of involution groups.

This case yields a greater temporal variability with respect to each individual subject.

D. ACCELERATION-GROUPS

Schemes of thematic sequence based on progressive symmetry are diversified enough to be used in temporal uniformity. In the cases of extreme refinement, however, other forms of temporal regularity may be used.

Example:

Thematic sequence: $A+(A+B) + (A+B+C) + (B+C) + C$.

Here each subject appears three times, and the total number of terms is 9. For this reason any temporal group consisting of 9 or 3 terms, and therefore not causing interference, can be used.

$T^{\rightarrow} = T$;

$T^{\rightarrow} (A, B, C \text{ progressive}) = A_1T + (A_2T + B_1T) + (A_3T + B_2T + C_1T) +$
$\qquad\qquad\qquad + (B_3T + C_2T) + C_3T$.

$T^{\rightarrow} = 1 + 2 + 3$;

$T^{\rightarrow} (A, B, C \text{ progressive}) = A_1T + (A_22T + B_13T) +$
$.. + (A_3T + B_22T + C_13T) + (B_3T + C_22T) + C_33T$.

In this case: $A_1 = T$; $A_2 = 2T$; $A_3 = T$;
$\qquad\qquad B_1 = 3T$; $B_2 = 2T$; $B_3 = T$;
$\qquad\qquad C_1 = 3T$; $C_2 = 2T$; $C_3 = 3T$.

$T^{\rightarrow} = (2+1+1)^2$;

$T^{\rightarrow} = (A, B, C \text{ progressive}) = A_14T + (A_22T + B_12T) +$
$\qquad + (A_32T + B_2T + C_1T) + (B_32T + C_2T) + C_3T$.

In this case: $A_1 = 4T$; $A_2 = 2T$; $A_3 = 2T$;
$\qquad\qquad B_1 = 2T$; $B_2 = T$; $B_3 = 2T$;
$\qquad\qquad C_1 = T$; $C_2 = T$; $C_3 = T$.

Figure 43. Application of involution groups.

The last case offers a characteristic rank arrangement of the individual subjects.

This discussion gives the student sufficient information to enable him to use his own initiative in evolving more elaborate forms of temporal coordination of the thematic sequence. Forms of temporal regularity coming from different sources and different series should be thoroughly analyzed and studied.

CHAPTER 13

INTEGRATION OF THEMATIC CONTINUITY

IN order to integrate thematic continuity in accordance with a temporally-coordinated form of thematic sequence, it is necessary to transform thematic units into subjects (themes) and their modifications, and to correlate such thematic groups with a group of key-axes.

Each of the above defined operations can be performed by means of special techniques.

A. TRANSFORMATION OF THEMATIC UNITS INTO THEMATIC GROUPS

An exposition of a subject (theme) or its modification constitutes a *thematic group*. The subject itself, or *theme*, can be defined as the *maximal thematic unit*, i.e., a thematic unit at its maximal duration.

As we have seen before, the period of a subject varies in its different expositions. If the subject is composed as the maximum of a thematic unit appearing in respective continuity, it can later be subjected to temporal modifications, such as shortening of its period.

In the thematic sequence with 3 subjects and 9 thematic groups in proportionate distribution, each subject has 3 thematic groups corresponding to 3 expositions. Thus, in a scheme: $(A_14T + B_12T + C_12T) + (A_22T + B_2T + C_2T) + (A_32T + B_3T + C_3T)$, A_1 constitutes subject A; B_1 constitutes subject B; and C_1 constitutes subject C—since all three subjects have their maximal temporal coefficient in their first exposition (indicated by the subnumeral 1). Hence: A_2 and A_3 are the shortened variants (temporal modifications) of subject A; B_2 and B_3 are the shortened variants of the subject B; and C_2 and C_3 are the shortened variants of the subject C.

Let us assume that the T of this scheme corresponds to 4 measures, or $T = 4T''$. Then subject A must be composed from its respective thematic unit as $A16T''$; subject B, from its respective thematic unit as $B8T''$; and subject C has, in this case, the period equivalent of B, i.e., $C8T''$.

If the case under discussion is evolved on the basis of $\frac{4}{4}$ series, then the actual transformation of thematic units into subjects may be realized in the following form:

$$A16T'' = 4(4T'');$$
$$B8T'' = 2(4T''); \quad B8T'' = 4(2T'');$$
$$C8T'' = 2(4T''); \quad C8T'' = 4(2T'').$$

Let us take another scheme having different proportions from the one we have just discussed. Let it have two subjects whose time ratio is 3. Then: $A_19T + B_13T + A_23T + B_2T$. Here, too, A_1 and B_1 constitute the original subjects (as having maximal coefficients of duration), and A_2 and B_2, their respective modifications. Thus A_2 and B_2 appear to be the temporal contractions of A_1 and B_1.

Assuming $T = 4T''$, we obtain the following thematic groups:

$$A = 36T''; \; A_2 = 12T'';$$
$$B = 12T''; \; B_2 = 4T''.$$

The transformation of thematic units into subjects may be realized in the following form:

$$A = 9(4T''); \quad B = 3(4T'')$$

Now we shall take a case where the full subject does not appear in its first exposition. Let the scheme of thematic continuity be: $(A+B+C) + (B+C+A) + (C+A+B)$, and the temporal coefficient-group be: $3 + 1 + 2$.

Then: $(A_1 3T + B_1 T + C_1 2T) + (B_2 3T + C_2 T + A_2 2T) +$
$+ (C_3 3T + A_3 T + B_3 2T)$.

In this case: $A_1 = 3T; \; A_2 = 2T; \; A_3 = T \;$;
$ B_1 = T \;; \; B_2 = 3T; \; B_3 = 2T;$
$ C_1 = 2T; \; C_2 = T \;; \; C_3 = 3T.$

Thus each thematic unit has a maximal duration in a different exposition.

Therefore:

$$A_1 \equiv A; \; B_2 \equiv B; \; C_3 \equiv C.$$

This means that the full form of subject A appears in its first exposition, after which modification of this subject takes place; that the full form of subject B appears in its second exposition, and therefore B in its first and third expositions is a temporal contraction of the original B; that the full form of subject C appears only in its last (third) exposition, and therefore C in its first two expositions appears in the form of temporal contractions of the original C.

B. Transformation of Subjects into their Modified Variants

A subject can be modified with respect to its two basic components: time and pitch.

1. Temporal Modification of a Subject.

Temporal modification of a subject affects its period, but not the form of its temporal organization. The various thematic groups of a subject, corresponding to the different expositions of it in thematic continuity, are the temporally-contracted variants or portions of the original.

Our immediate technical problem lies in the definition of the method by which temporally-contracted versions of the original subject may be obtained. The shortening of the subject can be accomplished in two different ways:

(a) by reducing the value of the duration-unit;
(b) by dissecting the subject into its original thematic units, or even shorter fragments, and by using such units instead of the entire subject.

The first technique must be applied in full accordance with the style of temporal organization of the subject. If such style is associated with 2 or any multiple thereof, the coefficient of contraction must be 1/2, 1/4, . . .; if it is associated with 3 or any multiple thereof, the coefficient of contraction must be 1/3, 1/9, . . .; in the case of hybrid series, any of the multiples constituting such a series can be used as the coefficient of contraction. For example, if the set of coefficients controlling temporal organization of thematic continuity is associated with 6, not as the determinant of the $\frac{6}{6}$ series but as a product of 2 by 3, either 1/2 or 1/3 may be used as the coefficient of contraction. It is also appropriate to rely on any of the members of one summation-series if one of its members is the determinant.

For example, a temporal organization evolved from $r_{5 \div 3}$ can be contracted by means of such coefficients as 1/3, 1/5, and also 1/2 or 1/8, as 2 and 8 participate in the same (first) summation-series.

Empirically this form of temporal contraction can be performed directly in musical notation. In *Symphonic Rhumba** by Paul Lavalle, a student of this system, the entire subject consisting of 64T″, is contracted in its second exposition by the coefficient 1/2, thus resulting in a 32T″ structure. The style of the temporal organization of this composition is a hybrid of $\frac{8}{8}$ and $\frac{4}{4}$ series.

The second technique consists of *fragmentation of the subject*. Such fragmentation must be performed in accordance with the characteristics of the respective temporal structure. In some cases the thematic unit itself may be dissected further into the units of measures (T″). The most perfect results of fragmentation of the subject are obtained in all cases where temporal coefficients are the terms of an involution-group.

While performing the fragmentation of a subject, it is important to consider which particular fragment is most appropriate for a certain exposition. With regard to this, we offer the following method of selection: if a fragmentary exposition of the subject is at the beginning (or close to the beginning) of the entire thematic continuity, it is preferable to use its *first fragment;* if such an exposition of the subject is located in the center (or close to the center) of the entire thematic continuity, it is preferable to use the *middle fragment* of the subject; if a fragmentary exposition of the subject appears at the end (or near the end) of the entire thematic continuity, it is preferable to use the *last fragment.*

We shall demonstrate this technique in practical application. Let us apply it to the case of three subjects in direct recurrence where the temporal coefficients are $(2 + 1 + 1)^2$. Then:

$$(A_14T + B_12T + C_12T) + (A_22T + B_2T + C_2T) + (A_32T + B_3T + C_3T).$$

This calls for the following forms of fragmentation:

$$A2T = \frac{A4T}{2}; \; BT = \frac{B2T}{2}; \; CT = \frac{C2T}{2}.$$

*Performed by the N. Y. A. Symphony on WNYC 8-11-40 and later by the NBC Sym- phony under Frank Black, and by the NBC Symphony under Leopold Stokowski.

Then, considering the requirements stated above, we acquire the following scheme of fragmentation, related to the sequence of thematic groups:

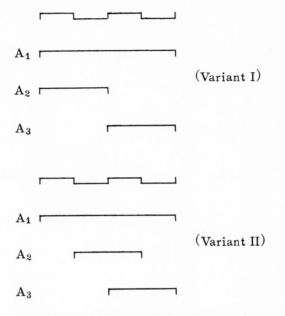

(Variant I)

(Variant II)

Figure 43. Fragmentation schemes.

This can be expressed as follows:

Var. I: $A_14T + \ldots + A_2(T_1 + T_2) + \ldots + A_3(T_3 + T_4)$
Var. II: $A_14T + \ldots + A_2(T_2 + T_3) + \ldots + A_3(T_3 + T_4)$

Variant I may be preferable because of its symmetry. Likewise:

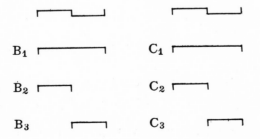

Figure 44. A symmetrical variant.

The entire thematic continuity (using Var. I for A) can be expressed as follows:

$$(A_1 4T + B_1 2T + C_1 2T) + (A_2 T_1 T_2 + B_2 T_1 + C_2 T_1) +$$
$$+ (A_3 T_3 T_4 + B_3 T_2 + C_3 T_2).$$

We shall now apply this technique to three subjects in circular permutations, and have $T = (1+2+1)^2$. Then: $(A_1 T + B_1 2T + C_1 T) + (B_2 2T + C_2 4T + A_2 2T) + (C_3 T + A_3 2T + B_3 T)$.

This scheme requires the following forms of fragmentation:

$$AT = \frac{A2T}{2}; \ BT = \frac{B2T}{2}; \ CT = \frac{C4T}{4}$$

These forms of fragmentation may be graphically presented as follows:

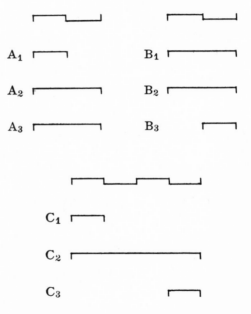

Figure 45. Forms of fragmentation.

The entire thematic continuity can be represented as follows:

$$(A_1 T_1 + B_1 2T + C_1 T_1) + (B_2 2T + C_2 4T + A_2 2T) + (C_3 T_4 + A_3 2T + B_3 T_2).$$

Forms of progressive symmetry yield perfect results from the subjects of equal period, like $T(A) = T(B) = T(C) = \ldots$; nevertheless fragmentation is applicable to such cases as well.

Let us take the form of progressive symmetry based on three subjects, and let us subject A, B and C to the same form of fragmentation: $2 + 1 + 1$. Then:

$$A_1 = 2T = T_1 + T_2; \ A_2 = T = T_3; \ A_3 = T = T_4;$$
$$B_1 = 2T = T_1 + T_2; \ B_2 = T = T_3; \ B_3 = T = T_4;$$
$$C_1 = 2T = T_1 + T_2; \ C_2 = T = T_3; \ C_3 = T = T_4.$$

The entire continuity assumes the following appearance:

$$A_1T_1T_2 + (A_2T_3 + B_1T_1T_2) + (A_3T_4 + B_2T_3 + C_1T_1T_2) +$$
$$+ (B_3T_4 + C_2T_3) + C_3T_4.$$

One of the most fruitful forms of fragmentation is the one which creates individual characteristics in the temporal behavior of the subject and, at the same time, offers temporal symmetry for the entire thematic continuity. For example:

$$A_1 = 2T; \ A_2 = T \ ; \ A_3 = T \ ;$$
$$B_1 = 4T; \ B_2 = 4T; \ B_3 = 4T;$$
$$C_1 = T \ ; \ C_2 = T \ ; \ C_3 = 2T.$$

This scheme of fragmentation can be arranged into a form of sequent temporal symmetry. For example:

$$A_1T_1T_2 + (A_2T_3 + B_14T) + (A_3T_4 + B_24T + C_1T_1) + (B_34T + C_2T_2) +$$
$$+ C_3T_3T_4.$$

In this case subject A, in its consecutive groups (expositions), undergoes an increasing fragmentation (decline); subject B remains constantly at its maximal duration (period) in all its consecutive groups (expositions); and subject C, in its behavior, reciprocates subject A, i.e., its consecutive groups (expositions) undergo a decreasing fragmentation.

Many other schemes of fragmentation can be evolved for the various forms of thematic sequence. The preceding illustrations are sufficient to start the future composer on his way to further exploration.

2. Intonational Modification of a Subject.

The process of fragmentation of a subject can be combined with intonational modification of it. Intonational modification takes place even in the absence of fragmentation. The experience of our musical past shows that when a subject has several expositions, in the course of the entire thematic continuity, it usually undergoes intonational modification. These modifications depend on the character of the musical culture, on its technical equipment in harmony, composition, etc. In plain chant, for example, intonational modification results in the modal variation; in the 18th Century—in "musical curls" of the Baroque, i.e., in the excessive use of melismas; in Wagner and his successors—in reharmonization; and even before Wagner—in modulatory key-changes. Thus, in the traditional sonata form of the early 19th Century, the second subject, usually appearing in the key of dominant in the exposition, reappears in the key of the tonic in the recapitulation.

With the technical equipment in the possession of a student of this theory, numerous intonational modifications can be applied to the successive expositions of a subject, thus making possible a sufficient variety even when the same subject reappears many times.

Among the techniques devised for the intonational modification of a subject, these are most essential:

(a) permutation of pitch-units within thematic units or within the entire subject; such permutations affect M, H and $\frac{M}{H}$, as well as CP;

(b) modal transposition and scale-modification in general; this is accomplished by direct change of accidentals;

(c) tonal expansion;

(d) quadrant rotation: geometric and tonal inversions;

(e) variations achieved by means of directional units and other resources of melodic figuration (chromatization of the original, which is not chromatic, is one of the most important techniques);

(f) variation of $\frac{M}{H}$ tension, which is equivalent to reharmonization.

It is advisable to use the above resources very sparingly in order not to overwhelm the listener, to whom an overabundance of technical devices may appear chaotic. The best path to follow within such limitations is to leave some of the subjects without any intonational modifications, and to subject others to individually specialized techniques. For instance, a certain theme A may be modified in the course of its various expositions with respect to quadrant rotation; another theme B may be left without any changes whatever; while a third theme C may be subjected, in its consecutive expositions, to modal variations, etc.

Besides the temporal and the intonational modifications of a subject, other forms of modification take place in the course of thematic continuity. These other modifications are based on the techniques of instrumental resources, and are inevitable in every composition. As this matter was sufficiently discussed in the *Composition of Thematic Units*,* and as we are now not discussing the technique of orchestration, initiative in using instrumental resources, as the technique for modifying a thematic group, must be left to the composer. He can make his decision on the matter of distribution of density, instrumental forms, dynamics, attack-forms, etc.

*See p. 1279 ff.

C. Axial Synthesis of Thematic Continuity

Axial synthesis corresponds to intonational coordination of thematic continuity on the basis of the selection of key-axes for all thematic groups as they appear in final continuity.

In classical music the key-axes followed what are known as tonic, dominant, subdominant, mediant, etc. Academic theorists prescribe such a key-selection. But the point is that a great many classical themes were based on the arpeggio forms of major and minor triads, i.e., $S_1(5)$ and $S_2(5)$ and their inversions, and for this reason such rules are of no consequence today when the forms of tonality are so diversified. Yet in the case of classical composers, rules or no rules, such a key-selection is *thematic;* and that is what really counts.

As an example we may refer to Beethoven's "Pathetique" piano sonata where the second subject of the first movement is based on $S_2(\begin{smallmatrix}6\\4\end{smallmatrix})$; the first subject of the second movement has a harmonic arrangement in the three upper parts of an $S_1(\begin{smallmatrix}6\\4\end{smallmatrix})$; and the first subject of the final movement is also based on an arpeggio of $S_2(\begin{smallmatrix}6\\4\end{smallmatrix})$. This in itself would not be of any consequence. But it is to be noted, first of all, that it is very typical of Beethoven to build important melodic patterns on the instrumental forms of $S(\begin{smallmatrix}6\\4\end{smallmatrix})$; and secondly, such a choice on his part is thematic and not based on any academic prejudice. Indeed, in the above mentioned Sonata in C-minor, the key-sequence of the first movement follows the pitch-units of $cS_2(5)$, i.e., c, eb and g. The first subject is in C-minor (with c-axis as the pedal point in the bass); the second subject is in Eb-minor; the third subject is in Eb-major—and so is the following subject. At the end of what is usually called an exposition, there is a bridge in G-minor. The introduction is in C-minor.

This type of evidence leads us to the conclusion that to regard any system of key-axes as universal, is basically wrong. The only correct way to select a key-axis system is to derive such a system from the thematic material of intonation, which, being individually different in each particular case, results in an individual key-axis system for each individual composition. The intonational interdependence between some important thematic unit, or master-pattern of melody or harmony, and the sequence of key-axes is a necessary characteristic of intonational unity of style. An excellent example of such unity—overlooked by all critics and analysts—is the intonational interdependence between the key-sequence of the second section of the first subject and the master-pattern of the subject with which "Venusberg" music begins in Wagner's overture to *Tannhäuser*. The pattern is based on the symmetry of the $\sqrt[4]{2}$ (four tonics), or a diminished seventh-chord, if you wish.

To follow such a principle of thematic interdependence of intonations between the part and the whole, is to select a set of pitch-units from a characteristic thematic unit, and to assign such a set as a system of key-axes.

It is necessary to indicate at this point that the real key-axes do not always coincide with the officially established tonalities. If a subject or a thematic group appears in the d_0 of a natural C-major, and the next portion of continuity, or the next thematic group, represents the position ⓓ of that group, key-axes are on c in both cases, though the second thematic group acquires four additional accidentals (4♭). The reason for this is our definition of scale and axis-transposition, as offered in the *Theory of Pitch-Scales.** We consider a scale with a c-axis, though read c − d♭ − e♭ − f − g − a♭ − b♭, which happens to be Phrygian (i.e., d₂), in the key of C.

So long as the composer adheres to the method of key-axis selection, through thematic interrelation of intonations, the concrete choice of an individual key-system is his.

CHAPTER 14

PLANNING A COMPOSITION

THE chief practical advantage of scientific planning over intuitive creation lies in the fact that, regardless of the value of intuition *per se*, scientific planning can be accomplished at any time and is independent of inspiration. For this reason, scientific method is more to be associated with professional performance, as such performance requires the achievement of high quality with regard to time consumed. Intuitive creation is beyond the artist's control. He cannot guarantee the amount of time which will be required in order to write a certain composition, nor can he guarantee the quality of the prospective work; moreover, even though the first two requirements may be satisfactorily fulfilled, the character of the work, when completed, may not possess the required characteristics.

The elements of an intuitively conceived composition, in actuality, are not elements, but *a priori* synthesized complexes. Their fitness is a matter of chance, and the remolding or fitting of such complexes, in order to meet specific requirements, usually calls for considerable effort.

Planning of a musical composition begins with "time." But "time" is one of the most elusive notions of humanity. Contemporary physics is lost in the maze of "times" it has created to solve its problems—the maze of definitions and classifications of time with respect to motion. But in addition to all these concepts of "subjective" and "objective" time (with which the student may acquaint himself through the lucid presentation by Sir Arthur Eddington in *The Nature of Physical World*) there is a concept of "psychological time" which we encounter in our daily existence.

Empirical time with which the composer has to deal, like everything else the composer has to deal with, has two sides. One aspect is physical, constitutes the excitor and is subject to measurement; the other, psychological, constitutes the reaction and is subject to experience. The quasi-objective, physical or clock-time, as encountered by the composer, is but an artificially isolated fragment of temporal manifold. This form of empirical time constitutes a concept by which events and their sequence are measured. It is conceived as one-dimensional and empirically irreversible.

When we think we reverse time, in actuality we only reverse the course of events. The direction of perceptible time remains irreversible. In the end, everything is subjective, as we cannot perceive time as such, but only as temporal configurations (events), taking their course in time. We perceive music as motion because there are in music continuous changes of temporal configurations. But we know from physics that motion perceived as "continuous" (in the mathematical sense) actually consists of an infinite number of phases, each of which, taken by itself, is stationary.

[1351]

The physical constitution of music, as perceived temporally, is not the composer's concern, as he deals with the perceptive side of music, its psychological form, which is always a continuum. The only knowledge of practical importance to a composer, involves two concepts of time: the physical and the psychological. The physical time of musical composition is measured by the clock. The psychological time of musical composition is measured by the *degree of saturation of physical time, by the temporal configurations of sound (or sound in its relation to silence).*

We know from a study of psychology that the intensity of a reaction is in direct relation to the frequency of impulses stimulating such a reaction. Experience shows that it is equally true of reactions to impulses of a more complex form. If we look upon the subjects of a musical composition as complex impulses, the frequency of such "thematic impulses" has a similar effect upon the formation of psychological reactions. The effect of hearing a few thematic groups, each characterized by a relatively high temporal stability in a relatively long period of "physical" time, produces an effect of psychologically "empty" time, i.e., time during which few events take place, or "uneventful" time. The opposite may also be true. The effect of time being eventful is due to the presence of many thematic impulses in a relatively brief period of clock-time. In this case, time appears to be saturated with events.

It follows from this reasoning that the length of a relatively short musical composition (as measured by the clock) psychologically largely depends upon the *degree of its thematic saturation.* This is the basis on which rests the quantitative characteristic of musical composition, i.e., the number of subjects and thematic groups necessary to produce certain effects contemplated by the composer.

Crowding of events into a relatively brief time-period was successfully accomplished in the polyphonic compositions of the 18th Century in the form of *stretto*, which is a form of thematic overlapping. In J. S. Bach's Fugue No. 5, *Well-Tempered Clavichord*, Vol. II, the entire composition consists of successive groups (expositions) with systematically progressive overlapping. The interval between the theme and the reply contracts itself in the following way: $12t + 8t + + 4t + 2t$; this contraction is carried out in both major and minor, major preceding minor.

Temporal saturation achieved by means of overlapping of the thematic groups is quite an ancient device. It was successfully employed by the Roman, Lucius Apuleius in his novel "The Golden Ass."

Thirty years of my own life have been devoted to a study of temporal structures as they appear in various phenomena, including literature, plays, cinema, and music. I would like to refer to two examples of the temporal saturation of musical form, as they appear in two of my compositions for piano. One of them is "Heroic Poem" from "Five Pieces, Op. 12."[*] In this composition, which requires only three minutes of performance, events are so crowded that even experts greatly overestimate the actual clock-time of performance. In

[*]Published by U.S.S.R. State Publishing Dept. and in Universal Edition of Vienna.

another composition, "Sonata-Rhapsody, Op. 17," events, besides being numerous, temporally overlap one another and merge one into another—one event taking another's place (like the "dissolve" in cinematic montage). This composition, in its temporal structure, more resembles a novel than a sonata. It attempts to project a whole epoch into 9 minutes of performance.*

I shall add to the observations above that it is a virtue to make a brief composition appear more eventful than its clock-time period would seem to permit, but that the opposite is the greatest sin a composer can commit.

The planning of a musical composition can be generally accomplished in 10 successive stages:

(1) Decision as to the clock-time duration of the entire composition.
(2) Decision as to the degree of temporal saturation.
(3) Decision as to the number of subjects and thematic groups.
(4) Decision as to the form of thematic sequence.
(5) Temporal definition and distribution of thematic groups.
(6) Organization of temporal continuity.
(7) Composition of thematic units.
(8) Composition of thematic groups.
(9) Intonational coordination (axial synthesis) of thematic continuity.
(10) Instrumental development.

A. CLOCK-TIME DURATION OF A COMPOSITION

Clock-time duration of a composition represents its dimensional aspect.

In architecture we define the space needed for a structure by the type of structure we plan to design. It may be an office building of many stories, it may be a cathedral, it may be a one-family house, or it may be a tent.

Likewise, in music, we define the necessary amount of clock-time, depending on the type of composition. An opera may occupy several hours of performance; a cantata or an oratorio may occupy a half or a whole of the concert program; a symphony usually lasts between 20 and 40 minutes; short instrumental or vocal compositions range from one to ten minutes; cues in radio-plays often are only a few seconds long. Thus, the first decision the composer has to make concerns the temporal dimension of a composition. If the form is "cyclic," i.e., consisting of several movements (like sonata, suite, symphony, oratorio, opera), the duration of the total composition must be determined first.

The next step consists of the definition of a common duration unit. It is my belief that in order to achieve perfect temporal coordination of the whole, it is necessary to work out the entire composition from homogeneous temporal units instead of the customary "tempo" modifications. It is over-optimistic for a composer to expect a performer or conductor to achieve the tempo he had in mind. Most performers are neglectful of the metronome indications provided

---

*Sonata-Rhapsody, Op. 17 for piano solo, has been widely acclaimed by critics (since its first performance in 1925) as 'a composition of overwhelming power, and has been performed on symphonic programs. (Ed.)

by the composer. For this reason the most practical thing to do is to establish *one tempo* for the entire composition (even if it consists of several movements), and to produce the *apparent effects of mobility* by assigning different coefficients of duration to the common duration-unit (t). Thus, one subject, or movement will appear in a fast tempo because the coefficient of duration is one, i.e., $t' = t$; another subject will appear in an intermediate tempo due to the respective value of the coefficient of duration ($t' = 2t$; $t' = 3t$); . . . In the same way the effect of a very slow tempo can be achieved by using a still greater coefficient of duration, such as $t' = 4t$; $t' = 5t$; $t' = 6t$; . . .

I used this form of notation instead of the tempo changes in my Symphonic Rhapsody, *October* (1927), and found it very profitable. In this particular composition, the shortest $t' = t = $ ♪ and the longest $t' = 16t = $ ♩ . Of course, ultimately, t (the original duration-unit) has to be defined by the clock and, together with all forms of t' (derivative duration-units), translated into the appropriate symbols of musical notation. Thus, for example, if the total duration of a composition is 3 minutes, and t = 1/4 second, such a composition contains $180 \cdot 4 = 720$ t.

B. TEMPORAL SATURATION OF A COMPOSITION

Temporal saturation is in direct relation to the *quantity of thematic groups*. This is true of both monothematic and polythematic continuity.

Thus, a monothematic composition consisting of one thematic group has a minimum of temporal saturation. Among the numerous compositions of this kind, J. S. Bach's *Aria on the G-string* for Violin can be mentioned as an outstanding example. Such forms belong to the category of "through-composed" music and have been extensively exploited by our outstanding contemporaries.

It must be obvious to students of this system that an extensive temporal form, which is monothematic and homogeneous, can be easily accomplished by means of various forms of interference. Its intonation can be evolved from any of the sources, such as MP designed from a scale or a set of scales, from a plotted melody (in this case being the entire composition), from melodization, rhythmicized harmony, counterpoint, etc.

Higher degrees of temporal saturation can be achieved either through the development of thematic groups, or through introducing more subjects.

Temporal saturation of a subject depends on the quantity of attacks. Subjects containing more attacks must be considered more saturated subjects. Thus, for example, if two adjacent movements of the same composition (as in a suite) have the same total period and are both monothematic, there is still a way to make one of them appear longer, i.e., by assigning to this particular movement a greater number of attacks.

In order to produce an effect of considerable saturation in a monothematic composition, it is necessary to evolve a number of thematic groups from the subject. This can be accomplished by various means, such as geometrical inversions, modal transpositions, tonal expansions, reharmonizations, instrumental variations, etc.

In polythematic compositions, a considerably higher degree of temporal saturation is due to the presence of a greater number of subjects. In this case, while each of the subjects may have a more limited number of thematic groups than is necessary in monothematic continuity, the appearance of a higher degree of temporal saturation may nevertheless be produced.

Further increase of temporal saturation in a polythematic composition can be accomplished either by increasing the number of subjects, or by increasing the number of expositions of each subject without increasing the number of the latter.

C. Selection of the Number of Subjects and Thematic Groups

After the composer has made his decision as to the form of temporal saturation of the prospective composition, his next step involves selection of the number of subjects and thematic groups. There are several situations which may be encountered in this selective process.

The first question is: shall all subjects have only one thematic group. The second question is: shall all subjects, or only some of them, have more than one thematic group. The next question is: how many thematic groups shall each subject have respectively. The last question implies the dominance of certain subjects over others, as the subject which has more thematic groups will *ipso facto* become a stronger thematic impulse.

Interrelations of the number of subjects and their respective thematic groups become a problem of temporal ratios. For example, the composer has decided to have two subjects: A and B. He wants A to dominate over B in $2 \div 1$ ratio. Then the number of thematic groups of A is 2, and the number of thematic groups of B is 1. Under the same ratio, however, the absolute quantity of thematic groups can be doubled, tripled, quadrupled, etc. Then the composer would have the following possible forms of selection:

$$2A, \quad B;$$
$$4A, \quad 2B;$$
$$6A, \quad 3B;$$
$$8A, \quad 4B;$$
$$\cdots \cdots$$

In each case there are several forms of distribution of the thematic sequence, but this we shall discuss later.

Now let us imagine that the composer has arrived at the decision to have four subjects: A, B, C and D. The next decision he has to make concerns the selection of a quadrinomial ratio. Suppose he chooses: $3 \div 1 \div 2 \div 2$ for A, B, C and D respectively. Then he may select any of the following schemes, representing the absolute quantities of thematic groups and equivalent to the above quadrinomial ratio:

$$3A, \quad B, \quad 2C, \quad 2D;$$
$$6A, \quad 2B, \quad 4C, \quad 4D;$$
$$9A, \quad 3B, \quad 6C, \quad 6D;$$
$$12A, \quad 4B, \quad 8C, \quad 8D;$$
$$\cdots \cdots \cdots \cdots$$

It is easy to see that either the number of subjects in a composition dominates the number of thematic groups, or the number of thematic groups dominates the number of subjects. In planning this particular aspect of a musical composition, we may arrive at various propositions which will prove valuable in different situations. For example, we may arrive at a condition (useful in a certain special case) in which the maximum number of thematic groups of one individual subject must not exceed the total number of subjects—so that in the event of three subjects, none of the subjects is allowed to have more than three expositions.

This is just an indication of the type of situation which the composer is compelled to work out for himself in each individual case. My system does not circumscribe the composer's freedom, but merely points out the methodological way to arrive at a decision. Any decision which results in a harmonic relation is fully acceptable. We are opposed only to vagueness and haphazard speculation.

Other illustrations of the conditions which control the relation of the number of subjects and their expositions.

(a) The quantity of exposition corresponds to the order of appearance of the subject:

Three subjects: A, B and C.

If the sequence is A + B + C for the subjects alone and does not involve the problem of temporal distribution of all thematic groups, then A, appearing first, is assigned to one exposition; B, appearing next, is assigned to two expositions; C, appearing last, is assigned to three expositions, i.e., A, 2B, 3C.

(b) The same proposition can be reversed: 3A, 2B, C.

(c) The quantity of exposition of each subject is one half of the total number of subjects:

Four subjects: A, B, C and D.
2A, 2B, 2C, 2D, as $\frac{4}{2} = 2$.

(d) The quantity of exposition for each respective subject is assigned on the basis of the arithmetical mean. Let us have 3 subjects, and let the number of expositions of the subject B be an arithmetical mean. Let A have four expositions, and let C have one half of this number; then B acquires 3 expositions, as: $\frac{4+2}{2} = 3$. Then the quantities of respective exposition are: 4A, 3B, 2C.

D. SELECTION OF A THEMATIC SEQUENCE

After the number of subjects and the quantity of their respective expositions have been defined, we obtain the total number of thematic groups. The next procedure deals with the form of thematic sequence into which all the thematic groups must be arranged.

Each individual case of the number of subjects and their respective expositions offers several possible forms of distribution. Let us start with a simple case first. Suppose the thematic selection is: 2A and B. In attempting to match the possible forms of distribution with the above quantities, we acquire the following solutions:

(a) $A_1 + B + A_2$;
(b) $A_1 + A_2 + B$;
(c) $B + A_1 + A_2$.

Obviously, case (a) is preferable because it offers a symmetric arrangement.

Under the same binomial ratio we may have: 4A and 2B. These can be distributed in the following manner:

(a) $(A_1 + B_1 + A_2) + (A_3 + B_2 + A_4)$;
(b) $(A_1 + A_2 + B_1) + (B_2 + A_3 + A_4)$;
(c) $(B_1 + A_1 + A_2) + (A_3 + A_4 + B_2)$;
(d) $A_1 + B_1 + B_2 + A_2 + A_3 + A_4$.

The first three cases are desirable since they are symmetric.

Let us discuss another case: 3A, B, 2C, 2D. This is a more elaborate quantitative group and requires a more elaborate distributive form. In order to evolve a symmetric form of distribution of the sequence, we must assign symmetric places to each letter individually:

$$A \ldots A \ldots A$$
$$B$$
$$C \ldots C$$
$$D \ldots D$$

In this case perfect symmetry is impossible, as B has no recurrences to reciprocate. But forms of nearly perfect symmetry are possible:

(a) $A_1 + C_1 + D_1 + B + A_2 + D_2 + C_2 + A_3$
(b) $A_1 + D_1 + C_1 + B + A_2 + C_2 + D_2 + A_3$
(c) $A_1 + C_1 + D_1 + A_2 + B + D_2 + C_2 + A_3$
(d) $A_1 + D_1 + C_1 + A_2 + B + C_2 + D_2 + A_3$

As soon as these quantities are doubled, symmetry becomes possible: 6A, 2B, 4C, 4D.

(a) $(A_1 + C_1 + D_1 + A_2 + D_2 + C_2 + A_3) + B_1 + B_2 +$
$+ (A_4 + C_3 + D_3 + A_5 + D_4 + C_4 + A_6)$
(b) $(A_1 + C_1 + C_2 + A_2 + D_1 + D_2 + A_3) + B_1 + B_2 +$
$+ (A_4 + D_3 + D_4 + A_5 + C_3 + C_4 + A_6)$
(c) $(A_1 + B_1 + C_1 + A_2 + D_1 + D_2 + A_3) + C_2 + C_3 +$
$+ (A_4 + D_3 + D_4 + A_5 + C_4 + B_2 + A_6)$
(d) $(A_1 + C_1 + C_2 + A_2 + B_1 + D_1 + A_3) + D_2 + D_3 +$
$+ (A_4 + D_4 + B_2 + A_5 + C_3 + C_4 + A_6)$

Let us now distribute the case: 4A, 3B, 2C.

$$A \ . \ . \ . \ A \ . \ . \ . \ . \ . \ . \ . \ . \ . \ . \ A \ . \ . \ . \ A$$
$$B \ . \ . \ . \ . \ . \ B \ . \ . \ . \ . \ . \ . \ B$$
$$C \ . \ . \ . \ C$$

From this we obtain the following forms:

(a) $(A_1 + B_1 + A_2) + (C_1 + B_2 + C_2) + (A_3 + B_3 + A_4)$
(b) $(A_1 + B_1 + C_1 + A_2) + B_2 + (A_3 + C_2 + B_3 + A_4)$

Inititative in constructing symmetric forms of distribution is the ability which composers must cultivate.

The composer can also make his choice directly from the forms of thematic sequence as they were presented in chapter 9 of Part Two of the Theory of Composition. Of course, such schemes have a pre-conceived quantity of exposition for each subject.

E. Temporal Distribution of Thematic Groups

The sum of durations of all thematic groups constitutes the duration of the entire composition. As each subject may have one or more expositions, the temporal coefficient of each subject, at first, must include all the expositions of such a subject. The temporal ratio consists of the number of terms corresponding to the number of subjects.

Thus, a thematic selection of A and B requires a binomial time ratio, regardless of the number of expositions of each subject. Temporal ratio in this case expresses the relation of the period of all expositions of A to the period of all expositions of B.

The simplest instance of temporal relations is that in which all the expositions of all subjects have the same period. In such a case, the dominance of some subjects over others is expressed solely through the number of expositions of such subjects in relation to other subjects.

In a scheme of $4A + 2B$, with identical periods for all expositions of A and all expositions of B, the ratio of temporal dominance of the subject A over subject B is still 2. Assuming that the thematic sequence of this composition is symmetric, we obtain the following as one of the possible schemes of temporal distribution:

$$(A_1T + B_1T + A_2T) + (A_3T + B_2T + A_4T)$$

Such a scheme can be expressed as: $\overrightarrow{T} = 4A4T + 2B2T$. The realization of this scheme consists of division of the period of the entire composition by 6. Assuming that $\overrightarrow{T} = 3$ minutes, we obtain the following period for each exposition: $\frac{180}{6} = 30$ seconds.

As the total duration of this composition consists of 4A and 2B, we can define the total duration of A as 4/6 and the total duration of B as 2/6.

In other words, if the temporal ratio is $2 \div 1$ for the two subjects, A takes 2/3 and B takes 1/3 of the entire composition. This reasoning is based on the fact that $2+1 = 3$, and therefore the $2 \div 1$ ratio belongs to $\frac{3}{3}$ series.

Now if we should decide that the total period of A equals the total period of B, such a decision would imply a different temporal distribution. In this case, then, $\overrightarrow{T}(4A) = \overrightarrow{T}(2B)$. Hence: $\frac{\overrightarrow{T}}{2} = \frac{180}{2} = 90$ seconds. Then the duration of each exposition of A is: $A = \frac{90}{4} = 22 \cdot 5$; the duration of each exposition of B is: $B = \frac{90}{2} = 45$. But this is true only if all the expositions of A have an identical period, and all the expositions of B have their own identical period. In some cases, the various expositions of one subject may have different temporal coefficients. Then the number of terms in such a ratio equals the number of expositions of its respective subject.

Let $3 + 1 + 2 + 2$ be the temporal coefficient group for the four expositions of A, and $3 + 1$, the coefficient group for the two expositions of B. As $3 + 1 + 2 + 2 = 8$ and the period of $4A = 90$, we find the following periods for the individual expositions of A:

$$T(A_1) = \frac{90 \cdot 3}{8} = \frac{45 \cdot 3}{4} = \frac{135}{4} = 33 \tfrac{3}{4};$$
$$T(A_2) = \frac{90}{8} = \frac{45}{4} = 11 \tfrac{1}{4};$$
$$T(A_3) = \frac{90 \cdot 2}{8} = \frac{45}{2} = 22 \tfrac{1}{2};$$
$$T(A_4) = \frac{90 \cdot 2}{8} = \frac{45}{2} = 22 \tfrac{1}{2};$$

Likewise the periods of the individual expositions of B appear as follows:

$$T(B_1) = \frac{90 \cdot 3}{4} = \frac{45 \cdot 3}{2} = \frac{135}{2} = 67 \tfrac{1}{2};$$
$$T(B_2) = \frac{90}{4} = \frac{45}{2} = 22 \tfrac{1}{2}.$$

Now we can represent the entire temporal scheme of this composition in seconds:

$$\overrightarrow{T} = A_1 33.75 + B_1 67.5 + A_2 11.25 + A_3 22:5 + B_2 22.5 + A_4 22.5$$

As the period of 4A equals the period of 4B, we can represent this also in the ratio equivalents, by multiplying $3+1$ by 2. $\overrightarrow{T} = A_1 3T + B_1 6T + A_2 T + A_3 2T + B_2 2T + A_4 2T$.

In chapter 11 (Temporal Organization of Thematic Sequence), we discussed many possible approaches in translating thematic sequences into temporal ratios. In the present discussion, we are primarily concerned with subdividing the entire period of the composition into temporal sections corresponding to the individual expositions, subordinated to a certain form of temporal organization conceived *a priori*.

This makes it possible to proceed with the planning of a composition in a different sequence. For example, we can take some temporal group, assume its total duration to correspond to the duration of the whole composition and its single terms, to the successive expositions. After this we can proceed with the selection of the number of subjects and their expositions. The latter must be in some simple correspondence with the number of terms of the temporal group. Often such groups offer more than one practical solution. In such a case the decision of the composer must be based on the desired degree of temporal saturation.

Many of the resultants of interference, particularly the r' which derives from ternary and quaternary synchronization, serve as practical temporal groups for such a procedure.

To illustrate this, let us take $r'_{3 \div 4 \div 7}$. This group consists of 12 terms, which permits numerous solutions for the different number of subjects and thematic groups. This resultant consists of the following terms: $r'_{3 \div 4 \div 7}$ = = $12+9+3+4+8+6+6+8+4+3+9+12$.

Assuming that our composition consists of two subjects, and both subjects have the same number of thematic groups, we acquire 6 expositions for each subject since $\frac{12}{2} = 6$. Then two basic forms of continuity become possible:

(a) direct recurrence:

$A_1 12T + B_1 9T + A_2 3T + B_2 4T + A_3 8T + B_3 6T + A_4 6T +$
$+ B_4 8T + A_5 4T + B_5 3T + A_6 9T + B_6 12T;$

(b) symmetric recurrence:

$A_1 12T + B_1 9T + A_2 3T + B_2 4T + A_3 8T + B_3 6T + B_4 6T +$
$+ A_4 8T + B_5 4T + A_5 3T + B_6 9T + A_6 12T.$

The same temporal group can be applied to three subjects, in which case each subject acquires 4 expositions, as $\frac{12}{3} = 4$.

Two forms of thematic continuity:

(a) direct recurrence:

$A_1 12T + B_1 9T + C_1 3T + A_2 4T + B_2 8T + C_2 6T +$
$+ A_3 6T + B_3 8T + C_3 4T + A_4 3T + B_4 9T + C_4 12T;$

(b) symmetric recurrence (taking the first two of the $\circlearrowleft$ circular permutations and inverting them about the axis):

$A_1 12T + B_1 9T + C_1 3T + B_2 4T + C_2 8T + A_2 6T +$
$+ A_3 6T + C_3 8T + B_3 4T + C_4 3T + B_4 9T + A_4 12T.$

As twelve is divisible by four, we can apply this temporal group to four subjects. This time, however, some subjects will dominate others.

We shall evolve our thematic sequences by arranging the letters in such a symmetry that four letters are supplemented by two of them, producing a group of six terms. By inverting this group about its temporal axis, we will obtain all 12 thematic groups for four subjects. In order to make A and B dominate over C and D, we shall repeat A and B after all four letters appear. This produces the following form of thematic sequence: $(A+B+C+D+A+B)$ + + $(B+A+D+C+B+A)$, in which there are 4A, 4B, 2C and 2D.

This thematic continuity assumes the following form:

$$A_1 12T + B_1 9T + C_1 3T + D_1 4T + A_2 8T + B_2 6T +$$
$$+ B_3 6T + A_3 8T + D_2 4T + C_2 3T + B_4 9T + A_4 12T.$$

In this case, the temporal dominance of A and B over C and D is due not only to the number of expositions of A and B but also to the total periods of these subjects:

$$T^{\rightarrow}(A) = 12T + 8T + 8T + 12T = 40T$$
$$T^{\rightarrow}(B) = 9T + 6T + 6T + 9T = 30T$$
$$T^{\rightarrow}(C) = 3T + 3T = 6T$$
$$T^{\rightarrow}(D) = 4T + 4T = 8T$$

An analogous treatment can be applied to the form of thematic sequence and continuity in which C and D become the dominant subjects. This requires the following arrangement of the thematic sequence: $(A+B+C+D+C+D) + (D+C+D+C+B+A)$. In this case, thematic continuity assumes the following form:

$$A_1 12T + B_1 9T + C_1 3T + D_1 4T + C_2 8T + D_2 6T +$$
$$+ D_3 6T + C_3 8T + D_4 4T + C_4 3T + B_2 9T + A_2 12T.$$

The temporal relations of the subjects appear as follows:

$$T^{\rightarrow}(A) = 12T + 12T = 24T$$
$$T^{\rightarrow}(B) = 9T + 9T = 18T$$
$$T^{\rightarrow}(C) = 3T + 8T + 8T + 3T = 22T$$
$$T^{\rightarrow}(D) = 4T + 6T + 6T + 4T = 20T$$

In this case the temporal dominance is more or less neutralized.

It is easy to see how such temporal groups, in their application of successive expositions, can be made useful in monothematic continuity—in which case they would influence the temporal relations of the different expositions of the same subject.

In all the above illustrations, T may represent any desirable duration-group.

One point concerning the general distribution of temporal groups remains to be discussed: *the distribution of climaxes.*

A musical composition may not contain any climaxes at all, or it may have one or more climaxes. Once it has one or more climaxes, proper distribution of the latter in thematic continuity becomes of utmost importance.

The problem of the distribution of climaxes is not limited to the climaxes appearing at the very beginning or the very end of a composition. It is the intermediate climaxes, appearing in the course of continuity, that require such distribution. The number of such climaxes (i.e., appearing in the course of continuity) is one less than the number of terms in the temporal ratio required for the respective distribution. Thus, a continuity containing one climax requires a binomial time ratio. The ratio itself must belong to the family to which the temporal structure of the entire composition belongs. Thus, in the $\frac{4}{4}$ series type of temporal structure, the position of the climax is determined by the ratio $3 \div 1$, i.e., the climax appears at the beginning of the last quarter of the entire composition. Likewise in a structure based on $\frac{8}{8}$ series, the ratio $5 \div 3$ determines the position of the climax, i.e., the climax appears at the beginning of the sixth eighth. It is always advisable to use the original form of the binomial—in which the first term has greater value than the second.

For the same reason two climaxes require a trinomial ratio, which ratio must be used in the form in which the values progressively decline.

In a structure based on $\frac{4}{4}$ series, the respective trinomial must be: $2 \div 1 \div 1$. Then the first climax appears at the beginning of the third quarter, and the second climax, at the beginning of the fourth quarter. Likewise, in a structure associated with $\frac{8}{8}$ series, the trinomial should be: $3+3+2$. The respective positions of climaxes in this case are: the first climax begins with the fourth eighth, the second climax, with the seventh eighth.

Indicating climax by the symbol Cl, we can express the two preceding cases as follows:

$$\text{(a)} \quad \frac{2T}{4} + Cl_1 + \frac{T}{4} + Cl_2 + \frac{T}{4};$$

$$\text{(b)} \quad \frac{3T}{8} = Cl_1 + \frac{3T}{8} + Cl_2 + \frac{2T}{8}.$$

The placing of the climax between the time-values means that the actual time for the climax (and its extension) is borrowed either from the preceding or the following term; and in some cases, the climax may itself extend over both (i.e., the preceding and the following) adjacent terms.

By taking temporal ratios with more terms, we can distribute more climaxes respectively. Thus, a temporal quintinomial becomes the tool for distributing four climaxes. For example, in the structure based on $\frac{8}{8}$ series, $2+2+2+1+1$ (which is one of the general permutations of the original quintinomial $2+1+2+ +1+2$ represented in declining values) offers the proper form of distribution of the four climaxes:

$$\frac{2T}{8} + Cl_1 + \frac{2T}{8} + Cl_2 + \frac{2T}{8} + Cl_3 + \frac{T}{8} + Cl_4 + \frac{T}{8}$$

Another basic form of the distribution of climaxes is based not on the individual ratios, but on proportions, i.e., *on the equalities of ratios*. This form of distribution of climaxes contributes the utmost temporal harmony to the entire composition.

Proportions are acquired in the forms of distributive involution-groups, i.e., squared and cubed binomials, trinomials, etc. In this case, the number of terms in the involution-group determines the number of climaxes.

In a temporal structure based on $\frac{4}{4}$ series, climaxes can be distributed as $(3+1)^2$, i.e., at $9T + Cl_1 + 3T + Cl_2 + 3T + Cl_3 + T$; in which case the common denominator of these values is 16.

In a temporal structure based on $\frac{8}{8}$ series, climaxes can be distributed as $(5+3)^2$, i.e., as $25T + Cl_1 + 15T + Cl_2 + 15T + Cl_3 + 9T$. Here the common denominator equals 64.

If the entire continuity is evolved from one or another type of acceleration-series, its climaxes can be distributed according to such a series. For example, a continuity consisting of 32T and evolved from the first summation-series can have its climaxes distributed as follows: $13 + 8 + 5 + 3 + 2 + 1$, i.e., $13T + Cl_1 + 8T + Cl_2 + 5T + Cl_3 + 3T + Cl_4 + 2T + Cl_5 + T$.

This discussion leads us to the conclusion that the composer has to make his decision with regard to desirability of climaxes, their number and distribution before he completes the final planning of the temporal organization of continuity.

The means by which the composition of climaxes can be accomplished does not belong to this section and will be discussed later.

F. REALIZATION OF CONTINUITY IN TERMS OF t AND t'

Subjects and their expositions vary not only in their temporal dimensions, but also in the dimensions of their duration-units. The dimension of duration-units may be in either *direct* or *inverse* relation to the dimension of the respective subject or its thematic groups. Nevertheless, once the dimension of a duration-unit for a certain subject is decided upon, it remains constant through all its expositions. As previously remarked, the duration-units from which the different subjects are constructed must be either identical or in simple relations with each other.

The original duration-unit (being at the same time the common denominator of the entire continuity) is designated as t, and all other duration-units of the same composition, as t'.

If the entire composition is associated with $\frac{2}{2}$, $\frac{4}{4}$, $\frac{8}{8}$, $\frac{16}{16}$, or other series of this class, the coefficients of duration for the various forms of t' usually acquire such factors as 2, 4, 8, . . . If the composition is associated with $\frac{3}{3}$, $\frac{9}{9}$, $\frac{27}{27}$, or other series of this class, the factors of t' usually are 3, 9, 27, . . . It is in this sense that one subject may be constructed from t as a duration-unit, another from t' = 2t as a duration-unit, and still another from t' = 4t as a duration-unit.

Once the respective t is translated into time equivalent, like 1/4 sec., all other forms of t' can be relatively defined, and ultimately, all forms of t and t' can be represented in musical notation.

Thus, for instance:

$$t'(A) = t = 1/4 \text{ sec.} = ♪ \ ;$$
$$t'(B) = 2t = 1/2 \text{ sec.} = ♩ \ ;$$
$$t'(C) = 4t = 1 \text{ sec.} = ♩ \ .$$

Before composing any rhythmic patterns of duration-groups for the respective subjects, we have to know the total number of duration-units in each particular subject taken at its maximal period.

Let us take a new scheme of three subjects; e.g.,

$$T^{\rightarrow}(A) = 16T; t'(A) = t = 1/4 \text{ sec.}$$
$$T^{\rightarrow}(B) = 16T; t'(B) = 4t = 1 \text{ sec.}$$
$$T^{\rightarrow}(C) = 16T; t'(C) = 2t = 1/2 \text{ sec.}$$

Then:

$T(A) = 16t;$
$T(B) = 4t';$
$T(C) = 8t';$

Hence:

$\overrightarrow{T}(A) = 16t \cdot 16 = 256t ;$
$\overrightarrow{T}(B) = 4t' \cdot 16 = 64t';$
$\overrightarrow{T}(C) = 8t' \cdot 16 = 128t'.$

In clock-time, all three subjects have the same period of 64 seconds; but psychologically the degree of temporal saturation varies with each subject, B representing the geometric mean of the remaining two subjects. Thus, psychologically, the most eventful subject (if we use the same rhythmic pattern of durations for all three subjects) is A and the least eventful is B.

To illustrate this in the simplest imaginable way, we shall assign $T = r_{4 \div 3}$ to be the thematic duration-group for all three subjects. Then:

$T'(A) = 16T$
$T'(B) = 4T$
$T'(C) = 8T$

This means that A has a recurrence of the thematic rhythmic pattern 16 times. Such a recurrence can be of exact or modified form. The 16 modifications can be evolved on the basis of four circular permutations of the second order:

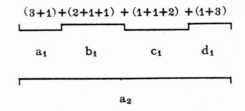

$$(3+1)+(2+1+1) + (1+1+2) +(1+3)$$

$a_1 \qquad b_1 \qquad c_1 \qquad d_1$

a_2

Figure 44. $T'(A) = 16T$.

Subject B has only 4 recurrences of the thematic rhythmic pattern. The latter may have either 4 direct recurrences or four circular permutations of the first order.

Subject C has 8 recurrences of the thematic rhythmic pattern. The latter may have either 8 direct recurrences, or four circular permutations of the first order with symmetric duplication:

abcd, bcda, cdab, dabc,
dabc, cdab, bcda, abcd   Or:
abcd, bcda, cdab, dabc,
cbad, badc, adcb, dcba.

If we count the number of impulses (which correspond to the individual terms or attacks of the thematic rhythmic pattern) in each subject individually, we acquire the following comparative table of temporal saturation for A, B and C.

As $T \equiv 10a$, the respective quantities of attacks (impulses) appear as follows:

$$T'(A) \equiv 10a \cdot 16 \equiv 160a;$$
$$T'(B) \equiv 10a \cdot 4 \equiv 40a;$$
$$T'(C) \equiv 10a \cdot 8 \equiv 80a.$$

Similar reasoning can be applied to subjects constructed from different thematic rhythmic patterns as well.

G. COMPOSITION OF THEMATIC UNITS

We have had a thorough discussion of this matter in chapter one of this book.* Here we simply approach the subject from a different angle. In our first discussion of the composition of thematic units, we put stress on the flexibility and the adaptability of thematic units to temporal expansion and contraction. When we approach the temporal structure of thematic groups from the viewpoint of the entire continuity of the composition, we have to evolve rhythmic patterns of duration-groups in such a manner that they will satisfy the total duration of a respective thematic group as it is expressed in terms of t'. This means that the form of a duration-group, in its total period, must equal the total time-period assigned for the respective thematic group. The same concerns the possible number of attacks which may result from the application of a thematic duration-group expressed in definite t'-units.

For example, if a thematic group consists of $20t'$, only certain forms of duration-groups are satisfactory. The easiest way to find such duration-groups is by finding the possible multiples producing 20 as a product. Such multiples are:

(a) $5 \cdot 4 = 20$; hence: $r_{5 \div 4}$;
(b) $2(5 \cdot 2) = 20$; hence: $2r_{5 \div 2}$;
(c) any 5T of the $\frac{4}{4}$ series;
(d) any 4T of the $\frac{5}{5}$ series.

The composer may also use his initiative in modifying various duration-groups in such a way that the sum of duration-units satisfies the case.

For example:

$$r_{5 \div 3} = 3+2+1+3+1+2+3 = 15;$$

The modified version achieved by the addition of 5, and distributed symmetrically $(2 + 1 + 2)$:

$$T = 3 + 2 + 3 + 4 + 3 + 2 + 3;$$
$$\text{or: } r_{7 \div 2} = 2 + 2 + 2 + 1 + 1 + 2 + 2 + 2 = 14;$$

*See p. 1279 ff.

the modified version achieved by the addition of 6, and distributed symmetrically
(2 + 1 + 1 + 2):

$$T = 4 + 2 + 2 + 2 + 2 + 2 + 2 + 4.$$

Examples of section F may serve as additional illustrations.

In a composition which contains climaxes and in whose scheme of temporal organization such climaxes are distributed *a priori*, it becomes necessary to pre-compose such climaxes for the respective subjects.

We have seen in the *Theory of Melody** that the melodic climax is a pitch-time maximum and is preceded by a resistance. We shall discuss here other important resources which produce climaxes.

As the main forms of resistance consist of rotary or centrifugal patterns, such patterns may be conceived as the bass of harmony (expressing some constant harmonic function and, thus, defining the tonal cycles, for instance); they either remain as bass or may be transferred into soprano (after the respective har-monization is completed). Another form of resistance produced by harmony consists of a group of tensions and releases, with an ultimate tension for the climax. Since centrifugal forms represent some of the most powerful forms of resistance, harmonic climaxes can be achieved by using such progressions as produce the respective configurations—for example, all cases of upper harmony ascending against a descending bass, or a pair of diverging harmonic strata. This, by the way, is one of the favorite devices of Beethoven, an example of which can be found in the third theme (E♭-major) of the first movement of the piano-sonata, *Pathetique*. In such forms, harmonic climax is represented by the max-imum interval between the strata, usually coupled with a high dynamic degree (f or f).

In addition to growth of tension of the harmonic structure and the diverging patterns of strata in motion, density plays an important role as a climax-builder. As the form of resistance, density either grows consistently or with delays, but reaches its climax at its maximum (i.e., the highest degree of density corresponds to a climax). As tension can be expressed not only through the growing com-plexity of harmonic structures, which appear in sequence, but also through harmonic intensification of melodic climaxes (i.e., by making such climaxes become higher harmonic functions), the latter also become the climactic resources of the entire thematic texture.

Dynamics as such is a powerful tool for building resistances and climaxes. The first is accomplished by the progressive or delayed growth of dynamic degrees (such as crescendo or $pp < mf + p < f + mf < ff$); and the second, by sustaining the highest dynamic degree reached (ff in this case) by the resistance.

The ultimate climactic effect can be achieved through a combination of the above described devices, such as high tension of harmonic structure accompany-ing melodic climax (which in itself represents a high degree of harmonic tension) coupled with high dynamics and high density.

*See Vol. I, p. 279.

Counterpoint can be successfully used for developing resistances in the form of a group of diverging melodic trajectories.

The oblique patterns in both harmony and counterpoint are useful in building the intermediate, secondary climaxes.

The period of a climax must represent a definite portion of the respective thematic group, and may even occupy the entire group.

To sustain a climax means to sustain the climactic conditions. Nevertheless, it is psychologically unavoidable that the intensity of climax goes into decline, as the receiving apparatus accommodates itself to the respective degree of the impulse relatively quickly. For this reason prolonged climaxes, in actuality, cannot be continuously climactic.

Since time periods, preceding climaxes, usually contract with each successive climax, the climactic periods themselves, though gaining in power, must necessarily contract.

H. COMPOSITION OF THEMATIC GROUPS

In a thematic continuity which is planned from the duration of an entire composition, the chief problem of the composition of thematic groups lies in the distribution of intonational modifications. These, as stated before, are approached from the point of view that each subject, in its successive expositions, is varied through one specified technique. The main point to be discussed here is that the planning of the number and forms of intonational modifications depends upon the pre-set form of thematic continuity.

If each subject appears in the entire composition only once, no modifications have to be planned at all. If a certain subject has three expositions, another subject has two, and still another subject has one, the planning of intonational modifications concerns only the first two subjects—and even then there are only two modifications to be planned for the first subject and only one for the second.

Thus, the composition of thematic groups for a pre-planned form of thematic continuity can be carried out with a minimal expenditure of the composer's time and energy.

When intonational modifications require an increase of attacks in certain expositions of a subject, the individual duration-values of the original become a split-unit group. This permits retention of the rhythmic characteristic of the respective subjects.

All the necessary techniques by which intonational modifications can be performed have been fully described in the preceding chapters.

The sequence of modifications of each subject as it appears in its successive expositions must grow from simple to complex.

I. COMPOSITION OF KEY-AXES

This subject, having been previously discussed, concerns us for the present only insofar as the number of key-axes has to be defined and distributed.

The number of thematic groups does not have to equal the number of key-axes. After the number of thematic groups is established and the form of continuity specified, the composer has to make his decision about the number of key-axes. Such a decision should be based on some one of the three fundamental approaches: either (a) vary the key-axis with each Thematic Group; or (b) vary the key-axis with each recurrence of the same Thematic Group; or (c) change the key-axes at points determined by some structural subdivision of the entire continuity; for example, according to the symmetric groupings of the various recurrences (i.e., expositions) of the various Thematic Groups.

Although its exploitation so far by composers has been very limited, the technique of symmetric recurrence of key-axes produces effective results. Examples of such symmetry would be: (a) Key I + Key II + Key I; or (b) Key I + Key II + Key II + Key I; or (c) Key I + Key II + Key III + Key II + + Key I. All that is required is that the recurrences of the same key be symmetrically arranged.

In composition of systems of key-axes all the methods previously discussed for use in handling thematic sequences are applicable: direct recurrence, symmetric recurrence, modified recurrence, and progressive symmetry. Note that such thematic sequences applied to key-axes need not be the same schemes (although they *may* be) as those controlling recurrence of other Thematic Groups; it is only the *method* of composition of sequences that need be the same.

Here are some examples of the ways in which conditions of the three basic approaches mentioned above can be met by synchronizing a sequence of Thematic Groups with a sequence of Key-Axes:

(a) *The key-axis changes with the entrance of each Thematic Group*
(Supposing that the sequence of Thematic Groups is one of direct recurrence of A + B:)
　　A in Key I + B in Key II + A Key III + B Key IV + ... (etc.)
(Supposing that the sequence of themes were a modified recurrence scheme, or (A + B + C) ↻ (permuting clockwise), the requirement could be met by either of the following variations: Var. I below, changing to a new key each time; Var. II, exhibiting five different keys recurring symmetrically; that is to say, the sequence of keys is symmetric, while the sequence of themes is one of modified recurrence, and the two are superimposed:)
Var. I: (A Key I + B Key II + C Key III) + (B Key IV + C Key V + A Key VI) + (C Key VII + A Key VIII + B Key IX);
Var. II: (A Key I + B Key II + C Key III) + (B Key IV + C Key V + A Key IV) + (C Key III + A Key II + B Key I).

(b) *The key-axis does not change until a Thematic Group reappears*
For a direct recurrence sequence of themes, A + B + C:
Var. I: (A + B + C) Key I + (A +B +C) Key II + (A +B +C) Key III + ...;
Var. II: (A +B +C) Key I + (A +B +C) Key II (A +B +C) Key I;
For a progressive symmetric scheme of thematic sequence: A + (A +B) + (A +B +C) + (B +C) + C:
Var. I: A Key I + (A +B) Key II + (A +B +C) Key III + (B +C) Key IV + C Key V;
Var. II: A Key I + (A +B) Key II + (A +B +C) Key III + (B +C) Key II + C Key I.

(c) *The key-axis changes at points determined by some structural subdivision of the whole continuity*
For a modified recurrence group, (A +B +C) ↻ , the key-changes might be pre-set for every Third Thematic Group, for instance, and the pattern of key-change could either be a single series (Var. I below) or exhibit symmetry (Var. II below):
Var. I: (A +B +C) Key I + (B +C +A) Key II + (C +A +B) Key III;
Var. II: (A +B +C) Key I + (B +C +A) Key II + (C +A +B) Key I.

J. INSTRUMENTAL COMPOSITION

Instrumental composition of the entire musical piece in detail depends a great deal on its purpose and instrumental combination. For example, the idea of a composition being an "etude" or a "concerto" implies that a high degree of virtuosity is required of the performer (whether individual or collective). A composition written for a beginner must be instrumentally simple. The idea of an ensemble or orchestra implies richness and diversity in the utilization of instrumental resources.

The basic approaches to instrumental composition of the entire continuity are as follows:

(a) the degree of complexity of the instrumental form of a subject is in *direct* relation to the complexity of its other components;

(b) the degree of complexity of the instrumental form of a subject is in *inverse* relation to the complexity of its other components;

(c) the degree of complexity of the instrumental form of a subject is in *oblique* relation to the complexity of its other components.

The meaning of the term "oblique," as it is used in paragraph (c) of this discussion, represents a variable instrumental form (variable with respect to its complexity) applied to a subject whose other components are of constant complexity.

The degree of instrumental complexity can be determined by the number of attacks, by the variety of their forms and by the general diversity of instrumental resources. The degree of complexity of other components is determined by the complexity of temporal and intonational forms in a broad sense.

Empirically, it is never difficult to determine whether the subject is simple or complex, and to what degree, when we make such an evaluation on the basis of comparison with other subjects participating in the same composition.

It is highly desirable to specify the characteristics of instrumental forms with respect to each subject and its successive expositions individually. Then we may arrive at highly diversified schemes of instrumental composition where one subject, being simple, acquires a progressively increasing instrumental complexity; another, being of intermediate complexity, acquires instrumental forms of corresponding complexity; still another subject, being complex, acquires a progressively decreasing instrumental complexity, etc.

Much of the success in composing depends upon the extension of the general method used in all branches of this theory, i.e., the method of *regularity and coordination*, and that is what the Theory of Rhythm basically represents.

The next two chapters are devoted to practical applications of this theory to monothematic and polythematic composition.

CHAPTER 15

MONOTHEMATIC COMPOSITION

A MONOTHEMATIC composition, having one subject and one or more expositions, can be evolved from any technical source, which in this case contributes its major component. The major component must be looked upon as the dominant characteristic of the subject. The selection of minor components, their style and form of coordination with the major component, is subject to the composer's choice.

A monothematic composition, with one exposition constituting the entire piece, hardly requires the use of any elaborate form of variations. A monothematic composition with more than one exposition obviously depends on the variations. Variations, as such, come from different sources, and may influence temporal, intonational or textural patterns. The selection of quantities and types of variations, as well as the distribution of the latter, are left to the composer's discretion, as by now the potential composer is sufficiently equipped to use his own initiative in selection.

I shall illustrate the final synthesis of monothematic composition in such a way that the student will be supplied with samples based on different technical sources. For such illustrations, I shall use my own compositions which have been produced through the use of this system. I shall supply the student with technical data only to the extent to which it is necessary in each individual case, as these compositions should serve also as material for analysis.

My own compositions will be supplemented by reference to the works of my students, whose compositions were also produced through the use of this system.

A. "SONG"*FROM "THE FIRST AIRPHONIC SUITE" (1929)

(Composed for the space-controlled theremin with sound amplification and a large symphony orchestra. It had its premiere in November 1929 in the Masonic Hall in Cleveland and was later performed in Carnegie Hall in New York. Both performances were given by the Cleveland Symphony under Nicolai Sokoloff, with Leon Theremin as soloist.)

The "Song" is a monothematic composition, with one exposition and a partial recurrence of the beginning of the subject. The subject is "through-composed" music, for it is based on one continuous melody, originally plotted, and then harmonized. Here melody is the major component.

*In the original sketch for piano and the version for Thereminvox and Piano, this is called "Melody" instead of "Song". (Ed.)

MELODY
for Thereminvox and Piano

Joseph Schillinger

Figure 45. Monothematic composition with melody as major component.

New York, Aug. 28, 1929

Figure 45. Monothematic composition with melody as major component (concluded).

B. "MOUVEMENT ÉLECTRIQUE ET PATHÉTIQUE" (1932)
(Composed for the space-controlled theremin and piano).

This piece is a monothematic composition, whose subject derives from a plotted melody. Later the melody was subjected to harmonization. The features of melodic structure are: pedal points, successive climaxes, temporal expansions and contractions of the thematic rhythmic patterns and a few geometrical inversions.

Pedal points have special significance in this case, as the theremin provides a tone of infinite duration without renewal of attack.

Copyright 1945 by Carl Fischer, Inc.

Figure 46. A monothematic composition whose subject derives from a plotted melody.

Figure 46. A monothematic composition whose subject derives from a plotted melody (continued).

Figure 46. A monothematic composition whose subject derives from a plotted melody
(continued).

Figure 46. A monothematic composition whose subject derives from a plotted melody (continued).

Figure 46. A monothematic composition whose subject derives from a plotted melody (continued).

Figure 40. A monothematic composition whose subject derives from a plotted melody (continued).

March 15, 1932, New York

Figure 46 A monothematic composition whose subject derives from a plotted melody (concluded).

C. "FUNERAL MARCH" FOR PIANO (1928)
(American premiere by the League of Composers in 1930).

In this monothematic composition, the major component of the subject is harmony. There is no independent melody. What appears to be the melody is a combination of instrumental and melodic figuration. There is a partial recapitulation of the beginning, only in a climactic form. The harmonic structure itself is a symmetric superimposition of the $\sqrt[4]{2}$: S_I is B♭ and S_{II} is C♯. The building up of the strata occurs gradually thus giving the listener an opportunity to adapt himself to the Σ. For this reason, the beginning, based on S_I, seems to be in B♭ and the very end, based on S_{II}, seems to be in C♯ Minor.

MARCHE FUNEBRE

Joseph Schillinger

Figure 47. A monothematic composition with harmony as major component (continued).

Figure 47. A monothematic composition with harmony as major component (continued).

Figure 47. A monothematic composition with harmony as major component (continued).

Figure 47   A monothematic composition with harmony as major component
(continued).

Figure 47. A monothematic composition with harmony as major component
(concluded).

D. "Study in Rhythm I" for Piano (1935)

This monothematic composition is based on a subject consisting of 12 measures in 7/8 time, and has four expositions evolved in quadrant rotation: ⓐ + ⓓ + ⓒ + ⓑ. All expositions have the same period.

In spite of the title, the subject's major component is strata-harmony: $\Sigma = 2S$. The structure of the lower stratum is: $S_I = 4+3$ (used in clockwise positions); the structure of the upper stratum is: $S_{II} = 5+5$. The progression consists of a random arrangement of 4i and 3i, made to produce 12 H: $1^{\rightarrow} = 4+3+3+4+$ $+3+4+4+4+3+4+4$. The transformations in S_I are consistently clockwise, and the transformations of S_{II} consist of binomial regularity of the clockwise and the counterclockwise alternation.

The chords, reading by the lower stratum, are: F + Db + Bb + G + Eb + + C + Ab + E + C + A + F + Db.

Quadrant rotations were obtained from F as the axis of inversion.

T_1 represents an introduction consisting of H_1; the next 12 Tⓐ represent the first exposition; the following three expositions ⓓ 12T + ⓒ 12T + ⓑ 12T are followed by a coda, which consists of 5T and represents a repetition of the preceding measure in a slowing down pace; it is based on one H, which is the first chord of the subject.

The temporal thematic pattern of this composition is evolved from the simplest elements of $\frac{7}{8}$ series. Melody, which in its first three expositions uses only the chordal functions of S_{II}, is based on T = (4+2+1) + (2+1+4). If we designate the first trinomial as a and the second as b, the whole subject appears as follows: (a+b+b+a) + (b+a+a+b) + (b+a+a+b). The harmonic accompaniment follows the same scheme as melody. Its temporal thematic pattern is: T = ($\boxed{1}$ + 1 + 1 + 2 + 1 + 1) + (1 + 1 + 2 + 1 + 1 + $\boxed{1}$); its instrumental form is based on single attacks throughout the entire composition. In the third exposition, it is varied by the split-unit groups. Melody has three instrumental forms. The first form, consisting of single-attack sequence of S_{II}, is followed by the second form, which is a double-attack sequence, combined with octave-coupling. These two forms are evenly distributed in the first exposition. The second exposition is based on the first form. The third exposition is based on. the second form. The fourth exposition is a variation combining the first two forms with the split-unit groups. The tones which appear as auxiliary, in reality are the chordal functions of S_I; the presence of leading units combined with splitting of durations attributes to the last exposition the character of melodic figuration.

(1) $\Sigma^{\rightarrow}$ of the subject.

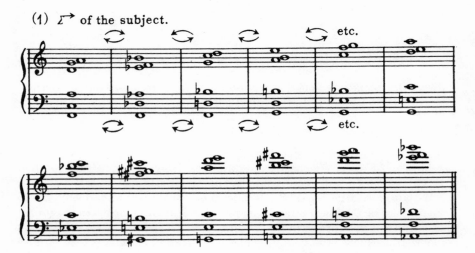

Figurè 48. $\Sigma^{\rightarrow}$ of the subject.

"STUDY IN RHYTHM" I

Joseph Schillinger

Figure 49. Major component is strata-harmony Σ = 2S (continued).

Figure 49. Major component is strata-harmony $\Sigma = 2S$ *(continued).*

Figure 49. Major component is strata-harmony Σ = 2S *(continued).*

Nov. 16, 1935, New York

Figure 49. Major component is strata-harmony $\Sigma = 2S$ (concluded).

E. "Study in Rhythm II" for Piano (1940)

A two-part instrumental interference is the major component of the subject in this monothematic composition. Its source is the $r_{5 \div 3}$. Each term of the resultant is broken into single t-units. Thus the attack-group appears as follows: $A = 3+2+1+3+1+2+3$. By distributing the attacks through two parts and through the durations, we obtain a double cycle of $r_{5 \div 3}$; $\frac{7}{2}$ interference makes the 7 terms of r appear twice:

(a) preliminary scoring:

(b) final scoring:

The entire continuity is based on the circular permutations of single terms:

$$\overrightarrow{T} = 7r_{5\div3} \, \circlearrowleft = (3+2+1+3+1+2+3) + (2+1+3+1+2+3+3) +$$
$$+ (1+3+1+2+3+3+2) + (3+1+2+3+3+2+1) +$$
$$+ (1+2+3+3+2+1+3) + (2+3+3+2+1+3+1) +$$
$$+ (3+3+2+1+3+1+2).$$
$$\overrightarrow{T}' = 7r_{5\div3} \cdot 2 = 7 \cdot 15 \cdot 2 = 210 \text{ t}.$$
$$T'' = 15 \text{ t}; \text{ hence: } NT'' = 210 \div 15 = 14.$$

In the form of two-part instrumental interference, this continuity appears as follows:

Figure 50. Source $r_{5\div3}$. *Attack distributed through 2 parts (continued).*

Figure 50. Source r₅÷₃. Attack distributed through 2 parts (concluded).

After accomplishing this, I came to the decision that the rhythmic exuberance of this setting is apt to horrify almost any performer. I then re-wrote the same setting into 3/4 time with t = ♩ , thus extending this setting to 70 measures. This gave the scheme an "easy" optical appearance:

Figure 51. Material of figure rewritten in 3/4 time (continued).

Figure 51. Material of figure 50 rewritten in 3/4 time (concluded).

This two-part setting was transformed later into continuous two-part counterpoint. The same pitch scale was used in both parts, but in the $\sqrt[3]{4}$ relation to each other, thus producing counterpoint of type III. The axis of the upper part was fixed on *c* and the axis of the lower part, on *e*.

After the counterpoint was written, couplings were added. The fundamental scheme of couplings (four to each part) was used in systematic permutations, employing one coupling at a time.

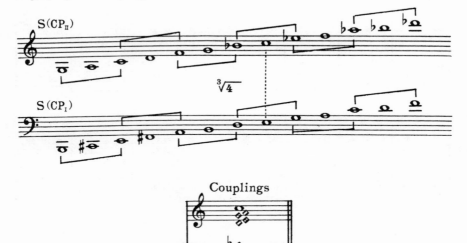

Figure 52. Two-part setting transformed into continuous two-part counterpoint.

Figure 53. Coupling (continued).

Figure 53. Coupling (continued).

Figure 53. Coupling (concluded).

The rhythmic scheme itself serves as an introduction and consists of 10 T. This is followed by the first exposition, based on the entire rhythmic scheme. Instrumental forms change in each 10 T subdivision of the subject. The last 10 T of the first exposition are used as a rhythmic modulation to the second exposition. This is accomplished by introducing split units progressively. The second exposition, lasting as long as the first, is based on juxtaposition of couplings in the upper part, in the original rhythm, and couplings transformed into single-attack instrumental forms (by means of split-unit groups) in the lower part.

"STUDY IN RHYTHM" II

Joseph Schillinger

Allegro molto

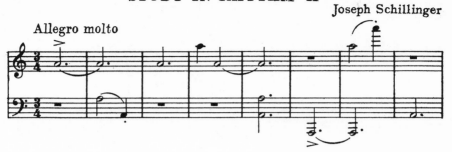

Figure 54. Study in Rhythm II (continued).

Figure 54. Study in Rhythm II (continued).

Figure 54. Study in Rhythm II (continued).

Figure 54. Study in Rhythm II (continued).

Nov. 10, 1940, New York

Figure 54. Study in Rhythm II (concluded).

Other examples of *monothematic composition* written by the students of this system:

Will Bradley: *Nocturne* for flute and piano. The subject is based on symmetric melodization and has one exposition. The melody has no recurrences and is of exceptional quality.

Edwin Gerschefski: *Solfeggietto*, etude for piano. This piece represents a through-composed music evolved from Σ4S4p in the form of unaccompanied melody. It was meant to be, according to the composer's intentions, a modern counterpart of Karl Ph. E. Bach's *Solfeggietto*.

Paul Lavalle: *Symphonic Rhumba* (one version is written for a 23-piece radio-orchestra; another, for a full symphony orchestra). The subject is based on symmetric melodization of harmonic ostinato: Phrygian descending tetra-chord in S(9) connected in sequence in identical progressions three times through the $\sqrt[4]{2}$ and producing four groups 16 T each. The total length of the subject is 64 T. In the second exposition, the whole subject is accelerated twice. The introduction is a build-up of instrumental interferences in $\frac{8}{8}$ series. The middle section consists of a fugal exposition, whose theme is the basic rhythmic trinomial of $\frac{8}{8}$ series, used in circular permutations. Melodically, it is identical with the bass of the Phrygian harmonic ostinato.

Rosolino De Maria: (a) *Prelude* No. 1 for piano.* The subject consists of several sections of different instrumental form, and strictly speaking, has only one exposition. Coupled two-part counterpoint was used as major component (type II). The attacks of the original counterpoint were $\frac{A(CP_{II})}{A(CP_I)} = \frac{4a}{a}$.

(b) *Etude* in C for piano.** This composition represents an elaborate use of harmonic strata, combined with high mobility. It is a sample of virtuosity in composition, and a challenge to the virtuoso performer.

Nathan Van Cleave: (a) *Improvisation and Scherzo**** for string orchestra. The improvisation is a through-composed subject, based on harmony and melodic figuration.

(b) *Etude for Orchestra*****. This composition is evolved from a three-unit scale, its modifications and derivative scales for the family. The through-composed melody is coupled by a full Σ 13. Rhythmic modifications are achieved by doubling the speed. Intonational modifications are achieved by quadrant rotation. A counterpart was included *a posteriori*. There is a great variety of instrumental modifications. The thematic sequence is based on the triadic progressive symmetry, but the three thematic groups are merely quadrant-modifications of the same subject.

*Published by Ricordi.
**Published by Ricordi.
***Performed on CBS on May 27, 1940 by string ensemble conducted by Alexander Semler. Available at Boosey & Hawkes, Inc. on rental.

****Performed by Robert Russell Bennett and his orchestra on June 13, 1941 on "Robert Russell Bennett's Notebook." Available at Boosey & Hawkes, Inc. on rental.

CHAPTER 16

POLYTHEMATIC COMPOSITION

W E shall illustrate the process of assembling a polythematic composition with materials presented in the preceding chapters.

Our first decision will concern the style of temporal organization. We shall assign $\frac{4}{4}$ as the determinant of the series.

The style of intonation will be based on the Persian (Double-Harmonic) scale.

We shall select three subjects, and plan our composition in such a way that the degree of mobility will be highest for A, lowest for B, and intermediate for C.

Let the thematic unit of A be: Fig. 8.

Let the thematic unit of Fig. 15 (melody with couplings) be assigned to B, and let the thematic unit of Fig. 16 be assigned to C.

Our next step will be to define the form of thematic sequence. Let it be evolved in the form of progressive symmetry, as we learned it in reference to three subjects:

$$A_1 + (A_2 + B_1) + (A_3 + B_2 + C_1) + (B_3 + C_2) + C_3.$$

Next comes the temporal organization of continuity. We shall arrange it in such a way that A, in the course of its expositions, will be a growing subject; B will be the dominant subject appearing in its maximal period through all three expositions; C will be, in the course of its expositions, a declining subject.

We shall assume the maximal period to be equal for A and C, and designate this value at 16 T''.

We shall select the form of growth and decline for A and C to be in $1 \div 2 \div 4$ ratio. Then we acquire the following temporal scheme for all three subjects:

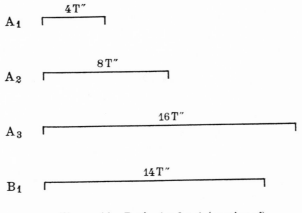

Figure 55. Ratio 1÷2÷4 (continued).

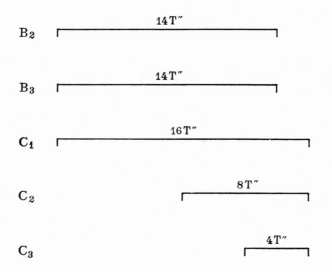

Figure 55. Ratio 1÷2÷4 (concluded).

From this we find: $T^{\rightarrow}$ (A) = 4+8+16 = 28 T''
                                $T^{\rightarrow}$ (B) = 14·3   = 42 T''
                                $T^{\rightarrow}$ (C) = 4+8+16 = 28 T''

Hence: $T^{\rightarrow}$ (A, B, C) = A28T'' + B42T'' + C28T'' = 98T''

Temporal relations of the subjects appear as follows:

$$\frac{B}{A+C} = \frac{42}{56} = \frac{3}{4}; \ \frac{A}{B} = \frac{28}{42} = \frac{2}{3}; \ \frac{C}{B} = \frac{28}{42} = \frac{2}{3}.$$

Hence: $T^{\rightarrow}$ (A) ÷ $T^{\rightarrow}$ (B) ÷ $T^{\rightarrow}$ (C) = 2 ÷ 3 ÷ 2.

Assuming t = 1/8 sec. = ♪ , we obtain the following duration-units for all three subjects:

t'(A) =   t = 1/8 sec. = ♪
t'(B) = 4t = 1/2 sec. = ♩
t'(C) = 2t = 1/4 sec. = ♪

        Then:
T''(A) = 16t = 2 sec.
T''(B) = 4t' = 2 sec.
T''(C) = 8t' = 2 sec.

The quantities of the respective duration-units in each subject appear as follows:

$$T^{\rightarrow}(A) = 28T'' = 448t$$

$$T^{\rightarrow}(B) = 42T'' = 168t' = 672t$$

$$T^{\rightarrow}(C) = 28T'' = 224t' = 448t$$

Since every $T'' = 2$ sec., the duration of the entire composition is: $T^{\rightarrow} = 96 \cdot 2 = 196$, or 3 minutes, 16 seconds.

The form of continuity of this composition appears as follows:

$$A_1(T_1 - T_4) + [A_2(T_1 - T_8) + B_1 14T] + [A_3 16T + B_2 14T + C_1 16T] +$$

$$+ [B_3 14T + C_2(T_9 - T_{16})] + C_3(T_{13} - T_{16}).$$

We shall distribute the key-axes in such a way that:

(a) they will be symmetric;

(b) they will change with each term of pentadic symmetry, which this form of thematic sequence represents.

Let the sequence of key-axes be based on the E_1 ($S^{\rightarrow}d_0$): C — E — G — E — C Further, let each term of pentadic symmetry appear in the different geometric positions; and let these positions be: ⓐ — ⓓ — ⓐ — ⓒ — ⓑ.

We shall select our dynamic forms in the following way:

$$\dot{A}_1P; \ A_2MF; \ A_3F \ \ ;$$

$$B_1F; \ B_2P \ \ ; \ B_3MF;$$

$$C_1F; \ C_2MF; \ C\text{-}P \ \ .$$

Under such a form of selection, A and C reciprocate dynamically in time-continuity, while B changes from one extreme degree to another and balances itself on an intermediate degree.

Now we can express the entire continuity with respect to intonational, axial and dynamic synthesis: $A_1 C$ⓐ$P + (A_2MF + B_1F)E$ⓓ$+ (A_3F + B_2P + C_1F)G$ⓐ$+ (B_3MF + C_2MF)E$ⓒ$+ C_3 C$ⓑP.

We shall select the instrumental forms in such a way that A and C will have the same form in their respective expositions, while B will appear in a different instrumental form in each exposition.

Example of Polythematic Composition

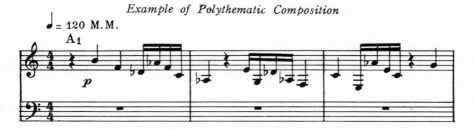

Figure 56. Polythematic form (continued).

Figure 56. Polythematic form (continued).

Figure 56. Polythematic form (continued).

Figure 56. Polythematic form (continued).

Figure 56. Polythematic form (concluded).

The miniature form in which we evolved the above composition must serve as a sample for such exercises. The student will find it more expedient to get acquainted with the various forms of composition by executing the most ambitious tasks in miniature form. These miniature forms will serve him as models for future works of greater temporal and instrumental dimensions. This method is comparable with the execution of stage models before the actual sets are constructed. It saves the artist's time, develops his initiative and technique, and helps him to visualize projects of a greater scope.

I shall refer for analytical purposes to a few compositions in *polythematic form* composed by students of this system.

Will Bradley: (a) *String Quartet*

    (b) *Duet for Two Clarinets and Piano.*

Carmine Coppola:

    (a) *Quintet for Wind Instruments:**
    (b) *Concerto for Oboe;*
    (c) *Pagan Dance* for Orchestra.****

Edwin Gerschefski: *Fanfare for the New York World's Fair of 1939* for Brass Septet.†

Rosolino De Maria: (a) *String Quartet;*

    (b) *As I Remember* Symphonic Impressions for large orchestra.

Of my own works, two may serve as examples of unusual and diversified forms of polythematic composition:

    (a) *Sonata-Rhapsody* for Piano (1925);††
    (b) *October*, Symphonic Rhapsody (1927) for large orchestra.‡

This concludes Part Two of the *Theory of Composition.*

---

*Chamber work for flute, oboe, clarinet, bassoon and horn in three movements. Performed by Detroit Symphony Woodwind Quintet in Detroit, March 17, 1941. (Ed.).

**Written in the summer of 1938, it was performed by the Rochester Philharmonic, Jose Iturbi conducting, on January 19, 1939. It has also been performed by the Michigan Symphony and by the Detroit Symphony. (Ed.)

†Performed over the CBS network in January 1939.- (Ed.).

††Performed in Russia by Alexander Ka-mensky, in Berlin by Irene Westermann, in Milan by Antonio Russolo, in New York by Nicolai Kopeikine, and in Washington, California, Mexico City by Keith Corelli (Ed.).

‡Performed in Moscow in 1927 and in Leningrad in 1928. Premiere in the United States by Leopold Stokowski and the Philadelphia Orchestra in 1929 (Ed.).

PART THREE

SEMANTIC (CONNOTATIVE) COMPOSITION

CHAPTER 17

SEMANTIC BASIS OF MUSIC

A. EVOLUTION OF SONIC SYMBOLS

THIS discussion requires on the part of the student complete familiarity with the semantics of melody and the connotative meaning of configurations, which information can be found in the Theory of Melody.*

Our present task is to include all the technical resources of composition in the field of connotative music. This inclusion of all forms of musical expression increases the range of admissible associations, thus enriching music as the *language of sonic symbols*.

All symbols are configurations. Graphic symbols are perceived by sight, sonic symbols are perceived by hearing. Sonic symbols are modifications of frequency and intensity. At the early stage of human evolution, there was only one language of sonic symbols. Later on it gradually differentiated into two sonic languages: speech and music. Early forms of speech greatly rely on the intonation (modification of frequency) as an idiomatic factor: words of the same etymological constitution, spoken with a different intonation, acquire different meanings, i.e., they become new symbols. Music, i.e., what we know now as music, emancipated itself from the fore-language of sonic symbols through the dominance of intonation over other sonic forms and through the crystallization of fixed frequency units.

Modifications of frequency and of durations are the basic components of sonic configurations. Further refinement of symbols is achieved by modification of intensity (which also includes the form of attack) and quality (which is physically the product of frequency and intensity). All other configurations, such as those produced by modifications of density, take place only when complex sonic symbols participate.

Sonic semar 'ics is altogether possible because of the configurational interdependence of the activating (stimulative) and the reactive patterns. All components of sound work in similar patterns, and these patterns are similar in all sensory experience. Identical patterns exhibit a tendency of mutual attraction, and the latter stimulates association. The meaning of music evolves in terms of physico-physiological correspondences. These correspondences are quantitative, and quantities express form.

We can easily imagine that at its early stage the language of sonic symbols existed in the form of larynx reflexes, caused by certain forms of physiological activity. As these sounds, stimulated by somewhat similar experiences, repeated

*See Vol. I, p. 279.

themselves in somewhat similar reactive forms, these reactive forms eventually began to crystallize. The crystallized sonic patterns could be intentionally repeated. Being associated with definite stimuli, they became symbols. As the response to sonic forms exists even in so-called inanimate nature in the form of sympathetic vibrations, or resonance, it is no wonder that even primitive man inherited highly developed mimetic responses. From this we can conclude that a great many of the early sonic symbols probably originated as imitation of sonic patterns, coming as stimuli from the surrounding world. We must not forget that echo (as a physical pattern-response) existed on this planet before any auditory receptor was developed. It is also true that tactile responses to pressure in general, as patterns of compression and rarefaction coming from the generalized cutaneous, i.e., skin-receptor, preceded the development of a more specialized auditory receptor.

The next stage of the evolution of sonic symbols is characterized by the use of intonational patterns as symbols of ideas and concepts. We find such use of musical symbols in ancient China, just as we find graphic symbols in the sand-paintings of the Navajo. At this stage, both sonic and graphic symbols are in competition with linguistic, i.e., etymological symbols. *Oxford History of Music* (Vol. 6, p. 111) defines this stage in the following way: "Program music is a curious hybrid, that is, music posing as an unsatisfactory kind of poetry."

Finally, we arrive at the stage where the forms of musical expression become confined to their purely configurational meaning. In this aspect sonic symbols may be looked upon as generalized pattern-stimuli. The first formulation of this meaning of music comes from Aristotle: "Rhythms and melodious sequences are movements quite as much as they are actions." "Musical motion," when projected into spatial configurations, possesses characteristics similar to that of motion, action, growth, or other "eventual" processes. It particularly resembles the mechanical trajectories and the projections of periodic phenomena, i.e., the processes which are characterized by a high degree of regularity. As mechanical trajectories are the inherent patterns of "musical motion," *music is capable of expressing everything which can be translated into form of motion.*

B. Configurational Orientation and the Psychological Dial

The interaction which we call "association," and which permits the formation of reactions, sensations, and emotional and mental attitudes, is based on an inherent capacity which we may term "configurational response." This capacity appears to us to be a special case of configurational responses in general. It extends itself to the entire range of the knowable, including physical and chemical reactions, various types of reflexes (including articulatory responses of speech), emotional, mental and even telepathic reactions.

The associative power of musical configuration depends upon three basic conditions: first, the selection of a configuration which is in proper correspondence with the configuration of the state or process to be expressed; secondly, the selection of a musical form which adequately corresponds to the selected configuration and which operates in media comprehensible to the listener; and finally, a favorable state of reactivity on the part of the listener, i.e., his disposition to react and comprehend at a particular moment.

So far we have dealt with sonic symbols in the form of linear configurations taken individually (*Theory of Melody*)* or in combinations (*Theory of Correlated Melodies*).** In the latter case the component melodies still remained linear patterns. The extension of configurational semantics into other simple and complex components of music constitutes the subject of the present discussion.

We shall consider linear configurations as simple and group configurations as complex. Linear configurations consist of individual components. Group configurations represent assemblages of conjugated components. Simple configurations are produced by melody and possess a greater configurational versatility than the complex configurations. The latter are produced by harmony and, compared to melody, are relatively inert.

The degree of configurational versatility of melody depends on the technique employed. When configurational versatility becomes the chief factor of expression, the Theory of Melody (plotting technique***) must be preferred to the Theory of Pitch-Scales† (variation technique).

The degree of configurational versatility of harmony partly depends on the number of conjugated parts in-the respective assemblage, partly on the number of simultaneous assemblages, and partly on the number of transformations employed. Harmonic progressions, as they derive from the permutations of intervals or from direct transposition of pitch-scales, have relatively limited configurational possibilities. In comparison with this, transformations and cycles employed in the *Special Theory of Harmony*†† offer a great many configurations. Configurational versatility of harmonic progressions reaches its maximum with the use of all transformations of the *General Theory of Harmony*.†††

The versatility of expression depends on the number and the forms of configurations. While the number of conjugated parts in an assemblage defines the possible number of transformations (which grows from p to 2p, 3p, 4p to Σ), it is also true that the stability of configuration, under all conditions being equal, grows with the increase of configurational elements: *the denser the assemblage, the greater its configurational inertia.* The patterns of S2p are more alert than the patterns of S3p, and the latter are more alert than that of S4p.

The discussion of this subject, i.e., the spatio-temporal patterns of simple and complex trajectories, brings us closer to an understanding of music in terms of motion and action. We have already seen that pattern stimuli activate *configurational response.* We shall use this term as a complex concept emphasizing all partial responses of the entire reactive chain. It includes *physico-physiological* (chemical, neurological, psychonic) and *psychological* reactions (associational, emotional, mental). Since we react as a unit, dissociation of the partial responses is impossible in actuality. For this reason there is a great advantage in using one concept which can emphasize reflexes, associations and judgments. We shall

*See Vol. I, p. 228; also p. 1432.   **See Vol. I, p. 708.   ***See Vol. I, p. 299.   †See Vol. I, p. 115.
††See Vol. I, pp. 368, 378, 382.   †††See pp. 1068, 1106 and 1127.

define *judgment* as the self-evaluating partial response of the entire reactive group. Its function consists of associating current configurational responses with past configurational responses, with which it has pattern-similarities. The association itself is a form of attraction (like that of sympathetic reactions) existing between the pattern-similarities. Thus, judgment may be looked upon as a form of *configurational orientation*. The evaluation of event, as a process, in terms of mechanical efficiency, i.e., in terms of performance (action), crystallizes the configurational response into an *attitude*. The relativity of forms (standards) of mechanical efficiency corresponds to the relativity of forms (standards) of configurational orientation and results in the corresponding attitudes.

To illustrate this, we shall demonstrate the translation of events into actions; and to accomplish this, we shall resort to the *scale of configurational responses*, as it was presented in the *Theory of Melody*,* i.e., in the form of a *psychological dial*.

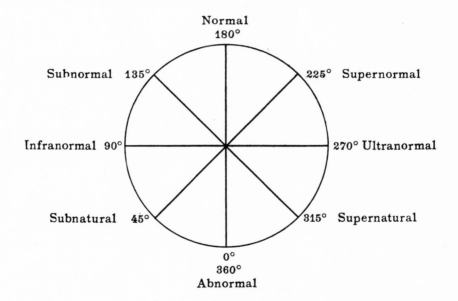

Figure 57. Psychological dial.

Here, infranormal represents the lower limit of normality and corresponds to ultimate depression; ultranormal represents the upper limit of normality and corresponds to ultimate ecstasy. The 0°, when arrived at by counterclockwise motion on the circumference, represents the lower limit of performance; the 360°, when arrived at by clockwise motion, represents the upper limit of performance. These two coinciding points are both in the range of the improbable.

*See Vol. I, p. 232 ff.

To facilitate our further discussion, we shall use a graphic representation for each response by the respective hand-position on the dial:

Figure 58. Hand-positions on the dial.

This scale, if necessary, can be developed to a further degree of refinement by introducing the intermediate hand-positions, in addition to those offered above.

The psychological dial may be looked upon as a form of bifold symmetry, having the ordinate for its axis. There is a configurational reciprocation of patterns symmetrically located on both sides of the axis. The reciprocating pairs are: ⏀, i.e., normal-abnormal; ⊘, i.e., subnormal-supernormal; ⊖, i.e., infranormal-ultranormal; ⊘, i.e., subnatural-supernatural. This implies that the reciprocating responses are activated by stimuli of mutually converse patterns.

The left half of our dial represents the differentiated forms of the original *defense-response;* the right half, the differentiated forms of the original *aggression-response.* The first response is characterized by *contraction-patterns;* the second, by *expansion-patterns.* Either of the two may be *active* or *passive,* depending on the presence of "resistance," which psychologically is the effortful feeling of striving. The presence of resistance in the activating pattern intensifies the configurational response. It "dramatizes" the response and is based on the amplitude-evaluation.

As we have seen in the "Semantics of Melody," this resistance in the response-pattern has its counterpart in the mechanical resistance-pattern. As aggression psychologically corresponds to *inducement,* and defense, to *submission,* we shall consider the right half of the dial as *positive* and the left as *negative.* The positive zone is associated with the *gain of energy and growth,* the negative, with the *loss of energy and decline.* The inducement in association with resistance becomes *dominance,* or the active form of inducement. The submission in association with resistance becomes *compliance,* or the active form of submission.

Now, we come back to the *evaluation of performance.* It is not difficult to see how mechanical performance can be put on a quantitative basis. Application of such-and-such amount of energy is expected to produce such-and-such result. When the result of the application of energy is what we expect, the response-pattern is *normal.* When the result is below our expectations, i.e., *less* than we expected, the response-pattern is *subnormal.* When the result is above our expectations, i.e., *more* than we expected, the response-pattern is *supernormal.* Further extension of the performance beyond these limits produces *subnatural* for the first group and *supernatural* for the second group. The final limit for both groups, merging one into another, produces the response-pattern of *abnormal* (absurd).

The concepts of normal, subnormal, supernormal, etc., are integrated and crystallized response-patterns, and as such, are capable of stimulating associations with other response-patterns and their integrated and cystallized conceptual forms. It is on the basis of these associations that it becomes possible to translate the original configurational response of *accumulation-discharge* into *tension-release, anticipation-fulfillment*, etc. It also becomes possible to form an attitude in each case on the basis of evaluation. The evaluation refers to pattern-similarities by associating them with past experiences, and the response-pattern becomes an attitude as the result of evaluation. The attitude demonstrates whether the outcome of a certain process (course of events) is below or above expectations, or is exactly what was expected. Thus, the fulfillment of anticipation may be *equal* or *smaller* or *greater* than is expected.

C. ANTICIPATION-FULFILLMENT PATTERN

In the chapter on "Climax and Resistance" (*Theory of Melody*),* we analyzed the various responses to the discus-thrower. These responses formed attitudes as a result of evaluation of the athlete's mechanical performance. We shall analyze now a group of responses and attitudes on events which do not contain any apparent motion or action, but merely the anticipation-fulfillment pattern.

For our first illustration, we shall employ a case which involves quantities, that is, a case in which evaluation can be based on some obvious quantitative relations.

Let it be a man who comes to a drugstore to buy an article for which he expects (owing to his previous experience) to pay one dollar and ninety-eight cents, and, perhaps, two cents tax. Suppose the customer gets the article he wants for the price he expects to pay. The response-pattern in this case is $\left(\,|\,\right)$, and the customer's attitude is either indifference or acknowledgment of the fact: he got neither more nor less than he expected, i.e., the response-pattern is *normal*. Now let us move to the negative zone. It is an assumed increase in price that would produce it. Suppose the price went up to $2.49. It undoubtedly would disappoint the customer and, whether he bought the article or not, it would stimulate the response of regret. Now if we continue our venture further into the negative zone, we might set the price for the same article at $2.98 or even more. If the article is of great importance to the customer, and if the customer is poor and cannot afford the purchase, depression would be the response. He may not be inclined to commit suicide in this case. But imagine a father whose beloved child has to undergo a surgical operation, for which the poor man cannot afford to pay, because of the increased cost. In this case, depression reaches its maximum and the response-pattern is $\left(-\right)$ (infranormal). The continuation of this venture through the negative zone may suggest such illustrations as one of an imaginary customer coming to a drugstore, or even better to a "five and ten cent" store, to buy a fountain pen, and being told that the pen costs several hundred dollars.

*See Vol. I, p. 279.

As this is in the category of loss that is so incredible, the response-pattern will be not that of disappointment or depression, but rather of humor. The owner of the store may even tell the customer that the pen is made of platinum, or maybe even studded with diamonds. Still the price would appear ridiculous to the customer, as he is conditioned to definite expectations at the drugstore, which are quite different from those which, let us say, he would expect at Tiffany's. Such a situation puts the response-pattern somewhat like this: ⟨⟩ (subnatural).

To bring this case to the pattern of the abnormal or the absurd, we shall imagine that an ordinary fountain pen at Woolworth's, which the imaginary customer picks from the counter, is not for sale and belongs to the Maharaja of Jodpur. The response-pattern to be expected in this case is ⟨⟩ (abnormal) and represents astonishment.

Let us resume our purchasing venture from the balance point and move into the positive zone. In that zone, the pattern of gain will reciprocate the loss-patterns which we have already described with respect to the negative zone.

Coming back to the prospective purchaser of the $1.98 article, we find him at a drugstore on a day of a special sale: the current price is then only $1.49. The customer buys the article and enjoys the acquisition of it at such an advantageous price. He would hardly jump for joy, but there would be a response-pattern of satisfaction, expressing the dial position at ⟨⟩ (supernormal) or less. The relative limit of satisfaction, which theoretically is at the point of esctasy, might occur for the same article at a "penny-sale"; that is, when by paying one more cent, the customer acquires two identical articles for the price of one. Carrying this incident further into the positive zone, somewhere around ⟨⟩ (supernatural), we must imagine a case where the store owner says to the customer: "I value your patronage of many years and I wish to give you a present. Choose anything you like within the range of $25." The situation is quite improbable, of course, but not entirely impossible. However, it exceeds all the possible expectations of the unsuspecting customer.

To bring this case to the point of the absurd ⟨⟩ in gain we might imagine something which would be diametrically opposite to the zero position with the Maharaja's pen at Woolworth's. Such a situation might occur when the store owner offers his entire store and a good sum of cash to the astounded customer who expected merely to get a pen and to pay for it. Thus, gain may extend itself to the degree of the absurd, in which case the pattern-response is one of astonishment. After the subject recovers from this stage, he undoubtedly fluctuates into one or another of the adjacent zones. But the latter are associated with humor; therefore, the subject will accept the incredibly-generous offer as a joke.

In this group of episodes, or imaginary events, we have based the evaluation process on the tangible figures of quoted price in relation to expected price.

We shall now present a case in which no obvious quantities are involved. We shall base this illustration on a *moral* instead of *material* evaluation. And in this case, the evaluation will be based on moral loss or gain.

Mr. A knows Mr. B for many years as an honest wage earner. One day Mr. A discovers to his regret that Mr. B is a petty thief. Mr. A does not find it tragic; but his response-pattern is sorrow and can be located on the psychological dial as ⊘ (subnormal). Mr. A does not believe any human being is perfect and with regret, makes allowances for such a weakness. One fine day however, Mr. A learns that Mr. B had actively participated in a bank robbery. This comes to Mr. A as a very depressing bit of news and his response-pattern becomes ⊙. But Mr. A is positive that Mr. B cannot be a killer. Yet, at a later date, Mr. B is accused of murder. This comes to Mr. A as a great surprise and his pattern-response becomes ⊖ (infranormal). As everything beyond this point of the negative zone is associated with an incredible loss (moral loss in this case), we would have to compel poor Mr. B to assassinate at least one or two families—and we can't afford to spare even the little children.

In order to find a proper response-pattern for the deeds of Mr. B, we would have to move the dial-hand to position ⊘ (subnatural). Remember that Mr. B is not known to be a maniac; otherwise, such actions might have been expected. To conclude the unfortunate venture of Mr. B, we shall collect sufficient evidence in order to prove beyond doubt that Mr. B, during his absence from town, exterminated cold-bloodedly and methodically the complete population of several small and remote communities.

The response pattern of Mr. A to such actions of Mr. B, and we sympathetically join Mr. A in his reaction, is ⊙ (abnormal); his attitude can be described as complete astonishment, from which it is not easy for him to recover. The concepts associated with such gruesome and cruel actions of Mr. B are: incredible, unbelievable, impossible, insane, nonsensical, etc.

Now to cheer up Mr. A and ourselves, we shall start a new life for Mr. B. Mr. B has just moved into a new neighborhood, where he makes new acquaintances, one of whom is Mr. A. The latter thinks he is "all right," but does not suspect what a nice fellow Mr. B really is. One day Mr. B pays a visit to Mr. A and brings him a gift. As time goes on, Mr. A. learns that the present was a token of true friendship and that Mr. B did not expect anything in return. The evaluation of such an action on the part of Mr. B can be expressed as moral gain. It places the response-pattern in position. ⊘ (supernormal). To put Mr. A into a state of real ecstasy, we shall compel Mr. B to perform an act of real sacrifice in favor of Mr. A. We may let Mr. B save Mr. A's drowning child, in which action he subjects himself to real danger. Thus, we reach the stage at which the response-pattern becomes ⊖ (ultranormal). Beyond the heroic action in saving his friend's child from drowning lies the field for incredible and fantastic actions that call for a superman.

Mr. B is not a superman, and for this reason his attempt to save a whole family of dogs from a burning house, which he succeeds in accomplishing, causes our response-pattern to become ⊘ (supernatural), as the whole affair seems in our evaluation to be incredible and fantastic. An unnecessary self-sacrifice on the part of Mr. B would also do as well to illustrate this response-pattern.

Such a case might have occurred if Mr. B had started some sort of business enterprise, and Mr. A, at some later date, had entered into competition with him. We find both competitors at a stage where Mr. B, who had established himself first, makes his enterprise a success while Mr. A fails to accomplish anything. Then, one day, Mr. B feels it such a pity to see Mr. A struggling and decides not only to move to another town, in order to get out of Mr. A's way, but even gives his whole enterprise and all the accumulated profits to Mr. A. The response-pattern to such actions of Mr. B, naturally, would come close to position ⊘. To make the situation completely absurd, we would have to induce Mr. B, in addition to the sacrifices he has just made, to commit suicide. This type of action on his part certainly would be unnecessary and abnormal. Our gain from this ridiculous action is that we obtain an illustration of the response-pattern associated with position ⊙ (abnormal).

As all our evaluations are relative, some of Mr. B's actions in the negative zone would have been quite normal for a criminal or a maniac. Likewise, were Mr. B a saint, we might evaluate his dog-saving expedition as quite normal. In other words, all our evaluations and response-patterns have been based on the assumption that Mr. B is an ordinary (i.e., 180°) man.

These illustrations are offered in order to demonstrate that response-patterns and the resulting evaluations depend upon the estimated realization of event; that the evaluation itself evolves from associations of loss and gain; that such loss and gain may pertain to either physical or moral actions.

These illustrations may serve the student as analytical examples for finding the corresponding response-patterns of events and locating them on the psychological dial. The next stage, after this has been accomplished, is to translate the response-patterns into geometrical configurations, i.e., trajectories.

D. TRANSLATING RESPONSE PATTERNS INTO GEOMETRICAL CONFIGURATIONS

The configurations, which represent both stimuli and responses, and are identical for both with a certain degree of approximation, form two basic groups. These two configurational groups correspond to negative and positive zones of the psychological dial. They also can be arranged in a bifold symmetry, in which case there is always a reciprocal pattern in one zone for any given pattern in another. Hence these patterns are geometrically convertible.

The balance point ⊙ corresponds to simple harmonic motion, i.e., to a *sine-wave* pattern, which at its zero amplitude is a straight horizontal line. Any oscillation about the point of balance increases the amplitude accordingly. Thus, absolute balance is a motionless state. All other forms of balance appear in the form of slight oscillation (compare this with the behavior of a magnetic needle).

The forms expressing gain (the positive zone) are directed away from balance. All forms expressing loss (the negative zone) are directed toward balance. Here the amount of gain or loss corresponds to the value of the angle of the axis-pattern in its relation to the line of absolute balance (that is, the abscissa, or horizontal line, which corresponds to primary axis).

We can ow represent the scale of configurations in their correspondences with the dial positions.

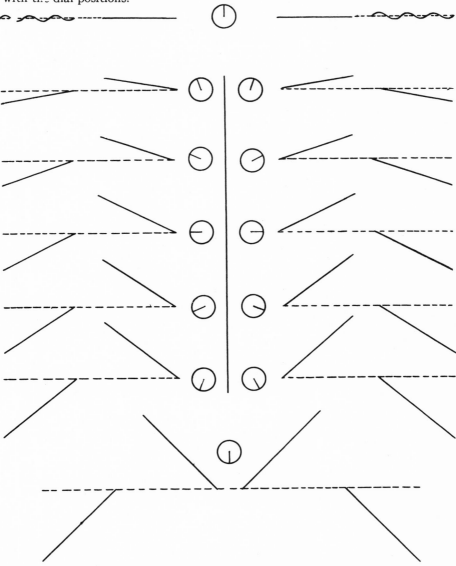

Figure 59. Basic scale of stimulus-response configurations.

The above scale represents configurations not containing resistance. Earlier, in the *Theory of Melody*, we defined the resistance-pattern as a geometrical projection of rotary motion. Its trajectory is that of a sine-wave (originally a circle; later extended into a cylindric spiral and, finally, into a sine-wave). By combining each of the above patterns with oscillatory motion in a sine-wave projection, we obtain the resistance forms of the stimulus-response configurations.

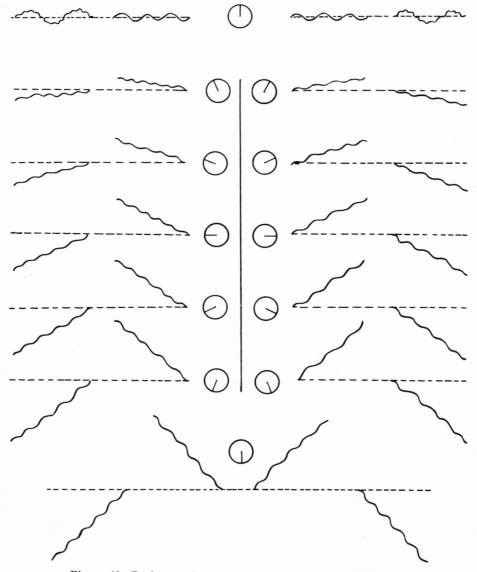

Figure 60. Resistance forms of the stimulus-response configurations.

E. Complex Forms of Stimulus-Response Configurations

Further intensification of resistance forms derives from combinations of the basic patterns. All positive forms become diverging and all negative, converging. We shall consider the basic patterns to be *fundamental* and the auxiliary patterns, *complementary*. Thus in the $\frac{a}{0}$ axial combination, a is fundamental and 0, complementary. In all oblique patterns, i.e., where 0 participates with the converging or diverging axes, the 0-axis is always complementary. In the case of a pair of converging or diverging axes, the axis which leads to a climax becomes fundamental.

A certain amount of intensification can be obtained by two or more parallel patterns, which in this case act as forces of the same direction; the addition of such forces increases the energy. This is true of mechanical phenomena; the intensification (growth or increase) of the amplitude which results from the addition of two or more identically directed phases (like the addition of sines or cosines) offers a purely physical illustration. Complex patterns resulting from several parallel configurations may be designated as $\frac{a'}{a}$, $\frac{a}{a'}$, $a \div a' \div a''$, $a' \div a \div a''$, $a' \div a'' \div a$, etc., in which cases they represent intensified variants of a.

The intensification of a pattern as a stimulus of configurational response depends on two main factors:

(1) the numbers of axes;

(2) the value of angles between the axes and the abscissa (primary axis).

The greater the number of axes employed simultaneously to produce one complex configuration, the more intense the response. An increase in the value of the angle (increase of its obtusity) stimulates an increase in the intensity of the response.

1. Parallel Forms

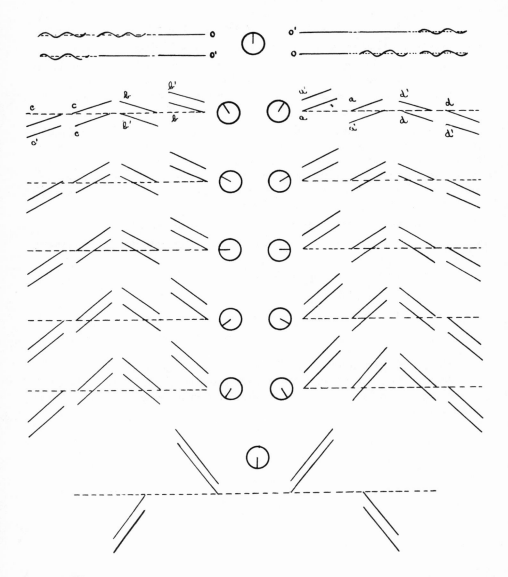

Figure 61. Binary forms of the stimulus-response configurations.

2. Oblique Forms

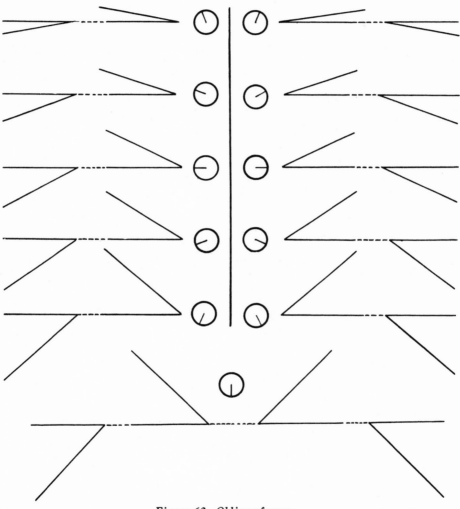

Figure 62. Oblique forms.

3. Diverging-Converging Forms

The angle of divergence or convergence between the fundamental secondary axis and the primary axis is equal to or greater than the angle of divergence or convergence between the complementary secondary axis and the primary axis: $\alpha \geqq \alpha'$.

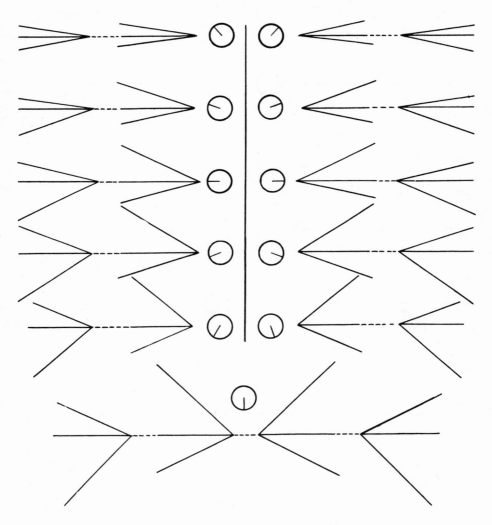

To all the above patterns of Fig. 61 (A, B and C) further resistance may be added by means of oscillatory sine-wave motion.

Figure 63. Diverging-converging forms.

Only diverging-converging forms are included in this table.

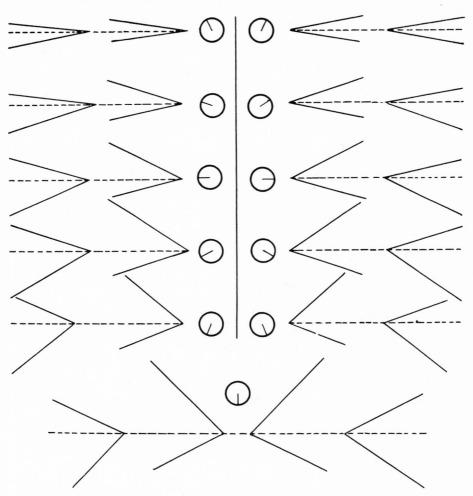

Figure 64. Ternary forms of the stimulus-response configurations.

To all the above patterns, further resistance may be added by means of oscillatory sine-wave motion.

Still more complex stimulus-response configurations can be included by means of a group of converging-diverging secondary axes which, in this case, produce a variety of angle values with the primary axis. Such configurations are of the radiating type. The angle value decreases with proximity to primary axis. This permits avoidance of overlapping when such configurations are transformed into harmonic strata. The outer strata must be expressed through S2p; the intermediate, through S3p; the closest to primary axis, through S4p.

All such complex diverging-converging patterns are characterized by extreme intensity and are applicable mostly to the last quadrants of the negative and the positive zone of the psychological dial.

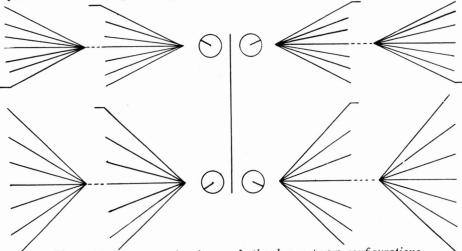

Figure 65. Some complex forms of stimulus-response configurations.

Further resistance may be added to all the above forms by means of oscillatory sine-wave motion. This form of resistance can be realized by means of combined (upper and lower: $\vec{\underset{\rightarrow}{E}}$) directional units.

The degree of angular divergence-convergence can be modified by the respective selection of tonal cycles for Sp, S2p, S3p and S4p, as each cycle has a different divergence-convergence tendency. The horizontal segments define the position of a climax for each configuration.

F. SPATIO-TEMPORAL ASSOCIATIONS

The responses we have dealt with thus far are of the inherited type. Other responses are inherited only as a tendency or inclination. These can be cultivated further. New uninherited associations can be conditioned and cultivated. These associations enter into the response-system by means of sense-organs. The latter may be activated simultaneously by the different stimuli entering the system, and also by self-stimuli already present in every sense-organ. The impulse-groups combine themselves in some fashion with those which are already present and which are integrated with self-stimulated groups.

The responses we have dealt with thus far are of the *eventual* (i.e., pertaining to event or process) type. · We shall discuss now the semantics of responses of the *essential* (i.e., non-eventual) type. These are primarily associated with intensity and quality.

One group of such responses belongs to spatio-temporal associations. These responses associate the auditory with the visual in terms of dimension, distance, form, luminosity and visible texture. These essential characteristics of the visual are mutually convertible with their auditory counterparts; that is, if a certain visual *symbol* has its auditory *counter symbol*, both symbols become interchangeable.

Another group of essential responses pertains to extra-visual-auditory perception. Sensations like the olfactory (smell), the gustatory (taste) and the thermic (temperature) belong to this group. These sensations can also be cultivated to a high degree of discrimination and, eventually, become hereditary, like the olfactory discrimination of canines. However, at present human beings in most cases are equipped with greater discriminatory power over the visible and the audible. All other sensations are less developed and therefore less crystallized.

Responses which are less concentrated than in the case of the visual and the auditory have a lower, i.e., a weaker associative capacity. In such cases the response-patterns and the associations they stimulate are often not capable of crystallizing beyond the "unpleasant-pleasant" diad. Individually, this is sometimes true of auditory discrimination as such. There are still some listeners who are not capable of auditory pattern-discrimination beyond the two biologically basic forms of response, which are characteristic of the undifferentiated universal fore-sense, i.e., the unpleasant (or unsatisfactory) and the pleasant (or satisfactory).

We shall return now to an analysis of the spatio-temporal associations. These include: dimension, direction, density of structure, form and luminosity.

Texture, i.e., the molecular structure of matter, as it can be perceived, is partly in visual and partly in tactile perception. Dimension, which in perception is closely associated with distance, corresponds to the intensity (volume) of sound. The close (near) appears to be loud, and the remote (far) appears to be soft. Including the dimensional characteristics, we acquire the following parallelisms of association:

close   —   big — loud
remote — small — soft

These associations are basic because they correspond to the space-perception of sounds in which intensity decreases with distance.

The association of spatial directions with sound seems to be pretty well established so far as high and low, or up and down are concerned. There may be a number of sources and reasons for the development of such associations in our civilization. But it may be questionable that such associations are either basic or rigid. For example, our basic pitch-scale motion is associated with increasing frequencies, in spite of the fact that in vocal execution it is the direction of increasing effort. On the other hand, the same pitch-scale motion among the primitive and past civilizations represents just the reverse, i.e., it is associated with decreasing frequencies (the biological pattern of exhaling or sighing). At any rate, for our purposes the following associations are acceptable:

high (above the point of observation) corresponds to high frequency of sound;

low (below the point of observation) corresponds to low frequency of sound.

Variation between the two opposites corresponds to respective frequency variation:

ascent—increasing frequency;
descent—decreasing frequency.

There are no right-left associations with any component of sound. Immediate associations with the *direction of the source of sound* can be obtained through the positioning of such sources, through the positioning of loud-speakers, as was done, for example, in the first presentation of Walt Disney's *Fantasia* in New York. Under such conditions the source of sound can be projected from any direction in relation to the listener. This possibility, however, has nothing to do with the expression of direction by any configuration of the components of sound.

Density of structure corresponds to the density of musical texture, which includes tone-quality, and instrumental and harmonic density. There is a general correspondence between the dimensional quality, i.e., size, and density. Large spatial extensions correspond to large frequency-ranges; small spatial extensions correspond to small frequency ranges. As the density of matter corresponds to the density of musical texture, different degrees of the density of matter, which have the same dimensional range, can be expressed by corresponding variations of textural density.

For example, S3p, distributed through two octaves, would associate itself with matter of lower density than S6p distributed through the same range. Thus, a wide area of cumulus clouds can be associated with the middle-high and high register of relatively low density. On the other hand, the sinister dark rain clouds can be associated with the middle and middle-low register of a considerably higher density.

As we have seen before, some spatio-temporal associations are mutually convertible. One of such mutually convertible associations is the association of continuity and discontinuity of space with the continuity and discontinuity of time. This capacity permits us to associate continuous durations with continuous extensions, and discontinuous durations with discontinuous extensions. Thus we arrive at the following correspondences:

continuous extension — curvilinear spatial form — continuous durations (smooth attack followed by legato);

discontinuous extension — rectilinear spatial form (angular form) — discontinuous durations (accented attack followed by non-legato or portomento);

discontinuous configuration — configuration consisting of dissociated elements — abrupt durations (abrupt attack corresponding to staccato).

It follows from the above group of correspondences that the musical expression of smooth or round or spheric configurations such as sky, domes, rolling hills, lakes, cotton-like clouds, etc., must assume the form of *legato*; that buildings, bridges, elementary rectilinear geometrical patterns, partitioned interiors, squarely landscaped grounds or gardens, etc., must assume the form of *portamento* which corresponds to broad strokes; that stars, raindrops, snow-flakes, birds in flight, planes in group-formation and other patterns produced by dissociated elements must assume the form of *staccato*, whose attack form, i.e., whose durability and intensity, corresponds with the dimensions of the elements producing the respective configuration.

The *texture* of matter can be defined as its molecular structure. The perception of textures is partly visual, partly tactile. They appear to our senses as a group of gradations from smooth to rough. In a smooth texture the structural units are imperceptible. Such a texture associates itself with sound whose physical components of the partials are also imperceptible. It can be associated musically with a pure "tone". An exceptionally good tone-quality on such instruments as flute, french horn, clarinet, violin corresponds to the sensation of smooth. In a rough texture, on the contrary, the structural units are perceptible. Such a texture associates itself with sound where either a vibrato is present, or certain partials noticeably stand out (as in the double reed instruments), or a certain harshness of tone-quality is due to the presence of inharmonic elements (such as noises produced by the friction of the bow over the strings as in mediocre violin playing).

Smooth and rough, when associated with the pleasant and the unpleasant, may also be expressed by the degree of musical harshness, which is one or another form of tension, i.e., of dissonant quality. A melody coupled in octaves or other simple harmonic relations appears smooth; on the other hand, a melody coupled in dissonant or complex harmonic relations appears rough. In all cases, there is a scale of gradations between the two extremes.

The associations of *luminosity* (the intensity of light) have a basic correspondence with the frequency-intensity components of sound. The intensity of light, its brightness, generally corresponds to high frequencies, i.e., to high register or a timbre composed of high partials, which render the brightness of tone quality. Flutes, french horns (in their high register), chimes and harmonics as such belong to this group. Concentrated light associates itself with intense sound, and diffused light, with a moderate or low intensity combined with the same bright tone-quality.

Light of low luminosity, dimmed light, sombreness and darkness correspond generally to low frequencies, i.e., to low range and to sombre timbres composed of middle-range or low partials. All brass in the low register, all double-reed woodwind instruments in the middle-low or low register, all single-reed woodwind instruments in the low register and all stringed-bow instruments, either in the low register or muted (if the register is not high), belong to this group. Concentrated light of low intensity can be best expressed by instruments with saturated timbre, such as trombones and particularly tuba. Diffused light of low intensity or darkness can be best expressed by the low register of saturated string timbres, such as 'celli and particularly basses.

So far as *color* associations are concerned, such associations with musical pitch (or tonalities), as verified by serious investigation, belong entirely to the individual type of conditioning and, therefore, cannot be generalized. However, the inherent luminosity of the different spectral hues (for example, yellow is more luminous than red at the same intensity) generally associates itself with the respective high and low frequencies of sound (i.e., the higher the luminosity, the higher the sound-frequency). In other words, there is apparently an *intensity-frequency correspondence.* It is easy to understand such a correspondence, if we take into account the data of psychology, which show that the *intensity of a sensation* is the result of the *number of impulses.* As this holds true for any sensation, we can produce an intensification of response by increasing the number of identical impulses, i.e., by repetition. As we have seen before, in our applications of this process to melody, the repetition of an impulse produces resistance and intensifies the anxiety-response.

Saturation is another factor of intensity. A saturated tone-quality is the result of the addition of several components (partials in this case). As identical phases of many components add up, this addition increases the amplitude. For this reason a dense sound is at the same time a loud sound.

Intensity of *all sensations* parallels the amplitudinal intensity of sound, i.e., stronger responses associate themselves with the louder sound. The sensation of high pressure, for instance, associates itself with high intensity of sound. Of course, the reverse is also true. The reason for such correspondences is that pressure is in direct association with force. We respond to pressure as a sort of "passive force".

In tactile form pressure appears as a kinaesthetic sensation of the "opposition" type, which comes from the receptors in the muscles. The latter permits us to judge the relative hardness or softness of an object and associates itself with the corresponding forms of attack (hard: pesante, portamento; soft: non-legato, legato).

Thermic sensations have not yet crystallized into any rigid associations with sonic forms. A general tendency may be observed, however, to associate "warm" with saturated tone-qualities and middle or middle-low register and particularly with the tone of brass instruments; and "cold", with unsaturated tone-qualities and high register. "Vibrato" also produces the effect of "warm" just as the "non-vibrato", that of "cold". Of course, some of the thermic forms can be associated with sonic forms through association with other sensations, in which case the latter become pattern-stimulating impulses. For example, an impression of boiling may be associated, not with temperature, but with the kinetic characteristics of the process of boiling and the sound pattern it produces.

The non-cutaneous sensations (i.e., the sensations not originating in the skin, which may be considered the basically biological sensations, such as hunger, thirst, pain, sexual urge) associate themselves with sonic patterns through the parallelism of pleasantness-unpleasantness. Some extreme forms of non-cutaneous sensations become so intense that they stimulate resistance associations. Then their configurations fall into the general class of kinetic patterns (as expressed in our psychological dial), i.e., the patterns of motion and action, as they include the striving for a goal of relief and satisfaction.

The *kinetic* patterns are immediate and self-sufficient symbols, and have a universal significance as elements of language. Nevertheless, as was stated before, the intonational forms which the kinetic patterns assume, are of local significance. In this sense, for example, a certain state of melancholy, corresponding to a certain response-pattern, may assume the intonational form of Chinese or of Roumanian music, precisely in the same way as "I feel sad" can also be said in the Chinese or Roumanian language, stimulating the same association-pattern.

The non-kinetic, or rather "extra-kinetic" patterns are not self-sufficient and therefore, not as universal in their association stimulating intensity. As in the case of gestures, when words alone do not seem to be sufficient, the extra-kinetic patterns have their value only as an auxiliary stimulus parallel to some other form of stimulation which is more universal as a symbol.

Such patterns are a good supplement to a script or a program, and serve as intensifiers of the basic symbols. Sonic symbols of music usually supplement verbal symbols, and as such are universally used in the theatre, cinema, radio and television.

CHAPTER 18

COMPOSITION OF SONIC SYMBOLS

THE principles disclosed in the preceding chapter constitute an application of my General Theory of Configurational Semantics to music. Now we arrive at the practical application of this theory to the composition of sonic symbols.

The maximum success with which such an application may be met depends upon the optimum of response, which is a reactive pre-disposition, and geometrically corresponds to congruence, i.e., configurational identity (or at least to a close approximation to it). This congruence exists between the stimulus and the response configurations and, in turn, is conditioned by the congruity of the dial of stimuli (i.e., phasic stimuli) with the dial of responses (i.e., self-stimuli and reactive pre-disposition). Thus the response optimum is achieved when all points of the response-dial adequately correspond (i.e., geometrically coincide) with the respective points of the stimulus-dial.

Such a condition exists when the listener is in a state of balance (180° position on the dial) before he is subjected to musical stimulation.

For the individual whose normal state of balance is a state of depression (to any extent), the stimulus which would bring him to what we would generally consider normal, must be above normal, i.e., in the positive zone, at an angle which equals the individual's deviation from normal in the negative zone.

For an under-stimulated Mr. Hypochondriac whose normal is at 150°, that is, 30° below normal, the stimulus which would appear to him as normal and which would bring him to our balance at 180°, would have a pattern corresponding to 180° + 30°, i.e., of 210°. On the contrary, an over-stimulated Mr. Highstrung, whose normal is at 210°, would require 180° − 30°, i.e., 150° stimulus-pattern, in order to bring him to our balance. In other words, the corresponding dial-adjustment must be made for each individual case deviating from normal. That is, the stimulus-dial must be turned to the right or to the left (clockwise or counterclockwise), on the angle of deviation from normal, and in the *opposite* direction from the individual's point of balance.

Indicating the response-clock by R and the stimulus-clock by S, we can illustrate the two cases discussed above as follows.

First, we have the case of the under-stimulated individual and the stimulus-clock adjusted to produce the intended response of balance:

R   S

Figure 66. Stimulus-clock adjusted to understimulated individual.

[1432]

Next, we have the case of an over-stimulated individual and the stimulus-clock adjusted to produce the intended response of balance:

Figure 67. Stimulus-clock adjusted to overstimulated individual.

In both cases, N indicates the point of normal for the respective individual and the stimulus which would affect him as our normal.

This process of the stimulus-dial adjustment for each individual case of response which does not coincide with this dial, may be looked upon as psycho-physiological coordination, or synchronization, of the two dials.

Each component produces its corresponding configuration for each dial-point. However, it is not necessary to have *all* components of one sonic symbol in exact correspondence with one another. For example, a melodic trajectory corresponding to ⬦ may have a pitch-scale corresponding to ⬦, and still produce the general character of ⬦. Naturally, an exact correspondence of several components of one sonic symbol intensifies the latter. But such an intensity of pattern is not always necessary.

A. NORMAL: ⬦

Associations: Balance, Repose, Quiescence, Passive Contemplation, Uniformity, Eventlessness, Inactivity, Monotony.

The stimulus-patterns of this group tend themselves toward uniformity, which must be expressed through all the participating components. As the point of absolute balance is imaginary rather than actual, most of the patterns of this group have a certain degree of oscillatory tendency and fluctuate to a certain degree about the balance point. The direction to the right (clockwise) from the balance point expresses the tendency of unbalancing and the direction to the left (counterclockwise) from the balance point expresses the tendency toward balancing. It is correct to think of the patterns of this group as trajectories of a pendulum or a magnetic needle.

Technical Resources:

(1) **Temporal Rhythm:** Durations ranging from very long to moderately long, depending on the degree of activity, in uniform or nearly uniform motion. Alternation of such durations with rests possessing similar characteristics. Uniform or nearly uniform attack-groups.

(2) **Pitch-Scales:** Scales with a limited number of pitch units and a fairly uniform distribution of intervals. In extreme forms of inactivity, one-unit scale.

(3) **Melodic Forms:** Only stationary and regularly oscillating forms, within a moderate pitch-range for associations with small dimensions, and a

wide range for associations with large dimensions. A good example of the latter is one-unit oscillation through three octaves in Verdi's scene on the Nile from *Aida*. The violins play *g* on all four strings, through an oscillating instrumental form of single attacks and uniform durations.

The typical trajectories are:

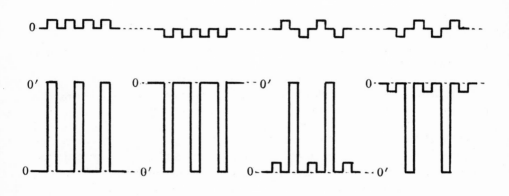

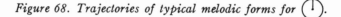

Figure 68. Trajectories of typical melodic forms for $\left(\!\begin{array}{c}\text{|}\end{array}\!\right)$.

(4) **Harmonic Forms:** Either a complete absence of harmony or one H which remains constant. The instrumental form is either sustained (stationary) or slightly oscillating in uniform durations. The most suitable structures are tonal expansions of the participating pitch-scale. Only one harmonic stratum should be employed. If harmony is employed without melody, its structures must consist of fairly uniform and consonant intervals. The latter is necessary in order to secure tranquility.

(5) **Contrapuntal Forms:** None, as the presence of a group of trajectories suggests activity.

(6) **Instrumental Resources:**

(a) *density:* uniform density which is conditioned by the
(b) *range:* which depends on the dimensional associations;
(c) *dynamics:* uniform and either low or medium; no sporadic accents;
(d) *attacks:* smooth; legato, non-legato and light staccato (uniform and continuous) are appropriate;
(e) *tone quality:* open, i.e., approaching the sine-wave form as far as possible: Flute, Violin (non-vibrato), particularly its harmonics, high French Horn (pp), sub-tone Clarinet, Double-Bass on open strings and particularly harmonics;
(f) *register:* depends on luminosity associations; night, darkness—low; sunrise, shining moon or stars—high; for neutral associations, like a peaceful landscape or quiet lake—middle register.

The following fragments have a recapitulating construction

(1) A moonless night in the desert

(2) Summer landscape of farmland; no action

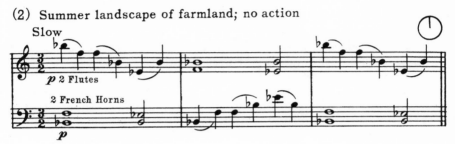

(3) Starry sky over Grand Canyon

(4) Contemplation

Figure 69. Musical examples for normal clock stimulus

B. Upper Quadrant of the Negative Zone: ◗

Associations: Dissatisfaction, Melancholy, Weakness, Sadness, Depression, Pain, Suffering, Despair.

The stimulus-patterns of this group tend themselves toward loss of energy and balancing. In their extreme and intense form, they assume anticlimactic configurations. The basic patterns of this group are *b* and *c* axes.* The degree of intensity of the stimulus-form corresponds to the amplitude of the respective configuration. The degree of dramatic tension corresponds to the respective form of resistance.

Technical Resources:

1 Temporal Rhythm:

⬭ Uniform and fairly uniform duration-groups, followed by one or two long durations; the weariness effect is achieved by frequent cadencing; moderate or slightly animated tempo. Many waltzes and mazurkas of Chopin will serve as suitable illustrations. Slow syncopation and upbeat-groups; also false syncopation produced by rests.

⬭ Configurations corresponding to the loss of momentum: (a) decreasing number of attacks in the successive groups; (b) increasing duration-values. The latter may correspond to either rhythmic (i.e., containing resistance) or progressive (i.e., direct) rallentando. Moderate tempo.

These characteristics, when they increase progressively, ultimately lead to an anticlimax:

⬭ This stage is the conclusive form of the preceding development. It signifies ultimate despair, exhaustion, loss of power and, finally, death. Use extremely long durations, often dissociated from one another by long rests, and obtained as a result of direct or indirect (delayed, i.e., rhythmic) rallentando. Slow tempo.

2 Pitch-Scales:

⬭ Uniform or fairly uniform intervals, arranged in such a way that the smaller intervals are below the larger ones. For example:

$1 + 2 + 1 + 2 + 1 + 2 + 1 + 2$, i.e.,

$c - d\flat - e\flat - f\flat - f\sharp - g - a - b\flat - c$;

$c - e\flat - g - b\flat - d - f - a - c - \ldots$; $(3 + 4) + \ldots$,

$c - f - d\flat - g\flat - d\natural - g - e\flat - a\flat - e \ldots (5 + 8) + \ldots$, i.e.

Also use the above scales combined with descending directional units.

⬭ Further increase of contrast between the upper and the lower interval placed adjacently. For example:

$(1 + 5) + \ldots$, i.e., $c - d\flat - f\sharp - g - c$;

$(3 + 8) + \ldots$, i.e., $c - e\flat - b - d - b\flat - c\sharp - a - \ldots$;

$(1 + 3) + \ldots$, i.e., $c - d\flat - e - f - g\sharp - a - c$.

---

*The b and c axes are balancing axes. The b axis is the descending direction toward the primary axis. The c axis is the ascending direction toward the primary axis. See Vol. I, p. 252 (Ed.)

Also several small intervals appearing in succession and followed by one large interval. For example:

$(1 + 1 + 3) + \ldots$, i.e., $c - c\sharp - d - f - f\sharp - g - b\flat - b\natural - c - e\flat -$
$\ldots$; $(3 + 3 + 5) + \ldots$, i.e., $c - e\flat - g\flat - b - d - f - b\flat - d\flat -$
$f\flat - a$
$(1 + 1 + 2 + 6) + \ldots$, i.e., $c - c\sharp - d - e - b\flat - b\natural - c\natural - d - a\flat - \ldots$

Such scales usually represent a combination of the scales referred to in ⟨↗⟩ and their crystallized descending directional units, in which case the latter become neutral units.

As the predominant configuration of this zone is one of decline, and is associated with descending tones, it is practical to think of scales belonging to this zone as being constructed downward (as in the primitive and archaic civilizations).

3 Melodic Forms:

⟨↗⟩ Balancing axes (b and c). Balancing binary parallel axes $\left(\dfrac{b'}{b}, \dfrac{b}{b'}, \dfrac{c'}{c}, \dfrac{c}{c'}\right)$. Only weak forms of resistance.

⟨↘⟩ Balancing axes with a strong form of resistance; often beginning with a climax and evolving into anticlimactic forms. Binary converging axes $\left(\dfrac{b}{c}\right)$. All forms have resistance. Ternary converging axial combinations ($b \div 0 \div c$ and $c \div 0 \div b$). Longer time-period is necessary for more extreme forms.

4 Harmonic Forms:

⟨↗⟩

(a) *Structures:* consisting of balanced or nearly balanced consonant intervals, with smaller intervals being placed below the larger ones (downward gravity effect). These structures are similar to or identical with the pitch-scales of this zone and can be used in any tonal expansion. Also balanced structures of the consonant type, with one lowered function (descending alteration), like the minor ninth in a diminished S(9). Casual descending directional units used in moderate quantities.

(b) *Progressions:* containing moderate downward motion. For example: Sp in C_{-7}; S2p in C_{-3}, C_5 (this pattern contains a certain amount of resistance); S3p in C_{-3} ↷, C_5 ↶ ; S4p in C_3 ↶ , C_5 ←↦, C_7 ↷ .

⟨↘⟩

(a) *Structures:* of the lower gravity type, containing *dissonant* descending alterations (one or more). Such structures can be obtained by altering some of the functions in a balanced or nearly balanced structure. For example, a balanced structure $4 + 3 + 4$, i.e., $c - e - g - b$, altered into $3 + 3 + 4$, i.e., $c - e\flat - g\flat - b$, by lowering its gravity, i.e., by aggregating smaller intervals in the lower part of the structure. Likewise, $5 + 5 + 5$, i.e., $c - f - - b\flat - e\flat$, can be altered into $4 + 6 + 5$, i.e., $c - e - b\flat - d\sharp$, or into $4 + 5 + 6$, i.e., $c - e - a - d\sharp$. Also strata consisting of structures possessing lower gravity. Needless to say, the intensity of the pattern grows with the addition of the respective characteristics.

(b) *Progressions:* containing extreme (i.e., rapidly progressing) downward motion, or delayed downward motion with resistance; the latter is caused by the motion-pattern of transformations, which is inherent in some structures. Examples of cycles and transformations: SpC_3, C_5; $S2pC_7$; $S3pC_7 \circlearrowleft$, S4p all general transformations producing rapidly descending or delayed descending patterns. For extreme effects: aggregations of rapidly descending strata; converging strata.

(5) $\frac{M}{H}$ **Tension Forms** (i.e., forms pertaining to harmonization and melodization: functional relations of melody and harmony):

$\oslash$ Descending directional units whose neutral units represent lower chordal functions. For example, in $S_2(5)$ such melodic steps as: $ab \rightarrow g$, $f \rightarrow eb$, $d \rightarrow c$, against C–chord; in $S_1(7b)$, i.e., large, such a melodic step as: $db \rightarrow c$, against C–chord.

$\ominus$ Descending directional units whose neutral units represent higher chordal functions. For example, in $S_1(7b)$ such melodic steps are: $eb \rightarrow db$, $bbb \rightarrow ab$, against C–chord. In extreme cases, symmetric superimpositions of $\frac{M}{H}$, where both M and H have the lower gravity characteristics; also the same type, combined with descending directional units. For example, $\frac{M}{H} = \sqrt[12]{2}$:

$$\frac{S_{II}}{S_I} = \frac{db - fb - ab}{CS_2(5)} \; ; \; \frac{M}{H} = \sqrt[12]{2} : \; \frac{S_{II}}{S_I} = \frac{db - gb - cb}{bb} \atop {S: \frac{\overline{f}}{c}}$$

6. Contrapuntal Forms:

$\oslash$ Oblique balancing forms: $\frac{b}{0}$ and $\frac{c}{0}$; binary parallel forms leading to balance: $\frac{b}{b}$ and $\frac{c}{c}$. The same in slightly converging angles:

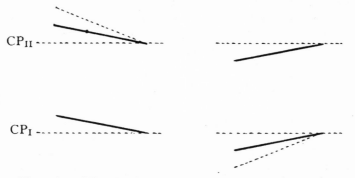

Figure 70. Oblique balancing axes and binary parallel axes.

Identical balancing axes in a more extreme convergence:

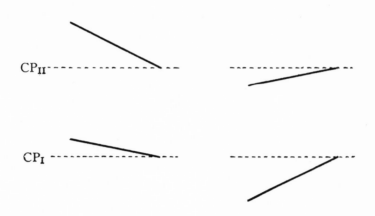

CP_{II}
CP_{I}

Figure 71. Identical balancing axes.

Simple versus complex axial groups of the same (balancing) direction:

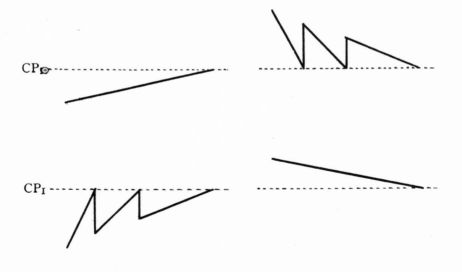

CP
CP_{I}

Figure 72. Simple versus complex balancing axial groups.

Non-identical converging axes, often containing resistance: $\dfrac{b}{c}$ and $b \div 0 \div c$

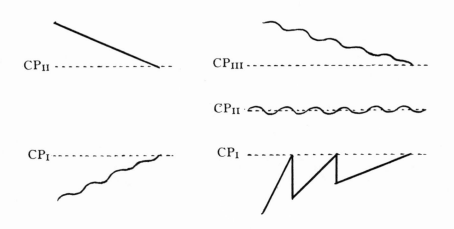

Figure 73. Non-identical converging axes.

For more extreme cases, convergence of many parts.

7. Instrumental Resources:

(a) *density:* ⟨ ⟩ low; ⟨ ⟩ medium; ⟨ ⟩ high; in extreme cases, variable density of the following forms:

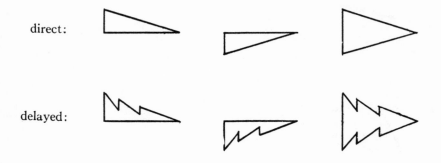

Figure 74. Variable densities.

(b) *range:* partly depends on the dimensional associations; more generally is associated with the intensity of the stimulus-pattern:

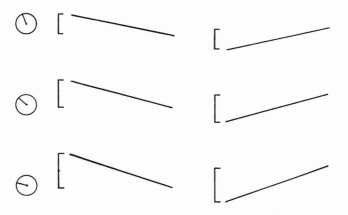

Figure 75. Stimulus-patterns.

(c) *dynamics:* either low (p, pp) or decreasing; the intensity of the stimulus-pattern is associated with the period of its diminuendo and with its dynamic range:

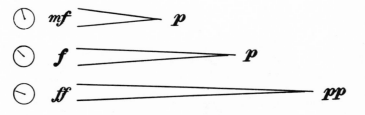

Figure 76. Dynamic ranges.

also groups of sfp with a gradual decline: sfmf + sfp + sfpp; the initial dynamic energy derives from the preceding climax;

(d) *attacks:*

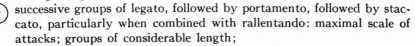 short legato groups starting with an accent; short staccato groups starting with an accent; mixed short legato-staccato groups starting with or without an accent: minimal scale of attacks;

alternate legato and portamento groups in which portamento follows legato, particularly when combined with rallentando; groups of an average length;

successive groups of legato, followed by portamento, followed by staccato, particularly when combined with rallentando: maximal scale of attacks; groups of considerable length;

(e) *tone-quality:*

⟨⟩ the single-reed quality: clarinet, violin (vibrato), French horn in its middle register, a mellow trombone at low intensity and in its high register (as in Tommy Dorsey's performance of "I'm Getting Sentimental Over You");

⟨⟩ the double-reed (nasal) quality in the middle or the high register: violin on the G-string, viola in general, 'cello (high or middle register), high oboe and high bassoon, muted trumpet;

⟨⟩ the muted quality: all stringed-bow instruments muted, low oboe, English horn, low bassoon, low trombone (also muted, the entire range) low and middle register of the bass clarinet, low French horn (also stopped), tuba, gong;

(f) *register:* the intensity of the stimulus-pattern in relation to range:

⟨⟩ middle or middle-low;

⟨⟩ middle and middle-low;

⟨⟩ middle, middle-low and low;
      the basic characteristics of the stimulus-pattern in relation to register:

⟨⟩ middle; ⟨⟩ middle-low; ⟨⟩ low.

(1) Moderate

(2) Slow

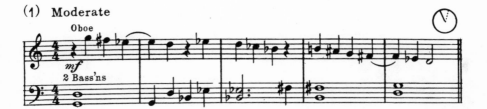

Figure 77. Musical illustrations for upper quadrant of negative zone ⬤
(*continued*)

(3) Moderate

(4) Moderate

Figure 77. Musical illustrations for upper quadrant of negative zone (*concluded*)

C. UPPER QUADRANT OF THE POSITIVE ZONE:

Associations: Satisfaction, Well-being, Strength, Accomplishment, Happiness, Joy, Gaiety, Challenge, Aggression, Conquest, Success, Triumph, Exuberance, Elation, Exaltation, Jubilation, Ecstasy.

Technical Resources:

1 Temporal Rhythm:

Uniform or fairly uniform duration-groups; groups of longer durations followed by groups of shorter durations; binomials with stress on the first term $(2 + 1; 3 + 1; 5 + 3; \ldots)$. Duration-groups characteristic of regimental marches and folk-dances. Down-beat patterns and down-beat accentuation. Only the simplest forms of syncopation, such as $1 + 2 + 1$, or $1 + 2 + 2 + 1$, or $1 + 2 + 2 + 2 + 1$. Fairly animated tempo.

(⟋) Configurations corresponding to the gain of momentum: (a) increasing number of attacks in the successive groups; (b) decreasing duration-values. The latter may correspond to either rhythmic (i.e., containing resistance) or progressive (i.e., direct) accelerando. Animated tempo.

These characteristics, when they increase progressively, ultimately lead to a climax:

(⟋) This stage is the conclusive form of the preceding development. It signifies a climax, i.e., the state of ultimate joy, exuberance, jubilation, and finally, ecstasy. It is characterized by an energetic overabundance resulting in groups which consist of many attacks and minimal durations. The total effect is vibrant and scintillating. The approach to short durations (often in the form of a rapid arpeggio, or tremolo, or frulato*) is accomplished by direct or indirect accelerando. A climax cannot be sustained for any appreciable length of time as the response automatically goes into decline (defense-reflex of the sense-organs and of the entire response-system is the probable cause of it; refer to the Weber-Fechner psycho-physiological law). Fast tempo.

2 Pitch-Scales:

(⟋) Uniform or fairly uniform intervals arranged in such a way that smaller intervals are above the larger ones. For example: $(4 + 3) + \ldots$, i.e., $c - e -$ $- g - b - d - f\# - a - c\# - e - g\# - b - \ldots$; $(5 + 4) + \ldots$ i.e., $c -$ $- f - a - d - f\# - b - d\# - g\# - c\# - \ldots$; $(8 + 7) + \ldots$, i.e., $c - ab -$ $- eb - cb - gb - d - a - \ldots$ These scales may be combined with ascending directional units.

(⟋) Further increase of contrast between adjacent upper and lower intervals. For example: $(3 + 1) + \ldots$, i.e., $c - d\# - e - f^\times - g\# - b - c$; $(4 + 1) + \ldots$, i.e., $c - e - f - a - bb - d - eb - g - ab - c - db - \ldots$; $(8 + 3) + \ldots$, i.e., $c - g\# - b - g\natural - bb - gb - a - f - ab - \ldots$

Also several small intervals appearing in succession and following one large interval. For example: $(3 + 1 + 1) + \ldots$, i.e., $c - d\# - e - f - g\# - a -$ $- bb - c\# - d - eb - \ldots$; $(5 + 3 + 3) + \ldots$, i.e., $c - f - g\# - b - e -$ $- g - a\# - d\# - f\# - g^\times - \ldots$; $(6 + 2 + 1 + 1) + \ldots$, i.e., $c - f\# -$ $- g\# - a - a\# - e - f\# - g - g\# - d - e - e\# - f\# - \ldots$

Such scales usually represent a combination of the scales referred to in (⟋) and their crystallized ascending directional units, in which case the latter become neutral units.

Since the predominant configuration of this zone is one of growth and is associated with ascension, it is practical to think of scales belonging to this zone as being constructed upward (in terms of the conception of civilized musical contemporaries).

*See p. 1458.

3 Melodic Forms:

① Unbalancing axes (a and d). Unbalancing binary parallel axes $\left(\dfrac{a'}{a}, \dfrac{a}{a''}, \dfrac{d'}{d}, \dfrac{d}{d'}\right)$. Weak forms of resistance.

② Unbalancing axes exhibiting a strong form of resistance and leading to a climax. Binary diverging axes $\left(\dfrac{a}{d}\right)$. All forms have resistance. Ternary diverging axial combinations ($a \div 0 \div d$ and $d \div 0 \div a$). A longer time-period is necessary for more extreme forms. In extreme cases, a development of several successive climaxes.

4 Harmonic Forms:

①

(a) *Structures:* consisting of balanced or nearly balanced consonant intervals, with smaller intervals being placed above the larger ones (upward gravity effect). These structures are similar to or identical with the pitch-scales of this zone and can be used in any tonal expansion. Also balanced structures of the consonant type, with one raised function (ascending alteration), like the augmented fifth in an augmented S(7♮). Casual ascending directional units used in moderate quantities.

(b) *Progressions:* containing moderate upward motion. For example: Sp in C_7; S2p in C_3, C_{-5} (this pattern contains a certain amount of resistance); S3p in $C_3 \circlearrowleft$, $C_{-5} \circlearrowright$; S4p in $C_{-3} \circlearrowright$, $C_{-5} \leftarrow\!\!\uparrow\!\!\rightarrow$, $C_{-7} \circlearrowleft$.

②

(a) *Structures:* of the upper gravity type, containing *dissonant* ascending alterations (one or more). Such structures can be obtained by altering some of the functions in a balanced or nearly balanced structure. For example, a balanced structure $4 + 3 + 4$, i.e., $c - e - g - b$, altered into $4 + 4 + 3$, i.e., $c - e - g\sharp - b$, by raising its gravity, i.e., by aggregating larger intervals in the lower part of the structure. Likewise, $5 + 5 + 5$, i.e., $c - f - - b\flat - e\flat$, can be altered into $6 + 5 + 4$, i.e., $c - f\sharp - b\natural - d\sharp$. Also strata consisting of structures possessing upper gravity. The intensity of the pattern grows with the addition of these characteristics.

(b) *Progressions:* containing extreme (i.e., rapidly progressing) upward motion, or delayed upward motion with resistance; the latter is caused by the motion-pattern of transformations, which is inherent in some structures. Examples of cycles and transformations: SpC$_{-3}$, C$_5$; 2SpC$_{-7}$; 3SpC$_{-7} \circlearrowleft$; S4p all general transformations producing rapidly ascending or delayed ascending patterns. For extreme effects: aggregation of rapidly ascending strata; diverging strata.

(5) $\frac{M}{H}$ **Tension Forms** (functional relations of melody and harmony):

Ⓛ Ascending directional units whose neutral units represent lower chordal functions. For example, in $S_1(5)$ such melodic steps as: $b \rightarrow c$, $d\sharp \rightarrow e$; $f\sharp \rightarrow g$ against C–chord; in $S_2(7\natural)$, i.e., the first augmented, such melodic steps as: $f^\times \rightarrow g\sharp$, $a\sharp \rightarrow b$, against C–chord.

Ⓛ Ascending directional units, whose neutral units represent higher chordal functions. For example, in $S_2(7\natural)$ such melodic steps are: $c^\times \rightarrow d\sharp$, $g^\times \rightarrow a\sharp$, against C–chord. In extreme cases, symmetric superimposition of $\frac{M}{H}$ where both M and H have the upper gravity characteristics; also the same type, combined with ascending directional units. For example,

$$\frac{M}{H} = \sqrt[4]{2}: \quad \frac{S_{II}}{S_I} = \frac{d\sharp - f^\times - a^\times}{CS_3(5)};$$

$$\frac{M}{H} = \sqrt[3]{2^2}: \quad \frac{S_{II}}{S_I} = \frac{g\sharp - b\sharp - d\sharp}{CS_1(5)}; \quad \frac{M}{H} = \sqrt{2}: \quad \frac{S_{II}}{S_I} = \frac{f\sharp - b - e}{b\flat}$$

$$S: \frac{\overline{f}}{c}$$

6   Contrapuntal Forms:

Ⓛ Oblique unbalancing forms: $\frac{a}{0}$ and $\frac{d}{0}$; binary parallel forms leading away from balance: $\frac{a}{a}$ and $\frac{d}{d}$. The same in slightly diverging angles:

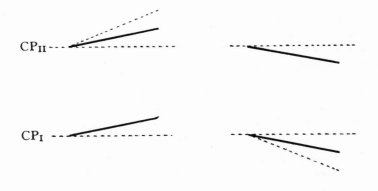

Figure 78. Oblique unbalancing axes and binary parallel forms leading away from balance.

Identical unbalancing axes in a more extreme divergence:

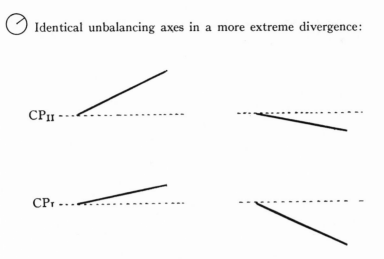

Figure 79. Identical unbalancing axes.

Simple versus complex axial groups of the same (unbalancing) direction:

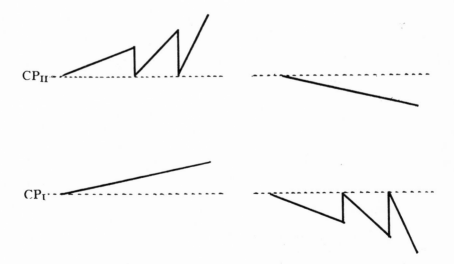

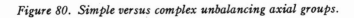

Figure 80. Simple versus complex unbalancing axial groups.

Non-identical diverging axes, often containing resistance: $\frac{a}{d}$ and a $\div$ 0 $\div$ d.

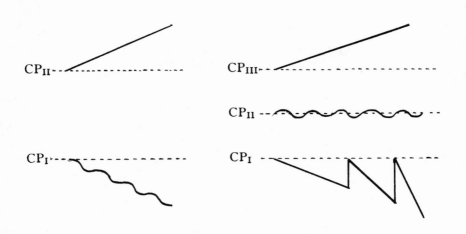

Figure 81. Non-identical diverging axes.

For more extreme cases, divergence of many parts.

7 Instrumental Resources:

(a) *density:* 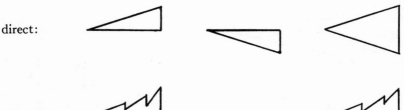 low; medium; high; in extreme cases, variable density of the following forms:

direct:

delayed:

Figure 82. Variable densities.

(b) *range:* partly depends on the dimensional associations; generally is associated with the intensity of the stimulus-pattern:

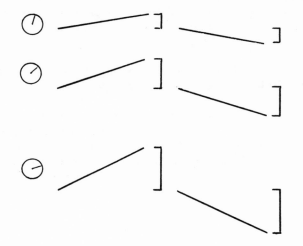

Figure 83. Stimulus patterns.

(c) *dynamics:* either high (*f*, *ff*) or increasing; the intensity of the stimulus-pattern is associated with the period of its crescendo and with its dynamic range:

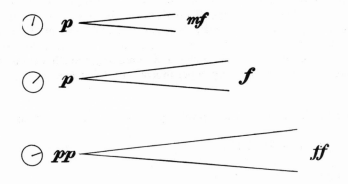

Figure 84. Dynamic ranges.

Also groups with rapid crescendo in a gradual growth: ppf + pf + mf-f; mp < mf + p < f + pp < ff; the dynamic energy grows through resistance.

(d) *attacks*

(*/*) short legato groups ending with an accent; short staccato groups ending with an accent; mixed legato-staccato groups (often two-attack groups of legato-staccato: ♩♪ ; also upbeat-downbeat two-attack groups: ♪♪ ♪♪ etc.); generally, minimal scale of attacks;

(*⟋*) alternate portamento and legato groups in which legato follows portamento, particularly when combined with accelerando;

(*⌐*) successive groups of staccato, followed by portamento, followed by legato (which often falls on the climax point) and combined either with accelerando (momentum gain) or with rallentando (suspension of a discharge, immediately preceding the climax); the portamento forms often become marcato or pesante in this case; maximal scale of attacks; groups of a considerable length;

(e) *tone-quality:*

(*/*) open and single-reed quality: flute, clarinet, violin, French horn; piano, harp, celeste, chimes, high-pitched drums, castagnets, wood-blocks, orchestra bells, tamburin;

(*⟋*) brilliant and open brass quality: mixtures of high stringed-bow and woodwind instruments; open trumpets and trombones; high register of 'celli for "passionate" effects; cymbals (*mf*) and kettle-drums;

(*⌐*) scintillating quality: tremolo, trills and rapid arpeggio forms on stringed-bow and woodwind instruments; extreme high register of trumpets and trombones; xylophone (also with abundant glissando and multiple attacks); frulato, trills and multiple tongue of flutes; multiple tongue (also sustained, for the climax) on trumpets; chimes and cymbals *ff*; kettle-drums, tremolo; brilliant qualities obtained by superimposition of harmonics;

(f) *register:* the intensity of the stimulus-pattern in relation to range:

(*/*) middle or middle-high;

(*⟋*) middle and middle-high;

(*⌐*) middle, middle-high and high;
The basic characteristics of the stimulus-pattern in relation to register:

(*/*) middle; (*⟋*) middle-high; (*⌐*) high.

(1) Fairly animated

(2) Animated

(3) Moderate

(4) Moderate

Figure 85. Musical illustrations for upper-quadrant of positive zone.
(continued).

(5) Moderate

Figure 85 Musical illustrations for upper-quadrant of positive zone (concluded).

D. THE LOWER QUADRANTS OF BOTH ZONES: ◓

1. Negative Zone

Both lower quadrants represent an exaggerated version of the respective patterns of each of the upper quadrants. As the negative (left) zone corresponds to decline, its patterns are that of decomposition. When such decomposition exceeds its natural maximum, the pattern begins to appear discontinuous and the formation of an image, greatly retarded. The normally unobservable details become apparent and begin to obstruct perception of the pattern as a whole. Such an effect is comparable to the extremely magnified optical images seen through a microscope. As we can observe only an insignificant part of an image, which part is greatly magnified, we cannot reconstruct the image as a whole.

For example, a very small portion of a man's arm, appearing as skin surface with some hair growing on it, under magnification may look like a fantastic jungle forest. It would be difficult to stretch the observer's imagination so far as to reconstruct the image of the entire arm, as the dimensional scale is too large. A similar situation exists with regard to the so-called "slow motion" of cinematic projection, in which an image, photographed at 128 frames per second, is cast on the screen at 24 frames per second. In temporal phenomena this extreme magnification of time-period obscures the image, or the process, as a whole, bringing out too many details, and dissociating the observable links of the image, or the process. With an increase in the number of images in recording (taking), the projected image becomes more and more stationary. Imagine a pugilist delivering a blow to his opponent at the rate of 2 minutes per blow. Such a rate, according to standards with which it would be associated, would appear subnatural. Thus it would be perceived as either fantastic or humorous.

As it follows from the above illustrations, in the temporal projections of an image or a process, the rate of mechanical speed is the basic source of extending a time-period. For this reason, sound images, recorded for performance at a certain rate of speed and played back at a considerably lower rate, are bound to produce an effect analogous to cinematic "slow motion". In both cases (i.e., optical and acoustical) of projection, the perceived image appears to be psychologically (i.e., as an associative group) more discontinuous, but physically approaches continuity, even in observation, as more intermediate points or events become noticeable.

As a consequence of this, phonograph records, made to be played at 78 R.P.M. and performed at 33.3 (i.e., taking mechanical speeds which are standard for the phonograph turntable at the present time) appear to be subnatural in effect. Depending on the association with the anticipated stimulus-pattern, such a performance activates the response of fantastic or humorous. The obvious character of "mechanical inefficiency" taking place during the process of formation of an image, makes such an image appear humorous. Further disintegration of perceptible image, caused by a still lower rate of projection, makes such an image appear fantastic.

Different rates of speed for a phonograph record using the standard turn-table speeds, can be obtained through duplication, triplication and even quadru-plication of the original from one speed to another, i.e., from 78 R.P.M. to 33.3 R.P.M., or vice versa. Beyond this, further variation of speed becomes im-practical, as the sound frequencies extend beyond the range of audibility, or beyond physical continuity.

Many ordinary recordings of fairly animated music, when recorded at 78 R.P.M. and played back at 33.3 are, for any practical purpose, humorous. How-ever, the presence of certain physical characteristics in the musical performance, when exaggerated by "slow motion" of the acoustical (i.e., mechanical) per-formance, sometimes increases the effect of humor. For example, "The Mad Scene" from *Lucia di Lamermoor* by Donizetti, as performed by Amelita Galli-Curci (a Victor red-seal record), appears incredibly hilarious when played at 33.3. The special reasons in this case are a lack of rhythmic unison (synchro-nization) with the accompaniment (normally associated with beginners and not with accomplished artists), and the other, a considerable deviation from the required intonation (also associated with beginners who are not able to exert sufficient control over their vocal apparatus), which is also a form of mechanical inefficiency pertaining to the control of frequency.

Nevertheless, the basic effect of humor in this case is mainly due to the straining of the anticipation-fulfillment chain conditioned by the pre-conceived image of an accomplished coloratura, from whom a high degree of alertness and mechanical efficiency are expected.

In another case, the effect of humor arises from: an exaggerated form of vibrato, appearing at a low rate of speed, and a quick fading of sound (the decrease of amplitude) following each attack and combined with the afore-mentioned vibrato. Such an effect can be observed in Bing Crosby's performance of *My Honey's Lovin' Arms* (accompanied by Mills Brothers on a Decca record), when the record is played at 33.3 R.P.M.. A secondary association contributing to the effect of humor is the anticipation-fulfillment chain, as, under such con-ditions of performance, Mr. Crosby's voice acquires the characteristics of piano or Hawaiian guitar (i.e., strong attack, quick fading, exaggerated vibrato, which characteristics are non-vocal, but generally typical of jazz.)

Music of slow pace and of middle-low or low register, triplicated from 33.3 R.P.M. performance to 78 R.P.M. recording and played back at 33.3, gives approximately 1/5 of the original speed. Under such conditions, this type of music appears to be so extended in time as to produce an extreme effect of the subnatural, i.e., fantastic. Something like the beginning of the Overture to *Tannhäuser* by Wagner is apt to produce this effect at 1/5 of its normal speed.

Among my own numerous experiments in this particular field, a record of singing canaries, played at 1/13 of its normal speed (quadruplication of the original from 33.3 R.P.M. performance to 78 R.P.M. recording), is as fantastic and unimaginable as any effect of music can be.

2. Positive Zone

We shall return now to an analysis of the lower quadrant of the positive zone. As the positive zone (right) corresponds to growth, its patterns are that of composition. When such a composition exceeds its natural maximum, the pattern appears not only continuous but extremely precipitated. At extreme velocities, the whole is more observable than the details. A comparable effect may be observed in the case of an extremely reduced optical image (seen through the reverse side of a binocular or a telescope for instance) or in the appearance of extremely remote images, however big in size (the moon, the planets, remote details of a landscape, etc.). In cinematic projection, such a situation occurs when a film exposed at 8 frames per second (as in the early days of the cinema) is projected at 16 or 24 frames per second. Today the old films (or similar use of "accelerated motion" for special effects) infallibly produce a humorous effect when projected at 24 frames per second, and the photographed motion itself appears to be fantastic.

The period of a given movement becomes so short that the observer can only see its initial and its final phases, and misses all the intermediate ones. As such speed is inconceivable for human beings, automobiles, trains and even airplanes, the "accelerated motion" appears supernatural. For this reason, it is perceived as either fantastic or humorous. Animated cartoons use a great deal of this technique of over-efficiency, as it means, besides the intended effect, economy in the number of individual drawings required to represent individual phases of given movements.

Thus, varying the rate of speed of the temporal projection of an image is, in this case, the basic device for contracting a time-period. For this reason, sound images recorded for a performance at a certain rate of speed and played back at a considerably higher rate, are bound to produce an effect analogous to the cinematic "accelerated motion". Phonograph records made to be played at 33.3 R.P.M. and performed at 78 R.P.M. appear to be supernatural in the effect of mechanical over-efficiency, and activate responses of the fantastic or humorous. In case of music, these effects are associated with the performing skill of individual artists. For example, no pianist can move his fingers at a speed which is several times greater than the known speed of a virtuoso pianistic performance, yet music recorded at 33.3 R.P.M. and played back at 78 R.P.M. gives all details of musical images, and including all the individual attacks, with full clarity. This translation of speed produces a miracle of technical accomplishment for even an unaccomplished performer. A smile is the usual form of response to such a speed translation: the performance, as it appears to the listener, is too good to be true.

Other forms of acceleration achieved by triplication and quadruplication from 78 R.P.M. to 33.3 R.P.M., each duplicated version to be played at 78 R.P.M., become incredibly fantastic. Besides exceeding any imaginable mechanical efficiency, such versions change pitch and tone-quality to a considerable extent. Any male speech in the first duplication becomes that of the Disney character "Donald Duck; any female speech, that of "Minnie Mouse". Male singers, particularly in choirs, produce a hilarious impression which cannot be verbally described. Female singing in its triplicated version (approximately a quintuple speed when played back at 78 R.P.M.) approaches very closely the singing of birds. However, my experiment in slowing down chirping of canaries produces a grotesque effect of howling wolves rather than female singers. This merely shows that our discrimination of tone-qualities of very high frequencies is quite poor, because physically such forms should be reversible.

The late tenor Enrico Caruso sounds at half speed like a cow (particularly when the consonant "m" is combined with an open vowel). I did not have an opportunity to convert a cow into Caruso by reversing the process. In my quadruplicated version of the Overture to *Tannhäuser* (approximately 13 times the speed of the original), the entire composition runs one minute. The incredibly fantastic character of this version is due to three factors: first, the unbelievable mechanical efficiency of performance *per se*; second, reversal of the anticipated dignified character of this composition in its original form   (all versions were made from my own recording of Arturo Toscanini conducting the National Broadcasting Symphony Orchestra); third, the physical image of frequencies, which episodically vanish beyond the audible range.

A study of music written by the recognized experts of the humorous, such as Modeste Moussorgsky, and of the responses of listeners to such music, show that the problem of creating humorous music has not been solved. Music combined with words (i.e., vocal music) in some cases stimulates the response of humor not by virtue of the music, but by virtue of the words which activate humorous associations. This is easily proved by playing such music on some instrument (or instruments) to somebody who has never heard it before and is not familiar with the accompanying text. Likewise instrumental music which is programmatically humorous, does not generally appear as such to a listener unaware of the program.

On the other hand, in many public performances we have witnessed audiences laugh, and laugh very heartily, at music which was not intended to be humorous. Such is the case on occasion of the first performances of new and very original, i.e., unconventional, compositions. Just about ten years ago, at a chamber concert sponsored in Town Hall by the League of Composers of New York, a Chamber Suite by Anton von Webern (for 14 instruments) was performed by a group of very skilful musicians under the direction of Eugene Goossens. Such concerts are generally attended by an audience which can appreciate and often enjoy extreme contemporary creations. Yet in the case of Mr. von Webern's Suite, the audience rolled in laughter as if it were extremely humorous.

On the basis of the theory, which I have advanced, it is easy to explain why a certain composition which is intended to be humorous does not appear as such at all, and why a composition, as serious as possible, may make people laugh. The explanation is very simple: *music is humorous when it gives the impression of extremely low or extremely high efficiency.* In von Webern's case, both these forms were present. On the one hand, the durations were very long or staccato, followed by very long rests; on the other, there were so few attacks to each movement of the Suite that each movement lasted only a few seconds, during which very few things happened; finally, the range was extremely wide, while the frequencies followed the course of extremely sudden changes from one end of the whole range (low pitches of Bassoon) to the other (high pitches of the Flute and Piccolo). The reaction to this piece as being humorous, of course, was the result of previous conditioning. From a philosophical standpoint, there is nothing inherently humorous in a vacuum. And this piece was a vacuum, since very few material sound-particles, or sound-images, appeared in a very broad range. But then the whole astronomical universe, which is a greater vacuum than we can produce artificially in any laboratory, must appear to be still more hilarious. Yet there is a reason why this does not happen. While the vacuumatic quality of the von Webern's Suite is immediately apprehensible auditorily, the vacuumatic quality of the universe is not immediately apprehensible visually. Besides we are not conditioned by any previous experience to a less vacuumatic universe.

What composers of supposedly humorous music have missed is that effects of the humorous and of the fantastic are primarily *agogic* (i.e., pertaining to speed) and cannot be expressed by purely intonational devices, such as melody, harmony, counterpoint or even tone-quality, unless such tone-quality is an imitation of sounds associated with the humorous (like the wow-wow trumpet effect in jazz music, or Rubinoff's laughing violin), or is a product or a result of an agogical process. By the latter, I mean tone-quality which appears to be humorous, owing to the excessive speed of projection, as in the case of a bass-clarinet performed at double speed.

It is true that a melody which is overloaded with resistances and does not move to a considerable climax, as well as a melody having extreme climaxes not adequately prepared by resistances (or, better, by any resistance at all) does appear humorous—but only to a slight degree and only to a highly discriminating audience.

The real sources of stimuli activating spontaneous responses of the humorous or the fantastic are, as we have seen, purely agogic. As our frequency-response (we mean the regular auditory response to sound-frequencies) is at the same time an intensity-response, the loudness of perceptible sound becomes an important component of the lower half of the psychological dial.

The right approach in composing sonic symbols, which are intended to stimulate reactions of the fantastic and the humorous, is to reproduce characteristics associated with extreme forms of acoustical projection. It is for this reason that we discussed the subject of recording and reproducing speed.

3. Technical Resources:

Still considering the mechanical extremes of acoustical projection to be the best means for this purpose, we offer, nevertheless, a parallel table of the common technical resources which, in the absence of technical facilities, will serve as the next best choice.

Low register. Extremely low speed. Low intensity.

Suitable instruments: Double-Bass; Contrafagot; Tuba; low register of the Harp or Piano; low register of the electronic instruments, or of the pipe-organ.

The lowest audible register. Still lower speed and longer durations. An extremely slow vibrato, artificially obtained either by producing slow beats in the low register or by very slow semitone trills. Very low intensity.

Suitable instruments: the 32′ pedal of the pipe-organ or its electronic equivalent; the lowest register of Double-Bass, Contrafagot and Tuba.

Percussion: gong.

Rests, when inaudibility is to be represented. This may affect only the lower parts of musical texture, such as harmony.

Music almost stops altogether. 0° One pitch unit is formed in the form of a trill, which is extremely slow and alternately stops and moves.

High register. Extremely high speed. High intensity.

Suitable instruments: Flute Piccolo; high register of the Clarinet Piccolo; high register of the electronic instruments, or of the pipe-organ.

The highest audible register. Still higher speed and faster durations. Abundance of staccato and accents. An excessive and extremely fast vibrato, artificially obtained by trills or frulato (flutter-tongue); in some cases by beats caused by minor seconds in high register. Very high intensity.

Suitable instruments: highest pipe-organ registers or their electronic equivalents; the highest register of Flute, Piccolo, Harp and Violin (for vanishing sounds approaching the high limit of audibility).

Percussion: triangle, clavis (Cuban), etc.

Partial inaudibility effect can be achieved by eliminating the upper parts of musical texture, leaving the bass as the only audible part.

Intonations changing with ultimate velocity (such as scalewise 360° grace-note groups on Flute, Piccolo): glissando of the highest Violin positions; also glissando of the highest positions on the space-controlled Theremin, or its equivalent; rapid passages in the highest ranges of the pipe-organ or electronic organ.

Figure 86. Table of resources for producing humorous and fantastic effects.

All other sonic symbols pertaining to the lower quadrants of both zones are produced on the basis of *association by contrast*. Such contrast can be achieved only through another stimulus pattern, executed in a different medium from sound. The most immediate forms of the basic stimuli are optical images and verbal symbols to which sonic symbols are composed as counterstimuli.

The basic associations by contrast, with respect to the lower quadrants of both zones, pertain to mechanical efficiency, power, dimension and density. The selection of a counterstimulus to a given stimulus must be performed on the basis of dial-reciprocity. For example, if the symbol can be located on the psychological dial as ⟨⟩, the countersymbol must be ⟨⟩, i e., it must have the same angle as the symbol only in the opposite quadrant. This proposition controls both quadrants in their entirety until they reach the 0° and 360° point.

The basic symbols appear as images on the stage or the screen (cinema, television), or as ideas stimulating imaginary optical forms, as in the play, the poem, the narrated story received through a broadcast.

The humorous effect results from the anticipation conditioned by an actual or imaginary situation, and the conflict created by fulfillment. For example, the symbol of a giant conditions anticipation of a powerful, low voice, for the dimensions of a giant, by previous conditioning, suggest large vocal cords. Therefore, in order to create an effect of humorous, it is necessary to compose a counterstimulus of the opposite character, i.e., a high frequency and low intensity sonic symbol. This sonic countersymbol would create conflict between anticipation and fulfillment, i.e., between the optical symbol and the inversely corresponding sonic countersymbol.

As the quadrant positions are reversible for symbol and countersymbol, we can put a mouse in place of a giant, and supply the tiny creature with a powerful basso, in which case the resulting effect will still be humorous.

In both these illustrations, the associations were based on *dimension-frequency and dimension-intensity inverse correspondence*. As a result, the density association is also affected, since a powerful basso is more saturated sound (by implication of its physical characteristics) than a weak high-pitched sound. We could also introduce an association by contrast on the basis of mechanical efficiency by adding agogical characteristic to both our illustrations: the giant has a weak high-pitched voice and, besides, speaks very slowly or stutters; the mouse, on the other hand, in addition to having a powerful low-pitched voice, speaks at such a high speed that it makes his speech almost incomprehensible.

More remote forms of association producing an effect of more subtle humor, require a considerably greater degree of refinement in the responses of an audience. For example, the counter symbol for a giant raging in furious violence, is quiet and pleasing lyrical music; or in a scene suggesting serenity, peace, silence and contemplation, the accompanying sonic countersymbol is crude, harsh and noisy music. But such countersymbols are effective only in the case of an audience equipped with highly developed associational responses.

Not only frequency and intensity can serve as a medium for creating humorous effects through association by contrast, but also the forms of attack in their inverse correspondence to movements and actions. For example, angular and abrupt movements can be accompanied by sonic symbols of extreme fluidity (legatissimo). Such an approach can be successfully applied to the staging of a humorous dance. The opposite, i.e., fluent movements accompanied by music with abrupt (staccatissimo) attacks, would produce an equally humorous effect.

Associations by contrast can be applied with the same amount of success to effects of the supernatural. For example, a poor and simple herdsman gets a horn or a pipe as a present from a stranger. The pipe looks like a very ordinary one, but in actuality it is enchanted. When the poor man begins to play, it sounds like a large and glorious orchestra with harps, human voices and an organ. Thus the conflict between anticipation and fulfillment is created on the basis of inverse correspondence between the primitive crudeness of the pipe ⟋ and the sonic countersymbol of rich and glorious music ⟍.

All other forms of associations by contrast, which do not pertain to the lower quadrants, will be discussed in the following exposition.

Figure 87. Varying the tempi.

The above must sound one octave higher and may be accompanied by a high pizzicato of strings, with a fill-in by the glissando of xylophone, also high.

CHAPTER 19

COMPOSITION OF SEMANTIC CONTINUITY

SONIC symbols, acting as associational stimuli, may assume numerous forms of simultaneous and sequent coordination. In many instances, contrasting and even conflicting patterns may become simultaneously or sequently adjacent. Under no circumstances should this deprive the continuity of its stylistic unity. The conflicting character of patterns does not imply conflicting systems of intonation and temporal organization of durations. Just as tranquility and excitement may be expressed in a poem written in one language, unity of the forms of musical expression is a necessary esthetic condition. In cases where the very nature of association requires hybrid forms, such hybrid forms must be unified by some one component. For example, in a rapid transition of reminiscences associated with different countries and nationalities, it may be desirable to express the different corresponding intonational forms through melody; yet a sequence of such melodies, bearing no resemblance to each other, i.e., based on the pitch-scales belonging to totally different families, may be stylistically unified by a certain form of harmonization applied to the entire continuity. As we have learned before, symmetric harmonization provides such a unifying technical resource.

The form of semantic continuity may be either *uninterrupted* or *interrupted*. The first takes place in a program composition, such as an opera or a symphonic poem or background music written for the stage, screen, radio or television production; the second is characteristic of fragmentary and often isolated sonic symbols serving as musical cues in the same types of production.

As the temporal organization of the plot of a play or a script is in the hands partly of the playwright and partly of the director, there is very little that the composer can do in this particular direction. In most cases the composer is called to do his job when it is too late, as the temporal organization of a plot is in the hands of people who know too little, if anything at all, about such matters. On the basis of principles evolved and disclosed in my major work, *Mathematical Basis of the Arts*,* it is possible to evolve the temporal structure of a plot and to coordinate it with the temporal structure of music into one organic whole by a purely scientific method. As such a luxury is not to be found in contemporary production-units yet, the composer can only try to do his best under the circumstances. For this reason we shall not discuss the technique of the temporal coordination of plot-music at present.

For the composers who intend to write music to their own program, we would like to offer a few basic suggestions.

Select a plot. Distribute the plot over a group of events (episodes). Analyze the sequence of episodes on the basis of our semantics (i.e., establish the relationship of episodes to balance, tension and release, anticipation and fulfillment, climaxes, etc.). Classify the episodes according to their importance. Give the

---

*To be published shortly.

episodes of primary importance the longest time-periods. Give the secondary and tertiary episodes shorter time-periods. Organize the entire temporal scheme according to such a selection. Write a continuity of sonic symbols to satisfy the temporal scheme of the plot.

Our main problem lies in the field of techniques pertaining to modulation and coordination of sonic symbols, by which the production of semantic continuity is accomplished.

A. Modulation of Sonic Symbols

The character of transition may be either sudden or gradual, and its technical forms either temporal, intonational or configurational.

Sudden transition introduces adjacent contrasts, characterized by the lack of commonness. Technically, such a transition is the negation of graduality. Gradual transition represents the transformation of one sonic symbol into another. The degree of graduality depends on timing. Modulation of one symbol into another can be accomplished through any technical component (i.e., temporal, intonational, configurational), by means of a common or a neutral form, i.e., such a form which is common or neutral, with respect to pre-modulatory and post-modulatory character of the respective sonic symbol.

1 Temporal Modulation

Transition of one stimulus-pattern to another often requires a change from one temporal pattern to another in the respective sonic symbol. Sudden transition implies only negative requirements: the absence of common characteristics. Gradual transition necessitates either neutralization of the preceding duration-group by introducing *uniformity* of t for the modulatory period, or by introducing a recurrence of the last *duration-pattern* of the pre-modulatory temporal group if such a pattern can be accepted as common for both (i.e., pre-modulatory and post-modulatory) groups. The commonness of a duration-pattern does not necessarily mean the commonness of T''.

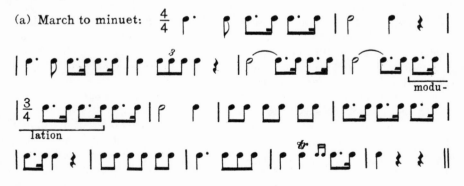

Figure 88. Temporal modulation (continued).

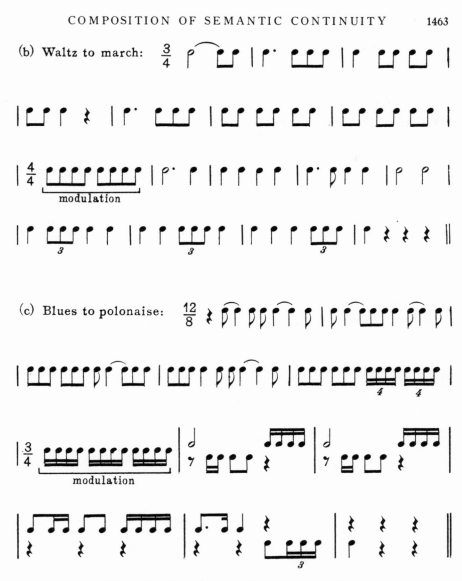

(b) Waltz to march:

(c) Blues to polonaise:

Figure 88. Temporal modulation (concluded).

2 Intonational Modulation

All problems pertaining to intonational modulation received full attention in the respective chapters of various branches of this theory.

Modulatory forms of melody are accomplished either by modal transposition, or by permutation of intervals, or by one of the modulatory techniques proper (common tones, chromatic alterations, identical motifs). Modulatory forms of correlated melodies (counterpoint) are obtained either by harmonic or by contrapuntal technique of modulation (sequent modulatory coordination of melodies). Modulatory forms of harmony consist of the following techniques: computative technique (see: Application of the Generalized Symmetric Progressions to Modulation)* applied to the distribution of the interval-group between the pre-modulatory and post-modulatory harmonic groups; direct modulation by altering the units of a modulatory chord, as described in the chapter on modulation in the *Special Theory of Harmony;*** indirect modulation (i.e., a modulation containing intermediate keys), as described in the same chapter.

Since in the modulations from one sonic symbol to another, axis-modulations are less essential, in most cases, than the modulations of the structural pattern of intonation (i.e., the modification of a chord-structure achieved by the redistribution of intervals), the latter are accomplished mostly by means of a C_0. Direct transitions are based on the uncommonness of pitch-units in the adjacent assemblages. For this reason, C_7 and C_{-7} is one of the most suitable resources and particularly in the symmetric forms ($\sqrt[6]{2}$ and $\sqrt[12]{2}$). Instantaneous change from positions ⓐ and ⓑ to ⓒ and ⓓ is another excellent device for a sudden transition.

3 Configurational Modulation

Sudden change from one pattern to another does not require any technical considerations, as each pattern is a definite associative stimulus, and we are conditioned to produce instantaneous changes in our responses when such changes take place in the stimulus.

Gradual modulations from one configuration to another are based on two fundamental techniques: (1) neutralization of a pattern and (2) introduction of a common pattern.

The *first technique* consists of gradually depriving the pre-modulatory pattern of its individual characteristics, such as the axial combination and the trajectory. This technique is based on the assumption that the neutral pattern is that of balance, i.e., of uniform periodic motion, associated with the 0-axis and the sine-wave. Thus, the growing dominance of the 0-axis constitutes a neutralization of any other form of stimulus. In this sense 0-axis is a neutralizer of all characteristics but repose, and for this reason is expedient as an "inter-eventual" link. The most gradual forms of neutralization are those in which the effect of the 0-axis is such that it influences the decrease of amplitude in the pre-modulatory axis (or axial combination), whatever such combination might be. In this case the pre-modulatory pattern (mostly its last axis) repeats itself with decreasing amplitudes (a fading effect).

---

*See Vol. I, p. 492.   **See Vol. I, p. 524.

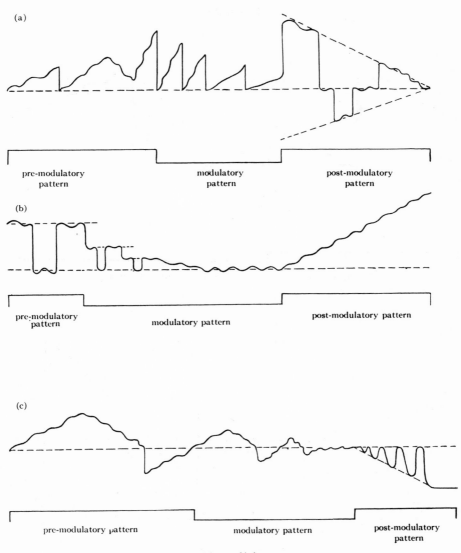

Figure 89. Neutralizing a pattern.

The *second technique* is based on recurrence of the pattern which is identical for both, the ending of the pre-modulatory and the beginning of the post-modulatory group. Such a common pattern is an axis (or axial combination) and a trajectory.

Examples

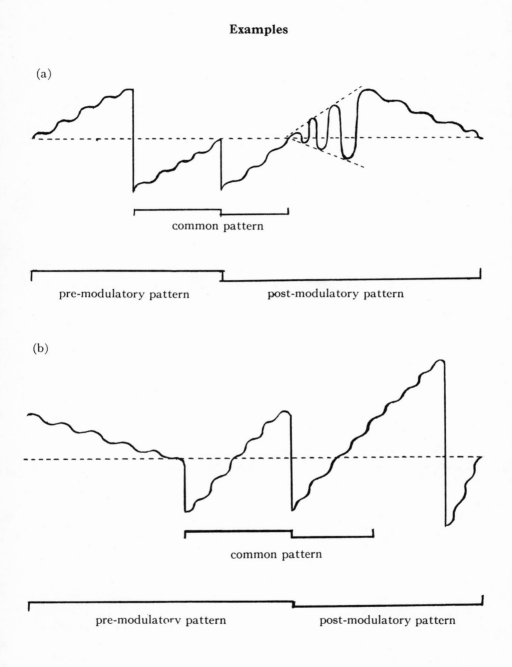

Figure 90. Introduction of a common pattern.

Configurational modulation is a resource by which one stimulus-pattern can be changed into another through the increasing dominance of one pattern over another. We have encountered such situations in the *Theory of Melody*,* where rhythmic resultants were applied as coefficient-groups controlling the rise of one axis and the decline of another.

For example: 4a + b + 3a + 2b + 2a + 3b + a + 4b produces the declining dominance of a and the increasing dominance of b, which situation illustrates a configurational modulation from the stimulus "a" to the stimulus "b":

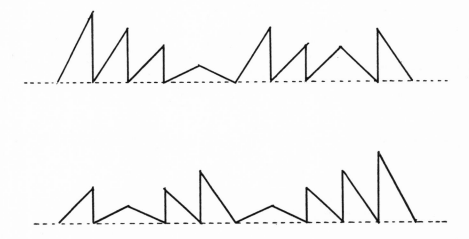

Figure 91. Graphic representation of 4a + b + 3a + 2b + 2a + 3b + a + 4b.

This case may psychologically correspond to a transition from dominance to compliance.

Configurational modulation is applicable in its respective forms to melody, harmony, counterpoint. In all these cases, patterns correspond to melodic trajectories, whether self-sufficient as in melody, or conjugated as in harmony and counterpoint. Configurational modulation can also be applied to the patterns of density and dynamics. The method of application remains the same as in the intonational patterns, but the meaning of balance or neutral configurational equilibrium lies in the center between the two extremes of density and dynamics. Neutralization of the extreme forms of density (low or high) is accomplished by resorting to *medium density*, which forms a general primary axis of the density-patterns. Neutralization of extreme dynamic forms (pp and *ff*) is also accomplished by the use of the *intermediate dynamic degree* (mf) acting as a neutralizer.

Common patterns of density and dynamics, linking together the otherwise contrasting or conflicting pre-modulatory and post-modulatory configuration-groups, serve as another technique of transition from one stimulus to another.

*See Vol. I, pp. 261 and 275.

Examples of neutralization

(a) density:

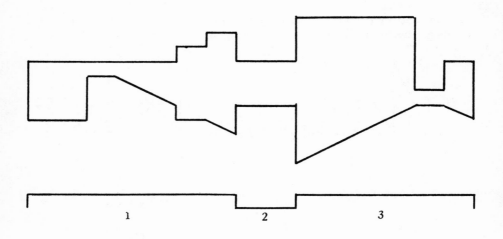

1. pre-modulatory pattern
2. modulatory pattern
3. post-modulatory pattern

Figure 92. Neutralization of density.

(b) dynamics:

$$sfp + sfpp + pp < f + f > mf + mf + ff$$

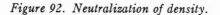

1. pre-modulatory pattern
2. modulatory pattern
3. post-modulatory pattern

Figure 93. Neutralization of dynamics.

Examples of a common pattern

(a) density:

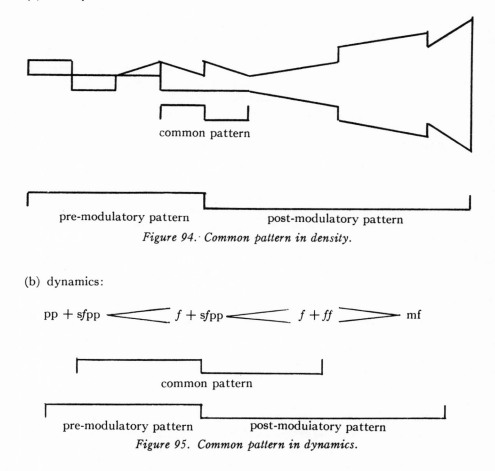

common pattern

pre-modulatory pattern   post-modulatory pattern

Figure 94. Common pattern in density.

(b) dynamics:

pp + sfpp ⟍⟍ f + sfpp ⟍⟍ f + ff ⟋⟍ mf

common pattern

pre-modulatory pattern   post-moduiatory pattern

Figure 95. Common pattern in dynamics.

Finally, configurational modulation can be applied to tone-quality, instrumental forms and attack-groups. Here, too, either neutralization of extreme patterns or configurational similarity serves as a modus of transition from one stimulus-pattern to another.

Instrumental forms which I view as essentially generalized arpeggio forms combine melodic and density configuration. In them a modulation from one stimulus-pattern to another is performed either by neutralization of the arpeggio form by changing it gradually into a sustained chord, after which a new post-modulatory form begins, or by transition through a common pattern. If the arpeggio forms are alike in the pre-modulatory and the post-modulatory groups, the modus of transition is confined to amplitudinal variation: technically it corresponds to the transition from one form of tonal expansion to another. Modulations representing a variation of density in an arpeggio form are performed by a gradual increase or decrease of the number of simultaneous attacks in the arpeggio.

Tone-quality modulations are also configurational modulations in the physical sense, as they represent a transition from one pattern to another. These modulations therefore are subjected to the same principles, as all other configurational modulations which we have already discussed. Empirically speaking, the change in the configuration of a tone-quality is accomplished, not by a physical transformation of one pattern into another* as they can be seen on the screen of an oscillograph, but by the pure techniques of orchestration, i.e., by the increase of timbral ingredients of one kind and by the decrease of timbral ingredients of another kind.

For example, a gradual transition from q_I (on a 5q scale) to q_V may be illustrated as follows:

$$2 \text{ Fl. } (q_I) + \frac{Fl}{Cl} \frac{Cl}{Cl} (q_{II}) + \frac{Cl}{Fr. H} + \frac{Fr. H}{Fr. H} (q_{III}) +$$

$$+ \frac{Fag}{Fr. H} + \frac{Fag}{Fag} (q_{IV}) + \frac{Fag}{Tromb (\bullet)} + \frac{Trump (\bullet)}{Tromb (\bullet)} (q_V).$$

A greater graduality as we have seen before can be accomplished by the human voice, where the modulation of a pattern may be performed by the modification of vowels.

Finally, configurational modulation of the attack-forms (embracing the legatissimo-staccatissimo scale) can also be performed, either through neutralization of the patterns possessing extreme characteristics (like legato or staccato) through introducing the neutral pattern of portamento, or by connecting the pre-modulatory and the post-modulatory groups by means of a common pattern. In addition to this, as in the case of amplitudinal variations, a gradual transition through the scale of attack-forms, from one extreme pattern to another, constitutes a modulation. For instance, a pre-modulatory pattern being staccato may gradually be transformed into legatissimo: $a_{IV} + a_{III} + a_{II} + a_I$ (i.e., staccato, portamento, legato, legatissimo), in which case legatissimo is the form of the post-modulatory pattern.

Range and register, as configurational stimuli, provide their own forms of transition and may serve as links connecting otherwise different patterns. For example, the commonness of range or register may bridge different intonational or timbral forms. On the other hand, gradual trransitions from one register to another, as well as amplitudinal range-variation, can serve as modulatory techniques.

---

*This will undoubtedly be done in the near future; I did it in 1932 by means of a special electronic organ built by Leon Theremin.
—J.S.

B. COORDINATION OF SONIC SYMBOLS

As all our differentiated sensations developed in the course of biological evolution from c..ie general tactile fore-sensation, so did our music develop from monody into the complexity of contemporary scoring. And though at one time or another a certain sensation may dominate over another, in actuality we have no pure sensations. The dominant sensation stands out by its intensity though it is conjugated with other sensations. The gamut of sensations can be compared to 1 certain extent with the acoustical phenomenon of timbre, where one frequency dominates over other frequencies with which it is conjugated and which are its partials. Of course, the sensational mechanism is much more complex than this, as it contains not only simultaneous and sequent processes, but also overlapping ones. As one sensation is in progress, another may be just activated and still another may be in its decline.

It is only natural that the art   music, which, in its present state of complexity, is employed as a connotative 'anguage of sonic symbols, should be flexible enough to produce a worthy counterpart of human sensations, not only in their isolated but also in their combined forms. Combined pattern-stimuli activate combined responses. And such stimuli may be created by simple or complex conjugated sonic symbols, each symbol being represented by the individual or by the group-components. Complex stimuli may also be produced through coordination of various art media where music, in all its complexity, becomes only one (simple or complex) component of the whole.

It is not our purpose to discuss here the semantics of other arts than music and their possible forms of correlation with music. For this reason our analysis of processes involving complex stimuli shall be confined solely to music. Let us suppose that the source of sonic symbols, simple or complex, is a text. The complexity of combined stimuli would derive from a certain treatment of the same text. For example, we may choose two dissociated events from a scenario and present them as two simultaneous conjugated sonic symbols. In this case, one symbol may parallel the present event, while the other may stimulate the presaging or premonition of another event to come. A scene of gaiety, taking place on the stage or screen, may be combined with a group of parts in the musical score, which have the same gaiety pattern. At the same time, a certain thematic counterpart of the same score may reflect the impending disaster, of which there is no sign in the respective scene.

As scripts and scenarios nowadays cover almost any imaginable situation, the composer must be so well equipped that he would never be caught unawares. Instead of the romantic "love in moonlight" he may face the problem of connoting a "day in an insane asylum" or "rush-hour at the Times Square shuttle", which cases call for all the dial positions to be employed simultaneously, as the gamut of associations in such cases ranges from normal to abnormal.

The correlation of sonic symbols pertaining to various pattern-stimuli, first, implies the selection of such stimuli as a combination and, second, discovering of the conditions under which such coordination can be performed.

In actual application, the stimulus-response scale, as represented on our psychological dial, can be greatly increased by our usual method of inserting intermediate forms between the basic forms already represented on the dial. Thus, the configurational scale can be extended to 12 or more patterns. Such details must be left to the initiative of the composer. Our present problem is to classify as simply as possible the combinations of the different patterns with each other in order to establish the basic procedure for producing scales of the combined complex stimulus-patterns and their corresponding combined complex sonic symbols.

For this reason we shall confine ourselves to the eight-pattern scale, which corresponds to an eight-point dial. Thus, mathematically, the entire problem is to compute the number of combinations possible out of 8 elements.

Table of Combinations of the Sonic Symbols Evolved in Accordance with an Eight-Point Stimulus-Response Dial.

$$_8C_1 = \frac{8!}{1!\,(8-1)!} = 8$$

$$_8C_2 + \frac{8!}{2!\,(8-2)!} = 28$$

$$_8C_3 = \frac{8!}{3!\,(8-3)!} = 56$$

$$_8C_4 = \frac{8!}{4!\,(8-4)!} = 70$$

$$_8C_5 = \frac{8!}{5!\,(8-5)!} = 56$$

$$_8C_6 = \frac{8!}{6!\,(8-6)!} = 28$$

$$_8C_7 = \frac{8!}{7!\,(8-7)!} = 8$$

Figure 96. Combinations of sonic symbols.

Thus there are 8 cases when 1 pattern out of 8 is used at a time; 28 cases when 2 patterns out of 8 are used as a combination; 56 cases when 3 patterns out of 8 are used as a combination; 70 cases when 4 patterns out of 8 are used as a combination; 56 cases when 5 patterns out of 8 are used as a combination; 28 cases when 6 patterns out of 8 are used as a combination; 8 cases when 7 patterns out of 8 are used as a combination. Then the total of all these combinations which are at the composer's disposal, when he is limited to an eight-point dial, amounts to: $8 + 28 + 56 + 70 + 56 + 28 + 8 = 254$. To this, we can add one combination of all 8 elements, thus making the total: $254 + 1 = 255$.

Of course more complex forms of the above combinations are used rather seldom. Strata harmony is the most suitable technical resource for evolving more or less complex combinations of sonic symbols.

Our next stage is the method of classifying configurational characteristics as they appear in combined patterns.

All patterns belonging to one quadrant must be considered as *identical patterns of different intensities*. The growth of intensity follows the clockwise direction in the positive zone and the counterclockwise direction in the negative zone. Thus, for example, the pattern of ⊘ is identical with, but more intense than, that of ⊘. Such reasoning is applicable to all quadrants.

Patterns belonging to different quadrants may also vary in intensity, but they are to be considered *non-identical*.

C. CLASSIFICATION OF THE STIMULUS-RESPONSE PATTERNS, TO BE REPRESENTED AS COMBINED SONIC SYMBOLS, ON THE BASIS OF THEIR INTENSITY OF CONFIGURATIONAL IDENTITY

(1) identical patterns of identical intensities;
(2) non-identical patterns of identical intensities;
(3) identical patterns of different intensities;
(4) non-identical patterns of different intensities.

Illustrations:

(a) Two craftsmen who are partners in the trade and are not rivals have a different degree of skill in making, let us say, Christmas tree ornaments. The problem of the composer is to produce a combined sonic symbol of two identical patterns of different intensities. Superior accomplishment corresponds to the pattern of greater intensity. Thus expressing the less accomplished craftsman as A and the more accomplished craftsman as B, we can establish the following correspondence: $\frac{A}{B}$ = ⊘ / ⊘

The resulting symbol B may acquire a wider range, higher mobility and higher intensity (of sound) than symbol A. Both may be expressed as self-sufficient but correlated melodies, or as an accompanied counterpoint.

(b) The old story about a poor young man in love with a rich young girl: the girl's parents in a united coalition of the entire family clan create unsurmountable obstacles and the marriage is called off; both boy and girl are in despair. The positive pattern of love and hope (i.e., if our sympathy is on the side of the young couple) is counteracted by a more powerful negative pattern of the family's opposition. The composer's problem is to produce a combined sonic symbol of two non-identical

patterns of different intensities. Let the young couple be A and the
family—B. Now we can establish the following pattern-intensity cor-

respondence: $\dfrac{A}{B} = \dfrac{\text{(/)}}{\text{(\\)}}$. The evil forces (i.e., evil from our viewpoint)

pull counterclockwise, overpower and win, bringing A into the negative
zone. Here are the considerations for composing the corresponding
sonic symbols for A and B.

Symbol A modulates from the positive into the negative zone under the
pressure of B, which retains its constant characteristics of the negative pattern
of high intensity, high dynamics and density (coalition). The B pattern is
negative in the sense that it is a destructive and not a creative force. By virtue
of its characteristic, B pattern is a counteracting force and for this reason must
have the axial characteristic opposite to that of A. As the A pattern obviously
corresponds, in its initial phases, to a-axis, the B pattern must be expressed by
b-axis of greater amplitude than the first phase of A. The effect of the B pattern
upon the A pattern is such that a-axis gradually loses its momentum and goes
into decline, transforming itself into b-axis.

This can be represented diagramatically as follows:

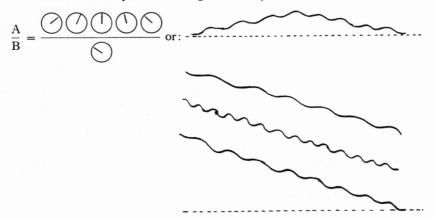

$$\frac{A}{B} = \frac{\text{(/)(/)(|)(\textbackslash)(/)}}{\text{(\textbackslash)}} \quad \text{or:}$$

Figure 97. Two non-identical patterns of different intensity.

The above identity-intensity pattern classification must now be supplemented further by the characteristic of *constancy* or *variability* of the pattern.
Then the original 4 forms become, in turn, quadrupled: $4^2 = 16$. The basic
classification represents the original phase from which the departure is made.

(1) identical patterns of identical intensities:
    (a) const. identity, const. intensity;
    (b) var. identity, const. intensity;
    (c) const. identity, var. intensity;
    (d) var. identity, var. intensity;

(2) non-identical patterns of identical intensities:
   (a) const. identity, const. intensity;
   (b) var. identity, const. intensity;
   (c) const. identity, var. intensity;
   (d) var. identity, var. intensity;

(3) identical patterns of different intensities
   (a) const. identity, const. intensity;
   (b) var. identity, const. intensity;
   (c) const. identity, var. intensity;
   (d) var. identity, var. intensity;

(4) non-identical patterns of different intensities:
   (a) const. identity, const. intensity;
   (b) var. identity, const. intensity;
   (c) const. identity, var. intensity;
   (d) var. identity, var. intensity.

In this table "constant" means a "constant form of relationship" with regard to the identity or intensity of the conjugated symbols; likewise, "variable" means a "variable form of relationship" in the same sense.

In the case of the unfortunate couple in love, the hope for marriage and happiness, represented by A, was a pattern of variable identity and variable intensity, while B was a pattern of constant identity and constant intensity. The basic relation of $\frac{A}{B}$ was that of non-identical patterns of different intensities. The fact that A was variable in both respects, made their relationship appear variable in the same respects.

The ultimate number of variations of all kinds, possible for each original relationship, depends on the number of individual symbols, conjugated into a combined complex symbol.

When sonic symbols are combined with script symbols or with each other into a combined complex symbol (the latter ultimately acquires the form of a score), their correlation assumes one of the following forms:

(1) parallel;

(2) contrary (inverse);

(3) oblique.

Parallel implies identity of symbols and is the most obvious and, for this reason, the most generally used form of association.

Contrary implies an association by contrast or juxtaposition, such as gay music to a sad scene or vice-versa; or two conjugated sonic symbols, each stimulating one of two contrasting associations.

Oblique implies either a deviation from identity to non-identity, or from non-identity to identity. This can be graphically illustrated as follows:

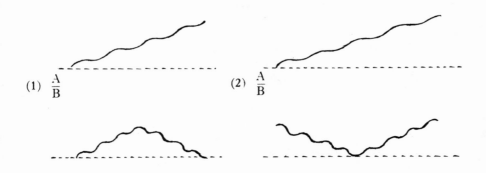

(1) $\dfrac{A}{B}$ (2) $\dfrac{A}{B}$

Figure 98. Parallel and contrary correlation.

Such is the case when friends gradually become enemies or enemies become friends; also when a gay scene is accompanied by music, modulating from gay to sad, or vice-versa.

In addition to all the previous relational classifications, there still remains the general category of *temporal congruence.*

Temporal congruence may emphasize either complete events, represented by sonic symbols, or their individual phases. Each event generally consists of five basic phases: generation (beginning, origination), growth, climax (goal, maximum), decline (anticlimax, balancing tendency), degeneration (completion, end).

As combinations of events take place in the interaction, *simultaneous* (synchronized) *associations* constitute only one form of temporal congruence. The two other forms represent the *anticipated* and the *delayed associations.*

The anticipated associations (i.e., that of presaging, premonition, etc.) represent the event to come, at a time when another event takes place (this other event may be executed as a different thematic component of the same score and can be carried out either in the same [music] or in a different [words, action] medium).

The delayed associations (i.e., that of recollection, reminiscence, etc.) represent a past event at a time when another event takes place.

From a technical standpoint, all forms of correlation of sonic symbols into their conjugated combined complex forms can be executed by identical, partly-identical, or non-identical groups of musical components.

Materials which illustrate the processes analyzed and systematized in this exposition are profusely scattered throughout all the program and operatic music, written by the competent composers of all ages. In my opinion, most of the so-called "great composers" produced in many instances impressive music because they had a high intuitive notion of configurational semantics, that is, they *felt music in terms of patterns*—which ability is lacking in most of our contemporaries. At the same time these men of the past had, in most cases, a very crude technique in handling special components, such as harmony, orchestration, etc., in which field our contemporaries are much more accomplished. Yet many of the present creations are born dead, as they lack the necessary qualities of associational stimuli.*

The field of connotative music is so broad and its applications so numerous that in this course of study we are only able to direct the student's attention toward the problems and the method by which they can be solved.

*The use of this system by Schillinger (as a staff composer of the Academic State Theatre of Drama, the Experimental Theatre of the State Institute of the History of Arts, both in Leningrad, and of the State Theatre for Children in Kharkov) and by his students in the U.S.A., who are active as radio, theatre, cinema and television composers, brought extremely fertile results . . . Among Schillinger students who made noteworthy use of the system are such men as Leith Stevens ("Columbia Workshop", "Tish", "Alice in Wonderland", "Big Town" and others); Paul Sterrett, Nathan Van Cleave (both at CBS, in the "Columbia Workshop" and other productions), Oscar Levant ("Nothing Sacred", "Charlie Chan at the Opera" and other motion pictures); Bernard Mayers ("Basin Street Chamber Music Society", NBC, where he made some very effective scores in the semantic sense: "Three Blind Mice", "Mary Had a Little Lamb", "The Bullfrog and the Robin" and others); Jesse Crawford ("Valiant Lady", CBS); Carmine Coppola ("Pictures in Music", CBS, where he wrote "G. B. Shaw"); Lyn Murray ("The Adventures of Ellery Queen", "26 by Corwin", opera "Esther", "This is War" and other CBS programs); Charles Paul ("City Desk", "The Adventures of Ellery Queen" and other NBC programs); and Rudolf Schramm [music to radio and cinema (U.S. government productions) in the field of education], just to mention a very few. (Ed.)

THE SCHILLINGER SYSTEM

OF

MUSICAL COMPOSITION

by

JOSEPH SCHILLINGER

BOOK XII

THEORY OF ORCHESTRATION

BOOK TWELVE

THEORY OF ORCHESTRATION

PART I

INSTRUMENTS

PART II

Instrumental Techniques

INTRODUCTION

WHAT has been known for the last couple of centuries as a "symphony orchestra" is a heterogeneous aggregation of antiquated tools. Wooden boxes and bars, wooden pipes, dried sheep's guts, horse hair and the like are the materials out of which sound-producing instruments are built.

The evolution of musical instruments, during their history of several millenia, followed the course of individual craftsmanship and of the trial-and-error method.

The instruments themselves are not scientifically conceived and not scientifically combined with each other. Some of the orchestral groups participate with others by virtue of tradition (like brass and string instruments which, in most cases, do not blend) and not by necessity. Nobody ever asks the basic question: why should there be such a combination as the stringed-bow, the wood-wind, the brass-wind and the percussive instruments; and why should the respective groups be used in the unjustified ratios which are considered standard?

It takes a long time to force upon the average normal human ear such combinations as piano and violin or strings and brass. And this imposition of unblendable combinations upon the selector called the human ear is termed "cultivation of musicianship". But eventually people begin to like it, as they begin to like smoking tobacco, which suffocates them at first. It is even possible to condition the human ear to hear the sound at a sustained intensity, while the sound is fading at its source. Such is the case with the piano. Ordinarily we are not aware of the fact that the piano tone fades very quickly. I once intentionally subjected myself (at the age of 30) to a forced isolation from the piano for three full months. The only sounds I heard during the time were that of an organ and of choral singing (i.e., durable sounds). I lived among peasants. When I returned to the city, the piano sounded to my ear as it really sounds, i.e., as a percussive instrument with exaggerated attack and quick fading. It took me fully two weeks to "recover" from this unconditioned modus of hearing.

The implication is that many of the orchestral tone-qualities and blends are gradually assimilated by our ear. Many of them are highly artificial and do not possess the appeal of natural beauty, as many natural forms and natural colors do.

The musician's argument against better balanced, more uniform tone-qualities, which are possible on the electronic instruments, is that they have not the individuality the old instruments have. But what *they* call "individuality" is often a group of minor defects and imperfections. A trombone, due to its acoustical design, has several tones (certainly, at least one) missing. While the composer can easily imagine those missing tones and imagine them in the trombone quality, he cannot use them in his score, since they cannot be executed. Now, take a bassoon. Its low b♮ is of a quality inferior to that of the surrounding tones. Why should one particular pitch be defective? No one knows.

A composer, due to his experience, can also imagine certain tone-qualities beyond the ranges of the respective standard instruments. He cannot use these qualities because there are no instruments to perform them.

Under such conditions, the art of orchestration amounts to a constant (and in most cases unsuccessful) struggle of the composer's imagination and inventiveness against the actuality of instrumental limitations and imperfections. The way things stand today, the composer must compose not in terms of tone-qualities, intensities, frequencies and attack-forms (if he does not want to live in a fool's paradise), but in terms of concrete instruments, each designed with no regard to any other instrument—each, therefore, having peculiarities of its own.

Musicians also have a sentimentally-childish attachment to the craftsman-ship of executing a "beautiful" tone on a violin or other instruments. Very few performers, indeed, can execute such a tone. But why is this self-imposed dif-ficulty and struggle necessary? Such an attitude has the flavor of sportsmanship and competition. Why not liberate the performer from the necessity of struggle to obtain the proper tone-quality, when such tone-quality can be achieved, and has been achieved, by means of electronic sound production?

The answer is that many good performers, once relieved of this struggle, would feel lost since, to them, the production of tone-quality is half of the problem of interpretation.

In 1918 I published an article ("Electrification of Music") in which I expounded my own ideas (at that time completely new and original) on the inadequacy of old musical instruments and on the necessity of developing new ones, where *sound could be generated and controlled electrically*. I thought it would be desirable to have tone-qualities, attack-forms, frequencies (tuning) and in-tensities under control, to be able to vary each component through continuous or discontinuous (tempered) scales, suddenly or gradually, and to determine the degree of the graduality of transition as well.

Though there is no universal use of electronic music yet, it is progressing very rapidly. Most of my dream has already come true. In 1920 Leon Theremin demonstrated his first primitive model of an electronic instrument before a con-vention of engineers in Moscow, Russia. On this model, pitch was controlled by movement of the right hand in free space (in actuality, in an electro-magnetic field) and volume, by a specifically designed pedal; the form of attack was con-trolled by a knob; the timbre was constant.

After a number of years of my collaboration with this inventor, the early history of electronic music culminated in 1930 in two Carnegie Hall (New York) performances in which participated a whole ensemble of 14 improved space-controlled theremins, manufactured by Radio Corporation of America on a mass production scale at the plant in Camden, New Jersey.

That first decade of electronic music, in which I am proud to have played the part of a musical pioneer, started the art of music on an entirely new road, which is in keeping with the engineering accomplishments of our industrial era of applied science. There is no turning back from this road, regardless of the absolute value of today's models of electronic instruments. The fact is that *a new principle of sound production and control* has been established, and this principle will bring further improvements and perfection.

It is important to realize that existing musical instruments and their combinations are not stabilized but ever-changing accessories of musical expression; that absolute knowledge of the functioning of the keys of a clarinet is of no basic value, as the design of such an instrument varies and the whole family of such instruments may vanish.

Thus, though in my description of standard instruments all the necessary information is given, the composer must not overrate the importance of it, as the entire combination of a symphony orchestra, with all its component instruments, may soon become completely outmoded and eventually obsolete. It will be a museum combination for the performance of old music. New instruments and combinations will take its place.

The moral of this *Introduction* is that it is more important for the composer to know the physical aspects of tone-qualities, frequencies, intensities and attack-forms *per se*, rather than the resultant forms as they appear on certain types of old instruments. It is a warning not to attach too much importance and confidence to certain types of instruments, simply because they are so much in use today.

In the *Acoustical Basis of Orchestration*, the student will find the type of knowledge which is *basic and general* and, therefore, can be applied to any special case. This system is devised with a point of view which will give lasting service and will not become antiquated with the first turn the history of this subject takes.

In order to broaden the student's outlook on the existing instruments, I am supplementing this Introduction with a chronological table borrowed from one of my other works, *Varieties of Musical Experience*.

Two items of this table deserve particular attention: (1) the chronological precipitation of progress and (2) the age of the new "electronic" era.

Scheme of Evolution of Musical Instruments

From Prehistoric Time
   I. Man utilizes his own organs: voice, palms, feet, lips, tongue, etc.

From 10-20 Thousand Years Ago Until Our Time
   II. Man utilizes finished or almost finished objects of the surrounding world: bamboo pipes, shells, bones of birds, animal horns and antlers, etc.

From 5 - 10 Thousand Years Ago Until Our Time
   III. Man processes raw material, giving it a definite form: from a piece of terra cotta and hunter's bow up to the Steinway piano and modern organ.

From 18th Century A.D.

    A. Man constructs automatically performing instruments: from 18th Century, mechanical musical instruments: from 19th Century, recording and reproducing musical instruments.

From the End of 19th Century

    B. Man develops transmission of sound waves over long distances: radio.

From the Beginning of 20th Century

    C. Man devises sound production by means of:
        1. Electro-magnetic induction
        2. Interference in electro-magnetic field.

CHAPTER 1

STRING-BOW INSTRUMENTS

CONTEMPORARY string-bow instruments have as their immediate ancestor the viol family. When the treble-viol, in the hands of Italian craftsmen, achieved its ultimate degree of perfection, it became the dominant member of the viol family: the treble-violin emancipated itself into the plain "violin". In this sense, the evolution of the violin family followed the downward (in the way of frequency) trend, i.e., the perfecting of the violin was followed by the perfecting of violas, 'celli and string double-basses (or contrabasses). This course of evolution was somewhat contrary to the development of the viol family, where bass-viol (later, violone) was the dominant instrument of the group, the patriarch of the family. Thus "violoncello" originated as the diminutive form of the "violone".

The more remote ancestor of this family is the Arabian "rebab", a primitive type of string-bow (often having only two strings, however, tuned in $3 \div 2$ ratio, i.e., in a perfect fifth) and having a resonating chamber. This ancient instrument leads us back to the "monochord", a one-string bow instrument with a resonating chamber, and, finally, to the actual source of the violin, which is the bow and arrow.

This remarkable evolution of a defense weapon into a musical instrument of high degree of perfection consumed not only millenia of astronomical clock-time, but also an incalculable amount of human energy lavishly spent by generations of craftsmen and musical performers.

But with so much said and written about violin-making and violin-playing, certain facts remain obscure. Since most of the time (between and during the eras of mutual mass-extermination), is spent by humanity in *creative mythology*, the history of the violin discloses a constant struggle between the glorification of violin-makers and violin-players. The fundamental question is: which factor is more essential in achieving perfection, the instrument or the player? Nobody would deny the importance of both. However, I am entitled to state, on the basis of experiments performed with Nathan Milstein and another highly accomplished, but not extraordinary, representative of the Leopold Auer school (which also contributed Heifetz, Zimbalist, Elman, Piastro, Seidel and many other virtuosi), that the player is a more important factor than the instrument. I draw this comparison particularly in reference to the quality of tone-production. In my experiment both performers were tested on the same two instruments: one was a violin made by Antonio Stradivarius and the other, a mediocre sample of mediocre craftsmanship. Milstein's tone-quality was superior on both violins and with less individual difference between the two instruments than that of the other violinist. This may be a good lesson to some parents and teachers: only a mediocre violinist needs a very expensive instrument.

As the best musical organizations of today have at their disposal some of the best string-bow performers (usually the potential soloists rejected by the market's maintenance of only the few best performers), the composer of our civilization may indulge in scoring which requires, on the part of the performer, a highly developed and versatile technique.

A. VIOLIN

1. TUNING

The entire range of the violin is written in treble clef.

The four strings are named g, d, a, e. From the physical standpoint all four strings have a different timbre. The timbre of the g-string is particularly different from the three upper strings. In the hands of an accomplished performer this timbral variance is greatly minimized. However, good playing does not affect the variance of the g-string with the three upper strings. This difference is due to the fact that g-string is a sheep's gut wrapped around with a metal wire, while d-string and a-string are sheep's guts which remain unwrapped. E-string only about three decades ago underwent a transformation: sheep's gut was replaced by a metal wire.

The violin is tuned in perfect fifths, i.e., in $3 \div 2$ ratio. The tuning begins with the a-string. Thus the ratios of the remaining strings are:

$$e = \tfrac{3}{2}; d = \tfrac{2}{3}; g = (\tfrac{2}{3})^2 = \tfrac{4}{9}$$

As the above ratios noticeably deviate from the corresponding pitches of the twelve-unit equal temperament, some of the more discriminating composers (Hindemith, for instance, makes it a rigid rule) avoid the use of open strings altogether, except in chords.

Figure 1. Tuning of the violin.

2. PLAYING

The Left Hand Technique

Intonation is controlled on the violin by means of shortening its strings, which is accomplished by pressing the string against the fingerboard. For this purpose the fingers of the left hand are employed. Strings vibrate between the two fixed points (nut and bridge) and transfer their vibrations to the bridge. The vibrations of the bridge stimulate sympathetic response from the body of the violin, which is a resonating chamber.

Four fingers of the left hand (thumb is excluded) participate in producing intonations. The various distances which the left hand occupies on the finger-board (while supporting the violin) in relation to the nut are called *positions*. Each position on each string emphasizes *four* pitch-units of the common diatonic scales. The positions begin with an *open* string. Such a position might be called the *zero position*.

Figure 2. The zero position.

Arabic numerals indicate the fingers employed. Major tetrachords are used here merely for convenience: other accidentals can be employed as well.

The first position begins with a whole tone from the open string.

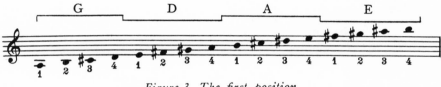

Figure 3. The first position.

If the first pitch-unit is only a semitone away from the open string, then such a position is called *half-position* or *semi-position*.

Figure 4. The half-position.

From here on, violinists do not discriminate any semi-positions, but consider only the *Second*, the *Third*, the *Fourth* and so on, positions, regardless of whether they are tone-and-a-half or two tones, two-and-a-half or three tones from the open string.

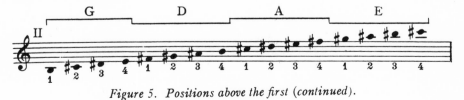

Figure 5. Positions above the first (continued).

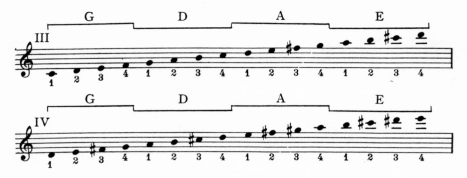

Figure 5. Positions above the first (concluded).

The three lower strings (G, D, A) are seldom used beyond the *eighth* position; the e-string is used even in orchestra-playing up to the fifteenth position (the beginning of Rimsky-Korsakov's opera *Kitezh*.)

All violin-playing is accomplished in most cases, including double-stops and chords, by means of standard fingering. Chromatic alterations are performed by moving the same finger a semitone up or a semitone down.

Insofar as the precision of intonation is concerned, it is always easier to move the fingers in the same position, making transitions from one string to another, than to change positions rapidly, particularly when such positions are not adjacent. It is to be remembered that though the use of the four fingers is analogous on all four strings and in all positions, the actual spatial intervals on the fingerboard contract logarithmically while moving upward in pitch. This means that a semitone in the first position is spatially wider than a semitone in the second position; the latter is wider than the semitone in the third position, and so on.

Musical intervals from the open strings can be defined in terms of positions, and positions can be defined in terms of musical intervals.

Position, where a given note is produced by the first finger, equals the number of the corresponding musical interval, minus one. For instance:

Figure 6. Position.

The given note g♯ to be played on a-string with the third finger requires the hand to be in such a position where *e* can be played on a-string with the first finger. As the musical interval from *a* to *e* (up) is a *fifth*, the position can be defined as 5 − 1 = 4 (i.e., it is the fourth position). This is so because the *first* position is produced by the interval of a *second* (i.e., 2) from the open string.

This proposition can be reversed. For example: what note is played by the *second* finger in the *sixth* position on the e-string?

The first finger in the sixth position produces an interval of a seventh (i.e., $6 + 1 = 7$); therefore the second finger, in the same position produces an octave. Thus the note to be found is *e*, one octave above the open string.

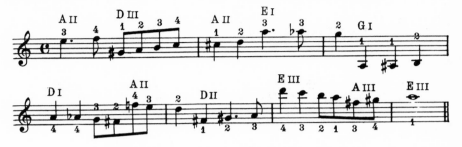

Figure 7. Example of fingering. Single notes.

Playing of S2p

The so-called "double-stops", i.e., couplings, harmonic intervals and two-part harmonies belong to this category.

S2ᴅ are played by means of standard fingering. Left hand is considered in an *open position* if the finger on the lower of the two pitches corresponds to a smaller number than that of the higher of the two pitches. The reversal of this proposition corresponds to a *closed position*. Open positions are easier to play. Closed positions can be used in double stops without particular difficulties, but preferably in a tempo that is not too fast.

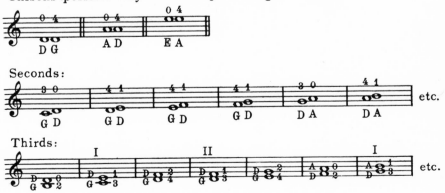

Figure 8. Fingering of S2p (continued).

Fourths:

Fifths: (are played with *one* finger pressing two adjacent strings):

Sixths:

Sevenths:

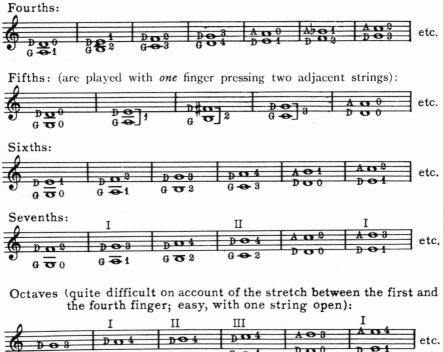

Octaves (quite difficult on account of the stretch **between the first and the fourth finger; easy, with one string open**):

Figure 8. Fingering of S2p (concluded).

Octaves are used mostly in solo playing. As a perfect acoustical octave (i.e., $2 \div 1$ ratio) sounds quite empty, soloists usually resort to playing an imperfect octave (somewhat more narrow in stretch than the acoustical octave), which sounds fuller. In scoring for an orchestra, octaves of violins are usually written *divisi* (i.e., both pitches are played by the different parts).

As octaves without participation of an open string require a stretch between the first and fourth finger, it becomes obvious that intervals wider than an octave can be performed only if the use of at least one open string is possible.

A special double-stop effect should not escape the attention of the orchestrator: passages on one string combined with another string remaining open. For example:

Figure 9. Special double-stop effect.

Such passages can be played at considerable speed.

Playing of S3p

Playing of triple-stops includes melody with two couplings and three-part harmony.

When employing 3 fingers at a time (i.e., without participation of open strings), only open position of the left hand can be used. In all other cases, previous considerations hold true.

Figure 10. Fingering of S3p

Playing of S4p

Playing of quadruple-stops includes melody with three couplings and four-part harmony. There is only one quadruple-stop with four open strings:

All other cases include 3, 2, 1 or no open strings. All left hand positions must be open. Such chords as S(5) in open harmonic ($\circlearrowleft$) positions are quite easy because only 3 fingers participate (as the perfect fifth is played with only one finger).

Three open strings:

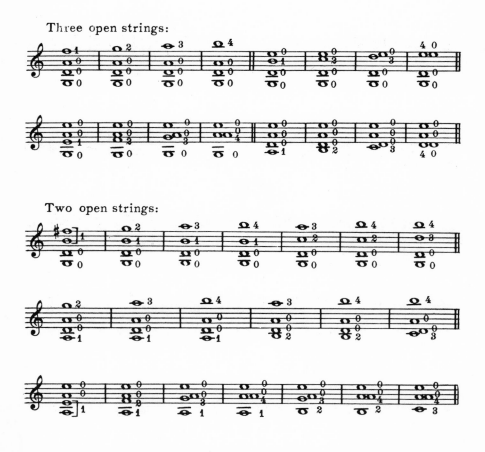

Two open strings:

Figure 11. Fingering of S4p. Three and two open strings (continued).

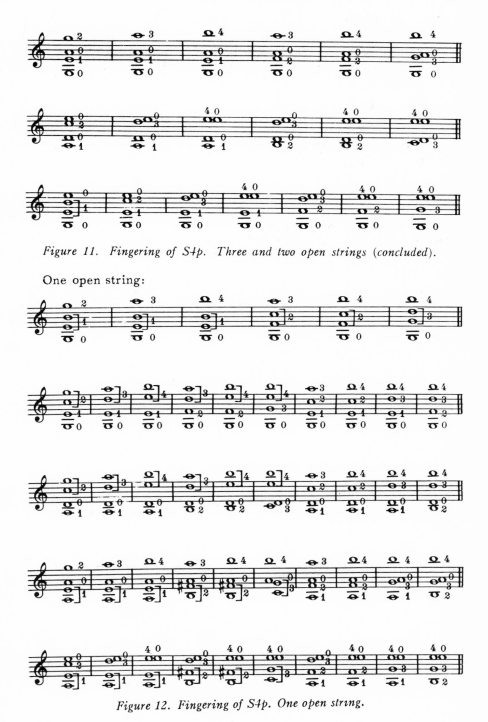

Figure 11. Fingering of S4p. Three and two open strings (concluded).

One open string:

Figure 12. Fingering of S4p. One open string.

No open strings:

Figure 13. Fingering of S4p. No open strings.

The above tables are merely samples of the systematization of the material on fingering; they can be extended to higher positions (with or without participation of the open strings). These forms of fingering are applicable to various instrumental forms.

As the bow can move simultaneously over not more than *two* strings (some exceptional virtuosi can bow three strings simultaneously in *forte*; but such an accomplishment is exceptional and we cannot count on it in writing orchestral parts for the violins), we see that:

I(2p) can be performed as:

ap and a2p in sequent combinations;

I(3p) can be performed as:

ap and a2p in sequent combinations;

I(4p) can be performed as:

ap and a2p in sequent combinations.

Figure 14. Examples of instrumental forms suitable for the violin (continued).

Figure 14. Examples of instrumental forms suitable for the violin (concluded).

B. THE RIGHT ARM TECHNIQUE

Bowing is a process by which friction is produced between the horse-hair of the bow and the string. The various techniques by which strings can be made to oscillate in different patterns, constitute the bowing attacks. Heavy bowing attacks cause large amplitudes, and light bowing attacks, small amplitudes. In order to produce a continuous sound, without a renewal of attack, the bow must move in one direction. The duration of a period depends upon the pressure of the bow on the string. Thus the period of continuous bowing in one direction in *piano* is greater than in *forte*.

We shall now classify the forms of bowing as the forms of attack in relation to the durability of sound. We shall assume that the total scale of attacks lies between the two limits: the lower limit corresponds to the most continuous form of attack, and the upper limit, to the most discontinuous, i.e., abrupt, form of attack.

The movement of the bow in the direction from g-string to e-string is considered *downward* and, when necessary, is indicated as ⊓ ; the movement in the opposite direction is considered *upward* and is indicated as ∨ . The upbeat groups are usually played ∨ and the downbeat groups are usually played ⊓ . Otherwise a composer must indicate the direction of the bowing which expresses his desire.

The Scale of Bowing Attacks

(1) *legato:* a group of notes united by a slur represents continuous bowing in one direction; *large legato* pertains to a long group, and *small legato*, to a short group;

(2) *non-legato* (detaché) or *detached* is indicated by the absence of slurs or any other signs: each note corresponds to an individual *smooth* bowing attack, i.e., the bow must be turned in the opposite direction after each note;

(3) *portamento* (in bowing) represents a group of slightly accentuated attacks, while the bow moves in one direction; it is indicated as follows: ♩♩♩♩ ;

(4) *spiccato:* abrupt bowing for each attack, while the bow moves in one direction: ♩♩♩♩ ; it sounds somewhat lighter than staccato;

(5) *staccato:* abrupt bowing for each attack and changing the direction of the bow after each attack: ♩♩♩♩ (no slurs);

(6) *martellato* (hammering): a vigorous downward or upward stroke indicated like this: ♩♩♩♩ (no slurs; bow changes its direction after each attack, unless specified otherwise);

(7) *saltando* (jumping): a bouncing group of attacks obtained by one stroke (usually two, three or four attacks, which can be described as throwing the bow from above; bouncing is caused by the resilience of the string and the bow; *saltando* has a light percussive character and is usually employed in accompaniments of the character of Spanish dances: this effect is a mild version of castanets; saltando is indicated like this: ♩♩♩♩ ;

(8) *col legno* (with the wooden part of the bow) is marked by these words above the part; no other indications are necessary; this effect is still more percussive in character than *saltando:* it is performed by an individual thrust of the bow downward upon the string, each throw corresponding to an individual attack; the general effect of *col legno* is that of pianissimo.

To continue the abrupt forms of attack, we may add, at this point, the various forms of plucking the strings.

From the orchestrator's viewpoint there are two basic forms of *pizzicato:* (1) *pizzicato legato,* where the respective finger of the left hand is moved on a small interval (usually a semitone or a whole tone), after the string is plucked (this effect resembles the so-called "Hawaiian guitar"); (2) *pizzicato* (the usual form), where each attack, single (one string) or compound (several strings; this sounds like an arpeggio) is produced by individual plucking. The regular pizzicato is marked *pizz.* and the pizzicato legato is indicated by a *pizz.* and a *slur:* pizz. ♩♩ . From the violinist's standpoint, there is also a distinction between the right-hand pizzicato and the left-hand pizzicato (the latter is indicated by a cross [+] above the note; it is mostly used on open strings, and can be easily executed amidst rapid passages of bowing).

Bowing positions in relation to the sections of the bow

Insofar as the manner of playing is concerned, the bow may be regarded as consisting of three sections: the nut (lower part), the middle section, and the head (upper part), which, in international musical terminology, corresponds respectively to: (1) *du talon,* (2) *media* (or: modo ordinare) and (3) *a punta d'arco.*

When specific sections of the bow are to be used, the composer must make corresponding indications. However, *du talon* is associated with *martellato; a punta d'arco* is associated with high-pitched *bowing tremolo* in pianissimo; and *media* simply serves as a symbol for cancellation of one of the previous special forms of bowing.

Bowing positions in relation to the fingerboard and the bridge

There are three such basic positions: (1) over the fingerboard (usually at its widest part), known and marked as *sul tasto;* this effect produces a delicate flute-like quality; (2) in the usual place between the fingerboard and the bridge (usually slightly closer to the bridge), indicated also as *media* or *modo ordinare*, used mostly for cancellation of the preceding or the following effect; (3) very close to the bridge, marked as *sul ponticello*, which is mostly used in *bowing tremolo;* this produces a nasal "double-reed" quality.

It is possible, while performing the bowing tremolo, to move the bow *gradually* from *sul tasto* to *sul ponticello* or back. This is a neglected but very valuable technique, by which a gradual modification of quality (*tasto* corresponds to flute; *ponticello*, to double-reed) can be obtained on all the stringed-bow instruments.

Bowing tremolo (i.e., rapid forward-backward movement of the bow) must not be confused with *tremolo legato*, which is a finger-tremolo (like the trill, only in a different pitch-interval).

3. RANGE

The range of the violin, as employed by composers, *grew upward* during the 18th and 19th centuries. It was the desire of some of the outstanding composers to extend violin pitch beyond the range known to their predecessors. This evolution of range must be considered now to be completed, so far as the known type of violin is concerned. The reason for this is that Rimsky-Korsakov employed (as a pedal point), at the very opening of his opera *Kitezh*, *b* of the *third octave* (the highest *b* on the piano keyboard), which happens to lie (that is, the point of finger-pressure) at the very end of the fingerboard. During Beethoven's time, the upper limit was at *c* of the same octave.

Only the e-string is used in such a wide range; all other strings are used within the range of a *ninth* (14 semitones); however, the range of g-string is frequently extended to a *twelfth* and even more (the purpose of this is to obtain the specific quality of high positions on that string).

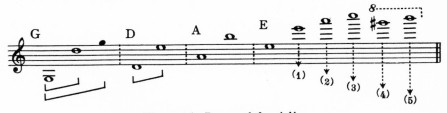

Figure 15. Range of the violin.

On the E string note the following:

(1) represents the limit for *cantabile* in unsupported unison (i.e., without octave doubling) and corresponds to the upper limit of the highest human voice, i.e., coloratura soprano; it is also the limit for pizzicato, after which limit the sound becomes too dry;

(2) Haydn's limit;

(3) Beethoven's limit; also the limit of *free orchestra-playing*, beyond which only easy passages in single notes and sustained notes (single or double) can be used;

(4) the limit in the early scores of Wagner reached *e* below this g#; the latter was introduced in the *Ring;*

(5) Rimsky-Korsakov's *Kitezh;* no fingerboard beyond this point.

4. QUALITY

The basic resources (besides those which we have already described) of special tone-qualities on the string-bow instruments and decidedly contrasting with each other are the *mute* (double-reed quality, marked *con sordino*) and the *harmonics* or *overtones* (purest quality: sine-wave; no vibrato). The mute can be put on (con sordino) or taken off (senza sordino) wherever the composer desires, providing he gives enough time to the performer to make such a change.

Harmonics are produced on the violin by touching instead of pressing the string. The scale of harmonics can be only approximated in our system of musical notation. Harmonics are a natural phenomenon corresponding to what is known in mathematics as "natural harmonic series", i.e., 1, 2, 3, 4, 5, 6, 7, 8, 9, ...

The sound of harmonics corresponds to simple ratios of frequencies and to the partial distribution of a sounding body. In the case of strings, harmonics correspond to the division of a string into uniform sections. These sections are in inverse proportion to the order of a harmonic.

Thus, in order to get the fundamental (which is considered the first harmonic), it is necessary to let the *entire string* vibrate. In order to get the second harmonic, it is necessary to let the two halves of the string vibrate separately. The zero point between the two halves is known as "node". The finger must touch (not press) at the point of the node. The higher the harmonic, the shorter the partial division of the string (and the higher the frequencies).

The correspondence between divisions of the string and the order of harmonics is as follows:

Division of the string	Order of the harmonic
1	1
$\frac{1}{2}$	2
$\frac{1}{3}$	3
$\frac{1}{4}$	4
$\frac{1}{5}$	5
$\frac{1}{6}$	6

Beyond this limit, harmonics produced on the string-bow instruments become impractical, except perhaps for the double-bass seventh harmonic. What violinists usually do not know, and what the composer should know is that *every node* in the same subdivision (denominator) produces identical harmonics.

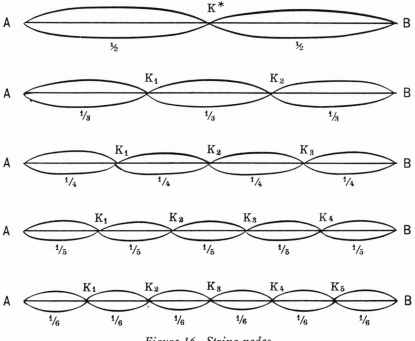

Figure 16. String nodes.

The practical consequences of this situation are the diversified ways of getting a harmonic in a passage where a violinist may think it impossible. Imagine a regular rapid passage which brings you to the upper (close to the bridge) part of the fingerboard. Now assume you want to use the third harmonic. A violinist might try to reach the point K_1 in Fig. 16 (2), while touching the string at the point K_2 would produce the same harmonic.

As more careful composers (Wagner, for instance) indicate in musical notation by a diamond-shaped note (♦, ♦, ♦, ♦,   etc.) the point of the finger-contact with the string, it is possible to carry out the above principle to a practical end.

Each string is subject to the same physical conditions, so far as harmonics are concerned. The longer the string, the more pronounced the harmonics. Thus, the *quality of harmonics increases* in the following order of instruments:

(1) Violin
(2) Viola
(3) Cello
(4) Bass

*Schillinger employed the word "knot" instead of "node." He therefore used the letter "K" as a symbol. (Ed.)

The lower the order of the harmonic, the richer it sounds. This means that lower harmonics still form physically their own harmonics (or the harmonics of the second order). Thus it is correct to state that, let us say, the third harmonic on the bass is denser than a third harmonic on the 'cello, and that the latter is denser than a third harmonic on the viola, etc. But a sixth harmonic on the 'cello may not be as dense as a second harmonic on the violin.

Here is a complete table of harmonics for the string tuned in c, which can be transposed to any other tuning. The large notes indicate the sound of the open string, the diamond notes indicate the point of finger-contact with the string and the small notes indicate the resulting pitch of the harmonic.

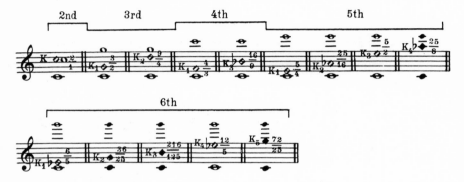

Figure 17. Table of harmonics for "c" string.

Fractions indicate the frequency ratios. All black notes indicate impractical cases.

With regard to equal temperament, the corresponding contact points (K) are practically exact:

$$\frac{2}{1}, \frac{3}{2}, \frac{4}{3}, \frac{16}{9}$$

$\frac{16}{9}$ is very slightly lower

$\frac{5}{4}, \frac{25}{16}, \frac{10}{4}$ are slightly lower

$\frac{6}{5}$ and $\frac{12}{5}$ are slightly higher

In addition to all these harmonics, usually called "natural harmonics", there are harmonics produced by pressing the string with one finger and touching with another. The latter are called by the violinists "artificial harmonics". In reality harmonics cannot be artificial. What would you think of an "artificial sunset"?

The pressing finger shortens the string, and the touching finger produces the respective partial subdivision. There is only one harmonic which is practical under such conditions: *the fourth harmonic. The pressing finger is always the first finger and the touching finger is always the fourth.* The practical advantage of this device is its chromatic universality, which permits the performance of any melodies in the form of harmonics.

Figure 18. Melodies in the form of harmonics.

B. VIOLA

The viola differs from the violin mainly in its tone-quality and in the possibilities for virtuosity. Its tone quality is "somber" as compared to that of the violin. The technique of performance is more difficult than on the violin. The reason for this is that though the dimensions of the viola are greater, the system of fingering remains the same. Thus, playing the viola requires greater stretching of the fingers. In most cases, the unsuccessful but broad-handed and practical minded violinists become violists. It is interesting to note that one of the best composers of today, Paul Hindemith, is one of the best violists of today. For many years he was the leader and the violist of the excellent "Amar-Hindemith Quartette". He has composed works for this neglected instrument in the form of a concerto, sonata and unaccompanied suite.

The tuning of the viola is one fifth lower than that of the violin. The alto and the treble clefs are used in the notation of viola parts.

Figure 19. Tuning.

The range of viola in orchestral use does not exceed a ninth from each of the lower three strings (C, G, D) and not more than a twelfth from the upper string (A). In writing for viola solo, the upper string can be used within a range of two octaves.

Figure 20. Range.

It is correct to say that the *viola is related to the violin as two to three.*

All forms of technical execution correspond to that of the violin. Except with regard to range, the parts written for the viola need not be limited in any respect in which the violin parts are not limited.

C. Violoncello

Violoncello means a small *violone*, which was the *bass viol* of the viol family. This is why it has a diminutive name in spite of its size. This instrument is commonly called *cello*, which does not make any sense, but conveys the association through the established use of this word. It is more correct to write " 'cello" (with an apostrophe in front).

Being held in a different position from the violin and the viola, and exceeding the latter in size (the 'cello is related to the viola as one to two and to the violin as one to three), the 'cello requires a different type of technique in fingering. The intervals on the fingerboard are wider, and the stretching is greater. Though the thumb does not have to support the instrument, it seldom participates in playing and is used on special occasions only (mainly for pressing the string while playing harmonics). The thumb is indicated as " ρ ". All other fingers are numbered in the same way as on the violin.

The 'cello is tuned in fifths and one octave lower than the viola. Bass (F), tenor (C) and treble (G) clefs are commonly used. Contemporary composers in most cases have abolished the tenor clef; but the 'cellists have to know it well because most composers of the past have used it in their scores.

Figure 21. Tuning.

The range of the 'cello in orchestral use does not exceed a ninth from each of the lower three strings (C, G. D) and a twelfth from the upper string (A). In solo playing, however, the latter can have a two-octave range.

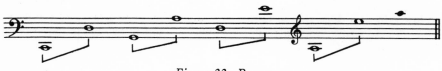

Figure 22. Range.

It is customary in ordinary passage-playing to make transitions from string to string in one position, rather than to change positions on one string. In case of chromatic scalewise passages, positions are frequently changed.

The usual fingering for the lower positions is based on the following principle:

(1) semitones are played by adjacent fingers;

(2) whole tones by alternate fingers;

(3) chromatic scales are played with continuous changes of positions, each position emphasizing three fingers: the first, the second and the third;

(4) all executions of double-stops, chords and rapid arpeggio are based on the above forms of normal fingering; as a consequence, the chords which are easy to play are either in open positions or contain open strings;

(5) perfect fifths are played with one finger on two adjacent strings;

(6) all "artificial harmonics" are played with the thumb (pressing) and the third finger (touching).

Figure 23. Examples of fingering.

All the forms of bowing, practical for the violin, are practical for the 'cello. As the bow of the 'cello is proportionately shorter than that of the violin, the composer must use long durations of single notes and of passages emphasized by the bow moving in one direction with discrimination.

One of the 'cello's features are harmonics. Owing to long strings, they are very sonorous. For the same reason pizzicato is richer on the 'cello than on the violin. Pizzicato glissando (marked: *pizz.* and a slur over the two bordering notes), produces a colorful effect similar to Hawaiian guitar. (See *Four Hindu Songs* for voice and orchestra by Maurice Delage).

Glissando of harmonics is another effect to which the 'cello is particularly suited. In order to execute it, touch the string at the nut and move the finger quite fast toward the central knot of the string. This causes a sequence of harmonics from high to low ones. Moving in reverse, i.e., from the central (node) knot to the nut, causes the reversal of the sequence of harmonics. There is no need to move the finger beyond the central knot (node) as the string has an axis of symmetry for all the knots (nodes), and such a finger movement would produce the same harmonics as when moved from the central knot (node) back to the nut. The resulting effect has great color value and has been used by the best orchestrally-minded composers. It sounds like a rapidly moving arpeggio of a large seventh-chord.

A combination of such harmonics glissando played by several 'cellists on different strings, and also in different directions if desired, produces a shimmering effect of fantastic harps, subtle and fragile.

The adopted notation of this effect is as follows (black notes show the *main points* of the actual sounds as all the points cannot be expressed in our musical notation).

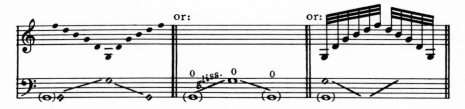

Figure 24. Harmonics glissando.

See Rimsky-Korsakov's opera *Christmas Night*.

D. Double-Bass (Contrabass)

The double bass (corresponding to the antiquated violone) has *four* strings usually. They are tuned in fourths.

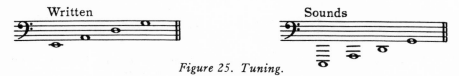

Figure 25. Tuning.

In the 18th and 19th centuries when a lower note was required, the bassists re-tuned the lower string to E♭ or to D. In the 20th century the problem has been solved by the addition of a fifth string (below the fourth regular string), which is tuned in C. All large symphonic and operatic organizations have at least half of their string basses equipped with five strings.

High positions are used less frequently on the string bass than on any other string-bow instrument.

The range, practical for orchestral use, is as follows: Double bass always sounds one octave lower than the written range.

Figure 26. Range.

All forms of bowing and effects, including the use of mutes, *pizz.*, glissando, harmonics and harmonics glissando, are perfectly suitable for the bass, though they are sometimes unjustly neglected.

Fingering technique and intonation are the chief difficulties of this instrument. The fundamentals of fingering are as follows:

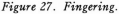

Figure 27. Fingering.

The last case is quite difficult and must be avoided, unless absolutely necessary.

As higher positions require closer spacing, it is easier to play the bass in the higher positions. The purity of intonation increases, but it becomes more and more difficult to get a pleasing tone. It is best not to use the double-stops at all as they sound muddy in low register anyway. However, certain forms of pedal and strata can be used.

Figure 28. Forms of pedal and strata.

Chords are impractical even when possible. Some composers have written solo passages and phrases for the bass, and have exceeded on such occasions the established orchestral range. See Rimsky-Korsakov's opera *Coq D'Or* in which a bass solo is written in the alto (C) clef.

There are very few outstanding bassists who appear as soloists. Probably the best of all bassists in the whole history of this instrument is Sergei Koussevitsky (at present the conductor of the Boston Symphony Orchestra). When Koussevitsky was younger, he frequently gave recitals on the double bass as well as played concertos with his own orchestra (which was known as the Koussevitsky Orchestra in Moscow, Russia). As bass literature is limited, Koussevitsky often played his own transcriptions of concertos written for some other neglected instruments. Thus, one of his favorites was Mozart's concerto for a bassoon (Fagotto) with orchestra. Another accomplished bassist (at present with the Radio City Music Hall Orchestra in New York) also comes from Russia. His name is Michel Krasnopolsky.*

When used as a solo instrument, the double bass must be tuned a tone higher and read a minor seventh down. It really becomes a bass in D. Some of the outstanding violin-makers in Italy made a few excellent basses, which are slightly smaller in size and permit the tuning one tone higher. They are better in tone too.

In jazz, the double bass is used mostly as a percussive instrument: it is plucked (pizzicato) and slapped. It is interesting to mention that in jazz playing, where virtuosity on some orchestral instruments leaves the classical way of playing far behind, the development of the performer's technique influenced mostly the right and not the left hand and, even then, not in bowing. This particular form of virtuosity produced some proficient performers. There are two duets for piano and double bass on Columbia records: *Blues* and *Plucked Again* (Columbia, Jazz Masterwork, 35322), with Jimmy Blanton (bass) and Duke Ellington (piano).**

---

*In Russia, he played among other things Schillinger's own "Suite for Double-Bass and Piano" composed in 1921. (Ed.)

**The catholicity of Schillinger's interest and the range of his information always astounded Schillinger's students. (Ed.)

CHAPTER 2

WOODWIND INSTRUMENTS

A. The Flute Family

1. FLAUTO GRANDE (FLUTE)

This instrument, known as a "large flute" in contrast to the smallest member of this family known as a "small flute," or Flauto Piccolo, or just plain "Piccolo" (which is as bad as "cello"), is a D-instrument without transposition. This means that, whereas its natural tones, i.e., the tones produced by modification of blowing and not by using holes and keys, have D as their fundamental, the tones sound as they are written. Tones which are not in the acoustical scale are produced by means of six holes and a number of keys (depending on the make). Opening of the holes from the foot-joint up shortens the air column and produces the tones of the natural major scale in D, i.e., d, e, f♯, g, a, b, c♯. The following d is the second natural tone (harmonic) from which the scale can be executed further in a similar fashion. All chromatic intervals are filled out by means of keys. The two (in some makes, three) tones below the fundamental d are executed by extending the bore with a pair of specially designed keys, which close instead of opening the holes.

Being cylindrical on the outside, the bore of a flute may be an inverted cone inside although with a very slight deviation from a cylinder. The shape of the bore and the form of exciting the air column directly (through an open hole), instead of through a mouth-piece of any kind gives the flute its whistle-like tone-quality.

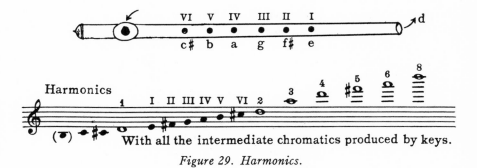

Figure 29. Harmonics.

As a consequence of this construction, the easiest keys for the flute are D, A, G, etc., i.e., keys adjacent to D through their signatures.

The flute is particularly suited for scalewise passages (which can be played at any practicable speed) and close forms of arpeggio (E_1). Finger technique is highly developed among flutists. All forms of *tremolo legato* (arpeggio of couplings), *trills, rapid grace-note scalewise passages* are typical of the flute.

Another flute specialty is the multiple-tongue effects: double, triple and quadruple, which as the name shows, are accomplished by a rapid oscillatory tongue movement. There is no special notation for this effect, and every flutist knows it should be used when there is a rapidly repeating pitch.

It must be understood that the term "legato" (indicated by a tie), as applied to flute as well as to *all wind instruments* (including woodwind and brass), means a group of notes executed in one breath. As non-legato, staccato, etc., are also executed in one breath for a group of notes, legato means one breath without a renewal of the tongue-attack.

Increase in the number of attacks augments the volume of the instrument and should be used in all cases when the natural volume is weak; yet harder blowing may produce the next natural tone. As a special device for both increasing the volume and giving the tremolo effect, *frulato* (flutter-tongue) is used. In order to execute *frulato* (which is only practical in the high register), it is necessary to pronounce (in a whispering manner) a continuous rolling of frrr. The notation for *frulato* is: ⌇⌇⌇ for the period of duration of the note.

Because blowing the flute is immediate, the air column in the bore is quite unstable. This causes great sensitivity of registers. Each register has its own dynamic characteristics. Consideration of the latter is of the utmost importance in orchestration. Contemporary manufacturers are constantly seeking a scientific solution for equalization of registers. To put it plainly, each register, unless very skilfully handled, sounds like a somewhat different instrument. When one melodic group occupies more than one register, the contrast between the registers becomes very undesirable. Some old-fashioned minds think it desirable to have nearly each tone in a different flavor, because they believe it attributes individuality to the instrument. This assumption is psychologically wrong because each sound does not sound *per se*, but in connection with preceding and following sounds. Imagine a book where each character is printed in a different type. It certainly attributes individuality to each letter, but at the same time makes the process of reading far from pleasurable.

Uniformity of tone-quality throughout the entire range is the main weapon of attack against electronic instruments because such instruments have a much greater qualitative stability than woodwind instruments. In other words, electronic instruments are condemned by the reactionaries while great string instrumentalists try hard to conceal bow changes from one string to another (which is equivalent to the change of registers).

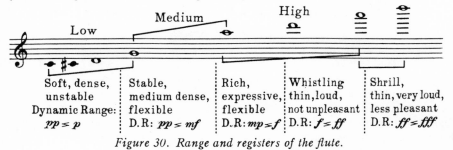

Figure 30. Range and registers of the flute.

2. FLAUTO PICCOLO (PICCOLO)

This is a diminutive flute and possesses all the main characteristics of the large flute. Its acoustical scale is also in D, but its range is much more limited. The lower register is practically useless, except for some humorous effects. The agility of this instrument is truly remarkable, and particularly so in the scalewise passages.

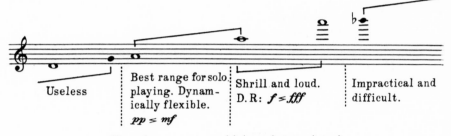

(Sounds one octave higher than written)

Figure 31. Range and Registers of the Flute Piccolo.

3. FLAUTO CONTRALTO (ALTO FLUTE)

This comes in two sizes (or types):

(1) Fl. Contralto in G.
(2) Fl. Contralto in F (used less than the one in G).

Both types are used a great deal in operatic and symphonic scoring.

The main value of the alto flutes lies *not in extending the range below the ordinary flute, but in giving a better quality and a more stable range* corresponding to the low register of flauto grando.

Fl. Contralto in G sounds a perfect fourth (5 semitones) lower than the written range.

Fl. Contralto in F sounds a perfect fifth (7 semitones) lower than the written range.

The first of the two has a better tone quality.

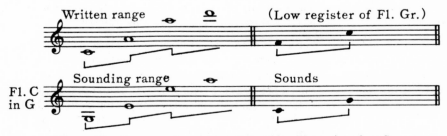

Figure 32. Range and registers of the Alto Flutes (continued).

Figure 32. Range and registers of the Alto Flutes (concluded).

There is no need to use the high register of alto instruments as the regular type gives a better tone-quality.

Other types, such as Bass Flutes, are obsolete nowadays. They produce tones in quality somewhere between the *ocarina* and an *empty bottle*.

B. THE CLARINET (SINGLE-REED) FAMILY

1. CLARINETTO (CLARINET) IN B♭ and A

This instrument has a cylindric bore, which causes, according to Helmholtz, the appearance of only odd (1, 3, 5, 7, 9, . . .) harmonics. The even-numbered harmonics are absent. This situation creates a gap of 18 semitones between the fundamental and the next (i.e., the third) appearing harmonic. Somehow the designers of this instrument succeeded in reducing the number of holes and keys considerably (usually to 13) though theoretically 18 holes are necessary in order to produce a chromatic scale covering the gap.

From the performer's angle, the clarinet is a difficult instrument to master. However, this should not worry the composer as accomplished clarinetists are really in abundance. The main consideration for the composer to bear in mind is that while approaching the third harmonic, the tone of the clarinet weakens for about the last 6 semitones. The register between the fundamental and the third harmonic is known as *chalumeau* (French, from Latin "calamus"—reed; originally, a single reed instrument with a built-in reed, now obsolete; probably the ancestor of clarinet). A special tone-quality, in addition to the usual one, and one which is hard to produce, corresponds to the chalumeau register and is known as *subtone* (soft, delicate and tender). Starting with the third harmonic and going up, the tone-quality of the clarinet changes noticeably. Of course, it is the task of an accomplished performer to neutralize this difference.

The sound on the clarinet is produced by blowing into a detachable mouthpiece to which a reed is attached. A complete chromatic scale is produced by means of various types of keys and by holes which are covered by the fingers (special keys on the bass clarinet). The clarinettists of American dance orchestras are able to produce a *glissando* (i.e., continuous pitch modulation between two frequencies). This is accomplished by the *embouchure* (which usually means "the assumed position of lips combined with lip-pressure"). Symphonic and operatic clarinettists are not trained to play glissando.

The scale of natural tones on the clarinet is *written* as follows (and sounds as written when played on a clarinet in C):

Figure 33. Natural tones of the clarinet.

The clarinet in C was discarded a long time ago because its tone quality was not as satisfactory as that of the clarinets in Bb and in A (some contemporary manufacturers make an extra hole and key to compensate the lower semitone on the Bb-clarinet; thus it can play the parts written for the A-clarinet; in other instances, mechanical adjustments have been made in order to obtain a combined version of the Bb and the A clarinets).

Though some individual performers get far beyond the common range, there is an unwritten international code of ethics by which composers limit themselves to the written *g* of the second octave.

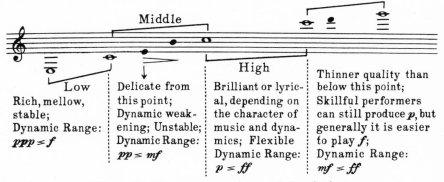

Figure 34. Range and registers of the clarinet.

For the clarinet in Bb the above table *sounds one tone lower*. This means that the composer must write his parts for the Bb instrument *one tone higher* than he expects to hear the actual sounds. For instance, the part which sounds in the key of *C* must be written in the key of *D*. Thus, the clarinet in Bb acoustically is a *D* instrument, as its fundamental tone (by sound) is *d*.

Likewise, parts for the clarinet in A must be *written three semitones higher* than they are expected to sound. Thus the above table sounds three semitones lower. Parts expected to sound in the key of *C* must be written in the key of *Eb*. Thus clarinet in A acoustically is a *C♯* instrument, as its fundamental tone (by sound) is *c♯*.

It was believed in the 19th century that the Bb-clarinet represented the masculine quality, and that it was more substantial but less delicate than the feminine quality of the A-clarinet. However, today skilful performers can obtain both characteristics on the B♭-clarinet.

Considering the quality of manufacture and the skill of contemporary performers, we may say that the clarinet can play practically everything. Its specialties are: rapid diatonic and chromatic passages, tremolo legato and trills. Staccato is preferable in its soft form. Arpeggio of the E_1 form is very grateful both ascending and descending.

2. CLARINETTO PICCOLO IN D AND E♭

The first instrument (D) is used in symphonic and operatic orchestras and the second (E♭), in military bands. Both these instruments are inferior in their tone quality as compared with the clarinets in B♭ and A.

The acoustical range of the D-clarinet is in F♯. It is *written one whole tone lower* than it is expected to sound. The parts which are written in the key of B♭ sound in the key of C.

The acoustical range of the E♭-clarinet is in G. It is *written three semitones lower* than it is expected to sound. The parts which are written in the key of A sound in the key of C.

Except for tone-quality, the piccolo clarinets can be favorably compared with the regular clarinets: their mobility is as high.

3. CLARINETTO CONTRALTO (ALTO CLARINET) and CORNO DI BASSETTO (BASSETHORN)

Clarinetto contralto is usually an E♭, but sometimes an F instrument. Thus its part should be written a *major sixth* and a *perfect fifth* higher, respectively, than the sounding keys. The F instrument is so constructed that its lowest written note is *c* below the usual *e*. The tone-quality of each of these instruments can be described as more "hollow" than the tone of a regular clarinet.

Corno di bassetto has a smaller bore than the clarinet. It looks somewhat like a miniature version of the clarinetto basso (bass clarinet). Its tone-quality is more "reedy" than that of the clarinet. The bassethorn is an instrument in F: it is *written a perfect fifth higher* than it sounds. Today the bassethorn is becoming more and more obsolete: the alto clarinet in E♭ takes its place.

4. CLARINETTO BASSO (BASS CLARINET) in B♭ and A

The A instrument is seldom used outside of Germany. Both these instruments sound one octave below their respective regular clarinets. This means that the B♭-basso is written a major ninth higher than it sounds; A-basso is written a minor tenth higher than it sounds when the treble clef is used. In German scores, both treble and bass clef are often used.

The rule is that in using the bass clef, *write one octave below* the corresponding note of the treble clef: that is, the transposition of sound from the bass clef is only a whole tone, or a tone-and-a-half down instead of the major ninth or minor tenth as in the treble.

Both these instruments are manufactured with and without the lower extension from *e* to *c*. The B♭-basso without lower range extension is used by dance orchestras, whereas the B♭-basso which reaches the lower c (*b♭*– by the sound) is used in symphonic and operatic scoring. These instruments have quite a sinister tone in their lower register. It is wise not to write for the bass-clarinet above *d* of the second octave. The bass-clarinet possesses somewhat less mobility than the smaller clarinets.

There is also a *contrabass* or *pedal clarinet*, a monstrous affair which has to be suspended on special stands and which is very hard to play. Richard Strauss used one in his *Electra*, but apparently only the Germans could play it. It sounds one octave below the bass clarinet (it is also in B♭) and has an awe-inspiring quality.

C. The Saxophone (Single-Reed) Family

The saxophone is one of the numerous creations of Adolf Sax, an eminent instrument designer of the 19th century. This instrument is a crossbreed between the oboe (owing to its conic bore) and the clarinet (owing to its single-reed mouthpiece).

Very few composers used this instrument in the 19th century (one of them was Georges Bizet) and eventually it became quite obsolete, with the exception of its use by military bands in France and Belgium, which have emplc ed saxophones widely.

The original saxophone family consisted of instruments in C and in F.

Soprano Saxophone in C
Alto   "   " F
Tenor   "   " C
Baritone "   " F
Bass   "   " C

American manufacturers rejuvenated interest in this instrument. They succeeded in constructing saxophones of a more improved design. American saxophones as played by American saxophonists have introduced a whole new style of music and musical execution.

American-made saxophones are so flexible that any type of part can be written for them. Rapid scales, arpeggio, tremolo legato, trills, staccato, glissando are all possible and grateful on this instrument. The last two or three decades have produced a number of outstanding virtuosi, many of whom are Negroes and many of whom are skilful improvisers. It is due to the wide influence of jazz and jazz-playing that saxophone manufacture has become a considerable industry.

Standard dance-band combinations customarily use 4 or 5 saxophones. In some instances this number varies. It is quite common for a saxophonist to double as a clarinettist. Some performers are equally good on both instruments.

In the earlier days of American jazz (and also in some instances in Europe) there were some ensembles consisting only of saxophones, but they have not survived.*

The American family of saxophones is tuned in B♭ and E♭.

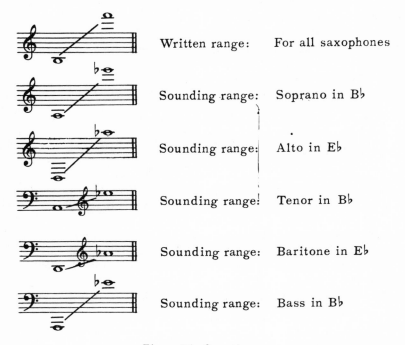

Figure 35. Saxophones.

The soprano and the bass are seldom used today. All saxophone parts are written in the treble clef. There is no noticeable difference of registers in a good performance, and it is for this reason that we have omitted range subdivisions.

D. THE OBOE (DOUBLE-REED) FAMILY

1. OBOE

The oboe is an instrument of ancient origin. In its primitive form it was in wide use throughout Asia. One of the oboe's ancestors was the Hellenic *aulos*, which was used for the expression of passion.

Blowing through the narrow opening of the flatly folded reed (usually called double reed) requires strong lungs and a peculiar technique of breathing. Some of the Asiatics (Persians, for example) can play the oboe-like double-reed instruments with uninterrupted sound (like the Scottish bagpipe). These performers

*Recently a well-known band leader, Shep Fields, organized a large, successful dance orchestra which consisted, apart from several percussion instruments, wholly of saxophones. (Ed.)

usually hold a reserve supply of air in one cheek, which is exhaled, i.e., blown into the reed, while the lungs are inhaling a new supply of air.

The contemporary oboe has a conic bore, which characteristic permits the appearance of the full scale of natural tones (harmonics).

Without additional keys, the oboe acoustically can be considered an instrument in D, like the flute. The oboe, like the flute, is not a transposing instrument. Most oboes of European manufacture have *b* of the small octave as their lowest tone. American-made oboes reach *bb*, immediately below it. It is customary not to use the oboe above *f* of the second octave. Owing to its construction the oboe is a slow-speaking instrument. Only passages of moderate speed are possible on this instrument. The oboe is valued mainly for its characteristic tone-quality, which can be described as "nasal" and "warm."

All types of passages are possible, including tremolo legato and trills, providing they are executed at a speed which seems moderate compared to flutes and clarinets. One of the most valuable characteristics of the oboe is the versatility and distinct character of the attack forms. The legato, the portamento, the soft and particularly the hard staccato appear on the oboe with clear distinction.

The density of the oboe's tone decreases considerably in the upper part of its range. The low register is somewhat heavy and has a natural volume increase in the direction of decreasing frequencies. The most flexible and expressive part of the range is the middle register. High tones are thin and shrill.

The density of the oboe's tone decreases considerably in the upper part of its range. The low register is somewhat heavy and has a natural volume increase in the direction of decreasing frequencies. The most flexible and expressive part of the range is the middle register. High tones are thin and shrill.

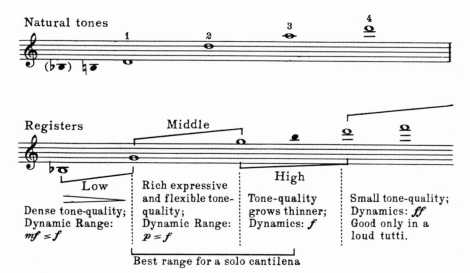

Figure 36. Range and registers of the oboe.

2. OBOE D'AMORE

A mezzo-soprano type of oboe which is now rarely used. J. S. Bach used it in his *Christmas Oratorio*. It was revived by Richard Strauss in his *Sinfonia Domestica*.

This is a transposing instrument in A♭.

Figure 37. Range of Oboe d'Amore.

3. CORNO INGLESE (ENGLISH HORN)

The immediate predecessor of this instrument is the *oboe da caccia* (hunting oboe), now obsolete. The contemporary version of corno inglese (also known as *oboe contralto*) represents an instrument similar in most respects to the oboe, but sounding a perfect fifth lower. It is a transposing instrument in F.

The middle octave is its best register for an expressive solo. The low register is denser and heavier than that of an ordinary oboe. The high register is seldom used beyond the written d (sounds g) of the second octave. All other characteristics correspond to oboe. It is still a somewhat slower-speaking instrument than the oboe.

The English horn is exceptionally suitable for the expression of passion and suffering. In orchestral scoring it is often given a solo. One of the famous solos is in Wagner's *Tristan and Isolde* (Prelude to the third act).

Figure 38. Range of corno inglese.

4. HECKELPHONE (BARITONE OBOE)

The baritone oboe is an instrument of German manufacture (made by Heckel) which, in its perfected form, was introduced about 1905. The tone has a quality of overwhelming richness and expressiveness. Richard Strauss used it first in his opera *Salome;* Ernst Krenek also employed it in his opera *Sprung Ueber den Schatten* ("Leap Over the Shadow"). It is an instrument well deserving wide use together with the oboe and English horn.

The heckelphone is made to sound one octave below the oboe; it sounds one octave below the written range. Its size is so big that the bell of the instrument rests on the floor, while the performer is playing it from a sitting position.

The key and hole system is designed to resemble that of an ordinary oboe, which construction makes it easy for an oboist to master the heckelphone.

As the range and the registers of this instrument correspond exactly to that of an oboe (the lowest tone is $b\natural$), but sound one octave lower, there is no need for a table of range and registers.

E. The Bassoon (Double-Reed) Family

1. FAGOTTO (BASSOON)

The name "fagotto" derives from "faggot": a bundle of sticks; the name "bassoon" from the association with bass register.

The bassoon is an instrument with a very long conic bore (about eight feet), which is folded upon itself, somewhat in the manner of the letter "u". This u-shape makes it possible to, have a system of accessible holes and keys. Some of the key-holes produce only one tone (the lower keys) and some, two (octave variation is easily produced by lip-pressure).

Being an instrument with a conic bore and a double-reed mouth-piece, the bassoon may be considered a bass of the double-reed group, i.e., it is a natural bass to the oboes.

The main difference between the oboe and the bassoon lies in the fact that the latter has an additional section, which extends its low register.

Under the same conditions of fingering (with the basic six holes closed), the bassoon is a perfect twelfth below the oboe, i.e., under the conditions which produce the middle d on the oboe, the bassoon produces the g one twelfth below.

The range of the bassoon (for all practical purposes) begins with the $b\flat$ of contra-octave and ends with d of the first octave. The $b\natural$ tone at the lower end is of somewhat poorer quality than all the other tones of the low register.

This instrument is capable of mobility, noticeably greater than that of an oboe. Various forms of arpeggio (practically in all expansions), octaves and leaps in general, as well as rapid scalewise passages, tremolo legato and trills constitute the versatile technique of this instrument. The attacks are distinct. Legato, portamento, soft and hard staccato (the latter being the bassoon's specialty and possible at a considerable speed) can be executed with quick changes.

Bassoon parts are written in the bass and the tenor clefs (though alto-clef may be used as well). It is not a transposing instrument.

The dynamic peculiarities of the bassoon require particular attention on the part of the composer. The low register (from $b\flat$ of the contra-octave to c of the small octave) is the most powerful part of the bassoon's range. It weakens slightly toward the middle register (this begins with c of the small octave and ends with c of the middle octave), which is considerably weaker than the low register. The high register, from c to g of the middle octave, is somewhat harsh; it becomes very mellow from g of the middle octave to d of the first octave. Stravinsky is one of the few composers who has utilized this upper region effectively (the opening bassoon solo at the beginning of the *Rites of Spring*).

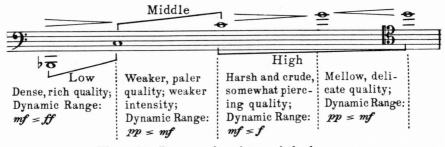

Figure 39. Range and registers of the bassoon.

2. FAGOTTINO (TENOROON, QUINTFAGOTT, TENORFAGOTT)

This instrument (now practically obsolete) was built a perfect fourth and a perfect fifth above the regular bassoon. Both types are transposing instruments: tenoroon in E♭, sounding one perfect fourth higher than written and tenoroon in F, sounding one perfect fifth higher than written. The tone-quality of these instruments is inferior to that of the regular bassoon.

3. CONTRAFAGOTTO (DOUBLE-BASSOON, CONTRA-BASSOON, CONTRAFAGOTT)

This instrument, still of greater dimensions, is meant to be the lower octave-coupler to an ordinary bassoon. The engineering quality of this instrument, being inferior to that of a bassoon, causes inferior tone-quality and less exacting intonation. The tone of this instrument is somewhat dry and does not sound as healthy as the tone of the bassoon. Its alertness is also somewhat lower.

As the contrabassoon is an instrument built mainly to produce low frequencies, it must not (except for some special purposes, such as creating associations of a "humorous" or "painful" nature) be used beyond its regular middle register.

The contrabassoon is a favorite instrument with many composers. Its sounding range is one octave lower than written. Its lower register is considerably weaker than that of a bassoon.

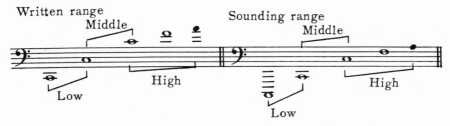

Figure 40. Range and registers of the contrabassoon.

CHAPTER 3

BRASS (WIND) INSTRUMENTS

A. CORNO (French Horn)

THE horn is an instrument with a long and rich history. The immediate predecessor of the contemporary three-valve chromatic French horn was the so-called natural horn, capable of producing only the natural tones. All other tones on the natural horn were obtained by putting the fist of the left hand into the bell and varying the depth of its position within the bell. The deeper the fist is set, the lower the sound of the respective natural tone. This manner of altering natural tones is based on the physical principle of *open* and *closed pipes:* an open pipe sounds one octave higher than the same pipe closed. As the gradual conic pipe (which is coiled around itself) extends in a horn to about seven feet, the partial closing of this pipe by a fist, at the bell, lowers the respective natural tone only by one or two semitones. This device does not cover all steps chromatically, as the acoustical gaps between the second and the third, and between the third and the fourth tones are too great. It is for this reason that the parts written in the 18th and early 19th centuries were predominantly fanfare-like.

Eventually natural horns became practically obsolete. Rimsky-Korsakov used natural horns in his opera *May Night* (when chromatic horns were universally in use) for the sake of his own amusement, which he called "self-discipline".

In order to read scores by such composers as Mozart and Beethoven, not to mention Bach or Händel, it is important to have at least some basic information about the sizes and the transposition-keys of the various horns which were used in not such a remote past.

Natural horns were constructed in two main size-groups: the *alto* horns and the *basso* horns. All horns transpose downward, i.e., they sound below the written range. Alto horns transpose directly to a designated interval, indicated by the transpositional name of the instrument. Basso horns, in addition to the alto transposition, sound one octave lower (compare with the clarinet in B♭ and the bass-clarinet in B♭).

The alto horns were constructed in all chromatic keys except G♭. The selection of a particular horn was in correspondence with the key in which a certain piece was written. Basso horns were used, where it was essential to reach the lower register. Basso horn parts are known only in three transpositions: the B♭ – basso, the A– basso and the A♭– basso. There was no octave confusion in interpretation of the scores because it was the alto horns that were usually meant. The use of basso horns was quite exceptional. An instance of their use may be found in Beethoven's *Fourth Symphony* (written in the key of B♭).

Except for the use of valves, which secure the entire chromatic scale, there is no noticeable difference in the construction of the present day French horns .(including the conic mouth-piece).

Blowing through a long narrow channel creates conditions under which it is easy to "overblow" the fundamental tone of the scale. That is, the air-column tends to break into two halves. For this reason, the officially recognized range of the horn begins with the second tone. From there on, all pitches are practical up to and including the twelfth natural tone. The sixteenth tone is seldom used nowadays. As the frequency increases, the tone-quality becomes brighter.

We shall represent now the scale of natural tones for the hypothetical French horn in C. As the chromatic horns used today are in *F*, the actual sounds appear a perfect fifth below the written range when the part is written in the treble clef; in using the bass clef, write the parts a fourth below the intended pitch, or, to state it differently, one octave below the treble clef. Thus the transposition of the French horn, when written in the treble clef, is exactly the same as that of an English horn.

Thus: [musical notation] and [musical notation] sound alike: [musical notation]

This cumbersome octave-variation as well as the whole idea of pitch-transposition is a survival of an old tradition. The sooner it is abolished, the better; no one gains by this transpositional technique, which is a constant source of complications and confusion.

During Wagner's time and later, chromatic French horns in E were used together with those in F. They are abolished today, because of the superior tone-quality obtainable on the horns in F.

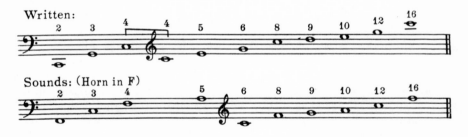

Figure 41. Scales of natural tones of the French horn.

Only in very exceptional cases is the French horn part written one or two semi-tones above the twelfth tone. The best tone-quality for solos lies between the fourth and the twelfth natural tones. The French horn provides a direct continuation of the tuba's timbre in the lower portion of its range. From the fourth to twelfth tones it acquires a gradually growing characteristic of lucidity; in its upper range, the French horn blends well with clarinets and particularly with flutes; in its lower range, with trombones, tuba and bassoons. In this sense, the French horn is an intermediary between the wood-wind and the brass groups.

The chromatic scale, as already stated, is obtained by operating the three valves. All three-valve instruments are designed on the same general principle.

The first valve (operated by the upper key) lowers the natural tone by two semitones.

The second valve (the middle key) lowers the natural tone by one semitone.

The third valve (the lower key) lowers the natural tone by three semitones.

Valves are indicated by the respective Roman numerals:

$$I \text{ lowers by } 2 \text{ semitones}$$
$$II \quad '' \quad '' \quad 1 \text{ semitone}$$
$$III \quad '' \quad '' \quad 3 \text{ semitones}$$

These indications are not used in scores or parts, but merely for reference, when necessary.

The operation of valves is such that while blowing the written middle *c*, for example (the 4th tone which sounds *f*), and pressing key I, one obtains b♭ (sounds e♭); blowing the same tone and pressing key II, one obtains b♮ (sounds e♮); blowing the same tone and pressing key III, one obtains a♮ (sounds d♮).

All other intervals, by which a natural tone can be lowered, are obtained by a combined use of keys controlling the operation of valves. Thus: I + II lowers the natural tone by 3 semitones;

I + III lowers the natural tone by 5 semitones;

II + III lowers the natural tone by 4 semitones;

the combination of all three keys lowers the natural tone by 6 semitones.

In the French horns of old make, there were some deficiencies of intonation when the combined valves were used. They are abolished in present manufacturing by a special interlocking of air columns in the valves, which device rectifies the corresponding frequency-ratios.

Valves themselves are additional short pipes, connected with the main channel by operation of the keys. The latter affect the *pistons* or the *rotary cylinders*. Cylinders are more common on the present French horn. So far as tone quality is concerned, it does not make any difference which particular mechanism is used. Thus keys open the valves, thereby connecting them with the main channel, which results in the lengthening of the air column and, for this reason, lowers the pitch of a given natural tone.

Since the change of *embouchure* (lip condition with respect to form and pressure) is never as alert as finger technique, it is preferable to write rapid passages when they can be produced mainly through the operation of keys. It is for this reason that the composer must have an exact knowledge of the key-valve operations. Even trills and tremolo legato are possible when they are obtained through the use of keys.

It follows from the above that the valve system is acoustically opposite to the whole system used on all wood-wind instruments (i.e., on the brass instruments natural tones are lowered; on the wood-wind instruments they are raised).

The French horn is a slow-speaking instrument, and for this reason speed is not limited by the finger-technique but rather by slow tone-production. All forms of legato and staccato, as well as portamento, are available and distinct. The breathing process, as applied to this instrument, is normal and healthy. It is possible for this reason to execute sustained tones or passages of considerable period in one exhaling. Contrary to the double-reed practice, playing the French horn is a healthful occupation.

Owing to the conical shape of the mouth-piece, double-tonguing is not within the scope of this instrument. One of the French horn's specialties is the dynamic effect of *sforzando-piano* (sfp). This can be performed at any point from the 3rd harmonic upward. The French horn has a wide dynamic range but its lower part weakens considerably.

The French horn is played either *open* (indicated as o) or *stopped* (indicated +). The first indication is not used, except as a cancellation of the "stopped." Stopping is usually indicated above each attack.

Mutes are generally applicable to French horns, but used by performers only under compulsion: they think the stopping "will do".

In volume (intensity), the French horn occupies an intermediate position between the brass (in relation to which it is weaker) and the wood-wind instruments (in comparison with which it is louder, particularly when played high and ff).

B. Tromba (Trumpet)

The trumpet is a chromatic three-valve instrument. Depending on manufacture, either cylinders or pistons are used.

Of all types of trumpets, the soprano (ordinary) type in Bb and A is used more universally than the alto trumpet in G and F, the piccolo trumpet in D and Eb, and particularly the bass trumpet in Eb and Bb.

1. TROMBA (SOPRANO TRUMPET) in Bb and A

Of these two designs, preference is given to the Bb trumpet in the U.S.A., while in Europe both tunings are used for the respective parts. American dance-bands use the Bb trumpet exclusively.

Some of the Bb trumpets can be converted into A trumpets, by drawing a special telescopic slide which lowers the range of the instrument by a semitone.

The trumpet part as written sounds two or three semitones lower respectively, as in the case of the clarinets.

Its scale begins with the second natural tone and ends, for all normal purposes, with the eighth. Outstanding trumpeters are able to blow the ninth, the tenth and even the twelfth tones. In this case the use of the piccolo trumpet becomes unnecessary as the tone of the regular soprano trumpet is preferable. On the other hand, the composer must not rely on the presence of a virtuoso in every orchestra, even the performer playing the part of the first trumpet.

Natural tones are produced by the embouchure, and the pitches between them by fingers, i.e., by pressing the keys which control the valves. The trumpeters of American dance-bands produce many chromatic variations and glissando by the embouchure. These virtuosi very frequently go beyond the eighth tone. In writing "improvised" solos (which in most cases are actually written out and studied), it is best to test the individual performer's range first.

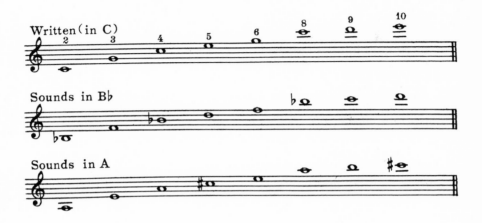

Figure 42. The range of the trumpet.

With the combined use of all three valves, the lowest tone of the trumpet is: f# (in C), e (in B♭), e♭ (in A). Tones below the second natural tone are generally weak. The natural intensity grows with the increase of frequency, but skilful performers have a considerable control over the dynamic range of this instrument.

The cup-shaped mouth-piece of the trumpet, the shape of the bore (slightly deviating from a cylinder to a cone) and the length of the bore make the transmission of tongue attacks more immediate. For this reason double and multiple tongue attacks become one of the main assets of the trumpeter's virtuosity (as in the case of a flute).

Rapid finger-work on the keys permits execution of trills and tremolo legato at a high speed, providing both component pitch-units are executed through the same natural tone (both pitch-units may be keyed, or one of them may be natural).

All forms of attacks are well defined on a trumpet: legato, portamento, soft and hard staccato. Scales and even arpeggio can be executed at a considerable speed. At one time the trumpet was considered as mostly suitable for a performance of signal-like and fanfare-like music, but this viewpoint (considered even by Rimsky-Korsakov) is completely outmoded. The prestige of this instrument has been amazingly restored and heightened by jazz.

2. CORNETTO (CORNET) IN B♭ and A

This instrument, also known under the French name of *cornet a pistons*; (i.e., a cornet with pistons; the name implies chromatic possibilities) does not, strictly speaking, belong to the trumpet family. Its bore is more conical than that of a trumpet; this makes its tone-quality more mellow. For this reason it is considered a more lyrical instrument than the trumpet. Today, however, the skill of performers is so great that accomplished artists are able to imitate the sound of a cornet on a trumpet and the sound of a trumpet on a cornet.

In most cases, American cornettists use the B♭ instruments. It is also customary for a trumpeter to play both trumpet and cornet. The scale of natural tones, the range and the whole mechanism of execution are practically identical with that of a trumpet. The cornet is generally considered to be somewhat less alert than the trumpet. Tone-quality on both trumpet and cornet can be altered by means of a mute inserted into its bell. The use of the mute is marked "con sordino"; the cancellation of this effect, "senza sordino".

American jazz created a real mute-o-mania, resulting in a great variety of new mutes (straight mute, cup-mute, harmon-mute, etc.). Another device, closely related to mutes is the "hat" (usually made out of metal, in the shape of a trench helmet or a derby). It is used for glissando "wow-wow" effects (acoustically, a transformation of the open pipe into the closed pipe).

This instrument is the prima donna of the brass band, but it has found its way into symphonic, operatic and particularly dance scoring.

3. TROMBA PICCOLA (PICCOLO TRUMPET) in D and E♭

This instrument is considerably smaller in size than the ordinary trumpet. The D-type is mostly used in symphonic scoring (for example, Stravinsky's *Sacre*), but relatively very seldom. The E♭ type is much more common in brass bands.

The tone-quality of both is decidedly inferior to that of a regular trumpet.

The transposition of this instrument is analogous to clarinet piccolo, i.e., two and three semitones up respectively. Thus the eighth natural tone (c) sounds d and e♭ respectively. As this instrument requires an excessive lip-pressure, it is very difficult to produce any tone above the eight harmonic. For this reason there seems to be no practical advantage in the further use of this instrument.

4. TROMBA CONTRALTA (ALTO TRUMPET) in G and F

This is a very useful instrument not only for the extension of the regular trumpet's range downward, but also (and mainly so) for obtaining better quality tones within the low register (from the third natural tone down) of a regular trumpet. Rimsky-Korsakov made a very extensive use of this instrument in his operas. It is a softer instrument compared to the B♭ and A trumpet.

The lowest possible pitch on the alto trumpet is the written f♯ (three keys pressed: all valves open), which sounds c♯ on the G trumpet and *b* on the F trumpet respectively, i.e., it transposes down like the alto flute.

It is quite customary for the performer of the third trumpet part to double on the alto trumpet.

5. TROMBA BASSA (BASS TRUMPET) in E♭ and B♭

Strictly speaking, this instrument is not a trumpet but a miniature tuba and, therefore, belongs to the so-called saxhorn family (the dominant brass group of the military bands). It is also known as tenor tuba or Wagnerian tuba.

In many instances the parts written for this instrument are played by the French horns. The E♭ instrument sounds eight semitones below the written range; the B♭ instrument, one octave below the soprano B♭ trumpet. Undoubtedly this instrument will become obsolete. There is also a bass trumpet in C basso which is very seldom used. It sounds one octave below the written range.

C. TROMBONE (TROMBONE)

The trombone is one of the most remarkable instruments in the orchestra. Its design is based on an ingenious yet very simple principle: it has an air column, whose length can be varied by means of **a** *slide*, which is a part of the instrument proper. As a result of this construction the trombone produces a complete chromatic scale consisting of *natural tones only.*

The pulling out of the slide increases the volume of the air-column and thus produces the additional six standard *positions.* When the slide is pulled all the way in, the trombone is considered to be in the *first position.* The opposite position, with the slide pulled out (to the limit, but still producing a continuous bore or air-column, as the slide can be pulled out completely, disjoining the instrument into two individual sections) is considered the *seventh position.* All other positions are between the two extreme positions. Thus the slide actually converts seven natural instruments into one chromatic instrument. As different positions possess different acoustical characteristics, we shall describe each position individually.

The first position has the following natural scale:

Figure 43. First, second, third and fourth positions of the trombone (continued).

The second, the third and the fourth positions have similar acoustical characteristics. See following page.

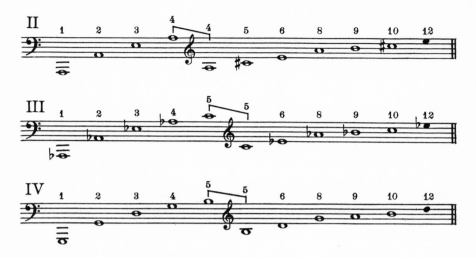

Figure 43. First, second, third and fourth positions of the trombone (concluded).

Tones produced by the fundamental are often called *pedal tones.*

Beginning with the fifth position, the air-column breaks up into two halves, thus making the production of the fundamental impossible.

The fifth, the sixth and the seventh positions have the following natural scale:

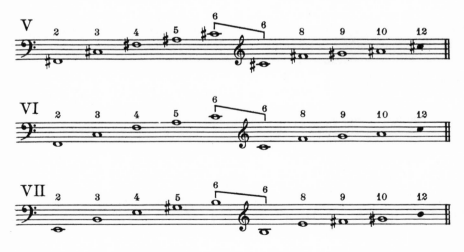

Figure 44. Fifth, sixth and seventh positions of the trombone.

It is easy to see that after the natural tones of all seven positions are combined, there appears to be a gap between the second natural tone of the seventh position and the fundamental of the first position:

Thus, the following pitches are not available on the trombone of this type:

Figure 45. Unavailable pitches on the trombone.

The ability to produce the natural tones above the tenth depends upon the skill of the performer. It is advisable, in writing orchestra parts, not to exceed the eighth harmonic, reserving the use of the ninth and the tenth for exceptional effects.

To compensate for the absence of pitches within the gap, an instrument with a special valve has been designed. This valve, operated by a string attached to a ring controlling the opening of the valve, lowers any natural tone by five semitones (perfect fourth). For this reason a trombone supplied with such a device is known as a *trombone with a valve.*

By means of this device, d♯, d♮, c♯ and c♮ can be obtained from the second natural tones of the III, IV, V and VI positions respectively.

Figure 46. Pitches produced by the open valve and slide.

The lowest pitch of the gap (b♮) still remains impractical owing to the fact that the air-column of the seventh position, augmented by the valve, becomes so great that it breaks itself into three thirds of the total volume, thus causing the third natural tone:

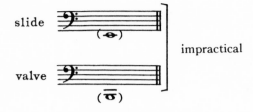

Figure 47. B impractical

It follows from this description that not only the entire chromatic scale is available, but that some of the pitches are even duplicated: they appear as the different natural tones of the different slide-positions. The preference in such cases depends on two conditions:

(1) the positional distance from the preceding to the following pitch; if such positions are too remote and there is a possibility of obtaining the same pitch on a different natural tone of a nearer position, it is the positional distance that becomes a decisive factor;

(2) the difficulty of producing higher natural tones in the lower positions as compared to lower natural tones in the higher positions; for example

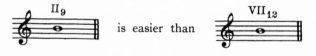

Figure 48. II_9 is easier than VII_{12}.

The trombone has a cup-shaped mouth-piece. Its tone-quality greatly depends on the manner of playing. Some trombonists have a bold, powerful tone; some have a mellow lyrical tone; and some have both. The character of the tone greatly depends on the form of vibrato (tremulant). All forms of vibrato on the trombone are vibrato by pitch (obtained by oscillating the slide within a small pitch interval as on the stringed-bow instruments). In comparison, trumpet vibrato is vibrato by intensity and is caused by variation of embouchure.

The trombone is an instrument of a sliding pitch par excellence, easily comparable to the 'cello. For a long time composers misunderstood the true nature of this instrument. American jazz recaptured the real meaning of the trombone, though in many instances dance-band trombonists overdo both the vibrato and the sliding, which renders a sugary character to the whole performance.

Glissando, which was first regarded (in the hearing of Stravinsky's scores) as an innovation, in reality is very basic on a trombone and today has become not only a commonplace resource, but also a source of annoyance. From the technical standpoint a true glissando can be executed *only on the same natural tone,* while the slide is being gradually moved through its *continuous* points (that is, not only the positional but also interpositional). All other forms of glissando are made by variation of embouchure and are not standardized.

A glissando can be performed either up or down. It is sufficient to indicate a glissando by showing the starting and the ending pitch of it, and to connect the two by a straight or a wavy line:

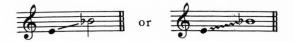

Figure 49. Glissando.

The term *gliss.* may also be added above the part, if desirable.

The passage just illustrated is executed on the eighth natural tone, while pulling-in the slide from the VII to the I position gradually. If a passage falls on the different natural tones, it is impossible to execute it in continuous, i.e., glissando, form. For example:

Figure 50. No glissando on different natural tones.

The execution of this passage is impossible because $e\flat$ can be only III_3, while if g is the third natural tone, its fundamental would be c and there is no such position on the trombone.

Mutes were very seldom used on the trombones in the symphonic music of the past. However, the development of jazz has led to a very extensive and diversified use of mutes (including "hats") in the same manner as they are being used on the trumpets.

Besides raising the standards of performance on this instrument, jazz has also created some outstanding virtuosi, among whom the greatest artist is Tommy Dorsey, particularly because of his unsurpassed tone-quality.

Some trombonists are capable of producing (as a special effect in the higher positions) simultaneously the fundamental and the third harmonic (actually sounding as a harmonic). In addition to this, some jokers sing the fifth harmonic, thus obtaining a whole triad.

Trombone parts are usually written in the bass and the alto clefs; 19th century composers preferred the tenor clef. Today it is practical to use treble clef for the higher register, as all trombonists can read these four clefs.

The trombone with a valve is usually employed as the third trombone in symphonic scoring, but is seldom used by dance-bands. All other types of trombones, such as alto trombone (in E♭, sounding a perfect fourth higher than written) or bass trombone (in F, sounding a perfect fourth lower than written) have become completely obsolete. The old three-valve trombones of various types were found unsatisfactory in their tone-quality, which was decidedly inferior to that of the natural (slide) trombone.

D. Tuba (Tuba)

This instrument is also known as bass-tuba and belongs to the sax-horn family, which is fully represented in the large brass bands. The tuba, which is used as a standard instrument in symphonic and operatic scoring, seldom appears in the dance bands. Dance bands mostly use the E♭ sousaphone bass (a three-valved instrument commonly used in the infantry).

The tuba, acoustically, is an instrument in F, but does not require transposition. Its parts sound exactly as written. Due to traditional use of a quartet consisting of three trombones and a tuba (usually the tuba part is written on the same staff as the third trombone), composers developed a habit of associating the tuba with trombones. However, the tuba comes closer to the French horn than to the trombone. Its pipe is conical, like that of a French horn, while the trombone's pipe is cylindrical until it reaches its bell. The mouth-piece of the tuba is closer in shape to that of the trombone than of the French horn.

The scale of the natural tones of the tuba is as follows:

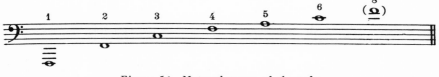

Figure 51. Natural tones of the tuba.

It is advisable to use the first six natural tones, and to resort to the eighth tone only in exceptional cases. The tone-quality of the French horn is preferable to that of the high register of the tuba and it bears a close resemblance to the latter.

Tones below the fundamental are difficult to execute as there is a constant danger of overblowing the fundamental. It is best not to write below *d* which lies three semitones below the fundamental.

There is an interval of a whole octave between the fundamental and the second tone and the design of the tuba requires four valves. These four valves are evolved according to the standard three-valve principle, the fourth valve being capable of lowering a natural tone by 5 semitones. In addition to this, tubas used in symphonic and operatic orchestras have a fifth valve. The purpose of his valve is to give an acoustically more satisfactory semitone-valve for the lower egister, as the second valve is not sufficiently large. Tubas of the type being described here have a valve operation on cylinders. Pistons are to be found in an instrument serving similar purposes in infantry bands, the ophicleide, which is carried over the shoulder while being played.

Thus the valve arrangement on the five-valve tuba is as follows:

   I lowers the natural tone by 2 semitones
  II lowers the natural tone by 1 semitone
 III lowers the natural tone by 3 semitones
 IV lowers the natural tone by 5 semitones
  V lowers the natural tone by 1 large semitone

Combined application of these valves produces any desirable interval between the first and the second tones.

The tuba is a slow-speaking instrument. Good intonation is one of the main difficulties of this instrument. The main asset of the tuba is its rich tone quality. All forms of attack are available, but the tuba is particularly suited for long sustained tones and slow passages in general. No mutes and no special effects are used on the tuba.

The Russian composer Shostakovich used, in his First Symphony, two tubas, instead of the customary one. As intonation on the tuba is usually less precise than on the other brass instruments, this score, at least when being performed in Russia, created considerable difficulties during rehearsal: one tuba is bad enough but two become unbearable.

CHAPTER 4

SPECIAL INSTRUMENTS

A. Arpa (Harp)

THE origin of the harp leads back to antiquity. In the bas-reliefs of ancient Egypt, dated as far back as 2700 B.C., court orchestras are represented which consist mostly of pipes and harps. In the last two or three centuries the harp has undergone many modifications. Some manufacturers have built chromatic harps and some, diatonic. Contemporary harps are diatonic instruments with a triple tuning.

The contemporary harp is originally tuned in a natural major scale in c♭. There are seven strings to each octave. All octaves are identical. The main feature of the contemporary harp is a set of seven pedals which control the tension of strings. The mechanism of the pedals is devised in such a manner as to produce modification of the same-named strings throughout all octaves. Thus, through the first step pressure-position of the c♭ pedal, the pitch of all the c♭–strings becomes c♮. Through the second pressure-position of the c♭ – pedal, the pitch of all c♭–strings becomes c♯. A similar mechanism affects the remaining six name-strings. The step-pressures are independent for each pedal. While one pedal is put into its first pressure-position, another pedal may be put into its second pressure-position. This is possible because all pedals have an independent operation. Pressure-positions are retained by the instrument until they are changed by the performer. This is possible because each pedal has a locking arrangement in the form of two inverted steps:

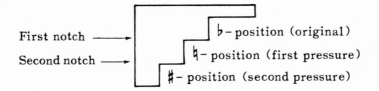

Figure 52. Pedal notches.

Looking at the harp from above, the pedals appear in the following arrangement:

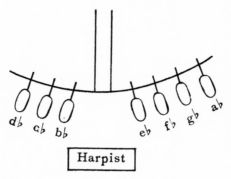

Figure 53. Pedals of the harp.

Accomplished harpists manipulate the pedals with great dexterity and can rearrange up to four pedals per second.

Harpists, as in the case of pianists, find the different strings by tactile distance-discrimination. However, in some cases, strings of red color are used for all the cb's, and of blue color, for all the fb's. This helps one to find the remaining strings.

The harp is played by either plucking a string, or a group of strings, with the individual fingers:

(1) in sequence (arpeggiato), which is the normal form of execution of chords on a harp;

(2) simultaneously (non-arpeggiato).

In addition to this, the harp is often played glissando, which is always a chord-glissando and is executed by sliding one of the fingers over the strings. As glissando affects *all* strings within its range, the problem of tuning glissando-chords becomes of major importance. Glissando can also be executed in octaves and other simultaneous intervals.

As a special effect, octave-harmonics can be used on a harp. This is executed by touching the string at its nodal point (geometrical center) with the palm and plucking with a finger of the same hand. If the interval is relatively small, each hand can produce harmonics in simultaneous intervals.

Dynamically the harp is a delicate instrument. It gains in volume considerably through the use of glissando. This effect can be executed in various degrees of the dynamic range (from pp to ff), depending on the pressure exerted on the strings and the speed of sliding over the strings: increase in speed and pressure results in the increase of volume.

It is important for the composer to understand that when pressure-positions are alike for all the strings, only natural major scales in the following three keys result therefrom: C♭, C♮, C♯.

Original position: c♭ — d♭ — e♭ — f♭ — g♭ — a♭ — b♭
First pressure-position: c♮ — d♮ — e♮ — f♮ — g♮ — a♮ — b♮
Second pressure-position: c♯ — d♯ — e♯ — f♯ — g♯ — a♯ — b♯

All other scale-arrangements require rearrangement of the pressure positions.

It would be of great advantage to the composer to know that all the 36 forms of Σ (13), tabulated in the *Special Theory of Harmony*,* are at his disposal. And any tonal expansions which derive from the above master-structures do not require any rearrangement of the pressure positions. This is possible because none of the above Σ (13) contains intervals greater than 4 semitones, which satisfies the pedal mechanism of the harp when tuned in E_0.

As the harp is a strictly diatonic instrument, it is desirable to use it as such. Quick modulations, containing several alterations, are quite impossible on this instrument. Many large scores contain two harp parts (used alternately for this purpose) in order to accomplish groups of modulating chords.

The part for the harp, like that of the piano, is written on two staves joined by a figured bracket. The clefs in use are the common bass (F) and treble (G):

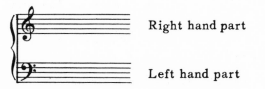

Right hand part

Left hand part

Figure 54. Harp clefs.

Instrumental forms suitable for the harp are quite similar to piano forms. Octaves in each hand can be executed only at moderate speed. Chords with wide intervals for both hands are more difficult than on the piano. Close positions are preferable to open ones, though the bass can be detached from the upper structures. Many effective passages can be accomplished by alternation of hands. Here the composer's inventiveness may bring many fruitful developments.

From the viewpoint of thematic texture, the harp can be looked upon as an instrument similar to piano, i.e., it can perform melody (in its various instrumental forms), harmony, accompanied melody, correlated melodies, and accompanied counterpoint.

In the orchestra it is frequently used as a coloristic instrument, which is due particularly to its capacity to execute effective and diversified forms of glissandi (upward, downward, combined, rotary, etc.)

*See Vol. I, p. 654.

There is a wide selection of structures which can be executed glissando (such structures often contain repeated pitches produced by the adjacent strings enharmonically tuned; but the speed of the slowest practical glissando is sufficiently great not to make these repeated pitches apparent to the ear). There is an easy way to determine whether a certain structure permits the performance of a glissando: *if the structure does not contain major thirds, built on the degrees of a natural major scale in Bb, then glissando is possible.* In other words, the structure in question cannot contain the following simultaneous intervals:

Thus the following chords are *possible* in glissando:

Figure 55. Glissando chords on the harp.

because they do not contain the major thirds referred to in Figure 55.

On the other hand the following chords are *impossible* since they contain such major thirds as are classified in Figure 55.

Figure 56. Impossible glissando chords on the harp.

The principle of major thirds of the Bb – scale saves the composer the trouble of empirical verification. For example, let us see why d — f# — a — c is impossible in glissando:

db — d♮
eb — impossible to stretch to f#.

In other words, the eb – string would be in the way, even if other strings could be tuned to the given chord.

On the other hand a chord like c — d — f — ab is possible:

cb — c♮
db — d♮
eb — e# (f♮)
fb — f♮
gb — g# (ab)
bb — b# (c♮)

There are several different forms in use, by which a glissando can be indicated. Here are the most common:

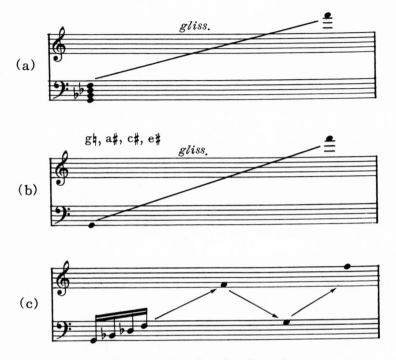

Figure 57. Notations for glissando.

The tuning of pedals in general, particularly when parts are harmonically simple, does not require any indication. Cautious composers, however, often indicate the pedal changes. For example:

Figure 58. Notation of pedal changes.

In the fourth measure b♮ and e♮ do not require any changes in tuning as b♮ = = c♭ and e♮ = f♭.

Octave harmonics, which are the only ones used on this instrument, are indicated by zeros above the notes, which notes should sound as harmonics in the same octave as written.

Figure 59. Notation of octave harmonics.

The forms of attacks on the harp correspond to that of a piano, i.e., legato, portamento, staccato, but the difference is less distinct than on the piano.

The basic timbre of the harp resembles the clarinet, owing to the method of playing (i.e., finger-plucking, instead of a hammer-attack, as on the piano; piano strings when played by fingers, without the medium of keys and hammers, also sound like the harp). The harp blends well with flutes and clarinets. The composer must not forget that the harp is a self-sufficient solo instrument of a diatonic type.

In the orchestra, of course, it is mostly used as an accompanying and coloristic instrument. It is also extremely effective as a semi-percussive rhythmic instrument.

Sometimes the harp, doubling wood-wind instruments, produces a more transparent equivalent of the pizzicato of stringed instruments.

Carlos Salzedo, who is probably the most accomplished and the most versatile harpist of all times, has invented a number of new effects for this instrument. He and some of his accomplished students (at the Curtis Institute in Philadelphia) are capable of executing these effects.

B. ORGAN (PIPE-ORGAN OR ITS ELECTRONIC SUBSTITUTES*)

The pipe-organ is a more self-sufficient instrument than any other instrument known. This is due to the number of tones which can be produced simultaneously and to their timbral variety.

The number of different tone-qualities depends upon the number of *stops*, which can be used individually or in combinations. More expensive organs usually have more stops, price also determines the quality. Organs range from two-manual to five-manual models, in addition to which every organ has a pedal keyboard, generally used for production of the lower pitches. The dynamic range of a pipe-organ is fully comparable with that of a full symphony orchestra.

This instrument underwent many evolutionary changes. The latest and most spectacular type of pipe-organ is the large theatrical organ. This type of instrument is furnished with a very diversified selection of stops (including many

*See p. 1544.

percussive effects like xylophone, chimes, etc.) not excluding all the essential stops of an ecclesiastic organ. There are a number of pipe-organs in the world which can be justly considered masterpieces of acoustical engineering.

As organs vary widely in design, number of manuals, selection of stops, etc., it is impractical to give a detailed description of a *pipe-organ*. Basically, however, all pipe-organs possess certain general characteristics in common. It is essential for the composer to know some of these common characteristics:

(1) The amount of pressure exerted by the performer on the keys has no effect on the intensity or character of the sound.

(2) Forms of attack are effective: legato, non-legato, staccato are quite pronounced.

(3) Physically, the tone is generated by a pipe or a group of pipes, which are often built-in at a considerable distance from the console; this produces an effect of *delayed action:* a very important detail to bear in mind in using the organ in combination with other instruments.

(4) Tone-qualities are classified into groups, representing timbral families: the strings, the flutes, the reeds, the chalumeaux, etc. Each family has a number of distinctly different stops (i.e., tone-qualities).

(5) Each stop has a set of pipes covering a definite range; organists look on ranges and registers as represented by the length of respective pipes. Thus they say: a 4′ string stop, or an 8′ reed stop, or a 32′ pedal stop. The longer the pipe, the lower the pitch. Certain timbres are available only in certain registers, while others cover the entire (or nearly the entire) range.

(6) The massive tone-qualities characteristic of the pipe-organ are due to single, double, triple, etc. octave-couplings. These couplings are executed by pushing coupler-keys. Under these conditions, an organist can produce a powerful and massive tone by using only one finger.

(7) Volume (the intensity of sound) is controlled in part by special pedals. Thus gradual dynamic changes are possible. A sforzando-piano (sfp) effect is also available on most organs.

(8) Composition of stops for the performance of a given piece of music is known as *registration*. Notation for the latter is seldom provided by the composer (unless he is an organist). Even when the composer or the editor of organ parts indicates the registration, it is quite traditional for the performer to change the indicated registration to one of his own choice.

(9) It is customary to mix the stops belonging to different timbral families as well as to couple them through several octaves.

(10) In addition to this, there are so-called organ-"mixtures", which are built-in combinations of *various couplings*. When such mixtures are used, one key pressed by a finger produces a whole chord structure of one or another type. Thus, melodies may be played directly in parallel chords. In some of the organs built in Germany in the second decade of this century, mixtures producing some less conventional chords were introduced (in one instance, the mixture added to *c* produced c — d♯ — f♯ — — b).

It is important for the composer to realize that as a consequence of couplings and mixtures accompanying each individual note, what reaches the ear of the listener (including the organist himself) is quite different from what is written on paper. Not only the respective octaves and registers (in the general sense of this word) can be different than in writing, but they also can be accompanied by whole sets of new pitches which do not even appear in parts. Often symphonic, operatic, oratorio and cantata scores contain an organ part.

The above-described characteristics of this instrument make it very difficult for the composer to use the organ in an orchestra or in a mixed vocal-instrumental combination properly, since the principle of clarity as a necessary quality of instrumental and vocal scoring often conflicts with the natural tendencies of the instrument. For this reason the organ is either misused in most scores, or it plays a purely decorative part. In the old scoring, the organ was used, according to ecclesiastic tradition, as a duplication of the choir, and its part was often written merely as a figured bass, which the organist had to fill in. This can be found in the scores of leading composers of the 19th century.

Another important characteristic of the organ is its tone-quality with respect to vibrato. The organ can produce non-vibrato or a *vibrato by intensity* (some instruments, particularly in the string-stops, have also a mechanical vibrato of beats, produced by simultaneous pitches which are set at slightly different frequencies). For this reason, organ vibrati are mostly of a different type from orchestra vibrati. Simultaneous use of both often creates conflicts and discrepancies.

Organ parts are generally written on three staves: the two upper staves refer to one or more manuals, and the lower to the pedal. Other manuals are *choir*, *solo*, *echo*, *etc.*

Figure 60. The three staves of the organ.

CHAPTER 5

ELECTRONIC INSTRUMENTS

THIS group of instruments is more diversified than all other groups combined. The term "electronic musical instrument" can be used to describe any instrument where electric current generates sound directly or indirectly. There are two basic subgroups of electronic instruments.

A. FIRST SUBGROUP. VARYING ELECTROMAGNETIC FIELD

The first subgroup consists of instruments whose sound (i.e., sonic frequencies) is generated by varying the capacity of an electromagnetic field created by two currents. The instruments invented and constructed by Leon Theremin are based on this principle. They include three basic models:

(1) Space-controlled Theremin (also known as Victor-Theremin; later: R.C.A. Theremin).
(2) Fingerboard-Theremin.
(3) Keyboard-Theremin.

Of these types, the first acquired far greater popularity than the other two models. Recitals are being given by various performers on this instrument. I was the first composer to use this instrument in a solo (concertizing) part with a symphony orchestra. The composition was called *The First Airphonic Suite* and was performed by Leon Theremin as soloist with the Cleveland Orchestra in Cleveland and New York in 1929. In 1930 a realization of an early dream came through. I scored, rehearsed and produced together with Leon Theremin and 13 other performers, two programs presented at Carnegie Hall in New York, in which an ensemble of 14 space-controlled theremins was presented for the first time.

1. SPACE-CONTROLLED THEREMIN

Each musical instrument displays some characteristics of its own. The chief characteristic of the space-controlled theremin is its extreme adaptability not only to pitch and volume variation, but also to the different *forms of vibrato*. In this respect it is so sensitive that the pleasantness or beauty of tone depends largely on the performer. In order to obtain a "beautiful tone" on this instrument, the performer must know what physical characteristics make a tone "beautiful". These can be briefly described as a combination of vibrato frequency and the depth of vibrato, i.e., pitch variation between vibrato points. As this text is meant for the composer or orchestrator, there is no need to elaborate on this matter further. In 1929 I wrote *A Manual for Playing Space-Controlled Theremin*, where these matters are discussed in detail.

Pitch on the theremin is controlled by the right hand, which is moved toward and away from a vertical rod (antenna). The spatial dimensions of pitch intervals vary with respect to total space range, which is adjustable either individually or for each performance. In other words, pitch is varied within the spatial boundaries of the electro-magnetic field. Depending on the stature of the performer and the length of his arms, spatial range may be practically adjusted (tuned by a knob control) somewhere between one and three feet.

The electro-magnetic field can be imagined as a three-dimensional invisible fingerboard. It is so sensitive that even the slightest move on the part of the performer affects the pitch. Spatially, intervals contract with the increase in frequencies, i.e., by moving the hand toward the right antenna (which is a physical generality; it works the same way on the regular fingerboards, air columns, etc.). Not having a fixed-length fingerboard, the thereminist faces, as it proved itself to be the case in many individual instances, much greater difficulty in pitch control than any string-bow performer. Yet some performers, who were not even professionals on any instrument, could master the pitch-control problem in about two weeks. Their reaction was that you control pitch mostly by "feeling distances", that you play as if you were singing.

I am not offering any description of the basic timbre of this instrument, as each model has a timbre of its own. Vaguely they all resemble a combination of a string-bow instrument (when bowed) at its best, if not better, and of an excellent human voice singing every tone on the consonant "m", which, of course, has its own basic acoustical characteristics.

The left antenna of this instrument serves the purpose of controlling the volume. The left hand moves vertically toward (decrease of volume) or away from (increase of volume) the loop-shaped left antenna. The intensity range can be also spatially adjusted by turning a knob, just as in the case of pitch-control. This permits any degree of subtlety in varying the volume, as in the case of the right antenna with respect to pitch.

Playing this instrument is a task in the coordination of both hands and arms moving through two space-coordinates. It would be just to say that this instrument is much more delicate and sensitive than any human being who has played it up to now. People with good coordination and sufficient sense of relative pitch turned out to be better performers than eminent musicians. Leon Theremin and his assistant, George Goldberg (also an engineer), proved this to be so.

The composer can have at his disposal the entire audible range, if necessary, and any volume, as sound is amplified electrically. All forms of attacks are available. The space-controlled theremin is a monodic (i.e., producing a single tone at one time) instrument par excellence and, therefore, particularly suitable for broad sustained cantilenas, pedal points, etc. Rapid passages of any kind can be executed by an accomplished performer at speeds comparable to that of an oboe. One of the first models of this instrument had a knob contact for producing attacks. By pushing the knob with a finger of the left hand abruptly, one could produce the most abrupt forms of staccato at any desirable speed.

The Philadelphia Orchestra, through the initiative of Leopold Stokowski, its music director, used a specially built model of the theremin. This instrument served the purpose of coupling and reinforcing orchestral basses of various groups. It had a pure (that is, sinusoidal) tone and immense volume amplification.

It is best not to compare the theremin with any other standard orchestra instruments, but to look upon it as the first instrument of the coming electronic era of music, having its own characteristics and being conceived and designed along entirely new principles of sound-production and sound-control. It is the first child of the electronic musical dynasty. Its first model dates back to 1921, when Leon Theremin demonstrated it in Moscow before a conference of electrical engineers and inventors. At that time it was in its early experimental stage. In the U. S. A. it was manufactured by R. C. A. Manufacturing Co., Camden, New Jersey.

2. FINGERBOARD THEREMIN

This instrument was designed and constructed for the purpose of supplying violinists and 'cellists with an electronic instrument, which they could learn to play in a very short time. Some violinists and 'cellists have played it with great success.

This instrument's main part is a cylindrical rod, about as long as the 'cello's fingerboard. While being played, it is held in position similar to the 'cello. The part which is touched by the fingers of the left hand (to which procedure all string-bow performers are accustomed) is covered by celluloid. Production of tone results from the contact of a finger with the celluloid plate. Thus pitch-control is very similar to that of a 'cello. Volume is controlled by a special lever, resilient and operated by the right hand. The greater the pressure on the lever, the louder the tone. This form of dynamic control allows not only gradual variations of intensity but also accents and sforzando-piano. All forms of attacks are available through direct contact with the fingerboard. Though the manner of playing this instrument more resembles the 'cello than the violin, violinists have found it easy to play.

The range of this instrument is adjustable, i.e., the same model can be tuned in high, low, or both registers. The tone quality of the fingerboard theremin resembles an *idealized* 'cello tone (i.e., one which is deprived of inharmonic sounds, usually resulting from the friction of horse hair over sheep's guts while bowing) and is more of a constant than on the space-controlled model. The usual type of 'cello vibrato gives a perfectly satisfactory result. The basic timbre is quite close to the double-reeds (nasal).

Of course timbre and other characteristics of this instrumeut could be easily modified. Some engineers in Europe, after Theremin, constructed instruments whose outer design resembled the violin, 'cello, or bass. Leon Theremin thought this pointless, because the dimensions and the shape of an electronic fingerboard instrument have nothing to do with its range or registers.

The fingerboard theremin is a *monodic* instrument. One of the advantages of having such instruments in the orchestra is tone-quality, which can be literally "made to order" by the engineer or manufacturer; another, is its range which offers a great economy: a passage, which generally starts on the 'celli and is completed by the violins, can be executed on one instrument and by the same performer.

3. KEYBOARD THEREMIN

Keyboard theremin is a *monodic* instrument, with a standard piano keyboard. It is a direct predecessor of the *solovox*, manufactured by the Hammond Organ Company today. Physically, though, the solovox does not belong to the *first subgroup* as piano strings, electromagnetically inducted, are the original sound-source. Nevertheless, the keyboard theremin operates physically on the same principle as other theremin instruments, i.e., by variation of the capacity of an electromagnetic field.

This instrument was designed with the purpose of supplying keyboard performers with an instrument which they could play without much additional training, yet which would possess such features as economy of space, any pre-conceived tone-quality, well expressed forms of attack, regulated forms of tremulant, fading effects with vibrato automatically performed (as on the Hawaiian guitar), and automatically pre-set varied degrees of staccato etc.

The business end of the Theremin enterprise was not properly handled. As a result there are not many space-controlled models to be found today, more than a decade since they were first built, not to mention the fingerboard and the keyboard theremins, of which there are very few, if any, left.

Leon Theremin built a number of other electronic instruments, among them various types of organs with micro-tuning and variable timbre-control (in the design of which I participated), but these instruments mostly served the purpose of research and have never reached the attention of the public at large.

The purpose of my directing the attention of the composer to these short-lived models is to show the direction in which lie the future stages of the field of orchestration, as there has never been any doubt in my mind that the present standard (non-electronic) instruments will soon be outmoded and superseded by perfected electronic models.

In this regard the composer will be confronted with new approaches and techniques of orchestration. He will have to think acoustically and not in terms of violins, clarinets, trumpets etc. This is just a note of warning.

B. SECOND SUBGROUP; CONVENTIONAL SOURCES OF SOUND.

The *second subgroup* of electronic instruments uses conventional sources of sound (strings, bars, oscillating membranes, etc.), but they are excited by means of *electro-magnetic induction* and amplified through a loud-speaker system.

While Theremin's models were entirely revolutionary and constituted a decidedly radical departure from all existing ideas of designing musical instruments, the instruments which I refer to as the second subgroup are decidedly a result of compromise, lack of vision and immediate commercial considerations. It is just to say that the theremin instruments are more refined as an idea though not sufficiently perfect in actual operation, while the existing models of the second subgroup are well designed, well-built, and are reliable in operation but are based on old-fashioned and often erroneous notions as to what a musical instrument should be. For this reason the instruments of the first subgroup eventually will be resurrected and will last longer in improved forms, while the instruments of the second subgroup will be considered too crude in comparison, and will die out the way the player-piano did when the perfected radio left no room for its existence. The instruments of the second subgroup are manufactured and sold on a mass production-consumption basis. They are widely used today, particularly in the field of radio and dance music.

The instruments of the second subgroup are generally called by their old original names, with the addition of the definitive "electrified". Thus we speak of such models as the electrified piano, electrified organ, electrified guitar, etc. The history of these instruments leads far back to Thaddeus Cahill, who in 1897 constructed the "Sound Staves", a clumsy instrument with oscillating membranes, effected by electric current.*

As electronic instruments of all types are in an early stage of development, and as the present models may soon become outmoded and obsolete, I shall offer only a brief description of the models which are most in use today, and only such a description as will provide the composer with information and ideas valuable *per se.*

1. ELECTRIFIED PIANO

This instrument consists of an ordinary piano and a system of electro-magnetic inductors connected with an amplified sound system. There are different designs of this instrument, but the resulting sounds have most characteristics in common. This instrument is usually known as electronic piano. In the U. S. A. the Miessner piano is better known; in Germany, the Bechstein (after the famous firm manufacturing the best pianos ever built). Some of the electronic Bechsteins are also in use in the U. S. A.

The main feature of all such instruments is the conversion of a regular piano into several different instruments. This is accomplished by a system of various pre-set forms of induction. The two characteristic extreme forms are: one, in which the duration of a tone is prolonged indefinitely and the volume of it can be increased even after the respective key has been released, and another, in which a pre-set form of quick fading, the sound of which resembles harpsichord, is produced. There are usually various intermediate effects between these two extremes. At the same time this instrument can be used without electrification, which is of great practical advantage. Any accomplished pianist or organist can master this instrument in a very short time.

*For more historical detail see my article "Electricity, the Liberator of Music" in the April issue of *Modern Music Quarterly*, published by the League of Composers in 1931 (Vol. 8). (U. S.)

2. SOLOVOX (manufactured by the Hammond Organ Co.)

Solovox is a monodic instrument, devised in the form of a piano-attachment. In fact, it is a monodic version of an electrified piano. The purpose of this instrument is to execute melody of a durable and, if desirable, tremulant tone directly from the piano (with the right hand playing the solovox) and the accompaniment being played by the same performer on the same piano (with the left hand). Whether such a combination is desirable, is a debatable matter. But this will be discussed in "Acoustical Basis of Orchestration".*

3. THE HAMMOND ORGAN

This instrument (manufactured by the same company and designed by Lawrence Hammond) is the most universally accepted of all the larger types of electronic musical instruments. The Hammond organ is a fairly complex piece of electrical engineering without being bulky.

The name "organ" is applicable to this instrument only insofar as the production of sustained simultaneous sounds is concerned. Otherwise, every organist or any experienced musician can tell, without seeing the instrument, whether he is hearing a pipe-organ or a Hammond organ. There is undoubtedly a general difference in the tone-qualities of the two instruments throughout their ranges, particularly in the pedal. The Hammond Co. expected to sell most of its instruments to cathedrals, churches and chapels. The instrument, however, approaches the theatre organ more closely than it does the church organ (particularly when used with a special tremulant speaker which, by the way, is not manufactured by the Hammond Co.). Today this instrument is widely used for dance music and "swing".

There are certain basic principles on which the instrument is designed and built, and they are important for the composer to know. The following information is not available elsewhere.

The first fact of importance is that this instrument does not sound like a pipe-organ in its tone-qualities. There are two reasons for this. The first is that the type of speaker and the whole sound system do not permit the high frequencies (the real partials of a tone) to come through. I verified this fact by connecting the Hammond speaker with a turntable. Good high fidelity recordings sounded completely "muffled". The second reason is that the Hammond instrument is not designed to include certain inharmonic sounds, which are the constants of many organ pipes. Whether such inharmonic sounds are desirable per se, is another matter.

The second fact, which is inseparable from the first, is that this instrument does not sound like a pipe-organ in its emission of sound. In a pipe-organ, the emission of sound is not instantaneous (particularly in old church organs) owing

*Vibratone, manufactured by Brittain Sound Equipment Co., Los Angeles.

to the necessary time interval required in transmission of an impulse from the keyboard of the console to the pipes and then to the ear of the listener. In the Hammond organ the transmission of sound is instantaneous, owing to the speed of electric contact. This particular characteristic adds one advantage to the Hammond organ, namely, the hard staccato of extreme abruptness. Organists complain that on the Hammond instrument "the sound appears before you touch the key".

The two factors are closely interrelated. The lack of real high partials on this instrument is due to the mechanical design of the Hammond organ which does not permit the use of better speakers and of a better sound system; high-frequency response would make the *key-contacts audible* (they would click loudly). Hence, the "muffled" tone, as the lesser of the two evils.

The speed of sound transmission could be easily modified by a special mechanism for delayed action. The inharmonic tones could be introduced electronically (such devices were used with success in the electronic instruments of the first subgroup type built by Dr. Trautwein in Berlin in 1928).

A valuable factor in applying electro-magnetic induction to oscillating membranes or revolving discs (as in the case of the instrument under discussion) is the stability of frequencies. So long as the electric current is relatively stable, i.e., of a constant voltage, the instrument, no matter how long it is in continuous use, remains in tune. This is not true of the instruments of the first subgroup, where warming up of the tubes eventually affects the pitch.

The Hammond organ, evaluated *per se* and not in comparison with other musical instruments, must be considered a valuable self-sufficient or auxiliary instrument. The chief asset of this instrument is its acoustical system of timbre variation.

The Hammond organ produces pitches of a twelve-unit equal temperament in simple (sinusoidal) waves. These simple components can be mixed at random at different intensities, which results in different tone qualities. The simple components are called by the names of the nearest tones of the natural scale. Each component is controlled individually and has *eight* graduated degrees of intensity. Actual control is exercised by pulling out the respective levers. There are *nine* levers corresponding to the nine components of each tone quality.

Figure 61. The nine levers of the Hammond organ.

The numbers in the circles indicate the levers as they appear from left to right.

① corresponds to the subfundamental, i.e., one octave below the fundamental;
② the subthird harmonic, i.e., one octave below the third harmonic;
③ the fundamental;
④ the second harmonic;
⑤ the third harmonic;
⑥ the fourth harmonic;
⑦ the fifth harmonic;
⑧ the sixth harmonic;
⑨ the eighth harmonic.

We shall consider such a set to be an acoustical system of components for production of one tone-quality at a time. All present models have two such systems for each of the two manuals. A special two-lever (two-component) system (the fundamental and the subthird) controls the pedal.

Once the levers of one system are pulled out into a certain pre-arranged position, such a position mechanically corresponds to a certain push-button. That is, the pre-arranged combination, producing a certain tone-quality, can be obtained instantaneously, by pushing the corresponding button. On the model E of the Hammond organ, the two systems correspond to push-buttons 11 and 12. The push-buttons are the same for both manuals.

All other push-buttons, numbered from 1 to 10, control pre-set combinations. The pre-set combinations are the most common stops of a church pipe-organ. However, these too can be re-arranged by changing some of the wire connections within the console.

The total number of tone-qualities for each manual individually (which would also absorb any of the pre-set combinations) equals the sum of all combinations by 2, by 3, ... by 9 out of nine elements (since there are nine levers). Each combination can be modified according to the different positions of intensity for each lever (of which there are eight). Thus, if it is originally one-lever setting, each of such settings has to be multiplied by 8. There are thus $9 \cdot 8 = 72$ one-lever settings. For a combination of two levers, the value 8 must be squared; for a combination of three levers, the value 8 must be cubed, etc.

There is no need to make a complete computation of all tone-qualities thus obtainable, as it would take several centuries to play them through. However, from a musical standpoint (i.e., from the standpoint of imperfect auditory tone-quality discrimination), there are not so many really distinctly different combinations since many modifications of the same combination sound quite similar to the ear.

Though components of tone-qualities on the Hammond organ are the tones which approximate harmonics in the twelve-unit equal temperament—but not real harmonics—the very principle of composing tone-qualities from elements and not from complexes (like the timbres of standard instruments) has a great educational value for any student of music in general and for the orchestrator in particular.

The Hammond organ is supplied with some controls adopted from the pipe-organ. Among these are the various couplers, the dynamic control swell-pedal, the tremulant-control, the "chorus", etc. The range of model E is from *c* of contra-octave to f♯ of the fourth octave (it has the frequency of approximately 6000 cycles and corresponds to lever ⑨ for f♯ of the first octave on the keyboard, which pitch is half an octave higher than the highest piano *c*).

Besides being a very diversified self-sufficient instrument, the Hammond organ is frequently used in small instrumental combination to supply the missing timbres.

The composer will make the best use of this instrument by realizing that the Hammond organ is an instrument whose specialty is production of controllable and highly diversified tone-qualities, combined with sufficiently versatile forms of attacks and an enormous dynamic range, without sacrifice of dynamic versatility. The Hammond organ keyboard has a very light action, which permits the production of rapidly repeating tones.

In order to assist the orchestrator with a method by which he can find the *basic timbral families* out of the enormous number of possible combinations, I have devised a simple system by which such families can be instantaneously arranged and easily memorized. This system is based on the *patterns of intensity* of the different components in relation to their lever-scale position (which *approximately* corresponds to the frequency position).

Scale of Basic Timbral Families on the Hammond Organ

Families: Patterns:

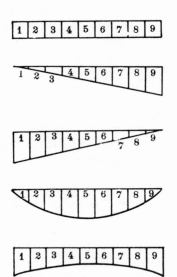

1. Uniform intensity of all participating components

2. Scalewise increase of intensity of all participating components.

3. Scalewise decrease of intensity of all participating components

4. Convex arrangement of intensities of all participating components

5. Concave arrangement of intensities of all participating components

Figure 62. Basic timbral families on the Hammond organ (continued).

6. Selective pattern of partials of uniform intensity based on odd-numbered levers.

7. Selective pattern of partials of uniform intensity based on even-numbered levers.

Figure 62. Basic timbral families on the Hammond organ (concluded).

This system helps the orchestrator to associate timbral families with the corresponding scale of visual patterns:

Figure 63. Visual patterns of the timbral families.

Verbal description of these basic qualities is highly inaccurate. For this reason I shall eliminate it altogether. The best way to get acquainted with these timbral families is by practical study of this system of timbral selection at the instrument. This practical study should be accompanied by further investigation of the dynamic variations within each timbral pattern. For instance, in the second family we may vary the angle representing intensities:

In the fourth family, we may modify the form of its convexity:

This study will be of great practical benefit to any composer or orchestrator, and particularly with regard to his study of my Theory of Orchestration.

4. THE NOVACHORD

The Novachord, another Hammond development, is a keyboard electronic instrument on which simultaneous sounds can be produced. The name is somewhat misleading, as "chorda" means "string", and, of course, there are no strings on this instrument.

The Novachord has the range of a combined string-bow group. It has one keyboard of the piano type. It is supplied with numerous timbre-controls and attack-controls. This instrument can be justly considered an improved and developed version of the keyboard theremin. One of the specialties of the Novachord is attack-forms whose fading periods can be automatically pre-set. The forms of vibrato can also be automatically controlled. Dynamic variation is controlled by pedal.

The timbres of the Novachord resemble closely (owing to the selective system of attack-forms) many of the standard orchestra instruments. Some Novachord timbres are of such high quality that only the very best performers on the original instruments can rival them.

The Novachord is a very valuable instrument as a substitute for missing standard instruments in an ensemble or orchestra. As a self-sufficient instrument, which it is meant to be, it is not quite satisfactory. The reason for this is that it is a simultaneously monotimbral instrument: only one tone-quality can be produced at a time. As the result of this characteristic, melody and accompaniment sound in the same tone-quality and, in addition to this, at the same volume. Thus, when melody is played with an accompaniment, it can be singled out by one means only: playing the accompaniment staccato.

CHAPTER 6

PERCUSSIVE INSTRUMENTS

W E shall adhere to the following definition of percussive instruments: *all instruments* whose sound is produced on a string, a membrane or a bar (often built of different materials) by direct attack and not by electro-magnetic induction. As a consequence of this characteristic, all percussive instruments naturally (and automatically, unless extended by some special devices) have a fading sound. Therefore the period of fading is in direct proportion to the intensity of sound, i.e., to the amplitude of its attack.

Since all the inharmonic (i.e., noise producing) instruments will be described as percussive instruments, though some of these really are not percussive, one distinction must be made clear: while on the percussive and inharmonic instruments sound is basically produced by *attack*, it is also produced by *friction*. For example, a drum can be played not only by a stick or a hand attack, but also by rotary motion of the palm of the hand over the skin of the drum. The same is true of the rubbing of surfaces of two emery boards, etc.

Some of the instruments known as self-sufficient, will be described here *specifically as orchestral and, therefore, as coloristic instruments*. Particular attention will be paid to their percussive possibilities, which are so often neglected.

Percussive sounds of the instruments, which originally are not meant to be percussive (such as string-bow instruments, when played pizzicato, col legno, etc.), will be discussed in the Technique of Orchestration*, in the chapter devoted to the Forms of Attacks.

We shall classify all percussive instruments in four groups:

Group one, where the source of sound is a string or a bar (metal or wood);
Group two,　where the source of sound is a metal disc;
Group three,　" 　" 　" 　" 　" 　is a skin membrane;
Group four, 　" 　" 　" 　" 　" 　is various other materials.

A. GROUP ONE. SOUND VIA STRING OR BAR.

1. PIANO

Piano (grand and upright) is a self-sufficient instrument, most universally used in our musical civilization. The range of a piano varies from concert grand manufactured by Bluethner in Germany (whose range extends from *g* of the subcontraoctave to *c* of the fourth octave) to American made five-octave miniature uprights. The standard range, however, can be considered $7\frac{1}{4}$ octaves, which comprises 88 keys (it extends from *a* of the subcontraoctave to *c* of the fourth octave).

The timbre of the piano, strictly speaking, cannot be uniform, as its strings are made of different materials, differently shaped and attacked by somewhat

*See Editor's note at the end of this book.

[1555]

differently designed hammers. The upper and the middle registers consist of straight steel strings used for each tone in groups of three. The middle-low and the low registers have coiled copper strings coupled in pairs. The lowest register has single copper strings for each tone.

It is to be remembered that the piano is a strictly percussive instrument, as strings are excited by the stroke of a hammer. The tone of the piano fades very quickly, as the oscillograph shows. It is our cultivated auditory imagination that extends the duration of a piano tone. Physically, a piano tone has a sharp attack and quick fading. The depressing of the right pedal extends the duration of a tone, as this releases the string, permitting it to vibrate. This, however, does not exclude the fading of a tone, but merely extends the time period of the fading. In musical terms this can be stated as: diminuendo is a constant of a piano tone.

The piano gets very quickly out of tune because its system of double and triple strings for each tone makes it physically difficult to maintain perfect unisons.

We had the description of piano possibilities in the Theory of Instrumental Forms*. Here we are primarily concerned with the unconventional uses of the piano as a percussive and coloristic orchestra instrument.

Igor Stravinsky made an interesting use of four pianos combined with an ensemble of percussive instruments in his *Les Noces*.

The real use of the piano as a percussive instrument comes mainly through the explorations of Henry Cowell, an American composer, who himself is an excellent exponent of his own techniques. Cowell has developed an exact and thoroughly developed system of playing piano with forearms and fists. Harmonically this device involves the use of "tone-clusters" (Cowell's term). Under such conditions the piano is capable of producing an amazing volume, uncommon to this instrument. My record library includes my own recordings of various Cowell devices, as they appear in his own compositions performed by himself. Unfortunately these are not on the market at present. There is, however, one Victor record of Ravel's *Bolero* arranged and played by Morton Gould. In this arrangement Cowell's forearm technique was employed. For more details on this subject see Henry Cowell's *New Musical Resources*.**

Apart from this specialized field of piano execution, rapid alternating tremolos of both hands involving the use of three or more fingers in each hand can be employed very effectively as a percussive device.

Another device which Henry Cowell uses and which is generally not unknown, consists of plucking the strings or sliding over them (with the right hand) while pressing the keys silently (with the left). Sliding over a group of strings permits the sound to come only from the strings whose keys are pressed. This produces a delightful harp-like tone.

Henry Cowell has also developed a highly coloristic effect which, so far as I know, he is the only one able to execute. It consists of sliding over the strings (in the back of the piano; somebody has to press the right pedal down continously) and sometimes plucking them. The sliding is done across an individual string

*See p. 1043 ff.   **Published by A. A. Knopf, N.Y.

and produces a most fantastic sound. Cowell often touches the nodal points of a string in order to get harmonics. He holds the string at a node with one hand and slides across it with the other. He has some compositions, like *Banshee*, entirely written for this technique. This device can be used with great success for wind and storm effects, as well as for fantastic and ghost-like effects.

The use of regular piano harmonics was made in Arnold Schoenberg's and my own compositions. Harmonics are particularly interesting as a variable timbre effects. By silently pressing a key (or a group of keys) which corresponds to the respective harmonic and by striking the fundamental (or a group of fundamentals) we obtain an actual harmonic. This is due to the sympathetic vibrations of the open string in response to the partial vibrations of the fundamental (which is executed staccato). The effect is that of an abrupt attack, followed by an extended fading harmonic. It is very interesting to note that under such conditions, each harmonic has a different timbre.

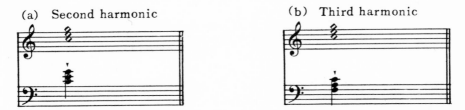

(a) Second harmonic   (b) Third harmonic

Figure 64. Second and third harmonics.

Cases (a) and (b) in the above figure have different timbres. Higher harmonics (preferably the ones which are used on a trumpet) can also be achieved.

The piano is also capable of producing *vibrato* (in single tones or chords). Not the imaginary vibrato, where a pianist is vibrating his finger while pressing the key (which is physically meaningless, as after the hammer strikes the string, no manipulation of the key has any effect upon the string), but a real physical vibrato by pitch.

This is my own device at which I arrived by the following reasoning. If we silently press the eleven lower keys (which is easily done with the palm of the left hand), then any keys we strike at an interval of an octave or more would stimulate the respective partials on the lower open strings. As the actual partials differ slightly in pitch with the corresponding keys we strike, the differences in frequencies produce *beats*, i.e., vibrato by pitch. I used this device with great success in the piano part of my Symphonic Rhapsody *October*. All sounds must be produced either portamento or staccato. They come out with special prominence on a concert grand piano, as there the strings are correspondingly longer and, for this reason, their partials are louder. This device can be applied either in long durations or in rapid arpeggio passages. For this effect the pedal must not be used.

The piano can be turned, for some special effects, into a harpsichord and other plucked instruments. For these effects, it is necessary to use paper (particularly wax-paper), placed right on the strings. When the hammer strikes a string covered with paper, it produces a buzzing effect. For a more drastic percussiveness, plywood boards may be used instead of paper. I made use of the latter in background music to *Merry Ghost*, a Japanese play by Kitharo Oka; this effect was used to produce a sound resembling that of the shamisen (a Japanese plucked instrument).

Finally the piano can be used as a sympathetic resonating (echo) system. The piano, when its right pedal is pressed, is able to reproduce sympathetically any sounds which are in its vicinity, i.e., any such sounds whose air waves can reach the strings with sufficient intensity. This concerns both the harmonic and inharmonic (noises) sounds.

Whistle into the piano and the response is the same pitch and the same tone quality. Sing, and the same sound continues as an echo. This device can be used specifically as an *echo generating device*. It is a natural phenomenon based on the physical pattern-response. It existed in nature before any animals inhabited this planet. Nobody can lay any claim to discovering the echo.

I suggested this device to all my students of orchestration, and it was Nathan L. Van Cleave who effectively used it in scores made for the Kostelanetz orchestra. This device can be utilized practically, in the alternation of staccato of an instrument or a group of instruments (preferably identical ones) and its echo; both should follow in uniform durations.

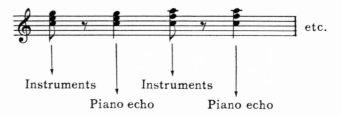

Figure 65. Piano echoes.

The alternation of such durations must not be too fast.

Many spectacular effects in orchestration can be achieved by a combined use of these piano devices. The *Harp, Novachord, Harpsichord, Guitar, Hawaiian Guitar* in many cases may be looked upon and utilized as percussive instruments. This does not require any additional description.

2. CELESTA

Celesta ("divine") is a keyboard instrument with soft hammers striking metal bars. These bars are made of precious and semi-precious metals. This instrument has a tone unsurpassed in delicacy and tenderness.

The most common design of this instrument includes four octaves (the small, the middle, the first and the second, usually starting from *c*).

Figure 66. Range of celesta. It sounds an octave higher.

The parts for this instrument are written on a two-staff system, the same as for piano. Standard bass (F) and treble (G) clefs are used.

It is a miniature self-sufficient instrument, on which melody, harmony, or both, can be executed simultaneously. Chords in their various instrumental forms, are frequently used on the celesta, as it produces a very delicate accompaniment suitable for melody played on the flute, the clarinet (particularly the subtone register), or in combination with the harp.

This instrument may be looked upon as a still more delicate version of chimes. It can be employed only in transparent (low density) textures and amid low dynamics (p, pp).

Debussy and Ravel used this instrument extensively in their scores. Chaikovsky made some effective use of it in his *Nutcracker Suite*.

3. GLOCKENSPIEL (Orchestra Bells; Campanelle)

This instrument is known in two basic models: the hammer and the keyboard types.

Hammer orchestra bells are played somewhat like the xylophone, i.e., by striking the bars with two hammers (usually made of wood) held in both hands. The bars, of semiprecious and common metals, are built in a portable closing box. The bars are arranged in two rows, similar to the arrangement of black and white keys on the piano. Often even the musical names of the individual pitches are engraved on each bar. This makes it easy for the performer to strike the right bar. Glockenspiels of both types are chromatic instruments. The keyboard model is of piano design.

The hammer instrument has a superior tone-quality to the keyboard model, which is clumsy and produces a less brilliant tone. Generally, the tone of this instrument is a harsher version of the tone of a celesta. The attacks, owing to unsoftened hammers, are more pungent. Some musicians describe it as having a "metallic" timbre.

The range commonly used for both models of orchestra bells is as follows:

Figure 67. Range of orchestra bells. Sounds two octaves higher.

Parts are usually written on one staff, in treble clef, but can be written, when necessary, on two staves.

As the sound of this instrument has a relatively long durability, it is not desirable to write rapid passages, unless such passages represent instrumental forms of one harmonic assemblage. However, the glockenspiel is a commonly used instrument. Its brilliance is due to the dominance of high partials.

4. CHIMES (Campane)

"Campane" means bells; the English term is "chimes". This instrument is used in large orchestras. It has a group of cylindrical metal bars suspended from a frame. The bars are struck by a wooden hammer (sometimes two hammers are used). This instrument has the sound of the church carillon and represents a more compact version of the latter. It is used for similar climactic or jubilant episodes, or, in some cases, for stimulating associations with a real carillon. The carillon, of course, is a totally different instrument, consisting of church bells and bars and played by fists, striking specially designed large keys.

Chimes usually have a set of bars covering one chromatic octave from c to c. The parts are written in the middle octave(treble clef) but there is such a predominance of higher partials that, strictly speaking, the pitches do not belong to one particular octave. Chimes blend well with the brass instruments.

5. CHURCH BELLS

This instrument is actually a group of several suspended church bells, matched in their pitches for each individual score. Such a set was used in Chaikovsky's overture "1812" where the church bells represented some of the standard Russian-Orthodox carillons and conveyed the idea of jubilation over the retreat of Napoleon Bonaparte from Moscow.

6. VIBRAPHONE (also known as Vibra-Harp)

This is a relatively new instrument, designed and manufactured in the United States. It is widely used at present in dance-bands. There are already several very eminent virtuosi, who appear as soloists with the dance-bands and small ensembles playing dance music (Adrian Rollini, Lionel Hampton and others).

This instrument is built on the general principle of the xylophone, but its bars, quite large in size, are made of metal, have resonating tubes under them and an extension of tone. The latter is achieved by means of electro-magnetic induction (which not only extends the durability of the tone, but also supplies it with an automatic vibrato by intensity); this effect is controlled by pressing a special pedal, built for this purpose. The execution of various dynamic effects, like sforzando-piano, is thus possible.

The vibraphone has a rich "golden" tone and differs from chimes in its timbral components: it has some similarity, in its basic timbre, with the "chalumeau" of the clarinet. Vibraphones, depending on their size, vary in range. Large concert vibraphones usually have the following range:

Figure 68. Range of vibraphones.

This instrument is played by special hammers, often even of a different design (to achieve different types of attacks). Some vibraphonists hold two, three and even four hammers in each hand. This permits execution of some self-sufficient solos in block-harmonies, following one another at a considerable, speed.

7. MARIMBA and XYLOPHONE

The marimba and xylophone are essentially the same kind of instrument. The difference between the two is chiefly in the resonating cylindrical tubes which are part of the marimba and are absent on the xylophone. Both types have the same kind of wooden bars and are played with special hammers. The xylophone is more traditional with the symphony orchestras, while the marimba is more used in dance-bands. It is interesting to note that many truly primitive African tribes use the marimba, i.e., even they have arrived at the necessity of using a resonating medium. The resonating tubes give the marimba a richer and a more sustained tone than the xylophone.

Music written for this instrument in a dance band is considerably more complex technically than parts written for the xylophone in symphonic scoring. One of the reasons for this is that in symphony orchestras one of the percussioners plays the xylophone part, but he is not expected to be a xylophone virtuoso. In the dance bands, quite the contrary, the marimbaist is a specialized soloist (often also playing the vibraphone) and is even capable of handling two, three and as many as four hammers in each hand. Some of these virtuosi handle the xylophone or the marimba as a very delicate instrument. This is accomplished by the use of special soft hammers. Some of such performers give a very refined rendition of Chopin's piano compositions. One very versatile xylophonist even built a dance band around the xylophone as a leading solo instrument. His name is Red Norvo, and recordings of his performances are available.

The range of the xylophone and the marimba varies. In writing for symphony orchestra, it is best to adhere to the following range.

Figure 69. Xylophone range.

In writing for the xylophone or the marimba used in present-day American dance-bands, the range can be extended as follows:

Figure 70. Range of xylophone in dance-bands

Full chromatic scale is available in both cases.

The alternate tremolo (like the plectrum tremolo on the mandolin) of both hands on the same bar (which is equivalent to the same note) is a common way of playing long notes on this instrument. All shorter durations are bound to sound staccato. It is an excellent instrument for execution of IS2p in any form and at practically any speed.

Glissando either on the naturals (c,d,e,f,g,a,b) or the sharps (c#, d#, f#, g#, a#) is another common device on this instrument. Combinations of both glissando forms, and in both ascending and descending directions may also be used.

Both the xylophone and the marimba have a wide dynamic range. The xylophone blends well with the flute; the marimba, either with the low register of the flute or with the "chalumeau" of the clarinet. Good combinations are also obtained by using the xylophone with the piano.

Parts for these instruments are usually written on the staff in the treble clef (G). In many French scores xylophone parts are written one octave higher than they sound. The reason for this is, probably, the dominance of upper harmonics which, in some cases, produces an impression that a certain tone sounds one octave higher. Many interesting effects may be achieved when parts for this instrument are written with full knowledge of the Theory of Instrumental Forms*.

The following percussive instruments of this group can be looked upon as more primitive or more simplified versions of the instruments already described.

8. TRIANGLE

This instrument consists of one long metal bar of cylindrical form and of relatively small diameter and is bent into an isosceles or an equilateral triangle (hence the name), not quite closed at its vertex. It is usually suspended on a string and is played by striking it with another straight metal bar of about the same length as each side of the triangle itself and of about the same (or smaller) diameter.

The triangle is rather like a single bar of a glockenspiel. Its high partials dominate to such an extent that it is considered to be an instrument "without definite pitch". Thus, the triangle can be used with any harmonic assemblage whatsoever.

*See Vol. I, p. 881 ff.

There are only two ways of using this instrument:

(1) individual attacks (all staccato) arranged in any desirable form of temporal rhythm;
(2) tremolo, which is accomplished by attacking alternately two adjacent sides of the triangle.

It is an instrument of limited dynamic range (generally mf) but can be made to sound very loud in tremolo. The latter also offers crescendo-diminuendo effects. The tone-quality of this instrument is very prominent and very "metallic". It blends well with all higher registers, as at such frequencies tone-qualities lose their timbral characteristics (owing to weakness or inaudibility of the high partials). Parts for this instrument are written on a single line. No clefs are used.

9. WOOD-BLOCKS

Wood-blocks are made in the form of a parallelepiped (rectangular solid) or, more frequently, in the form of a spheroid (eliptic solid). In both cases, some portion of the solid is carved out, and the hollowness thus formed contributes to the resonating quality of this instrument. Wood-blocks are made in different sizes to secure a selection of pitches, but these pitches are not too distinct.

A wood-block may be looked upon as a simplified version of the xylophone. The blocks are struck with sticks or hammers. Often (in dance combinations) an apparatus consisting of three, four or five wood-blocks is added to the usual combination of traps so that they can be handled by one performer. The wood-block is a purely rhythmic instrument. However, if a set of several is used, their parts may be notated on the regular five-line staff, where the pitches can be represented by the closest notes.

10. CASTAGNETTE (Castanets)

Castanets are an instrument of Spanish origin, and in most cases are used in music which is, if not truly Spanish, somehow associated with Spain. By tradition, castanets are an accompanying rhythmic instrument, played by the dancer and not by an outside performer.

Castanets are two small hardwood plaques (with the shape of the sole of an infant's shoe) loosely joined by a cord. They are held within the palm of a hand, with the string pulled over the middle finger. The actual execution of sounds is produced by finger attacks. Fingers strike one of the castanets and this, in turn, strikes the other. This produces a clicking and very brilliant high-pitched inharmonic sound. In some cases, two pairs of castanets are used (one pair for each hand). Some of the Spanish and Flamenco dancers are real virtuosi of this unpretentious instrument.

It is a highly developed (by tradition) rhythmic resource in orchestration and may be looked upon as a simplified version of the xylophone. It is particularly useful for animated high-pitched figures; wood-blocks are considerably lower in pitch and cannot be maneuvered at such a high speed.

The score for each hand occupies one line. Thus for two pairs of castanets, two lines must be used. The advantage of writing on two lines lies in the fact that it is simpler to score many complex interference rhythms, which are easily executed by two hands. It is well worth the time to make a study of traditional Spanish castanet rhythms.

11. CLAVES

The claves is a Cuban instrument consisting of two fairly thick sticks made of hardwood. The performer hits one stick with another. Both sticks are alike. This instrument is commonly used today as a rhythmic ingredient of Afro-Cuban dance forms (Rhumba, Conga, etc.) by our dance orchestras.

The sound of the claves is high-pitched, inharmonic and piercing. In rhumbas it usually performs the $\frac{8}{8}$ series trinomial (i.e., $3+3+2$, $3+2+3$, $2+3+3$). The part for the claves occupies one line.

The claves is ordinarily used with the so-called rhumba bands, but can be introduced into symphonic scoring, when Cuban character is desired in the music.

B. GROUP TWO. SOUND· VIA METAL DISC.

1. GONG

This instrument comes from Hindustan and China. It is made in two shapes: a circle or a rectangle. It is made of metal. It is usually very massive and large, at least the type used by the symphony orchestras. It is suspended from a frame to which it is attached by a pair of strings.

Figure 71. Two types of gongs.

It is the lowest-pitched inharmonic percussive instrument of the metal disc group. It is struck with a stick with a round soft end. The sound is very rich in quality and has a great dynamic range, combined with long durability of tone. It blends well with the low register of brass instruments.

The gong must be very moderately used, as it is the last resource of main climaxes. Too frequent use of this startling tone-quality neutralizes its character in the listener's impression. If the sound of the gong must be shorter than its natural fading period at a given intensity, it is damped out by the hand. Otherwise the term commonly used is written out above the note: "laisser vibrer" (let vibrate).

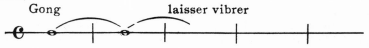

Figure 72. Allowing the gong to fade naturally

As the gong has a slow fading sound, successive attacks require considerable time-intervals between them.

2. PIATTI (Cymbals)

Cymbals consist of a pair of discs approximately 18" in diameter. They are made of semi-precious and precious metals. Each disc has a leather handle in the form of a short loop, by which it is held.

Cymbals are played in two basic ways:

(1) by striking one cymbal over the other (for louder and more prolonged sounds, with a certain amount of friction);

(2) by making a tremolo of alternating attacks over one suspended cymbal (held in horizontal position); for this purpose either hard drumsticks (result in harsher tone-quality and higher-pitched) or kettle-drum sticks (which are soft, and render lower-pitched softer tones) are used.

The range of the cymbals, the tone of which consists of rich inharmonic sound-complexes, varies depending on the form of attack. When the friction surface is small, the sound is higher-pitched. The partials cover approximately the range of trombones (excluding their pedal tones) and trumpets, with which they blend very well.

When cymbals are to be struck by one another, it is usually not necessary to indicate anything other than the temporal values and the dynamics wished. That a suspended cymbal is to be played tremolo is indicated by placing the sign ~~~~~~~ over the note. The use of hard sticks is marked: *colla bacchetta da tamburo*. The use of soft sticks is marked: *colla mazzuola*, or *colla bacchetta da timpano*.

This standard terminology is notoriously clumsy. I recommend that students use my own nomenclature, which is simple and economical, and permits a much more diversified use of the different types of attack:

a suspended cymbal:

    (a) hard sticks: —•

    (b) soft sticks: —○

two cymbals in hands: ○

I usually make footnotes at the beginning of my scores explaining the meaning of these symbols. I made the first use of this nomenclature in 1921.

An instrument which at once belongs to Group Two (discs) and Group Three (membranes) is the well-known

3. TAMBURINO (Tamburin)

This instrument consists of a circular wooden frame over which a skin membrane is stretched, covering one side of it. Thus the form of the membrane is a circle. In addition to this, there are small (about 1.5" in diameter) metal double discs, loosely mounted on perpendicular pegs in the frame of the tamburin. The tamburin viewed from above appears as follows:

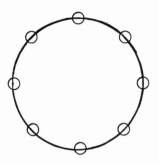

Figure 73. Tamburin

This instrument, associated with Italian and Spanish folk dancing, is played either by striking the skin with the palm, which at once produces a high-pitched inharmonic drum sound and the jingling of the discs (high-pitched "metallic" inharmonic sound); or by shaking the tamburin in the air (held by the left hand), which produces the jingling of the discs alone; or by producing an oscillatory frictional movement over the skin, with the thumb of the right hand, which results in a scintillating type of tremolo. Often these ways of playing the tamburin are combined in effective dynamic and rhythmic sequences. Much initiative in varying the attack forms is left to the performer.

The parts are commonly written on one line, and simply indicate durations and dynamics. Tremolo is marked as usual by: 〰〰〰

C. Group Three. Sound via Skin Membrane.

1. TIMPANI (Kettle-Drums)

Kettle-drums are the first percussive instrument to occupy a lasting place in symphonic scoring. It was Josef Haydn, who introduced them [*Sinfonie mit Paukenschlag* (Symphony with kettle-drums)]. Since that time, they have become a standard ingredient in symphonic and operatic scoring.

Kettle-drums are ordinarily used in groups of three and four. The original selection of three kettle-drums usually furnished the tonic, the subdominant and the dominant. Today they are used in any pitch-group combination that satisfies the harmonic need.

The kettle-drum consists of a hollow copper hemisphere, with a skin membrane stretched over its equatorial circumference. The tension of the membrane is adjustable: in other words, kettle drums can be tuned. This is accomplished by screwing in and out the handles (of which there are several around the skin surface) controlling the tension of the membrane. Tuning calls for a keen sense of pitch since it may have to be done quietly while the orchestra is playing. Kettle-drummers (or tympanists) usually know the parts of the neighboring instruments, from which they borrow the necessary pitch.

Each kettle-drum produces one pitch at a time. To obtain many pitches at a time would require as many kettle-drums. Berlioz, in one of his scores, used as many as 16 of them. Considering the usual equipment of the large symphony orchestra, it is advisable not to use more than four. In some instances two simultaneous tympanists can be used, in which case one may count on four or five instruments.

The three standardized sizes usually allow tuning within the following ranges:

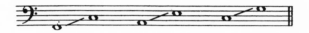

Figure 74. Ranges of the three standardized kettle-drums.

The total range may be considered practical even if one semitone is added at each end:

Figure 75. Total range of kettle-drums.

Rimsky-Korsakov ordered for his opera-ballet *Mlada* a small kettle-drum, which could be tuned up to *db* of the middle octave. He called it "timpano piccolo".

Contemporary American-made kettle-drums have a pedal device for automatic tuning.. This device is supposed to stretch the membrane at all points at an equal tension; it is not too reliable in actual practice. Performers still have to rely on their pitch-discrimination.

The tuning of kettle-drums is marked at the beginning of the score as follows, for instance: Timpani in F, Bb, C. When the tuning changes, the performer is warned by the composer in advance, as a certain amount of time is necessary for tuning of the instrument (the actual time period required largely depends on the performer's experience and skill). It is indicated like this, for example: *muta* in G, Bb, D.

The parts are written in the bass clef [F] on a regular five-line staff; two staves can be used if necessary. Kettle-drums are played by two special sticks having soft spheroid-like ends. The whole technique consists of individual and rolling attacks (i.e., alternating tremolo attacks; the latter may affect one or two instruments).

This instrument has an enormous dynamic range and in ff can pierce the entire tutti of an orchestra. Big crescendi are particularly effective in tremolo (marked: ~~~~~~~).

Sometimes, though very seldom, delicate sounds are obtained by muting. Flannel or other soft cloth is put over the skin of a kettle-drum. The use of such mutes is indicated by: timpani coperti (i.e., covered kettle-drums). To restore the normal effect, "modo ordinare" is used as a term.

The pitches of the kettle-drums leave something to be desired with respect to precision. This is due to the abundance of lower inharmonic tones. The instrument has a quickly fading tone. The pitch, owing to the presence of low inharmonics, seems lower to the ear than it is written.

2. GRAN CASSA (Bass-Drum)

This instrument usually has a cylindrical frame of very large diameter. The skin-membranes are stretched on both sides. It is considered to be an instrument without definite pitch, as the inharmonic tones predominate and all frequencies are very low.

The bass-drum is usually played with a special stick made for this instrument. The part is usually very simple, is written on one line, and consists of merely individual attacks. Of course other sticks can be used, and the execution of tremolo is also possible. Some of the bass-drums used by dance-bands have a narrow frame and only one membrane. The bass-drum blends naturally with low pitches.

3. TAMBURO MILITARE (Snare-Drum)

This is the most alert instrument in the entire third group. Although in shape it is the same as the bass-drum, it is considerably smaller in size. While the bass-drum is played in vertical position, the snare-drum is played in an almost horizontal position (there is a small angle to the horizon). It is played by a pair of hard sticks known as drum-sticks. The snare-drum derives its name from the snares, a pair of thin gut strings stretched across its lower head which produce a rattling sound. Sometimes the tamburo is used without snares (it is quite customary with dance bands), in which case a notation is made: "no snares".

This instrument produces middle-high inharmonic sounds. It has a wide dynamic range. The speed of rolling is the main feature of this instrument. Even the equivalent of grace-notes is often extended into rolls (marked: ♯♩   , i.e., the small note is the roll and the large note is the attack). It is suitable for the most intricate rhythmic patterns, which can be executed practically at any speed.

The jazz era has created many outstanding drummers in America. Yet the patterns of their improvised rhythms are still very one-sided and limited, as compared to their cannibal colleagues in Belgian Congo. The snare-drum has long been in use in military organizations. Its martial character by now is an inherited association. The part is written on one line. For students of this system, there are many opportunities to utilize the snare-drum as a two-part instrumental interference medium.

4. BONGO DRUMS

This usually consists of a pair of drums. The shape of the frame is a hollow inverted cone (it can be played on either side), which has skin membranes at its open ends. One of the drums is somewhat larger than the other, but there is no fixed ratio. Bongo drums are played by hand. Though probably of African origin, they are widely used in Cuban rhumbas and congas. Rhythmic patterns executed by the Cuban performers are often extremely intricate (mostly based on splitting of the $\frac{8}{8}$ series).

5. TOM-TOM

This instrument consists of a small cylindrical frame, which is relatively wide for its size. It has one skin membrane over its frame. It is ordinarily used (one or more) in jazz bands and played with a stick. Its inharmonic sound blends with the middle register of the ensemble.

D. GROUP FOUR. SOUND VIA OTHER MATERIALS.

No instrument can be considered standard in this group. All *special sound-effect* instruments belong to this group. It is neither necessary nor possible to describe all such instruments, as new types are being developed and introduced every year. Some of these instruments have a brief popularity, after which most of them become obsolete.

The purpose of bringing sound-effect instruments to the composer's attention is to stimulate his resourcefulness and to suggest that he too can use special materials for sound effects. It is also advisable for him to study the history of instruments and to attend the music departments of museums, as this will help him develop proper perspective and orientation in the subject.

One of the more commonly known instruments of this group is an ordinary *sheet of iron* (usually termed in French: *feuille de fer*). By holding such a sheet at one end and shaking it, one obtains thunder-like sounds. Single strokes and tremolo also can be executed on the suspended iron sheet, using different types of standard sticks.

Cow bells are used sometimes as a musical instrument for descriptive music of bucolic character. The bells can be either shaken or struck with a hard stick. Their tuning is unimportant, as the use of them is supposed merely to suggest the rural.

Emery boards (I used them in my Symphonic Rhapsody *October* to produce a steam engine effect) are sometimes used in symphonic and dance scoring. Rubbing of the surfaces of two emery boards (i.e., the sound is obtained by friction and not by attack) produces a powerful sound. It is an excellent descriptive medium for locomotive or train effects.

The *musical saw* was once very popular. It was used as an instrument of the melodic type. Two methods of playing were used: striking it with a stick or a small hammer, or stroking it with the bow (usually a long stroke ending with staccato). It is an extremely effective instrument, whose tone-quality resembles an idealized soprano voice and whose vibrato can be controlled by the performer. The handle is held rigidly between the knees and the end of the saw is supported by the middle finger of the left hand. While the finger presses the end of the saw, the entire saw bends: the greater the curvature, the higher the pitch. Bow or hammer produce attacks and either is held in the right hand.

Today composers have begun to use phonograph records with sound effects (birds, animals and other sounds of the surrounding nature); the latter are included as component parts of a score. Program and background music in radio and cinema utilize such recordings and often simply transfer them to a soundtrack. There are several sound-effect renting record libraries containing any imaginable sound effects (there are more than 10,000 items now). The firms are located in New York, but they supply the entire country.

1. HUMAN VOICES (Vocal Instruments)

The human voice is one of the original natural musical instruments. It is by no means standardized. There are too many types of voices and too many ways of using them. Each national culture has different types of voices and different methods of singing. Even different styles of music within one national culture often call for totally different manners of execution. Just to use a bold illustration, compare the bel canto style of operatic vocal art with popular crooning or "torch-singing" of today. The contrasts in singing of different nations are at least as great. Compare, for instance, French folk singing with Siamese folk singing or with Abkhasian choral singing (some of the Black Sea Caucasian shore; the mythical land of the Golden Fleece [Jason]) which has a unique instrumental character of its own.

Even in so-called European musical culture, we find such different styles as the Italian bel canto, the Russian vocal style (as in Chaliapine), the German lieder-singing, etc. Then we find such contrasting styles as vocal jazz ensembles and the plain chant of the Catholic Church. No doubt new styles will appear in the future.

Beside the necessity of considering all these stylistic and national differences in the voice as musical instrument, there are also biological differences and modifications, which take place as time goes on. One of such modifications is the appearance of greater differentiation of ranges and characters. Some time ago male voices were mostly tenor and bass. Later it became necessary to **single out** the intermediate type: baritone. Now we have bass-baritones, tenor-baritones etc. Standard parts of the classical repertoire are not written for them; so they have either to sing the parts which are too high or too low for them, or else to look for composers who would write for these new vocal instruments.

Sometimes we also encounter biological aberrations producing such voices as *altino*, which is not only higher than the male tenor, but also has a peculiar quality of its own, not to be confused with a boy's alto or a female's contralto. Rimsky-Korsakov even wrote a part for an altino (the astrologer in *Coq d'Or*), for which Russia found only two performers.

There are also other cases of vocal travesty, like the Russian Gypsy singer, Varia Panina, who possessed a genuine baritone; or another Russian singer, Anna Meichick, who had such a massive and wide-ranged contralto that she sang the part of the Demon, in Rubinstein's opera of the same name. Anna Meichick was the first contralto at the Metropolitan Opera House in New York for many years.

With all this in view, the problem of describing standard human voices seems insoluble. What the composer has to be aware of is that in writing for an oboe, he has a pretty well-defined auditory image in his mind, whereas in writing for a tenor, he can not know what he is likely to get in actual performance.

There are other considerations of equal importance. One of them is the effect of language upon the style of vocal execution. And this often involves such important considerations that the very nature of the Italian language (i.e., the type and the distribution of vowels and consonants) makes singing easy and natural and articulation clear, as compared with the English language. A number of good singers whose native tongue is English, *sing better* in Italian. Certain English sounds, like *th*, do not permit a proper air impact. On the other hand, the entire manner of singing in French, owing to its phonetic and articulatory nature, acquires a nasal character (on, en, un, in, etc.). All this naturally cannot be neglected by the composer. Thus, in order to present a somewhat practical description of human voices as orchestral instruments, I have to resort to somewhat specialized generalities.

Among these are the standard choral ranges, as they are traditionally used in our scoring for *a cáppella* or accompanied chorus. Soloists sometimes have wider ranges. But it is not always the case. Another generalization can be drawn with respect to basic timbres of vowels, in which case I shall use the Latin pronunciation of vowels.

No other components can be generalized, as all tone-qualities are individual; their forms of vibrato are also individual. Physically, each sound produced by the same voice on different vowels of the same pitch, or on the same vowel differently pitched, not to speak of different vowels differently pitched, has a different character. But this we cannot take into consideration, as even the violin changes its character (and in many instances even timbre) on different strings.

Among components which cannot be generalized is dynamics. The volume of voice and its dynamic range varies individually. Powerful voices, if combined with pleasing quality, are considered valuable, as such voices can produce a powerful impression by their dynamic versatility. Nowadays timbre, character and volume can be considerably modified either by using a microphone or by acoustical modification of the sound-track, which is constantly done in the radio and the cinema field.

Neither can individual articulating quality be generalized, (which, strictly speaking, belongs to the field of vocal attacks), even when we consider only one particular language. Some outstanding singers have magnificent articulation in addition to their vocal quality and general technique. I can mention two, as examples of perfect articulatory technique, though these singers belong to two different national cultures: one is Mattia Battistini (an Italian baritone); another, Feodor Chaliapine (the Russian basso).

Now after making all these necessary warnings, I can proceed with the description of choral ranges and basic timbres of the latinized vowels.

In some cases composers write certain solo, or even choral parts for a definite performer or a definite organization of performers. In such a case, of course, he can do a better job, as his parts are likely to fit the individual charateristics of the soloist or the ensemble.

Standard Choral Ranges

Female ranges:

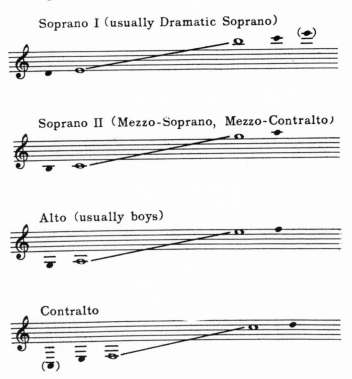

Figure 76. Standard choral ranges (continued).

Male Ranges:

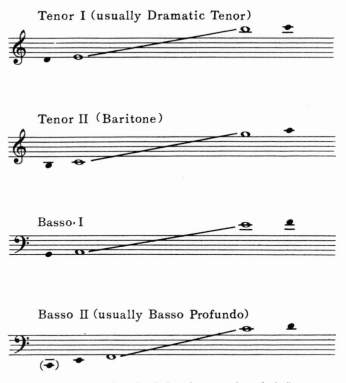

Figure 76. Standard choral ranges (concluded).

The parts for male voices, when written in treble clef, sound one octave lower than written. The so-called lyric sopranos and tenors usually have the range of soprano II and tenor II respectively, but with less developed lower register.

Latin	English Phonetic		Timbre
u	oo	open	O
o	oh	reed	R
a	ah	stopped	⊕
e	eh	double reed	RR
i	ee	closed	●

Figure 77. Timbral scale of the five basic Latin vowels.

This scale relates the vowels to five basic timbral groups, with which each vowel blends itself respectively. Thus, O corresponds to flutes, R to clarinets, ⊕ to horns, RR to oboes and bassoons, ● to nasal timbres and muted instruments (muted brass, celli, muted stringed instruments in general).

This scale can be extended to nine units, by means of combined vowels. The latter can be obtained by mixing the adjacent vowels of the basic scale. A nine-unit scale may be extremely helpful in evaluating general timbral characteristics of the English, French, German and Scandinavian vowels.

Latin	English	Timbre
u + o	u (up)	O + R
o + a	o (cod)	R + ⊕
a + e	a (as)	⊕ + RR
e + i	i (it)	RR + ●

Figure 78. Timbral scale of the four combined (intermediate) vowels.

Further supplements, which may still be necessary, derive from combinations of the non-adjacent vowels. The most important of these are somewhat common to Latin, English, French, German and Scandinavian.

Latin	English	(Phonetic)	French	German	Timbre
oe	e (alert) i (bird u (fur)	oe	eu	ö	R + RR
y			u	ü	O + ●

Figure 79. The two additional combined vowels.

All other u-vowels, as in the English word "you". or the sound of Russian character "Ю" (pronounced: you), have an attack of the attack of the English "y" (as in "yoke"), or German "j" (yot), or Russian "й" (brief "ee" [in Russian: ee kratkoye]) and the duration of the Latin "u", or English "oo".

This information is sufficient to guide the student in the field of basic vowel characteristics and to help him understand the reason for selecting one or another instrumental timbre in the accompaniment to vocal parts. Selection is based on coincidence (similarity) or juxtaposition (contrast) of the basic timbral characteristics, such as "u" (Latin), for flute, "o" (Latin), for clarinet, etc.

PART TWO: *INSTRUMENTAL TECHNIQUES*

CHAPTER 7

NOMENCLATURE AND NOTATION

THE following symbols represent a new system of notation, whose compactness and clarity may be of assistance in orchestral analysis and synthesis.

We shall use this system only if and when there seems to be a decided advantage in doing so. In the meantime, such notation will educate the composer to think of orchestral techniques through the medium of a unified system of concepts, thereby reducing his associational effort to a minimum.

The field covered by this system of symbols is as follows:

(1) orchestral forms (generalities);
(2) orchestral components (resources);
(3) orchestral tools (instruments);
    (a) groups;
    (b) families;
    (c) members;
    (d) auxiliary members

Some of the symbols, such as the last character of the Greek alphabet "ω" (omega) which is an equivalent of the Latin "o", are employed to designate the final stage of musical synthesis: orchestral form; thus, a symbol of finality is employed.

Other symbols are abbreviated idioms, like "q" for quality and "a" for attack. Still other symbols are simplified pictographs, like ⊟ for gong and ⊙ for tamburin.

In some cases it was necessary to resort to somewhat more complex symbols. Sometimes they are combinations of abbreviated idioms, such as ⊞ ("H" superimposed upon "O") for Hammond organ; and sometimes they are combinations of idioms and pictographs, as in ⊏✗⊐ for xylophone, ⊏Ṃ⊐ for marimba and ⊏Ṿ⊐ for vibraphone, where the pictograph of a bar is combined with the abbreviated idioms of X (xylophone), M (marimba) and V (vibraphone) respectively.

One group of symbols plays a particularly important part in the process of unifying the system. This group relates orchestral components (resources) to orchestral tools (instruments of execution). It is in this manner that the symbol of a simple open tone "○" becomes associated with the flute family, as its basic representative. The same concerns "R", the symbol of a single-reed quality, which becomes associated with the clarinet family.

Finally, the general use of horizontal lines added at different levels to basic idioms establishes range-register associations. Thus ○- is the flute quality, ○̄ is the highest-sounding member of the flute family (piccolo), ⊖ is the basic type (grande) and -○- is the lowest-sounding member (contralto). Similarly, the violin family is designated by Ⅴ for violin, Ⅴ̄ for viola etc.

[1575]

Greater accuracy in designating members of one family is hardly possible, as the range-register correspondences for the different families vary.

The nomenclature and symbols of *orchestral components* are identical with that of *instrumental resources* (see *Theory of Composition*, Part One*). For the present purpose this group of symbols must naturally be more complete. To make it more useful, each group is represented in the form of three- and five-unit scales. The latter can be extended still further if necessary.

It may be added that this system of nomenclature and notation is well worth studying as, quite apart from its use in this Theory of Orchestration, it has a methodological value *per se*, as the first system capable of designating, by means of its symbols and numerical coefficients, any situation to be encountered in the planning and execution of an orchestral composition.

A. Orchestral Forms (Generalities).

Musical synthesis results from three operational stages:

(1.) harmonic forms;
(2.) instrumental forms;
(3.) orchestral forms;

These three stages are interrelated through their density forms.

Symbols:

(1) harmonic:

p　　　　　$\rightarrow$part, a unit of an assemblage
S　　　　　—structure of an assemblage, stratum
Σ　　　　　—sigma, compound structure
Σ (Σ)　　—compound sigma

p　　　　　—a neutral unit
$p^{\rightarrow}$　　　　—a descending directional unit
$p_{\rightarrow}$　　　　—an ascending directional unit
$p_{\rightarrow}^{\rightarrow}$　　　　—a two-directional unit

$S^{\rightarrow}$　　　　—sequent assemblage, stratum
$\Sigma^{\rightarrow}$　　　　—compound sequent assemblage, sigma
$\Sigma^{\rightarrow}$ (Σ) —compound sequent sigma

H　　　　　—harmony, a group-unit of harmonic continuity, chord
$H^{\rightarrow}$　　　　—sequent harmony, chord progression

*See p. 1323.

(2) instrumental:

a   —an attack-unit
A   —an attack-group
I   —simultaneous instrumental form
$I^{\rightarrow}$ —sequent instrumental form
p   —simultaneous part
$p{\rightarrow}$ —sequent part

(3) orchestral:

p   —simultaneous part, simultaneous unit
$p{\rightarrow}$ —sequent part, sequent unit
ω   —simultaneous instrumental group, orchestral group (small omega)
$ω^{\rightarrow}$ —sequent instrumental group, orchestral group
Ω   —simultaneous instrumental combination, orchestra, tutti, (capital omega)
$Ω^{\rightarrow}$ —sequent instrumental combination, orchestration, orchestral score

Density:

d   —density unit
D   —simultaneous density-group
$D^{\rightarrow}$ —sequent density-group
Δ   —compound density-group
$Δ^{\rightarrow}$ —sequent compound density-group
$Δ^{\smallfrown}(Δ^{\rightarrow})$—sequent compound delta
φ   —phi, individual rotation-phase
        φ⟳ and φ⟲ in reference to t or T
        φ⟨⟩ and φ⟨⟩ in reference to p or P, or d or D
θ   —theta, compound rotation-phase

Density forms relating the three stages:

(a) harmonic density:

d (H)   —simultaneous harmonic density-unit
$d^{\rightarrow}$ (H)   —sequent harmonic density-unit
D (H)   —simultaneous harmonic density-group
$D^{\rightarrow}$(H)   —sequent harmonic density-group
Δ (H)   —simultaneous compound harmonic density-group, harmonic density
$Δ^{\rightarrow}$ (H) —sequent compound harmonic density-group, sequence of harmonic density

likewise:

$d\,(H^{\rightarrow}),\ d^{\rightarrow}(H^{\rightarrow}),\ D\,(H^{\rightarrow}),\ D^{\rightarrow}(H^{\rightarrow}),\ Δ\,(H^{\rightarrow}),\ Δ^{\rightarrow}(H^{\rightarrow})$

(b) instrumental density

d (I)	—simultaneous instrumental density-unit
$\overrightarrow{d}$ (I)	—sequent instrumental density-unit
D (I)	—simultaneous instrumental density-group
$\overrightarrow{D}$ (I)	—sequent instrumental density-group
Δ (I)	—simultaneous compound instrumental density-group, instrumental density
$\overrightarrow{Δ}$ (I)	—sequent compound instrumental density-group, sequence of instrumental density

likewise:

$$d\,(\overrightarrow{I}),\ \overrightarrow{d}\,(\overrightarrow{I}),\ D\,(\overrightarrow{I}),\ \overrightarrow{D}\,(\overrightarrow{I}),\ Δ\,(\overrightarrow{I}),\ \overrightarrow{Δ}\,(\overrightarrow{I}).$$

(c) orchestral density:

d (Ω)	—simultaneous orchestral density-unit
$\overrightarrow{d}$ (Ω)	—sequent orchestral density-unit
D (Ω)	—simultaneous orchestral density-group
$\overrightarrow{D}$ (Ω)	—sequent orchestral density-group
Δ (Ω)	—simultaneous compound orchestral density-group, orchestral density
$\overrightarrow{Δ}$ (Ω)	—sequent compound orchestral density-group, sequence of orchestral density

likewise:

$$d\,(\omega),\ \overrightarrow{d}\,(\omega),\ D\,(\omega),\ \overrightarrow{D}\,(\omega),\ Δ\,(\omega),\ \overrightarrow{Δ}\,(\omega)$$
$$d\,(\overrightarrow{\omega}),\ \overrightarrow{d}\,(\overrightarrow{\omega}),\ D\,(\overrightarrow{\omega}),\ \overrightarrow{D}\,(\overrightarrow{\omega}),\ Δ\,(\overrightarrow{\omega}),\ \overrightarrow{Δ}\,(\overrightarrow{\omega})$$
$$d\,(\overrightarrow{\Omega}),\ \overrightarrow{d}\,(\overrightarrow{\Omega}),\ D\,(\overrightarrow{\Omega}),\ \overrightarrow{D}\,(\overrightarrow{\Omega}),\ Δ\,(\overrightarrow{\Omega}),\ \overrightarrow{Δ}\,(\overrightarrow{\Omega})$$

Generalization:

harmonic forms:	p, S, Σ
density forms:	d, D, Δ
instrumental forms:	a, A, I
orchestral forms:	p, ω, Ω
density forms relating the three stages:	Δ (H), Δ (I), Δ (Ω)

Musical Synthesis:

transformation of harmonic density into instrumental density and, finally, into orchestral density: Δ (H) → Δ (I) → Δ (Ω)

B. Orchestral components (Resources)

Five orchestral components constitute omega (Ω)

D —orchestral density
V —orchestral volume (loudness)
Q —tone-quality
I —instrumental form of orchestration
A —instrumental form of attack

$$\Omega = D \div V \div Q \div I \div A$$

Scales of units in relation to their groups:

$$D = d, 2d, 3d, \ldots nd; d_I , d_{II} , d_{III} , \ldots$$
$$V = v, 2v, 3v, \ldots nv; v_I , v_{II} , v_{III} , \ldots$$
$$Q = q, 2q, 3q, \ldots nq; q_I , q_{II} , q_{III} , \ldots$$
$$I = i, 2i, 3i, \ldots ni ; i_I , i_{II} , i_{III} , \ldots$$
$$A = a, 2a, 3a, \ldots na; a_I , a_{II} , a_{III} , \ldots$$

Scales of orchestral components

(a) Scales of D:

$D = 3d$:

d_I	low	solo
d_{II}	medium	group
d_{III}	high	tutti

$D = 5d$:

d_I	low	solo
d_{II}	medium-low	solos
d_{III}	medium	group
d_{IV}	medium-high	groups
d_V	high	tutti

(b) Scales of V:

$V = 3v$:

v_I	low	pp	p
v_{II}	medium	mf	mf
v_{III}	high	ff	f

$V = 5v$:

v_I	low	pp
v_{II}	medium-low	p
v_{III}	medium	mf
v_{IV}	medium-high	f
v_V	high	ff

(c) Scales of Q:

$Q = 3q$:

			A.P. (*Amplitudes of Partials*)	H.L. (*Hammond Organ Levers*)	
q_I	low	○			open
q_{II}	medium	⊕			stopped
q_{III}	high	●			closed

$Q = 3q$;

			A.P.	H.L.	
q_I	medium-low	R			single-reed
q_{II}	medium	⊕			stopped
q_{III}	medium-high	RR			double-reed

$Q = 5q$:

			A.P.	H.L.	
q_I	low	○			open
q_{II}	medium-low	R			single-reed
q_{III}	medium	⊕			stopped
q_{IV}	medium-high	RR			double-reed
q_V	high	●			closed

(d) Scales of I:

$I = 3i$:

i_I	low	ap	ap
i_{II}	medium	aS	anp
i_{III}	high	aΣ	aS

$I = 5i$:

i_I	low	ap
i_{II}	medium-low	anp
i_{III}	medium	aS
i_{IV}	medium-high	anS
i_V	high	aΣ

(e) Scales of A:

A = 3a:

a_I	low	legatissimo	legato
a_{II}	medium	portamento	portamento
a_{III}	high	staccatissimo	staccato

A = 5a:

a_I	low	legatissimo
a_{II}	medium-low	legato
a_{III}	medium	portamento
a_{IV}	medium-high	staccato
a_V	high	staccatissimo

C. ORCHESTRAL TOOLS (INSTRUMENTS)

Groups:

SB	stringed instruments bowed
SP	stringed instruments plucked
W	wood-wind instruments
B	brass-wind instruments
P	percussive instruments

Families, members, auxiliary members:

Stringed Instruments:

(a) Violins:

∇ violin
∇ viola
∇ violoncello
$\underline{\nabla}$ double-bass

open: $\overset{\circ}{\nabla}$; muted: $\overset{\bullet}{\nabla}$

bowing (arco):

D	bowed	
$\overline{D}$	head	(punta)
$\ominus$	middle	(media)
$\underline{D}$	nut	(talon)

bowing in relation to fingerboard:

$\mathcal{D}$	fingerboard	(tasto)
Φ	middle	(media)
$D|$	bridge	(ponticello)

plucking, striking, slapping:

$\int$	plucked	(pizzicato)
$\mathbb{C}$	struck	(col legno)
λ	slapped	

(b) other instruments:

P   piano (grand or upright)

PE   piano (electronic)

◤   harp

⊓   guitar (Spanish)

⊓E   guitar (electronic)

⏀   mandolin

△   balalaika

Wood-Wind Instruments:

(a) flutes:

   ☌   piccolo
   ☌   grande
   ⊖   alto
   Ⴔ   basso

(b) clarinets:

   R   piccolo
   R   soprano
   R   alto   R   bassethorn
   R   basso
   R   contrabasso

(c) saxophones:

   ⊞   soprano
   ⊕   alto
   ⊕   tenor
   ⊕   baritone
   ⊕   bass

(d) double-reed instruments:

R̄R̄   oboe

R̄R̄   English horn

R̄R̄   heckelphone

R̲R̲   fagotto (bassoon)

R̲R̲   contrafagotto (contrabassoon)

Brass-Wind Instruments:

(a) horns:

♁   horn (French)

(b) trumpets:

♁   piccolo

♁   soprano

♁   alto

♁   basso

(c) trombones

♀   trombone

♀   trombone (extra crook: fourth ↓)

(d) tuba:

♀   tuba (contrabassa)

Closing:

○   open

○   stopped

●
○   muted

Organs:

  pipe-organ

電E electronic organ(in general)

日 Hammond organ

Electronic Instruments:

N novachord
V solovox
T theremin (space-controlled)

Percussive Instruments:

(a) bars:

Ｃ celesta   ⊞ bells   ⌐ᴦ· orchestra bells
                    (chimes)   (glockenspiel)

╳ xylophone   ᴹ marimba   ᵂ wood-blocks

Ꮙ vibraphone

(b) plates:

日 gong   ∞ cymbals   ⊢⊢ iron sheets
                                    (feuilles de fèr)

(c) skins:

▽ kettle-drums   ⊖ snare-drum   ◌̑ tamburin
  (timpani)

                    ◎ snare-drum without snares

                    ◎ bass-drum

(d) rods and others:

⚐ triangle   ☽ castanets   ⚐ clavis

(e) auxiliary percussive instruments:

●— drumstick (hard stick)

○— soft stick (kettle-drums)

○— soft stick (gong)

◁— brush (brushes)

Human Voices:

S   soprano
SA   mezzo-soprano, mezzo-contralto
A   alto, contralto
           AT   altino
T   tenor
TB   baritone
B   bass; $\overline{B}$ bass-baritone; $\underline{B}$ basso profundo

CHAPTER 8.

INSTRUMENTAL COMBINATION

IN this age of progressively precipitating mutations of forms, it becomes necessary to think in terms of present mutations and of mutations to come. One of the attributes of current progress is the plurality of the individual. This concept implies versatility of a self-contained unit. While it has been considered a virtue for a creative artist to develop one particular style from which he could be recognized, it is no longer so—since the composer equipped with a scientific method of production (such as is offered by this *System of Musical Composition*) can afford to master a multitude of styles, and be equally proficient in all of them. We have accumulated sufficient factual evidence to this effect to substantiate this claim.

In view of this consideration it becomes apparent that a certain style not only may become outmoded and obsolete, but the very idea of a composer being confined to one style no longer holds true. The character of progress affects not only the creators but also their tools. Musical instruments as types become outmoded and obsolete not only with regard to their design in general, but also with regard to the type of functions they are called upon to perform. It is not only important that a new method of sound-production has been discovered and put to use, but also that this new method transforms an instrument of a certain individual type into a versatile self-contained unit.

Until very recently the piano was "just a piano". Now we have an electronic piano, an instrument with a versatile functionality. It may be percussive, yet it may have a sustained tone; it may sound like a harpsichord and again it may sound like an organ. Not only its attack-characteristics become variable, but also its tone-qualities. It was formerly impossible to control the tone after a stroke of the hammer. This, in the case of an electronic piano, is no longer true.

Mutations affect not only individual instruments alone, but also the ways in which they are selected and combined in an instrumental combination. In view of this, hardly any combination can be considered standard, as what appears to be "standard" today, eventually may become an obsolete model of the vogue 1942.

This situation, over which we have no control, requires a broader basis for selecting individual instruments (though some of them may be of the plural type) and for combining them into groups.

A. Quantative and Qualitative Relations between Individual Members and the Group in an Instrumental Combination.

1. *Quantitative relations of members belonging to an individual timbral group or family.*

Members of the flute family are represented either by an individual instrument or by a pair of identical instruments, in which case the characteristics of both members with respect to timbre, intensity, attack-forms and range are identical, providing that both members are used in unison or at least in close intervals. Opening of a harmonic interval destroys correspondences of registers and partly of intensities.

The addition of a third flute, which is usually the piccolo, adds an upper octave-coupler which, for practical purposes, has a satisfactory correspondence of components with the large flutes.

In certain rare cases symphonic and operatic scores include an alto flute which, in some instances, alternates with the piccolo. It is important to realize that the range of the alto flute is located a fourth or a fifth below the large flute. It is in such relations that this instrument corresponds to the large flute. Thus the quantitative and the range relations within the flute family may be represented as follows:

$$
\text{Fl.;}\quad \text{2Fl.;}\quad 8\begin{bmatrix}\text{Picc.}\\[4pt]\text{2 Fl.;}\end{bmatrix}\quad 5\begin{bmatrix}\text{2 Fl.;}\\[4pt]\text{Alto}\end{bmatrix}\quad 8\begin{bmatrix}\text{Picc.}\\[4pt]5\begin{bmatrix}\text{2 Fl.}\\[4pt]\text{Alto}\end{bmatrix}\end{bmatrix}
$$

Figure 80.   Flute family

Such quantitative relations are quite different in the oboe family. As there is no piccolo type of oboe, there are only the following possible combinations:

$$
\text{Ob.;}\quad \text{2 Ob.;}\quad 5\begin{bmatrix}\text{2 Ob.}\\[4pt]\text{E.H.}\end{bmatrix}\quad 8\begin{bmatrix}\text{2 Ob.}\\[4pt]\text{B.O.}\end{bmatrix}\quad \begin{bmatrix}5\begin{bmatrix}\text{2 Ob.}\\[4pt]\text{E.H.}\end{bmatrix}\\[4pt]4\begin{bmatrix}\text{B.O.}\end{bmatrix}\end{bmatrix}8
$$

Figure 81. Oboe family

The clarinet family, on the other hand, besides the lower octave-coupler (B.C.) has a special type of diminutive clarinet (in D and in E♭), which is an upper second-or third-coupler. The quantitative relations of this family appear as follows:

$$
\text{Cl.;} \quad \text{2 Cl.;} \qquad 8 \left[\begin{array}{l} \text{2 Cl.} \\[1.5em] \text{B.C.} \end{array} \right. \qquad 3 \left[\begin{array}{l} \text{Picc.} \\ \text{2 Cl.;} \end{array} \right. \qquad 3 \left[\begin{array}{l} \text{Picc.} \\ \text{2 Cl.} \\ 8 \end{array} \right] \text{B.C.}
$$

Figure 82.   Clarinet family

The bassoon family uses only two types at present. In this case there is only the basic type and the lower octave-coupler.

$$
\text{Bssn.;} \quad \text{2 Bssn.;} \qquad 8 \left[\begin{array}{l} \text{2 Bssn.} \\[1.5em] \text{C.B. (Contrabssn.)} \end{array} \right.
$$

Figure 83.   Bassoon family

Thus we find no identical relations in four families of the wood-wind instruments, unless the basic types are used alone and only in even quantities.

The comparative tuning-range characteristics of the wood-wind group appear as follows:

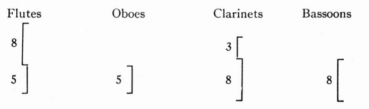

Figure 84.   Wood-wind tuning range.

In the absence of tuning-range correspondences, composers select the quantity and the type of supplementary instruments at random. In some cases an upper octave-coupler is added, in some a lower; in some other cases, the lower fifth-coupler is added, without adding any other couplers. More pretentious scores include four and even five members belonging to one group so that the quantitative relations of types vary greatly. Thus, we see that the quantitative relations within the wood-wind group are not based on any definite system of correspondences, unless only the basic types are used in equal quantities in each family.

The lack of a system of quantitative correspondences is equally as noticeable in the group of brass-wind instruments. There are 2, 3 or 4 French horns ordinarily used. In spite of the fact that they have identical tuning-range, they are often used as mutual octave-couplers. The quantitative and the range relations of the horns appear as follows:

H.;   2 H.;   3 H.;   4H.

Figure 85.   French horn family

As we are not discussing the use of instruments at present, we shall not include horns as mutual octave-couplers. A natural octave-coupler to this group is the tuba. It is customary to couple two horns with one tuba because the quality of the latter is so dense.

Trumpets, in their quantitative and tuning-range relations, represent a mixture of the flute and the clarinet family. The piccolo coupler is located a major second or a minor third above the basic type (as in the clarinets) and the lower coupler is an alto type (as in the flutes).

The quantitative and range relations of trumpets are as follows:

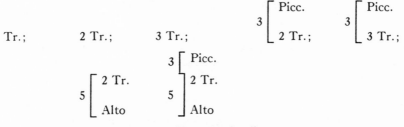

Figure 86:   Trumpet family

The trombone family consists of identical type-instruments only. Their quantities vary but their tuning-range relations are identical, though variable:

Tromb.;   2 Tromb.;   3 Tromb.

Figure 87.   Trombone tuning range

In the customary type of symphonic scoring, 3 trombones are generally used —and ordinarily in association with the tuba as lower octave-coupler of the third trombone.

The comparative tuning-range characteristics of the B.-W. group appear as follows;

Horns	Trumpets	Trombones	Tuba
0	$3\begin{bmatrix}\\ \\ 5\end{bmatrix}$	0	0

Figure 88. Brass tuning range.

These relations apparently do not disclose any system.

Quantitative and tuning-range relations in the string-bow group possess their own characteristics. It is customary to join groups of instruments of one type for the unison playing of one part. Thus from the composer's standpoint, one flute or one clarinet usually corresponds to a whole group of violins playing in unison. Whether such a method is justified is another matter.

It is customary to arrange the S.-B. instruments into four-part harmonies with a coupled bass (octave coupling). Their actual tuning-ranges, however, appear as follows:

$$\begin{array}{cl} 5 & \left[\begin{array}{l} \text{1st Vlns.} + \text{2nd Vlns.} \\ \\ \text{Violas} \end{array} \right. \\ 8 & \\ & \left\lceil \begin{array}{l} \text{Cellos} \end{array} \right. \\ 8 & \\ & \left\lfloor \begin{array}{l} \text{Basses} \end{array} \right. \end{array}$$

Figure 89.   String-bow tuning ranges.

In actual use, however, 1st Vlns. are frequently placed at some interval with 2nd Vlns. Inasmuch as string-bow instruments are of identical design and identical sound production, they can be considered to be of one type, though of a different tuning-range.

2. *Quantitative relations between the different timbral groups or families.*

We shall consider our classification on the basis of single, double, triple, etc., participation of each type of instrument in its respective group.

Coefficients of coupling are not used ordinarily with the lower octave-couplers—and very seldom with other couplers.

In the single combination there is only one representative of each family for each tuning-range. The assortment for a single instrumental combination, including the three orchestral groups (S., W.-W. and B.-W.) assumes the following form.

Fl.		
Ob.		
Cl.	Quartet	Quartet
Bssn.		
Horn		
Tr.		⌈Trio
Tromb.	Quartet	8
Tuba		⌊Coupler
Vlns.		
Violas		⌈Trio
Cellos	Quartet	8
Basses		⌊Coupler

Figure 90.   The single instrumental combination.

The second reading is considered because it is commonly used.

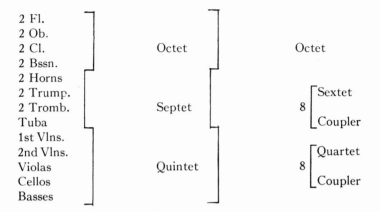

Figure 91. The double instrumental combination.

Here all types appear in two's, except for the tuba. Of course, the subdivision of violas and cellos into two parts each (but not the basses) is also acceptable and in some cases is actually used.

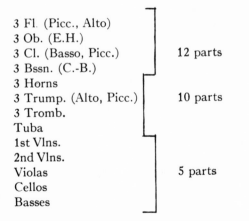

Figure 92. The triple instrumental combination.

Here W.-W. may have two or three octave-couplers (C.-F., Cl.-B., Fl. Picc.); B.-W. may have one or two octave-couplers (Tuba, Horn or Tromb.) S.-B., one octave-coupler (Basses).

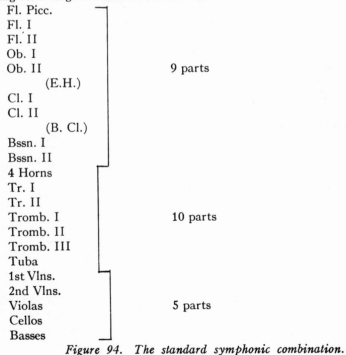

4 Fl. (Picc. and Alto)
4 Ob. (E.H. and B.O.)   16 parts
4 Cl. (Picc. and B. Cl. [Bassethorn])
4 Bssn. (Contrafag.)
4 Horns
4 Trump. (Alto, Picc.)   13 parts
4 Tromb.
Tuba
1st Vlns.
2nd Vlns.
Violas   5 parts
Cellos
Basses

Figure 93. The quadruple instrumental combination.

Upper and lower octave-couplers can be used as in the previous combination.

These classified instrumental combinations do not always correspond to the actual selections of instruments, which sometimes are a matter of tradition and routine, and sometimes the result of a random selection by the composer himself. As a result of this, many combinations used during the last century are of the intermediate, mixed type. In the latter, some groups contain only one member, while other groups consist of two, three and even four members.

One of the most standardized instrumental combinations of symphonic scoring for a large orchestra is as follows:

Fl. Picc.
Fl. I
Fl. II
Ob. I
Ob. II   9 parts
        (E.H.)
Cl. I
Cl. II
        (B. Cl.)
Bssn. I
Bssn. II
4 Horns
Tr. I
Tr. II
Tromb. I   10 parts
Tromb. II
Tromb. III
Tuba
1st Vlns.
2nd Vlns.
Violas   5 parts
Cellos
Basses

Figure 94. The standard symphonic combination.

In some cases the English Horn and/or the Bass Clarinet are added to this standard combination. Extra players may be required for these instruments but more often the second oboist is left free to play the English Horn as the second clarinet-tist plays the Bass Clarinet.

Radio orchestras are often reduced and modified versions of the symphonic combinations. They are by no means standardized. However, certain instrumental combinations are preferred by leading radio stations. We refer to the following combination merely as a prevailing one:

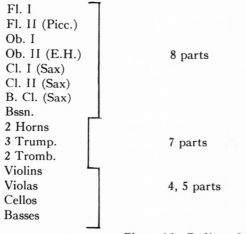

Fl. I
Fl. II (Picc.)
Ob. I
Ob. II (E.H.)   8 parts
Cl. I (Sax)
Cl. II (Sax)
B. Cl. (Sax)
Bssn.
2 Horns
3 Trump.   7 parts
2 Tromb.
Violins
Violas   4, 5 parts
Cellos
Basses

Figure 95. Radio orchestras.

Since the development of jazz, doubling on a saxophone has become quite customary. In addition to the plural aspects of an individual instrument, performers begin to develop plurality in mastering several instruments. All accomplished saxophonists are expected to play clarinets of various types, and some of them play also the double-reed instruments.

The distribution of groups in a score has undergone a number of modifications. It is somewhat standardized in each type of scoring, but different for the different types.

In symphonic scoring, at present, the parts for the wood-wind instruments are written at the top of the score; brass-wind parts appear below these; the percussive and solo parts (harp, piano, voices) follow; the lowest section is reserved for the string parts. The customary distribution is shown in Figure 94.

It is easy to see that the quantitative diversity of instrumental combinations poses a great many problems for the orchestrator or the composer. Since combinations vary, it is not sufficient simply to master any specific combination, as is required in the existing academic training. It becomes more and more important, as the diversity of instrumental combinations grows, to master the principles of this art.

3. Qualitative relations of members and groups or·families.

In addition to *quantitative diversity*, there is a great *qualitative diversity* which is noticeable even in one instrument of a certain type, not to mention the different types and, particularly, the different families of instruments. We shall now discuss these *qualitative relations* which concern correspondences of *timbre, intensity, attack-forms* and *pitch-range*.

In the wood-wind group, we find a close timbral similarity between the members of one family. The density of the timbre varies with the individual types, the lower instruments being denser than the higher, This, of course, is due to the fact that when more partials are within the audible range, the resulting quality appears denser. Timbral density, as a consequence, decreases in all instruments as frequencies increase.

The following subgroups of the wood-winds are those that are most homo-geneous:

> flutes and clarinets;
> oboes and bassoons;
> clarinets and oboes;
> clarinets and bassoons.

There is a greater timbral similarity between the two families of the double-reeds than between any other combinations. We can establish, for purely meth-odological reasons, a *scale of decreasing timbral similarities* for combinations of wood-wind families by two:

> oboes and bassoons;
> clarinets and bassoons;
> flutes and clarinets;
> clarinets and oboes;
> flutes and bassoons;
> flutes and oboes.

Timbral characteristics of the brass-wind group are more homogeneous than that of the wood-winds.

Trumpets have at least as much timbral similarity with trombones, as oboes with bassoons. In addition to this, it is more common to find several brass instruments of one type (like 3 trumpets, 3 trombones, 4 horns), than it is to find several wood-wind instruments of one type, except in very large com-binations. The French horns used today are all of one type. Their timbral characteristics can be considered as corresponding with trumpets and trombones to at least the same extent as that of flutes when combined with clarinets. The tuba bears a great timbral similarity to horns, but its quality is considerably denser. Thus we acquire two naturally blending subgroups:

> trumpets and trombones;
> horns and tuba.

The scale of decreasing timbral similarities, which is less pronounced in the case of brass instruments, appears as follows:

> horns and tuba;
> trumpets and trombones;
> trombones and tuba;
> horns and trombones;
> trumpets and horns;
> trumpets and tuba.

Of course, in the case of brass-wind instruments, timbral similarities are often variable, since they largely depend on execution. As mentioned in the description of instruments, trombonists can produce a very mellow tone, which remaining rich in the content of its partials, approaches the timbre of a French horn. The same is true of trumpets, which can be made to sound like cornets.

Though the individual timbral differences between the different strings of one string-bow instrument exist, they are not sufficiently pronounced to produce an undesirable timbral heterogeneity. Although the different strings are differently tuned in the sense that the degree of the tension in a string varies, depending on whether its material is gut, metal, or metal-wrapped gut, these different string-bow instruments can be accepted as members of one timbral family.

It follows from this discussion that though there is a relative timbral correspondence between the various families of one instrumental group, such correspondence is very remote between the three basic orchestral groups, i.e., the strings, the wood-winds and the brass-winds.

But then such a lack of similarity or correspondence may be very beneficial for producing contrasts. It is not only a matter of basic timbral characteristics but also of the manner of tone production. In this respect there are really two basic groups: the wind instruments and the string instruments. Both groups of the wind instruments give closer blends with each other than they give (particularly the brass group of higher register) with strings.

B. CORRESPONDENCE OF INTENSITIES.

The next problem to discuss is the correspondence of intensities within families, groups and instrumental combinations.

At this point we are not interested in the physical aspect of intensities, but merely in their basic relations which are conditioned by the various types and families of instruments.

The general characteristic of intensity in the flute family is such that there is a gradual increase of intensity in the direction of increasing frequencies and a broader dynamic range available in the middle register.

In the clarinet family there is an increase of intensity in both frequency-directions, with a sufficiently broad dynamic range. The exception is the upper part of the chalumeau where the sound is weak and weakening toward the upper end of that register.

The oboes must be described apart from the bassoons as these two types of double-reeds have different dynamic characteristics. The lower register of oboes has naturally increasing dynamics in the direction of decreasing frequencies. From the middle range upward the dynamic range is quite flexible, but that flexibility gradually disappears in the higher register which is loud, though the sound loses its density.

Bassoons have a powerful and dynamically flexible low register; they weaken gradually toward the higher register, which again becomes fairly strong, though lower in density and harsh in quality; this harshness disappears toward the upper end of the whole range, where the dynamics are quite narrow in range and of a low intensity.

It is to be remembered that outstanding performers succeed in neutralizing the registral differences of dynamics.

The dynamic correspondences of the wood-wind group as a whole appear as follows:

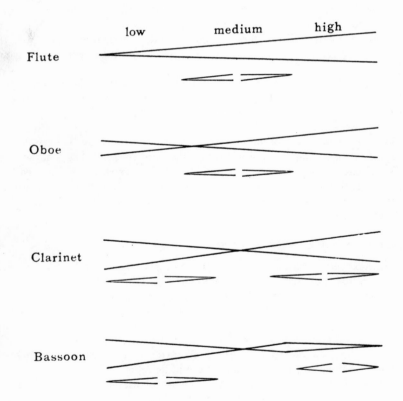

Figure 96. Dynamic correspondences of wood-wind group

There is a greater dynamic correspondence among the different types of brass-wind instruments.

Trumpets have low intensity in their lower register with a fairly wide dynamic range in the middle register and a high intensity in the high register. Thus the general tendency of the range is increasing intensity in the direction of increasing frequencies, with a fairly stable middle register and a fairly wide dynamic range.

Trombones grow in natural intensity with the increasing order of natural tones. The dynamic range of the middle register is fairly wide and stable. The pedal tones are weaker than the rest of the range.

French horns have the same natural tendency of increasing dynamics in the upward pitch direction. It is the upper half of the range that is dynamically most flexible.

The tuba has similar characteristics. Its lower register appears to be relatively loud, but this impression is really due to the high density of its tone in the lower register.

Summing up the dynamic characteristics of the brass-wind instruments, we obtain the following group of correspondences:

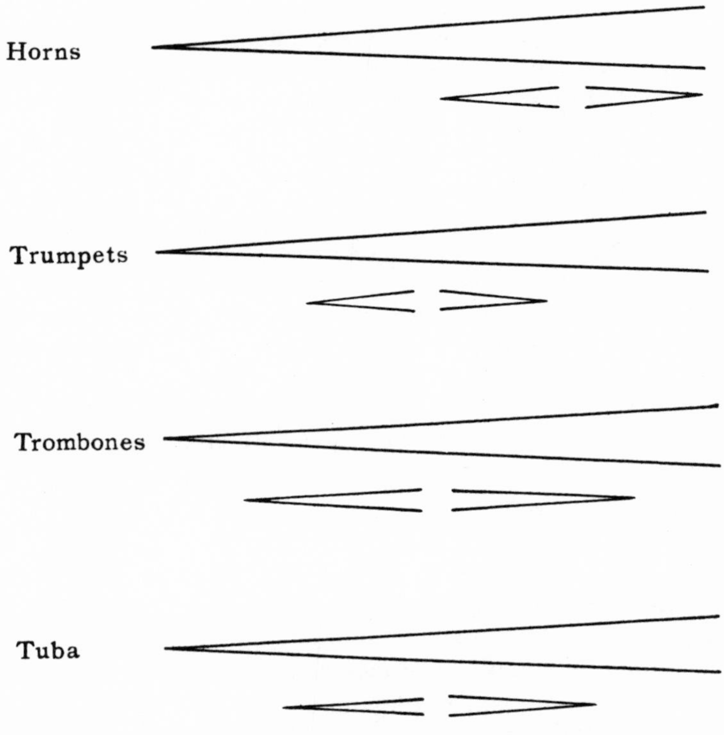

Horns

Trumpets

Trombones

Tuba

Figure 97. Correspondences of intensity in brass-wind group

As in the case of wood-winds, a great deal depends on the performer's skill.

All types of string-bow instruments have generally corresponding dynamic ranges, which give in all registers the same degrees of intensity and the same dynamic range. This statement, of course, is a simplification of the actual physical situation, but it is sufficiently accurate for the purposes of orchestration. In practice, the dynamic balances of string parts are often accomplished by selecting identical instruments (playing one part) in appropriate quantities. Here, however, we are chiefly interested in the correspondences of dynamic characteristics and not their equivalence with regard to the composition of balances.

It follows from the above discussion that string-bow instruments dynamically constitute the most homogeneous group. Strings, in homogeneity of dynamic correspondences, are followed by the brass-winds; the wood-winds, in this respect, occupy the last place.

C. Correspondence of Attack-Forms.

Next we shall be concerned with correspondences of attack-forms which exist between the different families of one group and among the groups.

Different families of the wood-winds have different attack characteristics. The flutes have legato, portamento and staccato. The latter is of one kind but can be obtained in piano and in forte, thus approaching only to some extent the distinctly different soft and hard staccato of the double-reeds. Two other special forms of attacks are available on the flute: the flutter-tongue (frulato) and the multiple tongue (double, triple etc.) The latter are not found in common with any other wood-wind instrument.

Clarinets have a perfect legato, a well-expressed portamento and a good soft staccato. The hard staccato is not characteristic of this instrument. It is more pronounced on the saxophone.

Oboes and bassoons have identical attack-characteristics but different mobility. Oboes are generally slower than bassoons. All double-reeds have an excellent legato, a perfect portamento and two distinct forms of staccato: the soft and the hard.

The attack characteristics of the wood-wind group may be summarized as follows:

Flutes: legato, portamento, staccato, frulato, multiple tongue
Clarinets: legato, portamento, staccato
Oboes: legato, portamento, soft stacc., hard stacc.
Bassoons: legato, portamento, soft stacc., hard stacc.

In the brass-wind group we find the following attack characteristics.

French horns have an excellent legato, a perfect portamento and a staccato which is closer to soft than to hard. The latter is due to the time period necessary for the transmission of attack through the long air column.

Attack-forms available on the trumpet are similar to those available on the flute; in addition to legato, portamento, and staccato (the trumpets somewhat emphasizing the distinction among these forms) trumpets, like flutes, can execute multiple-tonguing and flutter-tongue attacks.

Trombones offer only the first three of these forms, i.e., legato, portamento, and staccato; the individuality and distinction they bring to these attack-forms is analagous to that of the trumpets.

Attack-forms for tuba resemble those available on the horns.

In tabular form, attack-forms available from the brass and wood-wind instruments may be summarized as follows:

> *Horns*: Legato, portamento, staccato.
>
> *Tuba*: the same as above!
>
> *Trombones*: the same as above except that the subdivision between the soft and hard

staccato is more pronounced.

> *Trumpets*: the same as above except that, in addition, multiple-tonguing and flutter-

tongue (*frulato* or *flatterzunge*) are also available.

Richest of all in attack-forms is the string group, all instruments of which afford the same attack-forms. In nearly all cases, each attack-form available from the brass and wood-wind instruments is paralleled by *more than one* attack-form available from the strings—it is as if it were a question of two different languages, one of which might have but one word for a certain concept, while the other would have more than one word in order to describe minor shadings of meaning.

String attack-forms* w˙re classified in the chapter on the violin, the whole manifold forming a series that can be arranged into a decreasing scale with respect to tone duration: starting with the legato and proceeding through the detached (detaché, or non-legato), the portamento, spiccato, staccato, martellato, saltando, and sometimes the col legno to the pizzicato at the extreme of minimum duration. Strings can imitate all the attack-forms available from the brass and wood-wind instruments (although the imitation of the frulato is least exact); certain attack-forms available from the strings, on the other hand, cannot be obtained from the wind instruments. In establishing correspondences, then, between the attack-forms available from the strings on the one hand and the wind instruments on the other, the strings will exhibit a greater variety of form and of terminology than the wind instruments. It should be useful to establish a table of these correspondences, listed as to general characteristics.

> *Legatissimo* in general: obtained from the strings (S) wood-wind (W) and brass (B)

playing very *legato*.

> *Legato*: obtained from the S, W and B by producing several notes with the same bow

or breath.

> *Detached* (or detaché) available from S, W and B with a separate attack on every note.
>
> *Portamento*: obtainable from S, W and B.
>
> *Staccato* (soft): from the S in spiccato, mezzo-staccato, saltando or col legno; also from

the W and B.

> *Staccato* (hard): from the S in staccato, martellato, pizzicato; also from the W and B.
>
> *Multiple-tongue* effects: from the S by measured tremolo in mezzo-staccato; from the W

(flute) or B (trumpet) as double, triple or multiple-tonguing.

> *Flutter-tongue* effects: the nearest approximation on the S is obtained from an unmeasured

tremolo; from the W (flute) by flutter-tonguing or frulato and from the B (trumpet) by frulato.

Figure 98. Correspondence of attack-forms

*See p. 1499.

D. CORRESPONDENCE OF PITCH-RANGES.

The last form of correspondences to be discussed concerns instrumental pitch-ranges.

The individual range-characteristics of the different instruments, families and groups are the main source of difficulties encountered by the composer. or the orchestrator in his work on a score. If all instruments had been designed to produce the same range (in different zones of the general acoustical range, of course) and had the same register-distribution characteristics, such difficulties would be completely eliminated, and the composer would have felt greater freedom in conceiving an orchestral work. But with present instrumental combinations, such is not the case.

To get a clearer picture of ranges, we shall represent them in *semitones*. We shall confine all ranges to the practical limits in which the respective instruments are used.

Flutes:

Alto	Grande	Piccolo
31	38	27

Clarinets:

Bass	Alto	Soprano	Piccolo
38 (34)	34	39	39

Saxophones:

Bass	Baritone	Tenor	Alto	Soprano
30	30	30	30	30

Oboes:

Baritone	Alto	Soprano
27	28	31

Bassoons:

Contrabassoon	Bassoon
34	40

Figure 99. Semitone range of wood-winds

As we can see, only the saxophones have a balanced assortment of ranges. . No other family gives such a correspondence and there is no definite correspondence between the families.

Horns:

44

Trumpets:

Bass	Alto	Soprano	Piccolo
25	25	32	30

Trombones:

Tenor-Bass (with valve)	Tenor-Bass (without valve)
3 + (-1[gap]) + 38	3 + (-5[gap]) + 34

Tuba:

39

Figure 100. Brass-wind ranges in semitones

As we can see, no obvious correspondences of ranges exist in this group.

The stringed-bow instrumental group, though homogeneous in other respects, is entirely heterogeneous with regard to the instrumental ranges of its members.

		Orchestra	Solo		Pizzicato
Violins:		52	52		33
Violas:		33	40		28
'Cellos:		40	47		40
Basses:	(31)	27	41	(28)	24

Figure 101.   Range of string-bow group

It follows from the above three tables that a definite range-correspondence is not to be expected when instruments are combined in families and groups as they appear in a standard instrumental score.

It is particularly important to note the extreme difference between the violins and the basses; however, since basses are primarily used as octave-couplers to cellos, they have very little range similarity with the latter.

E. Quantitative and Qualitative Relations Between the Instrumental Combination and the Texture of Music.

1. Quantitative relations

One of the chief obstacles the composer encounters in translating his music into orchestral form is the lack of *quantitative correspondences between the harmonic and the density forms* of music, on the one hand, and the *instrumental combination*, on the other.

In scoring of the Mozartian type, where harmony consists of two parts with added bass, the problem of quantitative correspondences is very simple. Instruments of identical type are matched by pairs, thus supplying the two harmonic functions. On the other hand, the same pairs, when functioning in the low register, are assigned to represent the harmonic bass.

Unfortunately this happy situation does not exist in more developed forms of orchestral writing. Existing forms of harmony seldom correspond to the se lection of members in a family, to combinations of families and groups. Often double instrumental combination is used to represent so-called four-part harmony, which, as we know, in actuality is 3p + p. Such a harmonic structure basically requires a homogeneous instrumental combination of three with the addition of one instrument which is of the same or of a different timbral family from the first three.

My purpose in discussing this matter now is to call the student's attention to the fact that harmonic forms of music have developed independently of the quantitative aspect of instrumental combinations. It is natural for this reason to expect all kinds of quantitative discrepancies in translating music into orchestral language. From the subjective view of the composer, this discrepancy becomes a source of never-ending struggle. The elimination of quantitative discrepancies and the establishment of quantitative correspondences between the harmonic and the density forms of music, on the one hand, and the instrumental combinations, on the other, is one of the major tasks of my Theory of Orchestration.

All such problems in this system are solved by a different methodological approach, which in this case is the *translation of special harmony into a specified form of general* (strata) *harmony* in correspondence with the selected instrumental combination. This methodological approach also allows for the use of new harmonic forms, as well as new instrumental combinations. Thus the problem is solved both for the orchestration and the orchestral composition. This method gives a fully satisfactory solution to all the situations concerned with the balance within harmonic groups (i.e., the balance of p's within S) and between such groups (i.e., the balance of S's within Σ).

2. Qualitative Relations

Qualitative relations between the harmonic and the density group, on the one hand, and the instrumental combination, on the other, often compel the composer to draw his musical texture from the instrumental combination instead of from its own components.

For example, a high density harmonic group which would at its best be represented by a homogeneous timbral group, cannot be properly assigned because a certain (more or less) standard instrumental combination does not contain as many members as are necessary in a certain specified timbral group.

The reverse is true: in some cases there may be more members in a homogeneous timbral group than is required by the status of a harmonic structure and its presupposed density. Of course such situations are easily solved by employing only some of the members belonging to one timbral family. But suppose this situation is more or less prevalent in a given score. Then it would result in an unjustified waste of instruments and performers, which just does not agree with the universally accepted idea of the economy of resources necessary in artistic expression.

To refer to one of the previous discussions of composition (Theory of Composition: Part Two) it is important to estimate the qualitative relations between the musical and the orchestral texture. This means that any composition achieves its optimum only under a certain group of corresponding conditions, which affect both the musical and the orchestral textures. Otherwise it may happen that the selected instrumental combination is not capable of expressing a certain tonal texture. For example, it may not be possible for the French horns to execute a highly mobile fugato even if such timbre is desirable; or it may not be possible for a small instrumental combination of monodic instruments of any type to execute a diversified texture of high harmonic density.

Generally speaking, musical textures and instrumental combinations are closely interrelated. And though nearly every piece of music can be adapted, arranged or orchestrated with varying degrees of skill, the optimum of a synthesis can be achieved only under a certain specified group of conditions for nearly every instrumental combination that has been more or less standardized.

CHAPTER 9

ACOUSTICAL BASIS OF ORCHESTRATION

The problem before us is to define and describe the *material of orchestration*. But in what terms can such a definition and description be adequately accomplished? Certainly not in terms of violins, clarinets, trumpets and drums. To do so would mean to repeat once more the methodological error made by music theorists of the past. The description of orchestral devices in terms of musical instruments leads to the dogmatism of assorted recipes which presuppose a certain type of musical texture. If the composer is fortunate enough to apply them to just such a texture, he may meet with success. In all other cases he is bound to be a failure. Should then the elements of orchestration be described, perhaps, in *physical terms*, i.e., as frequencies, amplitudes, phases, energies, air compressions, and rarefactions? In a way such a description would be highly accurate. Yet it would be erroneous to assume that frequencies, amplitudes and air compressions constitute the material of orchestration. Such a viewpoint would be very one-sided, and description based on it would be insufficient.

On the receiving end, phasic stimuli produced by instruments encounter a *metamorphic auditory integrator*. This integrator represents the auditory apparatus as a whole and is a complex interdependent system. It consists of two receivers (ears), transmitters, auditory nerves, and a transformer, the auditory brain-center. The response to a stimulus is integrated both quantitatively and selectively. The neuronic energy of *response* becomes the psychonic energy of *auditory image*. The response to stimuli and the process of integration are functional operations and, as such, can be described in *mathematical terms*, i.e., as synchronization, addition, subtraction, multiplication, etc. But these integrative processes alone do not constitute the material of orchestration either. The auditory image, whether resulting from phasic stimuli of an excitor or from self-stimulation of the auditory brain-center, can be described only in *psychological terms* of loudness, pitch, quality, etc. This leads us to the conclusion that the *material of orchestration* can be defined only as a *group of conditions under which an integrated image results from a sonic stimulus subjected to an auditory response*. This constitutes an interdependent tripartite system, in which the existence of one component necessitates the existence of two others. The composer can imagine an integrated sonic form, yet he cannot transmit it to the auditor (unless telepathically) without sonic stimulus and hearing apparatus. The transmission of a sonic form by an instrumental stimulus necessitates the existence of such a form and of a hearing apparatus capable of reacting to it. Finally, the hearing apparatus itself produces an auditory image out of a sonic form executed by an instrument.

The study of sound and hearing is not complete for the present. Since Helmholtz's work on *Tone-Sensations*, certain facts have had to be added and certain others rectified. Some aspects of acoustics require further experimental study and verifications. No final clarity has been achieved in the matter of subjective and objective. Yet too many processes of importance pertain to this field. Among them are the striking tone, the combination tones, the auditory illusions, etc. Under these circumstances our definition, classification and description of the components of an auditory image, must necessarily lack the precision which might have been attained if the physical and the psychological study of sound were more complete. Nevertheless, even with what can be offered now, the acoustical basis of orchestration can be considered established for any pr..ctical purpose. Our main achievement is a methodological one. The definition of auditory image as a function of physical stimulus and the integrative process of hearing, with further progress of physical and psychological knowledge, will become more accurate and will permit a more adequate description of the material of orchestration. The present description of this material and the deductions based upon it are true only within the scope of the present knowledge of sound.

EDITORS' NOTE:

The original manuscript of the *Schillinger System of Musical Composition* does not end at this point. But the editors, after consultation with the publisher, deem it wise to terminate at this point because the material that follows is not complete and because much of the material on orchestration has already been presented by Schillinger in earlier books.

In Book I, for example, the application of resultants to Instrumental Forms (Chapter 7) foreshadows the procedure for developing scores of unprecedented richness and complexity from rhythmic raw material. In Chapter 8, *Coordination of Time Structures*, Schillinger describes the synchronization of an attack group with an instrumental group. In Book VII, Chapter 5, Schillinger considers the composition of a counterpart to a given melody by means of axial correlation—a technique indispensable in modern "arranging" and in virtually all good orchestration.

Book VIII, *Instrumental Forms*, covers comprehensively one of the most important aspects of orchestration. As Schillinger himself described the purpose of this book: "Instrumental forms will mean, so far as this discussion is concerned, a modification of the original melody and/or harmony which renders them fit for execution on an instrument . . . Depending on the degree of virtuosity which can be expected from singers, instrumental forms may be applied to vocal music as well as orchestral." An examination of chapter headings in this book quickly reveals how basic the material is for orchestration: Chapter 5. Strata of Four Parts; Chapter 6. Composition of Instrumental Strata; Chapter 8. The Use of Directional Units In Instrumental Forms of Harmony, etc.

Book IX, *General Theory of Harmony*, likewise is concerned with matters fundamentally orchestral. "My general theory of harmony," Schillinger writes, "denotes the whole manifold of techniques which enable the composer to write *directly* for groups of instruments or voices . . ." In this book, Schillinger develops two of his most original orchestral techniques: the Σ concept as it relates to orchestral strata (Chapters 2, 7) and the composition of density as it relates to strata (Chapter 15). These techniques were largely responsible for the rich and arresting arrangements made by Schillinger students.

From Schillinger's notes, it is clear that he planned to integrate the ideas of Books VIII and IX in Book XII. Other matters which he planned to consider and had in part written down include: instrumental media for achieving variation of true color; forms of attacks (such as durable, abrupt, bouncing, oscillating, etc.) as they relate to instrumental forms; curvature of a melodic line in instrumental performance; and other related material. In addition to *Acoustical Basis of Orchestration*, Schillinger had planned to include a section called *Theory of Interpretation*.

As previously stated, the original manuscript contains some of these materials in incomplete form. The editors also had before them notes taken by students who had studied personally with him. These notes covered various topics included in a table of contents prepared by Schillinger for Book XII.

For a time the editors and the publisher considered the possibility of reworking all of these materials and including them in the present volume. Since the major aspects of Schillinger's theory of orchestration are covered in earlier books and in Book XII as it appears here, it was decided to confine the published work in its first edition to Schillinger's manuscript as he had completed it.

[L. D.-A. S.]

GLOSSARY

Compiled by LYLE DOWLING and ARNOLD SHAW

(Terms appearing in bold face within a definition are explained elsewhere in this glossary and will be found in alphabetical order. Students should consult the index in order to discover the pages on which terms appear in the text itself.)

A

A Symbol ordinarily used for **Attack.**

A⃗ Symbol for **Attack Continuity.**

a Denotes an *a* axis; see **Axes.**

a See **Attack.**

ⓐ Denotes one of the positions in **Quadrant Rotation.**

a ÷ b Symbol for **Resultant** of a and b. See the footnote: Vol. I, p. 4.

a ÷ b Symbol for another **Resultant** of *a* and *b*, fractioned with symmetry around an axis.

a, b, c, These letters frequently denote **Chordal Functions** when the exact name of the function need not be specified.

ABSCISSA. In the **Graphing** of music the measurements horizontally, left to right, denoting the time dimension.

ACCELERATION SERIES. Any series in which there is an increasing or decreasing differential between successive terms. The decreasing series is sometimes known as a **Retardation Series.** Prime number series, summation series, etc., are ordinarily used for this purpose. A positive series may be synchronized with its reverse to produce a **Resultant.**

ACOUSTICAL CLARITY. In **Orchestration,** the result of (a) differentiation of overlapping **Strata** by timbral and/or **Attack-Form** variety, and (b) proper relationship of **Clockwise** and **Counterclockwise** positions of strata.

ACOUSTICAL EQUIVALENTS. Intervals differently named in diatonic nomenclature but consisting of an identical number of semitones, hence sounding the same.

ACOUSTICAL PROPERTIES OF INTERVALS. The critical properties are **Density** and **Tension,** as applied to **Harmonic Intervals.** See Vol. I, p. 700.

ACOUSTICAL RANGE. The range of an instrument as it actually sounds.

ACOUSTICAL SET. A distribution of tones corresponding exactly or approximately to the series of **Harmonics.**

ALIEN MEASURE-GROUPING. The grouping of a durational continuity (especially, a **Resultant)** by measures consisting of a number of units which does *not* correspond to any generator or product of generators, used in making the resultant.

AMPLITUDE. A measure of intensity (loudness) of sound. When a sound wave is graphed, the amplitude is the distance between the highest and lowest points of the track of the sound wave, and the intensity of the tone is related to this measurement in a logarithmic ratio.

ANTICIPATED TONE(S). In harmony, a tone of one structure caused to sound before other tones of the structure, and while tones of the preceding structure are still sounding.

ANTI-CLIMAX. Not to be confused with *negative* climax; refers to a segment of a composition in which the tension or magnitude of a climax is relaxed; see **Climax.**

ARITHMETICAL MEAN. An average found in the ordinary way by adding a series of numbers, then dividing the total by the number of terms in the series.

ARITHMETICAL PROGRESSION. A series in which each term is the previous term plus some constant number, n. For example, 1, 3, 5, 7, 9 is an arithmetical progression in which the constant is 2.

ASCRIBED MOTION. A type of melodic movement produced by constructing the melodic steps on a graph so that they are *outside* the **Secondary Axis**, that is, so that the secondary axis is between the pitch-line and the primary axis. When the steps are constructed *inside*, the motion is called **Inscribed Motion**. More strictly, ascribed motion is *sine* motion; inscribed *cosine* motion.

ATTACK. In this system, a very general term meaning both an instance of some musical event and the moment in time when the event begins. It is not to be confused with **Attack-Form**, which is an instrumental matter. When one says "three attacks per measure," one means that there are three events—of whatever kind—occurring in the measure, without specifying in exactly what rhythm they occur. The term need not refer always to tonal material; two *attacks* of O_1 would mean "two instances or occurrences of orchestral group number one," for example. The abbreviation for attack is A or some form of it, often a. Attacks may be grouped into **Attack-Groups**, consisting of various numbers of attacks in series. Such attack-groups may further be grouped into **Attack Continuity**.

ATTACK CONTINUITY. A **Continuity** composed of Attack-Groups which are, in turn, composed of **Attacks**.

ATTACK-FORM. The pattern of tonal material assigned to an instrument: for example, an *arpeggio* is one of many attack-forms for a chord.

AUTOMATIC CHROMATIC CONTINUITY. Produced by subjecting an initial chord, usually in the diatonic system, to a process whereby one or more voices move by semitones in but one direction at a time. See Vol. I, p. 544.

AUXILIARY TONE OR UNIT. A type of **Directional Unit** consisting of a chordal tone (or **Neutral Unit**) preceded by a tone that is one semitone, or two semitones, or a diatonic step removed. Distinguished from other types by the fact that the auxiliary need not belong to any pre-set scale or harmonic structure.

AXES. In general, lines of reference. 1. *Key-axis*: the particular pitch-level representing the first tone of the **Real Scale** in which the music is written. A shift in key-axis involves **Modulation** in the *modern* sense of the term. 2. *Primary axis* is the pitch-level, not necessarily the same as the key-axis, around which a melodic line moves; it is usually the pitch sounded for the greatest total duration in the course of a melody; a shift in primary axis involves modulation in the 16th century sense, or *modal* modulation. 3. *Secondary axis* in melody is an axis that has a specific direction and that describes the movement of the melodic line: specifically; a axis, up from the primary; b, down to the primary; c, up to the primary; and d, down from the primary. 4. *Balancing axes* are those leading toward the primary, that is, the b and c axes. 5. *Unbalancing axes* (a and d) lead away from the primary. 6. *Binary* axes are simultaneous pairs of secondary axes. 7. *Ternary axes* are sets of three simultaneous secondary axes. 7. *Axis of symmetry* is the "center," or line of reference around which a symmetrical structure is constructed. 8. *Axis of inversion* is the line of reference from which inverted intervals are reckoned in **Inversion**.

AXIAL COORDINATION. In melody, the process of composing a continuity of **Secondary Axes**; in counterpoint, the composition of properly interrelated groups of secondary axes for two or more **Correlated Melodies**.

AXIS RELATIONS. In general, the relations between two or more axes of two or more simultaneous parts or strata in music. Hence it may refer to the relation between melody and harmony, or, in counterpoint, to the relations between any pair of correlated melodies; specifically: (1) UU, unitonal-unimodal, that is, same key-signature, same mode (displacement) for both melodies; (2) UP, unitonal-polymodal, same key-signature, different displacements; (3) PU, polytonal-unimodal, different key-signatures, same displacements; (4) PP, polytonal-polymodal, different key-signatures, different modes.

B

b   Denotes one of the secondary axes. See **Axes**.

ⓑ   Denotes a position in **Quadrant Rotation**.

B   Symbol used for *balancing* axis (see **Axes**).

BALANCING. The process of adding to a **Resultant** a duration such that, if the generators are *a* and *b*, the duration added is a (a—b); especially, in **Contraction Groups**.

BALANCING AXIS. See **Axes**.

BEAT TONES. See **Differential Tones**.

BINARY AXES. See **Axes**.

BINOMIAL. A group consisting of two elements.

BLOCK HARMONY. An arranger's term referring to the result of a process in which a melodic line is subjected to **Coupling** at the octave, after which the remaining functions, whatever they may be, of a chord—usually S(5) with the 13th added or S(7)—are inserted between the extremes of the octave.

C

c   Denotes one of the secondary axes; see **Axes**.

ⓒ   Denotes a position—backwards and upside down—in **Quadrant Rotation**.

C_0 Abbreviation for **Zero Cycle**.

C_3 Abbreviation for **Cycle of Thirds**.   ⎤   **Positive** C_{-3} ⎤   **Negative**

C_5 Abbreviation for **Cycle of Fifths**.   ⎟   **Cycles** C_{-5} ⎟   **Cycles**

C_7 Abbreviation for **Cycle of Sevenths**. ⎦ C_{-7} ⎦

CADENCE. A configuration in melody and/or harmony, used very frequently, which has the effect of halting or retarding the movement and which, hence, is used to mark ends of divisions and subdivisions of form. *Melodic*: essential form of a melodic cadence is the tone of the **Primary Axis** immediately preceded by the next lower or next higher tone. *Harmonic*: essential form of a harmonic cadence is the key-axis root (**Tonic**) immediately preceded by the next lower or next higher root in the particular cycle in which the roots are moving; thus, each cycle (C_3, C_5, etc.), has its own two essential forms of cadence: the root above, or the root below, in the particular cycle or, many times, in some cycle foreign to the continuity. *Combined forms*, either for melodic cadences or harmonic cadences, are made of some combination of these elements, but with the axial element always last. In cases of so-called *half-cadence* or *deceptive cadence*, an axis other than the normal one is used.

CANTUS FIRMUS. A term from old contrapuntal theory, now used to designate what is *given* in a contrapuntal problem, usually reduced to abstract form by noting it in whole notes.

CF Symbol for **Cantus Firmus**.

CHORDAL FUNCTION ③, ⑤. In a structure, or chord, each tone may be denoted in relation to the root by a number—for example, the 3rd by a 3, and so forth. The term *function* is used to denote a 3 or a 5 or some other such interval consistently, and is used especially when **Transformations** of structure make it important to be able to identify the same interval in a series in which the position of the function may be constantly changing.

CHROMATIC ALTERATION MODULATION. See **Modulation**.

CHROMATIC GROUP. The fundamental group of three chords in **Chromatic Harmony** in which the first is diatonic, the second is chromatic, and the third is diatonic but not necessarily diatonic with respect to the key of the first. Shapes of these three are S(5) or S(7) in **Special Harmony**, but the second is preferably of S(7) structure.

CHROMATIC HARMONY. Not to be confused with harmony of some other type that has been subjected to **Chromatization**. The essence of chromatic harmony is the group of three tones chromatically related, expressible by x — x♯ — y (or: x — x♭ — y). Around each tone a **Chord** is built, a requirement being that the middle chord be of the S(7) shape. Thus the motion of chords in the continuity is determined by these groups of three. The same technique may be applied to two chromatic lines simultaneously, to three, or, in exceptional cases, to four. The groups of three may be consecutive or may overlap or may, in special cases, be simultaneous. The first and third chords are ordinarily diatonic, although they need not be diatonic with respect to the same **Pitch-Scale**. From this arises harmonic **Modulation** as a special case of chromatic harmony.

CHROMATIZATION. A process in which all whole steps (two semitones) in a part, whether the part is melodic or harmonic, are broken into two steps of one semitone each by insertion of the required chromatic.

CIRCULAR PERMUTATION. A type of **Permutation** produced by *displacing* the original group one step at a time until the original returns, as when *abc* is permuted circularly to produce *bca*, *cab*, and again *abc*.

CLIMAX. This, in terms of any given continuity, is the point at which the quantities are at maximum magnitude (negative magnitude producing a *negative* climax), no matter what the continuity is. Generally, it is the segment or segments in a composition where one or more or all **continuities** reach a maximum magnitude. *Attack climax*: maximum number of **Attacks**. *Dynamic climax*: maximum volume of tone. *Harmonic climax*: maximum number of strata and maximum number of parts with maximum permissible **Tension**. *Melodic climax*: maximum in time and in distance of pitch from the primary axis (see **Axes**). The psychological effect of the climax is heightened if the maximum magnitude is reached in a series of increasing "waves," each "wave" being higher than the last but falling back only to be succeeded by a greater magnitude until the maximum is reached (see **Resistance Forms**). The reverse of **Climax** so far as this "wave" movement is concerned is **Anti-Climax**.

CLOCK TIME. Time as measured on the clock, usually in seconds.

CLOCKWISE $\circlearrowright$ Circular motion in the same direction as that of the hands of a clock; used to differentiate in **Transformations** those in which, for example, 1-3-5 changes to 3-5-1. which is *clockwise* (as in $\binom{1}{5\ \ 3}$ from those in which 1-3-5 changes to 5-1-3, which is counter-clockwise (as in $\binom{1}{5\ \ 3}$).

CLOCKWISE POSITIONS. These are positions of structures which correspond to so-called open positions of chords. The functions of a positive structure are reckoned downwards.

CLOSED TONE. **Timbre** characterized by presence of relatively high number of **Harmonics**.

COEFFICIENT. A number by which some element in a series (which element may or may not be a number) is multiplied. *Coefficients of recurrence*: a series of coefficients used to control the number of times some element in music—a theme, or duration, or interval, or timbre, etc.—recurs.

COMBINATION TONES. See **Differential Tones**.

COMBINED HARMONIC CONTINUITY. A form of harmonic continuity consisting of segments of the various basic types—diatonic, chromatic, symmetric, diatonic-symmetric—the segments being frequently linked in some pattern by other segments. A **Hybrid** form.

COMMON CHORD. A term used in modulatory technique to denote a common-*name* chord, i.e., a chord the *names* of the pitches of which are the same as the names of the pitches of another chord without regard to accidentals.

COMMON PRODUCT. In rhythm, the number obtained by multiplying two or more numbers together, especially when **Resultants** are being derived.

COMMON UNIT METHOD OF MODULATION. See **Modulation**.

COMPLEMENTARY FACTOR. In calculating **Resultants**, the number of times a particular **Generator** recurs; found by dividing the particular generator into the **Common Product** of all the generators.

COMPOUND SIGMA. Two or more **Sigmae** interrelated by some form of **Interval Symmetry**.

CONFIGURATION. A general term meaning about the same as pattern, but including a time dimension; a selection of a specific number of specific elements arranged in a specific design.

CONSTANT B TRANSFORMATION. A special case of **Transformation**. The function denoted by *b* (usually the 3rd) remains constant while the other functions permute.

CONSTANT STRUCTURES. In harmony, use of the same chordal structure (or S) throughout a continuity. Characteristic of some types of **Symmetric Harmony**.

CONSTANT TRANSFORMATIONS. A type of **Transformation** of three or more functions, according to which one or more functions remain constant (limited by the total number of functions minus 2) while the others permute.

CONTINUITY. In music, a sequence of elements organized in time, usually of the same kind. For example, *harmonic* continuity is the sequence of harmonies considered as a whole; *orchestral* continuity is the sequence of **Orchestral Groups** considered as a whole, *dynamic* continuity is the sequence of degrees of loudness or softness considered as a whole. The principal continuities of which a composition is composed are denoted as follows:

$A^{\rightarrow}$	Attack continuity.	$\Delta^{\rightarrow}$	Density group continuity.
$T^{\rightarrow}$	Durational or rhythmic continuity.	$\Omega^{\rightarrow}$	Orchestral group continuity.
$I^{\rightarrow}$	Instrumental attack-form continuity.	$V^{\rightarrow}$	Dynamic group continuity.

$\Sigma^{\rightarrow}$ Harmonic continuity, complete, or *sigma* continuity.

CONTINUOUS IMITATION. In counterpoint, what is meant by canonic imitation; a single melody coexisting in two or more different strata of the continuity in different phases and at a constant velocity. See p. 778.

CONTINUUM. A Continuity, but with special emphasis on the concept of the continuity as a whole.

CONTRACTION GROUP. A rhythmic group consisting of two parts, the first of which is the resultant of two uniform periodicities with fractioning $(r_a \div b)$ and the second of which is the resultant of simple synchronization $(r_a \div b)$. More generally, any complex rhythmic group in which movement is from a longer to a shorter duration group, which groups contain only durations derived from the same style series. An *expansion group* consists of the same two elements, but with the longer one coming after the shorter one.

$$E = r_a \div b + r_a \div b.$$

CONTRAPUNTALIZED HARMONY. Contrapuntal continuity produced by (a) writing a harmonic continuity; (b) controlling the entrance and dropping out of individual parts by various density patterns; (c) subjecting individual parts to various kinds of melodic figuration.

CONTRAPUNTAL OSTINATO. Persistent recurrence of a segment of counterpoint accompanied in each repetition by some changing set of other musical elements, usually harmonization or additional contrapuntal lines.

CONTRARY CORRELATION. See **Correlation.**

CONTRARY MOTION. Simultaneous movement of two or more melodic lines in contrary directions.

CORRELATED MELODIES. Sehillinger's term for counterpoint, but used in a somewhat broader sense including many types of counterpoint not known to classical writers on the subject. Two or more melodic lines correlated as to (1) rhythmic continuities; (2) axial and other melodic characteristics; (3) tonal and modal relations; (4) harmonic relations.

CORRELATION. There are three main types of correlation of (a) pitch-time ratios in melody; (b) density-time displacements in composition of variations of density groups. The three types are: *parallel* when quantities increase simultaneously at the same rate; *oblique* when one series of quantities increases or decreases while the second series remains constant; *contrary* when one series increases in value while the other series decreases.

CORRELATION OF PRIMARY AXES. The planning of the interval or intervals separating two or more primary axes (see **Axes**), especially in counterpoint. See **Axis Relations.**

COS MOTION. Means *cosine motion*; see **Sine Motion** and **Ascribed Motion.**

COSINE MOTION. See **Ascribed Motion.**

COUNTERCLOCKWISE $\circlearrowleft$ See **Clockwise.**

COUNTERCLOCKWISE POSITION. "Close" positions of chords; see **Clockwise position.**

COUNTERMELODY. A second melody written in counterpoint to a given melody; an arranger's term is counter*part*.

COUNTERPOINT. See **Correlated Melodies.**

COUNTERPOINT TO GROUND MELODY. See **Ostinato.**

COUPLING. Adding to any sequence of tones, usually a melodic line, a parallel sequence either at some diatonic or absolute interval. *Diatonic*: the particular diatonic scale in use controls the exact shape of the interval of coupling. *Absolute*: the interval of coupling is measured in semitones rather than diatonically and remains constant throughout. Playing a melody in octaves is diatonic coupling at the octave. *Inward coupling*: the coupling lies below the upper parts and above the lower. *Outward coupling*: the couplings are constructed downward from the lowest part and upward from the uppermost part.

CP. Symbol ordinarily used for *counterpoint* or *countermelody*; occasionally for **Common Product.**

CROSSWISE TRANSFORMATION $\overset{a}{\underset{c}{\longleftrightarrow}}$ Denoted by $d \overset{a}{\underset{c}{\longleftrightarrow}} b$; and, as the figure illustrates, function *a* transforms into function *c* while *c* transforms into *a*, the other pair, *b* and *d*, meantime changing places in the same way. See **Transformations.**

CYCLES. These are the C_3, C_5, C_7 and their negative counterparts in the system of **Diatonic Harmony** and, by extension, in **Symmetric Harmony** as well.

D.

d Denotes one of the secondary axes; see **Axes.**

ⓓ Denotes the fourth position—forward and upside down—in **Quadrant Rotation.**

Δ, δ, $\Delta^{\rightarrow}$ See **Delta**; symbols used in composition of **Density.**

D, d Symbols sometimes used in density formulae.

d_0 Symbol for "zero displacement" of a **Pitch-Scale.** See **Displacement.** The zero displacement is no displacement at all; d_1, d_2, etc., indicate successive displacements.

d_1 1. Ordinarily indicates a scale **Displacement.** 2. Occasionally used in **Correlated Melodies** to indicate a dissonance as part of a pattern.

DELAYED RESOLUTION. A reduction of tension of a pitch assemblage accomplished, in contrast to direct resolution, with some other assemblage intervening. For example, the direct resolution in counterpoint of a 7th may be to a 6th; when a 3rd intervenes between the 7th and 6th, the resolution is delayed.

DELTA. The Greek letter Δ, referring to **Density** (textural).

DENSITY. Aside from density in the general sense of **Saturation**, or of instrumental density as a part of **Orchestration**, the term refers very specifically to the patterns made by the **Strata** actually sounding in music from moment to moment, in relation to the maximum number of **Strata** in the **Sigma Continuity.** The simplest patterns, or **Density Groups**, are developed into compound density groups (denoted by the Greek letter, *delta*) and these in turn are composed into **Density Continuity** (denoted by $\Delta^{\rightarrow}$) which, when further compounded, becomes "the delta of a delta" (analogous to the **Sigma of Sigma**) denoted by $\Delta^{\rightarrow}$ ($\Delta^{\rightarrow}$). A density group or compound may be subjected to *phasic rotation* by techniques which are fully explained in the text. These rotations are symbolized by the Greek letter, *phi*, or ϕ. When compounded, the rotations are symbolized by the Greek letter, *theta*, or Θ. The technique permits utmost control over the texture of orchestral sound. Essentially, it is the **Displacement** technique applied to two dimensions rather than one.

DENSITY OF INTERVAL. A quality similar to sonority measured roughly by the *average* number of tones sounding per octave of total range.

DIAD. A structure in harmony of but two parts.

DIATONIC. Used as an adjective, it denotes that the **Pitch-units** in question all correspond to those in some one **Diatonic Scale.**

DIATONIC HARMONY. In general, any harmony all the pitch units of which are members of, at any one time, the same **Diatonic Scale.** Specifically, one of the main types of which **Special Harmony** is composed. This is a type of harmony in which both the progressions of chords and the structures of the chords themselves are derived from the first **Expansion** of whatever scale is in use (E_1). But the term refers not alone to the seven-tone scales in general use, but also to scales (usually primitive scales) of fewer than seven tones. *Root movement* in diatonic harmony takes place in positive (reckon downward) or negative (reckon upward) cycles, the cycles being: C_3 ("cycle of the third"), downward by diatonic thirds; C_5, downward by diatonic fifths; C_7, downward by diatonic sevenths—which is the same as upward by diatonic seconds, of course. Negative forms of these cycles are measured upward instead of downward. Selection of these cycles, and the proportions and pattern in which they are used, influence profoundly the harmonic style of the resulting music. Terminal roots in the cycles constitute **Cadences.** *Structures* or chord shapes are selected from the E_1 of the scale so that the pitch-units conform to the given scale, whatever it may be. Voice-leading is effected by **Transformations** and **Doublings,** with occasional use of special pre-set **Groups of Chords.**

DIATONIC INTERVAL. An interval denoted conventionally—as a *second*, or *third*, etc,—the number of semitones in it being determined by the particular scale in effect at the time.

DIATONIC NOMENCLATURE. Naming of intervals as *unisons, seconds, thirds,* etc., in the conventional way. See **Symmetric Nomenclature.**

DIATONIC SCALE. A **Pitch-Scale** with the following characteristics: (1) it has but one **Tonic;** (2) its range is not more than one octave, as a scale; (3) no pitch-name (A, B, C, D, etc.) is used more than once in the scale; (4) the scale may have any one set of accidentals in its **Real Signature** at a time. The conventional form is that of the seven-tone major or minor scale; but the definition also includes (a) scales of fewer than seven tones conforming to the requirements given above; (b) modal scales that conform to the requirements.

DIATONIC-SYMMETRIC HARMONY. A **Hybrid** form, in which the **Roots** move in the **Cycles** of **Diatonic Harmony** but the chordal structures, as in **Symmetric Harmony,** follow a pattern independent of the diatonic system, being chosen usually for their particular sonorities. Schillinger calls this harmony Type II and bases it on chord structures employing variants of the diatonic triad $4 + 3$—that is, $3 + 4$ (minor), $4 + 4$ (augmented) and $3 + 3$ (diminished).

DIFFERENCE TONES. See **Differential Tones.**

DIFFERENTIAL TONES. Tones produced by a pair of tones sounding together. The **Frequency** of a differential tone is equal to the frequency of the higher tone of the pair minus the frequency of the lower tone.

DIRECTIONAL UNIT. A group of tones attached to and including a **Neutral Unit** in **General Harmony.** A neutral unit is a chordal tone of a structure. The directional unit always has the neutral unit as a member and must consist of at least one other tone. This other tone is either a semitone, or two semitones, or a diatonic step removed from the neutral unit—and any additional tones in the directional unit must either lead into the neutral unit or into some other tone which itself is a leading tone. Using these directional units sequently, the requirement is that the neutral unit or chordal tone be sounded *last.* Directional units in various forms constitute the general form of all melodic figuration and, indeed, of melody itself. What is important about them, so far as style is concerned, is the answers to these questions: (1) which neutral units are equipped with directionals? (2) what is the interval or intervallic pattern of the directional unit? (3) in what direction (upward or downward) are they constructed?

DISPLACEMENT. The process of forming new groups by rearranging (permuting) the elements of the original group one place at a time, as when *cdefg* becomes *defgc.* Each element is shifted one place to the left, and the leftmost element is shifted to the extreme right. In this case *c, d, e, f, g* would be indicated by d_0, and called **zero displacement,** while *d, e, f, g, c* would, be indicated by d_1, called *first displacement.* Displacement scales of the natural major scale on C yield the various so-called ecclesiastic modes.

DISSONANT INTERVALS. In classical theory, the diatonic unison, octave, fifth, sixth and third (sometimes the fourth, especially when occurring in inner voices or when supported by a third below it) are regarded as consonant; all other intervals are regarded as dissonant. For these older concepts, however, Schillinger substitutes the notion of *tension* of interval; substitutes the notion of *reduction of tension* for the classical concept of *resolution;* requires reduction only of such intervals as are acoustically of higher tension than the diatonic third; and points out that conventionally consonant intervals become dissonant in low register and that conventionally dissonant intervals become acoustically consonant in high register.

DISTRIBUTIVE CUBE. See **Distributive Powers.**

DISTRIBUTIVE INVOLUTION GROUP. Groups of numbers consisting of a polynomial raised to some power and arranged distributively. See **Distributive Powers.**

DISTRIBUTIVE POWERS. A series of values derived by raising any polynomial to any power but keeping it in distributive form. For example, the *non*-distributive square of $3 + 2$ is 25, but the distributive square is $9 + 6 + 6 + 4$. The binomial $a + b$, squared is normally $a^2 + 2ab + b^2$, but *distributively* it is $aa + ab + ba + bb$. Distributive powers are used frequently by Schillinger as a means of controlling durations and other characteristics of music.

DISTRIBUTIVE SQUARE. See **Distributive Powers.**

DOUBLE PARALLEL CHROMATICS. One variety of **Chromatic Harmony.**

DOUBLING. When a **Chordal Function** appears twice in the same **Chord,** it is said to be **Doubled.** Not to be confused with **Coupling.**

DURABILITY OF TONE. In **Orchestration,** the characteristic of the tone that depends essentially on its duration, judged according to a **Scale** the extremes of which are *legatissimo* and *staccatissimo.*

DURATION. Extent in time, measured chronologically in **Clock Time** and musically in the time-values of notes; measured on a **Graph** by extension along the **Abscissa.**

DURATIONAL CONTINUITY. A **Continuity** composed of **Durational Groups.**

DURATION GROUP. A group of one or more durations in time.

DYNAMIC CONTINUITY. A **Continuity** composed of **Dynamic Groups.**

DYNAMIC GROUP. A group of degrees of volume, such as *pp-mf-ppp.*

DYNAMIC MARKS. Marks such as *pp, mf,* etc. Schillinger stresses that these marks now give directions to the performers, whereas in Beethoven's time they indicated the dynamics as experienced by the listener.

DYNAMICS. In orchestration, the adjustment of other factors to the desire for loudness or softness of tone. Schillinger differentiates between volume of tone as measured logarithmically by **Amplitude.** and the *psychological* effect of loudness which can be created by multiplicity of **Strata** and the resulting large number of upper **Harmonics.**

E.

E_0 Symbol for a **Pitch-Scale** in "zero expansion," i. e., the scale cannot be contracted in the given system of tuning. E_1, E_2, etc., ordinarily indicate further **Expansions** of a scale. See **Tonal Expansion;** also Vol. I, p. 133. These same abbreviations are used occasionally for various **Expositions** in **Thematic Continuity.**

ECCLESIASTICAL MODES. A system of denoting various diatonic scales worked out in mediaeval times on the basis of a misunderstanding of the much earlier Greek modal system. For both the Greek and the Ecclesiastical system, Schillinger substitutes the general procedure of **Displacement,** so that no matter what scale is used (denoted d_0, or "zero displacement") the successive displacements or modes (denoted d_1, d_2, etc.) may be readily derived and controlled.

ELEMENT. In a **Series** or **Sequent Group,** the single items of which the series or group is made, whatever may be the nature of these items, whether numeral or musical or both.

EQUAL TEMPERAMENT. A tuning system (developed by Andreas Werckmeister in 1691) according to which the octave is divided into 12 pitches by relating the frequencies of each pitch to a logarithmic series consisting of the twelfth root of 2, $(\sqrt[12]{2})$ which 2 is successively raised to the zero power, first power, square, cube, fourth power and so on up to the 12th power. Remaining pitches are derived by octave duplication. See pp. 101, 102 and 146.

EXPANSION. E_0, E_1, E_2, etc., denote a segment of music, especially a **Pitch-Scale,** subjected to **Geometrical Projection** so that the pitch is increased by some constant factor, the results being interpreted either exactly or tonally (diatonically). See **Geometrical Projections** and **Tonal Expansion.**

EXPANSION GROUP. See **Contraction Group.**

EXPOSITION. Essentially, a **Thematic Group,** or "setting forth" of a **Thematic Unit;** used especially in contrapuntal forms. Schillinger tends to substitute **Thematic Group** for this term in the latter portion of his manuscript.

F.

FORMS OF RESISTANCE. See **Resistance Forms.**

FRACTIONING. The process of splitting a **Duration** into fragments, usually in proportion to some polynomial of the **Style Series.**

FRAGMENTATION. In composition of thematic continuity, the use of a selected fragment of the total theme in order to shorten the duration of a particular thematic group.

FREQUENCY. In acoustics, the rate of vibration of a vibrating medium; expressed in terms of vibrations per second.

FRULATO. Flutter-tonguing.

FUNCTION. See **Chordal Function.**

FUNDAMENTAL HARMONY SCALE. See **Harmony Scale, Fundamental.**

FUNDAMENTAL TONE. In acoustics, the pitch produced by vibration of the whole of the vibrating medium, in contrast to **Harmonics** produced by vibrations of segments of the medium.

G.

G6 In **Diatonic Harmony** a special **Group of Chords** used as a unit. See p. 415.

G$\frac{6}{4}$ A special **Group of Chords** used as a unit. See p. 427.

GENERAL HARMONY. Schillinger's term for his technology for the development of **Pitch-Assemblages** and for organization of these into sequent groups. It is a technology embracing all the *tonal* material of music—*tonal*, as distinct from temporal (rhythmic) or instrumental material. A pitch-assemblage is any set of **Pitch-Units** or tones taken together; it means what is meant by *chord*, except that (1) a pitch-assemblage frequently includes a great many more tones than are found in the chords of conventional harmony. (2) the arrangement of these tones need not correspond to the conventional structures built on diatonic thirds. The tones of a pitch-assemblage may sound sequently—one after the other—as well as simultaneously. The complete harmonic continuity is denoted by $\Sigma^{\longrightarrow}$ (to be read, "sigma continuity"). It is made up of a series of individual pitch-assemblages, each denoted by the Greek letter, *sigma*, Σ. Each sigma is, in turn, composed of a number of substructures or *strata*, each denoted by S, and each S consists of one or more *units* (usually called **parts**, denoted by *p*). The significant factors are: (1) the movement of the root tones of each stratum; (2) the pattern of intervals by which the various tones of each stratum are grouped around the root; (3) the spacing of strata; (4) the **Transformations** to which strata are subjected; and, finally, (5) the presence or absence of **Directional Units** within each stratum. Special aspects of general harmony are discussed under **Special Harmony** and under other subheadings in this glossary.

GENERATOR. A pattern of durations (usually a monomial) used in combination with another pattern to produce a new durational pattern, known as a **Resultant.** More simply, a series of sounds, notes or attacks of given duration.

GEOMETRICAL MUTATIONS. See **Geometrical Projections.**

GEOMETRICAL PROJECTIONS. A fundamental technique for variation. Any theme may be subjected to **Quadrant Rotation** to produce four forms: the original; the original backward in time; the original upside down as to pitch and backward in time; and the original upside down as to pitch and forward in time. The pitch may be multiplied by some factor, such as 2, 3, 4, etc., resulting in **Expansion.** The reverse process results in **Contraction**; but often this cannot be realized in our tuning system. Durations may also be increased or contracted. When the process of pitch expansion is done precisely, that is, with a graph divided into semitones, the results are called *geometrical*; when it is done diatonically, that is, with a graph divided according to some diatonic scale, the results are called tonal. The special forms resulting from these processes are thus: **Geometrical Expansion, Geometrical Contraction, Tonal Expansion, Tonal Contraction, Quadrant Rotation.** Temporal contraction and expansion are terms for operations on the time dimension as noted above.

GRAPH. A means of representing music by denoting the pitch of each tone according to the distance measured vertically and the duration of each tone by the distance measured horizontally. Paper ruled in small squares is usually used. Graphing may be (and preferably should be) *absolute*, that is, pitches should be measured in semitones in the 12-tone system; but it may be done diatonically, that is, having each pitch-line represent a tone of a **Diatonic Scale.**

GRAPHING. Specifically, notation of music in graph form, with the ordinate (up-down coordinate) representing pitch and the abscissa (left-right coordinate) representing time.

GROUND BASS. See **Ostinato.**

GROUND MELODY. See **Ostinato.**

GROUP. Used in the usual sense, except that it should be kept in mind that a group may consist of but one element and even, under some circumstances, of zero elements.

GROUP OF CHORDS. In **Diatonic Harmony** and occasionally in **Symmetric Harmony,** a *group* is a pre-set sequence of chords handled outside the prevailing system of cycles. They represent progressions influenced strongly by contrapuntal considerations. See page 415 ff.

H.

H Symbol used ordinarily for a harmonic structure, or chord.

$H^{\rightarrow}$ Symbol used for **Harmonic Continuity.**

HARMONIC. Used to refer to tonal materials in their mathematical connotation, i.e., pertaining to simple ratios. Not to be confused with "harmony" in its musical connotation, i.e., simultaneous pitch-assemblages varied in sequence.

HARMONIC CONTINUITY. A series of sequent **Pitch-Assemblages** arranged after each other in time in a certain order. Denoted either as $H^{\rightarrow}$ or, more fundamentally, as $\Sigma^{\rightarrow}$.

HARMONIC CORRELATION. See **Correlation of Primary Axes.**

HARMONIC INTERVALS. Two tones sounding simultaneously, in contrast to Melodic Intervals.

HARMONIC PROGRESSION. The pattern in which **Pitch-Assemblages (Chords)** follow one another, controlled especially by the pattern of roots; see **General Harmony.**

HARMONICS. Subcomponents of a sound wave, often called **Partials,** resulting from physical factors which convert a simple sound wave (or **Sine** wave) into a wave of more complex form. In music the term is used ordinarily to refer to one or more members of the **Natural Harmonic Series** in relation to a particular **Fundamental Tone,** and, in orchestration, to tones produced by stringed and certain other instruments.

HARMONIZATION OF HARMONY. A process by which, to a given harmonic continuity, one or more additional *harmonic* continuities are developed.

HARMONY. In the composition of music, the science of **Pitch-Assemblages** treated both individually (one by one) and in sequent groups (one after another). The foundation of Schillinger's harmony is **General Harmony,** which is the technology of all possible systems of harmony. A special variety of **General Harmony** is the kind of harmony usually (but not exclusively) found in Western music. **Special Harmony** in turn consists of four main types: **Diatonic Harmony; Diatonic-Symmetric Harmony; Symmetric Harmony;** and **Chromatic Harmony.**

HARMONY SCALE, FUNDAMENTAL. The E_1 (first **Expansion**) of any scale in *b* position as to **Quadrant Inversion**; from this are derived the various cyclic forms of root progression. If E_0 is *c-d-e-f-g-a-b-c*, then E_1 is *c-e-g-b-d-f-a-c*, and E_1 ⓑ is *c-a-f-d-b-g-e-c*.

HARMONY, TYPES OF. Schillinger classifies harmony by types as follows: Type I. Diatonic; Type II. Diatonic-Symmetric; Type III. Symmetric; Type IV. Chromatic.

HETEROGENEITY. Characteristic of **Groups** when the timbres in a single group are different, in contrast to **Homogeneity.**

HEXAD. A chord of six tones.

HOMOGENEITY. A characteristic of **Groups** of timbres when the timbres are similar, in contrast to **Heterogeneity.**

HYBRID. A term used to denote mixtures of type, as in *hybrid rhythmic style* (a mixture of groups deriving from more than one style-series); *hybrid harmonic continuity* (a mixture of more than one type of harmonic continuity). *Hybrid 5-part harmony* ordinarily consists of normal 4-part harmony to which an extra stratum (of one part; Sp = 1) has been added.

HYBRID HARMONIC CONTINUITY. Continuity composed of more than one main type of harmonic continuity; as in the mixture of diatonic and chromatic, for example.

i Abbreviation for *interval*.

I Abbreviation ordinarily used for **Instrumental Group.**

IDENTICAL MOTIF   One of three methods of melodic **Modulation**; a melodic pattern
in one key is followed by the same pattern in the new key.

IDENTITY OF INTERVAL METHOD. A means of deriving from a given **Pitch-Scale** one
or more additional scales that possess the same intonational characteristics; the intervals of
the original scale are permuted so that all appear in the derivative scale but in a different
order.

IDENTITY OF PITCH-UNITS METHOD. A method of deriving additional and related
Pitch-Scales from a given scale. Some or all of the pitch-units of the given scale are used,
but in different sequence. **Displacements** ("modes") of scales, for example, have the same
pitch-units as the scales from which they are derived, but in a different order.

INDIRECT MODULATION. Any type of sequence in which the ultimate **Key-Axis** is reached
by way of one or more intermediate keys in some fashion *other than* that by which the intermediate keys represent a one-by-one accumulation of flats or sharps. The one-by-one movement toward a "sharp" key is along the pattern, C - G - D - A - E - B - F♯ - C♯ - G♯, and there
is a similar pattern, in fifths downward, rather than upward, for "flat" keys. Any modulatory movement that *departs from* this pattern is called *indirect.*

INDIRECT RESOLUTION. See **Delayed Resolution.**

INSTRUMENTAL FORM. Schillinger never uses this term to indicate what is commonly
known as "musical form," but rather to suggest the modification of a tonal continuity by
various sequences of attack for actual performance on an instrument. It is a factor of great
importance in composition. See **Attack-Form.**

INTERFERENCE. A phenomenon observed in all fields of wave motion—sound, light, radio.
It refers to the crossing or synchronization of two waves which results in a third wave that
is the summation of the two. Schillinger uses the term to refer to the combination of two
continuously repeating sounds of different durations. *The Theory of Rhythm* (Book I) is
based on this phenomenon .... Interference is also used by Schillinger in another sense.
When two or more groups of elements consisting of nonidentical numbers of terms are combined by pairing, the two do not "come out even," so that the process must be repeated a
number of times until the two terminate together. This is the fundamental form of interference and may be applied on many levels in music.

INTERLUDE. Although Schillinger occasionally uses this term in the conventional way to indicate a "bridge" or "passage" connecting two **Expositions** of a **Thematic Unit,** he prefers
to treat all segments, no matter how episodic, as **Thematic Groups.**

INTERVAL SYMMETRY. Used of **Strata** or **Sigmae,** this term means that two or more
strata or sigmae are separated as to pitch level so that the pattern of intervals determining
the degree of separation is *symmetrical.*

INTONATION. Schillinger regards the fundamental material of music as being essentially *temporal* (that is, consisting of time elements), or *tonal* (that is, dealing with frequencies or pitches).
Intonation or "intonational" are used throughout the text to refer to the pitches and pitch
material in contrast to the temporal or durational material.

INTONATIONAL MODIFICATION. A generalized description of the several techniques of
producing variations based on changes in the **Pitch-Units** of a **Thematic Unit,** specifically
permutation of pitch-units; modal transposition or other scale modification by change of
accidentals in **Real Signatures**; **Tonal Expansions, Quadrant Rotation** and **Geometrical
Projections** in general; development of **Directional Units**; change in range of **Tension** in
relation between harmony and melody, or **Reharmonization.**

INVARIANT OF INVERSION. In inversions (see **Geometrical Projections**), especially of
chords, the element (tone) which does not change—i. e., the axis around which inversion
takes place.

INVERSION. See **Quadrant Rotation, Geometrical Projections** and **Tonal Inversion.**

K.

KEY-AXIS. See **Axes.**

L.

LEADING TONE. A tone which inevitably moves to an adjacent tone, especially to a **Tonic,** a primary axis (see **Axes**), or a **Neutral Unit.** See p. 1169.

LINEAR COMPOSITION. Assembly of **Pitch-Units** and **Durations** into a **Melody** by the axial method, usually by **Graphing.**

LOGARITHM. A mathematical term referring to the **Power** to which a certain constant base must be raised to produce a given number.

LOGARITHMIC RELATION. Interrelation between two series corresponding to the interrelation between the series of cardinal numbers and their logarithms.

M.

M Symbol used ordinarily for a melodic form, or **Sectional Scale.** Also used occasionally to indicate a *major tetrachord.*

M₁ M, meaning *melody,* is used with subscript numerals when more than one melody is in question, as in **Correlated Melodies.**

m₁, m₂ Abbreviations for two minor tetrachord forms.

MAJOR GENERATOR. In the making of **Resultant** rhythms, the larger of two generators.

MANIFOLD. A set of elements which is itself the result of selection and from which further selection can be made; the manifold determines the limitations on musical material of some kind.

MEAN, ARITHMETICAL. See **Arithmetical Mean.**

MELODIC FIGURATION. A process by which a **Harmonic Continuity** is converted into continuity having some characteristics of counterpoint but less highly organized; used by Schillinger in contrast to **Melodization.** The technique consists of subjecting one or more parts of the continuity to alteration by means of **Directional Units** developed for each **Neutral Unit.** The elements of melodic figuration may be classified according to 1) direction (ascending, descending), 2) chordal function (1-13), 3) adherence to scale, and 4) number of elements employed simultaneously.

MELODIC INTERVAL. Two tones considered as sounding one after the other.

MELODIC PATTERN. Specifically in Schillinger's system, the pattern of secondary axes (see **Axes**) in melody without special regard to the pitch and time dimensions; denoted by **MP.**

MELODIZATION. Construction of a melodic continuity in correlation with a given harmonic continuity.

MELODY. A special case of a **Pitch-Scale** possessing a higher degree of organization, especially a primary axis and a number of secondary axes (see **Axes**) arranged with a view to **Climax** and with a view to certain general forms of **Trajectorial Motion.** Melodies may differ as to the degree of organization introduced into them; they may take complex forms related to the patterns used for **Thematic Continuity.**

MINOR GENERATOR. In the synchronization of two generators (usually two uniform periodicities), the generator of lower numerical value.

MODAL TRANSPOSITION. Alteration of the mode (or scale displacement), effected practically by changing the **Real Signature.**

MODERNIZED PRIMITIVE. An **Original Primitive** scale subjected to development by a technique that converts the span of the original scale into a span for a symmetrical harmonic scale.

MODIFIED RECURRENCE GROUP. In composition of thematic sequences, a sequence in which some one polynomial group recurs but with the elements of the polynomial subjected to permutations in each recurrence.

MODULATION. A general process for shift of primary and/or key-axes (see **Axes**). Melodic modulation affects the melodic line only and may involve only a change or **Displacement** of mode. Harmonic modulation involves a shift of key axis and of **Real Signature.** The general process is called configurational modulation, aiming at neutralization of the previous key and establishment of the new; it takes practical form in three general methods: (1) **Common Unit Method,** emphasis of tones common to the two keys; (2) **Chromatic method,** singling out of the tones not in common and chromatic alteration of these; (3) **Identical Motif Method,** sounding of a conspicuous motif in one key and then in the second key, uniting the two by the common motif. In harmony the method takes practical form in (1) chromatic modulations, discussed as a variety of **Chromatic Harmony**; and (2) symmetrical modulations. Choice of key-axis is determined by pattern; see **Indirect Modulations.**

MONOMIAL. A group consisting of but one element.

MONOMIAL PERIODICITY. A series composed of a repetition of the same (**Monomial**) number, applied usually to **Durations.**

MONOTHEMATIC. A composition with but a single **Thematic Unit.**

N.

NATURAL HARMONIC SERIES. This is the set of overtones or partials produced by a single tone, the original tone (or fundamental) being included in the series as the first term.

NEGATIVE CYCLES. The standard cycles of diatonic harmony, but measured in an upward direction rather than downward. See **Cycles.**

NEGATIVE FORMS OF STRUCTURES. A chord reckoned downward instead of upward. In harmony of negative cycles, negative forms are used; they derive from positive-cycle harmony in the b (backward) quadrant inversion. See **Negative Cycles.**

NEUTRAL MELODIC FIGURATION. Melodic figuration achieved without regard to any pre-set melodic forms, but rather developed by selection of devices used in any combination. A term used in contrast to **Thematic Melodic Figuration.**

NEUTRAL UNIT. A *chordal* tone in a **Structure** in **General Harmony.**

NOMOGRAPHY. Any scientific system of recording natural phenomena; in particular, graphic notation of music.

O.

ω Symbol for **Omega** (small). Ω Symbol for **Omega** (capital).

OBLIQUE CORRELATION. See **Correlation.**

OCTAVE DUPLICATION. Derivation of one pitch from another so that the derived pitch is distant by one or more octaves from the initial pitch.

OMEGA. The Greek letter used in its capital and small forms to designate orchestral groups and orchestral thematic units.

OPEN POSITION. A structure is said to be in *closed position* when the numbers of its functions when read downward proceed in a counter clockwise direction; any other distribution of these functions, especially in a clockwise direction, is called an *open position. Extra-open* position means that there is room for two such intermediate functions.

OPEN TONE. A timbral description, denoting a tone characterized by a very small quantity of partials, ideally with no partials at all.

ORCHESTRAL CONTINUITY. A **Continuity** formed of one or more sequent **Orchestral Groups.**

ORCHESTRAL GROUP. A group of timbres in orchestration, selected (a) with regard to **Homogeneity** or **Heterogeneity**; and (b) with regard to one or more of these three factors: 1, a type of a **Timbre**; 2, **Dynamics**; 3, **Durability of tone.**

ORCHESTRATION. In music, the science of individual characteristics of sound-producing instruments and ways of combining them; specifically, in this system, the science of composing **Orchestral Continuity** and correlating it with the other **Continuities** of which music is made. Subject to the limits of what is practically possible for the instruments used, **Orchestral Groups** are formed in various combinations or for various purposes. These are assembled into the continuity.

ORDER. A practical term referring to the way one thing comes after another, but difficult to define rigidly. *Higher order* refers to a process of any kind which is performed on the results of another process of the same kind; for example, *squaring a square*, or *grouping a group*, is a *higher order* operation.

ORDINATE. In **Graph,** the measurement vertically, up and down, denoting pitch in music.

ORGAN POINT. See **Pedal Point.**

ORIGINAL PRIMITIVE. A term denoting a **Pitch-Scale** or scales used in some type of primitive music, the scale being in its original form (usually of fewer than seven pitches) but being subjected, for purposes of contemporary music, to adjustment to equal temperament tuning.

OSTINATO. Persistent repetition of a group of any kind, while other musical components change; usually, a *melodic ostinato* (repeated melody with changing harmonic continuities), a *contrapuntal ostinato* (repeated contrapuntal continuity i.e., a repeated melody combined with changing countermelodies), a *harmonic ostinato* (repeated configuration of successive chords, variously melodized) or a *rhythmic ostinato* (repeated durational group).

P

ϕ See **Phi.**

p Symbol ordinarily used for part, either in orchestration or in harmony.

P Abbreviation occasionally for **Permutation.**

P. A. Abbreviation for primary axis; see **Axes.**

PARALLEL CHROMATICS. See **Chromatic Harmony.**

PARALLEL CORRELATION. See **Contrary Correlation.**

PART. In harmony, a specific layer in the harmony, such as the "second from the bottom", "third from the bottom," etc. A part (p) is an element of a **Stratum** in **General Harmony,** and also an element in instrumental continuity.

PARTIALS. See **Harmonics.**

PART-MELODIZATION. Use of one or more parts of one or more strata in general harmony, as a source of melodic shapes.

PASSING TONES. *Chromatic* passing-tones are the result of inserting a half-step movement into a **Melodic Interval** originally of a whole step; *diatonic* passing tones are tones inserted into an interval of a third or more, and converting the interval into seconds. All passing tones, whether diatonic or chromatic, are special forms of **Directional Units.**

PEDAL POINT. Used by Schillinger for the most part in the conventional sense, but with special observations as to *location* in the thematic continuity, use in producing **Climax,** and means of determining what structures are permissible for use in a pedal point.

PENTAD. A chord of five tones.

PENTANOMIAL. A group consisting of five elements.

PERIODICITY. The continuous repetition of notes, sounds, or attacks. *Uniform* periodicity means that the groups of attacks are of identical duration. Such groups may include one or more terms. When they include only one term—a series of quarter notes, eighth notes, etc., then we have monomial periodicity. Uniform periodicity may, however, involve groups of more than one term.

PERMUTATION. The process of rearranging the members of a group as to sequence. *General* permutations (or logical permutations) are exhaustive, that is, they involve every possible arrangement that can be made. Circular permutations constitute a special set within the general set involving clockwise or counterclockwise patterns of alteration; see **Circular Permutations.** Permutation is a fundamental process (applied to **Pitch-Units,** intervals, chordal structures, durations, or any element) for development of groups.

PHASIC ROTATION ( ) ( ) ↶ ↷. In the composition of densities, a process for variation by displacement of any given group, the displacement taking place along the time-axis, or along the density axis, or both.

PHI ϕ The Greek letter used to refer to phasic rotation; see **Density.**

PITCH. The "highness" or "lowness" of a tone as measured by its **Frequency.** "Concert *a*" today is 440.6 per second.

PITCH-AGGREGATIONS. See **Structure.**

PITCH-NAME. The name of a pitch in alphabetical terminology (A, B, C, etc.).

PITCH-SCALES. A sequence of pitch-units in order of increasing or decreasing frequency of pitch. Schillinger's classification of scales is in four groups. *Group One*: Scales with one tonic and not more than one octave in range. *Group Two*: Scales with one tonic and more than one octave in range; they are obtained by **Expansions** of scales in the first group. *Group Three*: Scales of more than one tonic and of not more than one octave in range. Scales are symmetrical, containing equal number of semitones between tonics. *Group Four*: Scales of more than one tonic, and more than one octave in range; these scales are symmetrical. In the most generalized form, scales of groups one and two are regarded as special cases of symmetrical scales in which the points of symmetry are one or more octaves apart. Groups three and four are further classified according to the number of tonics.

PITCH-TIME RATIO. In melody, the ratio between the maximum pitch to which a secondary axis (see **Axes**) rises or falls, and the time it takes the axis to reach this point. See also **Contrary Correlation.**

PITCH-UNIT. A **Pitch** or tone; any one of the tones that go to make up a **Manifold** of pitches, usually determined first by a **Tuning System** and then by **Pitch-Scale.**

PLOTTED MELODY. A melody constructed by the graphing (or plotting) method: one or more primary axes are located; groups of secondary axes are developed to the primary axis or axes; a rhythm is constructed; the rhythm is superimposed on the secondary axes, the result being interpreted in terms of a selected scale or of a given harmonic continuity.

POLYMODAL. In describing interrelations of two melodic lines, this term indicates that the two are not in the same mode or displacement. See **Unimodal.**

POLYNOMIAL. A group consisting of more than one element.

POLYTHEMATIC. A composition with more than one **Thematic Unit.**

POLYTONAL. In describing interrelations of two or more melodic lines, this term indicates that the **Real Key** of each line is different. Note that Schillinger's concept of *Polytonal* is somewhat different from the conventional use of the term to describe music in which different keys are used simultaneously.

POWER. The result of multiplying a number by itself a designated number of times. A *zero* power of any number is the number, 1. The *first* power of a number is the number itself. A *negative* power is the power of the number divided into the integer, 1. In Schillinger's system, powers are almost always used as **Distributive Powers.**

POWER SERIES. A **Series** in which the terms are successive **Powers** of some constant number.

PP, PU. See **Axis Relations.**

PRESELECTION. Same as **Selection,** but with emphasis on the fact that the decisions are made some time in advance of actual composition. See **Pre-Set.**

PRE-SET. This adjective, of considerable importance in Schillinger's system, means that the characteristics of some factor in a musical continuity are determined in advance of actual composition, the "settings" being chosen according to specific desired effects.

PRIMARY AXIS. See **Axes.**

PRIME NUMBER SERIES. A series composed of cardinal numbers which are divisible without remainder only by the integer 1 and themselves.

PRIMITIVE. See **Original Primitive, Stylized Primitive, Modernized Primitive.**

PROGRESSION. See **Harmonic Progression.**

PROGRESSIVE SYMMETRY. A form of **Thematic Sequence** in which the successive groups first "grow" by the addition of more and more themes, then "decline" by the subtraction of more and more themes, the whole being arranged symmetrically.

PYRAMIDS. An arrangers' term denoting an orchestral *arpeggio*, each tone of which, once sounded, is sustained—the whole being produced by successive entrances of instruments on various chordal tones.

Q

Q Symbol ordinarily used for *quality* in construction of **Quality Scales.**

QUADRANT ROTATION. Once music has been reduced to graph form, the original graph (denoted as ⓐ) will produce three additional forms. These are: ⓑ the original backward in time; ⓒ the original backward in time and upside down as to pitch; ⓓ the original forward in time but upside down in pitch. In this process the intervals are calculated exactly in semitones and they are reckoned from some specific tone selected as the **Axis Of Inversion**. When the intervals are calculated in the diatonic manner, the result is **Tonal Inversion**.

QUADRUPLE PARALLEL CHROMATICS. Special form used in **Chromatic Harmony**.

QUANTITATIVE SCALE. A scale developed from a chromatic (or occasionally symmetric) harmonic continuity, the scale consisting of a selected set of pitch units occurring in the continuity. It is enough that tones selected be frequent enough to afford a good choice in melodization; this means that in some cases a tone appearing frequently may be omitted in order to simplify the scale finally chosen. This is also a technique for diatonic melodization of chromatic harmonic continuity.

R.

r Symbol for **Resultant**.

R Abbreviation for single-reed tone in **Orchestration**.

RR Abbreviation for double-reed tone in **Orchestration**.

RANGE OF TENSION. In melodization of harmony or in harmonization of melody, the maximum variation permitted in **Tension**. Minimum tension is present so far as this relation is concerned when the melodic tone is a tone also present in the harmony. The range of tension may be **Pre-Set** as a means of controlling the harmonic style of the music.

REAL SCALE. See **Real Signature**.

REAL SIGNATURE. In conventional music notation, all signatures used are those associated with major diatonic scales, and these constitute the key-signatures as they appear on the staves. When scales other than major or natural minor are used, however, the written notes acquire a uniform set of accidentals which, if arranged in signature form, would constitute the *real signature*. A melody written in harmonic minor starting on *c*, for example, has a conventional signature of three flats (as for Eb major) but has a *real* signature consisting of Eb, and Ab *only*. There is no reason, except convention, for not making the real signature function as the actual signature on the staff—and, indeed, a very few composers sometimes do this. Real signatures may have both flats and sharps. See page 123.

RECTIFICATION. 1). Chromatic alteration of a chordal tone in chromatic harmony made necessary by the chromatic alteration of some other tone. The necessity arises from the need to avoid major seconds or augmented thirds (perfect fourths). The tone that has been rectified is not required to resolve, by a further semitone, in contrast to the requirement for the tone originally modified. 2). In rhythmic treatment of harmonic continuity, rectification refers to that point in time where all voices finally arrive together at the points required by the new chord, after various movements of voices and mixtures of adjacent chords resulting from different rhythms in the several parts have occurred.

RESISTANCE FORMS. Melodic or harmonic (stratum) motion that corresponds to the increases and decreases of movement characteristic of a specific force overcoming a specific resistance. Ordinarily, some type of **Rotary Movement**.

RESOLUTION OF DISSONANCES. In Schillinger's generalized contrapuntal technique, the practice of dividing intervals into hard-and-fast classes labelled "consonance" and "dissonance" is abandoned in favor of a graded classification according to tension. With this he introduced the principle of "resolution" of high-tension intervals by reduction of tension. Unless intentionally dissonant counterpoint is desired, intervals of a tension higher than the thirds need only to have their tensions reduced, not necessarily in the classical manner. But for production of counterpoint of the classical type, various additional procedures are to be followed, the set of procedures depending on the period-style of counterpoint desired. The main criteria are (1) judgments at various periods in musical history as to what intervals *require* resolution; (2) judgments as to the *period of time* in which the resolution must be accomplished; (3) judgments as to what movements of parts constitute an acceptable resolution.

RESOLUTION OF INTERVALS. See **Resolution of Dissonances**.

RESULTANT. In **Rhythm,** the pattern of **Durations** that results when two or more **Period-icities** (usually but not always **Monomial**) are **Synchronized.** The periodicities are called *generators.*

RESULTANT OF ACCELERATION. A special form of **Resultant** in which an **Acceleration Series** is synchronized with itself backwards.

RHYTHM. The organization in time of the durations involved in music. In Schillinger's system, rhythm refers not only to what is ordinarily called rhythm, that is, the division of time within a single measure or small group of measures (**Fractional Rhythm**), but also to the way in which the measures themselves are organized into groups (**Factorial Rhythm**). According to the *fractional* technique, a single duration of time of any length is subdivided binomially (into two parts), trinomially (into three parts), or polynomially (into *n* parts) according to one or more **Style-Series.** The results of this subdivision, or fractioning, are the rhythm. The results may be subjected to factorial technique, by which a group of durations is developed into larger groups. Such results may be distributed in a number of ways over a number of simultaneous instrumental parts. Every aspect of music is, in Schillinger's system, controlled fundamentally by his rhythmic techniques . . . . . Schillinger does not restrict the concept of rhythm to time and the durations of attacks. He deals also with 1). instrumental rhythm—the pattern according to which instruments enter and leave an ensemble; 2). intonational rhythm—the pattern of pitches in a phrase; and 3). harmonic rhythm—the pattern of harmonic groups in a sequence.

RHYTHM OF CHORD-PROGRESSION. The pattern that consists, one after the other, of the durations in which each successive chord or pitch-assemblage is being sounded, simultaneously or sequently. Practically, the rhythm of changes in the pitch of the root.

ROOT (ROOT TONE). The particular tone from which all other tones of a **Pitch-Assemblage** or **Pitch-Scale** are derived and/or reckoned. Used of a **Pitch-Scale,** it refers always to the **Real Key.**

ROTATION. See **Quadrant Rotation.**

ROTARY MOVEMENT. Movement of a melody or a stratum circulating above and below an **Axis** which, when graphed, produces a wave-like curve. May be based on simple circular or **Sine** forms, or on spirals of various sorts, mainly those representing some **Summation Series.**

RUBATO. An alteration in the durations of tones, ordinarily accomplished by the performer in deviation from the written notation. Regarded by Schillinger as best denoted in actual notation, and as best accomplished by introducing a standard unit of deviation, by which unit a balanced binomial may be unbalanced, or an unbalanced binomial may be balanced.

S.

Σ See **Sigma.**

S(5). A structure (chord) corresponding to the normal triad of conventional diatonic harmony. $S_1(5)$ is the *major* triad (a major third topped by a minor third, or, in **Symmetric Notation,** $4 + 3$); $S_2(5)$, *minor* triad; $S_3(5)$, *augmented* triad; $S_4(5)$, *diminished* triad.

S(7). This denotes a seventh-chord shape. In **Special Harmony** the specific varieties, correlated with their normal terminology and intervals (reading upward in semitones), are: $S(7)_1$ or $S_1(7)$, *major* seventh, 4-3-4; $S(7)_2$, *minor* seventh, 3-4-3; $S(7)_3$, *large* seventh, 4-3-3; $S(7)_4$, *small* seventh, 3-3-4; $S(7)_5$, *diminished* seventh, 3-3-3; $S(7)_6$, *augmented* I, 4-4-3; $S(7)_7$, *augmented* II, 3-4-4

Sp. To be read, "stratum equals (or consists of) one part."

S2p. A stratum consisting of *two* parts.

SATURATION. The degree of concentration of some element in a given continuity. Complete saturation refers to presence of the element in maximum possible quantity. Temporal saturation refers specifically to concentration of an element in time. See **Temporal Saturation.**

SATURATION OF WAVE. The degree to which **Harmonics** are present, taken along with their intensities, in characterizing **Timbre.**

SCALE. As used by Schillinger, scale does not necessarily refer to **Pitch-Scale,** but rather to any scalewise arrangement of elements according to increase or decrease in some characteristic, as, for example, a quality scale in orchestration—in which timbral elements are arranged according to increase of some timbral characteristic, such as closed tone.

SCALE FAMILIES. See **Pitch-Scales.**

SCALE OF TENSION. **Tension** as measured in harmony by the distance of the **Function** representing the melodic tone from the functions in the harmony on a scale 1-3-5-7-9-11-13 & . For a 1-3-5 chord, for example, lowest tension is 1-3-5, as functions in the melody; next higher are the adjacent functions, 7 and 13; with 9 next higher and 11 highest of all. Different ranges of tension result in different melodic styles.

SCORED INTERFERENCES. See **Interference.**

SECONDARY AXIS. See **Axes.**

SECTIONAL SCALE. A **Pitch-Scale** built in the symmetric fashion by selecting a number of **Tonics** that symmetrically split one or more octaves, then attaching to each such tonic an identical intervallic pattern of semitones and/or whole tones or larger intervals so that no pattern overlaps the next higher tonic.

SELECTION. Used in the usual sense of the word, but denoting the act in composition of music by which the composer, confronted by all possible choices arranged in a systematic way, decides which particular resources he will use. In a selective continuity of any kind, for example, certain elements are chosen deliberately by reason of their effects and are combined in proportions that correspond to the relative emphasis the composer wishes to give them.

SELECTIVE. See **Selection.**

SELECTIVE CYCLIC CONTINUITY. Harmonic continuity in which certain cycles are chosen and used in selected quantities in order to produce continuity of desired characteristics; used in contrast to non-selective or casual continuity, in which the "selection" is made literally from chord to chord, as in older music (16th century) which is, as to cycle, in general *non*-selective.

SELECTIVE SYSTEM. Music is composed by successive steps of selection, that is to say, from the total manifold of all possible frequencies, certain frequencies are *selected* to comprise the manifold known as the tuning system; then, from the tuning system itself, certain pitch-units are *selected* to form a scale; and from the scale, certain other selections are made. Schillinger refers particularly to two types of selective systems—primary and secondary. The primary system is a given system of tuning while the secondary system is a scale or melody within the primary or tuning system.

SEMANTIC. Used by Schillinger to refer simply to meaning, and not necessarily to the evolution of meaning.

SEQUENCE. A group or set of elements arranged and considered with special regard to the *order* in which they come after each other, and usually without regard to the **Durations** attached to each.

SEQUENT GROUP. A group of elements that occur one after the other in time.

SERIES. A group of quantities, one after the other; or a group of any elements consecutively; usually each element is related in some constant way to the other elements.

SIGMA. The Greek letter (Σ) used essentially to denote a large structure, as distinct from smaller structures (usually of not more than four tones or **Neutral Units**) in **General Harmony.** The *sigma* is the same as some **Tonal Expansion** (or, sometimes, **Geometrical Expansion**) of a **Pitch-Scale.** Ordinarily, the E_1 (either tonal or geometric, depending on the type of harmony) of a diatonic scale is used.

SIGMA CONTINUITY. Denoted by ($\Sigma^{\longrightarrow}$). A sequent group of *sigmae*, used to denote the full tonal score and frequently to denote the patterns in which instrumental **Attack-Forms** are grouped.

SIGMAE. Plural form of **Sigma.**

SIGMA FAMILIES. Denoted by Σ (13), these are sigmae which consist of a root, 3rd, 5th, 7th, 9th, 11th, and 13th, the thirds involved being of all possible shapes. The result of various patternings of intervals is a series of different sigmae, each of which may become the source of a complete harmonic style through application of the techniques of **General Harmony.**

SIGMA OF SIGMA. See **Compound Sigma,** Σ (Σ).

SIMPLE HARMONIC MOTION. Melodic motion corresponding to the simple harmonic series (as used mathematically), or, practically, scalewise motion.

SIN MOTION. *Sin* is the conventional abbreviation for the mathematical ratio, *sine.* In the Schillinger System, *sin motion* is the same as **Ascribed Motion.** Used in contrast to *cos motion,* meaning cosine motion, which is the same as **Inscribed Motion.**

SINE. A mathematical ratio used in analysis of soundwaves and other types of cyclic motion. See **Sin Motion.**

SPECIAL HARMONY. The harmony associated with most of Western music, based on the E_1 of those scales which use all seven **Pitch-Names** with but one set of accidentals at a time. Schillinger uses this term, in contrast to **General Harmony,** to denote a narrow range of harmonic techniques corresponding to "classical" harmonic practice, but with considerable amplification of the range of device. His **General Harmony** includes **Special Harmony** as one type, and it, in turn, embraces **Diatonic Harmony, Diatonic-Symmetric Harmony Symmetric Harmony** and **Chromatic Harmony.**

SPEED. The number of **Attacks** in relation to total time; specifically, the number of basic time units, t, contained in the total duration.

SPLIT UNITS. In rhythm, the result of dividing a single duration by some divisor; extended to a technique by which the selection of units to be split is controlled by permutation or by coefficients of recurrence.

STATISTICAL SCALE. See **Quantitative Scale.**

STOPPED TONE. In **Orchestration, Quality Scales** or **Timbral Scales,** one of three general timbre intermediate between **Open** and **Closed Tone.**

STRATA. Plural form of **Stratum.**

STRATA HARMONY. A term meaning harmonic continuity in which a large number of parts are grouped into **Strata** and handled accordingly. See **General Harmony.**

STRATUM. One of the elements in **General Harmony** (or strata harmony, as it is frequently called), A stratum consists of one or more **Neutral Units** (rarely more than four, however), each neutral unit being a tone. From one or more of these neutral units, **Directional Units** may be developed. The pattern of neutral units within a single stratum is denoted in relation to the root of the stratum itself.

STRUCTURE. In general, any pattern of elements, organized either in pitch or in time. or both. Specifically, when denoted by S, a Pitch-Assemblage or chord consisting of **Neutral Units** and sometimes **Directional Units,** with emphasis on the exact shape (pattern of intervals, binding together the **Neutral Units.** One or more such structures (which are, of course, the equivalent in **General Harmony** of **Strata**) constitute a **Sigma.**

STYLE. In the Schillinger system, the style of a composition is the result of the individual styles of the component continuities, the main factors being *intonational* style, controlled by **Pitch-Scale** and its expansions into **Sigmae;** and *temporal* style, or **Rhythm,** controlled by **Style Series.** But many other aspects are also factors in the final style, especially those connected with **General Harmony.**

STYLE SERIES. This is a series which functions, in the Schillinger system, as the source of all families of temporal or rhythmic style, and consists of the following:

$$\frac{1}{n} \cdots \cdots \frac{1}{4}, \frac{1}{3}, \frac{1}{2}, \frac{1}{1}, \frac{2}{1}, \frac{3}{1}, \frac{4}{1} \cdots \cdots \frac{n}{1}$$

It may be compressed into simply:

$$\frac{1}{1}, \frac{2}{2}, \frac{3}{3}, \frac{4}{4}, \frac{5}{5}, \frac{6}{6}, \frac{7}{7}, \frac{8}{8} \cdots \cdots \frac{n}{n}$$

The denominators control **Fractional Rhythm;** the numerators, **Factorial Rhythm.** The manner in which generation of a family of **Durational Groups** takes place is the following: a **Monomial,** such as 4 (for $\frac{4}{1}$ series), is split asymmetrically (or 3-1) by the smallest unit of deviation the number affords; it is then synchronized with itself run backward (i. e., 3-1 is synchronized with 1-3) to produce a trinomial (1-2-1). All permutations of the trinomial are combined to produce a new polynomial (in this case, 1-1-1-1). The terms of the new poly nomial (up to the point where uniformity is reached) are again permuted and "interfered"— and so on. The resulting durational groups constitute the raw material of the style. The numerators function as multiplicands in making larger continuities. Schillinger tends to use the term *time-series* of this process when it controls details of larger form, reserving the term *style-series* for fractional rhythms.

STYLIZED PRIMITIVE. An **Original Primitive** scale developed according to techniques that are essentially diatonic.

SUBTRACTION TONES. See **Differential Tones.**

SUMMATION SERIES. Any series of numbers in which the third and all subsequent terms are the total of the two immediately preceding terms; or, by extension, the total of any pre-set number of immediately preceding terms. *First summation series*: 1, 2, 3, 5, 8, 13, 21 etc. *Second summation series*: 1, 3, 4, 7, 11, 18 etc. Also known as Fibonacci Series.

SYMMETRICAL NOMENCLATURE. Naming of intervals by the number of semitones, rather than as seconds, thirds, etc. That is to say, what by symmetric nomenclature is a 5 would be a 4 (perfect 4) in diatonic nomenclature.

SYMMETRIC HARMONIZATION. Harmonization of one or more melodies, the resulting harmonic continuity being of the symmetric type.

SYMMETRIC HARMONY. A system of harmony in which the roots of the chords move by patterns outside the diatonic system and computed in semitones; more specifically, a variety of the above in which the roots move in typical patterns, the patterns being: movement by semitones, denoted as $\sqrt[12]{2}$; by whole steps, denoted as $\sqrt[6]{2}$; by minor thirds (3 semitones), denoted as $\sqrt[4]{2}$; by major thirds (4 semitones, denoted as $\sqrt[3]{2}$; by augmented fourths (6 semitones), denoted as $\sqrt[2]{2}$. Movement of the root by an octave or unison is also technically a symmetric movement under the most generalized form. With the root moving as described, the specific tonal structures or chords are pre-set without relation either to any diatonic scale or to the tonal material of the pattern of roots, the chord forms being chosen usually for their acoustical sonority. **Transformations** ("voice leading") take place by permutation.

SYMMETRIC ROOTS. Patterns of root movement in **Symmetric Harmony.**

SYMMETRIC SCALES. Pitch-Scales, frequently of more than one octave in range, formed by a series of **Tonics** arranged symmetrically to which tonics are added one or more additional tones in a standard, pre-set interval relation. Schillinger describes two types of symmetric scales: Group III: range of less than one octave and containing equal number of semitones (2, 3, 4, 6) between tones; Group IV: range of more than one octave and containing equal number of semitones (8, 9, 10, 11) between tones.

SYMMETRY. A characteristic appertaining to any pattern, requiring that the whole pattern be susceptible to reversal without the pattern being thereby changed.

SYNCHRONIZATION. The process of making two series (usually **Durational Groups**) occupy the same period of time; performed by reducing each to a common denominator. **Interference** results unless the series are identical.

T.

T. Symbol ordinarily used for time. Occasionally a symbol for **Tonic.**

Θ. See **Theta.**

τ. See **Tau.**

T→. Symbol used for **Durational Continuity,** or sequent group of durations.

TAU. The Greek letter (τ), used to denote a unit of deviation in the notation of durations, especially in calculating **Rubato, Fermata,** minor changes in tempo, etc.

TEMPORAL ORGANIZATION. The organization of all details of a composition or section thereof in time; in particular, the organization of factorial and fractional continuities; see **Rhythm.**

TEMPORAL SATURATION. See **Saturation** in general. In the Schillinger System, increasing temporal saturation is achieved by having more and more **Thematic Groups** in a given continuity. This sometimes involves contrapuntal arrangements of the groups of the type known as stretto in older counterpoint, in which the thematic group has not yet come to an end before another thematic group (usually the same as the first) begins.

TENSION. The degree of dissonance (1) in a **Harmonic Interval,** or (2) between melody and harmony. The latter varies as to **Range of Tension,** which may be set narrowly or broadly, and as to degree of tension, itself, which may be kept high—around the 7, 9, 11 functions— or low—around the 1, 3, 5. The harmonic aspects of tension derive from the simpler intervallic aspects.

TERNARY AXES. See **Axes.**

TETRAD. A structure in harmony of four parts.

THEMATIC CONTINUITY. A sequence of **Thematic Groups,** organized in some pattern: direct recurrence, modified recurrence, symmetrical recurrence, etc. It controls the fundamental *musical form* of the composition as well as the emphasis given to various types of **Thematic Units.**

THEMATIC GROUP. A **Thematic Unit** existing in one of its potential forms in a *specific* period of time.

THEMATIC MELODIC FIGURATION. A process for melodic figuration of harmony whereby pre-set melodic forms are introduced into the successive chords of the given harmonic continuity.

THEMATIC SEQUENCE. A **Thematic Continuity,** but with special emphasis on the serial order in which **Thematic Groups** follow one another, and without regard to the durations attached to each.

THEMATIC UNIT. A configuration of elements in music chosen for its susceptibility to temporal and intonational modification. It may or may not be composed exclusively of tonal elements; it may also consist of **Density** or **Orchestral** groups; or of any other element in music. It may be rhythmic, melodic, harmonic, or contrapuntal. It may consist of some combination of elements, in which case it will have one element as a major component, around which the other elements (minor components) are organized. It is the basic ingredient of **Thematic Groups.**

THEME. In a composition, a **Thematic Group** in which the **Thematic Unit** is exhibited at its maximum duration in time; a subject.

THETA. The Greek letter referring to a compound rotation group in **Density,** and in general, to a **Density Continuity** with emphasis on phasic rotation.

TIMBRAL. The adjective refers to *timbre.*

TIMBRE. The quality or "color" of tone resulting from the interaction of all frequencies and intensities constituting a sound wave.

TONAL EXPANSION. Expansion carried out in terms of a specific diatonic scale. Contrast with the result of carrying out the same **Expansion** process geometrically, i.e., measuring in semitones rather than in diatonic intervals. Various degrees of expansion are denoted as E_1 ("first expansion"), E_2 ("second expansion"), etc,. especially when referring to expansions of diatonic scales. The first expansion is obtained through circular permutation *over* one pitch-unit of the original scale; the second expansion, over two pitch-units; etc.

TONAL INVERSION. A process for variation proceeding in much the same way as that used in **Quadrant Rotation,** except that the intervals are calculated diatonically rather than absolutely, so that the result—in contrast to the result of some of the quadrant rotations— is adjusted to the key of the original.

TONE SYMBOLS. ◯ See **Open Tone.** ● See **Closed Tone.** ⊕ See **Stopped Tone.**

TONES OF THE DIFFERENCE. See **Differential Tones.**

TONIC. The first tone of a **Pitch-Scale** and, occasionally by extension, the first tone or root of a *sigma.* *Two-tonic system;* a system of **Pitch-Scales** or **Harmonic Progressions** based on two tonics, usually related as C to F♯ or $\sqrt[2]{2}$. *Three-tonic system:* relationship usually as C, E, A♭, or $\sqrt[3]{2}$. *Four-tonic system:* relationship as C, E♭, G♭, A, or $\sqrt[4]{2}$. A five-tonic system does not exist in equal temperament tuning. *Six-tonic system:* relationship usually as C, D, E, F♯, G♯, A♯, or $\sqrt[6]{2}$. *Twelve-tonic system:* relationship usually as all tones of the chromatic scale in succession, or $\sqrt[12]{2}$.

TRAJECTORIAL MOTION. Melodic motion analyzed from the viewpoint of the trajectories it outlines when graphed; more specifically, these trajectories analyzed in relation to **Primary Axes** and **Secondary Axes.**

TRANSFORMATIONS. The general form of what is conventionally called "voice leading," but used in a much broader sense of the transformation of any Pitch-Assemblage (abcde, for example) into another (a'b'c'd'e', for example). *Parallel* transformations lead each function in the initial assemblage to the corresponding function in the next assemblage; in all other transformations, the initial set of functions transforms to a set of functions that represents some **Permutation** of the second set. In so-called **Constant Function Transformations,** in which one (or more) functions lead by parallels, the remaining functions leading by permutation. In general, transformations are classified as **Clockwise** or **Counterclockwise,** with **Crosswise** appearing as a special form of both.

TRIAD. A structure in harmony of but three parts; conventionally, but not necessarily, the familiar triad of ordinary diatonic harmony.

TRINOMIAL. A group consisting of three elements.

TRIPLE PARALLEL CHROMATICS. One variety of **Chromatic Harmony.**

TRUE PRIMITIVE. See **Original Primitive.**

TUNING RANGE. The range of tones as they actually sound that an instrument can produce for orchestral use.

TUNING SYSTEM. In music only certain pitches from among all the possible pitches are utilized. The particular set of pitches selected for use is the *tuning system*, or primary selective system. Various systems have been or are in use, but the system known as **Equal Temperament** is the basis of the notation of most Occidental music and is the basis of the Schillinger system. See pp. 101, 102 and 144.

U.

U. Symbol used for *unbalancing* axis (see **Axes**).

UNBALANCING AXIS. See **Axes.**

UNIMODAL. Describes axial relations of two melodic lines when each is in the same mode of its particular key; the keys need not necessarily be the same, but the modes (displacements) must be identical.

UNITONAL. Describes interrelation of two or more melodic lines (especially in counterpoint) as to the **Real Key** of each, and means that each is in the same key, although not necessarily in the same mode. See **Polytonal.** See **Unimodal.**

UU, UP. See **Axis Relations.**

V.

V⁻→ Symbol for **Dynamic Continuity.**

V. A symbol used in orchestration for *volume*, or dynamics.

v. A dynamic unit, See **V.**

VARIABLE DIFFERENCE SERIES. A **Series** in which each term is composed of a base that increases to some pattern, to which is added a second number that also increases according to some pattern; essentially, the sum of two series.

VARIABLE DOUBLINGS. In harmony, a technique by which varying chordal functions (the 1, 3, or 5 usually) are selected for doubling.

VARIABLE STRUCTURES. In harmony, the use of more than one structure (or "shape") of chord in a continuity.

VOICE LEADING. The trajectory or path followed by a **Part**; see especially **Transformations.**

INDEX

A

abscissa, 1, 187, 245, 302
acceleration, in non-uniform groups, 93
  in uniform groups, 92
acceleration groups, 1341
acceleration series, XVII
accompaniment, harmonic, 1204
acoustical fallacies, 697
Alexander, Jeff, XII
alto clarinet, 1516
amplitudes, 2
anticipation-fulfillment pattern, 1415
anticipations, 579-83, 1296
Aria on the G-string (Bach), 1354
Aristotle, XVIII
arithmetical mean, 315, 317, 352
arithmetical progressions, 352, 365
  with variable differences, 91, 365
ascribed motion, 301, 303
As I Remember (R. De Maria), 1409
atonality, 247, 739
attack, forms of, 1323, 1327, 1598
attack-group, synchronization of an, 36
attack-groups, development of, 912, 951
  in two-part counterpoint, 726
  melodic, composing, 642
attacks, bowing, 1499
  composition of, 1281
  multiplication of, 883
Auer, Leopold, 1489
Auric, 173, 1265
auxiliary tones, 584-96, 1198
auxiliary units, application of, 1202
  distribution of, 1198
Ave Regina Coelorum, 368
axes, centrifugal, combination of two, 287
  centripetal, combination of two, 288
  of melody, 246
  secondary, 247, 252, 299, 302, 312
  secondary parallel, 290
  simultaneous combination of three, 289
axial combinations, 253, 1292
  polynomial, 757
axis, balancing, 252
  binomial, 259, 754
  monomial, 259, 753
  primary, 125, 246, 312
  quadrinomial, 260
  quintinomial, 261
  trinomial, 260, 756
axis-relations, 126, 758

B

Bach, J. S., 34, 145, 194, 211, 215, 217, 312,
  317, 374, 437, 461, 495, 552, 795, 796-
  801, 875, 1277, 1330, 1331, 1352, 1520, 1523
balance, 21
Banshee (Cowell), 1557
bass, setting of the, 1011
bass drum, 1568
bass clarinet, 1516
bassethorn, 1516
bassoon (fagotto), 1521
Battistini, Mattia, 1572
Beautiful Dreamer, 1460
Beethoven, 34, 112, 196, 211, 244, 247, 299,
  314, 374, 507, 561, 1349, 1366, 1523
Bellini, 283
bells, church, 1560
  cow, 1569
  orchestra (glockenspiel), 1559
Benedicta Tu, 369
Berg, 211
Berlioz, 1567
biner, 314
B-minor Sonata (Liszt), 211
binomials, reciprocating, 1297
  temporal, 1296
Blanton, Jimmy, 1510
Blues, 1510
Bolero (Ravel), 1556
boogie-woogie, 94, 1044
Bongo drums, 1569
Boris Godounov (Moussorgsky), 375
Borodin, 73, 495, 506, 508, 666, 686
Bradley, Will, XII
Brahms, 524
But I Only Have Eyes for You, 316

C

Caccini, Giulio, music example by, 369
cadences, 363, 370, 371
Cadman, 1255
Cahill, Thaddeus, 1548
canons, 777
  composition from strata harmony, 1216
cantus firmus, 708, 801
Caruso, Enrico, 1456
Casella, 173, 1265
castanets, 1563
celesta, 1558
Chaconne in D-minor (Bach), 375
Chaikovsky, 569, 586, 627

VITA

Joseph Schillinger was born in Kharkov, Russia, September 1, 1895, and died in New York on March 23, 1943. At the age of 5 he manifested interest in design, dramatics and verse; at 10 he was experimenting in play-writing and music. He was educated at the Classical College and entered the St. Petersburg Conservatory in 1914. In 1917 he was graduated from the class in composition, after which he studied conducting under N. N. Cherepnin.

In 1918 he was appointed senior instructor in composition at the Kharkov Academy of Music; in 1920 he was made professor, and the following year, dean of the faculty of composition. In the same period he served as head of the music department of the Board of Education of the Ukraine. From 1922 to 1926 he acted as consultant to the Leningrad Board of Education. Beginning in 1925, and for three years thereafter, he served as professor and member of the State Institute of the History of Arts at Leningrad. In 1927 he was commissioned to make phonograms of the folk music of the Georgian tribes in the Caucasus, and he succeeded in recording folk songs previously unknown to the world of music. In this period his pedagogical responsibilities multiplied and he also served as senior instructor of the State Central Technicum of Music. From 1926 to 1928 he was vice-president of the Leningrad branch of the International Society for Contemporary Music. During this period he organized and directed the first Russian jazz orchestra.

In November 1928 Schillinger came to the United States on invitation of the American Society for Cultural Relations with Russia. Shortly after his arrival he began collaborating with Leon Theremin on research in musical acoustics, and the application of electronics to tonal production. For six years, from 1930 to 1936, he taught at various American universities and schools of art and music. From 1930 to 1932 he was a lecturer at the David Berend School of Music. In 1932 and 1933 he lectured at the New School for Social Research. In 1934 he gave lectures at the Florence Cane School of Art, American Institute for the Study of Advanced Education, and American Institute of the City of New York. In 1934 he became a member of the faculty of Teachers College, Columbia University, serving in three different departments: music, fine arts and mathematics. The Mathematics Museum of Teachers College placed on permanent exhibition, in 1934, certain geometrical designs which he evolved as part of his Theory of Design. In 1936 he lectured at New York University. In July of the same year he became an American citizen.

Schillinger's major musical compositions include works for orchestra, voice, string instruments and piano. *March of the Orient*, Op. 11, was composed in 1924, and performed by the Leningrad State Philharmonic, as well as the Persymphans; during the seasons of 1926-27 and 1927-28 it was played by the Cleveland Symphony, Nikolai Sokoloff conducting. *Symphonic Rhapsody*, Op. 19, was composed on commission to celebrate the tenth anniversary of the Soviet Union. After performances in Moscow and Leningrad, it was given its premiere in the Western hemisphere by the Philadelphia Orchestra under Leopold Stokowski. In

1929 Schillinger wrote *First Airphonic Suite*, Op. 21, for RCA Theremin and orchestra. The first performances were given by the Cleveland Orchestra under Sokoloff. The following year, on commission by RCA, Schillinger wrote the *North Russian Symphony*, Op. 22, for radio performances.

Among his outstanding piano works are the *Five Movements for Piano*, Op. 12; *Excentriade*, Op. 14; *Sonata Rhapsody*, Op. 17; and Funeral March. His *Sonata for Violin and Piano*, Op. 9, received its first performance in Kharkov in 1922 with Nathan Milstein.

Schillinger's two major theoretical works are the *Mathematical Basis of the Arts*, and the *Schillinger System of Musical Composition*. The former work represents the first scientific theory of the arts, and presents the application of his foundation ideas to the spatial as well as tonal arts. *Kaleidophone*, a manual of pitch scales in relation to chord structures, was published in 1940. Articles on various subjects may be found in *Modern Music, Experimental Cinema, Tomorrow, Metronome, 1938 Proceedings of the Music Teachers National Association* and *1938 Annual Meeting Papers of the American Musicological Society*. Schillinger left in manuscript, essays and articles, including *Musofun* (a book of musical games) and *Graph Method of Dance Notation*.

The publication of the *Schillinger System of Musical Composition* has been long awaited because of Schillinger's influence on American music for radio and motion pictures—an influence exerted through the prominent composers, conductors, arrangers and music directors who studied privately with him.